Education in a New Society

Education in a New Society

Renewing the Sociology of Education

EDITED BY JAL MEHTA
AND SCOTT DAVIES

The University of Chicago Press
Chicago and London

The University of Chicago Press, Chicago 60637
The University of Chicago Press, Ltd., London

Published 2018
Printed in the United States of America

27 26 25 24 23 22 21 20 19 18 1 2 3 4 5

ISBN-13: 978-0-226-51739-1 (cloth)
ISBN-13: 978-0-226-51742-1 (paper)
ISBN-13: 978-0-226-51756-8 (e-book)
DOI: 10.7208/chicago/[9780226517568].001.0001

Library of Congress Cataloging-in-Publication Data
Names: Mehta, Jal, editor. | Davies, Scott, 1962– editor.
Title: Education in a new society : renewing the sociology of education / edited by Jal Mehta and Scott Davies.
Description: Chicago ; London : The University of Chicago Press, 2018. | Includes index.
Identifiers: LCCN 2017039550 | ISBN 9780226517391 (cloth : alk. paper) | ISBN 9780226517421 (pbk. : alk. paper) | ISBN 9780226517568 (e-book)
Subjects: LCSH: Educational sociology. | Educational sociology—United States.
Classification: LCC LC191 .E4248 2018 | DDC 306.430973—dc23
LC record available at https://lccn.loc.gov/2017039550

♾ This paper meets the requirements of ANSI/NISO Z39.48-1992 (Permanence of Paper).

CONTENTS

FOREWORD: A MUCH-NEEDED PROJECT

MICHÈLE LAMONT

Education in a New Society represents a timely pathbreaking effort to renew and recalibrate the sociology of education so that it is better equipped to understand education as it exists today. In this book, Jal Mehta and Scott Davies have invited a number of talented researchers to take stock of the field and think through its current limitations and the challenges ahead. They have also written an informative introduction that draws on a detailed empirical study of the field of education as it has manifested itself in the leading sociology journals over the last five decades. This contribution in and of itself is worth the price of admission. Their analysis reveals some of the blind spots of the field as it has grown around the seminal contributions of a handful of leading theorists: James Coleman, Randall Collins, John Meyer, Pierre Bourdieu, and others. Without downplaying the importance of these experts' work, Mehta and Davies show that the scholarship has left important stones unturned. They point to paths for future development that can be pursued by approaching the study of education through the prisms of culture, institutions, politics, knowledge, comparative education, and values. They want sociologists of education to build on their disciplinary strengths to develop a perspective on education that is different, but complementary, to that of economists of education. The latter remain too often unaware of many of the questions that our multimethod intellectual field is particularly well equipped to answer. Sociology should mobilize its unique analytical tools to flesh out a multidimensional framework for capturing the institution of education in all of its manifestations. This volume takes a huge step in showing the way forward.

Concretely, what does this mean? From the perspective of knowledge production, it means looking at education as it is pursued and achieved not only in school and college settings, but also in other contexts: family, daycare, religious organizations, leisure activities, and so on. It also means focusing not only on the inequalities produced in educational settings, but also on inequalities that result from other outcomes, whether the selection of partners or the development of moral worldviews. It also means developing a more finely grained understanding of the cultural processes involved in the production of inequality by connecting with relevant literatures not yet considered by the field of education (e.g., the literature on omnivorousness referenced by Davies and Mehta in chapter 3). Finally, it means taking on the challenge of thinking bigger and differently about the place of education in larger society; reconsidering the theoretical notions that sociologists of education most often use to make sense of phenomena; inventing a novel approach outside well-traveled paths; and choosing not to spend time writing papers that add additional bricks to an already well established paradigmatic wall, or papers whose conclusions utterly lack surprise.

Against this background, the contributors to *Education in a New Society* are responding to a call to arms from the coeditors to demonstrate the likely heuristic payoff from a broadening of the sociology of education. For this particular volume, the main anchors for creating new analytical bridges come out of neo-institutional analysis, cultural sociology, the sociology of knowledge, the sociology of professions, and the sociology of morality. The contributors to this book are acutely aware of the many ways in which their own research agendas have been enriched by considering questions that lie beyond the traditional terrain of the sociology of education. They make the gamble that the field as a whole would be strengthened by debalkanization and a greater engagement with the surrounding subfields. I find their arguments most convincing, especially given that each chapter makes the case for a specific area of empirical inquiry. But the devil is in the details; it falls to the reader to determine whether the authors deliver on their promises, and to evaluate where this new gamble is likely to lead.

In bringing these authors together, Mehta and Davies pursue one more objective: they crystallize a movement that has been building over the last decade as a number of important books and articles have laid the groundwork for an intellectual agenda for a renewal of the sociology of education. Here I have in mind award-winning books such as *Paying for the Party* by Elizabeth Armstrong and Laura Hamilton, *Becoming Right* by Amy Binder and Kate Wood, *The Best of the Best* by Rubén Gaztambide-Fernández, and *Creating a Class* by Mitchell Stevens, to name only a few. Such books have fed not only the sociology of education but also other research areas such as the sociology of evaluation, gender and sexuality, organizations, political socialization, and social movements. They have also looked backward and sideways, and have been in conversation with a growing American literature on race and class cultures: books such as Annette Lareau's *Unequal Childhoods*, Karyn Lacy's *Blue-Chip Black*, Lauren Rivera's *Pedigree*, and my own *Money, Morals, and Manners*, *The Dignity of Working Men*, and *How Professors Think*. It should be remembered that it is precisely when a subfield becomes generative—a point of reference—for other subfields that its status increases. While the sociology of education has been viewed as being a bit inward-looking or even insular at times, it may now be in a position to act as a point of reference for researchers who are working far afield. This is all for the best.

It is without hesitation that I put my money on *Education in a New Society* and on the set of creative minds who have contributed to the book. Together, they propose a welcome intellectual renewal of our thinking concerning one of the most important social institutions. This is a significant achievement, which could well become a crucial impetus for strengthening sociology as a distinct contributor to the broader enterprise of the study of education.

ONE

Education in a New Society: Renewing the Sociology of Education

JAL MEHTA AND SCOTT DAVIES[1]

This volume considers the development of the sociology of education over the past fifty years, beginning in the 1960s and continuing to the present day. Our argument is that the field needs to be renewed: specifically, that many of the dominant ideas, concepts, and theories in the sociology of education were created by a few well-known theorists in a highly generative period between 1966 and 1979, and that much of the work since has followed the tracks laid down by these giants. We argue both that over the intervening period the real world of education has changed considerably (often in ways that were not anticipated by the early theorists) and that the broader field of sociology has evolved in ways that have not been integrated into the sociological study of education. We also argue that there are new strands of sociological thinking about education which are not recognized within what is commonly known as "sociology of education," but which provide templates for fresh modes of study. Taken together, these developments suggest the moment has come to ask new questions and develop new theories, drawing together disparate strands of inquiry and creating new programs of empirical research.

The rest of this introduction seeks to develop that case. First, we examine the key ideas of James Coleman, Daniel Bell, John Meyer, Samuel Bowles and Herb Gintis, Paul Willis, Pierre Bourdieu, and Randall Collins, whose theoretical frameworks have proven so influential to this day. Second, we explore empirically which topics have been taken up in the sociology of education since 1965. We do this in part through an original content and citation analysis of *Sociology of Education, American Journal of Sociology, American Sociological Review*, and *Annual Review of Sociology*. We then suggest that this analysis of leading American sociology journals misses other visions of the sociology of education which also have wide followings; we delineate five sociologies of education that have succeeded in different niches of the academic landscape. Third, we examine key trends that have shaped the educational world over this period, and consider the ways in which these are or are not captured by either the theories or the empirical work examined above. Finally, we conclude by examining strands of newer work, including those by many contributors to this volume, which begin to meet the challenges we have outlined.

Given the potential scope of this enterprise, it is important to specify what we are and are not seeking to accomplish. Our work does not purport to be a comprehensive review of the sociology of education. There are a number of existing reviews which, in different ways, cover the field (Dreeben 1994; Sadovnik 2007; Hallinan 2006; Bidwell and Friedkin 1988; Karabel and Halsey 1977). Rather, we are attempting something more pointed: (1) to document the distribution of topics that have received scholarly attention within the sociology of education from American sociology departments and journals over the past 50 years; (2) to suggest that this analysis reveals that there are a few central topics, particularly status attainment research and school effects, that have been critical to establishing sociology of education as a legitimate and respected subfield, but which have also crowded out other potentially important topics and ideas; (3) to point to a range of other approaches which are well-developed in their own niches but are not well recognized within American sociology departments; (4) to argue that, in particular, that there has been a neglect of questions related to culture, institutions, politics, knowledge, comparative education, and values, which are critical to understanding education in all its manifestations in the twenty-first century; (5) to conclude, based on a summary of these points, that sociology of education is both highly fragmented and heavily reliant on a small number of classic theories from forty to fifty years ago, and that the moment has come for new, more integrative theorizing and research in the field.

We fully acknowledge that someone else might look at the field and see different strengths and lacunae; we would welcome other "sociologies" of the sociology of education. But whether or not readers accept our specific assessment, we hope to convince them that the time is long overdue to "get on the balcony" and map the ecology of the field as a whole. This view allows us to consider not only the debates *within* the field, but to look at the *contours* of the field—to take stock of which topics are explored, which are not, and why. More theoretically, we employ a sociology of knowledge approach to understand how the contexts of production and reception have shaped the kinds of sociological knowledge that have been produced, legitimated, and located.

Overall, since the modern field of the sociology of education was created under the influence of a small number of theories and methods in the 1960s and 1970s, the world has changed considerably, and the field has developed many more conceptual tools. The moment has come to develop a new sociology of education for a new society.

Sociology of Education on the Eve of the 1960s

While our main topic is sociology of education over the past fifty years, it is important to set the stage by describing the field as it stood on the eve of the developments we are about to describe. Roughly speaking, there were a few classic texts, specifically Durkheim's discussion of schooling as a moral enterprise, Waller's treatise on the conflict between student and adult visions of school, and Sorokin's studies of social mobility patterns (Dreeben 1994). Education was also a major theme in well-known community studies, such as the Lynds' *Middletown* and Hollingshead's *Elmtown's Youth*. However, most overviews of the sociology of education at the time were not kind in describing the field (Gross 1959; Brookover 1955; Floud and Halsey 1958). For instance, Harvard sociologist Neal Gross (1959: 128) took stock of the sociology of education in a prominent Robert Merton-edited volume, *Sociology Today*, and concluded: "The sociological analysis of education may be described as a relatively underdeveloped and unfashionable subfield of sociology. There are currently only a handful of sociologists who make this field their specialty. Relatively few students in graduate training aspire to be known as educational sociologists, and few courses are offered in this area in American universities."

Why was education such an "unfashionable" field? Gross continues: "With a few notable exceptions, the literature is characterized by an undue emphasis on description in contrast to analysis. Many of the research studies lack theoretical orientation, and they have yielded few hypotheses of sociological importance. In addition the majority of the studies have not met the methodological standards generally accepted as minimal criteria for competent research. Although these criticisms might be applied to the research literature in other subdivisions of sociology, they appear to be especially applicable to the literature in the sociology of education."

What accounted for this bleak state of affairs? Gross argued that one cause was the absence of even an effort to develop significant empirical scholarship on schools. Gross (1959:129) writes that much of the "literature published under the rubric of 'educational sociology' . . . has little or no sociological relevance, largely consisting of hortatory essays. Essays pleading for a reorientation of the goals of American education or reporting educational practices in foreign countries have their place; but they are not, as they have been termed, 'studies' in the sociology of education." As we will document later in this chapter, a review of the early years of the journal that would become the *Sociology of Education* supports Gross's analysis; the vast majority of contributions were essays rather than studies based on empirical research.

A related challenge, Gross argued, in what would become a familiar refrain, was that sociologists of education might become associated with or be employed by schools of education. "In most institutions of higher learning, the educational faculty ranks at or near the bottom of the academic prestige hierarchy." Connecting too closely with such "low-status colleagues" is to "risk further loss of prestige for members of a discipline which itself has not yet received full acceptance by many members of more entrenched departments." Additionally, the "traditional 'applied' emphasis in the field has not especially enhanced the prestige of sociologists who have been associated with it."

In retrospect, perhaps as interesting as Gross's analysis of the field were his predictions of what the next decade might yield. Reflecting the reigning influences of sociology in the 1950s, he argued that schools would be good sites through which Parsons' structural functional lens could be developed; he thought that Howard Becker's early work on the occupation and career trajectory of teaching might be extended; he thought that questions about teaching as a profession should be explored; he argued that Waller's work was worth revisiting and testing more systematically; and he thought that schools were intriguing organizational sites to study questions of organizational control and change. While some of these predictions would be born out, particularly the ones concerning school-as-organization and teaching as a profession, notably absent in retrospect was any interest in measuring the impact of schools versus family background, or in quantitatively understanding the roles that schools play in social reproduction and mobility.

Overall, sociology of education on the eve of the 1960s was neither strong on its own feet nor well respected within sociology. Viewed from this perspective, what was to come would be nothing less than a revolution in the study of education, one which yielded a growing science of schooling and which secured a significant place for the sociology of education in the broader sociological discipline.

Classics: 1960s and 1970s Theorizing and Its Influences

We begin the modern story of the empirical study of education with the Coleman report, which by many accounts was the single most influential document in the sociology of education in the second half of the twentieth century (Walters 2009). As is well known, the report emerged from a federal government request to analyze whether measurable school factors were creating inequalities, particularly between blacks and whites. Coleman found that family background and peer composition of classes were the most important two factors in predicting student achievement, while many of the measurable variables about schools were less influential in explaining student outcomes. In a similar vein, a Christopher Jencks–led study, *Inequality*, used a range of data sets to argue that schools were much less important than previously thought in predicting adult outcomes.

While the results themselves continue to be both cited and debated, in the longer run perhaps the most important consequence of the Coleman report was the template it offered for how to do sociological research on education. Its vision was methodologically individualistic; the dependent variable was individual student achievement, and the independent variables were features of schools or families that could be easily quantified and entered into a regression. Its core questions were about differences across groups—in this case blacks and whites—and the factors that predicted those differences. Its underlying normative ethos was convergent with a prominent strain of equal-opportunity liberalism, which suggested that the problem was less the distribution of wealth or economic power than whether the link between parents and children's life chances could be broken through quality schooling. It promised policy relevance, because policymakers, working within a similar normative paradigm, also wanted to know what factors were important in helping more students "get ahead." And, finally, it gave social scientists a tool that differentiated them from lay inquirers: any journalist could write about how large classes were worse than small ones, but the power of large quantitative data sets and the regressions they enabled seemed to allow social scientists to provide definitive evidence about whether such a claim was actually true.

A related line of work was developing at the University of Wisconsin and elsewhere, which came to be known as the status attainment school. Led by Peter Blau, Otis Dudley Duncan, William Sewell, and later Robert Hauser, this work took a methodologically similar stance to Coleman's, although with a less explicit focus on policy and more attention to patterns in intergenerational mobility. Drawing on the Wisconsin Longitudinal Survey and other sources, these scholars computed whether children's educational and occupational status exceeded that of their parents, as well as the role played by mediating factors, such as students' aspirations. While the initial research focused on white farm boys, over time as more and different data became available, the work expanded to explore different patterns of mobility by race and gender. The core empirical argument of these theorists also converged with Talcott Parsons's famous thesis that society was moving from a world of ascription to one of achievement—namely, that advantage was no longer directly passed on from parents to children, but instead was largely mediated by children's educational attainment. In mapping these dynamics, the status attainment theorists also won a place for the sociology of education in the larger sociological discipline by establishing empirically the importance of education to the broader processes of social reproduction and mobility.

At the same time, the success of the work of Coleman and the status attainment researchers meant that the attention of the field was directed to some dynamics and not others. In particular, what happened inside schools was largely a black box—the mechanisms and processes of schooling were not visible within the status attainment picture (see Karabel and Halsey 1977). Higher education was largely ignored, except for its contribution to measuring years of schooling. The focus was primarily on the American system, with little interest in comparative perspective. Questions of history and politics were abstracted away in favor of a macroscopic vision of schools as conduits of social reproduction and mobility. And in their focus on differences across groups and factors that produced individual social mobility, the status attainment theorists did not examine the broader question of the growing role that schooling as a whole would play in society.

After the Coleman Report, the 1970s became *the* golden age of theorizing about schooling and society. A series of ambitious works, written in a remarkably short time span, offered accounts of modern school systems in contemporary society. Each of these classics observed how the expansion of schooling since World War II, particularly at secondary and post-secondary levels, was reshaping life courses and labor markets. In individual ways, each challenged prevailing human capital and functionalist thinking both in the academy and in policy circles. These theories are still major touchstones, continuing to demarcate important issues in the field; they are regularly taught to this day, and are cited by the thousand forty years later.

In 1973, Daniel Bell published *The Coming of Post-Industrial Society*, a sprawling forecast which named schooling as the major engine of post-industrial society. In 1976, Bowles and Gintis published *Schooling in Capitalist America*, a Marxist treatise whose "correspondence principle" regarded schooling as a major instrument of social control in the historical evolution of capitalism, one that necessarily generated class inequalities. In 1977, the English translation of Bourdieu and Passeron's *Reproduction* offered a cultural variant of that thesis, coining Bourdieu's signature concept "cultural capital" to highlight processes by which schools necessarily reproduce social class inequalities. Across the 1970s, Basil Bernstein's three-volume set *Class, Codes and Control* focused on the linguistic dimensions of reproduction, arguing that the particularistic speech codes of poor and working-class children were largely incompatible with the norms of middle-class schooling, which favored the more universalistic codes of middle-class children. In 1977–78, John Meyer used organizational and institutional thinking to theorize about school expansion and explicitly reject both functionalist and Marxist accounts. And, in 1979, Randall Collins published *The Credential Society*, which linked the expansion of higher education to stratification and identified credential inflation as a key mechanism by which schooling reshaped status attainment processes in labor markets.

These theories offer a strategic reference point for charting subsequent empirical trends and thinking about evolving links between schooling and society. The study of stratification was reoriented by notions of reproduction, with structural variants elaborated by Bowles and Gintis and cultural variants elaborated by Bourdieu. Their main message was that school necessarily maintained inequality, despite massive educational expansion, due to its very design. The main mechanisms by which stratification was seen to reoccur were through structural processes (tracking, unequal school resources across neighborhoods) and cultural biases (teacher expectations, curricular bias). Soon afterwards, the notion of resistance (Willis 1977; MacLeod 1987) served to round out this argument by noting that working-class children had few aspirations for schooling in the first place and discounted themselves from educational competitions, sometimes in ways that could be interpreted as signaling a type of social protest. The study of school organizations was similarly reoriented by new institutional theory, which saw schools as legitimacy-seeking organizations, not efficiency-seeking organizations, in which loose coupling and isomorphism created increasingly standardized school organizations, first domestically and then internationally. The signaling function of credentials was similarly identified as a key process by which education connected to labor markets, challenging the human capital view. Daniel Bell's work highlighted ideas about knowledge and schooling, while Willis and Macleod's studies became staples in various analyses of cultures and subcultures.

Overall, the 1970s bore real fruit for educational theorizing of all varieties. The shift from an industrial to a knowledge economy, combined with the political turbulence of the 1960s, generated an array of theses about the current and future relationships between schools and society. These had profound impact not only on the sociology of education, but also on sociology as a whole: they provided key ideas to connect the study of education to broader thinking about stratification, organization, and culture. But what has happened in the sociology of education since?

We offer a detailed empirical answer to that question in the pages that follow. But to summarize in broad strokes: the quantitative methodological individualism that characterizes both the Coleman report and the status attainment tradition became the staple orientation for the field, a shift consistent with the broader turn towards quantitative methods and large-scale data sets in the social sciences. Substantively, the focus on reproduction and its mechanisms became the orienting question for the field; both quantitative and qualitative work has elaborated and further specified these patterns and the mechanisms which sustain them. A smaller body of work has built on New Institutional theory, with major currents applying it to World Culture theory, microlevel analysis (Inhabited Institutions), and to new private educational organizations. Perhaps surprisingly, Collins has not generated his own empirical branches. There has been little work advancing the themes of Bell or charting the evolution of schooling as a whole. Perhaps most consequential, there has been scant new theorizing. Many older theories have been operationalized, but very few new theories have been created.

Taking Stock: Sociology of Education over the Past Fifty Years

In this section, we explore the evolution of the sociology of education over the past fifty years. We do this in two very different ways. First, we conduct an empirical analysis of four of the major sites of American sociological research as conducted by scholars in American sociology departments: *Sociology of Education, American Journal of Sociology, American Sociological Review,* and the *Annual Review of Sociology*. Second, we consider more broadly the range of sociological writing on education over the period. From this view, there are at least five sociologies of education that have developed niches in different corners of the academic ecology. We suggest that more conversation across these strands would be intellectually generative; we also note that there are critical questions that are not addressed by any of them.

Sociology of Education: *A Content Analysis*

One way to explore how the sociological mind has taken up educational questions is to examine the major sociological journals over time. We begin with the discipline's flagship journal, *Sociology of Education*. We conducted two kinds of analyses. First, we examined all of the issues every fifth year, beginning in 1950 and continuing to 2010. We had two research assistants, Kyle Siler and Stefan Beljean, code these articles on a number of dimensions. Specifically, we recorded whether the articles were quantitative, qualitative, mixed-method, or essays, as a way of viewing the methodological bent of the field. We also used Steven Brint's (2013) categories for different topics to investigate whether his conclusions about the distribution of subjects in *Sociology of Education* would hold up over a longer period. Second, we used a citation analysis method to see which articles were the top-cited pieces in the journal each decade.

Sociology of Education *until 1963*

It is important to realize that what is now the *Sociology of Education* journal was until 1963 *The Journal of Educational Sociology: A Magazine of Theory and Practice*, a general-interest magazine published by New York University's Educational Sociology Program.[2] Some of the pieces in our sample between 1950 and 1960 were written by people who were not scholars, including pieces by undergraduates, chaplains, consultants, and members of labor unions. The topics were highly varied, including pieces on "what athletics means to me," "literature and human relations," and "popular hero symbols and audience gratification," as well as more familiar sociological topics such as "The Structure of Role and Role Conflicts in Teaching Situations." The modal method was the essay: of the 109 articles in our sample between 1950 and 1960, 79 percent were essays, 11 percent were qualitative, and 10 percent were quantitative.

As a whole, this period reflects a vision of the journal that was less academically professionalized and thus much more diverse in both topic and method. In contrast, in the articles we examined after 1963, only 13 of 187 samples articles were essays (7 percent); of 120 articles since 1980, only 1 was an essay. There also has not been a single article since 1965 which lists its author as anything other than a professor, lecturer, or graduate student at a university.[3]

Sociology of Education *since 1963*

In 1963, the journal was transferred to the American Sociological Association and renamed *Sociology of Education*. We coded the post-1963 articles using the Brint (2013: 9) codes. Brint uses the following categories: (1) inequality; (2) "non-structural" sources of achievement; (3) culture/ideology; (4) school effects; (5) state/politics; (6) labor market/labor market transitions; (7) comparative historical; and (8) methods. Brint distinguishes between major sources of inequality in American society (i.e., class, race, immigration status, and gender) and "non-structural" sources of achievement for social structures and behaviors that vary within this wide strata (such as effects of work effort or obesity on achievement). Culture/ideology includes articles on how culture influences schools as well as how schools influence culture. To this group we added one category, "professional culture," which captures how professional norms affect practice.

The patterns we found from 1965 to 2010 are very similar to those Brint observed in a more recent sample between 1999 and 2008. In our larger sample, 43 of the articles were on inequality (23 percent), 35 on nonstructural sources of achievement (19 percent); 28 on culture/ideology (15 percent); 23 on labor market mechanisms (12 percent), and 18 on school effects (10 percent). Less featured topics included 10 on professional culture (5 percent), 8 that were comparative/historical (4 percent), and 4 on states/politics (2 percent). Of the articles that could be clearly coded by level of education addressed, 147 were about primary and secondary education (91 percent) and 15 were on postsecondary education (9 percent). Reflecting the quantitative orientation of the post-1963 field, 154 of these later articles were quantitative, 19 were qualitative, 13 were essays, and 1 was mixed methods.

Table 1.1 compares our results to Brint's. These results suggest that his recent observations reflect much longer-standing patterns in *Sociology of Education*. Since 1965, publications in the journal have been largely quantitative and have focused on primary and secondary education. The key questions that have occupied the minds of sociologists of education are the major axes of stratification: both structural causes and more proximate features which affect achievement. Conversely, questions of politics, states, history, and comparative work have been much less prevalent.

Turning to citation counts, Table 1.2 presents the ten most-cited articles

Table 1.1 Sociology of education, distribution of topics

Sociology of Education, distribution of topics	1965–2010 (our coding) (%)	1999–2008 (Brint 2013 coding) (%)
Method		
Quantitative	89	82
Qualitative	11	18
Level		
Primary and secondary	91	78
Postsecondary	9	22
Topic/dimension[1]		
Inequality and schools	23	25
Nonstructural sources of achievement	19	17
Culture/ideology	15	16
Labor market mechanisms	12	7
School effects	10	20
Professional culture	5	N/A[2]
Comparative historical	4	10
State/politics	2	5

[1] The remaining 10 percent were distributed across a range of topics.
[2] Brint did not have a category for professional culture in his coding.

in *Sociology of Education* by decade. In the late 1950s and 1960s, the most referenced was Turner's famous argument about sponsored versus contest mobility, suggesting the importance of broad theory at the time. We can also see the influence of large-scale community studies of schools, such as Hollingshead's *Elmstown's Youth* (2) and Coleman's *Adolescent Society* (5), as well as synthetic, integrative works like W. Lloyd Warner et al.'s *Who Shall be Educated?* (4). Before the creation of large-scale national data sets, these were some of the most well-known sociological works, as indicated in the rankings. Philip Jacobs' synthetic book on how colleges shape the attitudes and values of their students (3), and Samuel Stouffer's book reporting on surveys of attitudes toward communism and civil liberties (6) also make the list. Making an appearance towards the bottom of the top ten are two of William Sewell's early status attainment studies, indicating the initial influence of that paradigm. Five of the top six are books, all of which were aimed at a broad public audience, a stark difference from the more focused scholarly discourse which would follow.

In contrast, citation counts from the 1970s were dominated by quantitative research on the impact of schools as well as the status attainment

Table 1.2

Top ten cited articles, by decade, in *Sociology of Education*

1956–69			1970–79		
R. Turner	"Sponsored and Contest Mobility," *ASR* (1960)	9	J. Coleman	*Equality of Educational Opportunity* (1966)	35
A. B. Hollingshead	*Elmstown's Youth* (1949)	8	P. Blau and O. D. Duncan	*American Occupational Structure* (1967)	25
P. Jacob	*Changing Values in College* (1957)	7	C. Jencks et al.	*Inequality: A Reassessment* (1972)	17
W. L. Warner	*Who Shall Be Educated? The Challenge of Unequal Opportunities* (1944)	7	W. Sewell	"Ed. and Early Occupational Status Attainment: Replications and Revisions," *ASR* (1970)	17
J. Coleman	*Adolescent Society* (1961)	6	J. Coleman	*Adolescent Society* (1961)	17
S. Stouffer	*Communism, Conformity & Civil Liberties* (1955)	5	W. Sewell	"Ed. and Early Occupational Status Attainment," *ASR* (1969)	16
C. Anderson	"Skeptical Note on Vert. Mobility," *AJS* (1961)	5	K. Feldman and T. Newcomb	*The Impact of College on Students* (1969)	16
W. Sewell and V. Shah	"SES, Intelligence and Attainment of Higher Ed," *Soc of Ed* (1967)	4	O. D. Duncan	"Path Analysis: Sociological Examples," *AJS* (1966)	15
W. Sewell	"Neighborhood Context & College Plans," *ASR* (1966)	4	R. K. Merton	*Social Theory and Social Structure* (1957)	14
B. Eckland	"Acad. Ability, Higher Ed & Occ. Mobility," *ASR* (1965)	4	R. Rosenthal and L. Jacobson	"Pygmalion in the Classroom," *Urban Review* (1968)	13
1980–89			**1990–99**		
S. Bowles and H. Gintis	*Schooling in Capitalist America* (1976)	30	S. Bowles and H. Gintis	*Schooling in Capitalist America* (1976)	25
J. Coleman	*Equality of Educational Opportunity* (1966)	28	J. Oakes	*Keeping Track: How Schools Structure Inequality* (1985)	24
J. Coleman, T. Hoffer, and S. Kilgore	*High School Achievement: Public, Catholic & Private Schools Compared* (1982)	25	J. Coleman	*Equality of Educational Opportunity* (1966)	20
K. Alexander et al.	"Curriculum Tracking and Ed. Strat.," *ASR* (1978)	23	P. Blau and O. D. Duncan	*American Occupational Structure* (1967)	19

P. Blau and O. D. Duncan	*American Occupational Structure* (1967)	22	J. Coleman, T. Hoffer, and S. Kilgore	*High School Achievement: Public, Catholic & Private Schools Compared* (1982)	16
B. Heyns	"Social Selection and Strat. within Schools," *AJS* (1974)	18	A. Bryk and S. Raudenbush	*Hierarchical Linear Models* (1992)	15
C. Jencks et al.	*Inequality: A Reassessment* (1972)	18	A. Gamoran	"The Stratification of H.S. Learning Opportunities," *Soc. of Ed.* (1987)	15
P. Bourdieu and J. Passeron	*Reproduction in Education, Society and Culture* (1977)	16	P. Bourdieu and J. Passeron	*Reproduction in Education, Society and Culture* (1977)	13
J. Rosenbaum	*Making Inequality: The Hidden Curriculum of H.S. Tracking* (1976)	16	R. Collins	*The Credential Society* (1979)	13
K. Alexander and E. McDill	"Selection & Allocation: Causes and Consequences of Curr. Placement," *ASR* (1976)	16	D. Featherman and R. Hauser	*Opportunity and Change* (1978)	12
	2000–2009				
A. Lareau and E. Horvat	"Inclusion and Exclusion: Race, Class and Cultural Capital in Family-School Relationships," *Social Problems* (1999)	17			
P. Blau and O. D. Duncan	*American Occupational Structure* (1967)	17			
J. Ainsworth-Darnell & D. Downey	"Assessing Oppositional Culture," *ASR* (1998)	16			
J. Coleman	*Equality of Educational Opportunity* (1966)	14			
A. Bryk et al.	*Catholic Schools and the Common Good* (1993)	14			
J. Oakes	*Keeping Track: How Schools Structure Inequality* (1985)	13			
S. Fordham and J. Ogbu	"Black Students' School Success: Coping with the Burden of 'Acting White,'" *Urban Review* (1986)	12			
J. Coleman	*Adolescent Society* (1961)	11			
A. Bryk and S. Raudenbush	*Hierarchical Linear Models* (1992)	11			
J. Hearn	"Academic & Nonacademic Influences on College Destinations," *Soc. of Ed.* (1991)	11			

tradition. The Coleman report (1) was the most cited piece; Jencks et al.'s *Inequality* study was also highly cited (3); and familiar status attainment authors Blau (2), Sewell (4 & 6), and Duncan (8) assumed prominent places in the rankings. *The Adolescent Society* (5) continued to be the most prominent work from outside the school-effects and status attainment traditions; it was joined by Feldman and Newcomb's (7) integrative book on the impact of college on students, Merton's (9) classic book on social theory and social structure, and Rosenthal and Jacobson's (10) famous Pygmalion study about the power of academic expectations.

The 1980s citation counts are more varied. Theory is important: the most cited work is Bowles and Gintis's *Schooling in Capitalist America* (1); Bourdieu and Passeron's *Reproduction of Education in Society* (8) also appears on the list. However, as Olneck (2012) and others have noted, much of this work in the sociology of education has operationalized Bourdieu's theory with variables for cultural capital, which means that while theory is cited, it is not being taken up in its fullest form. Tracking and curriculum placement were also increasingly of interest to sociologists of education, as no fewer than four of the works on the list—Alexander (4 and 10), Heyns (6), and Rosenbaum (9)—take up this issue. Coleman, Hoffer, and Kilgore's study comparing public, Catholic, and private schools (3) is also highly cited, and we can see the continuing influence of the Coleman report (2) and Jencks et al.'s work on *Inequality* (7).

The 1990s citation counts again reflect a mixed picture. Theory is again well represented, with Bowles and Gintis (1), Bourdieu (8), and Collins's *Credential Society* (9) making the top ten. Status attainment and school effects continue to be a concern for the field, with the Coleman report (3), Blau and Duncan (4), Coleman's work on Catholic schools (5), and Featherman and Hauser (10). Tracking continues to be a focus, as indicated by the placement of Oakes' *Keeping Track* (2) and Gamoran's quantitative examination of the distribution of learning opportunites (7). We also see the first methodological work on the list, Bryk and Raudenbaush's *Hierarchical Linear Models*, reflecting sociologists' increasing interest in disentangling the effects of different levels of schooling on academic outcomes.

The period from 2000 to 2010 revisits many long-standing topics and opens up some new ones. In the most cited work, Lareau and Horvat build on Bourdieu's work (and preview Lareau's later work) by offering a qualitative case study of the intersection of cultural capital, race, class, and schools' receptivity to parents' claims. (We do not present the results from 2010 to 2015 because the sample is small, but Lareau's *Unequal Childhoods* is at the top of that list.) We also see two pieces developing and then disputing the oppositional culture hypothesis, Fordham and Ogbu (7) and Ainsworth-Darnell and Downey (3). There is also the continuing influence of old favorites Blau and Duncan (2), the Coleman report (4), Oakes on tracking (5), Coleman's *Adolescent Society* (8), and Bryk and Raudenbush's work on HLM (9). Bryk et al.'s book on Catholic schools (5) is also highly cited.

Overall, the work published in *Sociology of Education* over the past fifty years is broadly consistent with what we might expect, but there are some exceptions. The vast majority of the research has been quantitative and focused on K–12 schooling. Status attainment and the Coleman report have been the two largest influences on the field. These conclusions are consistent with Brint's analysis of *Sociology of Education* between 1999 and 2008, and show that similar dynamics have governed the journal since the 1960s. At the same time, theorists like Bourdieu, Collins, and, more recently, Lareau, are consistently among the most-cited pieces. While, as Olneck (2012) points out, many of these citations occur in pieces which operationalize variables quantitatively in ways that may not be fully consistent with the original theories, their prevalence does suggest that these theorists are continuing to influence the field. The citations on tracking and oppositional culture indicate that the field at times becomes focused on particular debates, which generate widely referenced articles. Thus while school effects and status attainment are the most prominent strands, theory and substantive debates on specific issues do continue to play a role. The evidence suggests that the field is less monolithic than it appears, and that if new theory or different substantive debates were created, they could play an important role in the discipline.

Annual Review of Sociology, American Sociological Review, *and* American Journal of Sociology

We also explored how the sociology of education was represented in sociology as a whole—specifically in the *Annual Review of Sociology*, the *American Sociological Review*, and the *American Journal of Sociology*. This analysis enables us to see which parts of the subfields have been elevated to become part of broader sociological debates and arguments.

The *Annual Review of Sociology* is an invitation-only publication that asks selected scholars to review areas of the discipline. It began publication in 1975. We had our research assistant, Stefan Beljean, conduct a search using the word "education" in either title, abstract, or keyword. We then read these articles and excluded ones that related only tangentially to education. In total, we found twenty-three articles focused on education in the *ARS* from

1975 to June of 2015. We coded these with the Brint codes. Because they were review essays, many of them touched on multiple topics, and thus our totals do not add up to twenty-three.

We found that nineteen of the twenty-three were about inequality in schooling, showing the overwhelming interest in processes of stratification by scholars in the sociology of education and in the broader discipline. These included many of the major structural dimensions of stratification in society, including race, gender, class, and immigration status. Five of the reviews contained discussions of school effects, frequently in the context of the roles schools play in larger processes of social reproduction. Of the pieces focused less directly on inequality, one reviewed the Meyer/world-systems perspective; one on higher education by Stevens, Armstrong, and Arum considered the different roles institutions of higher education play in society; one focused on school reform; and one described the social and economic returns from college attendance. Judging by the *ARS*, the contribution that the sociology of education has made to the broader literature centers almost exclusively on the roles that schools play in processes of social reproduction.

We also coded all articles from 1950 to June 2015 that mention education in the *American Journal of Sociology* (*AJS*)) and the *American Sociological Review* (*ASR*). *AJS* yielded 59 articles. Of these, 52 were quantitative, 4 were qualitative, 1 was mixed-methods, and 4 were essays (several using quantitative or qualitative data). This result reflects the quantitative orientation of the broader field of sociology as well as of the sociology of education. Topically, 16 articles were about inequality in schools (27 percent), 14 were about the connection between schools and the labor market (24 percent), 11 were about group processes in schools (19 percent), and 10 were about school effects (17 percent). All of these topics are roughly consistent with the sociology of education field as a whole. Topics which made fewer appearances included 5 on culture and ideology (8 percent), 5 on comparative education (8 percent), and 5 on states and politics (8 percent).

A similar picture emerges from *American Sociological Review*. In *ASR* there were 117 articles on education between 1950 and June 2015. Of these, 103 were quantitative (88 percent), 8 were qualitative (7 percent), 11 were essays, and 2 were mixed methods.[4] Topically, 59 were on schooling and inequality (50 percent), and 26 were on school effects (22 percent), showing again the dominance of those two topics in the sociology of education. Less prominent categories included 18 that were comparative and historical (15 percent), 17 on culture or ideology (14 percent), 15 on labor market mechanisms (13 percent), 13 on nonstructural sources of inequality (11 percent),

9 on group processes (8 percent), and 8 on family structure (7 percent). Taken together, the findings in *AJS* and *ASR* suggest that the distribution of topics in the broader disciplinary journals parallels those in the subdiscipline.

Overall, if we compare the sociology of education as practiced in America today to where it was in 1960, we see that it has taken a quantum leap forward both as a subfield and in winning a place in the broader discipline. By embracing quantitative methods, using large-scale data sets, asking questions compatible with broad notions of reformist liberalism, and developing increasingly refined knowledge about the roles that schools play in social reproduction and mobility, the field has developed an identity, a cumulative knowledge base, and a solid place within sociology (see also Bills, DeLuca, and Morgan 2013). But it has also done these things at the expense of other topics and approaches, reifying a small number of theories, questions, and research methods as central to the sociology of education enterprise. It also has missed opportunities to connect to sociologies of education that have emerged in other sectors of the scholarly ecology. We turn to these next.

A Broader View: Five Sociologies of Education

While from the point of view of publication in American sociological journals, the sociology of education has been focused on status attainment, school effects, and a few other topics, that is not the only way to see the field. In the section that follows, we delineate five different "sociologies of education" that have emerged over the past fifty years: (1) the status attainment and social reproduction traditions, (2) an organizationally oriented sociology of education focused on school and policy improvement, (3) a critical sociology of education, (4) a sociology of higher education, and (5) the new institutionalist view of sociology of education (see table 1.3). Building on Frickel and Gross's (2005) view of the basis of intellectual movements, we suggest that each of these strands has been able to develop a set of core capabilities which have sustained its work, including an intellectual community, organizational resources, prominent scholars, a core technology for doing the work, and a constituency that is interested in what is being produced. If the previous picture suggested a heavy focus on one topic, this view suggests a much more pluralistic ecology, with different strands seeking out different niches in the intellectual landscape.

It is important to note that our goal here is to be illustrative and not exhaustive. We chose these five because they take up a range of issues, use a

Table 1.3 Five sociologies of education

	Intellectual community	Key journal	Prominent scholars	Resources	Core intellectual technology	Academic audience	Nonacademic audience
Status attainment & social reproduction	American Sociological Association	*Sociology of Education*	Coleman, Jencks, Blau & Duncan, Hauser, Lareau	NSF, Russell Sage	Regressions, path models	Sociologists in sociology departments	Policymakers
School improvement	American Educational Research Association	*American Educational Research Journal*	Bryk, Darling-Hammond, Elmore, Noguera, Schneider	IES, Gates, Spencer, Carnegie	Evaluation methods, case studies of schools, mechanisms	Education school scholars	Policymakers, practitioners
Critical sociology	International Sociology of Education Conference	*British Journal of Sociology of Education*	Giroux, Apple, Freire, McLaren	X	Interpretation, critical discourse	Critical scholars across fields	Radical actors, unions abroad
Higher education[1]	Association for Study of Higher Education	*Journal of Higher Education*, books	Kerr, Clark, Geiger, Gumport, Trow, Bok	Lumina, Gates, Teagle	Case studies, organizational histories of universities	Sociologists, education schools, business schools	Public audience, university administrators
New institutionalism	American Sociological Association	*American Journal of Sociology*	Meyer, Ramirez, Powell, DiMaggio	X	Theory, macro studies of political development	Sociologists in sociology departments	X

[1]This chart represents only strands of research on higher education that focus on the evolving broad public priorities of universities. A more complete discussion of the different strands within the study of higher education can be found in the text.

range of methodological and even epistemological approaches, and have emerged from varied university contexts that support and shape the sociology of education. There are others one could have picked, such as the sociology of school knowledge or the sociology of school life. Our intent is not to offer a comprehensive catalogue, but rather to illustrate how different sociologies of education have cornered different parts of the intellectual market. This review also points to the fragmentation of the field; we see newly formed "traditions" that have developed successful niches but see limited dialogue across them.

One: Status Attainment and Social Reproduction

As described above, the first sociology of education is the one most heavily practiced in American sociology departments and most frequently published in leading American sociological journals. It is primarily quantitative, primarily focused on K–12 education, and primarily interested in explaining the factors that predict educational attainment and achievement. Work over time has explored these questions in terms of both structural bases of inequality (race, gender, class, wealth) and more proximate factors which influence the allocation of educational opportunities (tracking, aspirations, parenting strategies).

This work has many of the needed features to become a successful intellectual movement. Technologically, the availability of large-scale data that included both background factors and student achievement, as well as the increasing number of longitudinal surveys of students, combined with the seismic advances in computing power that began in the 1960s, created the factors necessary to enable the work. The increasing quantitative sophistication of the methods was consistent with the broader quantitative turn in the social sciences, which helped secure legitimacy for the field and sociological employment for its practitioners. The status attainment work gave the sociology of education a significant place in the larger field's work on social stratification. In seeking to explain the gaps in test scores or rates of college attendance, the research also spoke to mainstream policymakers. Over time, its leading practitioners became key gatekeepers through their functions as reviewers, journal editors, and members of hiring committees for faculty positions. Thus it is not surprising that this strand of scholarship has had such a sustained run as the dominant form of the sociology of education in sociology departments.

There is also parallel qualitative research which investigates similar questions. Well-known works such as Willis (1977), MacLeod (1987), Fordham (1996), Carter (2005), Tyson (2011), and Paulle (2013) extend earlier literature on student subcultures, exploring—and mostly disputing—the idea that poor and minority students have developed an oppositional culture, and providing a textured examination of how disadvantaged students form their identities in highly stratified societies. Work by Annette Lareau (2003) builds on earlier studies by Bourdieu and Melvin Kohn to show in detail how different class habitus produces different approaches to child-rearing and socialization. Work by Ferguson (2000) and others shows how race shapes the ways in which schools interpret minority students' actions, label students, and shape their trajectories. While much of this work is published in books rather than articles, and thus is less represented in the journal counts shown above, there is a thriving qualitative strand in the sociology of education that explores the school and societal forces that create cycles of social reproduction.

Two: Sociology of School Improvement

Largely invisible from the point of view of American sociology departments, a second sociology of education focused on school improvement has become a thriving area of research in American education schools. The key questions here are about efficacy—what policies or school-level factors enable students to achieve academic success? Methodologically, this strand includes quantitative program evaluation (for example, of particular reading programs or particular charter schools), and qualitative studies that explore the mechanisms that underlie policy interventions or factors that lead to effective schools or classrooms. Because education is a field and not a discipline, these studies are conducted by scholars from a range of disciplines, but sociologists such as Pedro Noguera, Anthony Bryk, James Spillane, and Linda Darling-Hammond are prominently represented.

This sociology of education is heavily shaped by the context in which it is produced. Education schools differ from sociology departments in a number of respects, perhaps the most important of which are that (1) as professional schools, they are expected to speak to the field as well as to the variety of disciplines they house; (2) they admit, teach, and graduate many students who have been in, or are entering, the field; and 3) "clinical" faculty and students oriented towards questions of practice coexist with colleagues engaged in scholarship and research as more traditionally defined in the university context. Collectively, these facts imply that while the strand of the sociology of education under discussion here needs to connect to the imperatives of general knowledge production, it also needs to be actionable by people who are entering policy and practice roles.

The sociology of school improvement has a number of advantages as an intellectual movement. Normatively, as is true of the status attainment paradigm, it conforms to mainstream equal-opportunity liberalism; it presupposes that with the right set of policy and practices in place, schools can change the trajectories of many children (particularly poor and minority children). By virtue of being more applied than status attainment work, it has a wider audience among policymakers, who seek concrete levers they can pull to yield results. The obvious efficacy of this work also means that there has been significant funding available from both the federal government and private foundations. The research is published in the *American Educational Research Journal*, as well as in a variety of other journals interested in educational outcomes, and is the central focus at the main professional association conferences, such as the American Educational Research Association and the Society for Research on Educational Effectiveness.

The conception of this enterprise, coupled with well-suited technologies, has helped to build the cumulative knowledge base needed by any normal science. In a highly decentralized system with an endless appetite for school improvement, there is never a shortage of programs, initiatives, or new educational approaches to evaluate. Every graduate student who wants to do a case study can find a local school that is willing to host it; almost every university has a teacher-training program that can be explored; every district or state has policies and programs that can be evaluated. Each of the explorations is likely to yield results both similar to, and moderately different from, prior findings enabling researchers to integrate their work with previous studies while also making a claim to differentiation. The methods that one needs to conduct these studies—econometric methods, interviews, case studies, causal inference—are widely taught in graduate school. The result is a thriving enterprise that has all the ingredients it needs to succeed as an intellectual field.

As scholars in an interdisciplinary field, sociologists need to claim a place in a professional context which also includes large numbers of economists and psychologists, and a smaller number of political scientists and cognitive scientists. The applied nature of the field makes it conducive to work in these other disciplines, particularly economics, which has a part of the discipline which is particularly interested in creating strong identification strategies for estimating causal effects and is comparatively less interested in developing theory. Walters (2009) has shown how the larger ecology surrounding school improvement research has shifted towards randomized control trials, which also tend to privilege those studying policy or lab experiments. Economics and psychology are also higher-status disciplines in the broader academy, a ranking which empowers them to set standards for education schools, particularly for leading schools in research universities. Finally, to the degree that these schools hope to affect policy, the blunt levers available to policymakers—sticks and carrots—are a good fit with economic models that emphasize incentives and consequences.

At the same time, sociologists have a number of advantages in studying schools. Foremost among them is the reality that many of the factors that are most important for creating successful schools are fundamentally social: trust, culture, social capital, and coherent organizational design. As a consequence, many of the highly recognized theories have been offered by sociologists (Bryk and Schneider 2002; Bryk et al. 2010; Coleman 1988). At the level of policy, research suggests that policies designed top-down frequently fail to influence teaching practice; this reality brings to the fore sociological lenses on organizational loose coupling, practitioner sense-making, and street-level bureaucracy (Tyack and Cuban 1995; Bidwell 1965; Weick 1976; Coburn 2004;, Lipsky 1980; Cohen 1990). Work from the sociology of the professions has depicted teaching as an act of skill and judgment uneasily situated within a bureaucratic structure ill-suited to developing skillful practice (Lortie 1975, Mehta 2013, 2014). Research on professional learning communities has shown the ways in which intentional collaborative structures can overcome some of the isolation that classic theories have depicted as shaping teachers' work (Johnson 1990; McLaughlin and Talbert 2001; Bryk et al. 2010). Studies of social systems have suggested the importance of building an educational infrastructure that would counter many of the weaknesses in the field (Cohen and Moffitt 2009; Cohen 2011). Much of this research continues to link the struggles of schools to the social contexts in which they sit, showing the ways in which poverty and segregation stymie efforts at school improvement (Noguera 2003; Orfield and Eaton 1996). Tracking is another prominent subject which has been explored by both sociology departments and education schools (Oakes 1985). All of these studies support Stokes' (1995) observation that applied research and theory-generating research can be conjoined; perhaps because of their interest in theory, sociologists are particularly well-positioned among education school scholars to create this link.[5]

Stepping back, there is a nice complementarity between the sociology of school improvement and the status attainment tradition. Status attainment research is frequently faulted for treating schools like "black boxes," ignoring politics, policy, history, and context. Education school research on school improvement, by comparison, is much more institutional in its approach, foregrounding what actually happens in schools, evaluating the impact of particular policies and programs, and developing a richer and more historically grounded vision of the nature of American schooling (Tyack 1974; Tyack and Cuban 1995; Powell, Farrar, and Cohen 1985). Conversely, this research is less focused on patterns of intergenerational mobility and the relative weight of schools compared to other components of the welfare state; that area of study is the strength of the sociological research conducted in sociology departments. At the same time, perhaps precisely because both status attainment and school improvement strands are in their own ways compatible with a gently reformist vision of schools shared by many policymakers and the public, they privilege certain questions while ignoring others that are incompatible with their orientation. Which brings us to the critical research tradition, described next.

Three: Critical Sociology of Education

A third sociology of education is represented by the critical tradition. Dominated by figures like Michael Apple, Henry Giroux, Paulo Freire and others, each of whom can claim thousands of citations,[6] this school parallels the mainstream's focus on inequality, but does so in a very different voice.

This school was founded on a trinity of writings from the 1970s. Bowles and Gintis (1976) adapted structural Marxism to implicate schooling in the rule of capitalism, identifying it as a producer of ideological hegemony, docile workers, and unequal outcomes. At almost the same time, Paul Willis (1977) adapted the then new field of cultural Marxism to champion the hidden "resistance" of working-class youth. And Paulo Freire (1970) critiqued teacher practices that aimed merely to "bank" knowledge and called for a new liberating pedagogy. Together, these three themes provided the original critical trademark: schools "reproduced" inequality, which students sometimes "penetrated" or "resisted" and which could be challenged by a new "critical pedagogy." These themes coalesced into a self-identified "critical theory" of education in a series of well-known 1980s texts (e.g., Apple, 1979; Giroux 1983; Giroux and McLaren 1989). But this theory quickly evolved through the 1990s. Its empirical focus on class was soon widened to include gender, race, sexuality, and their intersections. Its neo-Marxist sensibility was broadened to include feminist, antiracist, queer, postcolonial, postmodern, and poststructural inflections. These developments increasingly steered the camp away from mainstream empirical research and toward metatheorizing and political critique. Importantly, critical theorists have combined critiques of educational inequality with strong condemnations of the major reforms that have emerged since the 1980s, including accountability regimes, high-stakes testing, school choice, and standards movements, portraying them as neoliberal ploys that deepen race and gender inequality, create ever more oppressive and less humanistic forms of education, and obscure the fundamentally public nature of schooling. They have criticized economistic language and metrics as veils for efforts to privatize and commodify learning while privileging Western colonialization, whiteness, and heteronormativity (e.g., Spring 2000).

Importantly, this evolution has served to increasingly separate critical sociology of education from the mainstream. The founders did connect to sociological discourse in several respects. Bowles and Gintis's reproduction theory was forged in dialogue with functionalism, human capital theory, status attainment research, and empirical studies on linguistic codes (Bernstein), labeling (Rist), and orientations to work (Kohn). Willis drew on a lengthy tradition of youth subculture studies (Coleman, Cohen, Stinchcombe, Downes) to reinterpret student responses as "resistance." The "new sociology of education" (see Karabel and Halsey, 1977) was used by Geoff Whitty and Michael Apple to implicate the curricula in the capitalist order. Thus, while sociology of education in the 1970s surely had different camps, as Karabel and Halsey's famous review attested, they did so in common arenas, knew each other's positions, and battled within the same journals, presses, departments, and meetings.

But the past thirty years have seen less and less communication between the camps. The critical pantheon—Giroux, Apple, Friere, and McLaren—is rarely cited in *Sociology of Education* or any other mainstream journal. Leading US sociology departments do not regard the strand as offering viable research options. In turn, major critical writings frequently do not refer to mainstream empirical studies, even in comprehensive international handbooks (e.g., Apple, Ball, and Gandin 2010), or official journals like *British Journal of the Sociology of Education*. And, when they do refer to the mainstream, they often portray it as complicit with domination and oppression.[7]

What accounts for this separatism? We see two important changes in the ecology of academia since the 1970s that set critical sociology of education on its own trajectory. The first was the creation of new units that compete for resources with established disciplines and specialist policy-oriented and applied fields (Jacobs 2013). Mainly beginning in the 1980s, a new array of what we call "studies" units was founded, including media studies, cultural studies, women's studies, and African-American studies. In many respects, these fields reflect the penetration of academic logics by those from states and social movements, as both activists and government officials encouraged the creation of programs that might give voice to underrepresented populations such as African Americans and indigenous peoples. What is important for our purposes is the relation of these fields to established disciplines. They sought to be interdisciplinary, multidisciplinary, transdisciplinary, and sometimes postdisciplinary. Unlike natural science units that merge disciplines (such as biochemistry), comparable units in the social sciences and humanities mostly eschewed established discipline-based knowledge in favor of alternate forms of theory and method.

Being newcomers in social science and humanities faculties, these fields needed to find distinct niches. In some places, simply working as interdisciplinary hubs was sufficient, and these departments, especially at leading research universities, hired scholars from the established disciplines. But at other universities, these fields not only sought to become topically distinct; they sought to establish a methodologically and even ontologically distinct stance. Frequently drawing more from the humanities than from the social sciences, these studies units featured large amounts of critical theory as well as antipositivist and postpositivist stances toward inquiry.

Importantly, critical sociology of education has been greatly influenced by these "postdiscipline" units. Even though the first generation was partly inspired by Bowles and Gintis (who strove to be empirically grounded) and some other mainstream sociologists of education, several threads were hostile to empirical sociology. Willis's Birmingham School of Cultural Studies rejected mainstream sociology in favor of emerging literary approaches. Freire was a lawyer and philosopher, not a social scientist. Giroux, positioning himself as a humanist rather than a social scientist, faulted many luminaries, even Marx himself, for their "positivist" inclinations. After the 1980s, these threads led critical sociology of education towards "critical theory." Critical theory is rooted in the humanities, oriented towards metatheoretical discourse about knowledge and/or the political identity of the theorist or the population under consideration. Whereas "sociological theory" (as found in *Sociological Theory* or *Theory and Society*) aims to combine conceptual thinking with the synthesis of empirical data and in some versions prizes the creation of hypotheses that can be tested by empirical research, critical theory gets its legitimacy by combining philosophical argument with political or social critique. Critical sociologists have adapted critical theory to the educational realm and in so doing have created a new brand of educational theory.

Critical sociologists have similarly eschewed the mainstream's concern with empirical technique. Since Bowles and Gintis, they have largely abandoned quantitative approaches in favor of certain qualitative approaches. Importantly, those approaches are distinguished more by their political framing than by their technique, as exemplified by the "critical ethnography" tradition (for examples, see Madison 2011). Even though these alternative methods have been sharply criticized for lacking rigor from the standpoint of traditional social science standards (e.g., NSF, AERA), they are widely practiced in some "studies" units and among some education faculties. Thus, by combining critical theory and alternate methods, critical sociology of education no longer attempts to compete with mainstream, empirically oriented explanations, and instead has pursued a different path marked by reflexivity, self-positioning, and critique of school reforms.

As a result, the orientation of critical scholars disqualifies them from publishing in mainstream outlets like *Sociology of Education* or gaining positions in leading sociology departments. In turn, the critical camp has established its own outlets and hiring venues. Established journals like *Teachers College Record* and the *Harvard Education Review* now accept critical articles, and newer journals have been established, such as *Discourse* and *Critical Studies in Education*. While renowned university presses may not publish critical treatises, presses like Routledge and Peter Lang have filled that void. Importantly, some education schools also hire large numbers of critical scholars. Thus, these scholars have created their own professional norms, outlets, and gatekeeping practices. Mainstreamers, including one of the authors of this introduction, may criticize their writing for its abstraction, jargon, overpoliticization, and lack of empirical grounding (e.g., Davies 1995; Sadovnik 2007), but critical scholars can ignore their views, since they are irrelevant and alien to their own postdisciplinary, antipositivist milieu.

A second ecological change in the university has been the growth of semiprofessional training. Fields like education, social work, and other social services have expanded their graduate programs, producing more and more MEds, EdDs, MSWs, and so on. Unlike classic professions, these semiprofessions combine societal welfare missions with highly uncertain status in the university. Importantly, they have yet to build knowledge bases that are firmly grounded in empirical science, as has medicine, or deep traditions of logic, as has law. This tension between strong public-service orientations and uncertain knowledge bases has served to bifurcate semiprofessional training into two distinct branches.

One branch is "technocratic," characterized by attempts to apply knowledge to address core issues of practice and policy. In education, this is exemplified by the school improvement camp described earlier in this chapter. A second branch, however, performs a far more symbolic or political role. This branch signals a field's commitment to its human service mission and its ability to speak to progressive causes. Scholars in this branch position themselves less as bearers of technical expertise and disciplined knowledge, and more as moral guardians, social trustees for the disadvantaged, and harbingers of new political stances (for this distinction, see Brint 1994).

In many respects, the symbolic and technocratic branches in any field are symbiotic. Semiprofessions can establish their value to the university by demonstrating their effectiveness, and also by portraying themselves as relevant and inspiring to society at large. Their technocrats can signal their commitment to pragmatism, incrementalism and utility; their symbolic branch can signal their commitment to broader ideals. Education as a field needs both branches because it combines a highly uncertain technology with a prominent position in society. School reform is incessant since educational ideals always outstrip educational realities (Labaree 2010). Yet practical disappointment seems only to fuel more idealized optimism. Just as Elmore and McLaughlin (1988) could proclaim school reform to be "steady work," criticism of schooling is also "steady work," reflecting a constant societal appetite for reimagining the possibilities of education. Just as technocrats "reform again and again" (Cuban 1990), the symbolic branch criticizes the assumptions that underlie mainstream reforms again and again.

Crucially, the critical camp has distinguished itself from both "technocrats" and discipline-based research by adapting its symbols to new idioms and populations. It has developed a distinct and prolific flair for developing state-of-the-art terminologies. Terms like "equity," "inclusion," "social justice," "racialization," "praxis" and "postcolonialism" each rapidly attained a broad currency in fields like education and social work, and, even when their precise meaning was unclear, some moved quickly from rarefied academic settings into widespread usage. This language is also particularly attractive to students, particularly students of color, LGBTQ students, and other minorities who feel that the mainstream incrementalism of the technocratic branch has been too silent on questions of institutionalized racism and other embedded inequalities of the system. For the university administrators, retaining both critical scholars and more mainstream school improvement researchers in professional schools enables them both to speak to policymakers and practitioners in concrete and scientific terms, and to meet the demands of students and other critics who are looking for the university to take a more critical stance towards the educational arena.

Four: Sociology of Higher Education

Particularly intriguing for this review is the sociology of higher education. The canonical reviews of the sociology of education (e.g., Karabel and Halsey 1977) ignore higher education almost entirely in favor of K–12 schooling. But the sociology of higher education is an especially useful window into the production of sociological knowledge about education because higher education shares some strands with K–12 but also features research about institutions, organizations, governance, professions, and the purposes of education which is much more developed than in the study of primary and secondary schooling.

To start with the similarities: the study of higher education has a number of direct parallels to the study of K–12. In particular, we see higher education research that is analogous to strands 1 and 2 described above. Similar to the study of social reproduction in primary and secondary schools, a large body of sociological work demonstrates how colleges perpetuate and reproduce inequalities of social background (see McDonough and Fann 2007 for a review). This research documents the ways in which the stratification of American higher education favors the privileged, points out the gaps by race and class in who goes to college and who graduates, and enumerates the ways in which the taken-for-granted logics of college admissions (Stevens 2007) and features of college organizational life (Armstrong and Hamilton 2013) favor those who enter with more economic, social, and cultural capital (Jack 2016). A complementary body of work shows how inequalities in primary and secondary schooling, as well as in guidance and college advising, structure college choices to the disadvantage of poor, minority, and first-generation college students (McDonough 1997). This research, which is consistent with the sociological discipline's concern with reproduction and stratification, is produced in sociology departments and some education schools, and is presented at ASA and AERA.

Parallel to the sociology of school improvement, a second strand of higher education research focuses directly on improving student outcomes in colleges and universities. This work, conducted primarily in education schools, explores how students' level of engagement and social integration, their course-taking patterns, and their choices of how to spend time and devote effort, as well as more structural features like university size and diversity, affect college persistence and other outcomes (e.g., Astin 1977; Light 2001). The research draws on sociological concepts (for example, Durkheim on social integration and anomie), but its primary purpose is to develop knowledge for the field rather than for sociological theory. There is also considerable research on financial aid, student employment, and other monetary factors important to student outcomes. As is true in the K–12 scholarship, this work complements some of the macrosociological studies in seeking to identify actionable means that university administrators can use to improve college outcomes (see Hurtado 2007 for a review).[8] Much of the research is presented at the Association for the Study of Higher Education conference (founded in 1976), a crossdisciplinary arena focused on higher-education issues in which sociological thinking is well represented, as well as at AERA.[9]

At the same time, what is intriguing about the sociology of higher education is that it includes another body of work to which there are few parallels in the study of K–12 education. This research offers a macro view of how universities are changing over time, what drives these changes in the shape and nature of the sector, how universities respond to these changes, and whether these developments are bringing universities closer to or further from particular educational purposes. Much of this strand of study takes as its departure points Clark Kerr's (1963) famous series of lectures about the emerging multiversity and Burton Clark's early review offering a typology of the field (Clark 1973). One branch of this work is in close conversation with organizational theory. As in organizational theory more generally, closed-systems perspectives have given way to open-systems views, with the key questions becoming how universities are adapting to major changes in the economic, political, cultural, and social environments. One review of this work suggests that there have been roughly four eras of development in American universities since World War II: 1950–1965, a period of expansion during which scholarly concerns focused on how universities would differentiate their systems to serve rapidly swelling numbers of students; 1965–1975, a turbulent decade focused on handling disruption and threats to order while maintaining commitments to access and to academic freedom; 1975–1995, a period when concerns centered on increased competition and reduced state funding; and 1995 to the present, a time when universities have been seeking to respond to a much greater diversity of institutional forms, including for-profit colleges, online universities, and other new entities (Peterson 2007). Scholars working in this vein have also explored the deprofessionalization of higher education, characterized by a massive increase in adjunct faculty, the growing number of nonfaculty administrators leading to an increasingly corporatized university, and the erosion of faculty power at all but the most elite institutions (Rhoades 2007). Some of this work has focused on describing these trends and explaining what drives them; other research, particularly that emanating from professional schools, has sought to delineate how university leaders should respond to and manage these developments (e.g., Keller 1983).

Particularly important in this literature have been a few recurring themes. One is the change from elite to mass to universal education (Trow 1973, 1988), and how this dual shift has affected the size, shape, institutional distribution, and standards of higher education. A second theme is the way in which an increased appetite for market principles and a rising skepticism about academic governance have led to a more corporate university (e.g., Slaughter and Leslie 1997; Tuchman 2009), with mixed institutional logics from different fields coming to shape the academic space (Gumport 2002). A third theme concerns the ways higher education shapes the people and world it interacts with, particularly as described in new institutional accounts of its role in organizing and cementing the modern order (Meyer et al. 2007). And a fourth theme focuses on the role played by the federal government, particularly the military, in shaping the nature of the university in the post–World War II era (e.g., Lowen 1997).

A second branch of work has been less interested in the scholarly debates about the forces shaping the organization and governance of the university than in whether universities are achieving important educational and public purposes. Scholarship in this vein has asked an array of fundamental questions: how much students are learning (Arum and Roksa 2011), whether universities are becoming overly commercialized (Kirp 2003; Bok 2003), whether big-time athletics are undermining the academic purpose of universities (Bowen and Levin 2003); whether the academic canon needs to become more multicultural or should be defended in its classic incarnation (Bloom 1987); whether research purposes have improperly supplanted teaching and compromised undergraduate education (Bok 2008), whether students have become too focused on accumulating credentials to the exclusion of defining a good life (Deresiewicz 2014), whether higher education has become overly vocational at the expense of the liberal arts (Brint 2002; Nussbaum 2010), whether affirmative action is an appropriate or successful remedy for societal discrimination (Bowen and Bok 1998); and how universities can shape political identities and potentially promote liberal values (Gross 2013; Binder and Wood 2013). Much of this scholarship has focused on a relatively small group of elite research universities and leading liberal arts colleges, although there has been some work on institutions in other parts of the spectrum (Professor X 2011; Brint and Karabel 1989). Some research has appeared in scholarly venues, such as Owen-Smith and Powell's (2002) work on universities and intellectual property or Espeland and Sauder's (2007) work on commensuration, but much of it has been published in books that have seen wide circulation and have been reviewed in non-academic venues like *The New York Times* and *The Atlantic*. While the authors include sociologists (i.e., Arum and Roska, Brint), some of the best-known sociological work has been contributed by university presidents (i.e., Kerr, Bok, Bowen), by scholars in the humanities who have turned their analytic eye on the institutions in which they work (Bloom, Dereseiwicz, Delbanco, Nussbaum), and by conservative and populist critics from think tanks or journalistic venues, writing about the problems with universities (Douthat 2005; Carey 2015).

Each of these two strands of work on higher education has been able to establish a niche which sustains it. For the more scholarly work on the development of universities as an organizational field, there is a lively concentration of scholars working in sociology departments, education schools, and business schools who draw on the tools of organizational theory to understand the changing shape of the university landscape. This research is presented at the Association for the Study of Higher Education and AERA, and is published in both higher-education journals and organization journals. In addition to the scholarly readers, there is also a large class of university administrators interested in this work. Significantly, the Association for American Colleges and Universities (AACU) sponsors a major conference that brings together scholars and practitioners to examine the past, present, and future of universities (recent conference title: "Liberal Education, Global Flourishing and the Equity Imperative"). Institutions like the Teagle Foundation, which focus on the future of liberal education, also gather researchers and practitioners to address the changing face of the university. Finally, there is a sizeable public audience for the accessible versions of the research.

Overall, the study of higher education offers an intriguing counterpoint to the three strands of the sociology of education previously discussed. While it, too, conducts research in the stratification and educational improvement traditions, higher-education scholarship also studies the broad ways in which universities are evolving. It then attempts to assess whether those shifts are consistent with the educational values we hold for universities. Much more so than in K–12, there is an interest in the intersection between what actually happens within universities and whether those experiences are consistent with the academic and public purposes that universities are supposed to realize. More theoretically, there is also a prominent area of organizational scholarship that seeks to explain the changing shape of the higher educational institutional field, a strand of research that has few parallels in the study of K–12. For those who would like to see the sociology of K–12 education become more attuned to questions of institutions, organizations, politics, values, and purposes, it is worth noting that there is a significant body of work in higher education which takes up these questions.[10] Perhaps for that reason, many of the contributions in this volume focus on higher education.

Five: New Institutionalism in the Sociology of Education

A fifth sociology of education is what eventually came to be called the "new institutional" school, but which at one time was simply the Meyer school. The initial version of this work, as developed by John Meyer and Brian Rowan (1977), famously argued that schools were constituted more by their "myths" and "ceremonies" than by an instrumental rationality organized to produce measurable outcomes. Schools were organized more by a "logic of confidence" than a "logic of results," enabling them to maintain institutional legitimacy despite the many expectations placed upon them. The loose coupling of the system that was observed by Karl Weick (1976) and others was explained in this view as a mechanism that protected schools' autonomy and freed district and state officials from the hard task of actually changing school results from afar.

This work on K–12 schools connects to Meyer's broader argument about schooling as a constitutive feature of modern Western life. In direct opposition to human capital views of schooling as a rational approach to economic development, the Meyer school argued that schools were avenues through which states convinced themselves and their citizens that they were part of the modern Enlightenment project. This early research was extended by DiMaggio and Powell (1983) and their successors, who argued more generally that under conditions of uncertainty organizations would imitate one another and create the external appearance of legitimacy rather than apply technical rationality. In so doing, the new institutional view of schooling has carved out a small niche in the sociological landscape, linked to those who utilize a similar perspective in other spheres of social life.

At the same time, the new institutional school in education has remained what Stevens (2008) incisively labeled an "archipelago," unmoored from much of the other research on education and playing a relatively modest role in the discipline as a whole. In particular, its lack of any explicit concern with inequality has left it segregated from much of the research in the sociological discipline; its explicit rejection of the possibility of technical rationality has segregated it from the school improvement literature; and its all-encompassing theoretical view has made it difficult to integrate with other branches of theorizing. For all of these reasons, the work remains quite disconnected from other research on education.

Nevertheless, in recent years there has been new scholarship in this tradition. In 2006, Heinz Dieter Meyer and Brian Rowan published an edited book on new institutionalism in education. In their introduction, they argue that the discussions of institutionalism in political science and political sociology have advanced considerably over the past few decades, opening up new avenues for theorizing and research. They document the major ways in which the world has changed since the 1970s: specifically, the tighter coupling of school organizations, the greater pluralism of providers offering schooling, and the increased importance of schooling in society. Rowan (2002) has also offered one of the rare pieces in the sociology of education to take a wide view of the organization of the sector as a whole, in which he argues that many of the most important players in the "school improvement industry" (such as textbook companies and professional development providers) are entirely invisible from the state-district-school perspective on schooling which often prevails. At a more theoretical level, recent work by Hallett (2010) argues that the "cultural dopes" vision of new institutionalism should be replaced by what he calls "inhabited institutionalism," which connects structure and agency in seeking to understand how real people respond to accountability and isomorphic pressures (see also Hallett and Gougherty, in this volume).

The new institutional view of schools departs from other traditions in offering a macro-level argument for the development of the K–12 field as a whole. From one vantage point, many of its initial founding assumptions, particularly the "logic of confidence" and the "myth and ceremony" view of schooling have been supplanted by more recent developments focused on accountability and the growth of the "audit" society (Power 1997; Meyer and Rowan 2006). At the same time, one might argue that we have just exchanged one set of myths and ceremonies for another—PISA scores and data-driven instruction are today what graduation robes were forty years ago (Yurkofsky, in progress). But these are questions that new institutionalists need to take up. For the perspective to grow and have impact, it will not only need to contend with questions of institutional change as well as ones of stability; it will need to incorporate more varied theoretical perspectives in order to understand the dynamic and pluralistic nature of the modern schooling enterprise.

Hitchhikers Looking for a Ride on a Highway: Some Protofields in the Sociology of Education

Understanding what builds and sustains intellectual movements can also help us to understand what we might call protofields in the sociology of education. These are recognizable areas of study which have some signature concepts and some well-known scholars, but which do not have the large-scale followings that characterize the sociologies of education described above. We consider three examples: the sociology of organizations, sociological study of the politics of education, and cultural sociology and education. Our goal here is not to cast aspersions on these areas (indeed, we are hoping to promote more work of this type), nor are they the only examples we could have picked. Rather, we chose them precisely because they represent the kind of research we would like to see more of, and so we seek to understand the institutional and ideological forces that, thus far, have prevented them from coalescing into full-fledged fields.

The sociology of school organization, as practiced in sociology departments, is an interesting case because it has had a few high-profile authors but does not have the large "middle class" of researchers that we see in established fields. Scholars such as Charles Bidwell, Robert Dreeben, Adam Gamoran, Barbara Schneider, Maureen Halloran, and Anthony Bryk are well-known figures who have sought to offer organizational analyses of schooling and its relationship to government and society. Prominent in these accounts are the ways in which schools are organized both as bureaucratic hierarchies (in terms of formal control of work) and as loosely coupled systems (in terms of lack of monitoring of the technical core). Other frequent topics have been the microsociology of classrooms as a battle over social order (Swidler 1979; McFarland 2001), and the ways in which teaching is and is not organized similarly to other professions. Some sociologists have also been interested in the Durkheimian view of schools as socializing rather than achievement-producing entities, and have explored how different normative ethics of schools are produced and shape schools' purposes and values (Bryk, Lee and Holland 1993; Bidwell 2001; Schneider and Stevenson 1999).

At the same time, despite what to us is a range of fascinating questions and insights produced by this work, the statistical counts above suggest that it has not won a prominent place at the American sociological table. Why is this? One reason seems to be the orientation of the discipline as a whole. The questions taken up by the scholars described above do not speak directly to issues of inequality and stratification, and thus are of only peripheral interest to the vast majority of American sociologists. The one strand of school organization which has gotten considerable play in sociology is the work on tracking, ability grouping, and opportunities to learn, which in turn connects back directly to questions of stratification. A second possible reason why the sociology of school organization is not welcomed by sociology as a whole is its weak appeal from the point of view of theory. A major axis of the larger discipline is development of sociological theory, and from this perspective an exclusive focus on schools is limiting: schools are simply one site in which to explore the larger dynamics of organizational function and change. In contrast, when research on school organization crosses over into what we have described above as the school improvement field, located mainly at education schools, studies on loose coupling (Weick 1976), trust in schools (Bryk and Schneider 2002), and weak professionalization (Lortie 1975; Darling-Hammond 2010) become integrally important because understanding these processes is critical to that field's central goal: improving our country's schools. Thus, scholars of school organization at education schools have comparatively higher status (and exist in much greater numbers) than do their counterparts in sociology departments.

Politics of education is another field that is betwixt and between in the sociology of education. While in the abstract there is recognition that schools are public entities and so need to be understood as political bodies, there are few significant works by sociologists about the politics of schooling. The best known scholarship in this field has been done by political scientists (e.g., Chubb and Moe 1990; Katznelson and Weir 1985) and, sometimes, by historians of education (e.g., Katz 1968; Tyack 1974; Loss 2012). Part of the explanation here, we surmise, is that political sociology has focused largely on broad questions of state building, civil rights, and the social insurance functions of the welfare state. In this light, education has historically been viewed skeptically by welfare state scholars as something the state provides in lieu of fulfilling its broader responsibility to protect citizens from the vagaries of capitalism. Furthermore, education has historically been a local and state function, meaning that until recently there have been few major pieces of national legislation to draw the attention of scholars. Given that education has become increasingly nationalized and, at least in the United States, is arguably one of the very few widely popular services provided by the state, more sociological attention would seem to be warranted, but thus far it has not been forthcoming.

A third field focuses on the intersection of culture and education. As noted above, work on culture and education that connects to questions of stratification, social reproduction, and oppositional culture (or its absence) has occupied a central place in the field. But scholars interested in other cultural aspects of schools have had a harder time finding a home for their research. Work by Mitchell Stevens (2003) on homeschooling, by Espeland and Sauder (2007) on commensuration of college rankings, by Binder and Wood (2013) on the ways in which colleges shape political styles, and by Khan and Gaztambide-Fernandez (2009) on elite schooling have all been well received by the discipline as high-quality scholarship, but retain the status of outliers within a field whose primary concerns lie elsewhere. We think it would be profitable if the sociology of education developed a more varied set of linkages: Espeland and Sauder's work, for example, connects to broader sociological questions about quantification, rankings, and status; Khan and Gaztambide-Fernandez's work connects to the field's longstanding concern with elites; Binder and Wood's work connects to questions of political socialization. We can imagine a map of our profession in which the roads between the sociology of organizations, politics, elites and other topics to the sociology of education would each be well traveled, as opposed to the current highway between education and stratification and the tiny lanes that point to other topics.

We could continue, but the point is clear. The way in which the larger sociological discipline is organized promotes certain topics and approaches at the expense of others. Such encouragements and dissuasions, in turn, create signaling mechanisms for the next generation of scholars, and play an important gatekeeping function in terms of both space in journals and access to openings in sociology departments. Scholars who study less common topics within the sociology of education—organizations, politics, culture, commensuration, history, elite schooling—are like hitchhikers seeking to attach themselves to a mainstream topic that the discipline has deemed worthy of study. The result, ironically, is that the field has its own mechanisms of social reproduction as one generation replicates itself in the next, and outliers are gradually weeded out. It also means that the successful scholars in these outlying fields function more as singletons than as a scholarly community. One goal of this volume is to bring that disparate scholarship together under one umbrella.

Renewing the Sociology of Education: Culture, Institutions, Knowledge, Politics, History, Comparative Education, Values

Taken as a whole, this review of the field(s) of the sociology of education reveals more pluralism than is commonly acknowledged, but also identifies swaths of questions that remain largely unexplored. As might be expected, status attainment continues to reign in sociology departments, while work on the improvement of schools and the policies that govern them remains the staple in education schools. As a result, we know much about what predicts inequalities of schooling by race, class, and gender; we know an increasing amount about why it is difficult to reform schools and about which factors can help them to improve. A critical branch of scholarship addresses the ways in which schools reflect and reproduce assumptions of the broader political economy, and interrogates the ways in which dominant assumptions about testing and quantification undermine more holistic approaches to schooling. The new institutional view helps to clarify the continuing isomorphism of schools across fifteen thousand districts, and directs our attention to the ways in which imperatives of legitimacy shape the actions of school actors. In all of these areas of investigation, we know substantially more than we did fifty years ago (Bills, DeLuca, and Morgan 2013).

At the same time, while we know much more about some issues, we know very little about others. In particular, with respect to K–12 schools, we have virtually no sociological research on the evolution of the sector as a whole to parallel the organizational and field-level views that have been prominent in higher education. This seems to be a particularly acute lacuna in light of the infusion into the sector of market, professional, and community-oriented logics, as well as the emergence of a pluralism of providers. There is little in the sociological literature about the politics of education. One could take a sociology of education course and hear no mention of critical groups like school boards, mayors, textbook companies, and many other actors who are clearly consequential for schooling. There is little work that seeks to appraise K–12 schools through any measure other than test scores in reading and math. In contrast to the thriving higher education literature that measures universities against a variety of academic and broader ideals and purposes, there is almost no serious sociological scholarship that evaluates primary and secondary schools against a basic yardstick: Are they giving students a powerful and well-rounded education? Much of the work on K–12 education remains highly decontextualized; one would need to go to the political science literature (i.e., Stone 1989) to understand the ways in which different cities and their racial orders shape consequential decisions about schools. Issues of immigration and diversity of language are taken up a bit in the school-improvement literature on English-language learners, but there is no broad reckoning of the way in which the much more diverse landscape of learners is reshaping longstanding visions of school. The work which is being done also remains highly US-focused. With the exception of the critical scholarship and some strands of the school improvement literature, there is little comparative work that explores how common sociological issues about schools play out in different countries and contexts. In short, there is a glaring absence of issues of politics, culture, history, institutions, comparative education, and values in major sociological writing about schools.

Theoretically, what is striking is that the K–12 field proceeds mostly along the tracks laid down forty to fifty years ago. Questions about gaps by race, class and gender, as well as about intergenerational mobility, today still heavily reflect the assumptions, questions, and methods of Coleman, Blau and Duncan, and Hauser and Sewell. New institutional theory reflects the assumptions of Meyer and DiMaggio and Powell. Critical work draws on ideas from Marx, Freire, and Bowles and Gintis. Work on social reproduction draws on many of the above theorists, as well as on Bourdieu.

This reality is particularly unfortunate because the past forty to fifty years have seen an explosion of theoretical tools in sociology. No listing could possibly do justice to these developments, but in brief: in culture, we have seen the work by Bourdieu and his successors on fields, by Swidler on toolkits and repertoires, by Lamont on cultural boundaries, by Espeland and Sauder on commensuration, by Alford and Friedland and by Boltanski and Thevenot on institutional logics, and by Hallett on inhabited institutionalism. On the relations between different spheres of life, we have Fligstein and McAdam on fields and Abbott on professions and, more recently, linked ecologies. With respect to institutions, we've seen writing on different kinds of institutionalism which increasingly explain both institutional stasis and institutional change; collectively, these arguments foreground history, path dependency, and contingency. In the study of organizations, we have the movement from closed to open and natural systems, and increasingly complex accounts that draw together logics, structures, and agency to depict the development of social organizations. On social movements, we have the role of frames, resource dependency, strategy, and opportunity structures. We could continue, but the idea is clear. With the exception of isolated articles here and there, none of these perspectives has made a substantial imprint on any of the sociologies of education. Hence, our view is that the field needs to be broadened and renewed.

Thinking Anew About Race, Stratification, Inequality, and School Reform

If one part of the agenda for the field should be to broaden its scope, another is to develop new ways of thinking about longstanding topics. What would a forward-looking agenda look like in confronting the dominant questions of race, stratification, inequality, and school reform?

To briefly recap, the field has made significant progress by deploying tools and lenses to explicate the reasons for inequalities between more and less advantaged groups. Quantitative sociologists have parsed the black/white gap and have delivered increasingly precise estimates of the role of parenting practices, other forms of home advantage, and teaching quality, among other factors. Qualitative research has uncovered a series of mechanisms that preserve these inequalities, including in-school factors like labeling and tracking; other research identifies the role of macro factors like structural inequalities, growing income inequality, and residential segregation. Researchers in the Bourdieu and Bernstein traditions have also discussed the kinds of capital students bring to school and the ways in which school norms privilege some forms of capital over others. Ethnographic accounts have captured how such factors intersect in the poorest and most segregated schools—showing how generations of neglect combine to produce what Paulle (2013) calls "toxic schools." These accounts have been among the most important sociological work of the past generation.

At the same time, if the present and future generations of sociologists are to do more than refine the ideas of the past generation, they will need to find some new directions to explore. There are many more ways to do this than we can state here; what follows are a few dimensions that are of particular interest to us and to the authors of this volume.

One development that seems to be largely unrecognized in the education literature is that many of the critiques of schools made by earlier generations of sociologists have now become institutionalized in much of the broader society, and particularly within the training of school personnel. As Dobbin and others have shown, acceptance of diversity is now the "new normal": schools are expected to try to diversify their hiring; teachers are expected to see their students as assets rather than deficits; and a "growth mindset" is now increasingly pervasive in American schools. Most teachers now know that they are expected to help all children to achieve to high levels, and that the emphasis should shift from "talent" and "ability" to "effort" and "growth." Many schools have moved away from tracking across all subjects and towards more flexible approaches to ability grouping (e.g., a student may be in an advanced class in one subject but not in another), in recognition of the pernicious effects of tracking. Schools have also made significant strides to become more inclusive to minority groups and particularly to LBGTQ students, who, largely invisible only a generation ago, now have clubs and associations.

Still, inequalities in outcomes by race, class, and many other lines of division persist. Understanding how old inequalities persist in this new environment requires careful investigation. Perhaps in some of the most disadvantaged schools the old underlying structural inequalities—particularly those created by income inequality and residential segregation—overwhelm the moves toward inclusion and equity in school practices. To understand inequalities in more advantaged schools, sociologists need to delve beneath the surface of seemingly equitable policies—investigating, for example, the way in which implicit bias or past experience may continue to shape teachers' expectations even as they profess to see all students equally. Building on the work on tracking, we need to see continuing work that explores variance across curriculum levels, the assignment of students to those levels, and the interaction of home advantage or disadvantage with opportunities to learn across different levels continue to be key to understanding how inequality continues to be reproduced. Such investigations need to include the ways in which dominant parents mobilize their cultural capital and resources to exploit the wiggle room that exists in curricular differentiation and other school decisions; the "opportunity hoarding" of advantaged parents has begun to be recognized in a literature that historically has focused primarily on the challenges of disadvantaged students and their parents (see Aurini and Hillier, this volume; Lewis and Diamond 2016).

Such investigations into the subtle dynamics of inequality within schools could also lead to a different vein of writing in the school-improvement literature. The leading accounts in that literature emphasize core qualities that are theorized to be present in good schools—instructional leadership, high expectations, social trust, instructional guidance, and coherence (Bryk et al. 2010). But schools faced with persisting inequalities, particularly racial inequalities, may need more than these conditions; they need ways to enable the adults in their systems to grow in their understanding of racial and socioeconomic inequalities, an understanding from which can come the will to learn strategies and use technical tools to reach racial minorities and other underserved students. While there is work on culturally responsive pedagogy (Ladson-Billings 1995), there is less on how whole-school or district efforts might build on singular initiatives to create more equitable systems. There are some practical resources to support such efforts, such as those provided by the National Equity Project, but there is as yet a limited scholarly literature on school or district efforts that specifically seek to highlight race and respond to ongoing inequalities.[11]

The authors of this volume highlight some potentially useful new directions. Natasha Warikoo's chapter reminds us that in the United States we are gradually moving away from a dominant-white, minority-black country, and toward a majority-minority nation, with growing Latino and Asian-American populations. Making sense of this new mosaic will be one of the central challenges of twenty-first-century American sociology. Sociologists, not just those in education, will need to make sense of the contradictions surrounding racial progress: on the one hand, we have become a country that is overtly less racist than it was fifty years ago, but on the other, that very shift seems to have produced a powerful nativist and racist backlash, most notably in the recent election of Donald Trump. John Diamond's chapter suggests that much past work in the mainstream of the sociology of education has categorized "race as a variable," but that future work will need to draw on developments in the sociology of race that view race as a "socially constructed category along which resources are allocated and interactions are shaped." Such work might attend more to the way in which certain organizational contexts are "raced" in the way that they are described (such as the idea that white parents think of "good schools" as schools with other white children in them), as well as continue to investigate the ways in which race has historically shaped patterns of opportunity (Anyon 1997). While Diamond foregrounds more attention to racism, Charles Payne emphasizes the ways in which sociologists have shied away from examining the good and bad choices that poor people make, because of the perceived risk of "blaming the victim." He suggests that future work be more willing to enter these politically charged waters.

We would also encourage the discussion of stratification, race, and inequality to move beyond the United States and become more deliberately international in its focus. Other countries without the US history of slavery have developed very different dynamics around race.

Finally, we wonder whether some scholars in this tradition might want to shift some of their efforts from documenting problems to investigating solutions. Currently, the educational sociology of inequality, race, and stratification, as practiced in sociology departments, is *depressing*. ASA meetings can feel like competitions to reveal different forms of inequality and the forces that produce them—each session more damning than the last. To a degree, this is an important enterprise—societies need social critics to tell hard truths, and policymakers and practitioners need to understand problems before they can attempt solutions. But by this point, it is clear both that (a) many of the identified problems are familiar; and (b) that there is a long journey from understanding a problem to developing a workable solution (see Payne, this volume). Hence, to the extent that educational sociologists in sociology departments wish to contribute not simply to documenting problems but also to addressing them, they may need to take a page from the education school book and focus on understanding the organizational and institutional features that characterize successful schools, districts, and initiatives. As Mitchell Stevens argues in the epilogue to this book, education is a productivity-enhancing as well as an inequality-generating force. Understanding more about how and under what conditions it generates positive outcomes would likely give the discipline more salience in the broader world.

Education in a New Society: Eight Big Developments

This need for reimagining the sociology of education is particularly acute because over the past fifty years the world of education has changed in many ways that call out for sociological attention. Here are eight big developments that require further investigation.

First, education has become more critical to welfare-state debates. While we may not quite have entered the era of the "human capital state" replacing the welfare state, a policy debate that has long focused on social insurance and social safety nets is increasingly including education as a central issue. There are a number of reasons for this shift: the centrality of education to good employment in the postindustrial economy; and the expectation, backed by research, that increasing the number of educated workers will enhance economic growth, decrease crime rates, improve health, enlarge the tax base, and have other positive spillover effects. Particularly in neoliberal countries, education's growing centrality has been accompanied by an ideological shift on the left—from seeing government as the entity that ensures individual social welfare to seeing it as the entity that supports individuals' opportunities for social mobility.

Scholarship on the subject needs to follow suit. While there is extensive writing in both political science and political sociology on health care, Social Security, and welfare, there is comparatively little on education as a welfare-state function. As discussed above, in part this reflects ideological skepticism: historically, education has been seen as something which politicians provided in lieu of social insurance for its citizens (Wilensky 1975; Flora and Heidenheimer 1981). However, the world is changing, and increasingly education is a central tool of policymakers on both the center-left and the center-right. Scholarship needs to reflect this change. There is some literature on the topic in political science (Thelen 2004; Iversen and Stephens 2008; Busemeyer 2015), but there is very little by sociologists on the subject.

Second, there has been a huge increase in economic inequality since its low point in the early 1970s. Many of the classics, particularly the status attainment paradigm, were birthed at what was, in retrospect, a particularly optimistic moment in the post–World War II period, when a rising tide was lifting all boats, racial equality was becoming law, and many measures were being initiated to equalize opportunity. We now find ourselves in a radically unbalanced political economy in which massive inequality in income and wealth bleeds over into other realms of social life. Perhaps not surprisingly, given sociological interest in processes of stratification and inequality, this is an arena that has seen considerable work, particularly with respect to the consequences for the disadvantaged (Wilson 1987; Duncan and Murnane 2011; Reardon 2011) and the mechanisms which perpetuate inequality (Lareau 2003). Less explored have been questions of how elites are able to maintain their privilege and "hoard opportunities" (Walters, in progress; Aurini and Hillier, this volume), a perspective which would link the understanding of inequality to longstanding sociological themes of exclusion and status.

Third, the United States in the twenty-first century is a much more diverse place; the majority of students in public schools are already nonwhite, and the same will be true for the population as a whole within several decades. Much of the scholarship in the past reflected the dominant black/white dynamics of the country, with questions focusing on integration and desegregation, oppositional culture or lack thereof among African-Americans, tracking, and residential segregation. The future is one in which a binary is in the process of being replaced by a complex mosaic; some urban districts have dozens of different nationalities and even languages among the students they serve. Within the four umbrella groups—white, black, Latino, and Asian—there is a tremendous heterogeneity of experiences, both across ethnic groups within those larger categories and across individuals. There are also many people, including one of the authors, who belong to more than one of these racial groups. These developments are generating tremendous complexity for scholars of race and immigration, and how this diversity interacts with schools will create a similarly expansive agenda for sociologists of education.

Fourth, the providers of education have become much more pluralistic over the past generation: vouchers, charters, CMOs, EMOs, for-profit and nonprofit out-of-school providers, and even home schoolers have challenged what was a long-standing monopoly by traditional public schools. Correspondingly, the organizational landscape around schools has become much more complex. Alternative teacher certification and teacher residency programs challenge traditional certification; new foundations like Gates, Walton, and Broad join older ones like Ford and Spencer; portfolio districts displace more traditional districts; and new advocacy groups emerge to support the new providers (Mehta and Teles 2012). All of these developments call for sustained sociological attention. Lenses from institutional change, social movements, and institutional logics might be useful in making sense of them. A renewed exploration of isomorphism might help to explain why so many of these schools look quite similar, despite their different structural locations.

Fifth, the goals of schooling, particularly K–12 schooling, are becoming more ambitious, and there is a desire to make these goals achievable for all students. In the United States and around the world, there is a push for schooling to encompass more than the old "three R's" of writing, reading and 'rithmetic; advocates hope that schools can teach students to think critically, work collaboratively, direct their own learning, and create as well as receive knowledge. There are efforts afoot to turn a late-nineteenth-century factory model of schooling (which emphasized transmission of a fixed body of knowledge by largely rote methods) into a twenty-first-century organization of schooling in which students are connected to the ever-expanding world of knowledge. At the same time, research on efforts to make this shift suggests that inherited structures change slowly, if at all; that policies that emphasize high-stakes tests of simple tasks only reify old assumptions; and that unlearning is difficult for individuals, organizations, and polities (Mehta and Fine 2015). These issues warrant considerably more examination. Lenses from organizational imprinting, path dependency, inhabited institutionalism, and Giddens's structuration might be useful here.

Sixth, higher education continues to grow and change. Economic shifts have made university degrees a necessity for most middle-class employment, an imperative which has contributed to the continued increase in higher education. As the field has grown, it has diversified, with more different kinds of institutions, more and more varied students seeking higher education, more subjects under the university umbrella, and more part-time and adjunct faculty. To try to make sense of the tremendous diversity of organizational forms, the functions that universities perform, and the relations between universities and other spheres of life is to create a huge sociological agenda (see Olneck, this volume). As outlined above, research tries to grapple with these changes, but it would be interesting for that scholarship to be more consciously focused on incorporating insights from different branches of sociology.

Seventh, relatedly, education is becoming a more omnipresent force in modern social life. As both the Baker and the Davies and Mehta chapters in this book detail, education has become a vitally important force in structuring contemporary society. Education is now a birth-to-death phenomenon, with children finding their preschools organized by the expectations of formal schooling, more people gaining high school, college, and professional degrees, and more adults taking classes alongside their jobs or in retirement. Schooling also increasingly structures other spheres of life, especially for the more advantaged, directing how families spend their leisure time, and where people buy houses and whom they marry. For those slightly lower on the educational ladder, formerly apprentice-based fields have moved under the university umbrella. Schooling and school forms have also become more prevalent outside of formal education; there is now a huge industry focused on training and retraining workers. We need much more sociological work that seeks to make sense of the role that education is increasingly playing in modern life.

Eighth, and finally, the emergence of the schooled society has also given rise to pushback against it. Prominent conservative political figures question or ignore findings made by mainstream scientists if those findings run counter to religious belief or commercial interest. In the United States, universities are also increasingly sites of political conflict, as those with connections to universities, particularly elite universities, have become targets in a culture war over who is a "real American." Much as Willis argued that those who were failed by schools were destined to resist them, on a larger scale the emergence of a schooled society has created a backlash among those who have lost the academic competition.[12] If school is now the primary arbiter of who gets ahead in contemporary society, it only stands to reason that it will also be the site on which central political and cultural battles play out. These developments are discussed in newspapers, on television and digital media, and sometimes in political histories, but they should be carefully investigated by sociologists, who have thus far largely ceded this ground.

Taken together, these developments suggest that education is becoming increasingly salient in a variety of ways—as the primary arbiter of life chances, as a critical political touchstone, as something central to policy debates, and as a shaper of other significant arenas of social life. They interact with other major trends, such as the growth of markets, increasing inequality, technological change, and the resurgence of a populist political culture, producing results that are intriguing and often unpredictable. A new sociology of education should seek to make sense of the varied and complex role of education in a new society.

Toward a More Integrated Field

As outlined earlier, the first problem with the sociology of education that we see is that there are critical issues which have not received enough attention. A second related concern is the need for more integration across the sociology of education landscape. As described in the section on the multiple sociologies of education, there is work on a number of different topics within the arena, but the balkanization of the field means that potential connections and insights across areas of study are missed. Following are a few examples that show what might be possible.

Consider the arena of comparative education. This could have been listed above as another sociology of education; it has its own journal and a group of scholars who are comparing and contrasting features of schools across nations. But this work has little conversation with the Meyer new institutional school described above, which takes a more macro view of the development of common policy dynamics and systems. That, in turn, would connect us to a set of questions that, thus far, have been taken up primarily by the critical theorists—namely the degree to which we see a worldwide isomorphism of schooling created by OECD, PISA, and other globalizing forces. We might then connect this potential integration to the political science literature, which is starting to develop an account of the internal and external forces that have led different countries to make different decisions about their educational policies and strategies. And then, of course, it would be good to connect all of this emerging work on divergent educational regimes to cross-national research on educational effectiveness. Each of these strands exists, but would be much richer if cross-fertilized with related scholarship by other researchers.

Another arena is the sociology of school life. Here there is one tradition, emerging mostly from sociology departments, that studies *students*. Work in this area explores student subcultures, oppositional culture, resistance, peer pressure and groupings, and the nature of adolescent society. This is a rich vein that has produced a number of well-known books and ethnographies, as well as some recent quantitative work on oppositional culture. At the same time, there is a thriving tradition, emerging from education schools, of studying school life, but that work focuses mainly on the *adults*. Here the questions are about how the adults create vision and mission, order and high expectations, professional learning communities and learning organizations. But rarely, since Waller, have we brought these two worlds into conversation, asking how students' orientation towards social life and one another confounds the efforts of adults trying to create academic purpose.[13] When scholars do integrate these worlds, as in the account of *The Shopping Mall High School* (in which the adults defer to the desires of the students), or in McFarland's description of the battle for order in the classroom, the work is revealing precisely because it shows the two major actors in schools shaping each other's actions. Could we have a sociology of school life that adds to the few intriguing works in this tradition, a scholarship that thinks about schools holistically from the perspectives of all of their inhabitants?

A third example might draw on parallels between the study of primary and secondary schools and the study of higher education. Both fields are being reshaped by many of the same dynamics—more and more new providers; the rise of online competitors; the increasing influence of philanthropy; and the incursion of market, efficiency and accountability imperatives. At the same time, preschools and out-of-school providers are also increasingly being expected to meet academic and test-score expectations. In each realm there is active contestation, as internal actors push back against what they see as external efforts to rationalize and commodify learning. An integrated sociology of education might consider these dynamics together, seeking to develop broader-reaching theories about the causes and consequences of, and resistance to, the early twenty-first-century rationalization of schools.

These are a few examples among many. The number of potential combinations between different parts of the sociology of education or between those parts and different theoretical lenses is very large. May we encourage some sociological speed dating? How might Bourdieu help us make sense of MOOCs? How might the study of elites help to explain the shape of the preschool market? How might "linked ecologies" help us understand the tension between Teach for America and its more traditional competitors? We'll never know, if we don't get out of our corners and meet some new people.

It is also the case that there are proliferating reasons to develop a more integrated view. As we argue in more detail in our chapter on interpenetration, increasing numbers of people are going to school for longer periods, a pattern which creates more linkages between preschools, primary and secondary schools, and higher education. Test scores commensurate and link schools across jurisdictions. PISA scores shrink the world by creating commensuration across countries. The Internet increases information flow and speeds new or different educational practices across jurisdictions and levels of education. In an interconnected world, we need an interconnected sociology of education.

What Lies Ahead

The chapters in this volume begin to show what this new and more integrated sociology of education might look like. Many of the authors are individually quite well known for doing this kind of work; one goal of producing the book was to bring these individual contributors together under one umbrella. As the reader might expect from what we have said so far, many of the chapters are about higher education, since that has been the field most amenable to varied kinds of intellectual treatment. Befitting a volume intended to provoke new perspectives, selections also vary in form: certain of the contributors present extended empirical results, others offer new theories, some synthesize literature, and a few offer short provocations. All are intended to show new ways of thinking in the sociology of education.

Part 1 of this book focuses primarily on developing or extending theory about education in a new society. David Baker's chapter draws on his 2014 book *The Schooled Society* to build on the ideas of Daniel Bell and John Meyer and show the myriad ways in which schooling and its logics infiltrate and structure many elements of modern life. Steve Brint's chapter offers an ecological perspective on what he calls "knowledge structures," exploring how knowledge can be produced and legitimated both inside and outside of academia, and mapping the way in which such knowledge structures can be imported and exported across those divides. Davies and Mehta's chapter on interpenetration takes a similar perspective, suggesting that, as schooling has expanded to cover more students and subjects, it has frequently been transformed by its contact with new populations, organizational forms, and logics. Tim Hallett and Matt Gougherty's chapter takes an inhabited institutional approach to managerial professional education, suggesting that what is produced there is a negotiated product between students and faculty. Many of these chapters, in different ways, explore questions of structure and agency, institutional stability and change, as well as the ways in which different forces come together to shape educational and knowledge landscapes, sometimes in unpredictable ways. Many chapters in this part of the book are also ecological in their vision, seeing schools, universities and professions as sited among other actors and fields, and trying to understand the dynamics that explain which forms and practices emerge and why.

Part 2 explores different substantive domains of education in a new society. Shamus Khan's chapter explores the topic of elites, asking whether what happens to elites is countercyclical to what happens to mass society, and extending his 2011 book *Privilege* to suggest that top boarding school students today see themselves less as an ascriptive class and more as members of a meritocratic elite. Richard Arum and Amanda Cook take up the topic of assessment, seeking to move beyond debates over testing; they focus on assessment's increasing influence as a political, technological, social, and cultural phenomena. Amy Binder's chapter, exploring the role of colleges as socializing agents, analyzes how different organizational features of colleges shape the nature and style of students' political socialization. Michael Olneck's chapter explores the phenomenon of "badging," or microcredentialing, in higher education, drawing on Basil Bernstein's work to argue that badging has the potential to fundamentally shift the core nature of the university enterprise, including "the organization and forms of knowledge, what teaching, learning and knowing *mean*, to what ends they are directed, how they are accomplished, and how they are evidenced and represented." John Skrentny and Natalie Novick analyze the worldwide explosion of universities seeking international students, particularly in graduate schools and STEM fields, suggesting that creating legitimacy, spurring economic growth, and finding cheap labor all drive this trend. While the substantive terrain explored in these chapters is varied, all of the authors focus on unconventional topics in the sociology of education and draw primarily on theoretical lenses from other subfields of the discipline to analyze their cases.

Part 3 returns to long-standing issues in the sociology of education, particularly inequality, race, immigration, stratification, and school reform, but consider them anew in light of more recent theoretical, substantive, or demographic developments. David Karen's chapter takes up the matter of the growing pervasiveness of schooling in an era of growing inequality; it points to the ways in which the popular image of school as a meritocratic institution is increasingly belied by the evidence, and suggests that we need to rethink the role that schools should play in a democratic society. Janice Aurini and Cathlene Hillier revisit long-standing questions about socioeconomic gaps in academic achievement and attainment, arguing that poor and working-class parents and students are making some gains at the lower reaches of the academic tournament, but that affluent parents are mobilizing to protect their advantages by advocating for their children in schools, placing them in higher tracks, and supplementing their children's schooling with out-of-school activities and tutoring. Doug Downey's chapter cites mounting evidence, from research on summer slide and other topics, that schools are not creating different trajectories for students of different socioeconomic levels, but instead may actually be *equalizing* agents. Therefore, he argues, we should broaden the sociology of education to investigate the role of out-of-school factors in producing differential outcomes, especially as the society becomes more unequal. John Diamond's chapter connects emerging work in the sociology of race to the sociology of schooling, suggesting new ways to connect the two fields. Natasha Warikoo's chapter explores the issue of race in the new millennium, urging scholars to develop a fresh agenda for the coming majority-minority nation, one that looks beyond black and white to understand ethnic differences, immigration and youth culture, and which uses tools from cultural sociology to make sense of this emerging mosaic. In the concluding chapter of part 3, Charles Payne argues that the conversation about how to address inequality in education has been hijacked by two self-congratulatory elite discourses: liberal scholars so afraid of blaming the victim that they often fail to consider the full range of possible levers for change, and mainstream scholars so rooted in conventional visions of methodological rigor that they define problems too narrowly to generate usable knowledge. Despite their different foci, the chapters in part 3 demonstrate that long-standing ways of analyzing stratification and race need new methodologies or theoretical approaches if they are to capture critical modern realities.

Finally, in an epilogue that in some ways parallels Michele Lamont's foreword, Mitchell Stevens urges sociologists of education to remember that education is a productive process as well as an inequality perpetuating one, that it is a site to study much of how people self-fashion their identities, and that it is fundamentally a moral enterprise, something sociologists should hold at the heart of their endeavor.

Conclusion

Education is one of the most powerful forces in modern life. It structures individual life chances, develops authoritative knowledge, organizes the professions, and, despite the charges of its critics, remains the most popular public institution that we have. Education deserves a sociology that is similarly varied and robust—one that draws on all of its tools and traditions to match the range and importance of its subject.

Notes

1. We want to thank Steven Brint, Michael Olneck, Christopher Jencks, and Amelia Peterson for very helpful comments in developing this chapter.

2. The *Journal of Educational Sociology* was founded at NYU in 1927. See http://steinhardt.nyu.edu/humsocsci/sociology/history.
3. The 1970s issues did not list their contributors' full affiliations.
4. Several of the essays also used quantitative methods; thus the numbers do not total 117.
5. Some of this strand of research overlaps with work on the sociology of school organizations as practiced in sociology departments (see Hedges and Schneider 2004 for a review). We discuss this in more detail in the text below.
6. The 2000 edition of Freire's *Pedagogy of the Oppressed* has been cited more than fifty thousand times; Michael Apple's 2004 edition of *Ideology and Curriculum* has been cited more than six thousand times, and Henry Giroux has eight publications, each having been cited at least one thousand times.
7. Interestingly, critical sociology of education is more dominant in English-speaking nations beyond the United States, including Canada, Great Britain, and Australia. McLaughlin (2005) has noted that critical approaches thrive in nations where mainstream sociology is weakly institutionalized. Sociology has a lengthy history in the United States, which has allowed it to stand firm alongside economics, psychology, and political science. But in those other nations the discipline has shallower roots, winning a presence in universities only in the late 1960s, just fifteen years before the rise of various postdisciplinary "studies" units. As a result, in those countries mainstream sociology continually battles with "studies" units for breathing space. Michael Burawoy, in contrast, argues that the reason why mainstream sociology fails to take root in many nations is that their cultures are less "positivistic" than is the United States. But his assertion provokes the question of why other "positivist" disciplines like psychology and economics are now so highly institutionalized all over the world. Since our volume focuses on sociology of education in the United tates, we do not further pursue these kinds of comparative questions in this chapter.
8. Much of the work in the first strand is published in sociology journals and the second in education journals. Consider the issue of college access, which straddles the two fields. A comprehensive analysis of all journal articles ($N = 114$) on college access published in leading sociology and education journals between 1973 and 2004 found that the most common topic in higher education journals was financial aid (40 percent), with only one article on financial aid appearing in a sociology journal. Conversely, the most common topic in the sociology journals was the role of family socioeconomic status in shaping student attainment (56 percent), consistent with the status attainment work described above (McDonough and Fann 2007: 57).
9. Patricia Gumport (2007: 339) notes a dynamic in the production of higher-education research similar to what we see in the first two strands of K–12 research. Specifically, she notes that sociology departments have different expectations from education schools in the production of higher-education research, and that this split creates limitations in what sort of knowledge is created in each context: "Higher education doctoral students are commonly encouraged to frame research as practice-driven questions—albeit with a conceptual framework, often at least nominally drawn from sociological constructs—leading to conclusions that help inform or shed light on educational problems. The conceptual risks therein include unduly narrowing the research question and framing it with too many taken-for-granteds about the current terms of practice. . . . In sociology, the message is for research to be framed to advance established lines of inquiry in the discipline, such that higher education, if an interest at all, is considered as an instance or site of study for sociological phenomena or

as a major social institution on a par with K–12 education, religion, the family, and the economy. The risk is a lack of historical awareness of higher education's legacies and complexities as a site of study. Moreover, sociologists tend not to locate their research within the corpus of work covered in higher-education journals. Thus, their research may not recognize propositions already substantiated by higher education researchers, and may not take into account or contribute to a line of inquiry already established in the study of higher education."

10. Interestingly, as early as 1958, Floud and Halsey (1958: 187) commented on the differences between the study of higher education and that of K–12: "The ahistorical, social-psychological bias characteristic of so much of the work on the sociology of schools is conspicuously absent from the literature concerned with the universities. On the contrary, the staple of sociological analysis here is the dialectical interplay of a distinctive corporate organization with the rationalizing pressures of advancing industrialism."
11. There is some work on these efforts in the critical pedagogy school, but there is less that is specifically intended for practicing educators who are not already steeped in critical approaches.
12. This chapter was drafted before Brexit and the election of Donald Trump, but these recent world events only underscore this point.
13. There is also a small sociological literature on the sociology of the classroom (Boocock 1972; Cohen 1972) which has not been well integrated into the broader sociology of education literature.

References

Anyon, Jean. 1997. *Ghetto Schooling: A Political Economy of Urban Education Reform*. New York: Teacher's College Press.

Apple, Michael W. 1979. *Ideology and Curriculum*. Boston: Routledge & K. Paul.

Apple, Michael W., Stephen J. Ball, and Luís Armando Gandin. 2010. *The Routledge International Handbook of the Sociology of Education*. New York: Routledge.

Armstrong, Elizabeth A., and Laura T. Hamilton. 2013. *Paying for the Party: How College Maintains Inequality*. Cambridge, MA: Harvard University Press.

Arum, Richard, and Josipa Roksa. 2011. *Academically Adrift: Limited Learning on College Campuses*. Chicago: University of Chicago Press.

Astin, Alexander W. 1977. *Four Critical Years*. 1st ed. San Francisco: Jossey-Bass Publishers.

Baker, David. 2014. *The Schooled Society: The Educational Transformation of Global Culture*. Palo Alto, CA: Stanford University Press.

Bell, Daniel. 1973. *The Coming of Post-Industrial Society: A Venture in Social Forecasting*. New York: Basic Books.

Bernstein, Basil B. 1971. *Class, Codes and Control*. London: Routledge and K. Paul.

Bidwell, Charles, and Noah Friedkin. 1988. "The Sociology of Education" in *Handbook of Sociology*, ed. Neil Smelser. Beverly Hills: Sage, 449–471.

Bidwell, Charles E. 2001. "Analyzing Schools as Organizations: Long-Term Permanence and Short-Term Change." *Sociology of Education* 74:100–114.

Bills, David B., Stefanie DeLuca, and Stephen L. Morgan. 2013. "Altered States of the Collective Mind: A Response to Brint." *Sociology of Education* 86 (4): 286–288.

Binder, Amy J. and Kate Wood. 2013. *Becoming Right: How Campuses Shape Young Conservatives*. Princeton, NJ: Princeton University Press.

Bloom, Allan. 1987. *The Closing of the American Mind: How Higher Education Has Failed Democracy and Impoverished the Souls of Today's Students*. New York: Simon and Schuster.

Bok, Derek. 2003. *Universities in the Marketplace: The Commercialization of Higher Education*. Princeton, NJ: Princeton University Press.

———. 2008. *Our Underachieving Colleges: A Candid Look at How Much Students Learn and Why They Should Be Learning More*. Princeton, NJ: Princeton University Press.

Boocock, Sarane. 1972. *An Introduction to the Sociology of Learning*. Boston: Houghton Mifflin.

Bourdieu, Pierre, and Jean Claude Passeron. 1977. *Reproduction in Education, Society and Culture*. London: Sage Publications.

Bowen, William G., and Derek Curtis Bok. 1998. *The Shape of the River: Long-Term Consequences of Considering Race in College and University Admissions*. Princeton, NJ: Princeton University Press.

Bowen, William G., Sarah A. Levin, and James Lawrence Shulman. 2003. *Reclaiming the Game: College Sports and Educational Values*. Princeton, NJ: Princeton University Press.

Bowles, Samuel, and Herbert Gintis. 1976. *Schooling in Capitalist America: Educational Reform and the Contradictions of Economic Life*. New York: Basic Books.

Brint, Steven G. 1994. *In an Age of Experts: The Changing Role of Professionals in Politics and Public Life*. Princeton, NJ: Princeton University Press.

———. 2013. "The "Collective Mind" at Work." *Sociology of Education* 86 (4): 273–279.

Brookover, Wilbur B. 1955. *A Sociology of Education*. New York: American Book Co.

Bryk, Anthony S., Valerie E. Lee, and Peter Blakeley Holland. 1993. *Catholic Schools and the Common Good*. Cambridge, MA: Harvard University Press.

Bryk, Anthony S., and Barbara L. Schneider. 2002. *Trust in Schools*. New York: Russell Sage Foundation.

Bryk, Anthony S., et al. 2010. *Organizing Schools for Improvement: Lessons from Chicago*. Chicago: University of Chicago Press.

Busemeyer, Marius R. 2015. *Skills and Inequality: Partisan Politics and the Political Economy of Education Reforms in Western Welfare States*. Cambridge: Cambridge University Press.

Carey, Kevin. 2015. *The End of College: Creating the Future of Learning and the University of Everywhere*. Riverhead Books.

Carter, Prudence L. 2005. *Keepin'It Real: School Success beyond Black and White*. Oxford and New York: Oxford University Press.

Chubb, John E., and Terry M. Moe. 1990. *Politics, Markets, and America's Schools*. Washington: Brookings Institution.

Coburn, Cynthia E. 2004. "Beyond Decoupling: Rethinking the Relationship between the Institutional Environment and the Classroom." *Sociology of Education* 77 (3): 211–244.

Cohen, David K. 1990. "A Revolution in One Classroom: The Case of Mrs. Oublier." *Educational Evaluation and Policy Analysis* 12 (3): 327–345.

———. 2011. *Teaching and Its Predicaments*. Cambridge, MA: Harvard University Press.

Cohen, David K., and Susan L. Moffitt. 2009. *The Ordeal of Equality: Did Federal Regulation Fix the Schools*? Cambridge, MA: Harvard University Press.

Cohen, Elizabeth. 1972. "Sociology and the Classroom: Setting the Conditions for Teacher-Student Interaction." ERIC (US Department of Education).

Coleman, James. 1988. "Social Capital in the Creation of Human Capital." *American Journal of Sociology* 94:S95–S120.

Coleman, James S. 1961. *The Adolescent Society: The Social Life of the Teenager and Its Impact on Education*. New York: Free Press of Glencoe.

Collins, Randall. 1979. *The Credential Society: An Historical Sociology of Education and Stratification*. New York: Academic Press.

Cuban, Larry. 1990. "Reforming Again, Again, and Again." *Educational Researcher* 19 (1): 3–13.

Cuban, Larry, and David B. Tyack. 1995. *Tinkering Toward Utopia: A Century of Public School Reform*. Cambridge, MA: Harvard University Press.

Darling-Hammond, Linda. 2010. *The Flat World and Education: How America's Commitment to Equity Will Determine Our Future*. New York: Teachers College Press.

Davies, Scott. 1995. "Leaps of Faith: Shifting Currents in Critical Sociology of Education." *American Journal of Sociology* 100 (6): 1448–1478.

Deresiewicz, William. 2014. *Excellent Sheep: The Miseducation of the American Elite and the Way to a Meaningful Life*. New York: Free Press.

Dimaggio, Paul, and Walter Powell. 1983. "The Iron Cage Revisited: Institutional Isomorphism and Collective Rationality in Organizational Fields." *American Sociological Review* 48 (6): 147–160.

Douthat, Ross Gregory. 2005. *Privilege: Harvard and the Education of the Ruling Class*. New York: Hyperion.

Dreeben, Robert. 1994. "The Sociology of Education: Its Development in the United States," in *Research in Sociology of Education and Socialization*, ed. Aaron Pallas. Greenwich, CT: JAI Press, 7–52.

Duncan, Greg J., and Richard Murnane. 2011. *Whither Opportunity? Rising Inequality, Schools, and Children's Life Chances*. New York: Russell Sage Foundation.

Elmore, Richard F., and Milbrey Wallin McLaughlin. 1988. *Steady Work: Policy, Practice, and the Reform of American Education*. Santa Monica, CA: Rand.

Espeland, Wendy Nelson, and Michael Sauder. 2007. "Rankings and Reactivity: How Public Measures Recreate Social Worlds." *American Journal of Sociology* 113 (1): 1–40.

Ferguson, Ann. 2000. *Bad Boys: Public Schools in the Making of Black Masculinity*. Ann Arbor: University of Michigan Press.

Flora, Peter, and Arnold J. Heidenheimer. 1981. *The Development of Welfare States in Europe and America*. New Brunswick, NJ: Transaction Books.

Floud, J., and A. H. Halsey. 1958. "The Sociology of Education (with Special Reference to the Development of Research in Western Europe and the United States of America)." *Current Sociology* 7 (3): 165–193.

Fordham, Signithia. 1996. *Blacked Out: Dilemmas of Race, Identity, and Success at Capitol High*. Chicago: University of Chicago Press.

Freire, Paulo. 1970. *Pedagogy of the Oppressed*. Edited by Myra Bergman Ramos. New York: Seabury Press.

Frickel, Scott, and Neil Gross. 2005. "A General Theory of Scientific/Intellectual Movements." *American Sociological Review* 70 (2): 204–232.

Gaztambide-Fernandez, Ruben. 2009. *The Best of the Best: Becoming Elite at an American Boarding School*. Cambridge, MA: Harvard University Press.

Giroux, Henry A. 1983. *Theory and Resistance in Education: A Pedagogy for the Opposition*. S. Hadley, MA: Bergin & Garvey.

Giroux, Henry A., and Peter McLaren, eds. 1989. *Critical Pedagogy, the State, and Cultural Struggle*. Albany: State University of New York Press.

Gross, Neil. 2013. *Why Are Professors Liberal and Why Do Conservatives Care?* Cambridge, MA: Harvard University Press.

Gumport, Patricia. 2002. "Universities and Knowledge: Restructuring the City of Intellect" in *The Future of the City of Intellect*, ed. Steven Brint. Stanford, CA: Stanford University Press, 47–81.

———. 2007. "Reflections on a Hybrid Field: Growth and Prospects for the Sociology of Higher Education" in *Sociology of Higher Education: Contributions and Their Contexts*, ed. Patricia Gumport. Baltimore: Johns Hopkins University Press, 325–362.

Hallett, Tim. 2010. "The Myth Incarnate: Recoupling Processes, Turmoil, and Inhabited Institutions in an Urban Elementary School." *American Sociological Review* 75 (1): 52–74.

Hallinan, Maureen. 2006. Introduction to *Handbook of the Sociology of Education*, ed. Maureen Hallinan. New York: Springer, 1–12.

Hurtado, Sylvia. 2007. "The Study of College Impact," in *Sociology of Higher Education: Contributions and Their Contexts*, ed. Patricia Gumport. Baltimore: Johns Hopkins University Press, 94–112.

Iversen, Torben, and John Stephens. 2008. "Partisan Politics, the Welfare State, and Three Worlds of Human Capital Formation." *Comparative Political Studies* 41 (4): 600–637.

Jacobs, Jerry A. 2013. *In Defense of Disciplines: Interdisciplinarity and Specialization in the Research University*. Chicago: University of Chicago Press.

Jencks, Christopher, et al. 1972. *Inequality: A Reassessment of the Effect of Family and Schooling in America*. New York: Basic Books.

Johnson, Susan Moore. 1990. *Teachers at Work: Achieving Success in our Schools*. New York: Basic Books.

Karabel, Jerome, and A. H. Halsey. 1977. *Power and Ideology in Education*. New York: Oxford University Press.

Katz, Michael B. 1968. *The Irony of Early School Reform: Educational Innovation in Mid-Nineteenth Century Massachusetts*. Cambridge, MA: Harvard University Press.

Katznelson, Ira, and Margaret Weir. 1985. *Schooling for All: Class, Race, and the Decline of the Democratic Ideal*. New York: Basic Books.

Keller, George. 1983. *Academic Strategy: The Management Revolution in American Higher Education*. Baltimore: Johns Hopkins University Press.

Kerr, Clark. 1963. *The Uses of the University*. Cambridge, MA: Harvard University Press.

Khan, Shamus Rahman. 2011. *Privilege: The Making of an Adolescent Elite at St. Paul's School*. Princeton, NJ: Princeton University Press.

Kirp, David L. 2003. *Shakespeare, Einstein, and the Bottom Line: The Marketing of Higher Education*. Cambridge, MA: Harvard University Press.

Labaree, David F. 2010. *Someone Has to Fail: The Zero-Sum Game of Public Schooling*. Cambridge, MA: Harvard University Press.

Ladson-Billings, Gloria. 1995. "Toward a Theory of Culturally-Relevant Pedagogy." *American Educational Research Journal* 32 (3): 465–491.

Lareau, Annette. 2003. *Unequal Childhoods: Class, Race, and Family Life*. Berkeley: University of California Press.

Lewis, Amanda, and John B. Diamond. 2015. *Despite the Best Intentions: How Racial Inequality Thrives in Good Schools*. New York: Oxford University Press.

Light, Richard J. 2001. *Making the Most of College: Students Speak Their Minds*. Cambridge, MA: Harvard University Press.

Lipsky, Michael. 1980. *Street-Level Bureaucracy: Dilemmas of the Individual in Public Services*. New York: Russell Sage Foundation.

Lortie, Dan C. 1975. *Schoolteacher: A Sociological Study*. Chicago: University of Chicago Press.

Loss, Christopher P. 2012. *Between Citizens and the State: The Politics of American Higher Education in the 20th Century*. Princeton, NJ: Princeton University Press.

Lowen, Rebecca S. 1997. *Creating the Cold War University: The Transformation of Stanford.* Berkeley: University of California Press.

MacLeod, Jay. 1987. *Ain't No Makin' It: Leveled Aspirations in a Low-Income Neighborhood.* Boulder, CO: Westview Press.

Madison, D. Soyini. 2011. *Critical Ethnography: Methods, Ethics, and Performance.* Thousand Oaks, CA: Sage.

McDonough, Patricia M. 1997. *Choosing Colleges: How Social Class and Schools Structure Opportunity.* Albany: State University of New York Press.

McDonough, Patricia, and Amy Fann. 2007. "The Study of Inequality," in *Sociology of Higher Education: Contributions and Their Contexts,* ed. Patricia Gumport. Baltimore: Johns Hopkins University Press, 17–50.

McFarland, Daniel A. 2001. "Student Resistance: How the Formal and Informal Organization of Classrooms Facilitate Everyday Forms of Student Defiance." *American Journal of Sociology* 107 (3): 612–678.

McLaughlin, Milbrey Wallin, and Joan E. Talbert. 2001. *Professional Communities and the Work of High School Teaching.* Chicago: University of Chicago Press.

McLaughlin, Neil. 2005. "Canada's Impossible Science: Historical and Institutional Origins of the Coming Crisis in Anglo-Canadian Sociology." *Canadian Journal of Sociology* 30 (1): 1–40.

Mehta, Jal. 2013. *The Allure of Order: High Hopes, Dashed Expectations, and the Troubled Quest to Remake American Schooling.* New York: Oxford University Press.

———. 2013." From Bureaucracy to Profession: Remaking the Educational Sector for the Twenty-First Century." *Harvard Educational Review* 83 (3): 463–488.

Mehta, Jal, and Sarah Fine. 2015. *The Why, What, Where and How of Deeper Learning in American Secondary Schools.* Boston: Jobs for the Future, accessed at http://www.jff.org/sites/default/files/publications/materials/The-Why-What-Where-How-121415.pdf.

Meyer, Heinz-Dieter, and Brian Rowan. 2006. *The New Institutionalism in Education.* Albany: State University of New York Press.

Meyer, John, and Brian Rowan. 1977. "Institutionalized Organizations: Formal Structure as Myth and Ceremony." *American Journal of Sociology* 83 (1): 340–363.

Meyer, John, et al. 2007. "Higher Education as an Institution," in *Sociology of Higher Education: Contributions and Their Contexts,* ed. Patricia Gumport. Baltimore: Johns Hopkins University Press, 187–221.

Noguera, Pedro. 2003. *City Schools and the American Dream: Reclaiming the Promise of Public Education.* New York: Teachers College Press.

Nussbaum, Martha Craven. 2010. *Not for Profit: Why Democracy Needs the Humanities.* Princeton, NJ: Princeton University Press.

Oakes, Jeannie. 1985. *Keeping Track: How Schools Structure Inequality.* New Haven: Yale University Press.

Olneck, Michael. 2012. "State of the Field of Sociology of Education in the United States." Unpublished manuscript, University of Wisconsin–Madison.

Orfield, Gary, and Susan E. Eaton. 1996. *Dismantling Desegregation: The Quiet Reversal of Brown v. Board of Education.* New York: New Press.

Paulle, Bowen. 2013. *Toxic Schools: High Poverty Education in New York and Amsterdam.* Chicago: University of Chicago Press.

Peterson, Marvin. 2007. "The Study of Colleges and Universities as Organizations," in *Sociology of Higher Education: Contributions and Their Contexts,* ed. Patricia Gumport. Baltimore: Johns Hopkins University Press, 147–184.

Powell, Arthur G., Eleanor Farrar, and David K. Cohen. 1985. *The Shopping Mall High School: Winners and Losers in the Educational Marketplace*. Boston: Houghton Mifflin.

Power, Michael. 1997. *The Audit Society: Rituals of Verification*. New York: Oxford University Press.

Professor X. 2011. *In the Basement of the Ivory Tower: Confessions of an Accidental Academic*. New York: Viking.

Reardon, Sean. 2011. "The Widening Academic Achievement Gap between Rich and Poor: New Evidence and Possible Explanations," in *Whither Opportunity? Rising Inequality, Schools, and Children's Life Chances*, ed. Greg Duncan and Richard Murnane. New York: Russell Sage Foundation, 91–115.

Rhoades, Gary. 2007. "The Study of the Academic Profession," in *Sociology of Higher Education: Contributions and Their Contexts*, ed. Patricia Gumport. Baltimore: Johns Hopkins University Press, 113–140.

Rowan, Brian. 2002. "The Ecology of School Improvement: Notes on the School Improvement Industry in the United States." *Journal of Educational Change* 3 (3): 283–314.

Sadovnik, Alan. 2007. "Theory and Research in the Sociology of Education," in *Sociology of Education: A Critical Reader*, ed. Alan Sadovnik. New York: Routledge, 3–21.

Schneider, Barbara L., and David Stevenson. 1999. *The Ambitious Generation: America's Teenagers, Motivated but Directionless*. New Haven, CT: Yale University Press.

Slaughter, Sheila, and Larry L. Leslie. 1997. *Academic Capitalism: Politics, Policies, and the Entrepreneurial University*. Baltimore: Johns Hopkins University Press.

Stevens, Mitchell. 2003. *Kingdom of Children: Culture and Controversy in the Homeschooling Movement*. Princeton, NJ: Princeton University Press.

———. 2007. *Creating a Class: College Admissions and the Education of Elites*. Cambridge, MA: Harvard University Press.

———. 2008. "Culture and Education." *Annals of the American Academy of Political and Social Science* 619:97–113.

Stokes, Donald E. 1997. *Pasteur's Quadrant: Basic Science and Technological Innovation*. Washington: Brookings Institution Press.

Stone, Clarence N. 1989. *Regime Politics: Governing Atlanta, 1946–1988*. Lawrence: University Press of Kansas.

Swidler, Ann. 1979. *Organization without Authority: Dilemmas of Social Control in Free Schools*. Cambridge, MA: Harvard University Press.

Thelen, Kathleen Ann. 2004. *How Institutions Evolve: The Political Economy of Skills in Germany, Britain, the United States, and Japan*. Cambridge: Cambridge University Press.

Trow, Martin. 1974. "Problems in the Transition from Elite to Mass Higher Education," in *Policies for Higher Education*, Paris: OECD, 55–101.

———. 1988. "American Higher Education: Past, Present, and Future." *Educational Researcher* 17 (3): 13–23.

Tuchman, Gaye. 2009. *Wannabe U: Inside the Corporate University*. Chicago: University of Chicago Press.

Tyack, David B. 1974. *The One Best System: A History of American Urban Education*. Cambridge, MA: Harvard University Press.

Tyack, David B., and Larry Cuban. 1995. *Tinkering toward Utopia: A Century of Public School Reform*. Cambridge, MA: Harvard University Press.

Tyson, Karolyn. 2011. *Integration Interrupted: Ttracking, Black Students, and Acting White after Brown*. New York: Oxford University Press.

Walters, Pamela Barnhouse. 2009. "The Politics of Science: Battles for Scientific Authority in the Field of Education Research." In *Education Research on Trial: Policy Reform and the Call for Scientific Rigor*, ed. Pamela Walters, Annette Lareau, and Sheri H. Ranis. New York: Routledge.

Weick, Karl E. 1976. "Educational Organizations as Loosely Coupled Systems." *Administrative Science Quarterly* 21 (1): 1–19.

Wilensky, Harold L. 1974. *The Welfare State and Equality: Structural and Ideological Roots of Public Expenditures*. Berkeley: University of California Press.

Willis, Paul E. 1977. *Learning to Labour: How Working Class Kids Get Working-Class Jobs*. Farnborough, UK: Saxon House.

Wilson, William J. 1987. *The Truly Disadvantaged: The Inner City, the Underclass, and Public Policy*. Chicago: University of Chicago Press.

Yurkofksy, Max. 2016. "The Restructuring of Educational Organizations: From Ceremonial Rules to Technical Ceremonies." Working paper, Harvard Graduate School of Education.

PART ONE

Theoretical Perspectives

TWO

Social Theory and the Coming Schooled Society

DAVID P. BAKER[1]

Theorizing about education and society is at an intellectual crossroads. Starting from humanistic descriptions of schooling, over the past half-century sociology of education has matured into an academically recognized field with an influential record of inquiry contributing to the pursuit of central questions. Naturally, success comes at the price of some inertia and specialization. This book addresses the fact that, since its zenith in the 1970s, the debate over contrasting theories of the role of education in society has become sparse; empirical inquiry in sociology of education, while technically impressive, is nearly exclusively focused on stratification and educational inequality. To avoid being a victim of its own past success, sociology of education could intellectually embrace the most transformative educational phenomenon across the entire human record: the education revolution and the coming of what can be called "the schooled society."

Dominant theoretical positions from the inception of a mature sociology of education all depart from the implicit assumption that education is a secondary social institution, and that its sociological role is largely determined by its subservient relationship to more primary institutions.[2] The functional branch of social theory, including human capital and socialization theories, assumes that education exists to fulfill political and economic functions, while the Marxist-conflict branch assumes that it exists to reproduce and legitimate power and material contradictions inherent in the capitalist system of production (e.g., Dreeben 1968; Schultz 1971; Bowles and Gintis 1973). Yet an assumption of subservience increasingly flies in the face of evidence that education has become a dominant institution in its own right, with considerable independent sociological influence on culture (Baker 2014; Brint 2006). Given this, social theory about education and society should be recast and empirical inquiry expanded if sociology of education is to carry its success into the future.

The current robust and extensive culture of education is chiefly a product of its own development as an institution. In other words, it is not a creation of an overeducation crisis, educational credential inflation, a fooled public, a plot to reproduce social class, runaway populism, technological advance, media hype, or any of the other external reasons often suggested. Like other social institutions currently at the center of human society, the massive undertaking of formal education commands a significant share of cultural understandings that influence life globally, deeply permeating many noneducational dimensions. Seen this way, the indefatigable expansion of schooling across the world's population and the rising normative levels of educational attainment over successive generations can enrich the understanding of ascendant aspects of late-modern society, plus many qualities of the subsequent postindustrial society, and likely scenarios for the future of global society.

Of course, the sociology of education already occupies itself with the study of educational expansion and its institutional development. Since John Meyer's key formulation of education as a social institution in the late 1970s, a stream of research has investigated the education revolution through analysis of growing primary- and secondary-school enrollments over the past century and a half (e.g., Fuller and Rubinson 1992; Meyer 1977). While this is an obvious and productive approach, the impression remains that the education revolution came out of midair with few cultural ties to prior developments, thus trivializing the study of the independent influence of an expanding education sector on society. Further, this research, accompanied by neo-institutional theory, has not been fully integrated into sociology of education; the field seems not to know what to make of either. (See also chapter 3, by Scott Davies and Jal Mehta, for a similar argument with additional important theoretical extensions.)

To remedy this problem, two heretofore underdeveloped theoretical questions must be addressed and become foci of future empirical research: What is the origin of the education revolution? And what are the societal consequences of a robust institution of education? As described in more detail below, theories about the origin of the education revolution and its ultimate impact on society are a high priority for the future. Neo-institutionalism offers the beginnings of one such theory, but there is much it does not yet include. Similarly, if theory from a Marxist-conflict vein is to remain viable, it also must address origins, as it is now clear from the empirical record that industrialization and large-scale capitalism, while contributors to the education revolution, were not its originators. Human-capital arguments also must consider the education revolution if they are to go beyond narrow and limited recognition of the impact of education on the nature of work, labor markets, and economic innovation (Baker 2014).

Like its origins, the constructive power of education in a schooled society is a major new avenue for theory and research. Education is becoming a master causal agent in society, demonstrably independent from other factors such as race, gender, material wealth, and so forth. And although sociology of education currently has useful literatures on some aspects of this process, the changing power of education is so dynamic and extensive that the field risks falling behind if there is not significant new theory and research. Failure to embrace fully the "So what?" question is, for example, a notable weakness in past scholarship motivated by neo-institutional theory. And, as empirical research from other fields across a vast range of outcomes for humans and their collectives already promises, if answering the impact question goes well beyond social class reproduction, elite legitimation, and simple human capital accumulation, then how will the Marxist-conflict and human capital perspectives account for this?

In partially abdicating the study of education effects, sociology of education is missing a major opportunity to inform social science about central individual and collective processes. This is in large part a result of how the subservient assumption traps the field into considering education either as a secondary function or as only reproductive. Early attempts to research the cognitive and psychological impact of absolute levels of schooling on individuals were mostly abandoned in the rush to focus on relative social status attainment processes. But the education revolution and the rapid coming of the schooled society represent an invitation for the sociology of education to grow intellectually in dynamic ways; the schooled society is ripe with new and exciting research opportunities.

Change and Social Theory

When societies radically change, weaknesses in social theories can become apparent. In a sense, social change represents an empirical challenge for current theoretical perspectives. And that is as it should be, if sociology is to continue being scientific. New ways in which humans organize society and derive meaning from its reality offer rare opportunities to assess and, if warranted, reject theory. As any treatise on scientific methods attests, an empirical chance to reject theory is the essential logic of scientific inquiry. Social change as theory testing must be embraced.

The usual rejoinder to this is, "The more things change, the more they stay the same." In other words, is a particular incidence of social change profound enough to test theory? Or does current theory predict it, rendering it relatively trivial? Profound social change—industrial capitalist process and the decline of "traditional society"; the rise and spread of nation-states and the death of empire; social movements, revolution, and other widely participatory political actions; and world society's intensive globalization—have motivated broad theory testing and retheorizing. Indeed, the genesis of sociology as a formal intellectual endeavor stemmed from all of these changes as they first occurred in Western society over the late modern and industrial periods. But early social theory's success in explaining the decline of traditional society and the rise of late modern society becomes a liability as times moves on. Much sociological theory reads as if little else has occurred since, or as if the change that has happened was fully predictable from existing theories of a past world.

Early social theorists and precursors to empirical social sciences, with their "discovery of society," or, better, their "invention of society," as a manifest entity worthy of intellectual inquiry formed a new way to conceptualize origins of human life and its nature as a collective reality (Collins and Makowsky 1998). And this conception has in turn fueled the grandest of intellectual endeavors about society: namely, to identify key causal factors behind the worldwide decline of traditional society in all its forms, and the rise, globalization, and greater differentiation of modern society. From the mid-nineteenth century on, this inquiry led to the founding of the discipline of sociology and other social and behavioral sciences. Creators of sociological inquiry, including Karl Marx, Émile Durkheim, and Max Weber, spent their careers trying to understand this transition, and their general insights set the leitmotifs of investigation for the expansion of the social sciences over the course of the twentieth century (Frank and Gabler 2006).

It is ironic, then, that these intellectuals' work came too early to recognize the implications of the growing institution of education. Instead, economic and political factors received the lion's share of credit. Of course, both Durkheim and Weber included some examination of the role of the university and science in their analyses of the great societal transition, but they could not have been expected to perceive formal education's independent and future role in this transformation worldwide (e.g., Durkheim 1938/1977; Weber 1958).

Real social change is notoriously difficult to identify. Everyday life in postindustrial society is so wedded to the notion of constant change that much trivia is heralded as profound. Also, one of the central insights of social science inquiry is that human society is organized around a remarkably common set of requirements and hierarchies, so that societal change probably has some upper bounds. Perhaps the best way to conceptualize change, particularly in an ever-universalizing world, is that common components of culture can become more or less prominent in meaning, and hence in social control and power, at different historical points. This is the point of the functionalist stream of social theory in its attempt to address the question: How is society possible? Specifically from the neo-institutional version of functionalism, change is assumed to exist in a process of institutionalization.

As a theory, neo-institutionalism essentially retools the older concept of social institution by placing far greater theoretical emphasis on institutions as producing widely shared cultural meanings instead of as only consisting of highly prescribed and structured social roles and norms (Meyer and Jepperson 2000). The deep institutionalization of capitalism was a substantial social change from earlier periods during which this particular economic process had less meaning. Conversely, military conquest as an economic strategy was heavily institutionalized, only to lose its legitimation and advantage. There are many components to social change, including technological and physical change, but all result in institutionalization, which is at the heart of a social construction of reality that undergirds neo-institutional arguments (Berger and Luckmann 1966).

Seen this way, one of the largest societal projects of institutionalization over the past 150 years or so is the development of, and widening access to, formal education from early in childhood up through the far reaches of the university and now into adulthood. Compared to past societies, the worldwide education revolution, as Talcott Parsons named it in 1970s, is profound social change (Parsons and Platt 1973). Formal education has been a social institution for at least several millennia, but its level of institutionalization (control of meaning) has steadily grown, first over the eight-hundred-year course of the successful Western version of the university, and then into the recent period of mass schooling and wide inclusion of the world's population and many social functions into the institution. As recently hypothesized elsewhere, the education revolution is the essential social change by which current theories of sociology of education, and, to a significant degree, general social theories must be assessed (Baker 2014). The central empirical challenge before sociology of education is to explain why the education revolution is happening, and its consequences for postindustrial world society. We can no longer treat expanding education and its role in society as a secondary institution that supports economic or political reproduction of the nineteenth-century version of social class; it is now a prominent constructer of social reality at the center of society.

The Education Revolution as Institutional Change

The demography of the education revolution is well known to sociologists of education, but what may be less clear is how the trend may have accelerated, both quantitatively and qualitatively, from about 1960 onward. Gross enrollment rates have risen consistently over the past 150 years; near-full enrollments have been attained, first in wealthier nations, and since the middle of the twentieth century, more globally (Benavot and Riddle 1988; Fuller and Rubinson 1992). Consequently, 80 percent of persons across the world age fifteen or older can both read and write a short statement about their life—a social change that would have been hard to imagine fifty years ago, and unthinkable one hundred years ago (UNESCO 2002). Along with the diffusion of mass education, the normative standard of educational attainment has risen with each new generation of schooled parents. For example, the United States has led the way in developing mass education. A hundred years ago, about half of all US school-aged children were enrolled in school, whereas the proportion rose to 75 percent within the next forty years and to almost 90 percent over the next twenty years. Today more than twelve years of schooling is the median attainment (US Department of Education 1993).

Over the past several decades, mass education has flowed into the higher education sector in many nations, and the beginnings of mass post-undergraduate education are observable (Schofer and Meyer 2005). In the academic year 2006–2007, for instance, the entire American higher education system graduated approximately 1.5 million students with a BA degree, and 755,000 students with graduate degrees, yielding a ratio of one graduate degree for every two BA degrees (US Department of Education 2008). Since the early 2000s, individuals earning advanced degrees have had the highest rate of increase in US history; over the past decade the number of new PhDs grew by one million (45 percent) and that of Masters by five million (43 percent) (US Census Bureau 2012). And what has already occurred in Northern Europe and North America is now occurring worldwide.

Beyond educational expansion progressing through established levels of schooling, there are a number of new ways education grows in postindustrial life. For example, currently one-third of the entire US labor force is required annually to enroll in continuing education as a condition for employment, and 40 percent of all American adults participated in some formal education for work or for reasons of personal growth (Hussar and Bailey 2011; Jacobs and Stoner-Eby 1998; US Department of Education, NCES 2003). Universities create programs for the inclusion of all in higher education. For example, a growing number of higher education institutions now have nondegree attendance programs for mentally challenged youth. Significantly more youth enroll in BA/MA degree programs, pursue dual majors, and earn multiple graduate degrees (US Department of Education, NCES 2007). Formal education for early childhood expands in its centrality to childhood (Schaub, 2013; Schaub, Henck, and Baker 2017); and the massive worldwide shadow education phenomenon is a prominent example of unprecedented private resources used to supplement and expand access to schooling (Aurini, Davies, and Dierkes 2013; Baker and Mori 2010).

What is often overlooked in accounts of the growing demography of education is the realization that it is itself a consequence of a major cultural process. The education revolution is a cultural phenomenon more than a material or political one, although it has major material and political consequences. Widespread education in a postindustrial society creates cultural ideas about new types of knowledge, new types of experts, new definitions of personal success and failure, a new workplace and conception of jobs, and new definitions of intelligence and human talent. At the same time, educational achievement and degree attainment have come to dominate social stratification and social mobility, superseding and delegitimizing forms of status attainment left over from the past. The global impact of formal education on postindustrial society has been so extensive that it can be argued that mass education is a founding social revolution of modernity (Meyer 1977; Parsons 1973).

A final part of the education revolution, also frequently unnoticed, is unprecedented historical change in the content, intent, and organization of schooling. The everyday image of education is that there was some past golden age from which it has steadily deteriorated in quality and goals. And, indeed there has been much change, but not in the way most would characterize it. The idea of a golden age is dubious, and a case can be made that the technical quality of education has actually increased. But most important sociologically is the qualitative change in education, particularly over the twentieth century. Schooling, including the university, has become more cognitive in content, less vocational in intent, more focused on broad human development, and increasingly connected to universal ideas of knowledge. Among these new social constructions of education, several illustrate the overall change.

The first trend is a growing culture of cognition in curricula that narrows the status of human capabilities towards cognitive performance. Of course, all education and knowledge at any point in history involve cognition, but a dominant curricular trend of the schooled society constructs and celebrates a particular set of cognitive skills and elevates them to a heightened status. Increasingly, academic skills, particularly higher-order thinking capabilities, are equated with intelligence as a generalizable skill assumed useful for all types of human activity. With the development and flourishing of this "academic intelligence," traditional schooled mental skills, such as recitation, disputation, memorization, formalistic debate, formulae application, rote accuracy, and authoritative text reading and exegesis have been pushed aside as problem-solving, effortful reasoning, abstraction and higher-order thinking, and the active use of intelligence take center stage. The latter skills have become the explicit, overarching epistemological leitmotif of modern education, and there is evidence that a culture of cognition continues to intensify in its importance both within and without schools and universities (e.g., Baker et al. 2015).

The second trend is the rise of a culture of science as the main truth claim, which extends into ever more domains of knowledge (Drori et al. 2003). Further, the rise of the social sciences in the university has shaped authoritative knowledge as a science about humans and their societies (Frank and Gabler 2006). This is not to say that all people, including intellectuals, read science, do scientific experiments, or consider themselves scientists or social scientists; in fact, the overwhelming majority do none of these. But the core ideas of science as an epistemological system—knowing as a rational process, and knowledge as something rationalized through the connection of theory and empirical evidence—transform all knowledge, even that which is not explicitly about science or social science.

Therefore, as mass schooling has spread, mathematics and science—including social and behavioral sciences—have become major components of the curriculum as never before. Before the advent of mass schooling, most people had little contact with this kind of knowledge, yet by the end of the twentieth century the world's secondary and primary students were routinely exposed to heavy doses of mathematics and science. Beyond general education in these subjects, across 163 national secondary systems, about a third has a large curricular stream that focuses intensively on mathematics and science (Kamens, Meyer, and Benavot 1996). Along with language skills, these subjects have come to dominate all types of primary and secondary schooling curricular programs. The three now make up the cornerstone of the mass school curriculum from the earliest grades on, and older notions of elitist classicalism have died out.

Another consequence of this internal change is the obsolescence of "vocationalism"—the earlier education goal of schooling for specific vocational preparation, usually as the working-class part of a bifurcated education system. The idea of vocationalism materialized in most nations in a range of vocational secondary schooling aimed at making new workers for the coming industrial age (e.g., Baker, 2009). By 1950, a third of all secondary students in North America and Western Europe were enrolled in vocational programs, and worldwide about a fourth of secondary enrollments were in vocational education (in Eastern Europe it was a full 50 percent). But this was the tipping point, as these were the largest enrollment shares vocational education was to have for the rest of the century. By 1975, that share had dropped worldwide to 16 percent, and it kept declining to where vocational training now makes up only about 10 percent of all secondary-school programs (Benavot 2006). Curricular models have shifted to general academic training for most students, and even on-the-job training curricula have turned decidedly academic in content (Scott and Meyer 1991).

The third trend is towards greater universalism of knowledge, and its reflection in school and university courses. When authoritative knowledge privileges universality, then the particular, the local, and the time-bounded qualities of knowledge become less important than the universal, the global, and the timeless truthlike qualities. The emerging epistemology assumes that all knowledge can and should take on universalistic qualities, and the university is chartered to study and apply its authoritative science and rationalized scholarship to everything (Lenhardt 2002). Also, authoritative knowledge based on universalism comes to include universalization of humans themselves (Frank and Meyer 2007). Widespread education imbues knowledge with an ideology of the equality of humans and societies, constructed along the norms of universal social justice, which have been widely observed over the past fifty years to be included in schooling curricula globally, regardless of the cultures of nations (Suárez 2007; Suárez and Bromley 2012). Steven Brint's essay in this volume thoroughly critiques the centrality of academic knowledge production in contemporary society; and it concludes, with some useful caveats, that while not all knowledge comes from the university, of course, the university is the "the ultimate cultural authority" on knowledge.

Formal education in all its various forms and expressions has become so intensely institutionalized in its demography, cultural impact, and internal qualities that we can refer to the "schooled society" as a new type of relationship between education and society (Baker 2014). Seen this way, the schooled society offers an unprecedented opportunity to test current theory, re-theorize, and develop new research agenda for the future of sociology of education.

A Sociology of the Origins of the Schooled Society

Often greater institutionalization of education is met with attempts to write it off as an incidence of overeducation, as merely a vehicle for reproduction of social class inequality, or with a collective "So what?" But analyses suggest that educational inflation is not the best way to think about the trend, and while there are many implications for stratification, such massive elaborate changes are unlikely explained only by reproduction factors. And without easy ways to dismiss all of this institutionalization of formal education, the "So what?" becomes, "Why is this happening, and what impact will it have?"

Understanding what ultimately causes institutions to ascend or descend is a major challenge for sociology. Why education as an institution has become so successful at this time is a central question for the future of social theory. Functional theories, including neo-institutionalism as an improved functional theory, are well known to be weak on causes of social change, though they are much clearer on sustainability of social systems (e.g., Schofer, Hironaka, and Frank 2012). And even the most expansive of conflict theories leave much of the world unexplained.

To date, we know most about what is not, or is only moderately, associated with the greater institutionalization of education, at least in terms of its demographic spread and some content changes. Various conflict processes of social class, ethnic groups, and religions are only modestly (and in some analyses, not at all) associated, and while industrialization is, to a degree, it is not associated with the recent expansion of upper levels of higher education. Several lines of research suggest that job content, workplace structure, and profit strategies of firms are symbiotically related (in mutual causal processes) to a growing access to education in populations; nevertheless, educational expansion does not follow capitalism in some mechanical way. Also, the speed and global nature by which the education revolution unfolds transcends specific national and regional characteristics, and instead follows a pattern of international diffusion. At the same time, though, access to elaborated education systems is considered a major national asset by all types of governments and political ideologies. Finally, the institutionalization of education in the postindustrial world also transcends narrow economic and vocational functions while embracing logics about human development, social justice, and overall societal progress.

Recent scholarship suggests that the origins of the education revolution were shaped over the long historical development of the Western university, and that the schooled society has deep roots in Western society (e.g., Frank and Gabbler 2006; Meyer et al. 2008). Forty-five years ago, Parsons (1971, 1973; see also Bell 1973) predicted that the university would become the central cultural institution in society because of its multi-tiered charter to generate the universal knowledge that forms basic ideologies and creates academic degrees and expertise around them. If that is true, then in the last fourth of the twentieth century the university would have to intensify its original charter to a level unimaginable even at the start of the education revolution. There is evidence that it has done precisely this. Parsons also prophetically theorized that postindustrial society's origins stem from the three major social revolutions of capitalism, democracy, *and* education. Substantial evidence has since rendered that plausible. Yet much scholarship remains to be done on this broad and exciting thesis. If education might be one of the three major pillars of postindustrial society, should not its origins receive the same amount of sociological research as the other two have over the past century? The emerging schooled society places the institution of education at the heart of sociological inquiry, and sociology of education should seize the opportunity to explore it.

A Sociology of the Culture of the Schooled Society

The cultural impact of the education revolution is less obvious than growing educational attainment because all successful institutions increase the "naturalness" and taken-for-granted quality of the concepts, values, and meanings that they construct. No doubt this also reinforces a persistent intellectual underappreciation of the cultural influence of the schooled society. Yet what has been dubbed a "quiet revolution" because of its relative absence from accounts of the origins of modern society, is in its totality of influence a very loud social phenomenon that requires full integration into new sociological models of the history of societal change.

With greater institutionalization comes greater control over meaning and the extension of meaning into other social institutions. The relentless inclusion of the world's population into formal education produces a culture where education influences all facets of life (Baker 2014). This powerful cultural impact justifies and intensifies the now widely held belief that formal education is the best way to develop all humans and their capacities: an idea that surpasses centuries-old notions unrelated to education about how to raise children, make productive employees, and create effective citizens. The schooled society has far-reaching implications for human life, some of which are seen as positive and others as disconcerting.

A substantial amount of research finds evidence of the institutional impact of the educational revolution on the ideas, values, and norms of other institutions, such as work and occupations (Baker 2009), parenting roles and normative behavior (Schaub 2010), the structure and processes of polities and civic culture in democratic societies (Kamens 2009), the valuation of central human capabilities (Baker et al. 2015; Martinez 2000), the organization of religious communities and theology (Schwadel 2011), definitions of personal success and failure (Smith 2003), the spread and dominance of formal organizations (Stinchcombe and March 1965), the rising belief in professionalism and "scientization" of society (Drori, Meyer, Ramirez, and Schofer 2003), and the foundational image of society itself (Frank and Gabler 2006). Well beyond merely training individuals for jobs, the education revolution has produced a world in which education is an independent social institution that shapes significant parts of all other core institutions. Consider three examples of the future theoretical and empirical opportunities for a sociology of the schooled society.

Narrowing Educational Road to Status

Increasingly, formal education has become the main—and perhaps soon the sole legitimate—route to adult social status. Educational achievement and degree attainment dominate social stratification and social mobility, superseding and delegitimizing all noneducational forms of status attainment. And while the investigation of education's role in status attainment, and particularly in the reproduction of status over generations, is a central theoretical and empirical endeavor of sociology of education, the field seems not to fully appreciate the profound theoretical implications of this change.

By the late 1960s, sociologists of education were well aware that educational attainment had become a causal factor in adult status attainment to a degree unique in human society, and the same pattern was subsequently evident in other heavily schooled nations. While older forms of intergenerational reproduction (i.e., parents directly passing on their status to their children) were still part of the process, formal educational attainment had become the main route to an individual's adult status, and this was happening in two ways once thought mutually exclusive (Hout and DiPrete 2006). Educational attainment was influenced by an individual's social origin, but also by schooling factors independent of social origin: namely, academic merit (success or failure at schooling based on effort, intelligence, and motivation).

The next historical shift witnessed an even greater saturation of education in the social mobility process, as the latter process intensified along with the education revolution. Hout's landmark study (1988) found that by the late 1980s, direct intergenerational influence of origin had completely vanished among individuals completing the BA degree, and had substantially declined among individuals with a high school degree. This finding was replicated and also reported in other heavily schooled nations. Thus, once one is in the higher education arena, success becomes based chiefly on educational outcomes such as better academic performance in college, majors selected, and perhaps the influence of educational and prestige differences among institutions of higher education. Of course there remains the influence of one's origin on educational attainment, even up through higher education; but parental socioeconomic status itself is increasingly a function of earlier educational attainment. Consequently, over just several American generations, education has thoroughly saturated intergenerational mobility; given the increasing homogenization of schooling's influence, the educational dominance of social mobility is also, or will soon be, global.

Often the shift towards education's role in status attainment is attributed merely to greater economic and social complexity, and certainly economies have changed; yet replacing age-old social mobility mechanisms so rapidly and totally takes far more sociological change than can be accounted for by greater economic and social complexity. The rise of education as the nearly sole arbitrator of access to adult status has been so complete that former noneducation processes—apprenticeship, sinecure, occupational inheritance, marriage, religious charisma, guild training, patronage, caste—appear now as exotic social relics. With the exception of apprenticeship, these other mechanisms of status attainment are not well known to most in postindustrial society, but before the education revolution they were deeply embedded within societies and were considered legitimate.

The "Hout effect" is the clearest harbinger of the cultural impact of the education revolution on a central question of sociology of education. The field is perfectly situated to investigate why this change has happened, and what it will mean for social stratification into the future. For example, how does greater institutionalized education change the social construction of merit and replace older valued constructions? Further, what happens to mobility as origin reproduction diminishes and educational effects ascend? Will the schooled society profoundly reshape the terms of mobility, and with what consequences to social stratification and new forms of inequality? The opportunity to examine these kinds of questions is not only essential for the future of the sociology of education, but if the challenge is met, it will place the subfield at the center of sociology. See, for example, Douglas Downey's chapter in this book for a penetrating analysis of how this process might look in the near future, and David Karen's essay on how expanded schooling could create greater inequality.

The Education Effect and the Ubiquitous Educated Individual

Obsessed with the search for between-school effects, the field virtually ignores schooling effects, while other social and behavior sciences churn out finding after finding of the independent impact of education on just about every conceivable dependent variable at the individual level. Net of all individual variables including wealth, educational attainment is the most robust predictor of a wide array of behaviors, attitudes, and values. For example, the education revolution is fundamentally shaping all the major demography processes—mortality, health, fertility, marriage, and immigration—worldwide. Widespread education also dramatically changes the polity of nations and the content and pace of political action. It transforms people's religious beliefs and their worldviews. In fact, one is hard pressed to find a research literature on individuals where education is not the leading predictive factor. Further, this massive amount of evidence suggests that education's absolute effect is far more dominant than a relative one.

Unfortunately, these literatures often end up with overly simplified or just plain wrong explanations of why education is such a powerful causal agent. It turns out, for example, that in addition to manifest curricula, which have transforming impacts themselves, formal schooling is a major neurological and cognitive developmental institution (see Baker, Salinas, and Eslinger 2012 for review of studies). As a result, the education revolution is one main cause of rising fluid IQ in many populations (Baker et al. 2015). Sociology of education is so wedded to examining achievement as an outcome that it misses out on the study of cognitive change from schooling as a major independent variable. This becomes painfully obvious when colleagues in other subfields conflate education with an old notion of social class. The schooling process renders far more dynamic qualities than this.

The same is true for the substantial psychological impact of schooling. The "new modern people" that Alex Inkeles and colleagues found in the 1960s among the peasantry in developing nations with rising exposure to basic schooling have since become the norm worldwide (1996). It is a distinctly different world when wide access to even a few years of primary school pushes most people away from sources of traditional authority, such as clans, tribes, and religious leaders, and instead leads them to believe that worldly authority is not absolute; that it is natural to apply instrumental (means-ends) rationality to all aspects of one's life; and that one should embrace the notion of social progress and refrain from fatalism, accept science as a major source of truth, and adopt a cosmopolitan and global perspective. The world's population is now made up of waves of individuals empowered along these dimensions—who, in comparison to members of past societies, have considerable academic cognitive skills, and who feel entitled to apply them. This is not to say that everyone does equally well in pursuit of formal educational attainment or is equally transformed. But, compared to a century ago, when most were unschooled and illiterate, today's educated world population changes society in many unexpected and substantial ways. The educated worker, citizen, and believer transforms the nature of labor, profit-making, politics, and religion. When most, and soon all, people in many parts of the world are heavily educated, these changes fundamentally reconstruct other institutions, although not often in the ways that the original enthusiasts of mass education predicted.

For those who are educated and already live in the advanced form of the schooled society, the teaching of a child to read, write, do some mathematics, and have a beginner's understanding of science and social science seems by comparison to the great complexity of society a relatively basic undertaking, even a sociologically trivial one. But in comparison to an unschooled traditional society, the schooling of whole cohorts permeates every facet of life. The relatively simple act of teaching basic academic skills has the unintended effect of creating a new type of societal member. And as there are now waves of such people, their combined presence changes society. The broad question of what happens to populations when most individuals are more highly educated is a central challenge of sociology of education into the future. The social construction of the educated individual and the rise of an academic type of intelligence call out for deeper sociological theory and research.

The Educational Transformation of Jobs and Work

Most current theory assumes that the economy, as an institution, significantly dictates the form and nature of formal education. As noted above, theoretical paradigms about the function of education in society rely on the subservient assumption that education follows the contours of society. Human capital theory assumes that education mostly imparts work skills determined by the economy, while Marxist theory assumes that education mostly indoctrinates workers to the conditions of capitalist production and its social-class inequalities. But while there is no doubt that formal education involves training for the labor market and is increasingly the arena in which social status is determined, these theories minimize what education has become, and overlook its full impact on society. If one steps back from the traditional perspective and considers the cultural power of education in the schooled society, these well-worn theories can be turned on their heads by hypothesizing that there is an educational restructuring of jobs, occupational credentials, and profitable skills (e.g., Baker 2009; Goldin and Katz 2008).

In its robust institutionalized form, education does not merely follow the demands of jobs, nor is it an out-of-control process expanding education into a pandemic of overeducation, nor does it only socialize students for work. A considerable amount of recent research on labor economics, firms and organizations, and neo-institutional analyses of education finds that the education revolution is changing the qualities, the ideas, and expectations about work, workers, and workplaces. This is evident in the rising cognitive complexity of jobs, managerial requirements, and professionalization, particularly in the growing sector of employment within large organizations (e.g., Drori, Meyer, and Hwang 2006; Luo 2006; Howell and Wolff 1991). So too, just as the education revolution transforms work, so does it transform the nature of the connection between educational degrees and occupational placement (Baker 2011). While education has been tied to access to occupations for some time, the pace of educational expansion and its cultural impact have vastly increased the strength and salience of the connection.

The sociology of education has so far mostly missed this transformation (see Bills 1988 for an early notable exception). Overreliance on the old triad of theoretical notions of overeducation, education as a myth, and credentialism increasingly makes little sense in light of new evidence; all three should be laid to rest. The forms of jobs have changed along the values of the schooled society; the field could be more involved in understanding the why and how of the educational transformations of labor markets, job content, workplaces, and profit strategies.

Toward a Sociology of the Schooled Society

There is an endless debate over whether the conditions of contemporary society are morally better than those of past societies or imagined future ones. While the debate is an important one for the future of society in general, it often spills over into sociological theorizing, causing confusion. Theory attempts to explain how society is, not how it necessarily should be. This confusion between scientific theory and a moral position on the education revolution and society is a barrier to a sociological appraisal of the schooled society. For example, since the Marxist-postmodern perspective considers education as a conductor of capitalist oppression, when neo-institutionalism rejects this argument on theoretical and empirical grounds, the latter theory is condemned in some quarters as morally bankrupt for embracing education and ignoring inequality. But neither of these accusations is true.

So too, if economics is the "dismal science," education research is surely the Pollyanna science. Because the many researchers, policymakers, and others who are intent on improving the techniques of schooling assume formal education to be such a positive good, skeptical intellectuals instinctually suspect them of excessive optimism in prophesying of some morally superior world to come. Of course, the positive belief in education is an outcome of the schooled society itself, but it does not mean that a strong culture of education is necessarily morally good or bad. This commingling of scientific theory and moral assertion is harmful to future scholarship and to a balanced assessment of the costs and benefits of the education revolution. As with all successful institutions, there are significant moral assumptions behind education's central values, but this does not mean that the scientific study of those values promotes a particular moral order. Normative orders are all oppressive by definition, and understanding their assumptions, values, and logic is central to understanding society.

In keeping with the overall argument here, to the degree that the educational institution is oppressive, it is so more on its own terms than as a conveyer of other institutions' oppressive power. This is readily observable in the schooled society's celebration of an academic type of intelligence. The education revolution devalues the institutionalization of other capabilities such as physical labor, acuity in warfare, religious charisma, craftsmanship, and sexual prowess, all of which have been dominant sources of power in earlier human societies. The stronger the cultural effects of the ideas and understandings generated by education, the weaker and delegitimized other types of meanings become.

For individuals, the costs are evident: those who do not do well within dominating institutions of society suffer. Hence, extensive activity and industry to meet the central pressures and demands of schooling have penetrated all strata of society, and include everything from old-fashioned tutoring to psychological intervention to pharmaceutically aided learning. The same motivation also drives the legitimating proliferation of what is known as "special education" within the operation of schooling and among the research interests of learning scientists—a form of schooling adapted to students who experience a range of challenges in developing academic intelligence (and now also to students who are very adept at academic intelligence, to gain extra advantages; e.g., Hibel, Farkas, and Morgan 2010). As the institution's normative pressures mount, norms of parenting, childhood, formation of the self, and even the operation of schooling are pressured to change, thus creating stress and cultural strain as education is ever more institutionalized (e.g., Schaub 2013).

Like all known societies, the schooled society produces and legitimates a social hierarchy along with unequal distribution of social and material goods, including scarce privileged rights. Indeed, in the coming schooled society, stratification is transformed from older forms into a form that follows the institutional logic of formal education; but it is hierarchical social stratification nonetheless. Furthermore, and intriguingly, the postindustrial culture now equates academic hierarchy with an expression of socially just merit, although this yields a number of consequences that may not be socially just. For example, the schooled society readily expands the demand and supply of high-end services such as financial, legal, and health services, often at the expense of basic services for all kinds of people. The growing professions supplying these services are among the best-paid positions in developed nations, thus increasing inequality among the upper parts of the labor market; variation across educational credentials is also a main causal factor in inequality among all salaries. This educational effect on creating endless demand also feeds into a growing capitalist system of consumption, which of course has some well known negative societal consequences. Expanding formal education helps to lift many out of absolute poverty, a feat that most economists find more beneficial to society than eliminating relative inequality. Nevertheless, advanced forms of the schooled society can create and maintain damaging inequalities (see the chapter by Karen in this volume). For instance, many would cast the rise of a creative class as a positive, but this obvious consequence of the schooled society also comes with considerable exclusivity among social groups (Florida 2001).

Overwhelmingly, the education revolution's main ideology is changing the terms of the social contract worldwide to include the educated sensitivities and capabilities of a far greater proportion of populations than ever before. Thus, as the sociology of education sits at the crossroad of past success and the future, it must consider a question: Will a broader sociology of education emerge to meet the profound change of the schooled society?

Notes

1. Author thanks Scott Davies and anonymous reviewers for helpful comments on an early draft, and HyJong Jang for bibliographic assistance.
2. The term "primary institutions" refers to those with greater cultural meaning and social power compared to lesser secondary ones; the old distinction between formal versus informal institutions does not apply here.

References

Aurini, Janice, Scott Davies, and Julian Dierkes, eds. *Out of the Shadows: The Global Intensification of Supplementary Education*. Vol. 22. Emerald Group Publishing, 2013.

Baker, David P. 2009. "The Educational Transformation of Work: Towards a New Synthesis." *Journal of Education and Work* 22, no. 3: 163–191.

———. 2011. "Forward and Backward, Horizontal and Vertical: Transformationof Occupational Credentialing in the Schooled Society." *Research in Social Stratification and Mobility: A Journal of the International SociologicalAssociation* 29, no. 1: 5–29.

———. 2014. *The Schooled Society: The Educational Transformation of Global Culture*. Stanford, CA: Stanford University Press.

Baker, David P., and Izumi Mori. 2010. "The Origin of Universal Shadow Education: What the Supplemental Education Phenomenon Tells Us about the Postmodern Institution of Education." *Asia Pacific Education Review* 11, no. 1: 36–48.

Baker, David P., Daniel Salinas, and Paul J. Eslinger. 2012. "An Envisioned Bridge: Schooling as a Neurocognitive Developmental Institution." *Developmental Cognitive Neuroscience* 2:6–17.

Baker, David, P., et al. 2015. "The Cognitive Impact of the Education Revolution: A Possible Cause of the Flynn Effect on Population IQ." *Intelligence* 49 (March-April): 144–158.

Bell, Daniel. 1973. *The Coming of Post-Industrial Society: A Venture in Social Forecasting*. New York: Basic Books.

Benavot, Aaron. 2006. "A Global Study of Intended Instructional Time and Official School Curricula." http://ns.worldbank.org.ru/ecaedu/bg/Global_Curriculum_text_Eng.pdf.

Benavot, Aaron, and Phyllis Riddle. 1988. "The Expansion of Primary Education, 1870–1940: Trends and Issues." *Sociology of Education* 61, no. 3: 191–210.

Berger, Peter, and Thomas Luckmann. 1966. *The Social Construction of Reality: A Treatise in the Sociology of Knowledge*. Garden City, NY: Anchor Books.

Bills, David B. 1988. "Educational Credentials and Promotions: Does Schooling Do More Than Get You in the Door?" *Sociology of Education* 61, no. 1: 52–60.

Bowles, Samuel, and Herbert Gintis. 1976. *Schooling in Capitalist America: Educational Reform and the Contradictions of Economic Life*. New York: Basic Books.

Brint, Steven G. *Schools and Societies*. Stanford University Press, 2006.

Collins, Randall, and Michael Makowsky. 1998. *The Discovery of Society*. New York: McGraw-Hill.

Dreeben, R. 1968. *On What Is Learned in School*. Reading, MA: Addison-Wesley.

Drori, Gili S., John W. Meyer, and Hokyu Hwang. 2006. *Globalization and Organization: World Society and Organizational Change*. Oxford, UK: Oxford University Press.

Drori, Gili S., John W. Meyer, Francisco O. Ramirez, and Evan Schofer. 2003. *Science in the Modern World Polity: Institutionalization and Globalization*. Stanford, CA: Stanford University Press.

Durkheim, Émile. 1938. "The Birth of the University." In *The Evolution of Educational Thoughts: Lectures on the Formation and Development of Secondary Education in France*, trans. and ed. Peter Collins, 75–87. Boston: Routledge & Kegan Paul.

———. 1938/1977. *The Evolution of Educational Thought: Lectures on the Formation and Development of Secondary Education in France*. Trans. and ed. Peter Collins. Boston: Routledge & Kegan Paul.

Florida, Richard. 2001. *The Rise of the Creative Class*. New York: Basic Books.

Frank, David, and Jay Gabler. 2006. *Reconstructing the University: Worldwide Shifts in Academia in the 20th Century*. Stanford, CA: Stanford University Press.

Frank, David J., and John W. Meyer. 2007. "University Expansion and the Knowledge Society." *Theory and Society* 36, no. 4: 287–311.

Fuller, Bruce, and Richard Rubinson, eds. 1992. *The Political Construction of Education: The State, School Expansion, and Economic Change*. New York: Praeger.

Goldin, Claudia, and Lawrence F. Katz. 2008. *The Race between Education and Technology*. Cambridge, MA: Harvard University Press.

Hibel, Jacob, George Farkas, and Paul L. Morgan. 2010. "Who Is Placed into Special Education?" *Sociology of Education* 83, no. 4: 312–332.

Hout, Michael. 1988. "More Universalism, Less Structural Mobility: The American Occupational Structure in the 1980s." *American Journal of Sociology* 93, no. 6: 1358–1400.

Hout, Michael, and Thomas A. DiPrete. 2006. "What We Have Learned: RC28's Contributions to Knowledge About Social Stratification." *Research in Social Stratification and Mobility* 24, no. 1: 1–20.

Howell, David R., and Edward N. Wolff. 1991. "Trends in the Growth and Distribution of Skills in the U.S. Workplace, 1960–1985." *Industrial and Labor Relations Review* 44, no. 3: 486–502.

Hussar, William J., and Tabitha M. Bailey, 2011. "Projections of Education Statistics to 2019 (NCES 2011–017)." Washington: National Center for Education Statistics, Institute of Education Sciences.

Inkeles, Alex. 1996. "Making Men Modern: On the Causes and Consequences of Individual Change in Six Developing Countries." In *Comparing Nations and Cultures: Readings in a Cross-Disciplinary Perspective*, ed. A. Inkeles and M. Sasaki, 571–585. Englewood Cliffs, NJ: Prentice Hall.

Jacobs, Jerry A., and Scott Stoner-Eby. 1998. "Adult Enrollment and Educational Attainment." *Annals of the American Academy of Political and Social Science* 559, no. 1: 91–108.

Kamens, David H. 2009. "The Expanding Polity: Theorizing the Links between Expanded Higher Education and the New Politics of the Post-1970s." *American Journal of Education* 116, no. 1: 99–124.

Kamens, David H., John W. Meyer, and Aaron Benavot. 1996. "Worldwide Patterns in Academic Secondary Education Curricula." *Comparative Education Review* 40, no. 2: 116–138.

Lenhardt, Gero. 2002. "Europe and Higher Education Between Universalisation and Materialist Particularism." *European Educational Research Journal* 1, no. 2: 274–289.

Luo, Xiaowei. 2006. "The Spread of a 'Human Resources' Culture: Institutional Individualism and the Rise of Personal Development Training." In *Globalization and Organization: World Society and Organizational Change*, ed. J. Meyer, G. Drori, and H. Hwang, 225–240. Oxford, UK: Oxford University Press.

Martinez, Michael E. 2000. *Education as the Cultivation of Intelligence*. Hillsdale, NJ: Erlbaum Associates.

Meyer, John W. 1977. "The Effects of Education as an Institution." *American Journal of Sociology* 83, no. 1: 55–77.

Meyer, John W., Francisco O. Ramirez, David F. Frank, and Evan Schofer. 2008. "Higher Education as an Institution." In *Sociology of Higher Education: Contributions and Their Contexts*, ed. P. Gumport, 187–221. Baltimore: Johns Hopkins University Press.

Parsons, Talcott. 1971. "Higher Education as a Theoretical Focus." In *Institutions and Social Exchange: The Sociologies of Talcott Parsons and George C. Homans*, ed. Herman Turk and Richard L. Simpson, 233–252. Indianapolis: Bobbs-Merill.

Parsons, T., and G. Platt. 1973. *The American University*. Cambridge, MA: Harvard University Press.

Schaub, Maryellen. 2010. "Parenting for Cognitive Development from 1950 to 2000: The Institutionalization of Mass Education and the Social Construction of Parenting in the United States." *Sociology of Education* 83, no. 1 (January 1): 46–66.

———. 2013. "Is There a Home Advantage in School Readiness for Young Children? Trends in Parent Engagement in Cognitive Activities with Young Children, 1991–2001." *Journal of Early Childhood Research*. DOI 10.1177/1476718X12468122.

Schaub, M., A. Henck, and D. Baker. 2017. "The Globalized 'Whole Child': Cultural Understandings of Children and Childhood in Multilateral Aid Development Policy, 1946–2010." *Comparative Education Review* 61, no. 2 (May): 298–326.

Schofer, E., Hironaka, A., and Frank, D. J. 2012. "Sociological Institutionalism and World Society." In E. Amenta, K. Nash & A. Scott, eds., The Wiley-Blackwell Companion to Political Sociology, 57–68. West Sussex, UK: Blackwell Publishing.

Schofer, Evan, and John W. Meyer. 2005. "The Worldwide Expansion of Higher Education in the Twentieth Century." *American Sociological Review* 70, no. 6 (December 1): 898–920.

Schultz, Theodore W. 1961. "Investment in Human Capital." *American Economic Review* 51, no. 1: 1–17.

Schwadel, Philip. 2011. "The Effects of Education on Americans' Religious Practices, Beliefs, and Affiliations." *Review of Religious Research* 53, no. 2: 161–182.

Scott, Richard, and John W. Meyer. 1991. "The Rise of Training Programs in Firms and Agencies: An Institutional Perspective." In *Research in Organizational Behavior*, ed. B. Staw and L. Cummings, 287–326. Greenwich, CT: JAI Press.

Smith, Thomas. 2003. "Who Values the GED? An Examination of the Paradox Underlying the Demand for the General Educational Development Credential." *Teachers College Record* 105, no. 3: 375–415.

Stinchcombe, Arthur L., and James March. 1965. *Handbook of Organizations*. Chicago: Rand McNally.

Suárez, David. 2007. "Education Professionals and the Construction of Human Rights Education." Comparative Education Review 51, no. 1: 48–70.

Suárez, David, and Patricia Bromley. 2012. "Institutionalizing a Global Social Movement:

Human Rights as University Knowledge." *American Journal of Education* 118, no. 3: 253–280.
UNESCO. 2002. "Education for All: Is the World on Track?" *EFA Monitoring Report*. Paris: UNESCO.
US Census Bureau. 2012. "Educational Attainment in the United States: 2012." Washington. www.census.gov/hhes/socdemo/education/.
US Department of Education, NCES (National Center for Education Statistics). 1993. "120 Years of American Education: A Statistical Portrait." Washington.
———. 2003. "Trends in High School Vocational/Technical Coursetaking: 1982–1998," ed. K. Levesque. Washington.
———. 2007. "Digest of Education Statistics 2006 (NCES 2007–017)." Washington.
———. 2008. "Digest of Education Statistics 2007 (NCES 2008–022)." Washington.
Weber, Max. 1958. "Science as a Vocation." In *From Max Weber: Essays in Sociology*, ed. H. H. Gerth and C. Wright Mills. New York: Oxford University Press.

THREE

The Deepening Interpenetration of Education in Modern Life

SCOTT DAVIES AND JAL MEHTA

This chapter presents a framework for charting and interpreting evolving connections between schooling and other societal fields over the past thirty to forty years. The topic of school-society connections is a foundational one for the sociology of education, yet we believe it has been underplayed in the field over recent decades. Many sociologists have discussed the expansion, diffusion and legitimation of schooling over the post–World War II era. But the full extent, variability, and reciprocal nature of school-society relations has not been fully theorized. Our goal is to re-stimulate research on this topic. In this chapter we argue that schools and society are more deeply "interpenetrated" than they were several decades ago. Today's schooling has not only extended its reach into other societal realms, but has at the same time itself also become increasingly influenced by those realms. It has become a hybrid institution more than ever before.

Our departure point is a series of classic and still influential theories that emerged in the 1960s, 1970s, and early 1980s—particularly the work of Daniel Bell, Talcott Parsons, Clark Kerr, John Meyer, and Paul DiMaggio and Walter Powell. This was an era of bountiful theorizing in sociology of education, and its major images of school-society connections continue to predominate today. Forecasting emerging times that Bell famously called "the post-industrial society," these theorists saw a world in which schooling was becoming the primary mechanism for individual mobility and an engine of economic growth, and, more broadly, one in which knowledge and expertise was becoming the chief currency of modern life. Knowledge and the professionals who carried it would become the ruling force in contemporary society. The norms and even the categories created by schooling would become constitutive for modern life, as schooling's influence expanded. Contemporary theorists like David Baker (chapter 2), whose work extends this tradition, argue that we now live in a "schooled society" in which schooling increasingly structures social life.

This chapter builds on Baker's ideas, but takes a more dialectical view. We use the term "deepening interpenetration" to capture reciprocal processes by which schooling and other social spheres shape each other. Through what we call an *intensifying logic*, we describe an extending reach of schooling into other fields. Ever younger children enroll in some form of school, more people graduate from high school and enroll in college, and more adults continue their formal education, creating a birth-to-death connection to formal education that was unfathomable in previous generations. Through this expansion, schooling increasingly structures other realms of life, including parenting practices, housing choices, and marriage markets, especially among the most advantaged in society. But this same shift has different consequences for less advantaged students. They too are lengthening their schooling, but they are doing so more in fits and starts, often mixing higher education with work and child-rearing. Because many mass-access institutions depend on these students as their primary enrollees, those institutions have altered their structures and practices to suit their students' needs. The result is what we call an *accommodating logic*: as schooling expands and touches new populations and enters new arenas, it becomes more of a hybrid institution—one that is less purely academic, and more responsive to the characteristics of the new populations. Interpenetration is the sum outcome of these twin processes. These logics combine to make schooling a less cloistered institution. Boundaries between school and non-school realms become more porous; new practices, culture, and forms of organization flow in both directions. What emerges is an increasingly thick web of school-society connections and mutual influence. These connections also trigger a third *logic of resistance*. There are two sides to this resistance. On one side is an aggressive skepticism of the cultural authority of schooled professionals and of the cognitive authority of schooled credentials. Resistors take populist stances on culture, practical knowledge, and democratic expertise. On another side, educators fend off these challengers, creating boundaries between their jurisdiction and populists and alternative practitioners. In combination, these logics of resistance serve as a brake on interpenetration, limiting the connections between education and other societal fields—though in aggregate, logics of resistance are weaker than those of intensification and accommodation.

Overall, since the 1970s, these logics of interpenetration have combined to increasingly conjoin schooling with realms of society that were formerly more separate. This thesis departs from previous theorizing in several ways.

Foremost, it emphasizes how modern education is increasingly mixing "institutional logics"; indeed, this process is *the* defining feature of contemporary school-society connections. Further, we see interpenetration as creating messy effects that do not necessarily generate more equality, legitimacy, or peace in education. As we elaborate throughout this chapter, various forms of schooling expansion and interpenetration tend to generate, if anything, new forms of inequality, disputation, and discord. We contend that thinking about new school-society connections offers good conceptual tools for understanding many of the struggles that have arisen in education over the past few decades.

Our Approach to Theorizing School-Society Connections

To articulate our ideas, we draw on a series of concepts that have emerged since the 1970s and have rarely been applied in sociology of education: those of "fields" (Fligstein and McAdam 2012), "institutional logics" (Alford and Friedland 1991; Thornton, Ocasio and Lounsbury 2012), and "knowledge imports and exports" (Brint, this volume).

First, we analyze schooling as a type of societal "field," a realm of social order set within a broader environment that consists of countless fields with varying relations to one another (Fligstein and McAdam 2012). Some social spaces are more closely linked than others, and some remain disconnected entirely. But Fligstein and McAdam are animated by Anthony Giddens's idea that modern social space is increasingly interconnected. Advanced technology, communications, and transportation have boosted the capacity of actors to monitor, influence, and react to events in once distant fields. Stevens et al. (2008), for instance, characterize contemporary universities as "hubs" that increasingly connect with a variety of social institutions. But the quality of interfield connections varies. Some connections are hierarchical, with one field being dependent on another; others are more interdependent and reciprocal (Fligstein and McAdam, 2012: 59). Several factors shape these links: *resource dependency*, in which actors in one field connect to those in another because they need something; *information flows*, whereby thickening channels of knowledge can tighten connections between fields; and *legitimating processes*, whereby changing cultural norms make it advantageous for actors in one field to associate with a formerly separate field. Using field theory, we argue that since the 1970s, schooling has reached further and further into society, encompassing younger and older age groups, and increasingly influencing other fields ranging from family life to housing markets to businesses to criminal justice, leisure, and health care sectors.

We adapt field theory to argue that education has generally tightened its connections to previously distant fields through a variety of new resource dependencies.

This argument rests on our holistic conception of schooling *writ large*. We see schooling as having become a polymorphic set of institutions. Whereas the classic theorists in the 1970s focused mainly on the major forms of schooling (K–12 public schools and universities), our theory encompasses *all* kinds of schooling—formal and informal, at all credential levels, in all kinds of sectors. To comprehend the sheer variety of schooling, our unit of analysis is what we call the "school form"—any set of recognizable instructor and student roles, curricula, and certifications. This inclusive definition offers analytic leverage for examining school-society links by being attuned to the varying amounts of institutionalization, structuration, and social recognition that schooling assumes as it spreads through society. Indeed, we emphasize how the *mutability* of school forms becomes readily evident once one looks beyond standard K–12 public schools, colleges and universities. Field theory puts a spotlight on forms of schooling that are less recognized and less easily "counted," and which have less societal authority and legitimacy. We argue that nonstandard schools forms have become far more predominant since the 1970s.

Second, we emphasize mutual influences between schools and society. Schools have certainly imposed their logics on adjoining fields, as Baker shows in chapter 2. But where school institutions depend on resources in other fields, they adapt some of their forms and practices to those fields. This process generates hybrid practices and organizational forms, an ongoing intermeshing of institutional principles. We articulate these ideas by building on Friedland and Alford's (1991) classic statement about institutional logics, and on those researchers who have extended those ideas to ponder the mixing of cognitive categories, social practices, and organizational forms across fields (e.g., Thornton, Ocasio and Lounsbury 2012; Scott 2014).

Third, we wish to underscore the *uneven* nature of interpenetration between schooling and other fields. Connections between fields vary; practices in one field may shape practices in some regions of other fields, but not others (Fligstein and McAdam 2012). Consider how social stratification continues to condition the influence of universities on childrearing. The dictates of competing for admission into elite colleges have powerfully altered the meanings and structuring of childhood among advantaged families, as we describe further below. But this influence is far weaker in other societal strata, where schools still plays a more limited and often negative role.

Social class continues to forge uneven connections between schooling and other fields.

Setting the Stage for Interpenetration: Three Dimensions of School Expansion

To set up our argument about interpenetration, we first describe three dimensions of school expansion.

Vertical expansion is the phenomenon of greater participation across tiers of schooling that serve to increase people's aggregate time spent in education. This expansion, so explicit in classic theories, has continued over the past forty years. Americans have continued to spend longer years in high schools and in post-secondary institutions. Between 1980 and 2013, the proportion aged twenty-five and older that had graduated from high school rose from 69 to 88 percent, while the proportion with a BA degree rose from 17 to 32 percent. These trends are projected to continue for at least another decade (National Center for Education Statistics 2013).

A second expansion takes the form of broadening curricula, which we think of as *horizontal expansion*. Randall Collins' (1979) foundational writings on credentialism described the proliferation of recognized fields and formal certifications up to the 1970s. Since then, even more realms of life have been "schooled," particularly in higher education, where the number of fields of study, courses, topics, and majors has continued to spiral. This expansion has occurred in three forms: new applied sciences, self-touted interdisciplinary areas, and new vocational fields. In many respects, the latter process has been most striking. Brint et al. (2005: 157) have charted a major shift towards the "practical arts" across all American college sectors between 1970–71 and 2000–2001, noting that almost all of the fastest growing fields were occupational in nature, including a tenfold growth in protective services and computer and information systems, a fivefold growth in fitness, recreation, and leisure studies, and a threefold growth in communications. Many community colleges now offer degrees, certificates, and licenses for areas ranging from security to bartending to golf, winemaking, gaming, and hospitality. Liberal arts colleges now offer more professional majors (Kraatz and Zajac 1996). Even major research universities offer an assortment of vocational programs. Elizabeth Armstrong and Laura Hamilton (2014: 70) list popular majors in a Midwestern flagship state university that include arts management, sports management, outdoor recreation and resource management, and tourism.

Another engine of horizontal expansion has been new applied sciences that are driven by a combination of rapid discovery and desires to convert them into marketable products. And in universities, the social sciences and humanities have been broadened by a series of interdisciplinary fields that include cultural studies, media studies, gender and sexuality studies, and African American studies (Jacobs 2013). In combination, these three motors of horizontal expansion have broadened the array of realms that are "schooled."

A third form of expansion takes the form of "school imports." This expansion occurs when school forms migrate beyond formal education sectors into other fields. Since the 1970s, an array of professions has imported school forms as alternate vehicles for their practice. Such forms have emerged in criminal justice, leisure, health, social work, and social services. These imports lack the institutional power of regular schools; their certifications lack currency beyond their own field, are rarely recognized by formal educators, and have no "charter" (in John Meyer's [1970] sense) that can bestow a new social recognition for their graduates. Yet they represent a form of school expansion since they allow core elements of schooling such as student-teacher roles and structured curricula to spread to adjacent fields. Imports are organizationally flexible, easily adapted or discarded elements of the school form depending on the context.

Each of these three forms of expansion—vertical, horizontal, and imported—has served to more extensively connect schooling to other fields since the 1970s. But what underlying processes have fueled this interpretation? And what social forces have sometimes served as brakes?

Twin Logics of Interpenetration . . . and a Logic of Resistance

Expansion has triggered three logics of interpenetration. First, continuing vertical expansion has set in motion what we call an "intensifying logic." Vertical expansion not only raises aggregate educational attainments, but also boosts premiums for society's most exclusive credentials. This process continually refuels itself through a feedback loop, as Collins (1979) noted long ago: as more people seek schooling, lower-rank credentials get devalued in a process of inflation, which in turn stimulates more demand. This expansion triggers the intensifying logic. Already selective schools mostly respond to heightened demand by becoming *more* selective, thus making their credentials even more scarce. Their actions spark a spiraling competition for admissions among actors who seek those credentials and thus attempt to align their practices with the dictates of educational competition. Importantly, this competition has strong ripple effects on other fields: it reshapes residential preferences, parenting choices, and leisure time, as we detail further below.

But not all populations are oriented towards this top-level competition, of course. The vast majority of higher education students enter less selective, mass-access institutions that have greatly expanded and have captured most of rising demand. Vertical and horizontal expansion has created a gallery of new credentials that are now required in occupations that previously did not require such credentials. Thus even mass-access institutions generate an aligning process, albeit a milder version, forcing actors to alter their life courses in the pursuit of schooling requirements, delaying or suspending family and job duties. But even a mild aligning can be extremely difficult for many would-be credential seekers, especially those who joined the race later in their lives and already have had jobs, families, and children.

The second logic—the "accommodating logic"—is set in motion when expanded schooling brings such new populations into the orbit of formal schooling. Lacking name-brand reputations and grand academic histories, less selective institutions typically appeal to untapped markets of students, largely by offering useful, if not top-tier, credentials. Thus, at the mass tiers of education, interpenetration operates in reverse. Those institutions depend on a key resource: students and their tuition dollars. Being less able to compete for traditional students at the upper end of the market, mass access institutions search for untapped markets. To capture those markets, these institutions adapt to their students' needs, altering their organizational templates and practices with newly flexible scheduling and timetabling, new (and often more vocational) content, more convenient locations, and new forms of instruction. For instance, the rise of GED providers and a host of proprietary, for-profit, and community colleges represent accommodating adaptations to previously excluded populations.[1]

The intensifying and accommodating logics combine to drive interpenetration: the former leverages change in other fields, and the latter sparks change in schooling provisions. Both bring schooling and other fields into closer contact. Yet this interpenetration is very uneven; unequal school outcomes have persisted despite a half century of expansion and a slew of accommodations (Murnane and Duncan 2011). Already-advantaged actors are best positioned to enact logics of intensification and align their practices with the dictates of educational competition. They continually populate the most desirable, prestigious, and lucrative segments of higher education (Gerber and Cheung 2008; Radford 2013). In turn, intensifying logics boost the prestige of upper tiers of schooling. By contrast, the disadvantaged have far less capacity to align with intensifying logics. Elite schools and poorer families remain disconnected from each other despite great systemwide expansion. As a result, the poor tend to enter institutions that can accommodate their life circumstances, and even those institutions suffer substantial attrition (Engle and Tinto 2008; Hermanowicz 2003). Moreover, accommodating logics can diminish the societal valuation of mass-access institutions. While those institutions survive by meeting the needs of their students, they also suffer status penalties and get tagged as inferior forms of education. In sum, different regions of fields are interpenetrated differently, and by doing so they generate a different kind of unrest.

Expansion itself triggers a third logic, that of "resistance," which serves as a partial brake on interpenetration. By resistance we refer not to general criticism or skepticism directed at formal schooling, but specifically to practices that serve to weaken connections between schooling and other fields. As schooling logics enter other fields, most local actors work with them, but some contest those invading logics. We identify several species of this resistance. One is populist in tenor. Populists challenge the cultural authority of educated elites, portraying the latter as disconnected from the core values of ordinary people. This resistance was foreseen by Michael Young and Richard Hofstadter in earlier eras, but has been strongly rearticulated and refueled in today's "culture wars." Another species is resistance to the extension of the intensifying logic into family life. Commentators are decrying the overly hectic and scheduled childhoods that are spawning "excellent sheep" rather than independent thinkers, and call for "free range parenting" that encourages children to develop according to their own pace and wants (e.g., Deresiewicz 2014). A third species embraces a "do-it-yourself" ethic that challenges the professional credentialing authority of schools along with their certified knowledge. These skeptics champion more open and democratic approaches to knowledge production, expertise, skill, and task authority. In combination, these three types of resistance tend to slow interpenetrating processes, though ironically, many prominent resisters (e.g., politicians and internet entrepreneurs) are themselves highly schooled.

We substantiate this broad argument over the next five sections. First, we further detail what we mean by intensifying and accommodating logics of interpenetration. Second, looking more closely at changing organizational forms of schools and universities, we show how horizontal expansion and other forces have fueled the mixing of institutional logics between education and other fields. Third, we examine the cultural life of schools and universities, suggesting they are less cloistered and more infused with extraschool norms, logics, and popular culture than before. Fourth, we consider the importing of school forms to nonschool fields as a more subtle instance of interpenetration. And fifth, we describe how the expanding orbit of schooling has had mixed effects on its societal legitimacy, sometimes provoking resistance.

Vertically Expanded Schooling: Intensification and Accommodation

Until the latter half of the twentieth century, school was a relatively brief life experience for most Americans. In 1960 the adult population had median school attainment of ten years; among nonwhites it was eight years (US Census Bureau 2009). Only one-quarter of adults had completed high school; only 7 percent had a four-year college degree. Among rural people, only 5 percent had a degree. Indeed, according to the 1960 census, Americans were likelier to have completed only four years of schooling than to have received a BA degree. Schooling was hardly a "lifelong" experience. Before the advent of early education, preschool and kindergarten, and before the expansion of higher and adult education, most people encountered schooling for about ten consecutive years and never returned. The undistinguished role of schooling in most people's life courses weakened schooling's influence on family life; few families rearranged their home schedules and activities to better their odds for educational rewards, whether by creating elaborate study schedules, engaging in private tutoring, pursuing valued extracurricula, or saving large sums for college. Schooling also generated less social homophily in relationships like marriage, friendship networks or choice of neighbors (Blossfeld 2009). Schooling was also less economically consequential: graduating from high school was generally sufficient for a middle-class wage in a factory or in other forms of manual employment.

But continued "vertical expansion" over the past forty years has made "birth-to-death" schooling less of an ideal and more of a reality. Early childhood has become more "schooled." Between 1970 and 2010, the enrollment rate for children ages three to four (typically in nursery or preschool) increased from 20 to 53 percent. Between 1990 and 2012, the percentage of five-year-old children in full day, pre-primary programs rose from 42 to 73 percent (NCES 2012). Preschool and kindergarten has become more academic in its goals and rationales, as expressed in the term "school readiness" (Booth and Crouter 2007; Schaub 2016). Schooling also has a stronger grip among older Americans. One striking indicator is the rising number of graduate degrees holders. About 8 percent of the population now holds master's degrees, the same proportion that held bachelor's degrees in the 1960s (NCES 2014). Formal adult education and job training has also grown significantly, as has schooling for leisure, personal interest, or an institutional requirement (https://nces.ed.gov/programs/digest/d14/tables/dt14_507.40.asp). As more Americans at all ages attend a "school" of some sort, school forms occupy more days, nights, weekends and years of their lives. American society is now far more crowded with formally educated people than it was in the 1970s. But this vertical expansion has had different consequences for different populations.

Intensifying Logics: How Schools Structure Other Fields

For the middle classes especially, vertical expansion has sparked a revolution in family life. Parents' mental maps of their children's futures have been redrawn, as far more expect their children to attend a postsecondary institution; in fact, nearly *all* college-educated parents have these expectations (Rosenbaum 2001; Davies 2005). This interpenetration is most intense among families competing for admission into top-ranked colleges. Prior to the 1960s, most students in top colleges came from elite origins (Karabel 2005; Lehman 1999). But family life, at least for those in the heat of the race, has been recalibrated since the 1970s. As rising aspirations among the broader middle class were met with efforts to open access to meritorious students, scholars began to observe frenetic and spiraling competitive strategies (McDonough 1994). Top-flight educational competition has spawned family practices that are increasingly planned, sequenced, and structured. Prepping children for this race has become an art, vocation, and preoccupation. Annette Lareau (2000, 2003) has charted these changes in her studies of "concerted cultivation," a style of parenting that often begins from birth, surges into preschool years (Chin 2005), and takes firm root in elementary school. Today's upper-middle-class parents are mixing more "educational" activities into their children's leisure time than did previous generations (Sayer et al. 2004; Murnane and Duncan 2011), consciously reshaping their weekends and summers to pursue effective study schedules, vitae-friendly internships, volunteering, and extracurricular and leisure activities (Stevens 2007; Rivera 2015). While often voiced in idioms of self-actualization, personal expression, and well-roundedness (see Aurini and Hillier, chapter 12), concerted cultivation illustrates how the dictates of education-aligning practices have altered children's upbringings. It signals the extension of intensified educational competition into the field of family relations.

This intensifying logic also penetrates other social relationships. This rising number of women with advanced degrees rise has made school attainment a more prominent basis of marital selection, assortative mating, and other forms of homogamy (Blossfeld 2009). Educational attainment is now a strong predictor of residential choice (Domina 2006). Real estate markets have been increasingly organized around school catchments; houses in the "right" districts with highly ranked schools fetch premiums of hundreds of thousands of dollars (Figlio and Lucas 2004). Schools are increasingly segregated by family income, which is highly correlated with parental education (Reardon and Owens 2014).

This interpenetration can be understood in terms of a reconfiguring of interfield resource dependencies and flows of information that has occurred since the 1970s. Spots in top-rank schools and colleges have become scarcer than desirable houses. Actors in the housing field change their practices to align with school dictates. Real estate agents seize upon data about high school test score averages, AP placement rates, class sizes, and college going rates that are prominently displayed in magazines and websites. This information flows not simply in a neutral and transparent fashion, but in a commensurated form (Espeland and Sauder 2007) that selects, abstracts, and converts certain qualities of schools into metrics, which in turn trigger new housing practices. As per field theory, reconfigured resource dependencies and information flows have tightened links between formerly distant fields, at least at the upper end of the marketplace. But what happens at the lower end?

Accommodating Logics: How New Populations Structure Schools

Compared to forty years ago, vertical and horizontal expansion has created, in aggregate, far more tiers, institutional types, and entry, exit, and re-entry points among different types of schools. While few disadvantaged students enter upper tier institutions, system-wide expansion has widened the "pipelines" by which these students flow in and out other kinds of schools. An increasingly-elaborate "second chance" system has forged alternate routes for students to earn high school credits and then access a variety of colleges or adult education. This system has generated intricate two-way flows between educational organizations and labor markets. Rather than proceeding in an orderly fashion from school to work, more students are entering and re-entering school with a multiple starts, stops, and restarts. While scholars debate whether these alternate routes and timings actually benefit the most disadvantaged (Elman and O'Rand 2004), they have clearly altered school-society connections from formerly orderly "pipelines" to increasingly complex "circuit boards."

These new pathways are facilitating greater proportions of "nontraditional" students who do not "front-load" their higher education in four-year residential universities during their late teens and early twenties. Rather, they are older, have had full-time jobs and family dependents, and have more checkered academic histories. These nontraditional students have been the fastest growing demographic in higher education for two decades (Kerr 2001). One-third of today's freshmen are older than twenty-four, half are part-timers, a quarter have dependents, only 13 percent live on campus, half commute, and one-third live with parents or other family (Deil-Amen 2015). Many have "messy vitaes" marked by repeated school and job interruptions, less than stellar academic grades, and few status-enhancing leisure and extracurricular activities. They juggle multiple roles, mixing family and job responsibilities with their studies. Being a student is not their master identity; they rarely regard higher education as unique life stage for engaging in personal exploration, inner growth, leisure or experimental living (Mullen 2010; Setterson 2015). Their lives are instead shaped by conventional demands of employment, family, and childcare, and they see college as an instrumental means to attain jobs that in previous generations did not require higher-education credentials (Deil-Amen 2015).

Nontraditional students are reshaping universities and colleges by triggering the accommodating logic. "Broad-access" institutions (Stevens and Kirst 2015) are adapting to them with more part-time studies, remedial courses, child care supports, loan and bursary programs, and vocational programming (Setterson 2015). This process was kick-started generations ago by community college administrators (Brint and Karabel 1989) but it has now reached a new level: two-year, proprietary and community colleges now house the majority of students in American higher education (Deli-Amen 2015).

The accommodating logic, the inverse of the intensifying logic, is triggered by a very different and new resource dependency. To sustain their growth (or to turn a profit, in the case of for-profit colleges), less selective colleges depend on untapped student populations, those who cannot align their lives with the dictates of selective colleges due to multiple role commitments, thin finances, nonlinear academic trajectories, and vocational expectations. Mass institutions adapt to their clients in a competitive marketplace, much as megachurches in the field of religion attract adherents by offering flexible hours of service, rock bands, and climbing walls. This accommodating logic tightens links between higher education and fields like child care and many semiprofessions. Without these organizational adaptations, vertical expansion since the 1970s would have been far less extensive.

Yet accommodations are a mixed blessing in terms of legitimacy: they are championed for bringing higher education to the masses while simultaneously being faulted for eroding academic standards. At least since the 1950s, widened access to higher education has been praised as a noble mission; politicians gain popularity by calling for it, and progressive educators have declared equity and inclusion to be core values. But at the same time, older notions of academic exclusivity continue to have a grip. Selective institutions gain prestige by rejecting most of their applicants. Members of the public, particularly those with power—most of whom are graduates of traditional four-year colleges—worry about inflated grades, falling standards, credential inflation, and attrition. Student engagement, if never ideally high, may have declined over recent decades (Arum and Roksa 2011; Cote and Allohar 2006, 2011). Mass-access colleges are often bemoaned for diluting the capacity of higher education to fully transform students' inner lives. As school forms are permeated by practices in previously distant fields, that influence is not welcomed by all.

Horizontal Expansion and Hybrid Organizational Forms: From Isomorphism to Mixed Institutional Logics

The classic theorists, particularly John Meyer and his colleagues, saw vertical expansion as a signal of education's deepened institutionalization in society, manifested first in the universalization of primary and secondary education, and then in the worldwide expansion of higher education (Schofer and Meyer 2005). This institutionalization created school organizations that were thoroughly bureaucratic, state-penetrated, professionalized, and ultimately isomorphic, and that gained legitimacy not by being demonstrably effective or by outcompeting other organizational forms, but by conforming to a requisite image of the proper "school." Indeed, modern schools were cited as prime examples of isomorphism and legitimacy in new institutional theory (e.g., Meyer and Rowan 1978; Powell and DiMaggio 1991; Meyer et al. 1997; Weick 1976).

This institutionalization of schooling has continued since the 1970s, but in new ways. Horizontal expansion has served to "school" more realms of social life, and by doing so it has brought new actors and institutional logics into education. As a result, many isomorphic and legitimating tendencies identified by new institutionalists have been undermined and even reversed.

Horizontal Expansion: How Schooling More Subjects Creates Hybridity

The touchstones analyzed what we call horizontal expansion as a form of credentialism, a process in which a proliferation of degrees, diplomas, and certificates serves both to generate greater demand for higher education and to reshape a widening array of job markets (Collins 1979). Since the 1970s, this process has continued: the number of formal fields of study, courses, topics, and majors has continued to multiply. This continued horizontal expansion is an outgrowth of intensified competition for students: as educational offerings continue to proliferate, fewer educators can continue to adopt isomorphic forms of schooling; more need to differentiate their offerings in order to vie for their share of students and funds.

This process has taken three guises. First, high-tech applied sciences have expanded as scientific discoveries have been converted into commercialized ventures. Second, the "academic disposition" has grown especially in the humanities and social sciences, in a process that parallels what Bourdieu called the "aesthetic disposition," wherein realms that were previously deemed unfit for legitimate academic study get consecrated and deemed worthy (we discuss examples in the next section of this chapter). Recently created interdisciplinary programs have established new courses, journals, and specialties. And in a third guise, colleges have continually created new vocational credentials, certificates, and licenses for areas ranging from security to bartending to golf, winemaking, gaming, police and security studies, event planning, personal care, and hospitality studies. These programs bring formerly disconnected job realms into the orbit of mainline higher education. In sum, the effect of these three kinds of horizontal expansion—scientific, aesthetic, and vocational—has been to deepen links between higher education and other fields. These links are products of entrepreneurial academics and administrators responding to competition and seeking new opportunities. They bring more activities under the purview of schooling, but also expose schooling to new actors and forms of organization.

Hybrid Fields: From Legitimate Isomorphism to Multiple Logics

Continued expansion requires resources like tuition dollars and fundraising. Mass access colleges need nontraditional students and employers, and reshape their offerings accordingly. The tendency of selective colleges to exclude those students opens spaces for for-profit colleges. In response to this situation, some public benefactors pour funds into higher education, and public colleges alter their offerings to compete with the for-profits. To attend either private for-profit or public colleges, many students require loans, which trigger complex loan systems (Kamenitz 2015; Ruch 2001). The aggregate impact of these varying actions is that large sectors of higher education get exposed to actors and institutional logics from other fields, including finance and investment, government regulation, business, and philanthropy. These influences tend to leverage change in some schooling practices, in ways that sometimes are not to everyone's liking.

Gumport (2002) has compared the "social institutional logic" of traditional academe with "industrial logics" from the business world. The former prizes traditional liberal arts disciplines, faculty autonomy, tenure, research leaves, and academic freedom, while the latter valorizes cost-effectiveness, market relevance, practicality, and application. Vocational higher education has long mixed these logics. But over the past two decades, the industrial logic has gained more traction in many realms of higher education, subjecting many "sacred" academic practices and norms to cost/benefit analyses (Collis 2002). More colleges are displacing liberal arts majors, tenured faculty, and academic missions in favor of applied fields, top-heavy administration, causal and contingent faculty, and rationalizing practices like KPI metrics and commercialized images (Kamenetz 2015). These examples dramatize the penetration of industrial logics into the very instructional core of colleges and universities.

Similarly, at K–12 levels, new accountability regimes have allowed state actors to further penetrate schools. While standardized testing initiatives are hardly new in American education (Mehta 2013), today they are particularly visible, providing new flows of commensurable information between fields, fueled by rankings that media broadcast to prospective parents, real estate agents, for-profit providers, and state regulators. Accountability regimes create two new resource dependencies for educators: by requiring accreditation from central government, the latter wins some leverage into classroom processes, and in areas with much school choice, they empower families who have the requisite resources, compelling educators to cater to some of their wants.

School choice movements, considerably stronger now than they were in the 1970s, have brought new organizational actors and practices into K–12 schooling, including homeschoolers, EMOs, charter schools, voucher programs, and an assortment of non-Catholic private schools. Choice has helped nurture the rise of other actors in the field, including testing bodies, state overseers, curricular designers, and an array of para-educational organizations like private tutoring companies and early childhood preschools (Aurini and Davies 2013; Burch 2009; Rowan 2006).

These changes in education are reversing some tendencies towards organizational isomorphism in the field. Once new logics are introduced, they generate feedback from established organizations. For instance, urban public K–12 schools are offering more curricular choice as a strategy to compete with charter and private schools. In higher education, established universities have developed MOOCs, online instruction, and technical/vocational offerings in order to compete with newer for-profits. Even if those universities successfully push for-profits into small and undesirable market niches, their success comes at the cost of altering many of their conventional practices according to an industrial logic. Over the past twenty years, even public institutions have embraced forms of "academic capitalism" that divert resources to applied research fields, vocational programs, and commercial activities (Slaughter and Rhoades 2004).

Overall, the field of education has more hybrid organizational forms and practices than it did in the 1970s. New kinds of schools, colleges, and programs bring educators into deeper contact with other institutional logics from other fields. But this interpenetration also plays out very unevenly. The most elite universities have changed the least; more than any other school form, they have retained long-standing academic norms such as faculty governance, residential housing, and (mostly) nonprofessional majors, that are so popular elsewhere. They can dictate change on their own terms because they possess a resource craved in other fields: highly sought-after credentials. Less selective institutions are far more dependent on resources in other fields, and so they have been much more permeated by efficiency-oriented logics.

This interpenetration since the 1970s has faced a mixed reception, and has not necessarily enhanced the legitimacy of educators. On the one hand, new fields of study have been applauded for making academe more relevant, up-to-date, and vital; for better aligning schooling content with public preferences; and for validating the experiences of the socially marginal. On the other hand, they have provoked a curious array of enemies. The infiltration of the humanities by pop culture studies has displeased those traditional humanists who mock them for a lack of scholarly seriousness. Old leftists have seen the arrival of postmodernist educators signal a retreat from real-world politics (e.g., Sokal and Bricmont 1998). Conservatives, in turn, have questioned the applicability of those fields to the job world. On the vocational front, academics worry over enrollment shifts away from the liberal arts, while government and business representatives are continually disappointed by the sluggish enrollments in the much-touted STEM fields, as least as compared to fields like psychology, education, and sociology (see Skretney in this volume). Horizontal expansion is both celebrated and sharply criticized, depending on the actors in question.

Changing Cultural Connections between Schools and Society

Interpenetration assumes a most intricate and subtle form in the realm of culture. Today there is more cultural porosity between schools and other fields than ever before. Schools used to sponsor somewhat distinctive practices, restraining popular influences in classrooms. But popular culture now has a much stronger presence, even in elite institutions. In turn, expanded higher education has helped spawned new aesthetic sensibilities, altering the production and consumption of popular culture.

Interpenetration Erodes Unique Daily Practices

To some degree, schools have always reflected their surrounding societies. In the Progressive era they sought to assimilate the waves of immigrants; in the Sputnik era they promoted STEM subjects amid fears of Russia winning the space race; and since the 1960s they have been much more sensitized to racial, gender, and sexual issues. They have largely dropped corporal punishment, mirroring shifting societal attitudes towards discipline. Kansas schools are more likely to question evolution than are Massachusetts schools, reflecting how schools as public institutions reflect their surroundings to some degree.

But in other respects, schools in the first half of the twentieth century were culturally cloistered. Their underlying norms were ascetic, disciplined, and orderly. Their in loco parentis authority mandated teachers to protect children from corrupting and profane cultures beyond school gates. While parenting too was stricter in those days, parents granted teachers far more authority than they do now. Traditional pedagogy was teacher-directed, combining chalk and talk, rote memory, and recitation methods with firm controls over student conduct (Cuban 1993). Classroom interactions were relatively centralized, and less participatory and responsive. Teachers controlled students through regimented physical spaces, orderly seating plans, regulated entry in and out of classrooms, and strict rules over speaking and movement. Students were to sit with formal posture and refrain from eating, drinking, and gum chewing; they had to adhere to dress codes and address teachers formally and deferentially. This interaction resembled what Collins (2004) calls "power rituals," scripted and repetitive "front-stage" acts relatively distinct from those in other societal fields. Schools did incorporate other ritual elements from society that were less somber and more kinetic, but relegated them to their periphery, such as in their assemblies, sports, and clubs. But school interactions have since become less distinctive. In their liberalization, what happens inside schools increasingly mirrors practices from other realms of life.

Since the 1960s, traditional pedagogy has been increasingly mismatched with its cultural surroundings, regarded as stodgy, creaky, stifling, numbing, irrelevant, and even oppressive. The emerging "adolescent society" among teens stood in tension with school-sponsored interactions and status (Coleman 1961). Microlevel interaction across most realms of society were undergoing a "Goffmanian revolution" in which everyday conversation, greetings, appearance, manners, and etiquette were "informalized" (Collins 2014). Old-style classrooms increasingly seemed forced and alien in a contest of increasingly casual interaction styles. Teachers with stiff and formal demeanors seemed out of step in a culture that prized more relaxed manners.

Schools in the post-Sixties era could no longer rely on the compulsion of tradition to engage their clients. Just as Christian denominations enlivened their religious ceremonies by incorporating music, call-and-response incantations, and topical sermons, school became more responsive, particularly to younger students. Fewer teachers today are strictly traditional; they alternate between traditional lecture-based instruction when they need to meet coverage goals, and livelier activities that seek to promote engagement and forestall student mutiny (Brint et al. 2001; Cuban 2008; Jackson et al. 1998; McFarland 2001). This strategy can take several forms, ranging from sprinkling pop or street culture references into curricula (Olisky 2007) to using evolving digital technology like computer tablets, gaming, and social media. In becoming less print-text based and increasingly digitalized and interactive, classroom activities increasingly resemble those in workplace, play, and leisure. Schooling's unique "technology" ("'chalk and talk" methods with live instructors, assisted by print media) has been penetrated by innovations from elsewhere; some are forecasting even more profound shifts to come, particularly in higher education (Stevens 2015).

Changing Status Culture Influences

In the 70s, Pierre Bourdieu characterized schools as valorizing upper-middle-class cultures in their humanities curriculum (prestigious literature, music, arts) and through approved manners and interaction styles (Bourdieu and Passeron 1977; Bourdieu 1998). Critics have long faulted Bourdieu's image as exaggerated and overly Paris-centric (e.g., Goldthorpe 2007; Lareau and Weininger 2003; Kingston 2001); it may also be dated.

The intensifying logic has eroded old status cultures in education. For instance, elite boarding schools are primes sites where one might expect to see stubborn vestiges of traditional status culture, such as conspicuous leisure (polo, rugby, cricket) or "finishing school" mores (stiff formal manners, etiquette, regimented appearance). But competition for admission to upper-tier universities has encouraged these schools to intensify their academics, prioritizing cramming for exams, and adopting curricula such as advanced placement and the international baccalaureate. These pressures have made these schools less "country-clubby" and less concerned with old-fashioned displays of high culture (Khan 2011; Baker 2014; Gaztambide-Fernández 2009; Mullen 2010). Their students now prep for elite colleges not by cultivating what Bourdieu (1998) dubbed "secret handshakes"—cultural cues like subtle manners, refined etiquette, exclusive apparel, and expansive vocabularies—but more by competing as measured by comparatively transparent, meritorious, and rationalized criteria like test scores and grades. Here is the intensifying logic at work in the realm of elite gatekeeping: since the 1970s, upper-class children have adapted their practices to align with academic dictates, despite being the most advantaged youth on earth.

This process reflects changing cultural hierarchies. Exclusive preferences for European music, art, food, and literature have ceded ground to what Peterson and Kern (1996) have dubbed "omnivore" culture. Omnivores have altered the *valuation* of cultures, demoting traditional high culture and its connection to certain ethnic, racial, and national categories; and they have reconfigured the boundaries between legitimate and popular expression. This process has shifted tastes for food, music, and entertainment away from older ideals of exclusive luxuriousness, and toward those of authenticity, experimentalism, tolerance, and openness (Johnson and Bauman 2010). While retaining an egalitarian self-image, these omnivores have redrawn cultural hierarchies, continuing to devalue "crude" tastes (Bryson 1996; Veenstra 2015), and now scorning "univores" for not being attuned to approved forms of diversity and inclusion (Khan 2012). Importantly, the omnivores have helped shift cultural hierarchies in schools.

Greater Porosity between Pop Culture and Education

Much of the cultural space in schools once taken by old-fashioned status cultures has been filled by pop culture. Traditional pedagogues once drew firm boundaries between education-worthy culture and unworthy pop culture, prioritizing the Western canon over TV shows, movies, and popular music. But today's curricula are far more polycentric and expansive, having been penetrated by a range of pop culture influences. Even among peers in elite institutions, popular culture has a strong currency (Khan 2012; Baker 2014). Corporate recruits from elite universities score points with gatekeepers when they participate in novel extracurricula like extreme sports and exotic foreign adventuring—activities *not* formally taught in schools (Rivera 2015). Intensified competition in an omnivore world has squeezed out old status cultures in elite institutions. Further, by promoting pop culture to be legitimate fodder for research and teaching, horizontal expansion has imbued educators with an interest in toppling and rebuilding cultural hierarchies. Despite changing definitions of "good taste," schooling continues to shape cultural consumption (Bryson 1996; Lizardo 2014; Veenstra 2015), and indeed, university graduates remain leaders in many realms of culture (Bauman and Johnson 2009; Coulangeon 2013; Khan 2012; Collins 2014, Lizardo 2014).

Changing Links between Education and Cultural Consumption and Production

Sociologists have long linked educational attainment to cultural tastes, an old topic revived in Bourdieu's landmark *Distinction* ([1979]1984). But since the 1970s, education and culture have been interpenetrated in new ways. Vertical and horizontal expansion has created mass audiences for ascending genres. Movies were transformed over the twentieth century from lowbrow mass entertainment to "art," and this promotion was facilitated by a then-new stratum of learned critics and a sizeable university-educated audience (Bauman 2001). More recently, "foodie culture" has become a mark of the highly educated (Bauman and Johnson 2009). In turn, educational expansion has transformed culture-producing industries. Universities have attracted and exposed keen recruits to creative circles and ongoing aesthetic developments in literature, theatre, and visual arts. They have armed their graduates not only with new cultural references and dispositions, but also with new credentials, allowing them to populate the creative ranks in all sorts of pop culture industries.[2] Horizontal expansion has restructured pathways between universities and formerly lowbrow cultural fields. Whereas entry into those fields was previously haphazard, new credentials have altered their patterns of recruitment and criteria for hiring and evaluating merit. Universities are now springboards for jobs in these fields, bringing to them a certain modicum of order. Thus, the infiltration of pop culture into classrooms and lecture halls has been reciprocated: university graduates now comprise many of the producers and consumers of cutting-edge pop genres, and have transformed their aesthetics and creative practices.

Cross-Field Expansion: Importing School Forms into Nonschool Realms

"School imports" represent a unique kind of interpenetration of fields. As in horizontal expansion, school imports reorganize activities that were once more informal and housed in other community settings. But imports are only partial school forms that rely mostly on institutional mimicry. Importers typically select some features of schooling, such as teacher-student roles, assignments, and a curriculum; but they also discard other elements, such as detailed grading procedures, certified instructors, or extracurricula. Their participants might be called "students" and "instructors" who gather in "classes," but who can do without formal enrolments, grades, or any recognized certification (for a related discussion, see Michael Olneck, chapter 9). Importers creatively reshape mutable features of school forms to create institutional hybrids, often in "interstitial" locations where fields overlap (Scott 2014). This cross-field permeation assumes a variety of guises: diversion and alternative sentencing programs and prison classrooms in the criminal justice system; hospital classes for expectant parents in health care; job searching; anti–drug-use, antiracism, anger-management, and conflict-resolution classes offered in social services; corporate training; and all sorts of leisure classes.

School imports are arguably the least institutionalized form of schooling. Imports receive little social recognition since they enact some schooling elements but lack others. They lack clear definition, or standardized or coherent structure. They are rarely regulated, counted, or even named by government officials. And they can be precarious. Whereas most public K–12 schools are stabilized by secure central funding—as long as they adhere to standard structures and scripts—imports often get soft-money funding from multiple and/or decentralized sources. Some school imports can endure if their practices "stick" and blend with prevailing organizational routines; but others can atrophy, doomed to a fleeting existence. But this precariousness offers a tradeoff: importers are free to be creative and not merely follow institutional scripts; they can reassemble practices anew. Facing relatively few lines of authority, and blurry organizational roles and boundaries, importers can experiment, blending coexisting organizational models and logics, though with varying degrees of success.

School importers can be motivated by the legitimacy associated with school forms. Some question imports: Should we really send arrested Johns to a "school" rather than sentence them? But as the new institutionalists argue, schooling can enhance legitimacy. Over the past forty years it now has become a taken-for-granted organizational form, recognized as a proper vehicle for undertaking educational tasks, but also as a palliative for an array of social problems. Building on the latter point, new institutionalists implicate schooling with an implicit image of "expanded personhood" (Scott and Meyer 1994). Large, modern organizations—governments, corporations, universities—have embraced structures like health and safety offices, human resource departments, and employee benefits programs. Underlying them is an implicit notion that organizational members—students, corporate employees, patients, and even prisoners—are complex beings in need of motivation, personal enhancement, or expanded opportunities. School imports tap into this individualism, allowing professionals in other fields to associate their practices with evolving notions of self-help, self-actualization, self-realization, self-identification, and expanding lifestyle choice, not to mention human rights and human capital. Corporations can proclaim themselves to be "learning organizations" by creating their own universities (as McDonald's, General Motors, and Dunkin Donuts, among others, have done), while criminal justice officials can justify a john's school as a humane and inexpensive alternative to incarceration and fines to help men make better choices (Wortley and Fischer 2002).

This legitimacy also comes with few strings attached. Imports are monitored less intensively than are other school forms. Importers can combine practices across fields, blending alien and host routines without engaging in turf battles with professionals in the "exporting" field. Since teachers lack professional authority beyond their own jurisdiction, would-be importers can establish "schools" in their field without having to hire credentialed teachers, obtain certification from regulatory agencies, or win the blessing of teacher unions. Most imports lie on the outer edges of mainline professional practice in adjacent fields. Rather than demanding rigid conformity, imports allow a multiplicity of action, often evading professional monopolies, accreditation procedures, and binding standards that might otherwise dictate practice elsewhere.

The Logic of Resistance: Contesting the Schooled Society

The intensifying and accommodating logics connect schooling to other fields. But another logic places a brake on interpenetration, limiting cross-field connections.

While populism in America is at least as old as Andrew Jackson, since the 1960s conservatives have continued to voice their distrust of higher education, portraying universities as spawning a corrupt and effete liberalism that affronts "real Americans." Today's populist resentment of educated elites is directed at the latter's cultural authority. The "culture wars" have been turbocharged by recent battles over Trump and Brexit, yet they link back to longer-standing status rivalries, including those brewing in antiglobalization sentiments for at least thirty years. Populists contest and reject cultural terms and embedded assumptions that they believe flow down from educational hierarchies, seeing them as arrogated, unfounded, and illegitimate. Their targets can include the language of human resource departments, the implications of climate change science for fundamentalist religion and for business, and various expressions of left-wing identity politics. Viewed from a distance, populism is a resistance to a certain modernizing and cosmopolitan culture that is sponsored by higher education, and it highlights a struggle over old versus new forms of cultural power and status rivalry.

Schooling has become a central axis in the ongoing culture war. While those wars invoke trivial symbols like preferences for lattes, arugula, or Grey Poupon mustard, they have deeper roots. Populists see universities as the home base of the political left, invoking the touchy politics of class. Their politicians downplay their own educational credentials (particularly those from the Ivy League) in order to give voice to a thinly veiled tension between education and social mobility: Democrats promise to help voters join the educated middle class, while Republicans want them to distrust the highly educated. This distrust has led to campaigns against selected forms of science, like climate change or evolutionary theory, that are seen to offend core values and provide cover for extending the power of big government (Mooney 2005; note that this move ironically allies conservatives with postmodernist scholars in a post-truth universe). While Bell and others believed in the 1970s that university-based scientists would enjoy ever-increasing autonomy and influence on other fields, populists have attempted to limit that influence.

A second kind of resistance challenges the distinct logic of professionalism and credentialism (Friedson 2001). Like many sociologists, "do-it-yourself" skeptics are portraying professions as simply rent-seeking monopolies. Their skepticism is a partly a product of crises that have originated in other fields, including a broader declining confidence in all public institutions since the Vietnam War (Lipset and Schneider 1986), and the greater ease by which the Internet allows the general public to access formerly restricted and esoteric professional knowledge (Gardner 2015). The interpenetration of various fields has spurred this resistance in education, as have rising levels of education, which encourage people to trust their own judgment rather than that of professional experts. Further, as more fields ranging from business, journalism, and real estate to hairdressing seek to semiprofessionalize, local actors in those fields voice their displeasure over the specter of becoming dependent on new credentials created in the education field. Unlike the esoteric knowledge of classic professions (medicine, law, engineering, academia), which is acquired only through lengthy university-based training, knowledge for semiprofessions—including teaching—can be more readily accessed; people can book their own flights, sell their own houses, write their own wills, or homeschool their kids. In a world of start-ups and bloggers, in which one can read a message board for everything from fixing a computer to raising a child, professionally certified knowledge seems unnecessarily monopolistic. Ivan Illich might be partly heartened by the efforts of ordinary people, even if they themselves are educated at unprecedented levels, to evade formal school institutions and consume knowledge through the Internet—something unthinkable forty years ago. These struggles echo older debates over the proper roles of school-based versus apprenticeship-based knowledge, in which many advocated for training conducted within their host field over training contracted out to the field of education. Ironically, the tendency of more fields to seek being credentialed by universities itself sparks a resistance to overly theoretical knowledge in the name of real-world practice (Schon 1983; Susskind and Susskind 2015).

The third type of resistance is against the extended reach of the intensifying logic. These resistors decry the impact of educational competitiveness on other fields, particularly family life, and aim to limit its influence in select spheres of social life. In the opposite direction, educators engage in their own resistance, fighting to protect schooling from unwanted influences of other fields, particularly the hybridizing of school logics with institutional logics from elsewhere. Many contest the imposition of neoliberal and populist influences in schooling, which they variously portray as philistine, commodifying, anti-intellectual, anti-equity, regressive, and intolerant. These educators reject funds from conservative foundations, protest conservative speakers, and denounce alt-right media. More traditional scholars decry many accommodations in higher education, seeing them as diluting standards and diminishing the college experience. Liberal arts educators fret over the vocationalizing turn in higher education. Humanists worry about incursions from what they deem to be "frivolous" fields like cultural studies. These various forms of school-based resistance commonly contest new hybrid logics in the name of retaining academic integrity.

But overall, these forms of resistance are fragmented, scattered, and uncoordinated. Many working-class supporters of populist candidates still want their children to go to college. Republican politicians who belittle climate change as fiction and professors as an arm of the liberal media still cite academic studies to support their positions. In this new world, the influence of schooled professions and certified knowledge is mostly welcomed in other fields, but is resisted when it threatens older forms of cultural authority, the autonomy of certain work fields, or even the sanctity of family life. Nonetheless, intensifying logics are fueled by their associations with status competition and material advantage in labor markets. Accommodating logics are powered by their lures of new resources and associations with evolving norms of equitable access. As schooled knowledge penetrates society further and further, these forms of resistance serve mainly as brakes on more powerful interpenetrating processes.

Conclusion

This chapter returns sociology of education to a big question that originally animated the field: how do schools connect to society? Our answer is that since the 1970s, schooling has been more deeply interpenetrated with other fields. Though an "intensifying logic," actors in other fields reconfigure their practices to better align with schooling dictates. Through an "accommodating logic," school forms reconfigure some of their core practices as they encounter new populations and organizational templates in other fields. Today's schooling borrows increasingly from other fields and sends more of its logics to others. Indeed, many of today's battles in education can be seen as reactions to this hybridizing of institutional logics, and sometimes these battles represent a resistance that slows the pace of interpenetration.

While our ideas build on the foundation laid by the touchstone classics, and are largely in agreement with schooled-society accounts (chapter 2), they place greater weight on reciprocal influences between education and other fields and on their mixed implications for legitimacy and equality. As schooling (writ large) influences a large range of fields, it too changes, shedding some of its traditional elements while adopting features of its new surroundings. As links between fields deepen, more claimants seek to influence schooling, sometimes with alien institutional logics and practices. This hybridity has mixed implications for legitimacy. As more realms of society get schooled (horizontal expansion) and as more schooling bends to the needs of nontraditional students (accommodations) and fields like business (hybrid logics), critics take notice. They voice a variety of worries, ranging from those about lowered academic standards, unserious subject matter, and neoliberal invasions into sacred public territory, to a politically-charged elitism. Incorporating logics from other fields can be hailed as giving schooling a new relevance and vitality, or as betraying its venerable values.

Similarly, deepening interpenetration has not equalized school provisions. Intensifying logics have raised the ante for educational competitions in ways that disqualify most nontraditional students. Accommodating logics bring new populations into advanced credential tiers, but often in lesser-ranked institutions. In many respects, interpenetration has made schooling an even "thicker" social divider than it was forty years ago. To paraphrase one of the authors of this volume: So much interpenetration, so little change. But to that we add a caveat: Since the 1970s, any inequality has occurred amid a multidimensional expansion of a more hybridized set of school institutions.

Notes

1. Because official high school graduation rates include older persons who attain GEDs, Heckman (2008) argues that they mask a dilution of secondary education, since GED holders tend to have cognitive skill profiles that resemble those of high-school dropouts more than those of graduates.
2. Television, long reviled as a cultural wasteland, has spawned a genre of critically acclaimed shows over the past fifteen years, such as *The Sopranos, Six Feet Under, Mad Men, Girls, Boardwalk Empire, Dexter, Homeland, House of Cards, Oz, The Wire*, and *Breaking Bad*. All the creators of these shows attended universities, including Columbia, Stanford, Princeton, and NYU, many with degrees in theater, fine and visual arts, film studies, and creative writing. Few creators of popular shows in a previous generation (*MASH, All in the Family, The Dick Van Dyke Show, I Love Lucy, The Twilight Zone, 60 Minutes, Sanford and Son, The Mary Tyler Moore Show, Get Smart*) graduated from university or formally studied arts; they instead entered the industry through other paths, often via happenstance (e.g., by working in media while serving in the military, or through personal contacts).

References

Armstrong, Elizabeth, and Laura Hamilton. 2013. *Paying for the Party: How College Maintains Inequality*. Cambridge, MA: Harvard University Press.

Arum, Richard, and Jospika Roksa. 2011. *Academically Adrift: Limited Learning on College Campuses*. Chicago: University of Chicago Press.

Aurini, Janice, and Scott Davies. 2013. "The Changing Organizational Field of Education: The Case of Canadian Supplementary Education." In *Out of the Shadows: The Worldwide Rise of Supplementary Education*. Bingley, UK: Emerald.

Baker, David P. 2011. "Forward and Backward, Horizontal and Vertical: Transformation of Occupational Credentialing in the Schooled Society." *Research in Social Stratification and Mobility* 29:5–29.

Baker, Jayne. 2014. "No Ivies, Oxbridge, or Grandes Écoles: Constructing Distinctions in University Choice." *British Journal of Sociology of Education* 35(6): 914–932.

Baumann, Shyon. 2001. "Intellectualization and Art World Development: Film in the United States." *American Sociological Review* 66:404–426.

Bell, Daniel. 1973. *The Coming of Post-Industrial Society: A Venture in Social Forecasting*. New York: Basic Books.

Blossfeld, Hans-Peter. 2009. "Educational Assortative Marriage in Comparative Perspective." *Annual Review of Sociology* 35:513–530.

Booth, Alan, and Ann C. Crouter. 2007. *Disparities in School Readiness: How Families Contribute to Transitions to School*. Mahwah, NJ: Lawrence Erlbaum Associates.

Bourdieu, Pierre. 1984. *Distinction*. Stanford CA: Stanford University Press.

———. 1998. *The State Nobility: Elite Schools in the Field of Power*. Stanford, CA: Stanford University Press.

Bourdieu, Pierre, and Jean Claude Passeron. 1990 (1977). *Reproduction in Education, Society and Culture*. Second edition. London: Sage.

Bowles, Samuel, and Herbert Gintis. 1976. *Schooling in Capitalist America: Educational Reform and the Contradictions of Economic Life*. New York: Basic Books.

———. 2002. "Schooling in Capitalist America Revisited." *Sociology of Education* 75 (2): 1–18.

Brint, Steven, Mary F. Contreras, and Michael T. Matthews. 2001. "Socialization Messages in Primary Schools: An Organizational Analysis." *Sociology of Education* 74:157–180.

Brint, Steven, and Jerome Karabel. 1989. *The Diverted Dream: Community Colleges and the Promise of Educational Opportunity in America, 1900–1985*. New York: Oxford University Press.

Brint, Steven, Mark Riddle, Lori Turk-Bicakci, and Charles S. Levy. 2005. "From the Liberal to the Practical Arts in American Colleges and Universities: Organizational Analysis and Curricular Change." *Journal of Higher Education* 76 (2).

Brown, David K. 2001. "The Social Sources of Education Credentialism." *Sociology of Education* (extra issue): 19–34.

Bryson, Bethany. 1996. "Anything But Heavy Metal." *American Sociological Review* 61 (5): 884–899.

Burch, P. 2009. *Hidden Markets: The New Education Privatization*. New York: Routledge.

Chin, Tiffany. 2000. "Sixth Grade Madness: Parental Emotion Work in the Private High School Application Process." *Journal of Contemporary Ethnography* 29 (2): 124–163.

Chin, Tiffany, and Meredith Phillips. 2004. "Social Reproduction and Child-Rearing Practices: Social Class, Children's Agency, and the Summer Activity Gap." *Sociology of Education* 77 (3): 185–210.

Coleman, James S. 1961. *The Adolescent Society*. Glencoe, IL: Free Press.

Collins, Randall. 1979. *The Credential Society*. New York: Academic Press.

———. 2002. "Credential Inflation and the Future of Universities," in *The Future of the City of Intellect: The Changing American University*, edited by Steven Brint. Stanford, CA: Stanford University Press.

———. 2004. *Interaction Ritual Chains*. Princeton, NJ: Princeton University Press.

———. 2014. "Four Theories of Informalization and How to Test Them." *Human Figurations* 3 (2).

Collis, D., 2002. New Business Models for Higher Education. In Steven Brint, ed., *The Future of the City of Intellect: The Changing American University*, edited by Steven Brint. Stanford, CA: Stanford University Press,.

Cote, James, and Anton Allohar. 2006. *Ivory Tower Blues*. Toronto: University of Toronto Press.

———. 2011. *Lowering Higher Education*. Toronto: University of Toronto Press.

Coulangeon, Philippe. 2013. "Changing Policies, Challenging Theories and Persisting Inequalities: Social Disparities in Cultural Participation in France from 1981 to 2008." *Poetics* 41 (2): 177–209.

Cuban, Larry. 1993. *How Teachers Taught: Constancy and Change in American Classrooms 1890–1990*. Second edition. New York: Teachers College Press.

———. 2008. *Hugging the Middle: How Teachers Teach in an Era of Standards and Accountability*. New York: Teachers College Press.

Davies, Scott. 2005. "A Revolution of Expectations? Three Key Trends in the SAIP Data." In Robert Sweet and Paul Anisef, eds, *Preparing for Post-Secondary Education: New Roles for Governments and Families*. Montreal and Kingston: McGill-Queen's University Press.

Davies, Scott, and Neil Guppy. 2013. *The Schooled Society*. Third edition. Toronto: Oxford University Press.

Deil-Amen, Regina. 2015. "The "Traditional" College Student: A Smaller and Smaller Minority and Its Implications for Diversity and Access Institutions." In *Remaking College: The Changing Ecology of Higher Education*, edited by Michael W. Kirst and Mitchell L. Stevens. Stanford, CA: Stanford University Press.

Deresiewicz, William. 2014. *The Miseducation of the American Elite and the Way to a Meaningful Life*. New York: Simon and Schuster.

Domina, T. 2006. "Brain Drain and Brain Gain: Rising Educational Segregation in the United States 1940–2000." *City & Community* 5 (4).

Dougherty, Kevin. 1994. *The Contradictory College: The Conflict, Origins, Impacts, and Futures of the Community College*. Albany, NY: SUNY Press.

Duncan, Greg J., and Richard J. Murnane. 2011. *Whither Opportunity: Rising Inequality, Schools, and Children's Life Chances*. New York: Russell Sage.

Elman, Cheryl, and Angela M. O'Rand, "The Race Is to the Swift: Socioeconomic Origins, Adult Education, and Wage Attainment," *American Journal of Sociology* 110 (1): 123–160.

Engle, Jennifer, and Vincent Tinto. 2008. *Moving beyond Access: College Success for Low-Income, First-Generation Students*. The Pell Institute, http://files.eric.ed.gov/fulltext/ED504448.pdf.

Espeland, Wendy Nelson, and Michael Sauder. 2007. "Rankings and Reactivity: How Public Measures Recreate Social Worlds." *American Journal of Sociology* 113 (1):1–40.

Espenshade, Thomas J., and Alexandria Walton Radford. 2009. *No Longer Separate, Not Yet Equal: Race and Class in Elite College Admission and Campus Life*. Princeton, NJ: Princeton University Press.

Figlio, David N., and Maurice E. Lucas, 2004. "What's in a Grade? School Report Cards and the Housing Market." *American Economic Review* 94 (3): 591–604.

Fisher, Berenice M. 1972. "Education in the Big Picture." *Sociology of Education* 45 (3): 233–257.

Fligstein, Neil, and Doug McAdam. 2012. *A Theory of Fields*. New York: Oxford University Press.

Frank, David John, and John W. Meyer. 2007. "University Expansion and the Knowledge Society." *Theory and Society* 36: 287–311.

Freeman, Richard B. 1976. *The Overeducated American*. New York: Academic Press.

Friedland, Roger, and Robert Alford. 1991. "Bringing Society Back In: Symbols, Practices, and Institutional Contradictions." In *The New Institutionalism in Organizational Analysis*, edited by Walter W. Powell and Paul J. DiMaggio. Chicago: University of Chicago Press.

Friedson, Eliot. 2011. *Professionalism, the Third Logic: On the Practice of Knowledge*. Chicago: University of Chicago Press.

Gardner, Howard. 2015. "Is There a Future for the Professions? An Interim Verdict." http://www.thegoodproject.org/is-there-a-future-for-the-professions-an-interim-verdict/.

Gaztambide-Fernández, Rubén A. 2009 *The Best of the Best: Becoming Elite at an American Boarding School*. Cambridge, MA: Harvard University Press.

Gerber, Theodore P., and Sin Yi Cheung. 2008. "Horizontal Stratification in Postsecondary Education: Forms, Explanations, and Implications." *Annual Review of Sociology* 34:299–318.

Goldin, Claudia, and Lawrence F. Katz. 2008. *The Race between Education and Technology*. Cambridge, MA: Belknap Press.

Goldthorpe, J. 2007. "Cultural Capital: Some Critical Observations." *Sociologica* 2.

Gumport, Patricia J. 2002. Universities and Knowledge: Restructuring the City of Intellect. In Steven Brint, ed., *The Future of the City of Intellect: The Changing American University*. Stanford, CA: Stanford University Press.

Hardt, Michael, and Antonio Negri. 2000. *Empire*. Cambridge, MA: Harvard University Press.

Heckman, James. 2008. "Schools, Skills and Synapses." UCD Geary Institute Discussion Paper Series.

Hermanowicz, Joseph C. 2003. *College Attrition at American Research Universities: Comparative Case Studies*. New York: Agathon.

Illich, Ivan. 1970. *Deschooling Society*. New York: Harper and Row.

Jackson, Philip W., Robert E. Boostrom, and David T. Hansen. 1998. *The Moral Life of Schools*. San Francisco: John Wiley and Sons.

Jacobs, Jerry. 2013. *In Defense of Disciplines*. Chicago: University of Chicago Press.

Johnston, Josée, and Shyon Baumann. 2010. *Foodies: Democracy and Distinction in the Gourmet Foodscape*. New York: Routledge.

Kamenetz, Anya. 2015. "DIY U: Higher Education Goes Hybrid." In *Remaking College: The Changing Ecology of American Higher Education*, edited by Michael W. Kirst and Mitchell L. Stevens. Stanford, CA: Stanford University Press.

Karabel, Jerome. 2005. The Chosen: The Hidden History of Admission and Exclusion at Harvard, Yale, and Princeton. Cambridge, MA: Harvard University Press.

Kerr, Clark. 2001. *The Uses of the University* . Fifth edition. Cambridge, MA: Harvard University Press.

Khan, S. 2011. *Privilege: The Making of an Adolescent Elite at St. Paul's School*. Princeton, NJ: Princeton University Press.

Khan, Shamus. 2012. "The New Elitists." *New York Times*, July 7.

Kingston, P. 2001. "The Unfulfilled Promises of Cultural Capital Theory." *Sociology of Education* 88–99.

Kirst, Michael W., Kristopher Proctor, and Mitchell L. Stevens. 2011. "Broad-Access Higher Education: A Research Framework for a New Era." Stanford University. Accessed at https://pdfs.semanticscholar.org/d26e/9c358a57b1f14d5d12e691bc09b9912d93ea.pdf.

Kraatz, Matthew S., and Edward J. Zajac. 1996. "Exploring the Limits of the New Institutionalism: The Causes and Consequences of Illegitimate Organizational Change." *American Sociological Review* 61 (5):812–836.

Lareau, Annette. 2000. *Home Advantage*. Second edition. Lanham, MD: Rowman and Littlefield.

———. 2003. *Unequal Childhoods: Class, Race, and Family Life*. Berkeley: University of California Press.

Lareau, Annette, and Eliot Weininger. 2003. "Cultural Capital in Educational Research: A Critical Assessment." *Theory and Society* 32:567–606.

Lemann, Nicholas. 1999. *The Big Test: The Secret History of the American Meritocracy*. New York: Farrar, Straus & Giroux.

Lipset, Seymour Martin. and William Schneider. 1986. *The Confidence Gap: Business, Labor and Government in the Public Mind*. New York: Free Press.

Lizardo, Omar. 2014. "Taste and the Logic of Practice in Distinction." *Czech Sociological Review* 50:335–364.

Lizardo, Omar, and Sara Skiles. 2016. "Cultural Objects as Prisms: Perceived Audience Composition of Musical Genres as a Resource for Symbolic Exclusion." *Socius: Sociological Research for a Dynamic World*. 2:1–17.

Lubienski, Christopher. 2003. "Innovation in Education Markets: Theory and Evidence on the Impact of Competition and Choice in Charter Schools." *American Educational Research Journal* 40 (2): 395–443.

Martin, Brett. 2014. *Difficult Men: Behind the Scenes of a Creative Revolution: From "The Sopranos" and "The Wire" to "Mad Men" and "Breaking Bad."* New York: Penguin.

McDonough, P. M. 1994. "Buying and Selling Higher Education: The Social Construction of the College Applicant." *Journal of Higher Education* 65:427–446.

McFarland, Daniel A. 2001. "Student Resistance: How the Formal and Informal Organization of Classrooms Facilitate Everyday Forms of Student Defiance." *American Journal of Sociology* 107 (3): 612–678.

Mehta, Jal. 2013. *The Allure of Order*. New York: Oxford University Press.

Meyer, John W. 1970. "The Charter: Conditions of Diffuse Socialization in Schools." In *Social Processes and Social Structures: an Introduction to Sociology*, edited by W. Richard Scott. New York: Rinehart and Winston.

Meyer, John W., John Boli, George M. Thomas, and Francisco O. Ramirez. 1997. "World Society and the Nation-State." *American Journal of Sociology* 103 (1): 144–181.

Meyer, John W., and Francisco Ramirez. 2000. "The World Institutionalization of Education." In *Discourse Formation in Comparative Education*, edited by Jurgen Schriewer. Frankfurt: Peter Lang.

Meyer, John W., and Brian Rowan. 1977. "The Effects of Education as an Institution." *American Journal of Sociology* 83:55–77.

Meyer, John W., and Evan Schofer. 2005. "The World-Wide Expansion of Higher Education in the Twentieth Century." CDDRL Working Paper, Stanford University. http://iis-db.stanford.edu/pubs/20801/Schofer-Meyer_No32.pdf.

Mooney, Chris. 2005. *The Republican War on Science*. New York: Basic Books.

Mullen, Ann. 2010. *Degrees of Inequality*. Baltimore: Johns Hopkins University Press.

National Center for Educational Statistics. 2012. *The Condition of Education*. US Department of Education. http://nces.ed.gov/pubs2012/2012045_2.pdf.

———. 2013. *Projections of Education Statistics to 2021*. Fortieth edition. Institute for Educational Sciences, US Department of Education. http://nces.ed.gov/pubs2013/2013008.pdf.

———. 2014. *Educational Attainment: Fast Facts*. https://nces.ed.gov/programs/digest/d14/tables/dt14_104.20.asp.

Olitsky, Stacy. 2007. "Promoting Student Engagement in Science: Interaction Rituals and the Pursuit of a Community of Practice." *Journal of Research in Science Teaching* 44 (1): 33–56.

Peterson, Richard A., and Roger M. Kern. 1996. "Changing Highbrow Taste: From Snob to Omnivore." *American Sociological Review* 61 (5): 900–907.

Powell, Arthur, Eleanor Farrar, and David Cohen. 1985. *The Shopping Mall High School: Winners and Losers in the Educational Marketplace*. Boston: Houghton Mifflin.

Powell, Walter W., and Paul J. DiMaggio, eds. 1991. *The New Institutionalism in Organizational Analysis*. Chicago: University of Chicago Press.

Professor X. 2011. *In the Basement of the Ivory Tower*. Viking Books.

Radford, Alexandria Walton. 2013. *Top Student, Top School? How Social Class Shapes Where Valedictorians Go to College*. Chicago: University of Chicago Press.

Reardon, Sean F., and Ann Owens. "60 Years after Brown: Trends and Consequences of School Segregation." *Annual Review of Sociology* 40:199–218.

Rivera, Lauren. 2015. "Go with Your Gut: Emotion and Evaluation in Job Interviews." *American Journal of Sociology* 120 (5): 1339–1389.

Rosenbaum, James E. 2001. *Beyond College for All*. New York: Russell Sage Foundation.

Rowan, Brian. 2006. "The New Institutionalism and the Study of Educational Organizations: Changing Ideas for Changing Times." In *The New Institutionalism in Education*, edited by Heinz-Dieter Meyer and Brian Rowan. Albany, NY: SUNY Press.

Ruch, Richard S. 2001. *Higher Education, Inc.: The Rise of the For-Profit University*. Baltimore: Johns Hopkins University Press.

Sayer, Liana C., Suzanne M. Bianchi, and John P. Robinson. 2004. "Are Parents Investing Less in Children? Trends in Mothers' and Fathers' Time with Children." *American Journal of Sociology* 110 (1): 1–43.

Schaub, Mary-Ellen. 2016. "The Expansion of the Child's Garden: Women's Education and Kindergarten Enrollment during the Twentieth Century." *American Journal of Education* 122 (2): 267–286.

Schofer, Evan, and John Meyer. 2005. "The World-Wide Expansion of Higher Education in the Twentieth Century." *American Sociological Review* 70:898–920.

Schon, Donald. 1983. *The Reflective Practitioner: How Professionals Think in Action*. New York: Basic Books.

Scott, W. Richard. 2011. "Higher Education in America: An Institutional Field Approach." Stanford University. Accessed at https://cepa.stanford.edu/sites/default/files/ScottWRichard.pdf.

———. 2014. *Institutions and Organizations: Ideas, Interests, and Identities*. Fourth edition. Los Angeles: Sage.

Scott, W. Richard, and John W. Meyer. 1994. "The Rise of Training Programs in Firms and Agencies." In *Institutional Environments and Organizations: Structural Complexity and Individualism*, edited by W. Richard Scott et al. Thousand Oaks, CA: Sage.

Setterson, Richard A. 2015. "The New Landscape of Early Adulthood: Implications for Broad Access Higher Education." In *Remaking College: The Changing Ecology of American Higher Education*, edited by Michael W. Kirst and Mitchell L. Stevens. Stanford, CA: Stanford University Press.

Slaughter, Sheila, and Gary Rhoades. 2004. *Academic Capitalism and the New Economy*. Baltimore: Johns Hopkins University Press.

Sokal, Alan, and Jean Bricmont. 1998. *Fashionable Nonsense: Postmodern Intellectuals' Abuse of Science*. New York: Picador.

Stevens, Mitchell L. 2007. *Creating a Class: College Admissions and the Education of Elites*. Cambridge, MA: Harvard University Press.

———. 2015. "Introduction: The Changing Ecology of US Higher Education." In *Remaking College: The Changing Ecology of Higher Education*, edited by Michael W. Kirst and Mitchell L. Stevens. Stanford, CA: Stanford University Press.

Stevens, Mitchell L., Elizabeth Armstrong, and Richard Arum. 2008. "Sieve, Incubator, Temple, Hub: Empirical and Theoretical Advances in the Sociology of Higher Education." *Annual Review of Sociology* 34:127–151.

Stuber, Jenny. 2011. *Inside the College Gates: How Class and Culture Matter in Higher Education*. Lanham, MD: Lexington Books.

Susskind, Richard, and Daniel Susskind. 2015. *The Future of the Professions: How Technology Will Transform the Work of Human Experts*. New York: Oxford University Press.

Thorton, Patricia H., William Ocasio, and Michael Lounsbury. 2012. *The Institutional Logics Perspective: A New Approach to Culture, Structure and Process*. New York: Oxford University Press.

Veenstra, Gerry. "Class Position and Musical Tastes: A Sing-Off between the Cultural Omnivorism and Bourdieusian Homology Frameworks." *Canadian Review of Sociology* 52 (2): 134–159.

Weick, Karl. 1976. "Educational Organizations as Loosely Coupled Systems." *Administrative Science Quarterly* 21 (1): 1–19.

Wortley, Scot, B. Fischer, and C. Webster. 2002. "Vice Lessons: A Survey of Prostitution Offenders Enrolled in the Toronto John School Diversion Program." *Canadian Journal of Criminology* 44 (4): 369–402.

US Census Bureau. 2009. "School Enrollment and Educational Attainment, for the United States: 1960–Detailed Tables." www.census.gov/hhes/socdemo/education/data/cps/1960/cp60pcs1-20/tables.html.

FOUR

An Institutional Geography of Knowledge Exchange: Producers, Exports, Imports, Trade Routes, and Metacognitive Metropoles

STEVEN BRINT

This paper examines knowledge exchanges between universities and other institutional arenas in American society.[1] It develops a vocabulary for understanding key principles underlying these exchanges, and illustrates the major concepts in that vocabulary with examples drawn from a variety of institutional settings. A premise of this paper is that academe is only one of many locations in which knowledge structures are generated, and that knowledge structures generated elsewhere can provide the raw material for academic work, just as academic work can be appropriated for use in institutions outside of academe. Among many possible examples, knowledge structures generated outside of academe include formulas for successful popular culture products, frameworks to improve effectiveness in business, spiritual practices of Eastern religions insofar as they are tied to health benefits, human-centered design thinking in architecture, and scenario planning in the military.[2]

Clark Kerr (1962) wrote of postwar research universities as "the service stations of society," meaning that universities generated knowledge and expertise that helped direct and improve a wide range of organizations in their environment. His conception broadened the "Wisconsin idea" of service to the state to a much wider range of constituencies. In Kerr's view, universities generate much new knowledge, and also provide assistance to other institutions in society. In the view I will develop here, the relationships between universities and other institutions are more reciprocal than Kerr suggested. In this respect, I see universities not as service stations, but rather as all-purpose cognitive production and processing plants. They create knowledge products on their own, while at the same time taking in conceptual material from a variety of external sources, rejecting some of this material, and in other cases feeding back tested and refined products, with greater or lesser impact, to the source institutions.

The approach developed in this paper is consistent with recent work in the economics of innovation that stresses the bidirectionality of influence between universities and industries and the multiple pathways by which universities influence industries and industries influence universities (see, e.g., Geiger and Sa 2008; Kenney and Mowery 2014; Powell et al. 2005). This work has led to a revision of the naive linear model of innovation in which universities (and other research units) discover and corporations produce. But so far, social scientists have offered little in the way of theorization that encompasses a wide range of institutional settings. My goal is to open avenues for this theorization by developing a conceptual vocabulary with which to understand the relationships and trade networks between research universities and other institutional sectors. In the absence of a large sample of knowledge structures that would allow for systematic study, I will illustrate applications of this approach with case studies drawn from a range of institutional settings.

In contrast to the position I will develop here, much of the best work of social scientists and intellectual historians has focused on knowledge produced in the disciplines and transactions among the academic disciplines (see, e.g. Abbott 2001; Gieryn 2008; Gorman 2010: Jacobs and Frickel 2009; Lamont 2008). We have many studies, for example, of how methods are borrowed from one discipline to expand the tools available to another. Abbott (2002) has discussed a number of such imports in sociology, including the borrowing of durational methods from biology, the borrowing of network modeling from physics, and the borrowing of alignment algorithms from the pattern-matching literature on DNA (p. 228). Similarly, Jacobs and Frickel (2009) discussed the permeability of boundaries among the disciplines, contesting the notion that disciplines are "silos" that resist important new ideas or methods from other disciplines. In subsequent work, Jacobs examined the diffusion of such ideas as postmodernism, actor-network theory, and social capital from their originating disciplines into neighboring disciplines (see also Jacobs 2014: 85–88).

Thus, many prominent academics see "true" knowledge as based in the verification processes, scientific and scholarly methods, and peer review found only in academe. They see knowledge that originates outside of academe as something less than authentic—not authoritative, not subjected to sufficient expert scrutiny, or not based on adequate verification.[3] I explicitly depart from this view that "true" knowledge structures are very nearly coterminous with academic production. I disagree, for example, with assumptions embedded in Abbott's (2002) observation that academic disciplines "provide models of learning and images of coherent discourse" that are "much better . . . than the competition" (p. 130). At their best, they are indeed much better than the competition, but being much better than the competition is rarely the point in the development of "images of coherent discourse."

Knowledge produced outside of academe can have a studied, systematic quality that, like academic knowledge, distinguishes it from folkways or mere opinion. Typically, its validity has been subjected to some degree of critical scrutiny—though usually not at the level that would pass muster at the highest levels of academe. The disciplines are consequently not the only important spheres of knowledge production or coherent discourse. At the same time, they play a central role in knowledge verification, criticism, and refinement.

An Important Context: The Expansion of Advanced Degrees

The growth of graduate and professional education is an important backdrop for the themes developed in this paper. More than twenty-five million Americans have master's or higher-level degrees, approximately the population of the six largest cities in the United States. More than three million people have doctorate degrees, the population of Los Angeles, the country's second largest city (US Census Bureau 2014: table 2–01). The idea of a post-industrial society dominated by "knowledge workers" has not yet come to pass, but it is clear that a number of important industries are populated disproportionately by people with advanced degrees and, further, that these industries are among the leading contributors to GDP. If we identify the industries in the "knowledge sector" using the criterion of 5 percent of employees holding master's level or higher degrees, the sector includes agricultural services, mass-media industries, chemicals, plastics, pharmaceuticals, computers and electronic equipment, scientific instruments, banking, accounting, consulting and other business services, medical services and hospitals, educational services (obviously including colleges and universities), legal services, and nearly all of government (Brint 2001, 2015; see also Powell and Snellman 2004). The knowledge sector, so defined, accounted for 43 percent of GDP by 2010 (Brint 2015).

Sociologists have speculated that one of the important outcomes of the growth of a "knowledge sector" populated by people with advanced degrees is a change in dominant thought styles. Baker (2014) has described these changes as "an epistemological revolution":

> The growth and intensity of science, rationalized inquiry, theory, [and] empirical methods [are] all influenced and reinforced. . . . [These changes can be] understood as . . . at the core of an epistemological revolution (Baker 2014: 189–190).

If Baker is correct, we should see a growing capacity, found primarily in those with advanced degrees, to think abstractly and to gather and weigh evidence in support of abstract conceptual frameworks, and thereby to order the world by these empirically anchored abstract conceptual frameworks.

Knowledge Structures

In this paper, I will be concerned with *knowledge structures*, rather than knowledge per se.[4] Knowledge structures are akin to Thomas Kuhn's (1972) paradigms; they provide a framework of interrelated concepts, results, and procedures within which subsequent work is structured. But knowledge structures, as I will use the term, do not necessarily originate in scientific achievements. Nor do they necessarily contain many inter-related parts or principles. Instead, they are coherent frameworks for understanding that regulate action within specific organizational and institutional contexts. They are based on empirical verification, or have the potential for such empirical verification. The "balanced scorecard," for example, is a knowledge structure that provides a framework for managerial accountability within many corporations. It is based on abstract thinking about the key constituencies required for successful unit operation and metrics for scoring how well a manager is performing in relation to these key constituencies (Kaplan and Norton 1996). The potential for empirical verification related to unit effectiveness exists. Because knowledge structures make claims that can in principle be verified, knowledge structures are distinguishable from conceptual structures. The potential for verification may or may not be relevant to a conceptual structure, but, as I will use the term, it is always relevant to a knowledge structure. Religious systems, for example, are conceptual structures that are not subject to empirical verification. Like paradigms, knowledge structures do not typically impose a rigid or mechanical set of understandings and operations, but can be used more or less creatively and flexibly.

I will not argue that knowledge structures are the most important type of knowledge that is exchanged across institutional sectors. However, because of its "chunked" quality, good samples of knowledge structures can be identified and studied more easily than the nearly limitless amount of knowledge bits that flow across conversations, the media, and the Internet every day.

The Metaphor of Commodity Trade

A second premise of this paper is that commodity trade provides an illuminating metaphor through which to explore the interactions of academic knowledge structures with knowledge structures originating in other institutional domains. Ideally, one would like to map the institutional geography of knowledge exchange comprehensively, identify the types of knowledge commodities that become exports from academe and imports into academe, and show why some trade routes are well-traveled and others are rarely traveled at all. This would be the work of more than one lifetime. In this paper, I will therefore limit myself to providing a vocabulary for understanding the primary forms of interaction between academic knowledge and knowledge originating in other spheres of society, substituting these illustrations for a more comprehensive analysis. Similarly, I will not attempt to describe all trade routes. These would include many routes that bypass universities altogether, such as the analytical systems that private consulting firms develop and then provide for a fee to corporations, governments, and nonprofit organizations. Instead, I will focus solely on the relation of universities to other institutional spheres.

A better understanding of cross-institutional knowledge exchange processes is important for the same reason that knowledge structures themselves are important: they provide an influential, empirically grounded understanding of the world in which we live. Although my analysis leads to a partial dethronement of academe as the center of empirically grounded knowledge structures, it also brings into sharper relief the distinctive contribution of academe to the cultural organization of other institutional arenas in modern societies, as well as the content that these other institutional arenas can provide for the development of academic knowledge structures. Anyone interested in the cultural morphology of the modern world should, I believe, wish to take cross-institutional knowledge exchange processes into account. The shape of our world is produced in large part by the traffic and direction of these interactions—and by what happens to cultural goods in transit.

A Basic Vocabulary

Commodity trade is a useful metaphor for the processes I wish to explore, because it conjures images of goods mingling in busy ports in preparation for loading onto ships that traverse the globe. But in the cultural realm, commodity trade is a metaphor only. Exchanges of cultural goods do not require agreement on mutual advantage. Unless they have a protected legal status, cultural goods can be appropriated without cost and recirculated without charge. Cultural goods are typically not priced on a market, but rather flow back into practices based on whether or not they can overcome the mental preference for following existing mental constructs linked to action.

With these important differences in mind, I will use the metaphor of trade to develop a number of concepts that I believe illuminate and suggest hypotheses for future, more systematic studies of the institutional geography of exchange in knowledge structures. The basic vocabulary includes the following terms: *knowledge-producing institutions, knowledge exports, knowledge imports, trade routes, corruptions and impositions,* and *metacognitive metropoles.*

Knowledge-producing institutions are any institutions that create bodies of knowledge that shape practice and are based on more than assertion, convention, or opinion. Knowledge exports and imports are bodies of knowledge that pass into new institutional arenas and either are appropriated wholesale or are subjected to processes of testing, refinement, and revision that are consistent with the practices and purposes of the adopting institutional arena. The primary knowledge imports into academe are study topics and tropes and metaphors that influence knowledge structures. The primary knowledge exports from academe are verification tests, refinements, formalizations, and critiques. Many exports are not widely or fully adopted by trade partners, but in rare cases academic conceptualizations and analyses are so convincing that they transform practice in importing institutional arenas. Trade routes describe the direction and heaviness of the traffic from one institutional arena to another. Barriers to fair trade create corruptions in knowledge products or prevent the circulation of academically tested knowledge structures. These corruptions are typically consistent with the receiving institution's preexisting practices and priorities. Conceptualizations associated with failed exchanges often tread too closely to fundamental ideological beliefs in the receiving institution's legitimation repertoire. Metacognitive metropoles are the centers of adjudication of truth claims.

I will begin my exposition of this basic vocabulary with a brief discussion of the ways that institutional purposes and work processes shape the development of knowledge structures. I will then illustrate the vocabulary I am developing to study the institutional geography of knowledge exchange using cases drawn from a variety of institutional settings. I also develop several hypotheses that would be susceptible to systematic empirical investigation using a larger sample of knowledge structures.

Institutional Goals and Knowledge Structures

All institutional arenas have an important incentive to create processes that achieve the ends of the institution—whether these have to do with winning wars, creating profitable products, building commissionable buildings, or filling movie theaters. Moreover, every institutional arena operates under historically developed rules and conventions linked to the achievement of these goals. Businesses are in competition with one another for long-term growth. They are consequently highly motivated to search for systems that sustain market share and foster long-term growth under conditions of competition. They are also highly motivated to ensure efficient and effective allocation of resources and effort. Similarly, the costliness of modern war has led to elaborate planning activities to limit uncertainty to the extent possible, both prior to engagement and in preparation for future conflicts through postmortems following the secession of hostilities. Creative teams, by contrast, must enter many competitions, because they will inevitably fail much more often than they succeed. Deadline pressures of these competitions have fostered efforts to maximize the likelihood of producing creative and winning design in tight time frames. Both academics and their external institutional partners have a particular interest in the testing and refinement of broadly adopted goal-oriented knowledge structures and the practices that derive from them.

The main implication of this assumption about incentives is that knowledge exchanges are heavily weighted toward the institutional goals of the exporting institution. Business firms are not interested in knowledge structures that lead to mediocrity and decline in profitability or reputation. Military officers have scant interest in how other countries with less sophisticated technology have fought wars, unless they have continuing relevance to modern warfare. Creative teams are not interested in products that fail to satisfy clients or customers. In sports, new statistical approaches are welcomed so long as they do not challenge the enterprise's fundamental commitment to improving the probabilities of achieving winning records. No institutionalized analytical tools in sports have focused on explaining the sources of prolonged periods of competitive mediocrity. Nor have any been developed to foster equality of competition.

Ideological resistance is the most common source of failure in knowledge exchange across institutional sectors. This resistance may be based on deeply held beliefs, or on an underlying sense of threat to the authority or prerogatives of elites. But the adoption and rejection of new knowledge structures is also influenced by (typically unexpressed) criteria relating to perceptions of fit and utility. Fit between the proposed model and the institutional environment is important (although difficult to measure in a nontautological way), as is efficiency and ease of use. For example, ranking systems of colleges that focus on raw retention, graduation, and employment rates are misleading, because they do not take into account the academic or sociodemographic characteristics of entering classes. Nevertheless, they have become popular among politicians, at least in part because they do not require statistical controls that may be difficult to obtain or difficult for the public (or politicians themselves) to understand.

Types of Knowledge Exchanges

Knowledge exchanges exist within this broader context set by institutional purposes and perceptions of fit and utility. In this section I illustrate the main forms of knowledge exchange: imports into academe, exports from academe, trade routes, and barriers to trade.

Imports into Academe

What sorts of knowledge structures are imported by academics from other institutional arenas? The most important clearly are study topics; academics very frequently take up knowledge structures developed in other institutional domains and subject them to study. But study topics are not the only imports. At a less visible level, academics have also imported organizing tropes and metaphors from other institutional domains. These less visible imports can have a deep structural importance when they shape the knowledge-generating and knowledge-adjudicating practices of academe.

Imported Study Topics. Narrow technical refinements are the bread and butter of many applied academic fields, such as toxicology and civil engineering. Study topics can be imported through referral when organizations lack the time or expertise to engage fully with problems of practice. An example of such a referral occurred in the late 1970s when a survey conducted by UNESCO indicated a global need for guidance about landslide hazard zonation. UNESCO suggested that the International Association of Engineering Geology carry out basic studies on landslide hazard zoning. Academic geologists were prominent in the compilation and organization of principles and practices for identifying unstable or potentially unstable areas (Varnes 1984). Following its publication, this document served as a guide for geological consultants, as well as government policy makers. Most standard setting work is undertaken by committees with mixed representation from professional groups, industry, government, and academe (see, e.g., Bureau of Consumer Protection 1983).[5] We can hypothesize that when governments insist on disinterested study, or when industry and government lack the expertise to study high-stakes outcomes properly, university researchers will become centrally involved. Clinical trials represent classical cases in which industrial self-interest and government insistence on rigor lead to a prominent role for university medical researchers, though one that does not invariably avoid the taint of partiality due to dependence on pharmaceutical companies for lucrative future opportunities (see, e.g., Washburn 2000: 110–136).

More often, study topics are simply appropriated by academics with an interest in the institutional domain from which they originate. Knowledge structures related to the achievement of institutional ends are frequently appropriated by academics for testing, refinement, and in some cases formalization. These sorts of problems appeal to the broader intellectual interests of academics in testing whether prevailing ideas do or do not stand up to empirical scrutiny. Take, for example, the wide variety of business management strategies and systems that have been developed to make businesses more efficient or more socially conscious, and therefore more profitable in the long run. These include "management by objectives" (Drucker 1954), "Theory Z" (Ouichi 1981), "total quality management" (TQM) (Deming 1982), "the triple bottom line" (Elkington 1997), and the "balanced scorecard" (Kaplan and Norton 1996). In a few cases, academics have played a role in the creation of these management frameworks. But the primary role of academe has been to determine whether or not the knowledge structures created by businesspeople produce the intended results. This requires collection of data from many different firms that have enacted the system, comparison of those who have adopted to those who have not, control for potentially confounding variables (such as starting market position), and finally support, revision, or rejection of the approach. Some management practices pass out of practice before academics have had a chance to pass judgment, because of the time, expense, or clearly mixed results of their enactment.

Total quality management (TQM) provides a well-documented example of an imported knowledge structure. It was inspired by principles developed by W. Edwards Deming (1982) and Joseph M. Juran. Deming was an industrial consultant who spent some time in academe; Juran was an engineer (Petersen 1999). TQM's processes date back to quality control procedures in postwar Japanese manufacturing (Powell 1995). In 1985 the US Navy introduced a system of operational improvement, formally labeled total quality management (Houston and Dockstader 1998). From there, the TQM was applied to other government agencies and private manufacturing and service firms (Powell 1995). While specific applications varied across industries, twelve factors were common in the TQM literature: committed leadership, adoption and communication of TQM, close customer relationships, close supplier relationships, benchmarking, increased training, open organization, employee empowerment, zero-defects mentality, flexible production, process improvement, and measurement (Powell 1995).

The primary role of academe was to determine whether TQM produced the results intended. Many studies found support for a relationship between TQM and business success (Easton and Jarrell 1998; Hackman and Wageman 1995; Watson and Rao Korukonda 1995) and others suggested revisions (Powell 1995; Reed, Lemak, and Montgomery 1996). TQM is no longer a dominant framework in business, in large part because later adopters were less likely than early adopters to customize its application, thus resulting in fewer benefits (Westphal, Gulati, and Shortell 1997). However, elements of TQM that were strongly supported by academic studies left a lasting impression on business practices and fostered new innovations, such as six-sigma and ISO certification (Miller, Hartwick, and Le Breton-Miller 2004).

These critical analysis and adjudication roles of academe are found in virtually every area of social innovation. In the field of educational studies, for example, state and national government officials, supported by the major philanthropic foundations, have championed knowledge structures that became embedded in national policy, such as the state testing required by the No Child Left Behind Act and the curriculum and assessment standards of the Common Core. Academic researchers investigated these politically dominant knowledge structures to examine their effectiveness in raising achievement and reducing gaps between subgroups, and to identify reasons for their successes and failures. Through their research on outcomes (Darling-Hammond 2007; Linn, Baker, and Betebenner 2002), academic researchers contributed to the negative verdict on NCLB that eventually emerged in the policy community. Even before the Common Core was fully launched, academics had developed testable criticisms related to whether its underlying learning theory was age-appropriate in early grades (Bomer and Maloch 2011), was or was not based on evidence (Cuban 2010), could reduce state variation when most variation was within rather than between states (Loveless 2012), or would reduce or add to achievement gaps between groups (Ravitch 2013). They also debated whether the liberal arts educational ideal on which it was based was appropriate for students whose interests and aptitudes vary widely (Carnevale, quoted in Goldstein 2012). These early criticisms will undoubtedly serve as hypotheses in studies of the outcomes of the Common Core curriculum when and if it is fully implemented.

Imported Tropes and Metaphors. A second important process through which nonacademic institutions influence academic production has to do with the search for metaphors and frames that can be used to illuminate scholarly and scientific topics. *Tropes* work at a deep, implicit level of cultural structuration. In perhaps the most sophisticated and wide-ranging demonstration of the role of tropes in the framing of academic work, the intellectual historian Hayden White (1973) famously identified four literary "emplotments" that characterized all history writing, even the most "synchronic": romance (the journey of self-identification), comedy (the harmony of the natural and social, including causes for celebration), satire (the opposite of romance; people are captives of a corrupt world), and tragedy (the failed effort to test the limits of the world, including the pathos of a hero's blind spots or limitations). Nor has the quest for metathematics been limited to the humanities and social sciences. Stephen Jay Gould (1978) posited that Darwinism showed an affinity to the politics of Victorian gradualism, whereas punctuated equilibrium, the theory inspired by his own work, reflected the underlying outlook on social change of the 1960s protest movements in which Gould participated. In sociology we find evidence of extensive metaphorical borrowing—for example, from the telecommunications industry (adapted for cybernetics and network theory), from the political arena (adapted for considerations of occupational jurisdictions) from stagecraft (essential to Goffmanian dramatism), and from religion (as elements in Durkheimian approaches to secular rituals), to name just a few.

Exports from Academe

Conversely, the knowledge exports of academia can exercise an imprint over knowledge practices in other institutional domains. Academe plays a central role in testing, criticizing, refining, and formalizing knowledge structures originating in other institutional arenas. It also has the capacity to "colonize" knowledge space and work practice in other institutional arenas, although this is a much rarer outcome.

Test Results. A primary function of academe is to serve as a relatively disinterested testing site for knowledge structures generated in other institutional domains and to feedback new approaches based on these tests. In areas related to the public and nonprofit sector, academe appears to enjoy a privileged role. In areas in which profit making is a possibility, particularly if profits are large, private firms can be stronger competitors.

Although we tend to think of academe's role in producing test results as being focused on more rationalized fields, such as medicine or business management, examples can be found throughout American institutional life, including in such unlikely places as the popular culture industries. Within the film industry, for example, formulas have long existed for predicting a film's success. One set of formulas makes predictions based on business variables, such as number of screens contracted, marketing budget, genre, release date, success rate of producers, and marquee value of directors and stars. Another set of formulas makes predictions based on the "emotional torque" of narratives. In one version of the story formula, the main structural elements are the protagonist who is attempting to reach a goal, the antagonist who places obstacles in the way of the protagonist, and the relationship character who accompanies the protagonist on his or her journey and is often not listened to. The story ends when the protagonist achieves or relinquishes her goal, defeats or is defeated by the antagonist, and reconciles with the relationship character. The closer these things happen together, the higher the emotional power (Anders 2011).

Academics have examined the business formula, often throwing doubt on the importance of star power while affirming the significance of budget summer and holiday release, and the popularity of the historically highest-grossing genres (Brewer, Kelley, and Jozefowicz 2001), or concluding that because of the heavily right-tailed distribution, with infinite variance, no predictions of exceptional box office success are possible (DeVany and Walls 1999). In recent years, more sophisticated modeling has developed in which neural network methodologies are used to consider much more fine-grained story elements, including, for example, locale of the setting, how well the film takes advantage of the dramatic potential of the setting, and whether or not a woman is brought into peril. The specific features of these empirically derived predictive models are closely held by commercial firms, some founded by former academics and most drawing on the statistical expertise of academics or former academics (Barnes 2013; Gladwell 2006). A parallel case exists in the popular music industry, where firms such as Music Xray measure the mathematical relationships among melody, harmony, beat, tempo, rhythm, octave, pitch, chord progression, cadence, sonic brilliance, and frequency to identify "hit" clusters and to predict the probable success of new songs by their closeness to one of these clusters (Gladwell 2006). Naturally, a major concern about these tools is that they will lead to ever greater levels of imitation in popular culture industries, rather than to creativity.

Another unconventional but revealing example comes from the world of spiritual practices. Maharishi Mahesh Yogi introduced transcendental meditation in the 1950s as a mental calming and spiritual development practice (Alexander, Boyer, and Alexander 1987). The first tests of the physiological effects of TM were conducted in the early 1970s by Herbert Benson and his associates at the Harvard Medical School (Benson and associates 1975). Since then, the transcendental meditation movement has gained traction throughout the Western world, with practitioners using it to reduce anxiety, improve health, and achieve a heightened level of spirituality. Hundreds of academic tests of the effects of transcendental meditation have yielded mixed results. A consensus has developed that regular practice can have benefits for relief of stress and anxiety and for cardiovascular health, and can be prescribed for hypertension (see, e.g., Bai et al. 2015; MacLean et al. 1997; Zamarra et al. 1996), though its benefits do not typically exceed those of other relaxation techniques or regular exercise. This medical support, while mixed, has helped to legitimize and expand the popularity of a practice that once appealed in the West only to a small segment of countercultural young people.

Refinements and Formalizations. Many industrial knowledge structures have been subjected to deeper scrutiny by university researchers, leading to improved practices. Less developed knowledge structures may give way to academically generated refinements when practical problems develop or persist. For example, frameworks and methods for separating compounds developed in university laboratories when it became clear that batch processing used in industry could not provide the quality or efficiency that would be desirable for many bulk goods. In some cases, these separations require total purification, as in electrolysis refining of bauxite ore for aluminum. In other cases, the separation process splits mixtures into other more valuable mixtures, as in crude oil refinery. Different techniques are suitable, depending on differences in chemical properties or physical properties such as shape, mass, density, or chemical affinity (Wilson, Adland, and Cooke 2000). Today, dozens of separation techniques exist, and most were developed in university laboratories.

Refinements of social knowledge structures may be less common, but they can be equally transformational. The evolution of user- (or human-) centered design (UCD) provides an example of the interplay of an early influential idea from industry and its refinement and formalization by academic researchers. In UCD the needs, wants, and limitations of end users are given centrality at each stage of the design process. The first seminal paper on the topic, by IBM engineers John D. Gould and Clayton Lewis (1985), identified several elements of user-centered design that remain central: early and continual focus on users; empirical measurement of usage; and iterative design whereby the product or system is developed, modified, tested, modified again, and tested again. Subsequent work by academic researchers led to elaboration of methods for understanding users, for prototyping, and for validating design. Affinity diagrams (compilations of user insights), personas, mental models, and use scenarios have been identified by academic researchers as valuable methods for probing the minds and practices of users (Wallach and Scholz 2012). The underlying ideas of UCD have been expanded well beyond their original focus on human-software interface to encompass a wide variety of products, processes, and organizational systems.

The engineering professor Donald A. Norman (1988) provided an adumbrated conceptual frame that focused on the broader world of design of "everyday things." In Norman's scheme, human-centered design focused on simplifying the structure of tasks, making things visible, getting the mapping of the product right, exploiting the powers of constraint, designing for error, exploring affordances (such as the historical connection between handles and pulling), and standardizing "when all else fails." By mapping, Norman meant following the relationship between intentions and required actions, between actions and the resulting effect, and between information that is visible and the interpretation of the system state. Academic researchers such as William Rouse (2007) extended similar ideas to organizational systems and processes. The International Organisation for Standardization has institutionalized basic principles of human-centered design (ISO 2015), while industry has added new interests in the sources of physiological and emotional pleasure in design, as opposed to mere utility and convenience (see, e.g., Jordan 2000). These could easily become future topics for academic refinement and formalization.

Similarly, scenario-planning methodologies were imported into academe from the military and industry, where they were subsequently formalized and exported back to the military and industry, albeit with mixed reception. Scenario planning is used as a strategic tool for individuals and organizations to imagine realistic possible future scenarios to improve planning and decision-making processes (Chermack, Lynham, and Ruona, 2001; Varum and Melo 2010). Scenario planning originated in military war game planning led by the military strategist Herman Kahn, and was quickly adopted by the oil industry as an aid to think through and cope with uncertain environments (Schwartz 1991). The theoretical framework of scenario planning was researched, refined, and formalized by academic thinkers from RAND, the University of Pennsylvania's Wharton School, and the University of Strathclyde (Georgantzas and Acar 1995). These scholars helped introduce alternative approaches to the generation of scenarios, such as mathematical models and algorithms, which did not rely solely on judgment and intuition (Georgantzas and Acar 1995). One of the pioneers of scenario planning, Kees Van der Heijden, moved from the Shell Oil Company to a university appointment in Scotland, where he formalized principles of scenario planning in a prizewinning book on strategy (Van der Heijden 1997). Although the methodology of scenario planning has become more sophisticated due to the work of academic researchers, the jury is still out with respect to whether scenario planning contributes to organizational learning or long-term stability (Chermack, Lyman, and Rouna 2001; Varum and Melo 2010). Nor is it clear how many business strategists and military planners faithfully follow Van der Heijden's formalizations in the design of scenarios.

Critique. Critique is part of the lifeblood of the academic system, and a prelude to any serious quest for improved understanding or action. Critique without testing or refinement is a common occurrence in academic encounters with knowledge structures produced in other institutional settings. Indeed, whole libraries could undoubtedly be constructed of books and papers subjecting social knowledge structures to critique.[6] Much of this work is irrelevant to understanding cross-institutional knowledge exchange because its impact exists solely within the community of academic commentators and critics. However, critiques can have influence even when refinements for use are not provided, when they induce rethinking in source institutions.

Prominent examples can be found in the world of knowledge structures surrounding hiring and promotion. Modern hiring practices attempt to control for racial-ethnic and gender biases by creating oversight offices concerned with equal employment opportunities (Dobbin 2009). We can consider these practices as knowledge structures because they have relied on elaborated criteria for evaluating applicants while incorporating articulated safeguards, and because they have included empirical testing for outcomes. Recent social-science studies have critiqued these knowledge structures for failing properly to account for "unconscious bias" or "implicit social cognition" that can influence the initial sorting of applicants' qualifications

(Greenwald and Banaji 1995). Similarly, management schemes such as the triple bottom line have been critiqued—in this case, by researchers who find applicable data difficult to find for the proposed social and ecological "bottom lines" (Slaper and Hall 2011). In most such cases of critique without refinement, researchers leave it up to actors in source institutions to devise refined knowledge structures to address their critiques—and of course, this often does not happen. The reconsideration of equal opportunity in light of "implicit social cognition" theory is a liminal case, because university researchers have developed tests, such as the Implicit Association Test (Greenwald, McGhee, and Schwartz 1998) to measure unconscious bias, but the tests have not at this time been accepted by employers—in part because other psychologists have criticized their validity (Azar 2008).

Colonization of Practice.[7] New knowledge structures generated in academic libraries and laboratories sometimes so clearly appear to represent advances that they transform nonacademic institutions in short order. The importation of knowledge structures from positive psychology into the training of military soldiers and officers is a notable recent example (Seligman 2011). The US Army's Comprehensive Soldier Fitness program derives from research on resilience conducted by psychologists associated with the Center for Positive Psychology at the University of Pennsylvania. The program includes tests for psychological fitness, online courses aiming to improve psychological fitness, and a master resilience training program for drill sergeants. The last component—the linchpin of the program, according to its director—focuses on building officers' mental toughness, "signature strengths," and capacity for strong relationships with troops in their platoons. More than one million soldiers have participated in the program. The focus on resilience is obviously appropriate in the context of military combat, though undertheorized in the past. The program, developed by Seligman and his associates, also meets efficiency criteria. It is easy to deliver, provides quick feedback on results, and builds on core competencies already required for military officers (Seligman 2011).

A more modest, and much less successful, example of the colonization process can be found in James Q. Wilson and George L. Kelling's "broken windows" theory of policing (1982). Wilson and Kelling posited that evidence of neighborhood deterioration, such as an increase in the number of broken windows on a street, provided a leading indicator of social disorder and consequent probable increases in the crime rate. The prescription of the "broken windows" theory was for police to put additional emphasis on neighborhoods that appeared, on the basis of physical deterioration, to be in danger of becoming high-crime areas and to encourage community members, working with government and nonprofit organizations, to improve the physical appearance and sense of social order in their neighborhoods. The broken windows theory influenced policing practices, notably in New York City, where it gave rise to the "zero-tolerance" policy of police commissioner William Bratton, but also in other large cities. One appeal of the theory lay in its connection to aspects of communities that police can influence, such as visible signs of physical deterioration, rather than those they cannot, such as the availability of jobs. Another source of its appeal was its promise to allocate resources in an efficient and seemingly progressive way by preventing future crimes from occurring rather than focusing resources exclusively on neighborhoods where crime was already rampant. However, the theory, as implemented, received stringent criticism from social scientists and community activists for, among other deficiencies, equating correlation with causation, ignoring underlying economic and social roots of crime, and contributing to higher levels of enmity towards police in closely monitored minority communities (see, e.g., Harcourt 2001; Sampson and Raudenbush 1999).

Trade Routes

Just as the traffic of finished goods is heavy from China to the United States and light between Iceland and sub-Saharan Africa, so too would it be possible to chart the movement of cultural goods, such as knowledge structures, across institutional sectors. In the absence of systematic study, we cannot identify the zones in which exchanges are common or those in which they are rare. We also cannot know why traffic on these routes is heavy or light. Consequently, hypotheses are the most that can be offered at this early stage of theorization.

Notwithstanding the political preferences of professors (Gross 2013), universities may engage in lower levels of exchange with institutional domains associated with political liberalism than with those associated with political conservatism. Politically conservative domains include manufacturing industries, small business, the military, the medical professions, finance, and other business services linked to the corporate economy (Brint 2015). Insofar as this hypothesis is correct, an important source of this variation will likely be found in the degree of congruence in analytical languages between academic scientists and participants in these politically conservative institutional spheres. All organizations have an interest in knowledge structures that lead to greater effectiveness in the achievement of valued outcomes, but only some institutional domains are likely to have verification methods in place to evaluate whether valued outcomes are being met.

Outlying cases tend to reinforce this view. In the liberal institutional sphere, the volume of exchange between academe and nonacademic scientific research firms is likely heavier than in any other trade route; in the conservative sphere, the volume of exchange between academe and small business is likely lighter than elsewhere. The difference that congruent and incongruent analytical languages make is clear in these cases. Academics and other scientific researchers share congruent analytical languages; academics and small business people for the most part do not.

The mass media is a special case. Here the trade with academe is very heavy, but unlike other trade routes, the relationship between academics and journalists does not depend on speaking a congruent analytical language. Instead, journalists are reliant on academic experts to provide sourcing for informed opinions and provocative or illuminating results that may be of interest to their audiences. This leads to heavy traffic between the two, but low levels of penetration into the workings of mass-media institutions themselves.

Another factor affecting the volume of inter-institutional exchange may be the existence of conferences or other meeting spaces that foster interactions and relationship building between academics and practitioners. When practitioners and academics attend the same conferences, results of academic research can be fed back quickly into practice. Medicine is a prime example. Academic medical researchers are prominent presenters at virtually all conferences of medical practitioners (Ionnaides 2012). By contrast, in less technical fields knowledge development has more to do with new fads and fashions, or with government regulatory policies, than with academic testing and refinement. K–12 education is a notable example. Practitioners and academics do not attend the same conferences, and most K–12 educators do not see themselves as part of a scientifically governed ecosystem; instead, what tend to count for them are their relationships with students and the growth they observe in them, and what the government requires them to do in relation to accountability for learning assessments (Darling-Hammond 2004). Government is the intervening regulatory party, and researchers consequently attempt to make their case through policy makers rather than to educators. For this reason, the results of academic research are fed back much more slowly into the field, when they are fed back at all.

Barriers to Trade

We can think of successful cross-institutional exchanges as instances in which knowledge structures are handled without distortion, and in which barriers are not raised against the free flow of knowledge structures. I will briefly discuss three barriers to successful cross-institutional trade. In order of severity, they are (1) corrupted knowledge goods, (2) failed exchanges, and (3) blockades.

Corrupted Knowledge Goods. Often academic exports are selectively appropriated so that evidence that supports the agenda of an interest group or institutional value structure is adopted, while caveats and qualifications are not. The relationship between social-science evidence on marriage as a benefit and conservative religious institutions provides an example (e.g., Waite and Gallagher 2001). Conservative Christian groups have taken up supportive findings on marriage benefits, both because of the legitimacy of science and because of the value of empirical evidence for the success of their "family values" agenda (Klemp and Macedo 2009). At the same time, they have downplayed or ignored evidence that nonspouses can fulfill a role similar to that of spouses in single-parent families, and that some single-parent families succeed, provided that love and support exist in the household and behavioral norms for children are enforced (Entwistle, Alexander, and Olsen 1997). They have also ignored the evidence on the social and psychological difficulties faced by children whose parents are married but unhappy together (Sturge-Apple, Davies, and Cummings 2010).

We can analogize these processes to the dilution of medicine for profit by corrupt testing laboratories and commercial interests in the developing world. This is a common problem in global medical care. In the world of knowledge exports, we can hypothesize that corruptions occur both as a result of selective retention of ideologically harmonious findings and of simple corner-cutting and profiteering. Academic knowledge exported into political and religious institutions may be particularly prone to selective retention on ideological grounds, while academic knowledge exported into industry may be particularly prone to cost-saving corruption.

Failed Exchanges. Failed exchanges occur when one side of a potential exchange relationship determines that its priorities or interests will be harmed through the adoption of a new knowledge structure. Foundational beliefs linked to prerogatives of the powerful are a frequent source of failed exchanges. Disagreement within the community of experts can contribute significantly to failed exchanges, because dissenting views provide resources for opponents. The history of social indicators in the United States, led from the beginning by academic social scientists, illustrates these sources of failed exchanges. The social indicators movement started in the United States during the Depression era, but it never achieved institutionalization as an element of governmental policy (Cobb and Rixford 1998; Innes 1989). This stands in contrast to the acceptance of social indicators in Europe and in the developing world (Noll and Zipf 1994). In the United States, the social indicators movement was plagued by methodological issues and a proliferation of parameters of interest to investigators (Cobb and Rixford 1998). A proposal for a Council of Social Advisors and annual reports of social indicators, analogous to the Council of Economic Advisors, were opposed by the Reagan administration, and have not gained traction at the national level in the United States since that time (Cobb and Rixford 1998).

Failed exchanges also occur when university researchers propose knowledge structures that are misaligned with fundamental institutional purposes as perceived by gatekeepers. The theory of multiple intelligence provides an apt example. At the end of the twentieth century, buoyed by popular and scholarly skepticism, the academic psychologists Howard Gardner (1983) and Robert Sternberg (1985) developed theories of "multiple intelligences." These new theories were both critiques of existing knowledge structures focusing on a single dimension of intelligence, and attempted efforts to refine them. Both psychologists attempted to justify the theories on empirical grounds. However, these alternative conceptualizations could not gain traction either in public schools or with college admissions offices. Public schools were under increasing pressure to reduce tracking and to show learning gains for all students (Mehta 2013). The leading college admissions offices remained focused on academic aptitudes and major accomplishments, presumably reflecting the primary purpose of the institution: the identification and development of cognitively talented and highly motivated students.[8] In retrospect, this indifference to conceptions of multiple intelligences is impressive, given that these broader conceptions might have resulted in more diversified classes—a goal actively pursued by selective colleges and universities during the period. Perceptions of fit and utility may also have played a role. If tests based on multiple intelligence could have been proven to produce outstanding entering classes, at reasonable cost and without greatly complicating the admissions process, they would likely have received more attention from universities and the testing industry than they ultimately received.

Blockades. At an extreme, in highly politicized situations, all knowledge intercourse between institutional sectors may be blocked. The analyses and policies advocated by climate scientists ran into a wall of opposition from conservative business and political leaders during the time of the Bush and Trump administrations. These opponents distrusted the science and feared the costs that would be required to comply with new regulations on greenhouse gases (see, e.g., McCright and Dunlap 2010). Similarly, civil rights groups and their allies in the Democratic Party succeeded for two decades in blockading frameworks for understanding the contribution of family structure to the perpetuation of intergenerational poverty, by labeling such frameworks as tantamount to "blaming the victims" of poverty and racism (Patterson 2010). Blockades are commonplace in democracies whose parties require the support of powerful interest groups. In these circumstances, interest groups must be able to make it sufficiently costly for policymakers to depart from the interest groups' position. Yet I would hypothesize that in societies where scientific literacy grows more important and the scientific community is undeterred by political pushback, the accumulation of evidence has a way of overcoming the opposition of politicized interest groups—even if it may take decades to do so.

Communication across Institutional Boundaries

I will conclude by taking up the question how knowledge producers rooted in different institutional settings communicate across sector boundaries. The historian of science Peter Galison (1997, 2010) has developed a vocabulary to discuss the language development processes involved. I believe this work may have application to the larger cross-institutional canvas on which I have been working in this paper. Galison's focus has been on language development: the communicative mechanisms that develop within what he calls "trading zones," or areas in which the pursuit of interdisciplinary interests can be stymied by failures to share a common language.[9] For Galison, when issues of communication are solved, trading zones become, simply, trade. Galison discusses three mechanisms for the development of new languages: (1) inter-languages, strategically directed jargon that allows for sharing of key points of intersection, (2) pidgin, a more integrated language which nevertheless continues to contain elements of the specific expert languages of those contributing to a field, and (3) creoles, new languages developed through the selective adoption of features of the contributing expert languages. Nanotechnologists are still working through inter-languages, while biochemists have developed a full-blown creole that represents a freestanding language in its own right.

Along similar lines, Collins and Evans (2002, 2007) have highlighted the role of "interactional expertise"—people whose knowledge skills and intuitions are sufficient to allow for fruitful exchanges across expert community boundaries. These people are generally not capable of making substantive contributions to the work of experts in more than one interacting community, but they have the "translational" skills to understand both communities sufficiently to facilitate their joint progress. As Galison emphasizes, "Regularized and stripped down out-talk is not a lesser version of something else; rather, it is a register of scientific interaction that is supple and effective in its domain. The skills of someone versed in interactional expertise represent one specific register of scientific language" (Galison 2010: 48).

Certain capacities of the academic mind make it distinctive. These include its capacity to see problems whole, to capture key characteristics of problems, to assemble data from which authoritative evidence can be developed, and to subject these data to rigorous analysis. Those in other institutional realms develop conceptual knowledge, but they can rarely work with ideas in a way that allows them to identify key features capable of manipulation, or to investigate these key features in a systematic way. This is true for three reasons: (1) the self-selection of people capable of this work into the scientific domains of academe, (2) the training academics receive in making these types of judgments, and (3) the very different purposes of practitioners in other institutional arenas. Even if they are systematic in their thinking and are capable of comparing alternative approaches, practitioners do not typically have the time, or very often the inclination, to break up the whole into its component parts or to collect and study data carefully to develop conclusions about the advisability of specific understandings. In their use of knowledge structures, those who work in other institutional realms are inclined to satisfice rather than to inspect critically. When they are innovators, they may be inclined to sell their ideas, rather than to investigate them thoroughly. In the trade with academe, knowledge producers in other domains may simply hand over problems—this is a typical scenario—or allow them to be appropriated by academics for more careful analysis.

The ideas of Galison and his colleagues may prove useful in future studies of the trade in knowledge structures. We should be open to the discovery of cross-institutional interlanguages, pidgins, and creoles, as well as individuals who provide interactional expertise across borderlands. However, I doubt that these "languages" will be as important in cross-institutional studies as they are in the development of trade within expert communities in academe. Because those who communicate across institutional sectors do not share a common metacognitive orientation, new languages are less likely to develop. Academic expertise is the metacognitive orientation that sees problems in full, breaks down the elements of problems into categories that can be manipulated, interprets the key features of the problems as so classified, and collects data in a more or less systematic way to arrive at conclusions. Potential collaborators from outside academe must show the capacity to engage with this common metacognitive orientation in order to become full collaborators. Because relatively few do so, academics function both as investigators and translators, often aided by journalists in translational work.

In this respect, the centrality of academe in the world of knowledge production and trade can be reasserted—not as the sole, or perhaps even the principal, generator of knowledge structures, but as the home of the ultimate cultural authority (and the privileged work space) that permits knowledge generated both in universities and elsewhere to be examined, proven, deepened, revised, or rejected on the basis of evidence. As a feature in the cultural trade routes that crisscross institutional settings, academe alone is capable of functioning as the metacognitive metropole.

Notes

1. I would like to thank Sarah R. K. Yoshikawa for research assistance. I would also like to thank colleagues at the Radcliffe Institute working group on the new sociology of education and at the University of Oslo faculty of education, who provided valuable criticism of earlier versions of this paper. Special thanks to Michael Olneck, who sent a number of valuable references.
2. Academics have a natural desire to monopolize legitimate knowledge. To the extent that they can define academic knowledge as the only legitimate form of knowledge, the cultural capital of academe becomes a more valuable commodity, and the position of universities and professors gains in stability and status. Obviously, my position differs. It is important to separate the status and certification value of the institutionalized cultural capital of schools and universities from the more free-flowing (but nevertheless analyzable) intermingling of knowledge exports and imports in the cultural construction of the modern world. Among social scientists who have recognized that knowledge exists outside as well as inside academe, my position is distinctive in relation to its structural anchorage. I prefer to root my analysis in the core social structures of advanced industrial societies—particularly institutions, organizations, work settings, and interest groups—rather than in the more diffuse patterns of "bounded cultural units" in the Boasian tradition; the recipe knowledge of "ordinary social life," as in Schutzian phenomenology; or interpretations of political psychology, as in Mannheimian ideology analysis.
3. One fundamental question is "What is knowledge?" All agree that knowledge requires truth claims. Idioms and practices that do not make truth claims may play an important role in society (e.g., satire) or even in brain activity (e.g., instrumental music), but they are not knowledge. Recent discussions about knowledge tend to divide between social constructionists ("Knowledge is an institutionalized truth claim, verifiable or not") and positivists ("Knowledge is a truth claim that is subject to verification, and consequently refutation"). Both groups agree that knowledge

goes beyond mere information or opinion; it is an organized body of understandings connected to some section of the empirically existing world (including texts). Both also agree that knowledge systems generate understandings of how specific parts of the world work, and may include implications for how to live based on "facts" (or "institutionalized understandings"), principles, and recipes for action. Although the social constructionists make an irrefutable point (i.e., that ideas we believe to be real are real in their consequences), a positivist definition of knowledge is essential to the study of the institutional geography of knowledge exchange, for, as I argue here, one of the most important functions of academe is the verification, revision, and refinement of truth claims that are susceptible to verification.

4. If we look at research statistics, it is obvious that knowledge production takes place outside of academe. For decades, statistics from the National Science Board in the United States have indicated that only about half of basic scientific research is conducted inside universities. Moreover, only a small fraction of total applied research is conducted in universities (National Science Board 2014: chapter 4). Many of the most important inventions of the period, from the Internet and GPS to the birth control pill and the pacemaker, were developed in government laboratories and private corporations by university-trained doctorates, sometimes but not always building on basic research conducted in universities (see, e.g., Isaacson 2014 on inventions related to computing and digital media.)
5. There are tens of thousands of product standards in use in industry. Many hundreds of groups, with thousands of committees and subcommittees, set standards for manufactured articles ranging from screw threads and safety devices for steam boilers to computer software. The American Society of Mechanical Engineers alone publishes nearly six hundred codes and standards; its annual income from the sale of such publications is in the tens of millions of dollars (ASME 2015).
6. The idea of facts themselves has been subjected to relentless critique by postmodern scholars influenced by Michel Foucault and other social constructionists (see, e.g., Poovey 1998). These critiques, while important in the contextualization of historically contingent knowledge structures, have unfortunately contributed to a more general skepticism about whether objective understandings of observable phenomena are possible.
7. My view departs from the overgeneralized perspectives of Habermas (1984) on "the colonization of the lifeworld" and Foucault (1977) on "discursive practices" that construct the "carceral" institutions of modern societies. I focus instead on concrete instances of knowledge exports from academe that transform specific institutional practices outside academe.
8. This focus on academic aptitudes and major accomplishments has been offset to a degree by extra consideration given to applicants from families of alumni and especially donors, athletes, and minorities, among others (see, e.g., Soares 2007; Stevens 2007),
9. This is a phrase with obvious resonance to the vocabulary developed here, although I discovered Galison's work only after I was quite far along in applying the metaphor of trade and a new vocabulary based on trade imagery to cultural exchanges. My thanks to Michael Olneck for bringing this work to my attention.

References

Abbott, Andrew. 2001. *Chaos of Disciplines*. Chicago: University of Chicago Press.

———. 2002. "The Disciplines and the Future." In Steven Brint, ed., *The Future of the City of Intellect: The Changing American University, 206–230*. Stanford, CA: Stanford University Press.

American Society of Mechanical Engineers (ASME). 2015. *Standards and Certification*. https://www.asme.org/wwwasmeorg/media/ResourceFiles/AboutASME/Who%20We%20Are/Standards_and_Certification/ASME_Codes_and_Standards-Examples_of_Use_for_Mechanical_Engineering_Students.pdf.

Anders, Lou. 2011. *Writing Excuses: The Hollywood Formula*. http://www.writingexcuses.com/tag/lou-anders/.

Azar, Beth. 2008. "IAT: Fad or Fabulous?" *APA Monitor* 39 (7): 44.

Baker, David P. 2014. *The Schooled Society: The Educational Transformation of Global Culture*. Stanford, CA: Stanford University Press.

Bai, Z., et al. 2015. *Investigating the Effect of Transcendental Meditation on Blood Pressure: A Systematic Review and Meta-analysis*. www.10.10381 jhh 2015.6.

Barnes, Brooks. 2013. "Solving Equation of a Hit Film Script, with Data." *The New York Times*, May 5. http://www.nytimes.com/2013/05/06/business/media/solving-equation-of-a-hit-film-script-with-data.html?pagewanted=all&_r=0.

Benson, Herbert, and associates. 1975. *The Relaxation Response*. New York: HarperTorch.

Bomer, Randy, and Beth Maloch. 2011. "Relating Policy to Research and Practice: The Common Core Standards." *Language Arts* 89:38–43.

Brecher, Tony. 1989. *Academic Tribes and Territories*. Buckingham, UK: Society for Research into Higher Education and Open University Press.

Brewer, Stephanie M., Jason M. Kelley, and James J. Jozefowicz. 2009. "A Blueprint for Success in the US Film Industry." *Applied Economics* 41:589–606.

Brint, Steven. 1994. *In An Age of Experts: The Changing Role of Professionals in Politics and Public Life*. Princeton, NJ: Princeton University Press.

———. 2001. "Professionals and the 'Knowledge Economy': Rethinking the Theory of Post-Industrial Society." *Current Sociology* 49:101–132.

———. 2015. "Professional Responsibility in an Age of Experts and Large Organizations." In Douglas Mitchell and Robert K. Ream, eds., *Professional Responsibility*, 89–107. London: Springer.

Chermack, Thomas J., Susan A. Lynham, and Wendy E.A. Ruona. 2001. "A Review of Scenario Planning Literature." *Futures Research Quarterly* 17 (2): 7–31.

Cobb, Clifford W., and Craig Rixford. 1998. *Lessons Learned from the History of Social Indicators*. San Francisco: Redefining Progress Press.

Collins, Harry, and Robert Evans. 2002. "The Third Wave of Science Studies: Studies of Expertise and Experience." *Social Studies of Science* 32:235–296.

———. 2007. *Rethinking Expertise*. Chicago: University of Chicago Press.

Cuban, Larry. 2010 (July). *Common Core Standards: Hardly an Evidence-Based Policy*. www.larrycuban.wordpress.com/2010/07/25/common-core-standards-hardly-an-evidence-based-policy.

Darling-Hammond, Linda. 2004. "Standards, Accountability and School Reform." *Teachers College Record* 106:1017–1085.

———. 2007. "Race, Inequality and Educational Accountability: The Irony of No Child Left Behind." *Race, Ethnicity and Education* 10:245–260.

Deming, W. Edwards. 1982. *Quality, Productivity, and Competitive Position*. Cambridge, MA: MIT Press.

Dobbin, Frank. 2009. *Inventing Equal Opportunity*. Princeton, NJ: Princeton University Press.

Drucker, Peter F. 1954. *The Practice of Management*. New York: HarperBusiness.

Easton, G. S., and S. L. Jarrell. 1998. "The Effects of Total Quality Management on Corporate Performance: An Empirical Investigation." *Journal of Business* 71:253–307.

Elkington, John. 1997. *Cannibals with Forks: The Triple Bottom Line of Twenty-first Century Business*. Oxford, UK: Capstone.

Entwhistle, Doris, Karl L. Alexander, and Linda Steffel Olsen. 1997. *Children, Schools, and Inequality*. Boulder, CO: Westview Press.

Foucault, Michel. 1977. *Discipline and Punish: The Birth of the Prison*. New York: Random House.

Galison, Peter. 1997. *Image and Logic: A Material Culture of Microphysics*. Chicago: University of Chicago Press.

———. 2010. "Trading with the Enemy." In Michael E. Gorman, ed., *Trading Zones and Interactional Expertise*, 25–52. Cambridge, MA: MIT Press.

Gardner, Howard. 1983. *Frames of Mind: The Theory of Multiple Intelligences*. New York: Basic Books.

Geiger, Roger L., and Creso Sa. 2008. *Tapping the Riches of Science: Universities and the Promise of Economic Growth*. Cambridge, MA: Harvard University Press.

Georgantzas, Nicholas C., and William Acar. 1995. *Scenario-Driven Planning: Learning to Manage Strategic Uncertainty*. Westport, CT: Quorum Books.

Gieryn, Thomas F. 1999. *Cultural Boundaries of Science: Credibility on the Line*. Chicago: University of Chicago Press.

Gladwell, Malcolm. 2006. "The Formula." *New Yorker*, October 16. www.newyorker.com/magazine/2006/10/6/the-formula.

Goldstein, Dana. 2012. "The Schoolmaster." *Atlantic, October*. http://www.theatlantic.com/magazine/archive/2012/10/the-schoolmaster/309091/2/.

Gorman, Michael E., ed. *Trading Zones and Interactional Expertise: Creating New Kinds of Collaboration*. Cambridge, MA: MIT Press.

Gould, John D., and Clayton Lewis. 1985. "Designing for Usability: Key Principles and What Designers Think." *Association for Computing Machinery Magazine* 28:300–311.

Gould, Stephen Jay. 1978. "Flaws in the Victorian Veil." *New Scientist* 82 (September 28): 942–943.

Greenwald, Anthony G., and Mahzarin Banaji. 1995. "Implicit Social Cognition: Attitudes, Self-Esteem, and Stereotypes." *Psychological Review* 102:4–27.

Greenwald, Anthony G., Debbie E. McGhee, and Jordan L. K. Schwartz. 1998. "Measuring Individual Differences in Implicit Cognition: The Implicit Association Test." *Journal of Personality and Social Psychology* 74:1464–1480.

Gross, Neil. 2013. *Why Are Professors Liberal and Why Do Conservatives Care*? Cambridge, MA: Harvard University Press.

Habermas, Jurgen. 1984. *The Theory of Communicative Action, Vol. 1: Reason and Rationalisation*. Boston: Beacon Press.

Hackman, J. Richard, and Ruth Wageman. 1995. "Total Quality Management: Empirical, Conceptual, and Practical Issues." *Administrative Science Quarterly* 40:309–342.

Harcourt, Bernard E. 2004. *The Illusion of Order: The False Promise of Broken Windows Policing*. Cambridge, MA: Harvard University Press.

Houston, Archester, and Steven L. Dockstader. 1998. *Total Quality Leadership: A Primer*. Washington: Department of the Navy.

Innes, Judith Eleanor. 1980. "Disappointments and Legacies of Social Indicators." *Journal of Policy* 9:429–432.

International Organisation for Standardization (ISO). 2015. *Ergonomics of Human-System Interaction. Part 210: Human-Centered design for Interactional Systems*. Geneva: ISO. https://www.iso.org/obp/ui/#iso:std:iso:9241:-210:ed-1:v1:en.

Isaacson, Walter. 2014. *The Innovators*. New York: Simon and Schuster.

Jacobs, Jerry A. 2014. *In Defense of the Disciplines*. Chicago: University of Chicago Press.

Jacobs, Jerry A., and Scott Frickel. 2009. "Interdisciplinarity: A Critical Assessment." *Annual Review of Sociology* 35:43–65.

Jordan, Patrick. 2000. *Designing Pleasurable Products*. London: Taylor & Francis.

Kaplan, Richard S., and David P. Norton. 1996. "Using the Balanced Scorecard as a Strategic Management System." *Harvard Business Review* 74 (January-February): 75–85.

Kenney, Martin, and David C. Mowery. 2014. *Public Universities and Regional Growth: Insights from the University of California*. Stanford, CA: Stanford Business Books.

Kerr, Clark. 1962. *The Uses of the University*. Cambridge, MA: Harvard University Press.

Klemp, Nathaniel, and Stephen Macedo. 2009. "The Christian Right, Public Reason, and American Democracy." In Steven Brint and Jean Reith Schroedel, eds., *Evangelicals and Democracy in America*, Vol. 2, 209–246. New York: Russell Sage Foundation Press.

Kuhn, Thomas S. 1970. *The Structure of Scientific Revolutions*. Chicago: University of Chicago Press.

Lamont, Michele. 2008. *How Professors Think: Inside the Curious World of Academic Judgment*. Cambridge, MA: Harvard University Press.

Lemann, Nicholas. 1999. *The Big Test: The Secret History of the American Meritocracy*. New York: Farrar, Strauss, and Giroux.

Lester, Paul B., et al. 2011 (December).*The Comprehensive Soldier Fitness Program Evaluation: Report #3: Longitudinal Analysis of the Impact of Master Resilience Training on Self-Reported Resilience and Psychological Health Data*. http://dma.wi.gov/dma/news/2012news/csf5tech5report.pdf.

Linn, Robert L., Eva L. Baker, and Damian W. Betebenner. 2002. "Accountability Systems: Implications for the Requirements of the No Child Left Behind Act of 2001." *Educational Researcher* 31 (6): 3–16.

Loveless, Tom. 2012. "The Common Core Initiative: What Are the Chances of Success?" *Educational Leadership* 10:60–63.

MacLean, C. R. K., et al. 1997. "Effects of the Transcendental Meditation Program on Adaptive Mechanisms: Changes in Hormone Levels and Responses to Stress after 4 Months of Practice." *Psychoneuroendocrinology* 22:277–295. http://dx.doi.org/10.1016/S0306-4530(97)00003-6.

McCright, Aaron M., and Riley E. Dunlap. 2010. "Anti-Reflexitity: The American Conservative Movement's Success in Undermining Climate Science and Policy." *Theory, Culture and Society* 27:100–133.

Mehta, Jal. 2013. *The Allure of Order: High Hopes, Dashed Expectations and the Troubled Quest to Remake American Schooling*. New York: Oxford University Press.

Miller, Danny, Jon Hartwick, and Isabelle Le Breton-Miller. 2004. "How to Define Management Fad—and Distinguish It from a Classic." *Business Horizons* 47 (4): 7–16.

National Science Board. 2014. *Science and Engineering Indicators 2014*. Washington: National Science Board.

Noll, Heinrich Herbert, and Wolfgang Zipf. 1994. "Social Indicators Research: Societal Monitoring and Social Reporting." In I. Borg and P. Mohler, eds., *Trends and Perspectives in Empirical Social Research*. Berlin and New York: DeGruyter.

Norman, Donald A. 1988. *The Design of Everyday Things*. New York: Doubleday.

Ouichi, William. 1981. *Theory Z*. New York: Avon Books.

Patterson, James T. 2010. *Freedom Is Not Enough: the Moynihan Report and America's Struggle over Black Family Life*. New York: Basic Books.

Poovey, Mary. 1998. *A History of the Modern Fact: Problems of Knowledge in the Sciences of Walth and Society*. Chicago: University of Chicago Press.

Powell, Thomas C. 1995. "Total Quality Management as Competitive Advantage: A Review and Empirical Study." *Strategic Management Review* 16:15–37.

Powell, Walter W., and Kaisa Snellman. 2004. "The Knowledge Economy." *Annual Review of Sociology* 30:199–220.

Powell, Walter W., Douglas R. White, Kenneth W. Koput, and Jason Owen-Smith. 2005. "Network Dynamics and Field Evolution: The Growth of Inter-Organizational Collaboration in the Life Sciences." *American Journal of Sociology* 110:1132–1205.

Ravitch, Diane. 2013 (Feb.) *Why I Cannot Support the Common Core Standards*. www.dianravitch.net/2013/02/why-i-cannot-support-the-common-core-standards.

Reed, Richard, David J. Lemak, and Joseph C. Montgomery. 1996. "Beyond Process: TQM Content and Firm Performance." *Academy of Management Review* 21:173–202.

Rouse, William B. 2007. *People and Organizations: Explorations in Human-Centered Design*. New York: Wiley.

Sampson, Robert J., and Stephen Raudenbush. 1999. "Systematic Social Observation of Public Spaces: A New Look at Disorder in Urban Neighborhoods." *American Journal of Sociology* 94:381–414.

Schwartz, Peter. 1991. *The Art of the Long View*. New York: Doubleday.

Seligman, Martin P. 2011. "Building Resilience." *Harvard Business Review, August*. Retrieved from https:hbr.org/2011/04/building-resilience/ar/1/.

Shoemaker, Paul J. H. 1995. "Multiple Scenario Development: Its Conceptual and Behavioral Foundation." *Sloan Management Journal* 14:193–213.

Slaper, Timothy F., and Tanya J. Hall. 2011. "The Triple Bottom Line: What Is It and How Does It Work?" *Indiana Business Review* 86:4–8.

Soares, Joseph A. 2007. *The Power of Privilege*. Stanford, CA: Stanford University Press.

Sternberg, Robert J. 1985. *Beyond IQ: A Triarchic Theory of Intelligence*. Cambridge: Cambridge University Press.

Stevens, Mitchell L. 2007. *Creating a Class: College Admissions and the Education of Elites*. Cambridge, MA: Harvard University Press.

Sturge-Apple, Melissa L., Patrick T. Davies, and E. Mark Cummings. 2010. "Typologies of Family Functioning: Implications for Children's Adjustment during the Early School Years." *Child Development* 81:1320–1335.

United States Census Bureau. 2014. *Current Population Survey, 2014: Annual Social and Economic Supplement*. https://www.census.gov/hhes/socdemo/education/data/cps/2014/tables.html.

Van Der Heijden, Kees. 1997. *Scenarios: The Art of Strategic Conversation*. New York: John Wiley & Sons.

Varnes, David J. 1984. *Landslide Hazard Zonation: A Review of Principles and Practices*. Paris: United Nations Educational Scientific and Cultural Organization.

Varum, Cecilia. A., and Carla Melo. 2010. "Directions in Scenario Planning Literature: A Review of the Past Decades." *Futures* 42:355–369. http://dx.doi.org/10.1016/j.futures.2009.11.021.

Waite, Linda, and Maggie Gallagher. 2001. *The Case for Marriage: Why Married People are Happier, Healthier and Better Off Financially*. New York: Random House.

Wallach, Dieter, and Sebastian C. Scholz. 2012. "User-Centered Design: Why and How to Put Users First in Software Development." In A. Macdche et al., eds., *Software for People*, 11–38. Berlin and Heidleberg: Springer-Verlag.

Washburn, Jennifer. 2005. *University, Inc.: The Corporate Corruption of Higher Education*. New York: Basic Books.

Watson, John G., and Appa Rao Korukonda. 1995. "The TQM Jungle: A Dialectical Analysis." *International Journal of Quality & Reliability Management* 12 (9): 100–109.

Westphal, James D., Ranjay Gulati, and Stephen M. Shortell. 1997. "Customization or Conformity? An Institutional and Network Perspective on the Content and Consequences of TQM Adoption." *Administrative Sciences Quarterly* 42:366–394.

White, Hayden V. 1973. *Meta-History: The Historical Imagination in 19th-Century Europe*. Baltimore: Johns Hopkins University Press.

Wilson, James Q., and George L. Kelling. 1982. "Broken Windows: Police and Neighborhood Security." *Atlantic*. www.theatlantic.com/magazine/archive/1982/03/broken-windows.

Zamarra, John W., et al. 1996. "Usefulness of the Transcendental Meditation Program in the Treatment of Patients with Coronary Artery Disease." *American Journal of Cardiology* 77 (10): 867–870. http://dx.doi.org/10.1016/S00029149(97)89184-9.

FIVE

Professional Education in the University Context: Toward an Inhabited Institutional View of Socialization

TIM HALLETT AND MATT GOUGHERTY[1]

George W. Bush and Hudson La Force III.[2] David Petraeus and Ellen Johnson Sirleaf.[3] Michelle Rhee and Kevin Martin.[4] However one might respond to these names, be it with admiration, disdain, or something in between, they are uniquely accomplished people. Despite their uniqueness, the graduate degrees that they carry are becoming more common. Bush and La Force hold master's degrees in business administration (MBA). Petraeus and Sirleaf hold master's degrees in public affairs and public administration (MPAs). Rhee and Martin hold master's degrees in public policy (MPP). While the graduate schools that these people attended include elite institutions such as Harvard, Northwestern, Princeton, and Duke, the number of universities offering these degrees is increasing. The first business school, Wharton, was founded at the University of Pennsylvania in 1881, and as of 2015 there are 513 accredited business schools in the United States. The first MPA program opened in 1914 at the University of Michigan, and as of 2014 there are 163 accredited MPA programs in the United States. The first MPP program opened in 1967 at the University of Michigan, and as of 2014 there are 34 MPP programs in the United States.[5] This growth reflects the horizontal expansion of education and its interpenetration with the professions; just as universities have been central to the development, growth, and spread of the traditional professions of medicine, law, and the clergy, the same is true of the degrees that represent what have been termed the "managerial" professions.[6]

In this chapter we think broadly about the graduate degree programs that are coming to represent the managerial professions: the master's of business administration, master's of public administration, the master's of public affairs, and the master's of public policy. In doing so, we make two main contributions. First, we consider the social implications of the growth and expansion of the managerial professions and the MBA, MPAs,[7] and MPP, particularly as they relate to the increasing rationalization of organizations in the private, public, and nonprofit sectors of society. Second, we refresh and invigorate the research on higher education and the professions, and reconsider the sociological approaches that have been used to examine the connections between them. Pushing against both the functionalist and the power/jurisdictional approaches to understanding the professions, we discuss the conceptual and empirical merits of new institutionalism and symbolic interactionism. In doing so, we develop an "inhabited" institutional approach to understanding professional socialization, and we call for a fresh wave of research on professional education as a way to revitalize long-standing work that has focused on traditional professions.

Inhabited institutionalism represents a theoretical union between two traditions of research that both have a long history of engagement with education: new institutionalism (NI) and symbolic interactionism (SI). At first blush, this union may seem nonintuitive. NI is commonly viewed as a macro-sociological approach that examines how schooling and the cultural rationales associated with schooling structure society through the diffusion of common organizational forms.[8] SI is commonly viewed as a microsociological approach that examines how students interpret their educational experiences and infuse them with meaning.[9] We argue that both of these characterizations are too narrow, and there is rich meso ground between NI and SI. NI and SI are both cultural approaches in that they both examine social meanings, and taking an inhabited institutional view to professional socialization enables us to see how students in these programs are confronted with managerial rationales and how those rationales dominate the educational landscape, but also how students respond to these rationales at the local level, reinfusing them with meaning, reshaping them towards their own group and career purposes, and crafting their own notions of "professionalism."

Background: Describing the Degrees

While the degrees that are associated with the managerial professions are becoming more common, the general public has a much better sense of what the MBA is, in comparison to MPAs or the MPP. Generally, MBA programs prepare students for managerial positions in the private sector, but increasingly MBAs also go on to positions in the public and nonprofit sectors.[10] These programs typically draw from economics, accounting, finance, marketing, and organizational studies. Most MBA programs have a set of core requirements that commonly involve some combination of classes in accounting, business management, finance, leadership, managerial economics, marketing, operations, organizational behavior, and statistics and data analysis.

The master's of public administration and master's of public affairs are less well known, but if you were to ask someone involved in these degrees what the MPA "is," they might respond, "The MPA is like an MBA but for public organizations and nonprofits."[11] While the focus can vary, most of these programs exist at the boundaries between political science, economics, law, and management. Master's of public administration programs usually have required core courses that focus on topics including economics, law and public policy, policy analysis, budgeting and finance, public management, and statistics. The master's of public administration tends to focus on management and implementation, while the master's of public policy (MPP) tends to focus on policy research and evaluation.[12] MPP programs have more rigorous and more extensive course requirements in quantitative data analysis, although MPA programs commonly offer such courses—for example, cost-benefit analysis and program evaluation—as electives. The master's of public affairs exists between those two types of programs, combining administration and analysis.

Each of these degrees could be considered distinct, and there are important differences between them, but they also share many commonalities. They all focus on various aspects of management; they all emphasize the use of quantitative methods to strategically plan, measure, and evaluate organizational practices and policies; and increasingly, economics is a key part of their lingua franca.[13] Importantly, students who hold these degrees find employment in a broad range of jobs in all sectors of the economy: private, public, and nonprofit. As they do so, they take the rational models of management that they have learned in graduate school with them, potentially changing the operations of the very organizations in which they are employed.

For the students who earn these degrees, as well as for many of the faculty and administrators who work in these programs, the MBA, MPAs, and the MPP are considered "professional" degrees. However, this commonsense understanding flies in the face of traditional scholarly notions of professions. As such, we begin with a provocative, contrarian thrust, briefly reviewing two prominent research traditions that would suggest that these degrees, and the people who hold them, do *not* meet the definition of being "professional." This mismatch between common-sense understandings and scholarly notions highlights some of the problems with traditional research on professions in its conceptualizations, substantive scope, and empirical focus. This sets the table for our discussion of NI and SI thought regarding the professions and education, and how wedding NI and SI can revitalize the field through a dual focus on rationalization and local meaning-making. We develop an inhabited institutional approach as a third way for examining professions, professional education, and the socialization that occurs therein.

Up against Two Traditions: Functionalist and Power/ Jurisdictional Approaches to the Managerial Professions

Sociologists who study professions have developed multiple approaches. While these approaches vary, they commonly involve efforts to define what constitutes a profession. These definitions are often criteria-based, and usually rely on some combination of expert knowledge, technical autonomy, service norms, social trust, and high status, income, and rewards.[14] This was especially true in mid-century functionalist sociology, which reified professions as occupations with "special" characteristics and special rights based on their capacity to fulfill social needs. As this approach developed, it became a common trope to examine a range of occupations against the ideal-typical criteria, and to place them on a continuum of greater or lesser professionalization based on those criteria.[15]

Starting in the 1960s, numerous scholars challenged the functionalist tradition and the checklist approach it employed.[16] This second wave rejected functionalist notions of social needs and public trust, and criticized the "ex ante" approach of defining professions without sufficient attention to a relentless, historical, empirical process.[17] In this second wave, professionalization is an ongoing process that is full of conflict, a "project" in which occupations strive to gain control over a market for their services.[18] Prominent in this "power" approach to the professions was Freidson, who emphasized how professions dominate by creating monopolies through their relations with the state and educational systems.[19] Larson connected the professions to market control and social class. She understood professionalization "as a collective assertion of special social status and as a collective process of upward mobility" that is legitimized by the system of educational credentials.[20] For Abbott, the key focus is on how professions define and control their work tasks to construct a jurisdiction which they must police against other occupations in a linked-ecology of competition.[21] Would-be professions must either take over existing jurisdictions or identify gaps between jurisdictions in the larger ecology—gaps they can then leverage for status.[22]

The differences between the functionalist and power/jurisdictional traditions are evident and important. In both waves of research, however, the lure to study the highest-status professions of medicine and law proved irresistible, and those exceptional outlier cases determined or, worse, distorted their views of professions.[23] Moreover, as Stinchcombe notes, conflict theories maintain a functionalist rationale to the extent that the social processes that are examined serve to benefit a particular group, if not the whole of society. As in other areas of sociology, in the professions literature these two traditions resemble opposite sides of the same coin.[24] Likewise, Starr comments that such things as jurisdictional control and market shelters could be seen as part of a checklist, albeit a more critical one emphasizing domination and ideology.[25]

Given the similarities and differences between these two scholarly traditions, how do the MBA, MPAs, and the MPP measure up? Looking at the functionalist criteria, when one thinks of the MBA, one does not think of service norms and public trust, and this has been an issue for business schools.[26] MPAs and MPPs may do better in terms of service norms, and many of the students who enter those programs want to "do good,"[27] but they routinely go on to work inside of bureaucratic organizations, lacking the autonomy that functionalists see as central to professionalism.[28] While one might argue that MPAs and MPPs work to fulfill various social needs, they are not especially well rewarded economically for doing so (certainly not as much as MBAs, doctors, or lawyers), and they are not "special" in that regard.

Shifting to the power approach, what is the jurisdiction for these degrees? It is hard to say. These degrees are worthwhile credentials, but they do not assure access to a particular occupation. Alumni go on to fill many types of jobs across all of the sectors of the economy—private, public, and nonprofit—and while graduate education may be needed to advance in their careers, a specific degree is rarely required. There is little exclusivity and no monopoly of control. There are multiple pathways available for the jobs that these degree holders pursue. One need not have an MBA to go into business. MPAs go on to work for private companies, and MBAs go on to work for nonprofits.[29] The same is true for MPPs, and the holders of these degrees are not assured access to or limited by a particular occupation or economic sector. These degrees might be called *interjurisdictional,* which could facilitate broad employability, but would not promote an exclusive professional status. If these degrees are part of a professional project, that project remains in the very early stages or has yet to advance, and the jurisdictional vagueness and the competition between these degrees (as well as other degrees) might foreshadow trouble.

Captured by these traditional, academic conceptualizations, some scholars (but not practitioners or students) who work inside these programs are self-conscious about their "professional" status or lack thereof. Combining aspects of the functionalist approach and Larson's notion of a professional project, Khurana has written a masterful account of the history of American business schools. He documents how these schools initially embraced professional ideals of disinterestedness and trustworthiness, only to have these noble ideals eroded over time as schools slowly embraced a market logic in which the MBA became a product sold to student customers, thereby undermining professional ideals. Khurana and Nohria call for reform, and argue that the best way to restart the professional project is to change course and adopt a rigorous MBA code of ethics (or to check a different box on the checklist).[30] In the case of public administration, Schott argues that MPA programs are unlikely to achieve occupational control and the licensing of their practitioners, thus falling short of true professional status.[31] Regarding the MPP, the degree was developed in the late 1960s and early 1970s in part as a response to the vague knowledge base and lack of standards in MPA programs at the time. MPP programs crafted themselves as having a more specific knowledge base, emphasizing rigorous quantitative data analysis. This expert knowledge might promote professionalism, but quantitative analysis is not exclusive to the MPP, and such courses are now common in public administration and especially in public affairs programs (as they are in most social-science degree programs). Once again, there is little exclusivity or control.[32]

Scholars within these degree programs who use somewhat different criteria come to somewhat different conclusions,[33] but the point remains: If we hold these degrees up against the two main sociological traditions, claims of professional status are questionable. And yet, these ruminations aside, the people who work and learn in these programs generally conceive of themselves and the degrees as being professional. At our university, and, we suspect at others, when people refer to the business school and the school of public affairs, they call them "the professional schools," as a contrast to the college of arts and sciences. One does not have to go far into the materials of the top MBA, MPA, and MPP programs to see that people within the programs consider the degrees and resulting career paths as professional. For example, the Stanford University Graduate School of Business (currently the top-ranked MBA program) promotes its programs by arguing: "Our alumni are insightful, passionate *professionals* who are never satisfied with the status quo. Instead, they choose to employ their knowledge, talent, and ideas to create change."[34] Similarly, one of the top MPA programs (Syracuse University's Maxwell School) sees itself as professional:

> Recognized as the *professional* degree in the field of public service, the MPA is designed principally, but not exclusively, for those who plan to pursue careers in the public and not-for-profit sectors within the US and abroad. The Maxwell School's MPA program prepares individuals for careers as managers and policy analysts in government agencies and organizations closely associated with the public sector.[35]

The USC Price School, which has highly ranked MPA and MPP programs, advertises "a strong analytic core—economic analysis, quantitative analysis, and political analysis—with a *professional* focus that that ensures that students have the skills to be successful in our rapidly globalizing world."[36] These materials suggest that, if you were to approach one of these students and say, "You are not getting a professional degree and you are not going to be a professional," the student would be surprised, and you could be in for a surprise as well.

If we accept these traditional sociological understandings as correct, then the people involved in these educational programs—the faculty, administrators and students—who *do* think of themselves and their affiliated degrees as "professional" are just wrong, or are in the midst of a shaky professional project. This mismatch suggests that the traditional conceptualizations of the professions fail to account for important aspects of empirical reality.

Instead of holding these degrees up against the two traditional sociological approaches, we break from tradition and develop a third way. In doing so, we draw inspiration from research that uses a far less narrow definition of professions. For example, whereas the establishment of a market shelter has been seen as a vital aspect of professionalism, Timmermans questions this criterion, and shows how the comfort of a market shelter can actually undermine the ongoing cultivation of expertise upon which professions depend.[37] Removing this monopoly criterion opens new possibilities, and Brint denotes a broad "professional middle class" of people who, even without a market shelter, "earn at least a middling income from the application of a relatively complex body of knowledge." He labels this "expert professionalism," and emphasizes that universities are central to the creation and promotion of this expertise.[38] Drawing from Brint, Jason Owen-Smith defines professions as "any occupation in which experts draw on abstract bodies of knowledge to solve problems they might never have encountered before."[39] Likewise, MacDonald defines professions as "occupations based on advanced, or complex, or arcane knowledge."[40] These conceptualizations provide a better fit for the managerial degrees that we are interested in. With these more liberal definitions in mind, we turn to the possibilities evident in new institutional and symbolic interactionist research on professions and education. NI and SI add to the mix an important focus on rationalization and local meaning-making as they relate to managerial degree programs.

New Institutionalism: Education, Abstract Managerialism, and Rationalization

The traditional approaches to understanding the professions grew, in part, out of research on work and occupations.[41] In general, that research was interested in answering the question of why some occupations come to have an especially high stature. In other words, in both the functionalist and power/jurisdictional approaches, professional status was an outcome to be explained. In contrast, new institutionalism (NI) is interested in a different set of questions and puts the professions in a different place in a different causal chain. In its original manifestation, NI sought to answer questions such as: What accounts for the surprising level of conformity that can be observed across organizations? Why do organizations tend to adopt policies and structures that reflect common forms of rationality, even if organizations have their own, uncommon needs? How does this process of isomorphism operate?[42] NI's answers emphasized, in part, the role of university education and the professions. However, these scholars spoke of "professions" in a looser way than did the traditional literatures of their day. Perhaps they were able to get away with these looser conceptions because they were not trying to explain professions, but rather, organizational conformity. Regardless, this early NI work was prescient, and it foreshadowed the break from tradition.

An early example of this novel approach is evident in DiMaggio's research on art museums.[43] DiMaggio wanted to know why museums came to be defined as homes to "high" art instead of a variety of aesthetically pleasing artifacts. To answer this question, he focuses on university-trained experts in art appreciation—"art professionals," not professional artists. DiMaggio argues that these experts had a key role in the structuring of the art field, and as they became curators their definition of high art took hold. In the process, museums conformed to this understanding.

Likewise, in their seminal paper on organizational isomorphism, DiMaggio and Powell use the term "professional" colloquially, with a qualifier but not a definition, as they state: "The major recent growth in the professions has been among *organizational* professionals, particularly managers and specialized staff of large organizations."[44] In this way, NI began to shift focus away from the sovereign occupations of medicine, law, and the clergy, and toward occupations that incorporate abstract managerial knowledge and practices.

Within the NI framework, professional schools and managerial degrees such as the MBA, MPAs, and MPP are seen as important sources of isomorphism:

> Universities and professional training institutions are important centers for the development of organizational norms among professional managers . . . Such mechanisms create a pool of almost interchangeable individuals who occupy similar positions across a range of organizations and possess a similarity of orientation and disposition . . . In addition, individuals in an organizational field undergo anticipatory socialization to common expectations . . . socialization acts as an isomorphic force.[45]

The assumption is that these would-be professional managers enter degree programs and become socialized into managerial norms and dominant models of organizational rationality, and as they move into the workforce, they spread these norms and rational models, creating a convergence in organizational forms.

How big is this "pool of almost interchangeable individuals"? Data are spotty, but suggest that the pool is sizable and growing. Business degrees account for the largest volume in the pool by far: According to the *Digest of Education Statistics*, in the 2000–2001 academic year alone, US business schools conferred 115,602 master's degrees. In the 2009–2010 academic year, that number rose to 177,684 degrees conferred. These numbers are somewhat distorted, as they reflect all master's degrees conferred by business schools, and not just the MBA. According to the Network of Schools of Public Policy, Affairs, and Administration (NASPPA), in the 2001–2002 academic year there were 5,314 master's of public administration degrees conferred by accredited schools, rising to 5,621 in the 2009–2010 academic year. The master's of public affairs has seen some decline, from 586 degrees conferred in 2001–2002 down to 407 in 2009–2010. However, the master's of public policy is growing, from 441 degrees conferred in 2001–2002 to 910 degrees conferred in 2009–2010. These numbers are also problematic in that some prominent schools, including Harvard's Kennedy School of Government, do not participate in NASPPA and are not accredited by them. Nevertheless, taken together, these numbers are indicative of the size and the shape of the pool, and they exemplify the intensifying logic, horizontal expansion, and vertical expansion of education that Davies and Mehta examine in chapter 3 of this volume.[46]

According to NI, as this pool grows, it floods more and more organizational fields. In words that echo earlier research, Hwang and Powell argue that the "growth of managerial professionals represents a profound institutional change. This group shares common administrative or management training and similar occupational norms," and they "enhance the diffusion of common evaluative normative standards" across a variety of institutional sectors—private, public and nonprofit. They go on to state that, "by adopting formal, rational practices, these diverse individuals develop a *lingua franca*, and their disparate organizations are rendered more similar and brought into a common orbit."[47]

Hwang and Powell describe this professional training as an "abstract managerialism," and it consists of the very things common to the MBA, MPAs, and MPP: the use of quantitative methods to strategically plan, measure, and analyze organizational practices and policies, usually with an instrumental, economic sensibility reflective of cost-benefit analyses and program evaluation.[48] As Baker notes in chapter 2 of this volume, such practices are tied to the rise of science as the purveyor of truth and the increased universalism of knowledge. Oftentimes, and particularly for organizations that focus on substantive concerns that are hard to measure—for example, learning in schools, spirituality in churches, or community service in nonprofits—these techniques are not in fact "rational," but are nevertheless seen as important and legitimate managerial practices. Reflecting this apparent legitimacy, organizations and the professionals therein engage in "rationalization projects" by creating standardized systems and impersonal rules; and, in the process, substantive concerns are analyzed as technical issues.[49] This process often involves commensuration: the transformation of different qualities into a common metric, such that a range of organizational practices can be evaluated against stated standards and goals.[50]

In early NI research, these processes were conceived as "myth and ceremony": an organization might hire a managerial professional for the sake of appearances, and drape itself ceremonially in the myth of "rational" reform, but behind closed doors, practices would remain unchanged, precisely because these reforms do not address substantive needs.[51] For example, the existence of a standardized test does not help a teacher to determine how to get and hold the attention of impoverished students who come to school with empty stomachs. Recent work suggests, however, that this gap or loose coupling between organizational substance and formal ceremony is closing, in part because commensuration changes what organizations attend to and how they do so.[52] Accountability policies coerce schools into focusing on test scores, stomachs be damned. In this light it is notable that at least two high-profile champions of educational accountability hold these professional degrees: Hudson La Force III (Northwestern, MBA) and Michelle Rhee (Harvard, MPP).

Moving beyond educational policy, there is reason to believe that managerial professionals are also changing nonprofits. In their analysis of 190 nonprofits in the San Francisco Bay area, Hwang and Powell found that organizations that were managed by personnel with MBAs, MPAs, or degrees in nonprofit management were significantly more likely to adopt formally rational procedures such as strategic planning, independent audits, quantitative program evaluation, and the use of consultants. They note that while these practices promote transparency and efficiency in nonprofits, they also change the allocation of energy, resources and focus—in one case, the director of a religious training organization emphasized creating a measurable "market share for God" instead of scripture.[53]

Equipped with these techniques and the corresponding mindsets, these new managerial professionals become premier "carriers" of rationalization. Again, universities have a central role: "Professionalism is now carried by empowered and schooled individual persons equipped with scientized knowledge and embedded in training and occupational structures that are often themselves organizations."[54] This "scientized" knowledge is upheld as legitimate because of its university home and apparent quantitative rigor. As is evident in the case of accountability policies in education, it is a "technocratic logic" that emphasizes measurement-driven change.[55] Accountability is a rationalization project, but it is not, and never has been, limited to the educational field. This rationalization project is much wider in scope because performance indicators and accountability are central to this new form of managerial professionalism.[56]

As Mehta notes, there is increasing demand for accountability across the traditional "sovereign" professions and semiprofessions.[57] To this we add that the managers and policymakers who are holding the older sovereign professions and semiprofessions accountable are fashioning themselves as the new professionals, based not on a market shelter, or even on a particularly clear jurisdiction, but rather on their mastery and use of seemingly rational, scientized knowledge. At the same time, these new managerial professionals are subject to the very accountability that they promote: they are "both the governor and the governed." They are both sources of, and subject to, this type of modern surveillance.[58]

In sum, NI successfully breaks from criteria-based approaches, provides a fresh way to think about professions, and demonstrates the stakes and implications that these new managerial professionals can have for organizations. However, if taken to an extreme, this is a picture of soulless professionals, one in which managerial education fosters "common mindsets that, in turn, result in nearer to rote implementation of well-known rules and tools."[59] In this extreme, perhaps cynical interpretation of NI, if quantitative accountability is a more recent iteration of Weber's iron cage, then we have met our jailers, and they are the managerial professionals.

However, professions are not inhabited by soulless automatons, and a limitation of NI is its tendency to focus on molar units. The full title of DiMaggio and Powell's seminal article is "The Iron Cage Revisited: Institutional Isomorphism and *Collective* Rationality in Organizational Fields." As we have seen in the discussion above, NI repeatedly refers to these collectives as "carriers" of rationality. Binder argues that when NI takes this position, it assumes that isomorphic forces "are so strong that people in organizations have little choice but to adhere to these institutional scripts."—a position that "deprives people of generative creativity in their responses to their environments."[60]

Fortunately, NI scholars who escape this molar focus paint a more humanizing picture. In his exceptionally rich account of the development of equal-employment policies, Dobbin draws from historical, interview, and survey data to tell the surprising story of how these policies came to take their rather unusual form in the United States.[61] The story is surprising because it was human resource professionals, and not lawyers or politicians, who crafted these policies in practice. While these managerial professionals drew from their existing repertoires—adapting and reshaping earlier policies that had been developed to prevent discrimination against union members—they lead the way in interpreting President Kennedy's 1961 executive order and subsequent antidiscrimination laws, all of which were exceptionally vague. Although they were housed inside of organizations and were responding to external legal mandates, these personnel managers established best practices which the courts later used to define nondiscrimination for the broader environment—a classic example of "endogeneity of law."[62] In taking this more granular approach, Dobbin shows that managerial professionals are not mere carriers or automatons. Instead, they were responsible for "inventing" this distinctly American form of employment policy. By considering the important role that interpretation plays in institutional processes, Dobbin opens the door to a consideration of local meaning-making and the virtues of symbolic interactionism, although he himself does not walk through the door.

Symbolic Interactionism, the Meaning of Profession, and Professional Education

NI gives ample attention to education and the professions, but as Meyer was formulating the approach, he directed research away from the experience of socialization to instead focus on how education impacts society "over and above the immediate socializing experiences it offers the young."[63] Nevertheless, this prompts the question: How do these would-be "carriers" learn professional rationales and techniques? NI does not answer this question directly, but it adheres to an implicit model of professional socialization that is top-down and deterministic. Recall DiMaggio and Powell's comment about training institutions "creating a pool of almost interchangeable individuals" in which "socialization acts as an isomorphic force." Thus, even as NI has come around to the idea that professionals are not, in fact, "dopes" (as research by Dobbin and others would suggest), their implicit view of socialization lags behind and mirrors the dopey view of its "older" institutional brethren: a correspondence model in which people are appropriated into a profession as they practice roles and learn values in graduate school.[64]

A symbolic interactionist (SI) approach would start, instead, with the meanings that students, faculty, and administrators themselves associate with "professionalism" and how those meanings arise from various situations and sets of interaction. Whereas NI breaks from criteria-based approaches by expanding the conceptualization of profession, SI makes a break by taking local folk understandings of "profession" seriously. While few would argue that professionalism is only a folk concept—a pure social construction in which professionals are merely those who successfully label themselves as such—SI would view these local understandings as important empirical evidence for the development of sensitizing concepts, and would focus on what people in these programs actually do, and how they do it together.[65]

In taking this approach, one could use Blumer's three premises of symbolic interactionism as a starting point for analysis:[66]

1. People act towards things [professions] based on the meanings those things [professions] have for them.
2. The meaning of things [professions] is derived from, and arises out of, social interaction between people.
3. The meaning of things [professions] is handled in, and modified through, an interpretive process.

If Blumer were to examine the MBA, MPA, and MPP promotional materials that we referenced earlier—"passionate *professionals* who are never satisfied with the status quo," "the *professional* degree in the field of public service," "a *professional* focus that ensures that students have the skills to be successful in our rapidly globalizing world"—he would see people acting based on a variety of meanings (premise 1) subject to ongoing interpretation and modification (premise 3) that undoubtedly arise out of interaction (premise 2).

Becker, Geer, Hughes, and Strauss adopt this interactionist perspective in their classic 1961 study *Boys in White: Student Culture in Medical School.* As they began their ethnography of professional education at the University of Kansas Medical School, Becker et al. were open to the kind of deterministic and rote socialization envisioned by old institutionalism. In an earlier essay on medical education, Hughes (who was the senior scholar on the project) had suggested that medical education is "a set of planned and unplanned experiences" through which students *"become possessed* of some part of the technical and scientific medical culture of the professionals."[67] However, in focusing on groups of students and their actual interactions with each other and with faculty, the data did not fit a deterministic view. Instead, Becker et al. found that "the joints of the medical system have a great deal of play in them."[68] This was necessarily so because before the students could "possess" anything, they found themselves in problematic and ambiguous situations that they had to interpret, and only then could they act.

Specifically, the students were confronted with an overwhelming course load. At first they interpreted this situation idealistically; medicine was the "best of all professions," and they would work tirelessly to "learn it all." However, this effort was unsustainable, and they were soon confronted with another problematic situation: midterm exams. This was another ambiguous situation that needed interpretation because they did not know what the exams would cover, and they could not possibly digest all of the eligible material. Becker et al. found that groups of students interpreted the situation differently, depending on their interactional networks. Students who lived in fraternities (keep in mind that the data were collected in the late 1950s) focused on what they thought the "faculty most want us to know." In contrast, those who did not live in fraternities developed a different perspective, and focused on the material that they thought would be most useful for their future medical practice.

As the academic year continued, the students faced more situations that were new to them: final exams and the prospect of future crushing semesters, as well as evidence indicating that the students in fraternities did better on midterm exams. In interpreting this situation they settled, collectively, on what Becker et al. call the final perspective: We will work tirelessly but focus "on what the faculty wants." Throughout, the meaning of their endeavor changed from an idealistic one where they would join "the best of all professions," to a different meaning, in which they were sacrificing their ideals so they could survive. Becker et al. emphasize that this "fate of idealism" may appear cynical to outsiders, but it reflects a pragmatic response to the situation.[69] Moreover, as the situation changed and students left medical school, they regained a tempered, less naive idealism regarding the profession.

Importantly, the students' interpretation of their situation and the meanings that they ascribed to their activity (what Becker et al. refer to as a "perspective") did not accord with their professors' desires. The professors wanted them to focus on the whole, and not on their exams. As such, Becker et al. conclude that the students are agentic instead of passive:

> Students collectively set the level and direction of their efforts to learn . . . These levels and directions are not the result of some conscious cabal. . . . They are the working out in practice of the perspectives from which the students view their problems in relation to their long-term goals. The perspectives, themselves collectively developed, are organizations of ideas and actions. To these perspectives, we give the name *student culture*."[70]

Thus, instead of a picture of socialization that is top-down and deterministic, Becker et al. paint a picture in which students create a peer culture that shapes what they learn and how they learn it. In doing so, students take an active role in their own professional socialization.[71] They respond collectively but with a local rationality, and not the kind of collective macrorationality upheld by new institutionalism.

Boys in White inspired a range of interactionist studies of professional education throughout the 1970s, 1980s, and 1990s. Many of these studies focused on types of medical education as a way to modify or expand insights by Becker and his colleagues. Notable here is Haas and Shaffir's work, which incorporates Goffman's focus on impression management.[72] Haas and Shaffir argue that a key aspect of professionalization in medical school is the development of a "cloak of competence," which medical students use to convince various audiences of their trustworthiness. Additional scholars used interactionist frameworks to study professional education outside of the medical field, ranging from studies of teachers and psychiatrists to clergy and sociology graduate students.[73]

By the mid-1990s, interactionist research on professional education lost steam, perhaps because of its tendency to focus on occupations associated with the traditional professions and semiprofessions (for a fascinating exception, see Cahill's study of mortuary students).[74] Herein lies an irony of interactionist work: conceptually, it is unconventional in that it is open to, and even embraces, local meanings about professions, but it remains conventional in its site selection. In this regard, SI missed the opportunity to push the research in new directions and into the managerial professions.

As with the broader SI research on K–12 education, SI work on professional education become "an archipelago, robust in itself but linked only tenuously to the core."[75] Nevertheless, the approach has value for research on professional socialization in managerial degree programs. Chiefly, SI squares with empirical reality on the ground: that people associated with these programs conceive of themselves, and the degrees, as professional. It also draws attention to the ways in which expertise alone is insufficient; such expertise must also be successfully presented to relevant audiences, and impression management is part of professionalism. Moreover, it suggests that while the students who enter these programs may leave with less idealism, they are not destined to become robots that spread rationalization in unreflective, uncreative ways. Rather, they interpret and modify rationalization both as they learn about it in graduate school and as they use it in their jobs as they construct a professional career.

Toward an Inhabited Institutional Approach to Professional Socialization

While SI has many virtues for thinking about professional socialization in MBA, MPAs, and MPP programs, it is not without criticism, including longstanding (and at times overstated) charges that it is too micro, astructural, and ahistorical.[76] Working from within the approach, Snow argues that Blumer downplays "the extent to which symbols and the meanings they convey are often, perhaps routinely, embedded in and reflective of existing cultural and organizational contexts and systems of meaning"—the very things that are central to new institutionalism.[77] Although SI studies of professional socialization do well in their focus on situational imperatives and the largely informal student interactions that arise from situations, they have been criticized for failing to "cope with problems of knowledge and to produce a sociology of the curriculum."[78] The extent to which graduate programs reflect broader systems of meaning—or institutional rationales—particularly in their core curriculum, is not evident in SI studies of professional socialization. SI research to date is unconcerned with the "abstract managerialism" and "scientized knowledge" that are so central to new institutional research on the managerial professionals.

Inhabited institutionalism (II), a recent approach developing at the intersections of organizational sociology, cultural sociology, and social psychology, attempts to overcome these shortcomings by integrating and expanding aspects of SI and NI.[79] Instead of seeing NI and SI as competing approaches, II views them as largely complementary. The rationalizing ideals that NI focuses on are cultural meanings that script organizational activity. SI's view is less rigid, but it still focuses on meaning in the form of interpretation, especially as it is related to group culture.[80] II takes as its focus the meso-ground between SI and NI, where these different styles of meaning come into contact in the empirical and conceptual spaces in which culture, organizations, and interactions intersect. Standing in this meso ground, II looks "two ways at once": "outward, to the broader relationships and understandings that condition organizational life, and inward, towards the construction of meaning in organizational settings."[81]

Inhabited institutionalism examines the recursive connections between the rationalizing ideals that exist in the institutional environment (including the professions), and the interactions though which people—on the ground, inside of, and across organizations—respond to rationalizing ideals, and in turn shape and refine them. To quote Binder:

> Organizations are not merely the instantiation of environmental, institutional logics "out there" . . . where workers seamlessly enact preconscious scripts valorized in the institutional environment . . . Instead, they are places where people and groups (agentic actors, not "institutional dopes") make sense of, and interpret, institutional "vocabularies of motive" . . . and act on those interpretations—the central premise of symbolic interactionism.[82]

Adapting this quote to our purposes, we can say that professions and professional schools are not merely the instantiation of institutional logics, but places where students, faculty, and administrators make sense of and interpret rationalization projects.

Importantly, these rationalizing ideals are not "neutral," as Blumer might argue. For example, in his analysis of social change, Blumer argued that macro social changes such as industrialization are "neutral" in the sense that they are "indifferent to what follows socially" in their wake.[83] Rationalization is not neutral because it shapes (but does not completely determine) what social interactions are about, how they unfold, and the previous meanings that feed into ongoing interactions. This is especially evident in the curricular focus and the types of courses that are common across the MBA, MPAs, and MPP degrees: courses that use quantitative methods to strategically plan, measure, and analyze organizational practices and policies, usually with an instrumental, economic sensibility. These courses and the rationality therein set the terms for official school interactions. At the same time, these rationalizing ideals do not operate on their own. "Institutions are not inert categories of meaning; rather, they are populated with people whose social interactions suffuse interactions with local force and significance."[84] Rationality is not a specter; it is a form of institutional knowledge that is inhabited by people doing things together, at times in concert, and at times in conflict.

Much like SI and NI, inhabited institutionalism has developed through research on education. Using Meyer and Rowan's research on loose coupling in schools as a foundation, Hallett examines how administrators and teachers respond to the rationalized ideal of accountability by recoupling practices to policy, and how, through their social interactions, seemingly "rational" accountability policies are assigned an irrational meaning that creates organizational "turmoil." Taking a similar approach, Aurini examines the link between the market rationality that governs tutoring franchises and the actual, on-the-ground teaching practices that occur within them. Tutoring franchises are for-profit organizations, and we would expect that the teaching practices used by tutors would be tightly coupled to the market. Indeed, the market rationale flooded the organization, and, based on that environment, the franchise had a highly structured curriculum and a set of mandated practices that tutors had to follow. However, Aurini shows how the tutors create space for themselves even as they follow the letters of the franchise law. They do this by selectively interpreting, prioritizing, and blending the frameworks that govern their actions in order to meet the needs of the situation. In this way they are able to create structural looseness and avoid turmoil even within the confines of a tightly coupled organization. Whereas Hallett and Aurini use II to reconsider the coupling concepts that are central to organizational sociology, Nunn uses II to examine school culture and inequality. In a comparative study of three high schools, Nunn examines how schools and students within those schools formulate distinct "success identities" in response to broader cultural myths about hard work and intelligence, and how those success identities generate different college trajectories.[85]

All of these studies combine ethnographic observations and interview techniques to show how qualitative methods can be used to gather data on larger institutional pressures, local understandings, and the connections between them. Of particular interest for studies of professional socialization in MBA, MPAs, and MPP programs is Judson Everitt's recent research on teacher education and training.[86] Everitt expands II by engaging with research on early-childhood socialization and using that work to think about teacher training. Specifically, Everitt draws from Corsaro's conceptualization of socialization as "interpretive reproduction." Corsaro pushes against both deterministic models of socialization, and constructivist models that depict childhood as a blank slate. Instead, Corsaro argues that, as children spend time in organizations such as schools, churches, and families, they take features of the adult world and "play" with them both literally and figuratively. This play occurs during their interactions with adults, but also during their interactions among peers. Through those interactions with peers, children create robust cultures through which they incorporate aspects of the adult world, but in their own ways. Hence, socialization occurs through interpretation; and while those interpretations often reproduce the adult world, children can also create change, although such change occurs within, and is in response to, institutional parameters.[87]

Everitt notes the natural affinity between Corsaro's work and inhabited institutionalism. By viewing teacher training and socialization as interpretive reproduction, Everitt documents how novice teachers learn about accountability policies in their college classrooms, in their student teaching, and on the job. Confronted with this form of rationality, novice teachers are forced to respond in ways that generally conform to accountability dictates, but in doing so they interpret accountability and, through their own sense-making, they create their own novel "arsenals of practice." As a result, their teaching is tightly coupled to accountability, and yet their arsenals of practice are not homogeneous, and are subject to ongoing development.

With this framework in mind, we call for a new wave of research on professional socialization in managerial degree programs. In this research, professional socialization can be understood as an interactive process that both responds to and constitutes what is thought of as "professional," while in constant contact with disciplinary rationales that provide the grounds and subject matter for these interactions. Yes, socialization acts as an "isomorphic force," but what diffuses and how it spreads is collectively developed at a far more local level. Yes, this process occurs via interactions in which people do things together, and in this sense students are not "interchangeable individuals," but the environmental and organizational pressures that students face are not "neutral." Rather, they partially constitute the form and content of the interactions.

Given the centrality of interaction and meaning for II, these studies will likely be qualitative in orientation, and will use a combination of ethnographic and interview methodologies. However, these studies must also place their gaze on the environment and the broader forms of rationality that bear on professionalization at the local level. As such, interviews with people associated with these degrees must also inquire into the history and context of the programs, and should include faculty and administrators in addition to students. Additionally, scholarship using an inhabited institutional approach has examined organizational artifacts, historical documents, and archival materials to document the broader discourses that bear on local settings (see in particular Haedicke's research on cooperative grocery stores).[88] These data and methods will be useful for understanding the variety of tight and loose couplings that exist between the institutional environment, organizations, and interactions in professional degree programs. This new wave of research can ask and answer the following questions:

- How are abstract managerialism and scientized knowledge evident in the structure of the degree programs, and in particular the curriculum? How are these rationalities manifest in the material that is taught in the core classes, and how do administrators, faculty, and students respond to and interpret these rationalities?
- What is the diversity of knowledge represented in these programs, and does this diversity create segments within the programs? What conflicts exist between the types of knowledge promoted within these programs—quantitative, economic, political, organizational, legal, etc.—and how are those conflicts negotiated by the students, faculty, and administrators?
- What does abstract managerialism mean to the people who work and learn in these programs? What do students do with these understanding as they embark on their careers? What do students take away from these programs, how do they change, and how do they translate those understandings and experiences into new settings?
- What does professionalism mean to the people involved in these programs, and how and when are those meanings connected to, or disconnected from, the broader rationalities that bear on the educational context? What

accounts for those connections and disconnections? How does interpretive reproduction work in these settings, and what gets reproduced?

- How does the meaning of professionalism vary across groups (administrators, faculty, students), but also within those groups? What accounts for those differences? How do these meanings change over time, especially as students progress through their graduate careers and experience different situations? How are those situations structured by larger organizational concerns? How do informal interactions and group cultures reflect but also change these understandings?
- Given the meanings that become attached to professionalism, how is professionalism performed, and how does that performance change depending on the audiences? How do people justify their activities as professional, and on what bases do they do so? How, if at all, are those bases of justification reflective of the broader environment? How do people use meanings and performances to draw symbolic boundaries and status distinctions between groups and demarcate what is "unprofessional" or "not professional?"[89]
- Given that each of these degree programs can be seen as addressing multiple sectors (for-profit, nonprofit, public, health), how might these processes change or differ via sector or specialization within degree programs? How do these processes vary across degree programs?

Answering the last question, of course, would require multiple studies, and no single study could possibly answer all of these questions. Inevitably, as research proceeds, different questions and possibilities will arise. Regardless, taking this kind of an approach to study MBA, MPAs, and MPP degree programs can go far in revitalizing research on education, professions, and socialization, and in creating new connections among different research traditions.

Coda: From the Field to the Essay

We are currently engaged in such a project, and we have completed two years of field observations and interviews as part of an ethnographic study of a highly regarded master's of public affairs program. As we began the project, however, we did not begin with the conceptual framework that we have outlined above. Rather, our focus on professions and the conceptual framework developed out of an abductive process, based on our preliminary understanding of our data (having collected it firsthand) and our engagement with the literatures that are most relevant to the themes that emerged in the course of data collection.[90] Although we are not far enough into our analysis to provide definitive answers to the questions posed above, those are the types of questions that our data speak to or which merit further attention, and the conceptual framework that we develop in this essay is both an endpoint (of our research thus far) and the starting point for our ongoing analysis.

This is not to say that this essay is a result of pure induction, the myth of ethnographers entering the field with an empty mind and developing theory from data. We began with preliminary interests and ideas, but without a conceptual axe to grind. Our study grew out of Hallett's earlier ethnographic research on accountability and recoupling in an urban elementary school.[91] In that research, the principal charged with enforcing accountability at the school, "Mrs. Kox," often spoke in glowing terms about an intensive summer course she had taken at a prestigious *business* school, involving many of the rationales one might learn in an MBA program. Likewise, the "CEO" of the urban school district had a background in *public finance*, the kind of education that is offered in an MPA program. With this, we began to wonder if something interesting was happening in these programs as a site for the development and cultivation of various forms of accountability.

Initially we planned an ethnographic study of an MBA program, and we developed a Spencer Foundation small grant proposal to support the project, "Learning the Executive Way: Men and Women of the B-School." The title was a play on two sociological classics, Morrill's *The Executive Way*, and Kanter's *Men and Women of the Corporation*.[92] In the proposal we were interested in rationalization, but also in how MBA students acquire the savoir-faire and codes of honor outlined by Morrill, and how those processes might vary across male and female students (given that women are minorities in MBA programs but their numbers are rising). In developing these themes, we drew from Hallett's earlier work which created a dialogue between Bourdieu and Goffman to examine how forms of capital shape social interaction, and how those interactions are used to cultivate and deploy symbolic power.[93] For the MBA project, we were interested in the forms of cultural and social capital that students brought with them into the program, how the MBA program developed and expanded that capital, and how the students might acquire a form of human capital that would reflect and promote rationalization.

We identified an MBA program, gained preliminary access, and received the Spencer small grant to support the research. As we talked about the project with colleagues, we wondered about how students in MBA programs learn economic rationales developed in the for-profit sector and yet increasingly go into government, education, and nonprofits, changing those organizations. One colleague commented that if we were truly interested in that process, we might consider studying an MPA program, as MPA programs usually have core courses on microeconomics, and MPA students go en masse into government, education, and nonprofits.

Around that time, we hit a snag with the MBA program. The dean pulled the plug, because the school had unexpectedly dropped in the *Businessweek* rankings. He attributed this drop to the recent recession: students were not getting jobs, and they vented their frustration on satisfaction surveys, which are a large part of the *Businessweek* rankings. He feared that our presence would compel the students to complain more, which could show up on satisfaction surveys, and another drop would be a "death sentence." We were devastated but also intrigued, as this, too, spoke to institutional pressures, accountability, and rationalization processes.

We used the moment to reflect, and we followed our colleague's advice. With the blessings of the Spencer Foundation, we shifted our field site to an MPA program. As we navigated access, we were forthcoming about our foray into MBA programs and the fear of rankings. The associate dean of the MPA program agreed that rankings were always a concern, but they were subject to fewer ranking systems than MBA programs, and their rankings are "almost entirely reputation-based," so our study posed little potential harm. Like the MBA program, the MPA program was excited to see what their program looked like through the eyes of the students. The project was on.

At this point we were not particularly interested in professions and professionalization. This changed as we began to interview faculty and administrators during the summer of 2012. For example, we were able to interview the first dean of the School of Public Affairs, who also was involved in the establishment of NASPAA, and was formerly associate dean at a business school. In telling the story of both the school and NASPAA, he said:

> It seemed to me what the field really needed was a professional management program, and that's what I thought the school, this school, should be. And we structured it accordingly, so if you look at how we're structured fundamentally, a business school in the public sector in some ways—we never said that, but that's really what we were. (Interview transcript)

Unprompted by us, he described both the MPA and MBA degrees as "professional," as did other faculty and administrators whom we were interviewing. At the time, we found this curious. We had limited knowledge about the professions literature, but we sensed a disjuncture.

While this early round of interviews alerted us to the "professional" theme, it became ever more prominent as we started our fieldwork later that summer. Our first observations were during a week-long "mini-math course" for incoming students who were admitted into the MPA program with borderline GRE math scores. More generally, "mini-math" was encouraged for anyone who wanted additional, intensive math instruction before the start of regular classes, all of which was seen as necessary given the emphasis on economics and quantitative methods in the program. Notably, these types of introductory courses are common in MPA programs. In this case, the "mini-math" course was well attended, and our field notes describe a part of the orientation: "During his brief remarks, one of the directors of the program tells the students, 'Math is a tool, an important tool' for what they will be doing, 'as professionals . . . analyzing . . . interpreting . . . *managing*'" (field notes; emphasis in original).

The instructor of the course later echoed this link between math, professionalism, and management. Take, for example, how he introduced the topic for the day, substitution:

> The instructor tells the students: "In the professional world you are dealing with multiple equations." He uses the example of maximizing cost functions, and says that you end up with a system. To deal with those systems of equations, substitution can be used where what you have from one equation can be moved to another equation. (Field notes)

In another session, during discussion of an application of what the class had been learning using economics and oil prices, "the instructor told them, 'Finding the equation is just a dry matter'; but when it's put in context, it's different. 'All the time it's about application' and context. 'When you are a professional, it's about application.'" Later in the same class, the instructor emphasized that finding equations and integrals to understand scenarios and contexts is "what we do as professionals." (Field notes)

Finally, at the end of math camp and heading into orientation week, the director of Graduate Student Services told the students, "Monday is the start of your professional career" (field notes). These, and many other examples, raised our awareness of the importance of "professional" themes, and what those themes meant to people involved in the program. In the data collection that followed—spanning two academic years, approximately 330 days of fieldwork, 145 interviews with 71 different students (33 interviewed three times, 14 interviewed twice), and 21 interviews with members of the faculty or administration, we collected data on this theme and others. In many ways, as suggested by the excerpts presented above, the data fit the NI theme of scientized knowledge and abstract managerialism: professionalism as mathematical understanding of and application to contexts. Students also embraced this theme. During an interview, for example, one student described the degree as "professional" because "the way you're taught to quantitatively look at qualitative issues, it teaches you a way of thinking. And that's what a professional degree is; it's a discipline, a way of approaching a problem and the tools to do it." She went on to talk about microeconomics, program evaluation, and cost-benefit analysis (interview transcript).

However, and especially for the students, professionalism had additional, often divergent meanings. Take, for example, this field note from one of our *last* observations, at a group "bar night" to celebrate the completion of a capstone project:

> It was near midnight, and people were reflecting on the past two years before heading home. One of the students, "Pete," was getting riled up. He felt that people, both students and faculty, didn't really take the whole endeavor very seriously. In turn, he hadn't given it his best effort, and he criticized it all as "not professional." But his friend and capstone colleague, "Mary," responded curtly, "Pete, you can be unprofessional while getting a professional degree." (Field notes, late spring 2014)

We are still analyzing our data and working to unravel this paradox of being "unprofessional while getting a professional degree," but this type of data speaks to the situated, interactionist aspects of the material. Upon finishing our data collection with a final round of interviews in the summer of 2014 (after students had graduated), we found that this is indeed a story about professions, professionalism, and professionalization. With this preliminary knowledge, we returned to the literature on the professions with much greater vigor, and we believe that the inhabited institutional approach we have developed in this chapter provides the right kind of flexible conceptual framework for making sense of the data.

Conclusion

In this chapter we call for a new wave of research on professional education and the socialization processes that occur in the "managerial" degree programs, such as the master's of business administration, the master's of public administration and public affairs, and the master's of public policy. This call fits with broader calls for research on colleges and universities,[94] and a focus on professional socialization has much to offer for an expanded and revitalized sociology of education. The education of professionals is a key aspect of modernity, and it provides a window not only into processes of rationalization and adult socialization, but also into the interstices between universities, occupations, and organizations.

In making this call, we push against research that uses traditional theoretical approaches to study the traditional sovereign professions of medicine, law, and the clergy. Instead of focusing on functionalist criterion or the status of jurisdictional struggles, the approach that we advocate accounts for the recursive relationship between institutions and people by wedding NI's concern with rationalization to SI's focus on local activity and meaning-making in the university context of professional socialization. Compared to the traditional studies of the professions, NI provides a more liberal conceptualization of professions with special attention to abstract managerialism and scientized knowledge. By demonstrating the role that education and the professions have in promoting rationalization across a variety of organizations, NI sets the stage and establishes the stakes. However, it begs the question of how students learn the forms of rationality that characterize the managerial professions. Meanwhile, SI provides a subaltern tradition of research on professional socialization and group culture, one that is well equipped to deal with the local meanings that students, faculty, and administration ascribe to professions and professionalism, and how professionalism can be a type of performance. However, SI research neglects the curricular content of professional education and the broader institutional pressures that structure degree programs.

Inhabited institutionalism marries these approaches in a way that is prone neither to the "microchauvanism" of interactionism, nor the "macrochauvanism" of new institutionalism.[95] In this view, professional socialization can be understood as an interactive process that both responds to and constitutes what is thought of as "professional," while remaining in constant contact with the disciplinary rationales that provide the grounds and subject matter for these interactions. As a part of their socialization, MBA, MPA, and MPP students also engage in interactive displays of professionalism. These displays do not meet the criteria outlined by functionalists, and, given the ambiguous jurisdiction for these degrees, do not resemble a coherent professional project to advance an occupational status. Instead, these professional performances advance a rationalization project.

As promising as an inhabited institutional approach may be for studies of managerial degree programs, it is also useful for research on the sovereign professions, education, and occupational socialization more broadly. Education and socialization processes are implicated in the diffusion of organizational forms, but in institutional research those socialization processes have been presumed, and not interrogated empirically. By recovering the interactionist tradition of research on professional socialization and bringing it into dialogue with new institutionalism, inhabited institutionalism provides a flexible conceptual framework for examining these empirical matters.

Notes

1. This research is supported by funding from a Spencer Foundation Small Grant, the Indiana University Center for Evaluation and Education Policy, and an Indiana University Summer Stipend for Collaborative Research and Creative Activity. We thank Jal Mehta, Elizabeth Popp Berman, Clay Thomas, and Judson Everitt for their valuable comments.
2. Former chief operations officer, US Department of Education.
3. President of Liberia, Nobel Peace Prize winner.
4. Rhee is former chancellor of Washington, DC, public schools, and founder of the educational nonprofit organization StudentsFirst. Martin is former chairman of the Federal Communications Commission.
5. Rakesh Khurana, *From Higher Aims to Hired Hands*. AACSB, "2015 Business School Data Guide"; Alice B. Stone and Donald C. Stone, "Early Development of Education in Public Administration"; NASPAA, "2014–2015 Roster of Accredited Programs"; NASPAA, "Find Your Graduate Degree for Public Service"; Elizabeth Popp Berman, "Thinking Like an Economist."
6. Harold Wilensky, "The Professionalization of Everyone?"; Magali Sarfatti Larson, *The Rise of Professionalism: A Sociological Analysis*. On managerial professional degrees, see Steven Brint, *In an Age of Experts*; Rakesh Khurana, *From Higher Aims to Hired Hands*; Mitchell Stevens, Elizabeth Armstrong, and Richard Arum, "Sieve, Incubator, Temple, Hub." For the purposes of this essay we focus on the MBA, MPAs, and MPP, because these are general degrees that span the private, public, and nonprofit sectors of the economy. However, there are a variety of other degrees that could be considered "professional" in the sense we develop here. and which exist outside of law, medicine, and religion. These include, but are not limited to, degrees and programs in public health, urban planning, and education. The framework we develop in this essay will also be of use when considering these additional degree programs.
7. In what follows we use the abbreviation "MPAs" to refer to both the master's of public administration and the master's of public affairs.
8. John W. Meyer, "The Effects of Education as an Institution"; John W. Meyer, "World Society."
9. Howard Becker et al., *Boys in White*.
10. Hokyu Hwang and Walter W. Powell, "The Rationalization of Charity."
11. Tim Hallett and Matthew Gougherty, "Learning the Administrative Way."
12. NASPAA, "MPA and MPP FAQ."
13. Elizabeth Popp Berman, "Thinking Like an Economist"; Marion Fourcade, *Economists and Society*.
14. For a review of the professions literature, see Keith MacDonald, *The Sociology of Professions*; Michael Reed, "Expert Power and Control in Late Modernity"; Eliot Fried-

son, *Professionalism, the Third Logic*; Elizabeth H. Gorman and Rebecca L. Sandefur, "Golden Age."

15. Talcott Parsons, "The Professions and Social Structure"; Ernest Greenwood, "Some Attributes of a Profession"; William J. Goode, "Community within a Community"; Bernard Barber, "Some Problems in the Sociology of the Professions." For work on professionalization, see William J. Goode, "Encroachment, Charlatanism, and the Emerging Profession" and "The Librarian"; Harold L. Wilensky, "The Professionalization of Everyone?"
16. Symbolic interactionist work on the professions and professional education has existed alongside both the functionalist and jurisdictional approaches, but has been overshadowed by them. Later in this essay we bring the interactionist legacy out of the darkness and highlight it as a key part of an inhabited institutional approach. For examples of the interactionist work, see Rue Bucher and Anselm Strauss, "Professions in Process"; Everett Hughes, *Men and their Work*; Howard Becker, "The Nature of a Profession."
17. Andrew Abbott, *The System of Professions*; Andrew Abbott, "Linked Ecologies."
18. Magali Sarfatti Larson, *The Rise of Professionalism: A Sociological Analysis*; Elizabeth Popp Berman, "Before the Professional Project."
19. Eliot Freidson, *Professional Dominance* and *Professional Powers*.
20. Magali Sarfatti Larson, *The Rise of Professionalism*, xvi; Randall Collins, *The Credential Society*.
21. Andrew Abbott, *The System of Professions*.
22. Katherine C. Kellogg, "Brokerage Professions."
23. For examples related to law and medicine, see Robert Dingwall and Phillip Lewis, *The Sociology of Professions: Lawyers, Doctors, and Others*; Robert Granfield, *Making Elite Lawyers*; Dan Lortie, *Laymen to Lawmen*; For a critique of using law and medicine as the basis of comparison, see Julia Evetts, "The Construction of Professionalism."
24. Arthur L. Stinchcombe, *Constructing Social Theories*.
25. Paul Starr, *The Social Transformation of American Medicine* and "Professionalization and Public Health."
26. Rakesh Khurana, *From Higher Aims to Hired Hands*; Rakesh Khurana and Nitin Nohria, "It's Time to Make Management a True Profession."
27. Tim Hallett and Matthew Gougherty, "Learning the Administrative Way."
28. Indeed, even the traditional "sovereign" professionals are increasingly working in a variety of organizational settings, further problematizing the functionalist understanding. For a discussion, see Kevin Leicht and Mary Fennell, "The Changing Organizational Context of Professional Work." For an earlier statement on the topic, see Richard Hall, "Professionalization and Bureaucratization."
29. Hokyu Hwang and Walter W. Powell, "The Rationalization of Charity."
30. Rakesh Khurana, *From Higher Aims to Hired Hands*; Rakesh Khurana and Nitin Nohria, "It's Time to Make Management a True Profession."
31. Richard L. Schott, "Public Administration as a Profession."
32. Richard Campbell and George Rawson, "The "New" Public Policy Programs"; Joel Fleishman, "A New Framework for Integration."
33. Richard W. Campbell and George E. Rawson, "The "New" Public Policy Programs." Laurence E. Lynn Jr., *Public Management as Art, Science, and Profession*.
34. Stanford University Graduate School of Business, "Stanford GSB Experience"; emphasis added.

35. Syracuse University Maxwell School, "Master's Handbook and Course Guide 2014–2015"; emphasis added.
36. University of Southern California, "Price Degree Brochure 2014–2015," 15.
37. Stefan Timmermans, "Professions and Their Work."
38. Steven Brint, *In an Age of Experts*, 1 and 9. Brint also makes the apt observation that many occupations, "from cosmologists to watchmakers," require licensed credentials but do not have the stature associated with a profession (1994: 24).
39. Jason Owen-Smith, "The Institutionalization of Expertise," 65.
40. Keith MacDonald, *The Sociology of Professions*, 1.
41. Everett C. Hughes, "The Humble and the Proud."
42. John W. Meyer, "The Effects of Education as an Institution"; John W. Meyer and Brian Rowan, "Institutional Organization" and "The Structure of Educational Organizations"; Paul DiMaggio and Walter W. Powell, "The Iron Cage Revisited."
43. Paul DiMaggio, "The Cultural Entrepreneurship in Nineteenth-Century Boston, I," The Cultural Entrepreneurship in Nineteenth-Century Boston, II," and "Constructing an Organizational Field as a Professional Project: U.S. Art Museums, 1920–1940."
44. Paul DiMaggio and Walter W. Powell, "The Iron Cage Revisited," 152; emphasis added.
45. Paul DiMaggio and Walter W. Powell, "The Iron Cage Revisited," 152–153.
46. For information on these statistics, see http://nces.ed.gov/programs/digest/d13/tables/dt13_318.20.asp?current=yes; NASPAA, "Enrollment and Degrees Awarded Data 2001–2002" and "Program Almanac 2011."
47. Hokyu Hwang and Walter W. Powell, "The Rationalization of Charity," 269 and 288; italics in original. See also Gili Drori, John W. Meyer, and Hokyu Hwang, *Globalization and Organization*.
48. Elizabeth Popp Berman, "Thinking Like an Economist."
49. Steven Brint, *In an Age of Experts*, 141. Although Brint's work has some commonalities with NI, it is important to note that he does not call himself an institutionalist and has created his own robust work on professions.
50. Wendy Nelson Espeland and Mitchell L. Stevens, "Commensuration as Social Process"; Wendy Nelson Espeland and Michael Sauder, "Rankings and Reactivity."
51. John W. Meyer and Brian Rowan, "Institutional Organizations" and "The Structure of Educational Organizations."
52. Michael Sauder and Wendy Nelson Espeland, "The Discipline of Rankings"; Heinz Dieter Meyer and Brian Rowan, "Institutional Analysis and the Study of Education"; Tim Hallett, "The Myth Incarnate."
53. Hokyu Hwang and Walter W. Powell, "The Rationalization of Charity," 288.
54. John W. Meyer and Patricia Bromley, "The Worldwide Expansion of "Organization," 373. For a discussion of professions as carriers of rationality, see also W. Richard Scott, "Lords of the Dance" and *Institutions and Organizations*.
55. Jal Mehta, *The Allure of Order*; Arum and Cook, chapter 7 of this volume.
56. Michael Power, *The Audit Explosion*; Marilyn Strathern, *Audit Cultures*; Julia Evetts, "The Construction of Professionalism."
57. Jal Mehta, *The Allure of Order*.
58. Valerie Fournier, "The Appeal to 'Professionalism' as a Disciplinary Mechanism," 285. See also Michael I. Reed "Expert Power and Control in Late Modernity."
59. Jason Owen-Smith, "The Institutionalization of Expertise," 66.
60. Amy Binder, "For Love and Money," 550.
61. Frank Dobbin, *Inventing Equal Opportunity*.

62. Lauren B. Edelman, Chistopher Uggen and Howard S. Erlanger, "The Endogeneity of Legal Regulation."
63. John W. Meyer, "The Effects of Education as an Institution," 55.
64. Robert Merton, George Reader, and Patricia Kendall, *The Student-Physician*. New institutionalism does well with examining the intensifying logic that Davies and Mehta discuss in chapter 3 of this volume, but it does little to consider the accommodating logic: how education is forced to adapt to the populations it encounters. Symbolic interaction does much better in this regard, and by focusing on how people do things together inside of organizations it can also provide a means to consider the possible origins of the very rationales the are the focus of new institutionalism (Baker, chapter 2).
65. For an extreme constructionist perspective on professionalism, see Howard S. Becker, "Some Problems of Professionalization." For a discussion of sensitizing concepts, see Herbert Blumer, *Symbolic Interaction*. On the focus of people doing things together, see Everett C. Hughes, "The Making of a Physician" and Howard S. Becker, *Doing Things Together*. Abbott's work (1988) on the professions has been largely influential, and can be seen as Hughesian theorizing writ large. He argues that at the core of professional life is interprofessional competition and control of knowledge and work activities. Like Hughes, he views the professions in an interdependent system characterized by jurisdictional disputes. Abbott claims that he is "extending the Hughes logic to its limit and focusing on jurisdictional interactions themselves" (1988: 112). In doing so, however, he tends to lose focus on people doing things together. As Bechky notes, even in the case of Abbott's work, "in most of the studies of professions as institutional systems, one rarely sees the people within organizations, as evidence is drawn from field-level activities such as regulatory action and association lobbying. As a consequence, individual workplace action is often missing, and thus these frameworks lack conceptual grounding in the work itself" (Bechky 2011: 1160).
66. Herbert Blumer, *Symbolic Interaction*, 3; paraphrased and edited for brevity.
67. Everett C. Hughes, "The Making of a Physician," 22; emphasis added. See also Robert Merton, George Reader, and Patricia Kendall, *The Student-Physician*.
68. Howard Becker et al., *Boys in White*, 13.
69. See also Robert Granfield and Thomas Koenig, "The Fate of Elite Idealism."
70. Howard Becker et al., *Boys in White*, 435; emphasis in original.
71. Becker et al. actually eschew the term "socialization" because of its association with a deterministic, functionalist tradition.
72. Jack Haas and William Shaffir, "The Professionalization of Medical Students" and "Ritual Evaluation of Competence"; Erving Goffman, *The Presentation of Self in Every day Life*. See also Virginia L. Oleson and Elvi W. Whittaker, *The Silent Dialogue*; Basil J. Sherlock and Richard T. Morris, *Becoming a Dentist*; Charles L. Bosk, *Forgive and Remember*; Rue Bucher and Joan Stelling, *Becoming Professional*.
73. On teachers, see Dan Lortie, "Shared Ordeal and Induction to Work." On psychiatrists, see Donald Light, *Becoming Psychiatrists*. On the clergy, see Sherryl Kleinman, *Equals before God*. On sociology graduate students, see Sherryl Kleinman, "Collective Matters as Individual Concerns."
74. Spencer Cahill, "Emotional Capital and Professional Socialization."
75. Mitchell L. Stevens, "Culture and Education," 109. For examples of interactionist work on K–12 education, see Donna Eder, "Cycle of Popularity"; Peter Adler and Patricia Adler, *Peer Power*; David A. Kinney, "From 'Nerds' to 'Normals.'"
76. For critiques, see Rosabeth Moss Kanter, "Symbolic Interactionism and Politics"; and

Jürgen Habermas, *The Theory of Communicative Action*. For a defense of SI, see Lonnie Athens, "The Roots of 'Radical Interactionism.'"

77. David A. Snow, "Extending and Broadening Blumer's Conceptualization of Symbolic Interactionism," 371.
78. Paul Atkinson, "The Reproduction of the Professional Community," 234.
79. Tim Hallett and Marc Ventresca, "Inhabited Institutions"; Tim Hallett, David Shulman, and Gary Alan Fine, "Peopling Organizations"; Beth Bechky, "Making Organizational Theory Work."
80. Gary Alan Fine, *Kitchens*; Gary Alan Fine and Tim Hallett, "Group Cultures and the Everyday Life of Organizations."
81. Michael Haedicke and Tim Hallett, "How to Look Two Ways at Once."
82. Amy Binder, "For Love and Money," 551.
83. Herbert Blumer, *Symbolic Interaction*, 9; Herbert Blumer, *Industrialization as an Agent of Social Change*.
84. Tim Hallett and Marc Ventresca, "Inhabited Institutions," 213.
85. Tim Hallett, "The Myth Incarnate"; Janice Danielle Aurini, "Patterns of Tight and Loose Coupling in a Competitive Marketplace"; Lisa Nunn, *Defining Student Success*.
86. Judson Everitt, "Teaching Careers and Inhabited Institutions" and "Inhabitants Moving In."
87. William A. Corsaro, *The Sociology of Childhood*.
88. Michael A. Haedicke, "Keeping Our Mission, Changing Our System"; Michael Haedicke and Tim Hallett, "How to Look Two Ways at Once."
89. Michele Lamont, *The Dignity of Working Men*; Michele Lamont and Laurent Thevenot, *Rethinking Cultural Sociology*.
90. Iddo Tavory and Stefan Timmermans, *Abductive Analysis*; Haedicke and Hallett "How to Look Two Ways at Once." Abduction is "the creative inferential process aimed at producing new hypotheses and theories based on surprising research evidence" (Tavory and Timmermans, *Abductive Analysis*, 5).
91. Tim Hallett, "The Myth Incarnate."
92. Rosabeth Moss Kanter, *Men and Women of the Corporation*; Calvin Morrill, *The Executive Way: Conflict Management in Corporations*.
93. Tim Hallett, "Between Deference and Distinction" and "Symbolic Power and Organizational Culture."
94. Mitchell Stevens, Elizabeth Armstrong, and Richard Arum, "Sieve, Incubator, Temple, Hub"; Amy Binder and Kate Wood, *Becoming Right*; Neil Gross, *Why are Professors Liberal and Why do Conservatives Care?*; Daniel Chambliss and Christopher Takacs, *How College Works*.
95. Ronald Jepperson and John W. Meyer, "Multiple Levels of Analysis and the Limitations of Methodological Individualism."

References

AACSB. "2015 Business School Data Guide." Accessed May 26, 2015, at http://www.aacsb.edu/~/media/AACSB/Publications/data-trends-booklet/2015%20Business%20School%20Data%20Guide.ashx.

Abbott, Andrew. "Linked Ecologies: States and Universities as Environments for Professions." *Sociological Theory* 23 (2005): 245–274.

———. *The System of Professions: An Essay on the Division of Expert Labor*. Chicago: University of Chicago Press, 1988.

Adler, Peter, and Patricia Adler. *Peer Power: Preadolescent Culture and Identity*. New Brunswick, NJ: Rutgers University Press, 1998.

Athens, Lonnie. "The Roots of 'Radical Interactionism.'" *Journal for the Theory of Social Behaviour* 39 (2009): 387–414.

Aurini, Janice Danielle. "Patterns of Tight and Loose Coupling in a Competitive Marketplace: The Case of Learning Center Franchises." *Sociology of Education* 85 (2012): 373–387.

Atkinson, Paul. "The Reproduction of the Professional Community." In *The Sociology of Professions: Lawyers, Doctors and Others*, edited by Robert Dingwall and Philip Lewis, 224–241. New York: St. Martin's Press, 1983.

Barber, Bernard. "Some Problems in the Sociology of the Professions." *Daedalus* 92 (1963): 669–688.

Bechky, Beth. "Making Organizational Theory Work: Institutions, Occupations, and Negotiated Orders." *Organizations Science* 22 (2011): 1157–1167.

Becker, Howard S. *Doing Things Together*. Evanston, IL: Northwestern University Press, 1986.

———. "The Nature of a Profession." In *Sociological Work: Method and Substance*. 87–103. New Brunswick, NJ: Transaction Books, 1976.

———. "Some Problems of Professionalization" *Adult Education* 6 (1956): 101–105.

Becker, Howard, Blanche Geer, Everitt Hughes, and Anselm Strauss. *Boys in White: Student Culture in Medical School*. Chicago: University of Chicago Press, 1961.

Berman, Elizabeth Popp. "Before the Professional Project: Success and Failure at Creating an Organizational Representative for English Doctors." *Theory and Society* 35 (2006): 157–191.

———. "Thinking Like an Economist: How Economics Became the Language of US Public Policy." In progress.

Binder, Amy. "For Love and Money: One Organization's Creative Responses to a New Funding Environment." *Theory and Society* 36 (2007): 547–571.

Binder, Amy, and Kate Wood. *Becoming Right: How Campuses Shape Young Conservatives*. Princeton, NJ: Princeton University Press, 2013.

Blumer, Herbert. *Industrialization as an Agent of Social Change*. New York: Aldine de Gruyter, 1960 [1990].

———. *Symbolic Interaction: Perspective and Method*. Berkeley: University of California Press, 1969.

Bosk, Charles L. *Forgive and Remember: Managing Medical Failure*. Chicago: University of Chicago Press, 1979.

Bucher, Rue, and Anselm Strauss. "Professions in Process." *American Journal of Sociology* 66 (1961): 325–334.

Brint, Steven. *In an Age of Experts: The Changing Role of Professionals in Politics and Public Life*. Princeton, NJ: Princeton University Press, 1994.

Bucher, Rue, and Joan Stelling. *Becoming Professional*. Beverly Hills, CA: Sage Foundation, 1977.

Cahill, Spencer E. "Emotional Capital and Professional Socialization: The Case of Mortuary Science Students (and Me)." *Social Psychology Quarterly* 62 (1999): 101–116.

Campbell, Richard W., and George E. Rawson. "The "New" Public Policy Programs and Their Effects on the Professional Status of Public Administration." *Southern Review of Public Administration* 5 (1981): 91–113.

CEPH. "Accredited Schools and Programs." Accessed May 26, 2015, at http://ceph.org/accredited/.

Chambliss, Daniel F., and Christopher G. Takacs. *How College Works*. Cambridge, MA: Harvard University Press, 2014.

Collins, Randall. *The Credential Society: An Historical Sociology of Education and Stratification*. Orlando, FL: Academic Press, 1979.

Corsaro, William A. *The Sociology of Childhood: Second Edition*. Thousand Oaks, CA: Pine Forge Press, 2005.

DiMaggio, Paul. "Constructing an Organizational Field as a Professional Project: US Art Museums, 1920–1940." In *The New Institutionalism in Organizational Analysis*, edited by Walter W. Powell and Paul DiMaggio, 267–292. Chicago: University of Chicago Press, 1991.

———. "The Cultural Entrepreneurship in Nineteenth-Century Boston, I: The Creation of an Organizational Base for High Culture in America." *Media, Culture and Society* 4 (1982): 33–50.

———. "The Cultural Entrepreneurship in Nineteenth-Century Boston, II: The Classification and Framing of American Art." *Media, Culture and Society* 4 (1982): 303–322.

DiMaggio, Paul, and Walter W. Powell. "The Iron Cage Revisited: Institutional Isomorphism and Collective Rationality in Organizational Fields." *American Sociological Review* 48 (1983): 147–160.

Dingwall, Robert, and Phillip Lewis. *The Sociology of Professions: Lawyers, Doctors and Others*. New York: St. Martin's Press, 1983.

Dobbin, Frank. *Inventing Equal Opportunity*. Princeton, NJ: Princeton University Press, 2009.

Drori, Gili, John W. Meyer, and Hokyu Hwang. *Globalization and Organization: World Society and Organizational Change*. New York: Oxford University Press, 2009.

Edelman, Lauren B., Christopher Uggen, and Howard S. Erlanger. "The Endogeneity of Legal Regulation." *American Journal of Sociology* 102 (1999): 406–454.

Eder, Donna. "Cycle of Popularity: Interpersonal Relationships among Female Adolescents." *Sociology of Education* 58 (1985): 154–165.

Espeland, Wendy Nelson, and Michael Sauder. "Rankings and Reactivity: How Public Measures Recreate Social Worlds." *American Journal of Sociology* 113 (2007): 1–40.

Espeland, Wendy Nelson, and Mitchell L. Stevens. "Commensuration as Social Process." *Annual Review of Sociology* 24 (1998): 313–343.

Evaschwick, Connie, James W. Begun, and John R. Finnegan Jr. "Public Health as a Distinct Profession: Has It Arrived?" *Journal of Public Health Management Practice* 19 (2013): 412–419.

Everitt, Judson G. "Inhabitants Moving In: Prospective Sense-Making and the Reproduction of Inhabited Institutions in Teacher Education." *Symbolic Interaction* 36 (2013): 177–196.

———. "Teacher Careers and Inhabited Institutions: Sense-Making and Arsenals of Teaching Practice in Educational Institutions." *Symbolic Interaction* 35 (2012): 203–220.

Evetts, Julia. "The Construction of Professionalism in New and Existing Occupational Contexts: Promoting and Facilitating Occupational Change." *International Journal of Sociology and Social Policy* 23 (2003): 22–35.

Fine, Gary Alan. *Kitchens: The Culture of Restaurant Work*. Berkeley: University of California Press, 1996.

Fine, Gary Alan, and Tim Hallett. "Group Cultures and the Everyday Life of Organizations: Interaction Order and Meso-Analysis." *Organization Studies* 35 (2014): 1773–1792.

Flieshman, Joel L. "A New Framework for Integration: Policy Analysis and Public Management." *American Behavioral Scientist* 33 (1990): 733–754.

Fourcade, Marion. *Economists and Society: Discipline and Profession in the United States, Britain, and France, 1890s to 1990s*. Princeton, NJ: Princeton University Press, 2009.

Fournier, Valerie. "The Appeal to 'Professionalism' as a Disciplinary Mechanism." *Sociological Review* 47 (1999): 280–307.

Freidson, Eliot. *Professional Dominance: The Social Structure of Medical Care*. New York: Atherton Press, 1970.

———. *Professionalism, the Third Logic: On the Practice of Knowledge*. Chicago: University of Chicago Press, 2001.

———. *Professional Powers: A Study of the Institutionalization of Formal Knowledge*. Chicago: University of Chicago Press, 1988.

Goffman, Erving. *The Presentation of Self in Everyday Life*. New York: Anchor Books, 1959.

Goode, William J. "Community within a Community: The Professions." *American Sociological Review* 22 (1957): 194–200.

———. "Encroachment, Charlatanism, and the Emerging Profession: Psychology, Sociology, and Medicine." *American Sociological Review* 25 (1960): 902–914.

———. "The Librarian: From Occupation to Profession?" *Library Quarterly* 31 (1961): 306–320.

Gorman, Elizabeth H., and Rebecca L. Sandefur. ""Golden Age," Quiescence, and Revival: How the Sociology of Professions Became the Study of Knowledge-Based Work." *Work and Occupations* 38 (2011): 275–302.

Granfield, Robert. *Making Elite Lawyers: Visions of Harvard and Beyond*. New York: Routledge, 1992.

Granfield, Robert, and Thomas Koenig. "The Fate of Elite Idealism: Accommodation and Ideological Work at Harvard Law School." *Social Problems* 39 (1992): 315–331.

Greenwood, Ernest. "Attributes of a Profession." *Social Work* 2 (1957): 45–55.

Gross, Neil. *Why Are Professors Liberal and Why Do Conservatives Care?* Cambridge, MA: Harvard University Press, 2013.

Haas, Jack, and William Shaffir. "The Professionalization of Medical Students: Developing Competence and a Cloak of Competence." *Symbolic Interaction* 1 (1977): 71–88.

———. "Ritual Evaluation of Competence: The Hidden Curriculum of Professionalization in an Innovative Medical School Program." *Work and Occupations* 9 (1982): 131–154.

Habermas, Jürgen. *The Theory of Communicative Action: Life World and System: A Critique of Functionalist Reason*. Vol. 2. Boston: Beacon, 1987.

Haedicke, Michael A. "'Keeping our Mission, Changing our System': Translation and Organizational Change in Natural Foods Co-ops." *Sociological Quarterly* 53 (2012): 44–67.

Haedicke, Michael, and Tim Hallett. "How to Look Two Ways at Once: Research Strategies for Inhabited Institutionalism." In *The Handbook of Qualitative Research in Organizations*, edited by Kimberly Elsbach and Roderick Kramer. Forthcoming.

Hall, Richard H. "Professionalization and Bureaucratization." *American Sociological Review* 33 (1968): 92–104.

Hallett, Tim. "Between Deference and Distinction: Interaction Ritual Through Symbolic Power in an Educational Institution." *Social Psychology Quarterly* 70 (2007): 148–171.

———. "The Myth Incarnate: Recoupling Processes, Turmoil, and Inhabited Institutions in an Urban Elementary School." *American Sociological Review* 75 (2010): 52–74.

———. "Symbolic Power and Organizational Culture." *Sociological Theory*. 21(2003): 128–149.

Hallett, Tim, and Matthew Gougherty. "Learning the Administrative Way: Men and Women of the Policy School." In progress.

Hallett, Tim, David Shulman, and Gary Alan Fine. "Peopling Organizations: The Promise of Classic Symbolic Interactionism for an Inhabited Institutionalism." In *The Oxford Handbook of Organizational Studies: Classical Foundations*, edited by Paul S. Adler. Oxford, UK: Oxford University Press, 2009.

Hallett, Tim, and Marc Ventresca. "Inhabited Institutions: Social Interactions and Organizational Forms in Gouldner's *Patterns of Industrial Bureaucracy*." *Theory and Society* 35 (2006): 213–236.

Hughes, Everett C. "The Humble and the Proud." *Sociological Quarterly* 11 (1970): 147–156.

———. "The Making of a Physician: General Statement of Ideas and Problems." *Human Organization* 14 (1956): 21–25.

———. *Men and Their Work*. Glencoe, IL: Free Press, 1957.

Hwang, Hokyu, and Walter W. Powell. "The Rationalization of Charity: The Influences of Professionalism in the Nonprofit Sector." *Administrative Science Quarterly* 54 (2009): 268–298.

Jepperson, Ronald, and John W. Meyer. "Multiple Levels of Analysis and the Limitations of Methodological Individualism." *Sociological Theory* 29 (2011): 54–73.

Kanter, Rosabeth Moss. *Men and Women of the Corporation*. New York: Basic Books, 1977.

Kanter, Rosabeth Moss. "Symbolic Interactionism and Politics in Systematic Perspective." *Sociological Inquiry* 42 (1972): 77–92.

Kellogg, Katherine C. "Brokerage Professions and Implementing Reform in an Age of Experts." *American Sociological Review* 79 (2014): 912–941.

Khurana, Rakesh. *From Higher Aims to Hired Hands: The Social Transformation of American Business Schools and the Unfulfilled Promise of Management as a Profession*. Princeton, NJ: Princeton University Press, 2007.

Khurana, Rakesh, and Nitin Nohria. "It's Time to Make Management a True Profession." *Harvard Business Review* (October 2008): 70–77.

Kinney, David A. "From 'Nerds' to 'Normals': The Recovery of Identity among Adolescents from Middle School to High School." *Sociology of Education* 66 (1993): 21–40.

Kleinman, Sherryl. "Collective Matters as Individual Concerns Peer Culture among Graduate Students." *Journal of Contemporary Ethnography* 12 (1983): 203–225.

———. *Equals before God: Seminarians as Humanistic Professionals*. Chicago: University of Chicago Press, 1984.

Lamont, Michele. *The Dignity of Working Men: Morality and the Boundaries of Race, Class, and Immigration*. Cambridge, MA: Harvard University Press, 2009.

Lamont, Michele, and Laurent Thevenot. *Rethinking Cultural Sociology: Repertoires of Evaluation in France and the United States*. Cambridge: Cambridge University Press, 2000.

Larson, Magali Sarfatti. *The Rise of Professionalism: A Sociological Analysis*. Berkeley: University of California Press, 1977.

Leicht, Kevin T., and Mary L. Fennell. "The Changing Organizational Context of Professional Work." *Annual Review of Sociology* 23 (1997): 215–231.

Light, Donald. *Becoming Psychiatrists: The Professional Transformation of Self*. New York: Norton, 1980.

Lortie, Dan. *Laymen to Lawmen: Law School, Careers and Professional Socialization*. Cambridge, MA: Harvard University Press, 1959.

———. "Shared Ordeal and Induction to Work." In *Institutions and the Person*, edited by Becker et al. Chicago: Aldine, 1968.

Lynn Jr., Laurence E. *Public Management as Art, Science, and Profession*. Chatham, NJ: Chatham House Publishers, 1996.

MacDonald, Keith M. *The Sociology of Professions*. London: Sage Publications, 1995.

Mehta, Jal. *The Allure of Order: High Hopes, Dashed Expectations, and the Troubled Quest to Remake American Schooling*. Oxford: Oxford University Press, 2013.

Merton, Robert, George Reader, and Patricia Kendall. *The Student-Physician: Introductory Studies in the Sociology of Medical Education*. Cambridge, MA: Harvard University Press, 1957.

Meyer, Heinz-Dieter, and Brian Rowan. "Institutional Analysis and the Study of Education." In *The New Institutionalism in Education*, edited by H. D. Meyer and R. Rowan, 1–13. Albany, NY: SUNY Press, 2006.

Meyer, John W. "The Effects of Education as an Institution." *American Journal of Sociology* 83 (1977): 55–77.

———. "World Society, Institutional Theories, and the Actor." *Annual Review of Sociology* 36 (2010): 1–20.

Meyer, John W., and Patricia Bromley. "The Worldwide Expansion of 'Organization.'" *Sociological Theory* 31 (2013): 366–389.

Meyer, John W., and Brian Rowan. "The Structure of Educational Organizations." In *Environments and Organizations*, edited by John W. Meyer et al. San Francisco: Jossey-Bass, 1978.

———. "Institutional Organizations: Formal Structure as Myth and Ceremony." *American Journal of Sociology* 83 (1977): 340–363.

Morrill, Calvin. *The Executive Way: Conflict Management in Corporations*. Chicago: University of Chicago Press, 1995.

NASPAA. "2014–2015 Roster of Accredited Programs." Last modified September 1, 2014. https://naspaaaccreditation.files.wordpress.com/2014/08/annual-roster-of-accredited-programs-updated-09-01-14.pdf.

———. "Enrollment and Degrees Awarded Data: Masters Degrees: 2001–2002." Accessed May 26, 2015. http://www.naspaa.org/principals/almanac/Survey2002/mastersdegrees.asp.

———. "Find Your Graduate Degree for Public Service." Accessed June 20, 2015. http://naspaa.civicore.com/search/index.php?section=basic&action=new.

———. "MPA and MPP FAQ." Last modified July 2012. http://www.naspaa.org/students/faq/faq.asp#Whats_the_difference_between_an_MPA_and_an_MPP_degree.

———. "Program Almanac 2011." Accessed May 26, 2015. http://67.199.57.12/naspaa/DataCenter/Almanac/Almanac2010.cfm.

Nunn, Lisa. *Defining Student Success: The Role of Student Culture*. New Brunswick, NJ: Rutgers University Press, 2014.

Oleson, Virginia L., and Elvi W. Whittaker. *The Silent Dialogue: A Study in the Social Psychology of Professional Socialization*. San Francisco: Joessey-Bass, 1968.

Owen-Smith, Jason. "The Institutionalization of Expertise in University Licensing." *Theory and Society* 40 (2011): 63–94.

Parsons, Talcott. "The Professions and Social Structure." *Social Forces* 17 (1939): 457–467.

Power, Michael. *The Audit Explosion*. London: Demos, 1994.

Reed, Michael I. "Expert Power and Control in Late Modernity: An Empirical Review and Theoretical Synthesis." *Organization Studies* 17 (1996): 573–597.

Sauder, Michael, and Wendy Nelson Espeland. "The Discipline of Rankings." *American Sociological Review* 74 (2009): 63–82.

Schott, Richard L. "Public Administration as a Profession: Problems and Prospects." *Public Administration Review* 36 (1976): 253–259.

Scott, W. Richard. *Institutions and Organizations*. Los Angeles: Sage, 2014.

———. "Lords of the Dance: Professionals as Institutional Agents." *Organization Studies* 29 (2008): 219–238.

Sherlock, Basil J., and Richard T. Morris. *Becoming a Dentist*. Springfield, IL: Charles C. Thomas Publisher, 1972.

Snow, David A. "Extending and Broadening Blumer's Conceptualization of Symbolic Interactionism." *Symbolic Interaction* 24 (2001): 367–377.

Stanford University Graduate School of Business. "Stanford GSB Experience." Accessed May 26, 2015. https://www.gsb.stanford.edu/stanford-gsb-experience.

Starr, Paul. "Professionalization and Public Health: Historical Legacies, Continuing Dilemmas." *Journal of Health Management Practice* 15 (2009): S26–S30.

———. *The Social Transformation of American Medicine*. New York: Basic Books, 1983.

Stevens, Mitchell L. "Culture and Education." *Annals of the American Academy of Political and Social Science* 617 (September 2008): 97–113.

Stevens, Mitchell L., Elizabeth A. Armstrong, and Richard Arum. "Sieve, Incubator, Temple, Hub: Empirical and Theoretical Advances in the Sociology of Higher Education." *Annual Review of Sociology* 34 (2008): 127–151.

Stinchcombe, Arthur L. *Constructing Social Theories*. Chicago: University of Chicago Press, 1968.

Stone, Alice B., and Donald C. Stone. "Early Development of Education in Public Administration." In *Public Administration: Past, Present, Future*, edited by Fredrick C. Mosher, 11–48. Tuscaloosa: University of Alabama Press, 1975.

Strathern, Marilyn. *Audit Cultures: Anthropological Studies in Accountability, Ethics, and the Academy*. New York: Routledge, 2000.

Syracuse University Maxwell School of Citizenship and Public Affairs. "Master of Public Administration and Executive Master of Public Administration Master's Handbook and Course Guide 2014–2015." Accessed May 26, 2015. http://www.maxwell.syr.edu/uploadedFiles/paia/degrees/MPA%20Handbook%202014-15.pdf.

Tavory, Iddo, and Stefan Timmermans. *Abductive Analysis: Theorizing Qualitative Research*. Chicago: University of Chicago Press, 2014.

Timmermans, Stefan. "Professions and Their Work: Do Market Shelters Protect Professional Interests?" *Work and Occupations* 35 (2008): 164–188.

University of Southern California Sol Price School of Public Policy. "Price Degree Brochure 2014–2015." Accessed June 20, 2015. https://priceschool.usc.edu/files/2010/09/2255_2014DegreeBroUpdate_FNL-Oct6.pdf.

Wilensky, Harold L. "The Professionalization of Everyone?" *American Journal of Sociology* 70 (1964): 137–158.

PART TWO

Substantive Contributions

SIX

Talking Pigs? Lessons from Elite Schooling

SHAMUS KHAN

In comparison to the transformative rights movements of the 1960s, the question of what was happening among the elite seemed quaint. As women and nonwhites began to demand and acquire greater social integration and opportunities, the future appeared to be one in which marginalized groups would be integrated into the mass of society. The fattening middle, rather than the diminished tail, would be the object of our analysis. The changes were revolutionary: the household structure of Western nations radically changed, the economy transformed, cultural tastes were realigned, global dynamics seemed more pronounced, and the legitimacy of social barriers was undermined. In comparison to these processes, knowledge about the elite was rather unimportant. Indeed, we seemed to be moving away from elites and elite rule to a different, more just world. Our theoretical and methodological tools reflected this realignment. Regression analysis flattened out the extremes of distributions; trends were driven by the middle of society rather than the exceptional outliers. Scholars questioned how status was attained rather than maintained.

But more recent experience and the corresponding scholarship about both inequality and elites has pushed against these methodological and theoretical approaches. Elites are driving inequality, and within our winner-take all markets, the importance of these nonrepresentative outliers requires new social science approaches. Perhaps more than any other area, the sociology of education has led the charge in this new study of the elite. In this chapter I draw upon this work for important empirical lessons about the elite, as well as insights into the conceptual framework of sociology more generally.

The privileged place of education with respect to these developments is partly due to scholars in this research area being uniquely situated to study the elite. Whereas boardrooms are largely behind closed doors, academics inhabit and indeed run a central institution of elite formation and reproduction: schools.

Most schools are not elite, of course, and most academics are not in a position to walk out their door and observe the dynamics of elite reproduction. This trivial observation has an important implication. The difference between Harvard and a local community college in Cambridge, Massachusetts, may be so dramatic that to suggest they are part of the same category of phenomena borders on the absurd. Where many colleges have shrinking faculty, Harvard has faculty with shrinking teaching obligations. Whereas most colleges accept almost everyone who applies, Harvard is harder and harder to get into. Where most colleges are struggling to stay afloat, Harvard sits atop tens of billions of dollars.

This reveals a trend that goes far beyond schooling. Elites have tended to be countercyclical. When others have been economically mobile, elites been locked in place. And vice versa. Combining these insights—(1) that elite institutions are nonrepresentative, (2) that those institutions can reveal much about the workings of power in America, and (3) that such power is often not deployed for the good of all because those who are powerful experience different economic cycles—reveals core lessons for sociology.

In this chapter I begin by outlining what it means to study nonrepresentative institutions. Next, I discuss the idea of elites as "countercyclical," explicating the implications of this position. And finally I outline a cultural rhetoric that helps us better understand the practical implications of these first two points. Overall, I hope to show what general lessons sociologists can draw from the study of the nonrepresentative case of elite schooling.

Studying Nonrepresentative Institutions: New Classifications

Ivan Ermakoff has recently made the case for the epistemic contributions and normative expectations of studying "exceptional cases" (2014). Ermakoff's own work is far from our current concern; he writes on fascism and democratic abdications. Yet he provides keen insights into what we might learn from the study of the exceptional. Ermakoff draws upon Blumer (1986: 146) to think of a case as an "object of consideration." He suggests that there are three advantages to looking beyond the representative. First, exceptional cases reveal the limits of our standard classifications. Second, they outline new classes of objects. And third, they magnify relational patterns that are less visible in more mundane contexts.

While social scientists might think of nonrepresentativeness as a criticism, I seek to build upon Ermakoff and think of the virtues of the exception. In certain realms of social life, we know this well. Take, for example, the scholarship on extreme poverty (Desmond 2015). Beyond the importance of knowing about those who are suffering, extreme poverty gives us an exceptional case with which to challenge our classifications, generate new classifications, and magnify the relational patterns of inequality.

We can only push this analogy so far, however, as it would be an analytical mistake to assume that the tails of the distribution (the elite and the homeless) are ruled by the same inverted dynamics. They share their exceptionalism, and in this, their theoretic and methodological value. But we have far too little evidence to expand our analogy to imagine that poverty and wealth are the inverse of one another. And so we must study both.

To this insight we might add, further, that elites are not only exceptional, but are those with power. Definitions of elites—those with vastly disproportionate control over or access to resources that provide them with power (Khan 2012a)—suggest that while elites may well be nonrepresentative of others within society, their relative monopoly of power makes them ideal space for understanding the power dynamics of a society. While the findings about elites may not be generalizable to other populations, the implications of these findings are important for understanding the direction of society. These two observations—that there are advantages to studying exceptional cases, and that elites as an exceptional case allow us to better understand the dynamics of power within society—serve as a justification for taking the nonrepresentative phenomena of elites seriously.

Schools are places where we can see networks form, culture emerge, ideas created, symbols adopted, and knowledge adopted and transformed. In short, if we want to know of the dynamics of economic, knowledge, cultural, social, and symbolic capital—how they emerge, are experienced over time, transform, and are transmitted—then schools, and elite schools in particular, become critical sites of inquiry. Following Ermakoff, we might ask what sociology learns in general from the study of the rather unique process of elite schooling. That is, what do we learn about classifications, classes of objects, and relational patterns?

First, elite schooling reveals some of the limits of our standard classifications. Let us take the classic Weberian view that exclusion and boundary drawing are core dynamics for social groups, and that such processes are central to the reproduction of inequality (Lamont 1992; Lamont and Molar 2002). From this perspective, competition over scarce resources generates status groupings, wherein groups seek to align themselves with particular resources and define themselves in opposition to other groups. In the case of schools, this would mean having groups within a society align themselves with educational institutions in order to augment their social power, prestige, and advantage.

The sociology of elite education certainly provides evidence for this view. In his study of the history of admissions at Harvard, Yale, and Princeton, Jerome Karabel (2005) outlines how these schools sought to draw and redraw boundaries around the class of people who belonged within their walls. Deploying a deep anti-Semitism, admissions officers and key administrators sought to include white Protestants and exclude others. This drawing of boundaries aligns closely with Weber's, and its modern applications in work like that of Michele Lamont. But if we look at the second part of Karabel's story, a different picture emerges.

The system based in anti-Semitism, one which sought to admit students not on the basis of academics alone but instead on a range of attributes considered "character," is now deployed by elite schools to *include* those who had previously been excluded. Elite schools are more racially diverse than ever before (many are "majority minority"); women make up the majority of students, and more than half of each class is on financial aid. Elite schools express a deep commitment to diversity (Berrey 2015; Gaztambide-Fernandez 2009a, 2009b; Khan 2011). While these transformations can be overstated, it is important to note that they are not window dressing.

My own elite institution, Columbia University, accepted an incoming class of 2020 that is 40 percent white. Fifteen percent of the class are Latino; 13 percent are African American; 28 percent are Asian/Asian American, and 3 percent are Native American. This is a massive transformation in the composition of the school, compared to a generation ago. It marks ways in which elite schools may be some of the most diverse in the country. Racial, ethnic, and religious exclusion, once defining features of elite schools, are now aggressively rejected by these institutions. Indeed, there is clearly an intentional commitment to diversity that cannot be imagined away. The symbolic boundaries may have shifted, and if you ask the leaders of these institutions, they would suggest that boundaries in general are being dismantled.

At the same time, these changes haven't been associated with increases in equality. Work on diversity within such schools has indicated mixed results at best (Berrey 2015; Jack 2016). More broadly, elites have captured a greater share of the national income and wealth. The study of elite schools reveals something new about our standard understanding wherein exclusion drives inequality and inclusion generates opportunity. The picture is far more complicated, where certain dynamics of inclusion may well be coupled with increases in resource seizure.

Such an insight may already rest within the deeper reaches of our knowledge. Most sociologists, for example, would recognize both the potential emancipatory power of "free" markets, but also express concerns about how such open institutions can augment inequalities. Yet in general, our models of inequality rest on concepts like group exclusion. The literature on elite schooling throws critical light upon this, outlining how we can have things like democratic inequality or, better, how openness does not necessarily close the gap between people within a society.

As we reflect upon such open inequality, we also begin to see our second basic insight, gleaned from Ermakoff: Studies of elite schools help us outline new classes of objects. Through the study of elite spaces, we begin to see different patterns of inequality. For example, whereas little has changed within patterns of racial segregation in much of society, within elite schools racial diversity has blossomed (Espenshade and Radford 2009). Where most of the US economy has been stagnant, the economy of elite schools is one of massive growth. If the cost of a Harvard education tracked to inflation since 1970, tuition would cost about fifteen thousand dollars a year. Instead it currently costs around forty-five thousand (this does not include room, board, and fees, which brings the total cost to well over sixty thousand). This doesn't mean, though, that Harvard is more expensive for poorer students, as grants have made up for this massive rise in tuition. The openness we observe in elite schools is not mirrored across society; the economic growth they have enjoyed has not been shared; the mobility of new groups into schools does not represent a broader mobility of Americans. And so what we uncover when looking at elites, and in particular at elite schools, is something relatively unknown and obscured before: countercyclical economic and educational processes.

A "New" Object: The Countercyclical Character of the Elite

The broad story of inequality in America is that it declined in the postwar period, and then increased in the 1970s. Today, inequality is what it was at the tail end of the Gilded Age—which is to say that America is a very inequitable nation in comparison to other industrialized countries and to its recent past. One of the more specific takeaways from the account provided by economists Piketty and Saez is that the engine of inequality has been the rich rather than the poor or middle classes (2003). We cannot explain a variable by a constant. And while the level of inequality in America has varied considerably over time, the relative position of the poor and middle classes has remained roughly the same since the 1960s. The fate of the rich, however, has waxed and waned; this variation is what has driven inequality over the last fifty years. While both the rich and poor experience the same national levels of inequality, they experience it quite differently. Disaggregating the general trend reveals important patterns.

We can start to do this by drawing upon the work of economists Edlund and Kopczuk (2009, see also Kopczuk and Saez 2004; Kopczuk et al. 2010). Using estate tax return data, these look at dynastic wealth by focusing on the very wealthy in the America (0.01 percent). They find that wealth mobility into the elite *declined* from the 1940s through the early 1970s, only to increase in the subsequent period. Which is to say that elites have been the key drivers of inequality, but that simultaneously there has been *more mobility* into the elite in recent years, under high inequality regimes. By contrast, in the recent past (1960s), inequality was lower, but so too was mobility into the elite relatively low.

This brings us to a crucial point: Elites in America have recently experienced "countercyclical" dynamics. When most Americans experienced mobility, elites experienced stagnation; while most Americans have been locked in place, elites have experienced considerable mobility (Khan 2015).[1] The language we use when talking about economics often deploys the imagery of water: rising tides lift all boats, or resources trickle down. Yet this image of economic processes moving over terrain rather seamlessly, such that what happens in one area spills over into the next, may well be inaccurate. The terrain between the rich and the rest is fractured; the economic worlds might be more separate than connected.

We can ask ourselves: What is the experience of the world from 1945 until the 1970s for two groups—average Americans and very, very wealthy Americans? If you were an average American in the immediate postwar period, you would experience some of the lowest levels of inequality our nation has ever seen. As inequality is a national measure, by definition you would share this experience with all Americans. But in other respects you would be rather different from elites. You would enjoy substantial mobility over your lifetime, and be less hindered or advantaged by your parents' wages than your parents were by theirs. Hard-fought battles over racial and gender oppression also mean that the relative position of nonwhites and women began to advance. There would be variability among your group—with some members, particularly women and nonwhites, advancing more quickly than others, in no small part because they were so relatively disadvantaged that they had more space within which to be mobile. Still, in general, for the average American, the experience was one of mobility both inter- and intragenerationally. We often read our American experience through this moment: one in which rights were fought over and won, opportunity was relatively available, and inequalities were comparatively low.

But if we were to look within, say, the very rich, we would find something different. Elite wages were comparatively stagnant, and so too was the likelihood of new men joining the elite; dynastic wealth was the most dominant in this moment in the twentieth century. This means that movement in (and out of) the elite was comparatively rare.

The recent story of the last three decades is very different, yet the general point remains the same. The average American has experienced comparative wage stagnation and relatively stagnant mobility. However, if we were to look in the elite, we would observe something quite different. The likelihood of being in the top .01 percent is not so strongly related to having parents that were within that group as it was in the 1960s. There are more "new rich" today than in the immediate past. And the wage gains that we observe within the top .01 percent are so dramatic as to be startling to most scholars and social commentators.

My argument here is not that economic resources are finite or zero-sum, and that when one group does well other groups are thus necessarily constrained (which is to say that there are no rising tides). These trends extend over too short a time period, and are too conditional on how you define the beginnings and ends of time periods, to make such a grand argument. But there is an important implication nonetheless: there is no "economy" in the sense of a unified experience of market conditions. Instead, just as there are multiple different economies in different geographic spaces within national markets, or differences across subsectors of the economy (say, finance versus manufacturing), so too are there economies across different parts of the income distribution. This is certainly true across race and gender, where intersectional experiences create different dynamics. Yet we have been less attentive to how it is also true between class factions.

My own realization of such dynamics does not only emerge from my having read the economics literature on this subject. The story I have just laid out may be supported by the economics literature, but it is not one that is told by economists. Instead, we see it most clearly in comparing the nonelite and elite schooling. We can observe these countercyclical processes not simply on the economic level for individuals, but on the institutional level as well.

In her book *Unequal City*, Carla Shedd outlines how the practices of prisons have made their way into poor schools (2015). She shows students walking through metal detectors, being stopped and frisked in hallways, and subject to constant surveillance; behavioral issues are more often addressed by the police than by school administrators. The rise of what we might think of as the "incarceral school" generates distrust of authority and feelings of powerlessness. Shedd's work is consistent with many school ethnographies of middle-class and poor schools, which focus on the imposition of rules upon students, the challenges of managing authority, and systems of punishment. Further, such work notes the recent rise of such practices. Willis' classic *Learning to Labour* remains a powerful account of the relationship between class, culture, and schooling (1977). Yet if we compare it to Shedd's work, or to that of Bowen Paulle (2013), who explored high-poverty schools in New York and Amsterdam, we see a fairly radical transformation. Whereas Willis's "lads" were met with school disapproval at their acts of resistance, Shedd's young men and women are met by police officers and imprisoned.

We might compare this with the work of other scholars, such as my own work on elite schooling (2011), or that of Ruben Gaztambide-Fernandez (2009) on similar institutions. We both explored the lives of elite boarding schools at the same time Shedd was doing her research. Yet in our work there is almost no discussion of punishment. Instead of the imposition of surveillance, we note the rise of autonomy. We outline the work that schools do to encourage thinking outside rules to challenge received wisdom. Rather than distrust of institutions, students are taught to believe in the fundamental justness of the system; rather than the feeling of powerlessness, elite students are taught to feel the privilege of their own empowerment.

Further, while national school curricula move toward standardization and regulation, elite schools tout unique, tailored programming. While most schools are cutting back on arts education and funding for other kinds of programs, elite schools are building expertise in such areas to make their students distinct from the growing crowd of applications.

Just as the economic conditions are countercyclical, so too are the structure of elite schools. Whereas earlier scholarship on elite schools found that such institutions were "total"—regulating nearly every aspect of the lives of their members (Cookson and Persell 1985), recent work has suggested a considerable move away from such regulation. Whereas elite curricula were once highly structured around a set of texts and subjects that mirrored a narrowly defined elite culture and knowledge, today topics have proliferated to mirror a kind of omnivorous elite. Whereas most schools have remained stubbornly segregated, elite schools have become massively more diverse, racially. While most schools see their federal and state support dwindling, elite schools continue to benefit disproportionately from federal research dollars, growing endowments, tax exemptions for both donations and purchases, and the benefits of higher and higher tuition.

When we think of the economy or schooling as a singular system, we don't see such dynamics. It's only in parsing out economic elites and elite schools as a distinct ecosystem that we begin to see new processes and unique objects. In the final section of this chapter, I push this observation further. I show how studies of elite schooling help magnify relational patterns that are less visible in more mundane contexts.

The Political and Economic Impact of Elite Schooling

Americans are comparatively segregated in terms of where we live, not just racially but also economically. While we often think of such segregation relative to the dynamics of concentrated poverty and disadvantage (Edin and Shaefer 2015; Sampson et al. 1999; Sharkey 2013), we must also think about the experiences of concentrated advantage and wealth.

While the global character of the elite mobility is likely massively overestimated (Young et al. 2016), understanding the global worldview of elites provides us with a richer picture of how the concentration of advantage yields unique experiences and perspectives. Perhaps the best look at these processes comes from the journalist Chrystia Freeland (2012), whose access to elites provides the reader an acute view of a world that is often more imagined than observed. Traveling with elites from penthouses to boardrooms to the streets of Davos, Switzerland, Freeland combines ethnographic skill with journalistic prose in conveying how it is that they understand and live in the world. In her work, Freeland argues that the plutocratic elite think of neighborhoods not relative to physical proximity or national bounds; they think of them globally, in terms of those they feel closest to in spirit rather than geography. In this sense, the Upper East Side may be closer to Tokyo's Ginza district than it is Spanish Harlem. While elites may be proximally close to nonelites, their tendency to occupy different worlds means that encounters between the two groups are few and relatively unsustained. This is likely a cognitive perspective more than a lived experience, yet its consequences are significant.

If we are to follow our earlier story, one of the things we see is a radical change in the social conditions of the elite.[2] One of those aspects is their "opening"—by which I mean that there is more mobility into the group than before. But such an experience has been mirrored by other declines in what we might think of as social closure. We cannot underestimate these radical changes to society; access to opportunities from which the majority of the population (women, minorities) were once excluded is a major social transformation. This opening has not meant anything close to equality. But the impact of these changes on the ways in which people understand their worlds is profound.

Elite institutions are those that seem to have most forcefully embraced the language of openness. In the United States, the Ivy League has demonstrated a tremendous commitment to affirmative action; if you visit the website of any major corporation, all will have statements of their "diversity initiatives." Scholars like Ellen Berrey (2015) and Lauren Rivera (2015) have given us strong empirical evidence to be highly skeptical of such rhetoric. Yet, even in light of the potentially hollow character of the diversity within schools and organizations, the rhetoric around such a feature is deeply expressed.

Still, elites have been relatively blind to problems of increased inequality (Jencks 2002), and hostile to programs that might help alleviate it (Page et al. 2013). It has been the growth of wages of those at the top that has resulted in the rise of inequality in most of the Western world (Atkinson and Piketty 2007, 2010). The democratic embrace among the elite has been accompanied by a similar rise in their fortunes. Again, this is a rather curious phenomenon. How can it be that the rich have enjoyed increasing fortunes, while dismantling some of the most profound limits (gender, racial) on access to their most important institutions: schools?

The answer is twofold. First, there is no single elite. Instead, there are elites. Those with control over elite educational institutions are many—from wealthy trustees to administrators who often, earlier in their careers, were professors, faculty, or students themselves. Over the last fifty years, educational elites, particularly intellectuals, have insisted that their institutions participate in a more diverse social project. This, perhaps more than other dynamics, has driven the embrace of diversity (though we should not forget that corporations have similar, if weaker, commitments).

The second explanation lies within the broader cultural transformation that has undergirded this first explanation. There are many explanations to the rise of inequality, from the declines in unionization (Western and Rosenfeld 2011) and the financialization of the economy (Tomaskovic-Devey and Lin 2011) to the increased capacity for managers to leapfrog one another (DiPrete et al. 2010; but see also Gabaix and Landier 2009). Underplayed in this literature, and at the core of my interest, is the cultural rhetoric that has facilitated these processes. I outline such rhetoric through an account of my own work. The core of this rhetoric is the idea of the rise of the talented, deserving, meritorious individual. And the increasing mobility among the elite, as well as the diversity of elite institutions, supports such a cultural framework. Looking, then, at studies of elite schools, we can see the emergence of new cultural frameworks for elites' self-understandings. And this helps reveal more general relational patterns within society.

In my earlier work (Khan 2011), I argued that the culturally important shift in the elite identity has been from being a "class" to being a collection of individuals—the best and the brightest (see also Gaztambide-Fernandez 2009). Rather than identifying themselves as a group constituted through institutions and organizations (families, schools, clubs, a shared cultural and historical legacy, etc.), today's elites consider themselves as having become elite because of their individual talents. What "groups" elites is the fact that they have worked hard and gotten ahead; they are the cream that has risen to the top. In embracing this individual work rather than class narrative, elites draw upon and support the language of meritocracy (Lemann 2000; Young 1958). Yet this language of meritocracy has its own history; the concept of merit is socially defined, not objectively constituted.

The rise of diversity and equal opportunity has played a role in the changing conceptualizations of merit. During the collectivist movements of the 1960s, groups gathered together—blacks, women, gays, and immigrants—to argue that the properties that grouped them and were then used to explain or justify their disadvantage should not matter. It should be human capital that matters; we should all have opportunities based on our capacities, not on characteristics ascribed to us. Yet the continued embrace of this framework may well be strongest outside these groups, within institutions initially designed to keep such "diverse" people out. I developed this idea in the context of an ethnography of St. Paul's School—one of the most elite boarding schools in the nation, and my alma mater.

My research aim was to better understand a place that vigorously embraces the importance of being an "open" or representative institution in a context where inequality was increasing, and, as Espenshade and Radford have shown, where schools refused to take into account the disadvantages of poverty when making their admission decisions (2009). I found students at St. Paul's School to be very forthcoming and almost universally consistent about how they made sense of their success: through their own toil. Framing achievements as the result of hard work—whether consciously or not—

works against a common suspicion of entitlement and the nagging feeling that the rich succeed just because of who they are. St. Paul's students sought to replace the entitlement frame with one based on merit. Ascension was a goal that came through work, not a deserved acquisition that came from time spent at an institution, or by inheritance.

The students are not completely naive in building such a narrative. They know that not everyone who works hard gets ahead. They see many at their school who suffer this fate. These people are the staff—the men and women who make the school function day in and day out. Not surprisingly, students speak fondly of staff members. They are the caretakers and cheerleaders for students while parents are away. Gathering all of the interview responses together, we learn that the students explain the stagnation of the staff by suggesting that they are unlucky, have different priorities, or—most commonly—are casualties of an unjust era that we have since overcome. Throughout these accounts, students maintain a belief in meritocracy.

Students also know that being talented and hardworking may not make them the best at everything. In fact, they consistently bring up other students who are better than they are. Students told stories about a violinist on campus who might soon have a premiere at Carnegie Hall, a mathematician who would win one of the greatest prizes in that discipline (the Fields Medal), an artist who would sell paintings for millions, and a squash player who would soon take home a gold medal in the junior Olympics. There is, no doubt, a certain teenage mentality to this; students assume that the school is the whole world. But it was not simply that the students thought of themselves as having a potential, and that the world was theirs to contribute to; they also recognized that certain people had extraordinary talents and skills that far exceeded their own. At St. Paul's School, the students believed they were surrounded by such talents; as a result, that which was extraordinary became a part of their ordinary reality. Their school was a collection of some of the most talented and hardworking kids in the world.

This new world held promise and required more work; students simultaneously expressed a commitment to social justice and a narrative of just how far the world had come. The lessons from their accounts were of past injustices, present opportunities, and the necessity of work, discipline, and talent to make it. This did not mean the world was an equal place; some people were better than others, and their talents were important to recognize. The view was that inequalities were increasingly acquired by the action of individuals and decreasingly ascribed by class, race, or gender. There certainly still were privileges and unjust disadvantages. But these were rapidly being stamped out, and were less prevalent than thay had been a generation earlier.

The elite have vigorously adopted the stance of an open meritorious society. They look more diverse, including many of those they formerly excluded. And while they know that their individual traits, capacities, skills, talents and qualities are cultivated, they suggest that this cultivation is done through hard work, and that access is granted through capacity rather than birthright.

Elite culture today, then, is one of "individual self-cultivation." This cultural framework is not simply a delusional presentation of self or a hegemonic attempt to blind the masses, but instead has an experiential basis. Elites can maintain such a rhetoric in the face of overwhelming evidence against its general reality partly because they live in segregated spaces of concentrated advantage. Such spaces are radically different from those that most Americans occupy.

Sending their children off to colleges that are "majority minority," it's hard for elite parents to imagine a world of exclusion. Like most of us, elites suffer from availability bias—making erroneous judgments on the basis of biased information. Young people get into elite schools by "outcompeting" their local, often demographically very similar peers. They then enter elite institutions that look radically different from their homogeneous home environments. It may be inaccurate for them to think that they're part of a great project toward the building of equality, but it is not terribly naive, given their experience.

The narrative of openness and talent may help elites explain themselves to themselves, but as we have seen from our discussion of overall patterns of mobility and equality, it obscures the broader American experience. The result might not be pernicious, but the consequences are important. Society has recessed in the minds of the elite; if anything, it is a producer of social problems. What society did was create the biases of old institutions based in categorization—racism, sexism, and exclusion. The resulting view is one in which society must be as benign as possible, sitting in the background as we play out our lives in a flat world. And the result of such a stance is a new efficiency: the market.

Such a view suggests that social problems are the result of the times in which we think in terms of collectivities. With such barriers removed, market equality can take over. We live the results of this triumph today, and I would argue that it has been a world with less equality and mobility for the average American and a more empowered elite.

Conclusion

Meritocracy is a social arrangement like any other: it is a loose set of rules that can be adapted in order to obscure advantages, all while justifying them on the basis of shared values. Markets allow elites to limit investments in all by undermining public goods and shared, socialized resource allocations. This allows them to increase their own advantage by deploying their economic spoils in markets; they receive returns to these investments, while those without resources to invest are left behind. As Miles Corak has shown in his work (2013), those societies with higher returns to education tend to be less mobile. This is an associational finding, but it might be explained by high-inequality regimes wherein those with resource surpluses purchase additional education, thereby solidifying advantages for their offspring.

In suggesting that it is their work and not their wealth, and that it is their talents and not their lineage, elites do two things. First, they draw on a generally available cultural architecture to explain their own experiences, and overgeneralize from this. Elite schools have played a critical role in this cultural production. To look at the process of such schooling, from preparation and application, to being in residence and its consequences, we see the constant reification of individual self-cultivation. Such a cultural architecture is, of course, a rhetoric and not an explanation. Most elites have not achieved from nothing; only a few have done so, whereas most have achieved an enormous amount from the position of already considerable advantage. Yet the cultural architecture supported by elite schooling helps obscure this fact. Second, elites have applied the cultural view of *their* world to *the* world. From their biased available information, they have generalized to institutions and experiences not like their own.

As scholars, we might learn from this. As this chapter has argued, it may well be better to treat exceptional cases as exceptional, and to point to the advantages of such cases rather than couch them in a veneer of representativeness. Elite schools in particular are nonrepresentative; this does not make them unimportant. Indeed, the very fact that they do not represent a general trend may be what makes them the most interesting and important schools to understand.

The aim of this chapter was to show the reader what we can learn from looking at the exceptional case of elite schooling. Drawing upon the work of Ivan Ermakoff, it outlined three ways in which we can take advantage of the exception. First, exceptional cases reveal the limits of our standard classifications. Second, they outline new classes of objects. And third, they magnify relational patterns that are less visible in more mundane contexts.

The literature on elite schooling can and should remain a series of case studies of the exceptional. Through them we can better see the cultural dynamics and logics underlying a group that is driving our current patterns of inequality. I have interwoven the story of elite schools with the economics literature to help demonstrate the broad implications of such localized observations. Such implications do not mean that they apply to all classes of objects. Indeed, part of the point has been to show how different elite schools are from the rest, and how even though these are a tiny range of phenomena, they matter for revealing things far beyond what they narrowly represent.

During a conversation about generalizability of cases, a colleague once remarked to me, "If I showed you a pig that could converse in English, would you need to see a second one before you thought it was important?" Elite schools are hardly as remarkable as talking pigs. But their rarity may well be what makes them important. They are a class of objects that are knowable to scholars. And such knowledge tells us much about our social world that we are unable to see clearly in most other contexts.

Notes

1. The next few paragraphs borrow slightly from this paper.
2. In the following paragraphs I draw upon earlier published works, most deeply Khan 2011, 2012b; and Khan and Jerolmack 2013.

References

Atkinson, A. B., and T. Piketty. 2007. *TopIncomes over the 20th Century*. Oxford: Oxford University Press.

———. 2010. *Top Incomes in Global Perspective*. Oxford: Oxford University Press.

Berrey, Ellen. 2015. *The Enigma of Diversity: The Language of Race and the Limits of Racial Justice*. Chicago: University of Chicago Press.

Blumer, Herbert. 1986. *Symbolic Interactionism: Perspective and Method*. Chicago: University of Chicago Press.

Cookson, Peter W., Jr., and Caroline Hodges Persell. 1985. *Preparing for Power: America's Elite Boarding Schools*. New York: Basic Books.

Corak, Miles. 2013. "Income Inequality, Equality of Opportunity, and Intergenerational Mobility." *Journal of Economic Perspectives* 27, no. 3: 79–102.

Desmond, Matthew. 2015. "Severe Deprivation in America: An Introduction." *Russell Sage Foundation Journal of the Social Sciences* 1, no. 1: 1–158.

DiPrete, T., G. Eirich, and M. Pittinsky. 2010. "Compensation Benchmarking, Leapfrogs, and the Surge in Executive Pay." *American Journal of Sociology* 115, no. 6: 1671–1712.

Edin, Kathryn, and H. Luke Shaefer. *$2 a Day: Living on Nothing in America*. Boston: Houghton-Mifflin Harcourt.

Edlund, Lena, and Wojciech Kopczuk. 2007. "Women, Wealth, and Mobility." *American Economic Review* 99, no. 1: 146–178.

Ermakoff, Ivan. 2014. "Exceptional Cases: Epistemic Contributions and Normative Expectations." *European Journal of Sociology* 55, no. 2: 223–243.

Espenshade, T., and A. Radford. 2009. *No Longer Separate, Not Yet Equal.* Princeton, NJ: Princeton University Press.

Freeland, Chrystia. 2012. *Plutocrats: The New Golden Age.* Doubleday Canada.

Gabaix, X., and A. Landier. 2009. "Why Has CEO Pay Increased So Much?" *Quarterly Journal of Economics* 123, no. 1: 49–100.

Gaztambide-Fernández, Ruben. 2009a. *The Best of the Best: Becoming an Elite at an American Boarding School.* Cambridge, MA: Harvard University Press.

———. 2009b. "What Is an Elite Boarding School?" *Review of Educational Research* 79, no. 3: 1090–1128.

Jack, Anthony Abraham. 2016. "(No) Harm in Asking Class, Acquired Cultural Capital, and Academic Engagement at an Elite University." *Sociology of Education* 89, no. 1: 1–19.

Jencks, Christopher. 2002. "Does Inequality Matter?" *Daedalus* 131, no. 1: 49–65.

Karabel. J. 2005. *The Chosen: The Hidden History of Admission and Exclusion at Harvard, Yale, and Princeton.* Boston: Houghton Mifflin.

Khan, Shamus. 2011. *Privilege: The Making of an Adolescent Elite at St. Paul's School.* Princeton, NJ: Princeton University Press.

———. 2012a. "The Sociology of Elites." *Annual Review of Sociology* 38: 361–377.

———. 2012b. "Elite Identities," *Identities* 19, no. 4: 477–484.

———. 2015. "The Counter-Cyclical Character of the Elite." *Research in the Sociology of Organizations* 38.

Khan, Shamus, and Colin Jerolmack. 2013. "Saying Meritocracy and Doing Privilege." *Sociological Quarterly* 54:8–18.

Kopczuk, Wojciech, and Emmanuel Saez. 2004. "Top Wealth Shares in the United States, 1916–2000: Evidence from Estate Tax Returns." *National Tax Journal* 57 (Part 2): 445–487.

Kopczuk, Wojciech, Emmanuel Saez, and Jae Song. 2010. "Earnings Inequality and Mobility in the United States: Evidence from Social Security Data since 1937." *Quarterly Journal of Economics* 125, no. 1: 91–128.

Lamont, Michèle. 1992. *Money, Morals, and Manners: The Culture of the French and the American Upper-Middle Class.* Chicago: University of Chicago Press.

Lamont, Michèle, and Virág Molnár. 2002. "The Study of Boundaries in the Social Sciences." *Annual Review of Sociology* (2002): 167–195.

Lemann, N., 2000, *The Big Test: The Secret History of the American Meritocracy.* Macmillan.

Page, Benjamin I., Larry M. Bartels, and Jason Seawright. 2013. "Democracy and the Policy Preferences of Wealthy Americans." *Perspectives on Politics* 11, no. 1: 51–73.

Paulle, Bowen. 2013. *Toxic Schools: High-Poverty Education in New York and Amsterdam.* Chicago: University of Chicago Press.

Piketty, Thomas. 2014. *Capital in the Twenty-First Century.* Trans. Arthur Goldhammer. Cambridge, MA: Harvard University Press.

Piketty, Thomas, and Emmanuel Saez. 2003. "Income Inequality in the United States, 1913–1998." *Quarterly Journal of Economics* 118: 1–39.

———. 2006. "The Evolution of Top Incomes: A Historical and International Perspective." *American Economic Review* 96, no. 2: 200–205.

Rivera, Lauren A. 2015. *Pedigree: How Elite Students Get Elite Jobs.* Princeton, NJ: Princeton University Press.

Sampson, Robert J., Jeffrey D. Morenoff, and Felton Earls. 1999. "Beyond Social Capital: Spatial Dynamics of Collective Efficacy for Children." *American Sociological Review* (1999): 633–660.

Sharkey, Patrick. 2013. *Stuck in Place: Urban Neighborhoods and the End of Progress toward Racial Equality*. Chicago: University of Chicago Press.

Shedd, Carla. 2015. *Unequal City: Race, Schools, and Perceptions of Injustice*. New York: Russell Sage Foundation.

Tomaskovic-Devey, Donald, and Ken-Hou Lin. 2011. "Economic Rents and the Financialization of the US Economy." *American Sociological Review* 76:538–559.

Western, Bruce, and Rosenfeld, Jake. 2011. "Unions, Norms, and the Rise in American Earnings Inequality." *American Sociological Review* 76:513–537.

Willis, Paul E. 1977. *Learning to Labor: How Working Class Kids Get Working Class Jobs*. Columbia University Press.

Young, Cristobal, Charles Varner, Ithai Lurie, and Richard Prisinzano. Forthcoming. "Millionaire Migration and the Taxation of the Elite: Evidence from Administrative Data." *American Sociological Review*.

Young, Michael Dunlop. 1958. *The Rise of the Meritocracy*. Transaction Publishers.

SEVEN

What's Up with Assessment?

RICHARD ARUM AND AMANDA COOK[1]

Sociologists of education have a special relationship with assessment. While educational assessment has long been used by educators, schools, firms and governments to allocate rewards and opportunities, in recent decades sociologists have been at the forefront of social science efforts to apply measures developed by psychometricians to better understand and improve schooling. At the same time, as sociologists, we cannot help but be deeply aware of the historic moment that exists with respect to the social and cultural anxieties associated with standardized testing instruments. This chapter reflects on the relationship between educational assessment and sociology, as well as educational assessment and society.

One way to understand our current relationship with assessment is to appreciate the extent to which educational assessment is a technology—with its scannable scoring sheets, adaptive testing algorithms, percentile rankings, student subscore reports, value-added statistical estimates of learning, and analysis of integrated longitudinal data. Given the extent to which assessment is a technology, one finds that individuals are quick to project onto it either unrealistic aspirations for technical salvation or unfounded apprehensions about societal change.[2] Reformers in the progressive administrative tradition, drawing on a powerful technocratic logic, hold out hope that improved assessment will lead to more efficient school management and enhanced responsiveness to identifiable, differentiated student pedagogical needs.[3] Others, aligned with a pedagogical progressive tradition, appear to assign many of our educational ills to the over-use of assessment.[4] Like other technologies, assessment is able to conjure up ideologically and culturally our deepest hopes and fears.

In this chapter we hope to move beyond these stark and divergent views of assessment to address how the features and uses of assessment have changed over the past several decades and how, sociologically, we can understand the uses of and various actors' interest in assessment. We discuss how the assessment of student learning in K–12 and higher education has grown and evolved over the past century. In addition, we discuss how standardized assessment has become a prominent feature of the sociology of education, especially since the 1970s, as longitudinal data sets that include student performance measures have proliferated.

We argue throughout this chapter that assessment is not only a technological phenomenon, but also quite clearly a political one. That is to say, changes in the role of assessment in society are the result of a complex interplay between technological and political developments. To some extent, the technology of assessment (e.g., the ease with which an assessment can be administered, the ability to track student progress longitudinally, and assessments' predictive power) shapes political actors' understandings of how schools, educators, and students can—and should—be managed, monitored, and evaluated. To an equal extent, prevailing understandings of and philosophies about education and society, which are fundamentally political in nature, have a major impact on the kinds of assessments that are developed and how those assessments are used.

Historical Background

Over the past century, standardized assessments, with the support of private foundations, higher education associations, school systems, state governments, and the federal government, have become an increasingly important part of schooling in the United States. During the first half of the twentieth century, standardized assessments, bolstered by widespread enthusiasm for science and efficiency, were used to sort people into different ability groups, make admissions decisions at the college and graduate level, and certify levels of mastery. Starting in the 1960s and 1970s, however, the federal government began to use assessment data as a way to track national educational progress and inform policy decisions. Soon thereafter, states began to use it not only to track student outcomes, but also to hold schools and educators accountable for their performance. This trend toward test-based accountability attained national visibility with the passage of No Child Left Behind (NCLB) in 2002.

What follows is a brief summary of some of the key moments and trends in the history of standardized assessment in the United States.[5] This summary serves as an empirical backdrop for the next section, which offers a sociological analysis of the political and organizational factors that have shaped the role of assessment in primary, secondary, and postsecondary education.

Sorting, Selecting, and Certifying: Early K–12 Testing and the Rise of Admissions and Certification Tests

The history of standardized assessment in the United States reaches as far back as the mid-nineteenth century, when school administrators, legislators, and other authorities first began to turn to formal large-scale written testing as a way to sort children into ability groups and monitor school performance.[6] The demand for these tests "grew from a range of social and economic forces that produced similar calls for efficiency and compartmentalization in the workplace" and society at large.[7] Among the forces driving the perceived need for increased efficiency in schools were an increase in enrollments due to the universalization of education, dramatic population growth driven largely by immigration, and concomitant concerns that schools were struggling to cope with the challenge of educating students of widely varying skill levels. Standardized testing in K–12 helped educators handle larger populations of students more efficiently "without violating principles of fairness and equal access."[8]

Early efforts to improve the efficiency and effectiveness of schools used standardized measures of student achievement that were designed to reflect the curriculum of schools. According to a report from the US Congress Office of Technology Assessment, "It was believed that the kind of information provided by the standardized achievement tests could light the way to effective reform."[9] However, many school reformers eventually came to believe that poor student achievement was due not only to school-related deficiencies, but also to low levels of innate intelligence. If schools could sort students into different classrooms on the basis of innate intelligence, it was believed, they would be better equipped to deliver educational experiences that were tailored to students' needs, thus increasing the efficiency of the education system.

This idea paved the way for intelligence testing in schools. Instruments like the Stanford-Binet Intelligence Scale, published in 1916 by Stanford psychologist Louis Terman, soon became a popular means by which primary and secondary schools could sort students into ability groups. According to data collected by the US government, "by 1925, around 90 percent of elementary schools and 65 percent of urban high schools grouped students by ability, many on the basis of intelligence tests."[10] To this day, intelligence tests like the Stanford-Binet are adopted as scientific and efficient tools, and continue to be used to sort primary and secondary school students into special education and gifted and talented programs.

Itself an adaptation of a test developed by French psychologist Alfred Binet in 1906, the Stanford-Binet Intelligence Scale gave rise to a long and consequential line of other aptitude tests, including the Scholastic Aptitude Test, now known as the SAT. The SAT was initially used in the 1930s, with support from the Carnegie Foundation, as a screening device for merit-based college scholarship programs.[11] In the early 1940s, it made the leap from scholarship screener to general admissions test, replacing the College Boards, a battery of essay-based exams, as colleges and universities' admissions exam of choice.[12]

Soon, variations on the SAT were developed for graduate school admissions. The GRE, which initially consisted of the SAT plus a battery of achievement tests, was created in 1944.[13] In 1948, the College Board designed and administered the first iteration of the Law School Admissions Test (LSAT).[14] The first half of the century also gave rise to a large number of standardized certification tests, including the US Medical Licensing Examination (1916), the Uniform Certified Public Accountants exam (1917), and the GED (1942).[15]

Thus, in just a few decades, an elaborate suite of standardized assessments, many of which shared a common lineage, were developed and deployed to sort, select, and certify children and aspiring adults in the United States. Debates about the nature of intelligence and whether it was possible to assess aptitude (i.e., natural talent) separately from achievement (i.e., learning) were common, but the basic idea behind the tests—that it was possible and desirable to use examination reports to sort students into different educational tracks, make admissions decisions, and certify competency scientifically and efficiently—was generally uncontroversial.

The Rise of Test-Based Accountability

State-level test-based accountability policies first emerged in the late 1960s and 1970s, during a period of economic and political uncertainty that exacerbated the nation's longstanding concerns about the quality of primary and secondary education. In response to these concerns, several states embarked on efforts to raise their educational standards and track student learning outcomes using what were known as minimum competency exams (MCEs). By the 1980s, many states had gone a step further by requiring high school students to pass an MCE in order to graduate.[16] Exit exams, as they came to be known, spread across the country over the next two decades. According to Grodsky et al. (2008), "The number of states with high school exit exams rose gradually from zero for the class of 1978 to 22 for the class of 2006."[17]

In 1983, President Ronald Reagan's Commission on Excellence in Education published *A Nation at Risk: The Imperative for Educational Reform*, which provided powerful momentum to the country's nascent test-based accountability movement. Drawing on historical and comparative test score data, as well as a range of other data, the report argued that the quality of primary, secondary, and postsecondary education in the United States had declined since the early 1960s, and that US academic achievement was falling behind that of other industrialized nations. The report issued a set of recommendations for educational reform, including recommendations about educational standards and the use of standardized tests.[18]

In the years that followed the publication of *A Nation at Risk*, large numbers of states engaged in standards-based curriculum reform and administered standardized assessments to track schools' progress. Most of these assessments were low-stakes, but some, like high school exit exams, were high-stakes. State and federal efforts to design and implement standards-based reform policies proliferated throughout the 1980s and 1990s, laying much of the groundwork for the passage of NCLB, the largest test-based accountability policy in US history, in 2002. NCLB's unprecedented scale and scope sparked more than a decade of debate about the proper role of the federal government in educational policy, the proper role of testing in schools, and whether test-based accountability policies were actually able to improve outcomes. Later in this chapter, we offer a more in-depth analysis of the origins and impacts of NCLB, and we discuss why such a policy has yet to take hold in the postsecondary realm.

Race to the Top (RTT), a competitive federal grants program launched in 2009 with the support of President Barack Obama, built on NCLB in a number of important ways. One of the most visible aspects of the program was its requirement that participating states adopt common, as opposed to state-specific educational standards and assessments for K–12 education. The incentives put into place by RTT, combined with a generally pro-reform, pro-test-based accountability political climate, led more than forty states to adopt common educational standards (i.e., the Common Core State Standards, which were developed with private foundation funding). As of this writing, thirty of these states have also begun to implement assessments that were designed, with the help of federal RTT funding, to align with the Common Core State Standards. This trend toward national, as opposed to state-based, standards and assessments has not been without controversy.

Like NCLB, RTT has generated a significant amount of debate about the extent to which the federal government should influence states' educational policies, as well as debate about the speed with which educational reforms can be rolled out responsibly and effectively.

The Use of Assessments in Social Science

With Project TALENT in 1960 and the Equality of Educational Opportunity Study in 1964, the federal government began to sponsor large-scale efforts to collect and analyze standardized assessment data.[19] The largest and longest running effort of this kind has been the National Assessment of Educational Progress (NAEP). Launched in 1969 after several years of foundation-funded planning and development, the NAEP measures academic achievement among nationally representative samples of students in grades four, eight, and twelve. The program began by assessing math and verbal skills, but has since grown to include assessments of science, writing, the arts, civics, economics, geography, US history, and technology and engineering literacy. NAEP data have been used to track educational progress and inform national and state-level educational policy.[20]

In addition to the NAEP, several other large-scale national studies on education, many of which use standardized measures of academic achievement, and most of which were sponsored by the federal government, emerged in the 1970s. For example, the National Longitudinal Study of 1972, which included vocabulary, reading, and mathematics test score data, followed a group of twelfth graders as they made transitions to postsecondary institutions and the workforce. In subsequent decades, the number and complexity of these kinds of longitudinal studies has grown to include the following efforts (and start dates): the National Longitudinal Study of Youth (1979), High School and Beyond (1980), the National Educational Longitudinal Study (1988), the National Longitudinal Study of Adolescent to Adult Health (1994), the Early Childhood Longitudinal Studies (1998, 2010), the Educational Longitudinal Study (2002), the High School Longitudinal Study (2009), and more.

In the midst of all of this new data on education, computing technology and statistical analysis software were becoming more sophisticated and widely available. The first widely used statistical analysis software packages, including SAS and SPSS, were released in the 1960s and operated on mainframe computing systems. By the mid 1980s, these software packages, plus Stata, had been adapted for the emerging personal computer market, drastically increasing the ease with which statistical analyses could be per-

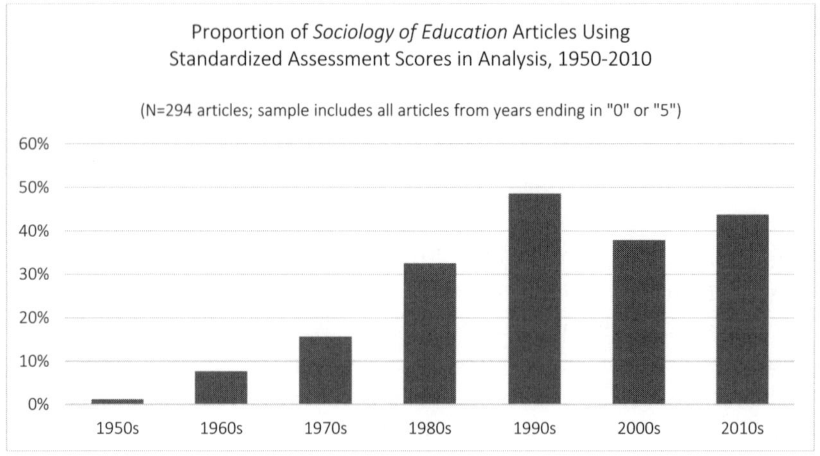

Figure 7.1.

formed.[21] As computer processing, storage, and data transfer capacities increased, so too did the ability of the education system and social scientists to perform complex analyses on large-scale, cross-sectional, and longitudinal educational data sets. These new data sets and improved data analysis software had several significant impacts on social science research on education, some of which are discussed elsewhere in this volume. One of these impacts was that social scientists began to use test score data in their research with increasing frequency. We illustrate this trajectory in figure 7.1, which shows the proportion of *Sociology of Education* articles from 1950 to 2010 that used test scores as part of their analytical framework.

Advances in the Technology of Assessment

In the second half of the twentieth century, advances in computing technology and data analysis software, along with the proliferation of federally subsidized data sets, changed the face of social science research on education. More recently, the technology of assessment itself (i.e., the means by which tests can be administered and the kinds of questions and tasks that are included on standardized assessments) has also undergone significant changes. Three major shifts—the advent of computer-based testing, a shift towards measuring more complex skills, and the rise of online education—have significant implications, not only for the future of assessment in education, but also for the future of social science research on education.

Computer-based testing, which first emerged in the 1980s and 1990s, has now become the primary means by which standardized assessments are administered. With computer-based testing, tests can be graded instantaneously and more complex types of questions, such as simulations, can be administered on a large-scale basis. Increasingly, computer-based tests use adaptive testing technology, which achieves greater precision in measurement by automatically adjusting the difficulty of test questions in response to test takers' performance.[22] Machine scoring of short written responses and longer essays, still in its early stages, is also being used with increasing frequency.[23]

Multiple-choice and true-false questions still make up the vast majority of standardized test items in the United States, but the underlying constructs that are being used to write these questions are evolving. Indeed, standardized tests like the AP are increasingly designed to measure test takers' analytical reasoning skills in addition to their mastery of content.[24] Likewise, the new Common Core–aligned assessments, SBAC and PARCC, also aim to have a particular focus on students' higher-order skills.[25] These changes are a reflection of broader changes in educational standards in the so-called Information Age, where skills like analytical reasoning and critical thinking are seen as increasingly important relative to the acquisition of content knowledge.

Finally, the rise of online education has presented new opportunities to assess student learning systematically, as essentially all aspects of students' experiences in online learning environments can be observed and analyzed. A leading example of work being done to assess student learning in online environments is Carnegie Mellon University and Stanford University's Open Learning Initiative (OLI). Founded in 2002 at Carnegie Mellon University, OLI builds online courses that use machine-learning technology to understand students' learning styles, strengths, and weaknesses and customize the lessons accordingly.[26] Other entities in the online education world are working on this as well. Nevertheless, the practice of using data from online learning environments to track progress and craft personalized learning experiences, often referred to as embedded assessment, is still in its infancy.

Together, these three major advances in the technology of assessment have in many ways paved the way for new and increasingly pervasive uses of educational assessment. In the next section we examine the use of standardized assessments in schools through the lens of organizational sociology, which allows us to see that assessment is not only a technological phenomenon, but also a political one.

Institutional Logics and the Rise of Assessment

Over time, the technological character of assessment has changed how students, teachers, and schools are measured, but political factors and normative organizational commitments are what have structured the adoption and implementation of assessments. In terms of political determinants of the use of assessments for accountability purposes, Richard Elmore has asserted that "the central fact of accountability systems as they presently exist is that they are political artifacts crafted out of relatively superficial and underspecified ideas to meet the demands of political action."[27] In the educational field, however, the adoption of assessment is not being driven solely by coercive institutional pressures, such as federal accountability mandates imposed by policy makers for reasons of political expediency. Rather, in addition to these coercive pressures for increased use of assessments, there are compelling normative and mimetic forces at play that are also driving adoption.

Systematic measurement of performance through the use of standardized assessments is an organizational practice that is very closely aligned with broader institutional logics associated with modernity. "Organizations are driven to incorporate the practices and procedures defined by prevailing rationalized concepts of organizational work and institutionalized in society," Meyer and Rowan have noted. "Technical procedures of production, accounting, personnel selection, or data processing become taken-for-granted means to accomplish organization ends. . . . Such institutionalized techniques establish an organization as appropriate, rational and modern."[28] Systematic assessment of students can be used to demonstrate to internal and external audiences the extent to which schools are committed to bureaucratic, rationalized, and efficient forms of organization. Performance of this type of ritual can enhance long-term institutional legitimacy, resource stability, and organizational survival; although these organizational practices in the short term can also undermine institutional legitimacy, as they subject the organization to outside scrutiny and inspection.

Standardized assessment of student learning also is closely aligned with what Wendy Espeland and Mitchell Stevens have termed *commensuration* (i.e., "the transformation of different quantities into a common metric") and *quantification*.[29] Espeland and Stevens have noted astutely that "quantification is a constitutive feature of modern science and social organization."[30] Given its alignment with larger societal commitments to rationality and objective measurement, it is unsurprising that the use of educational assessment is now widespread and has been growing cross-nationally. As a recent report noted, "Most OECD countries now see evaluation and assessment as playing a central strategic role, and are expanding their use."[31]

In the field of US education, this commitment to rationalization has long-standing roots. For example, reform efforts during the Progressive Era, led by a group of people who can be understood as "administrative progressive" reformers, were focused on replacing what they saw as inefficient school organization with professional management systems that abided by the principles of scientific management.[32] Efficiency in schools—and in business and society in general—was to be achieved through modern bureaucratic and rationalistic reforms. David Labaree has noted how this was to be accomplished through "restructuring the governance and organization of schooling in order to make it run more efficiently."[33] In addition to a wide array of financial accounting reforms, this administrative progressive approach rested heavily on implementing a differentiated curriculum (sorting students into ability groups and educational tracks) and increasing the use of assessments. Using this strategy, reformers hoped to match "differences in the [objectively measured] abilities of individual students with the different mental requirements of the vast array of occupational roles required by a complex industrial society."[34]

The growth of educational assessment thus has much broader and more diffuse roots than coercive mandates like NCLB. Nor is the rise of assessment a simple product of late-twentieth and early-twenty-first-century neoliberal pressures to increase scrutiny and provide improved accountability for public spending. More accurately, assessment's alignment with widespread and long-standing normative commitments to rationalization has allowed it, through both normative and mimetic forces, to assume an increasingly large role in US society. These broader commitments help explain why both Democratic and Republican administrations have pursued policies that have required more assessment. Even leaders of US teachers' unions, while opposing punitive test-based teacher evaluation systems, more often than not have otherwise supported standardized educational assessment.[35]

While the fate of particular components of accountability systems that rely on standardized educational assessment are uncertain and subject to ongoing political debate, make no mistake about it: technological developments and widespread normative commitments to rationalization will likely continue to drive the increased use of standardized educational assessments across the globe. In the following two sections, we illustrate this through an examination of the origins, features, and implementation of NCLB in K–12 education, and a discussion of the complex factors behind the use—or lack thereof—of standardized assessment in higher education.

K–12 Assessment

Looking closely at the historical context, the groundwork for No Child Left Behind (NCLB), a national test-based accountability policy, was in place long before its passage. Assessment technology had been refined and legitimized over the course of many decades and had become an integral part of US schooling, and the sense that US schools were underperforming had been percolating for decades.[36] According to policy analysts Frederick Hess and Chester Finn, in the years leading up to NCLB, Republicans and Democrats came to embrace "essentially the same analysis of what ailed U.S. K–12 education—and how to cure it."[37] Indeed, both President George H. W. Bush and President Bill Clinton encouraged states to "set explicit academic standards, deploy tests to determine whether and how well students and schools were meeting those standards, and create behaviorist 'accountability' mechanisms, whereby rewards would come to schools that succeeded, and interventions, embarrassment, and sanctions would befall those that failed."[38]

That there was bipartisan agreement about school problems and how to fix them is not all that surprising. The basic logic underlying both parties' analysis was the same one that had been driving school management for almost a century, ever since the advent of administrative progressivism: schools should be organized to deploy resources as efficiently as possible towards the goal of preparing the next generation for life and work in a complex, differentiated society. Using test scores to guide decision making, especially now that test data could be easily collected, stored, and analyzed, thanks to sophisticated computing technology, was from an organizational perspective a relatively inescapable imperative.

To be sure, there were many who voiced concerns that NCLB would do more harm than good. Worries abounded that an annual testing mandate would narrow the curriculum, take the joy out of teaching and learning, create incentives for cheating, and produce flawed and racially biased data.[39] In the end, the sense of urgency around needing to hold schools accountable for student learning proved considerably more compelling. Policymakers, with few exceptions, assumed that there was a problem; and to address that problem in an advanced, rationalized society, learning needed to be measured and tracked systematically.

In many ways, NCLB was similar to the national frameworks and state-based policies that preceded it. The policy's scale, scope, and ambition, however, were unprecedented. For this reason, NCLB put student learning, school performance, and assessment into the national spotlight like never before. NCLB not only had an impact on how people thought about schools in general and testing in particular, but also potentially affected pedagogical practices, the organization of schools, and student performance. NCLB, by putting test scores front and center, caused many to call the validity of such measurements into question. Increasingly, teachers, unions, and others began to argue that test scores were a fundamentally inadequate measure of the contributions teachers make to students' lives. Testing and test-based accountability, something that used to enjoy relatively widespread support, increasingly became a matter of complex and heated public debate.

In this political context, social scientists also were more explicitly critical about the biases, misuses and unintended consequences of assessment. For example, Joshua Aronson and Claude Steele demonstrated how stereotype threat biased test results, and the sociologist Jennifer Jennings found evidence of teachers teaching to the test, and of other unintended and undesirable school responses to assessment mandates.[40]

Higher Education Assessment

As discussed earlier on, higher education institutions incorporated standardized assessments into their admissions systems beginning in the early 1900s. Since then, tests like the SAT, ACT, GRE, LSAT, and MCAT have become a central, unavoidable feature of higher education. Standardized assessments for professional certification purposes have also become increasingly common. Notably absent or marginal in higher education, however, have been standardized assessments used to track students' academic progress.

How has higher education, by and large, avoided the same kind of assessment and test-based accountability policies that have been implemented in K–12? Perhaps the most compelling explanation is that colleges and universities serve multiple purposes, only one of which is to educate students. To be sure, primary and secondary schools also have multiple purposes—academic instruction, socialization, childcare, et cetera—but the primacy of academic instruction has been widely taken for granted. Take away the teaching and learning, and you no longer have a primary or secondary school. The organizational priorities of postsecondary institutions, by contrast, are considerably more diffuse. Teaching and learning are important, but so is research, and so is creating an elaborate space for social exploration and psychological development. In this complicated context, with so many different priorities and so many ways to measure success, it has been possible for colleges and universities to get by with proxy measures of learning such as grades, graduation rates, and, more recently, postcollegiate outcomes.

Another important reason why standardized assessments of academic progress have not become commonplace in higher education is that colleges and universities are fragmented into discipline-specific communities. In this context, there are no common standards for student learning. Because students are free to take courses from whichever departments they choose, students' paths through college are widely divergent. In light of this, colleges have had a difficult time coming to an agreement about what kinds of learning outcomes should be measured, not to mention coming to an agreement about whom should be held accountable for these outcomes within the institution.

Finally, the regulatory structure governing institutions of higher education in the United States has been weaker and more fragmented than the state and federal regulatory structure in K–12. Higher-education institutions receive their funding from a wide variety of sources, both public and private, which means that any single source of funding has only limited control over institutional practices.

Nevertheless, in recent years, efforts to articulate learning goals and measure students' academic progress have been on the rise. These efforts are propelled by concerns about the cost of college and the belief that colleges are not adequately preparing students for work and life after graduation. Publications like *A Nation at Risk* in 1983 and the *Spellings Report* in 2006, as well as comparative research by the Organisation of Economic Cooperation and Development, have given substantial weight to claims that colleges are not delivering on their promise to students, and pressure has grown to do something about it.[41]

In a few states, concerns about the quality and cost of higher education have given rise to early manifestations of test-based accountability policies.[42] Given higher education's multiple purposes and diverse revenue streams, however, it seems the prospects for such policies to become widespread are modest.

Even in the absence of testing mandates, some colleges and universities have begun to use standardized assessments like the Collegiate Learning Assessment (CLA) to monitor learning outcomes.[43] Too little is known about why these institutions have voluntarily embraced standardized assessments while others have not. Are they attempting to distinguish themselves from the competition by signaling a special commitment to student learning? Are they taking a normative stand against a system that has placed too much emphasis on nonacademic metrics? Are they trying to deter stricter, top-down accountability policies by being proactive? Regardless of their reasons, standardized measures of student learning occupy a relatively marginal place in higher education, at least for the time being. There are, however, a number of tests on the market, and given the general societal trend toward more assessment, it is very likely that more will be developed and adoption will spread in the future.

Learning Outcomes Assessment in Online Higher Education

As relatively new entrants into the higher-education field, online providers have been faced with the challenge of proving their worth, often to skeptical audiences. Given the fact that online education presents a wide range of opportunities to measure student learning systematically, one way for providers to demonstrate their value is to provide clear evidence of their students' learning outcomes. In reality, most online universities and courseware designers have opted to make a case for themselves by focusing on student-consumers' main concerns: affordability and career prospects.

There are some actors in the online space, however, primarily those with ties to traditional higher education institutions, who have put a great deal of effort toward finding ways to track and improve learning by making use of the plethora of student data produced in digital learning environments. For example, the Open Learning Initiative, founded at Carnegie Mellon University in 2002 and expanded to Stanford University in 2013, has designed adaptive learning courses that use students' responses to mid-unit and end-of-unit questions to craft customized learning pathways.[44] OLI courses have even been programmed to identify and correct common misunderstandings of the material.

Research on the effectiveness of adaptive learning environments is promising. It should be noted, however, that this technology has not been fully developed; nor is it widespread. Indeed, the assessment of student learning in most online learning environments has not been particularly innovative. Nevertheless, the potential to assess student learning in online environments is vast, and many individuals and organizations are working to move this technology forward.

Perhaps more importantly, online education providers have a great deal to gain if they can demonstrate an ability to produce positive learning outcomes. One can even imagine a future in which systematic learning-outcomes assessment becomes the norm in online education, thus exerting pressure on traditional institutions to do more to measure and demonstrate students' learning outcomes systematically.

Conclusion: Assessment and the Future of the Sociology of Education

Throughout, we have stressed that assessment is an increasingly prominent feature of schooling in the United States and worldwide. Given the centrality and growing importance of standardized educational assessment, sociologists of education are expected to continue to use these measures frequently in their work. We believe there are significant opportunities to utilize assessment in research, both to improve our understanding of how schools structure individual student outcomes and to explore how schools as organizations respond to the increasing use of assessment.

We expect that sociologists of education will continue to engage in research that uses standardized assessments to understand and improve pedagogical outcomes, as well as to identify and support efforts to address inequality in educational outcomes. Given changes in assessment-related technology, opportunities to engage in such efforts are growing rapidly. For instance, sociologists now have opportunities to engage in emerging efforts to make use of embedded assessment and other (big) data generated by new online instructional systems that make learning visible. They can also work to facilitate the development of research communities focused on improving instruction. Sociologists with an interest in engaging closely with practitioners can join or lead efforts to build networked improvement communities, bringing together stakeholders around schools to work together to foster data-driven continuous improvement.[45] Finally, sociologists can continue to play a leading role in organizing and advocating for access to local, regional, and national educational assessment data.[46] When pursuing research using these instruments, researchers should remain mindful of potential biases related to ascriptive characteristics and other factors that influence assessment measurement.

As many authors have argued in this volume, researchers should also be encouraged to ask questions about assessment that approach the topic with respect to organizational culture and practice. Organizationally, as assessment is increasingly integrated into accountability systems, a rich array of opportunities to study the politics of assessment and accountability has emerged. Rather than focus exclusively on official policy mandates, as sociologists we should examine how policies are actually understood and implemented in practice. In addition, more work on the complex historical, political, cultural, and institutional factors responsible for the emergence and implementation of these policies is warranted.[47]

Educational assessment is a prominent and powerful feature of our technological, political, and organizational landscape. As a data-generating technology, assessment presents myriad opportunities for sociologists with an interest in understanding educational processes and outcomes. As a complex feature of our political and organizational landscape, it also merits the attention of sociologists with an interest in modernity, rationalization, management, and the evolution of educational systems. As sociologists, we must continue to make use of educational assessments for what they can reveal to us as researchers, and not be deterred by what has been projected onto these measures as symbols of technology and rationalization.

Notes

1. Authors listed alphabetically; direct correspondence to rarum@uci.edu.
2. Claude S. Fischer, *America Calling: A Social History of the Telephone to 1940* (Berkeley: University of California Press, 1994).
3. Jal Mehta, "The Penetration of Technocratic Logic into the Educational Field: Rationalizing Schooling from the Progressives to the Present," *Teachers College Record* 115 (2013): 1–36.
4. See David Labaree, *The Trouble with Ed Schools* (New Haven: Yale University Press, 2004) for an in-depth account of administrative progressivism and pedagogical progressivism.
5. For more complete accounts of the history of assessment in the United States, see US Congress, Office of Technology Assessment, *Testing in American Schools: Asking the Right Questions*, Rep. *OTA-SET-519* (Washington: US Government Printing Office, 1992); Nicholas Lemann, *The Big Test: The Secret History of American Meritocracy* (New York: Farrar, Straus and Giroux, 1999); Randy Elliot Bennett, "What Does It Mean to Be a Nonprofit Educational Measurement Organization in the 21st Century?" (Princeton, NJ: Educational Testing Service, 2005); and Anya Kamenetz, *The Test: Why Our Schools are Obsessed with Standardized Testing—But You Don't Have to Be* (New York: Public Affairs, 2015).
6. US Congress, *Testing in American Schools*, 107.
7. US Congress, *Testing in American Schools, 114*.
8. US Congress, *Testing in American Schools*, 114.
9. US Congress, *Testing in American Schools*, 118.
10. Eric Grodsky, John Robert Warren, and Erica Felts, "Testing and Social Stratification in American Education," *Annual Review of Sociology* 34 (2008): 389; citing US Congress, Office of Technology Assessment, *Testing in American Schools: Asking the Right Questions*, Rep. *OTA-SET-519* (Washington: US Government Printing Office, 1992).
11. Lemann, *The Big Test*, 38.
12. Bennett, "What Does it Mean," 6.

13. Bennett, "What Does it Mean," 7.
14. William P. LaPiana, "A History of the Law School Admission Council and the LSAT" (Newtown, PA: Law School Admissions Council, 1998), 4.
15. For a history of the US Medical Licensing Examination, see National Board of Medical Examiners, "National Board of Medical Examiners: 100 Years," NBME, http://nbme100.org/#home (accessed June 8, 2015). For a history of the CPA exam, see S. David Young, "The Economic Theory of Regulation: Evidence from the Uniform CPA Examination," *Accounting Review* 63 (1988): 284. For a history of the GED, see GED Testing Service, "History of the GED Test," GED Testing Service, accessed June 10, 2015, at http://www.gedtestingservice.com/educators/history.
16. Anne Hyslop, *The Case against Exit Exams*, New America Policy Brief (Washington: New America, 2014), 5.
17. Grodsky et al., "Testing and Social Stratification," 396; citing Keith Gayler et al., *State High School Exit Exams 2003 Annual Report: Put to the Test* (Washington: Center for Education Policy, 2003) and John Robert Warren and Rachel B. Kulick, "Modeling States' Enactment of High School Exit Examination Policies," *Social Forces* 86, no. 1 (2007): 215–229.
18. National Commission on Excellence in Education, *A Nation at Risk: The Imperative for Educational Reform* (Washington: United States Department of Education, 1983).
19. Grodsky et al., "Testing and Social Stratification," 394.
20. Maris Vinovskis, "Overseeing the Nation's Report Card: The Creation and Evolution of the National Assessment Governing Board (NAGB)," (Washington: US Department of Education, 2001).
21. SAS, "Company Information: History," SAS, http://www.sas.com/en_au/company-information.html#history (accessed June 10, 2015); SPSS, "About SPSS, Inc.: Corporate History," SPSS, http://www.spss.com.hk/corpinfo/history.htm (accessed June 10, 2015); Nicholas Cox, "A Brief History of Stata on Its 20th Anniversary," *Stata Journal* 5 (2005): 2–18.
22. Stephen Sireci and Richard M. Luecht, "A Review of Models for Computer-Based Testing," (New York: College Board, 2012).
23. Michael Winerip, "Facing a Robo-Grader? Just Keep Obfuscating Mellifluously," *New York Times*, April 22, 2012.
24. Christopher Drew, "New Advanced Placement Biology Is Ready to Roll Out, but US History Isn't," *New York Times*, January 29, 2011.
25. "Frequently Asked Questions," Partnership for Assessment of Readiness for College and Career, http://www.parcconline.org/frequently-asked-questions (accessed July 1, 2015).
26. Open Learning Initiative, "Learn More About OLI," Carnegie Mellon University, http://oli.cmu.edu/get-to-know-oli/learn-more-about-oli/ (accessed June 10, 2015).
27. Richard Elmore, "The Problem of Stakes in Performance-Based Accountability Systems," in *Redesigning Accountability Systems for Education* (New York: Teachers College Press), 295.
28. John W. Meyer and Brian Rowan, "Institutionalized Organizations: Formal Structure as Myth and Ceremony," *American Journal of Sociology* 83 (1977): 340, 344.
29. Wendy Nelson Espeland and Mitchell L. Stevens. "Commensuration as a Social Process." *Annual Review of Sociology* (1998): 314.
30. Wendy Nelson Espeland and Mitchell L. Stevens. "A Sociology of Quantification." *European Journal of Sociology* 49, no. 3 (2008), 402.
31. Organisation for Economic Co-operation and Development (OECD), *Synergies for*

Better Learning: An International Perspective on Evaluation and Assessment (Paris: OECD Publishing, 2013), 13.

32. Mehta, "The Penetration of Technocratic Logic," 9.
33. Labaree, *The Trouble with Ed Schools*, 146.
34. Labaree, *The Trouble with Ed Schools*, 147.
35. See for example, Randi Weingarten, "How Useful are Standardized Tests?" *New York Times*, February 17, 2015.
36. For example, there were pronounced federal and local efforts to improve math and science education following the launch of Sputnik in 1957 and widespread public concern.
37. Frederick Hess and Chester Finn, *No Remedy Left Behind: Lessons from a Half Decade of NCLB* (Washington: AEI, 2007), 3.
38. Hess and Finn, *No Remedy Left Behind*, 3.
39. For a more detailed list of concerns, see Kamenetz, *The Test*, 13.
40. Claude M. Steele and Joshua Aronson, "Stereotype Threat and the Intellectual Test Performance of African Americans," *Journal of Personality and Social Psychology* 69, no. 5 (1995): 797–811; Jennifer Booher-Jennings, "Below the Bubble: 'Educational triage' and the Texas Accountability System," *American Educational Research Journal* 42, no. 2 (2005): 231–268; Jennifer L. Jennings and Jonathan Marc Bearak, "'Teaching to the Test' in the NCLB Era: How Test Predictability Affects Our Understanding of Student Performance," *Educational Researcher* 43 (2014): 381–389.
41. See for example, Organisation of Economic Co-operation and Development, *OECD Skills Outlook 2013: First Results from the Survey of Adult Skills* (Paris: OECD Publishing, 2013); and Organisation of Economic Co-operation and Development, *Time for the U.S. to Reskill? What the Survey of Adult Skills Says* (Paris: OECD Publishing, 2013).
42. For example, North Carolina is working on a mandate to implement assessment of generic competencies (see http://facsen.uncg.edu/Content/Forums/x.%202014-2015%20Faculty%20Senate%20%28other%29%20Information%20&%20Reports.pdf); and Tennessee has incorporated standardized assessment into its institutional performance funding system (http://www.state.tn.us/thec/Divisions/AcademicAffairs/performance_funding/PF%202010-15%20Overview.pdf).
43. See, for example, the Voluntary System of Accountability (voluntarysystem.org), a joint initiative of the Association of Public and Land-Grant Universities (APLU) and the American Association of State Colleges and Universities (AASCU).
44. See http://oli.cmu.edu or http://oli.stanford.edu/courses/.
45. See for example, Candace Thille, "Building Open Learning as a Community-Based Research Activity," in *Opening Up Education: The Collective Advancement of Education Through Open Technology, Open Content, And Open Knowledge*, ed. Toru Iiyoshi and M. S. Vijay Kumar (Cambridge, MA: MIT Press, 2008), 165–180. See also, Anthony S. Bryk, Louis M. Gomez, and Alicia Grunow, "Getting Ideas into Action: Building Networked Improvement Communities in Education," in *Frontiers in Sociology of Education*, ed. Maureen Hallinan (Dordrecht, the Netherlands: Springer, 2011).
46. See for example, Ruth López Turley's work as director of the Houston Education Research Consortium (HERC) and Meredith Phillips' work founding the Los Angeles Education Research Institute.
47. Jal Mehta, *The Allure of Order: High Hopes, Dashed Expectations, and the Troubled Quest to Remake American Schooling* (Oxford, UK: Oxford University Press, 2013), offers a sociological account of the political, cultural, and institutional factors behind

standards-based reform and assessment in US K–12 education in the twentieth century.

References

Bennett, Randy Elliot. "What Does It Mean to Be a Nonprofit Educational Measurement Organization in the 21st Century?" Princeton, NJ: Educational Testing Service, 2005. https://www.ets.org/Media/Research/pdf/Nonprofit.pdf.

Booher-Jennings, Jennifer. "Below the Bubble: 'Educational Triage' and the Texas Accountability System." *American Educational Research Journal* 42, no. 2 (2005): 231–268.

Bryk, Anthony S., Louis M. Gomez, and Alicia Grunow. "Getting Ideas into Action: Building Networked Improvement Communities in Education." In *Frontiers in Sociology of Education*, edited by Maureen Hallinan. Dordrecht, the Netherlands: Springer, 2011.

Fischer, Claude S. *America Calling: A Social History of the Telephone to 1940*. Berkeley: University of California Press, 1994.

Gayler, Keith, Naomi Chudowsky, Nancy Kober, and Madlene Hamilton. *State High School Exit Exams 2003 Annual Report: Put to the Test*. Washington: Center for Education Policy, 2003. http://www.cep-dc.org/displayDocument.cfm?DocumentID=251.

Cox, Nicholas. "A Brief History of Stata on Its 20th Anniversary." *Stata Journal* 5 (2005): 2–18.

Drew, Christopher. "New Advanced Placement Biology Is Ready to Roll Out, but US History Isn't." *New York Times*, January 29, 2011. http://www.nytimes.com/2011/01/30/education/30advanced.html.

GED Testing Service, "History of the GED Test." GED Testing Service. Accessed June 10, 2015, at http://www.gedtestingservice.com/educators/history.

Grodsky, Eric, John Robert Warren, and Erica Felts. "Testing and Social Stratification in American Education." *Annual Review of Sociology* 34 (2008): 385–404.

Hess, Frederick, and Chester Finn. *No Remedy Left Behind: Lessons from a Half Decade of NCLB*. Washington: AEI, 2007.

Hyslop, Anne. *The Case against Exit Exams*. Washington: New America Foundation, 2014. https://www.newamerica.org/education-policy/policy-papers/the-case-against-exit-exams/.

Jennings, Jennifer L., and Jonathan Marc Bearak. "'Teaching to the Test' in the NCLB Era: How Test Predictability Affects Our Understanding of Student Performance." *Educational Researcher* 43 (2014): 381–389.

Kamenetz, Anya. *The Test: Why Our Schools Are Obsessed with Standardized Testing—But You Don't Have to Be*. New York: Public Affairs, 2015.

Labaree, David. *The Trouble with Ed Schools*. New Haven: Yale University Press, 2004.

LaPiana, William P. "A History of the Law School Admission Council and the LSAT." Newtown, PA: Law School Admissions Council, 1998. http://www.lsac.org/docs/default-source/publications-(lsac-resources)/history-lsac-lsat.pdf.

Lemann, Nicholas. *The Big Test: The Secret History of American Meritocracy*. New York: Farrar, Straus, and Giroux, 1999.

Mehta, Jal. *The Allure of Order: High Hopes, Dashed Expectations, and the Troubled Quest to Remake American Schooling*. Oxford, UK: Oxford University Press, 2013.

———. "The Penetration of Technocratic Logic into the Educational Field: Rationalizing Schooling from the Progressives to the Present." *Teachers College Record* 115 (2013): 1–36.

Metz, Mary Haywood. *Classrooms and Corridors: The Crisis of Authority in Desegregated Secondary Schools*. Berkeley: University of California Press, 1979.

Meyer, John W., and Brian Rowan. "Institutionalized Organizations: Formal Structure as Myth and Ceremony." *American Journal of Sociology* 83 (1977): 340–363.

National Board of Medical Examiners. "National Board of Medical Examiners: 100 Years." Accessed June 8, 2015, at http://nbme100.org/#home.

National Commission on Excellence in Education. *A Nation at Risk: The Imperative for Educational Reform*. Washington: United States Department of Education, 1983.

Open Learning Initiative. "Learn More About OLI." Carnegie Mellon University. Accessed June 10, 2015, at http://oli.cmu.edu/get-to-know-oli/learn-more-about-oli/.

Organisation for Economic Co-operation and Development (OECD). *Synergies for Better Learning: An International Perspective on Evaluation and Assessment*. Paris: OECD Publishing, 2013.

Partnership for Assessment of Readiness for College and Career (PARCC). "Frequently Asked Questions." PARCC. Accessed July 1, 2015, at http://www.parcconline.org/frequently-asked-questions.

SAS. "Company Information: History." SAS. Accessed June 10, 2015, at http://www.sas.com/en_au/company-information.html#history.

Sireci, Stephen, and Richard M. Luecht. *A Review of Models for Computer-Based Testing*. New York: College Board, 2012. https://research.collegeboard.org/publications/content/2012/05/review-models-computer-based-testing.

SPSS. "About SPSS, Inc.: Corporate History." SPSS. Accessed June 10, 2015, at http://www.spss.com.hk/corpinfo/history.htm.

Steele, Claude M., and Joshua Aronson. "Stereotype Threat and the Intellectual Test Performance of African Americans." *Journal of Personality and Social Psychology* 69, no. 5 (1995): 797–811.

Thille, Candace. "Building Open Learning as a Community-Based Research Activity." In *Opening Up Education: The Collective Advancement of Education through Open Technology, Open Content, And Open Knowledge*, edited by Toru Iiyoshi and M. S. Vijay Kumar, 165–180. Cambridge, MA: MIT Press, 2008.

US Congress, Office of Technology Assessment. *Testing in American Schools: Asking the Right Questions*, Rep. *OTA-SET-519*. Washington: US Government Printing Office, 1992.

Vinovskis, Maris. "Overseeing the Nation's Report Card: The Creation and Evolution of the National Assessment Governing Board (NAGB)." Washington: US Department of Education, 2001.

Young, S. David. "The Economic Theory of Regulation: Evidence from the Uniform CPA Examination." *Accounting Review* 63 (1988): 283–291.

Warren, John Robert and Rachel B. Kulick. "Modeling States' Enactment of High School Exit Examination Policies." *Social Forces* 86, no. 1 (2007): 215–229.

Weingarten, Randi. "How Useful are Standardized Tests?" *New York Times*, February 17, 2015.

Winerip, Michael. "Facing a Robo-Grader? Just Keep Obfuscating Mellifluously." *New York Times*, April 22, 2012. http://www.nytimes.com/2012/04/23/education/robo-readers-used-to-grade-test-essays.html.

EIGHT

College and University Campuses as Sites for Political Formation: A Cultural-Organizational Approach

AMY BINDER

Many sociologists have approached the topic of higher education as if it were a simple input-output phenomenon.[1] One example of this tendency is our discipline's heavy focus on questions of who gets to go to college (access) using demographic measures such as race, gender, and class (as inputs) and who does best while they are there, using achievement as a measure of output.[2] A second way of conducting input-output research has been to study "college effects," in which scholars study changes in students' attitudes, beliefs, values, and behaviors as a measure of universities' discrete influence on them.[3] The bulk of this scholarship relies on a framework that makes the individual student, in the aggregate, the primary unit of analysis. Using either national-level or campus-level data sets, researchers use the input-output framework to measure college's net impact on a variety of students' ideas and activities, ranging from graduation rates, changes in their religious and political beliefs, and sexual behavior. This is the dominant way of understanding college's influence on students.

Whatever the merits of these approaches, the input-output model is thin; it takes insufficient stock of universities as central socializing agents. For example, in the area of politics, the college effects literature can tell us about overall patterns in how college-educated citizens are more likely to vote than their less educated peers, and how they are more inclined to identify as liberal rather than as conservative. However, survey research cannot tell us about the particular political issues students discuss on college campuses; where, how, and with whom they discuss them; or the types of political actions that students deem appropriate on their campus in light of these issues. In the absence of research that explores how the cultural and organizational dimensions of educational settings influence students' ideas and activities (a point underscored in the foreword and chapter 5 in this volume), we may be able to glean a general sense of the political, and even the liberalizing effects of college, but we are left guessing about the mechanisms, processes, and details of political socialization.

This lack of precision about the effects of college on students' political identity and action has led to many sociological oversights. But perhaps more importantly, it has left the way clear for leaders of the political right to make strong and relatively uncontested claims about how colleges indoctrinate young people to a leftist point of view (although see several publications by Neil Gross, among them his 2013 book).[4] In my own 2013 book *Becoming Right: How Campuses Shape Young Conservatives*, my coauthor Kate Wood and I used conservatives' liberal-indoctrination critique as our starting point, and explored how college campuses truly matter to conservative students' politics on two college campuses. In the book, we provide a rich cultural-organization analysis of students' experiences on college campuses as well as in national and local organizations that sponsor college-age conservatism. Our book, and other research that uses a similar conceptual framework for studying politics on campus—such as Daisy Reyes' study of Latino/a activism at three universities—is a model for better understanding the links between higher education and political actors and action.[5]

In *Becoming Right*, Wood and I found that college and university campuses have an enormous influence on the tone and tenor of right-leaning students' political thought and behavior, though perhaps not in the way most people would expect. Based largely on interviews with students, alumni, and others on campus (combined with institutional data and archival sources), we discovered that while conservative students' *ideological beliefs* may have been more or less shared across campus sites, students' political *styles* varied substantially from one university to the next.[6] By shared "ideological beliefs," we meant that students across university settings commonly held more or less consistent commitments to lowering taxes, creating more restrictive immigration policies, and downsizing social welfare programs, among other policies. By varied "political styles," we meant that students' discursive expression and performance of their politics diverged significantly between our case-study schools.

Comparing two universities that vary along some dimensions (the public/private divide, degree of selectivity in admissions, reputations as particular places to be) but which are similar to one another in other key aspects (both are Research I and secular, as well as often in the conservative spotlight for being "liberal bastions"), we found that a *provocative style* dominated conservative political action on a campus we called Western Flagship University, while a *civilized discourse style* prevailed at a university we called Eastern Elite Private. It may not seem surprising today that young conservatives would be split between "provocateurs" on the one hand and "establishment" styles on the other, since the presidency of Donald Trump has brought unprecedented stylistic ruptures into plain and often painful view for conservatives, liberals, and moderates alike. However, in 2007–2008, when Wood and I were collecting our data, the difference between these styles was still largely uncatalogued, since the extreme right Tea Party movement had yet to emerge. In addition, what was so fascinating about our findings was that each style was all but exclusive to just one of the two campuses. This boundary demarcating conservative styles in our case-study schools may point to significant selection effects among students on these different campuses—in which students who already were socialized to provocation by their families or prior school experiences chose to attend campuses like Western Flagship, while those socialized to the civilized discourse style selected (or were selected by) Eastern Elite. Or, this sharp division in conservative styles between universities may indicate that the campuses themselves played a large role in students' political expression. We found compelling evidence of the latter.

The provocative style used by conservatives at Western—staging controversial public events such as the now-familiar Affirmative Action Bake Sale or Catch an Illegal Alien Day,[7] or inviting such conservative entertainers as Ann Coulter to speak on campus—was meant to get under the skin of the left-leaning Flagship population—including students, administrators, and professors. Conservative students at Western tended to regard their professors as off-the-charts liberal, and they said that their "radical" faculty were prone to ridiculing conservative students and their beliefs in the classroom. If they could put on events that were media-ready and which forced confrontations between their supporters and opponents, conservative students considered themselves to have successfully pushed these and other issues—climate change denial, protection of gun rights—into the face of their adversaries. Their actions were designed to agitate, not to start conversations.

The civilized discourse style at Eastern Elite Private, conversely, was informed by students' high regard for their classmates' talents (if not also their politics), which campus conservatives believed gave them the luxury to have more reasonable conversations with their liberal peers, while also obliging them to refrain from a more confrontational style. Eastern Elite conservative students knew that conservatives in the larger political sphere had a tarnished reputation for being populist right-wingers, and these students sought to avoid being spoiled with that identity. Their deliberative stance was meant to ward off any such association. It is interesting to note that eight years after we collected our data, the Harvard and Princeton chapters of College Republicans (among others) declined to endorse Donald Trump for president in 2016, citing troubling aspects of the candidate's "temperament" and "character"—which are nothing if not elements of a political style.[8] The civilized discourse style also reflected Eastern conservative students' admiring attitudes toward professors as "experts in their field" who, as "consummate professionals," were not the kind of people who would sully the classroom with political bias, or treat students such as themselves with political contempt.

As such, the well-known critique issued by conservative pundits such as David Horowitz, or by Republican politicians striking anti-elitist poses, fell on relatively deaf ears at Eastern. Conservative students at Eastern did harbor some resentment against faddish humanities and social science faculty who teach postmodernism or feminist theory, or who seemed to regard right-leaning students as not as smart as their liberal peers in some general way. However, we found that conservative students' concern that they would not be seen to be as intellectually sophisticated as their liberal classmates further shaped Eastern Elite students' decisions to engage in intellectualized discourse and to forsake the more confrontational style, since the civil mode underscored their respectability.

What were the roots of these very different stylistic differences among conservative students on these two campuses? The argument Wood and I make in our book is that such stylistic expressions were not wholly, or even predominantly, inculcated in students when they stepped onto these two college campuses, but, rather, were to a large extent shaped by the kinds of experiences that students had in their college settings. This is not to say that students entered college with no preconceived stylistic inclinations or ideas about the university as a certain kind of political place. However, these background socialization experiences (or selection effects) were far from the whole story—as evidenced, for example, by the fact that several Eastern Elite students in our sample had grown up in places far from cosmopolitan coastal cities, had watched Fox News along with their parents, had participated in confrontational protests against abortion before coming to college, and, prior to matriculating, had read widely in and subscribed to the conservative critique about liberal bias at elite universities. Eastern students leaned heavily into the civilized discourse style once they got to Eastern, discovering that their past experiences with the more combative style were inappropriate for use in their new educational setting.

Meanwhile, at Western, students who had also grown up on a diet of Fox News and Rush Limbaugh's critiques of American universities as indoctrinators went much further in their provocative behavior than they had done before college, also in response to new circumstances at their university. They also were more likely to be targeted by, and active in, highly resourced national conservative organizations such as the Young America's Foundation (YAF) and the Leadership Institute (LI), both of which sponsor the highly confrontational conservative style for "Joe Average" college students, as promoted at YAF's national conferences and LI's "boot camps" designed to fight persecution through an activist mentality.[9]

What precisely is it about these two university settings that creates such differences in conservative styles, and how does our analysis add to a thicker description of campuses as places that socialize students to particular political styles?

Earlier sociologists of higher education, such as Kenneth Feldman and his colleagues, worked diligently to move beyond the college effects model by directing our attention to the campus environment and its "subenvironments" as the key objects of inquiry for understanding students' ideas and practices.[10] Campuses, in this light, are "arena[s] of social interaction in which the individual comes into contact with a multitude of actors in a variety of settings, emphasizing that through these social interactions and other social influences, the identities of individuals are, in part, constituted."[11] In our case, although conservative students participated in a national political culture of what it meant to be on the right, as articulated mostly by the Republican Party (and even a national College Republican framework one level down), the local culture of specific campus settings was where we found meaningful interaction to take place.

Using Feldman's observations as a departure point, Wood and I understood conservative college students as operating in a series of formal organizational arrangements and informal small groups on campus, most of which were not political in any obvious way, but which nevertheless helped to constitute students' ideas about how to act politically toward their peers and others. We analyzed such formal arrangements as whether the university offered students on-campus housing for all four years, or whether most students lived in apartments off campus. We asked them about their views of the general education courses they were required to take, looked at institutional data on the average size of students' classrooms and student-to-professor ratios, and the restrictive or unrestrictive registration procedures that students encountered when signing up for classes (potentially limiting their choices of electives). We analyzed the informal small groups such as the students clubs that undergraduates joined and the peer groups they moved in and out of. We also considered the larger symbolic level of these students' college lives, such as the distinctive college rituals, institutional reputations, and "organizational sagas" they participated in.[12]

The upshot of this more institutional approach to higher-education studies is that students—as they interacted with one another in a variety of college-level organizational structures—learned how to be active and creative members of their community, and to grasp appropriate styles of discourse and performance—in concert with their peers and other significant figures on their campuses. At Western Flagship University, students were socialized by the relative anonymity of being a Western student (off-campus housing, impersonal class registration procedures, some thirty-thousand-plus students on campus), where recreation and fun were reputationally known to be at a premium in their college experience. These institutional features at Western affected students' ideas about who they were and how they were expected to act, even in their politics. Exciting "gotcha" politics was designed to be over the top, and to snag attention from their classmates and professors. Since the students were relatively anonymous and spatially distributed in off-campus housing, there were few social barriers to being confrontational. Eastern students, on the other hand, who described living in a special "bubble" of fellow Easterners, were socialized to a kind of "collective eminence" or understanding of elite privilege and individual cultivation that led them away from such actions (see also Khan, chapter 6 in this volume).[13] Of course universities are not monoliths and do not generate singular norms of political appropriateness, but the point here is that ideas about one's political expression are based on culture in interaction on campus.[14] The college-age political identities we discovered were largely the result of shared understandings that were durable over time on these campuses, and which were significantly influenced by particular organizational and cultural opportunity structures at the two universities. We found that the political styles students engage with on any given campus emerge out of distinctive combinations of the ideas, beliefs, symbols, discourses, practices, and opportunities that are contained in cultural and organizational repertoires that exist at that university.

In our comparative case study of how culture and organization affected politics on campus, Wood and I provided a thicker account of college's influence on students than a large-*N* survey aimed at studying "changes in students' attitudes" could ever provide. Although Reyes's 2015 study of Latino/a activism on campus is as yet one of the only other studies to use this approach for studying politics in higher education, other sociologists of education are taking the general approach to get inside the black box of college life on a wide range of students' ideas and practices (see also Stevens and Gebre-Medhin 2016 for an overview of studies of this kind). Armstrong and Hamilton ethnographically researched a large state school's divergent influences on working-class and upper-class women's social lives and job possibilities, Mullen used comparative cases to study two institutions' effects on students' feelings of college fit and career aspirations, Stuber's two cases allowed her to explore how extracurricular activities could reproduce class position, and my own work with Davis and Bloom demonstrated the power of college campuses to funnel students toward particular occupational sectors.[15] If we add here Gatzambidé-Fernandez' research on elite formation in preparatory schools, Nunn's comparative case study of how high school students come to think of themselves as intelligent, and Mehan's account of the organizational, social, and cultural scaffolds needed to change first-generation students' academic habitus in the sixth through twelfth grades, there are still more good models of taking culture and organization seriously in studying meaningful school effects on students.[16] In each of these cases, scholars atttentive to schools' culture and organizational features have understood educational settings to be generative systems of meaning and action through collective interaction, which fundamentally changes and shapes students' orientations toward the world (see also chapter 5). This learning is collective and interactional. Informal group settings and formal organizational arrangements—where students learn, live, debate, party, have sex, think of themselves as talented and meritorious, and search for jobs together—lend cultural support for leaning into the dominant style of their school, and considerable constraints against branching off into unendorsed styles or choices.

To return to politics, one could imagine future scholars pushing this approach still further, by studying the links between higher education and politics in any number of ways. One important area for research would be to examine similarities and differences in political socialization between left-leaning and right-leaning students on campus. Another would be to take a longitudinal perspective and look at the longer-term influences of college styles on political behavior. Following the 2016 election, I would be surprised if culturally and organizationally minded educational researchers did not look at emerging issues of student political activity, including the rights of undocumented students, microaggressions and safe spaces, student debt and school cost, and many more. All of these would be welcome empirical topics for research on political socialization, and they are also needed correctives to the dominancy of input-output studies in the sociology of education. The future looks bright for continued energy in this area.

Notes

1. In a widely read forum published in 2013, Steven Brint laid out the dominance of quantitative methods in published articles from 1999–2008 in the journal *Sociology of Education*.
2. In an earlier observation of these trends in the field, published in 2008, Mitchell Stevens noted the dominance of stratification research in the sociology of education field.
3. See Pascarella and Terenzini 2005.
4. See Gross 2013.
5. See Reyes 2015.
6. When we say that conservative ideology is more or less shared, we do not mean that there are not any local differences. For instance, on one of our campuses, libertarianism had somewhat more of a hold on students' imaginations.
7. The Affirmative Action Bake Sale is a well-known piece of political theater in which conservative students sell baked goods at higher prices to white students than they do to African-American and Latino students. The idea is to illustrate how historically underrepresented students get unfair advantages on campus. During Catch an Illegal Alien Day, one or several students are delegated as "undocumented," and other students participating in the event must try to find the alien. Both of these events attract considerable negative attention and are often shut down by administrators—demonstrating once again (in the eyes of the conservative event planners) the bias of their campuses.
8. *Inside Higher Ed* ran an online article titled "College Republicans Split on Trump" in September 2016. https://www.insidehighered.com/news/2016/08/29/some-college-republican-groups-decline-endorse-trump-setting-debates.
9. For more information on these organizations, see Binder and Wood 2013.
10. See page 464 in Kaufman and Feldman 2004.
11. Ibid.
12. See Clark 1972 for the concept of organizational sagas.
13. Robert Granfield (1992) discusses collective eminence as a feeling state enjoyed by Harvard Law School students; Shamus Khan (2011) discusses the sense of privilege that is part of becoming elite at St. Paul's School.
14. See Eliasoph and Lichterman 2003, for an excellent analysis of culture in interaction.
15. See Armstrong and Hamilton 2013; Mullen 2010; Stuber 2012; Binder et al. 2016.
16. See Gaztambidé-Fernandez 2009; Nunn 2014; Mehan 2012.

References

Armstrong, Elizabeth, and Laura Hamilton. 2013. *Paying for the Party: How College Maintains Inequality*. Cambridge, MA: Harvard University Press.

Binder, Amy, Daniel Davis, and Nick Bloom. 2016. "Career Funneling: How Elite Students Learn To Define and Desire 'Prestigious' Jobs." *Sociology of Education* 89:20–39.

Binder, Amy, and Kate Wood. 2013. *Becoming Right: How Campuses Shape Young Conservatives*. Princeton, NJ: Princeton University Press.

Brint, Steven. 2013. "The 'Collective Mind' at Work: A Decade in the Life of Sociology of Education." *Sociology of Educaton* 86:273–279.

Clark, Burton. 1972. "The Organizational Saga in Higher Education." *Administrative Science Quarterly* 17 (2): 178–184.

Eliasoph, Nina, and Paul Lichterman. 2003. "Culture in Interaction." *American Journal of Sociology* 108:735–794.

Gaztambidé-Fernandez, Rubén. 2009. *The Best of the Best: Becoming Elite at an American Boarding School*. Cambridge, MA: Harvard University Press.

Granfield, Robert. 1992. *Making Elite Lawyers: Visions of Law at Harvard and Beyond*. New York: Routledge, Chapman and Hall.

Gross, Neil. 2013. *Why Are Professors Liberal, and Why Do Conservatives Care?* Cambridge, MA: Harvard University Press.

Kaufman, Peter, and Kenneth Feldman. 2004. "Forming Identities in College: A Sociological Approach." *Research in Higher Education* 45:463–496.

Khan, Shamus. 2011. *Privilege: The Making of an Adolescent Elite at St. Paul's School*. Princeton, NJ: Princeton University Press.

Mehan, Hugh. 2012. *In the Front Door: Creating a College Going Culture of Learning*. Boulder, CO: Paradigm Publishers.

Mullen, Ann. 2010. *Degrees of Inequality: Culture, Class, and Gender in American Higher Education*. Baltimore: Johns Hopkins University Press.

Nunn, Lisa. 2014. *Defining Student Success: The Role of School and Culture*. New Brunswick, NJ: Rutgers University Press.

Pascarella, Ernest, and Patrick Terenzini. 2005. *How College Affects Students. Volume 2: A Third Decade of Research*. San Francisco: Wiley and Sons.

Reyes, Daisy. 2015. "Inhabiting Latino Politics: How Colleges Shape Students' Political Styles." *Sociology of Education* 88:302–319.

Stevens, Mitchell. 2008. "Culture and Education." *Annals of the American Academy of Political and Social Science* 619:97–113.

Stevens, Mitchell, and Ben Gebre-Medhin. 2016. "Association, Service, Market: Higher Education in American Political Development." *Annual Review of Sociology* 42:121–142.

Stuber, Jenny M. 2012. *Inside the College Gates: How Class and Culture Matter in Higher Education*. New York: Lexington.

NINE

Digital Badges and Higher Education in a New Society: A Bernsteinian Analysis

MICHAEL OLNECK

A Google search for the term "MOOC" yields 66,300 hits for the year 2010, and 3,370,000 for the first ten and one-half months of 2016. Massive open online courses are a widely known and controversial phenomenon. It is almost certain that any reader of this volume has heard of them. In contrast, a search on "digital badges" yields only about 870 hits for 2010, and 15,700 for the first ten and one-half months of 2016. Despite growing interest in digital badges, it is very possible that a reader will not have heard of them. While digital badges have prompted puzzlement, ridicule, and a modest amount of criticism, they have not occasioned conflict or controversy (Olneck 2013). Nor have they drawn the interest of sociologists.

I first briefly introduce readers to digital badges. Next, I relate the study of digital badges to the aspirations of this volume, and argue that digital badges are a phenomenon that warrants the serious attention of sociologists of education. Third, drawing upon the perspective of Basil Bernstein, a British sociologist whose work has been inadequately capitalized upon in mainstream North American sociology of education, I examine the challenge that digital badging may pose to the autonomy and authority of traditional universities and colleges, and note the congruence of digital badging with features of the "new society" referred to in the title of this book.

What Are Digital Badges?

Digital badges are digitized records of an individual's achievements, skills, abilities, knowledge, competencies, and know-how. They can be presented visually as icons on a computer screen, hence the name "badges." Digital badges are unlike course grades or college degrees in that they can recognize at a much more granular level what individuals "know and can do." Also, unlike grades and degrees, badges can contain layers of metadata which describe the precise criteria for a badge having been earned, offer demonstrations of a badge earner's work, and include information about the badge issuer.

Digital badges were well established in video gaming prior to 2010. At Mozilla's Drumbeat Festival in 2010, a number of individuals with experience in digital media learning and with knowledge of gaming informally discussed the possibility of using badges to recognize a broader range of learning. Later, the MacArthur Foundation dedicated its 2011 Digital Media Learning (DML) competition to the development of badge prototypes, and funded thirty winners to develop them. Winners included various online and offline youth programs, online academic skills programs, programs to recognize occupational skills, and the University of California, Davis's Sustaining Agriculture and Food Systems major. The DML competition was administered by HASTAC, the Humanities, Arts, Science, and Technology Alliance and Collaboratory at Duke University. Simultaneously, the MacArthur Foundation funded Mozilla to build an "open badges" infrastructure which could technologically facilitate badge issuing and display.

The Mozilla Open Badge Infrastructure is now operational, as are several other options for storing digital badges. The HASTAC projects have been researched and reported upon (Grant 2014; Hickey, Willis, and Quick, 2015). And, as the Google figures show, digital badges are a recognizable and growing phenomenon. Badges are being used as credentials in a variety of fields, including, for example, human resource management and teacher professional development. A number of institutions of higher education are awarding badges in both for-credit and noncredit courses, and for demonstration of skills and qualities in co-curricular activities. Some institutions take account of badges in selecting from among applicants for admission. Badges can be shared on social media sites like LinkedIn. They are being used for recognition of accomplishments in voluntary activities. Badges are being awarded for successful performance in MOOCs, as well as for successful performance in online and offline courses for degree students. They have become a worldwide phenomenon. According to statistics provided by the Badge Alliance, through 2013, 235,100 total badges were issued utilizing Mozilla's Open Badge Infrastructure, while in 2014 an additional 68,800 were issued.[1] In 2015 and 2016, digital badges continued to grow in number (Ifenthaler, Bellin-Mularski, and Mah 2016; Muilenburg and Berge 2016).

An important potential and sometimes actual complement to digital badging is competency-based education, which defines learning as the acquisition of applicable competencies, and awards degrees and other credentials on the basis of their acquisition, rather than awarding credits for passing time-defined courses. Competency-based education is increasingly prominent in higher education policy-discussions, and increasingly enjoys the support of federal officials and others who are seeking ways to reduce both the costs of education and the purported "skills gap" among those attending and completing higher education (Kelchen 2015; Seymour, Everhart, and Yoshino 2015; Inside Higher Education 2016). Badges, as we will see below, are awarded for "competencies." Badge advocates recognize and promote the affinity between badging and competency-based education (Everhart 2014a; Roome and Willis 2015). While competency-based education programs do not necessarily award digital badges, the two innovations increasingly accompany one another. Institutions offering degree programs which combine competency-based education with digital badging include, for example, Brandman University (Credly 2015), Purdue University (Ashby et al. 2016), and Lipscomb University (Long and Clark 2013).

The Sociological Significance of Digital Badges

The accelerating adoption of digital badges since 2010 is a fascinating sociological story of institutional entrepreneurship, social and organizational innovation, category and classification construction and legitimation, and the dynamics of the relationships between the increasingly less distinct and less strongly bounded fields of education and economy. Badges and competency education are innovations which have the potential to reconfigure boundaries and positions within the organizational field of education, and to change the relationships between the fields of education and economy. These innovations could change the institutional categories which define and constitute structures, practices, identities, and social relations at the very core of educational processes. These include the organization and forms of knowledge; what teaching, learning and knowing *mean*; to what ends they are directed; how they are accomplished; and how they are evidenced and represented.

Digital badges offer sociologists new opportunities to address a number of the priorities outlined by Mehta and Davies in chapter 1 of this volume. These include enhancing the sociological study of higher education, promoting "more integrative theorizing and research within the field" (Mehta and Davies, chapter 1), advancing connections between sociology of education with other subfields within sociology and with disciplines outside of sociology, broadening applications of neo-institutional and field theories in the study of education, and diminishing the neglect in American sociology of education of forms and meaning of pedagogy, learning, and knowledge.

Enhancing the Sociological Study of Higher Education

While digital badging and competency-based education exist at PK–12 levels of schooling, it is because of their potential role in credentialing for the job market that their place in higher education is particularly important. And it is because of the *reciprocal* "interpenetration" of education and the world of work (Davies and Mehta, chapter 3) that the question of the challenge that digital badges and competency-based learning may pose to the authority and autonomy of higher education arises.

The challenge that digital badges and competency-based learning pose may extend even beyond their challenge to higher education's authority and autonomy to the very existence of a societal sector recognized as "higher education." The higher education "field" is, as Mehta and Davies (chapter 1) have pointed out, increasingly complex and diverse. Nevertheless, even recent analyses of the field concentrate on variants of familiar academic forms that can be denoted with institutionalized categories, such as "schools," "colleges," and "universities" (Scott 2015a,b; Scott and Biag 2016). Digital badging and competency-based learning may lead in directions that so blur, or even dissolve, the boundaries between what is recognizably "higher education" and other societal sectors that the category "higher education" could disappear from our vocabulary. This would depend not only upon the extent to which digital badging and competency-based learning became widely diffused and legitimated, but on the extent to which they depart from the "school form,"—that is, "any set of recognizable instructor and student roles, curricula, and certifications" (Davies and Mehta, chapter 3), and on the extent to which the "school form" can become unmoored from its existing organizational forms and still perpetuate conventional institutional designations like "higher education." For example, badge proponents ubiquitously refer to "learners" rather than to "students," signaling that learning does not require enrollment in something called a "school." And whether "competencies" can be subsumed under "curricular knowledge" is problematic.

So, in addition to asking how Davies and Mehta's (chapter 3) concept of "interpenetration" or Baker's (chapter 2) concept of the "schooled society" pertain to higher education, we should ask whether higher education as we know it may undergo various degrees and forms of "deinstitutionalization" through which institutionalized organizational activity or practice is eroded, discontinued, dissipated, rejected, or displaced (Oliver 1992: 563). Following the course of digital badging and competency-based education will help answer that question.

More Integrative Theorizing and Research in the Field of Sociology of Education

Diverse sociologists of education have long-standing interest in how and why academic credentials matter beyond the boundaries of education. This interest is exemplified by stratification and status attainment scholars who have long recognized education as a key variable in determining individual occupational and economic attainment, and in mediating between family of origin and adult status (Jencks et al. 1972; Jencks et al. 1979), by those interested in how credential dynamics (e.g., credential inflation) bear on the expansion, contraction, and structuring of education (Brown 1995; Collins 2002), by sociologists of education interested in the role academic credentials play in hiring and promotion (Bills 2004) and by sociologists and other social scientists interested in how schooling contributes to the structuring of power and control in the fields of production, consumption, politics, and culture (Bowles and Gintis 1976; Bourdieu 1984, 1991, 1996). Should badging persist, itself a question to which sociologists might attend, we can expect sociologists of education to add badges to measures of education attainment, to ask how badges are interpreted and rewarded by employers, as well as what role they play in status competition among groups and individuals. We can expect sociologists of education studying social reproduction and intergenerational transmission of status to ask to whom badges are awarded,[2] and how badges influence the structure of workplace authority.[3]

Digital badging, as an emerging phenomenon, is constructed at the macro-level of discourse, institutional logics,[4] and idealizations of practice and organization. At the meso-level, digital badging is established and enacted within and across organizational contexts, according to "vocabularies of organizing"[5] and categories of identity and practice. At the micro-level, interactions among individuals will entail pedagogy, learning, and assessment governed by what Bernstein has called "realisation rules,"[6] resulting in "learners earning badges." Sociologists of education studying digital badging might do well to examine interrelationships across these levels of analysis, which are not often investigated together.

Advancing Connections between Sociology of Education and Other Subfields within Sociology

The emergence, diffusion, and adaptation of organizational innovations, efforts to legitimize them, and the prospects for innovations being fully institutionalized have long been objects of sociological inquiry within organizational sociology, but they have not been so within sociology of education. With badges, in a very short time, a new *kind* of credential has been introduced into a field long dominated by academic grades, credits, transcripts, diplomas and, degrees, and to a lesser extent by occupational certifications and certificates. "Badges" have rapidly become a meaningful category. Although sociologists of education have analyzed changes in *extant* practices—for example, types of schooling (Collins 1981), curricular content and courses of study (Kamens, Meyer, and Benavot 1996; Frank et al. 2000; McEneaney and Meyer 2000; Frank and Gabler 2006), and college and university degrees (Brown 1995)—they have rarely examined the *emergence* and consequences of entirely new categories of practice. For example, although John Meyer introduced neoinstitutionalist arguments about the important legitimating functions of schooling and its categories of practice, including the designation of school subjects, age-level grades, and teacher certification (Meyer 1977; Meyer and Rowan 1978), he did not analyze the emergence of such practices. Study of digital badging offers sociologists of education the opportunity to pursue such inquiry while drawing on sociological accounts of organizational change.

Advancing Connections between Sociology of Education and Other Disciplines

As Mehta and Davies point out in chapter 1 of this book, sociologists have frequently raised challenges to economists' preferred account of why those with lengthier schooling get better jobs and earn higher income—namely, human capital theory. Proponents of digital badges as occupational credentials adhere to the theory that credentials are rewarded for the skills for which they are taken as proxies, and that badges can provide better and more useful information to employers than can degrees and diplomas. The increasing availability of digital badges offers opportunities to test tenets of human capital theory by examining how badges are interpreted and used by prospective employees and by employers in hiring and promotion processes, and by examining how well they predict on-the-job performance. If we find employers increasingly willing to hire or promote on the basis of badged competencies and to relax requirements for degrees or diplomas, we could conclude that human capital theory best explains the historical reliance on academic credentials. If, instead, we find continuing reliance on academic credentials, we could conclude that alternative sociological explanations for the rewards to education, such as an institutionalized "charter" defining graduates as deserving (Meyer 1970), credentialism (Collins 1979; Brown 1995) and status culture or cultural capital (Bourdieu 1986, 1996) remain tenable.

In reality, we are likely to find that badges as credentials will find greater acceptance in some occupational sectors than in others, that in some sectors badges will provide certification of skills for those who already hold academic credentials, and that in some cases badges will signify qualities not easily categorized as "technical" rather than "cultural," such as "leadership." Studies of digital badging thus provide opportunities for more nuanced inquiries into long-standing debates between economists and sociologists about why education is so closely associated with economic rewards at the individual level, and with occupational hierarchies at the structural level.

Broadening Applications of Neoinstitutional and Field Theories in the Study of Education

Sociologists define and use the concept of fields in a variety of ways. Perhaps most familiar is DiMaggio and Powell's (1983) definition of field as "those organizations that, in the aggregate, constitute a recognized area of institutional life: key suppliers, resource and product consumers, regulatory agencies, and other organizations that produce similar services or products" (DiMaggio and Powell 1983:148; see also Greenwood, Suddaby, and Hinings 2002). It is in this sense that Mehta and Davies (chapter 1) use field in referring to the proliferation of actors within the "education" field. Importantly, field boundaries are not settled and static. Rather, they are the object of contestation, and are subject to redefinition (Greenwood, Suddaby, and Hinings 2002). Boundaries of fields can be fuzzy and partial. This is particularly true "when organizational fields are in flux and audiences struggle to make sense of new organizations" (Ruef and Nag 2011: 3).

Important aspects of changes in fields are the emergence of new organizational entities and the development and incorporation of new practices and identities. While American sociologists have used a variety of criteria and methodologies to analyze categorical differentiations within the field of higher education (Brint et al. 2006; Brint 2013a; Ruef and Nag 2015; Scott 2015a,b), only Rawlings and Bourgeois (2004) have attempted to closely examine the dynamics by which new field positions emerge. Digital badges, along with competency-based education, are innovations with the potential to reconfigure the boundaries of and positions within the organizational field of education, and to change the relationships between the fields of education and business enterprise. Thus, they will be useful for exploring the applicability of field theory within the sociology of education.

We may count the kinds of organizations that award or curate digital badges as being among the "new organizations" that challenge the boundaries of the higher-education field. Examples include the for-profit firms Credly, Pearson, Blackboard, and Canvas. The extent to which such organizations become "naturalized" as part of the field of "higher education" will be a measure not only of whether their products and services become taken for granted in education practices, but of the extent to which for-profit organizations are no longer treated as interlopers within the field.

Fligstein and McAdam (2011, 2012) have extended the concept of "field" to pertain to a social terrain in which actors engage in strategic action. A strategic-action field may develop as actors pursue ends directed toward changing practices, positions, and identities within already recognized institutional fields. Individual and organizational actors involved in furthering digital badging have successfully established a new, recognizable "field of action," self-referenced as "the badge community." The "badge community" is important for its efforts to popularize the notion of digital badging, to secure legitimacy for badges, and to persuade organizations to issue badges or to accept them as credentials relevant to hiring, promotion, admission to education institutions, and as recognition of accomplishments in organizations and other purposeful communities.

The "badge community," however, is as important for whom it comprises as for what it does. Digital badging involves individuals and organizations whose organizational homes include lower and higher education, museums, libraries, philanthropic foundations, professional associations, credentialing and accreditation associations, workforce development agencies, government agencies, consultancy and research firms, established education technology firms, education start-up firms, education investors, and for-profit and not-for profit online learning "providers." The actors within the "badging community" are drawn from distinct organizational fields whose institutional logics and vocabularies of organizing are in some cases contradictory. This matters for the character and trajectory of digital badging, *and* for the ways in which badging may mediate relationships between distinct and competing broad institutional fields.

Wooten and Hoffman (2008) remind us to think of fields not as the "container" of organizations, but as "*relational spaces* that provide an organization with the opportunity to involve itself with other actors" (138; emphasis in original). Pierre Bourdieu's model of fields is the most thoroughgoing in its insistence of the relational character of fields (Martin 2003), with fields being characterized by both *positions* and effective *capitals*. It is important that, although they may be may be issued by schools, colleges, and universities, badges are not inherently "academic" credentials. The introduction of a new kind of credential into a crowded, expanding field of already differentiated, largely academic, credentials raises the interesting question of the *relations* between badges and other credentials. The *meaning* of particular credentials lies in their positions *in relation to* other credentials' positions within the field (Bourdieu 1996; Rawlings and Bougeois 2004), and in the relative strengths of *capital* they exercise (Bourdieu 1986). The positions that badges come to inhabit in the field of credentials, and the kinds of capital they authorize, should be of particular interest to sociologists of education.

Finally, badging and competency-based education have the potential to further shifts in the norms, regulations, and cognitive beliefs that constitute institutionalization (Scott 2008) and logics of action (Thornton and Ocasio 2008; Thornton, Ocasio, and Loundsbury 2012) characteristic of actors and practices within the field of education. For a considerable period, neoinstitutionalists concerned themselves more with the nature of stable institutions and institutional fields, and not with the emergence of candidates for institutionalization or with changes in institutions (DiMaggio and Powell 1991; Fligstein and McAdam 2012). Since the late 1980s (e.g., DiMaggio 1988), neoinstitutionalists, including sociologists of education (see H-D Meyer and Rowan 2006), have paid greater attention to the dynamics of institutional change, including processes of "deinstitutionalization" (Oliver 1992) and "reinstitutionalization" (Hinings et al. 2004). Thus, badging and competency-based education will also be fruitful avenues for expanding the application of neoinstitutional analysis within the sociology of education.

Diminishing the Neglect in American Sociology of Education of Forms and Meaning of Pedagogy, Learning, and Knowledge

Regrettably, North American sociologists of education have shown little interest in the sociology of school and university knowledge and curriculum (Brint 2013b; Mehta and Davies, chapter 1). In contrast, academic knowledge has been an important focus of British sociologists of education, notably Michael F. D. Young (1971b, 1998), Basil Bernstein (1977, 1990, 2000), and Geoff Whitty (1985, 2010), as well as of American curriculum theorists (Apple 1979, 1982, 1993, 1999, 2013). In their well-known assessment and compilation of the field as of the mid-1970s, Jerome Karabel and A. H. Halsey (1977), attempted to introduce the work of Basil Bernstein into mainstream sociology of education. Their effort was largely unsuccessful.

Only forty-three articles in *Sociology of Education* between 1977 and 2014 cite work by Bernstein. Fifteen of these occur in special issues of the journal, including several by authors from outside the United States. Very few of the citations are more than perfunctory. The overwhelming number of citations are to the sociolinguistic work Bernstein published in the 1970s. Only *one* article cites Bernstein's 1990 volume *The Structuring of Pedagogic Discourse, Volume IV: Class, Codes and Control*, and only *one* article cites his 2000 volume *Pedagogy, Symbolic Control and Identity: Theory, Research, Critique*. We may fairly conclude that Basil Bernstein's work has not in any substantial way guided research in American sociology of education.[7]

In view of expansive claims about the emergence of a "knowledge society" or "knowledge economy," and as political debates about the purposes of higher education become more contentious (Mehta and Davies, chapter 1), I believe that it is imperative to focus sociological attention on the learning and knowledge that institutions of higher education offer. The "social organization" of the curriculum (Young, 1971a), broadly speaking, organizes experience, perception, and dispositions in ways that "make people," albeit not automatically; and it stratifies knowledge and knowers along dimensions of power and prestige (Apple 1979, 1982, 1993, 1999). Basil Bernstein's later work (1990, 2000, 2001a, 2001b) offers a valuable framework and set of concepts with which to examine the nature of the learning and knowledge that digital badges will recognize, and the possible impact of badging on the autonomy and authority of traditional institutions of higher education.

In the next section of this chapter I endeavor to demonstrate the value of Bernstein's theory for analyzing the phenomena of digital badging and competency-based education, and I hope, for more broadly analyzing trends in higher education and the relationships between education and neoliberal society. In doing so, I hope to encourage recognition among American sociologists of education of the promise of Bernstein's later work to help us comprehend processes that are reshaping education in contemporary society.

Bernsteinian Analysis of Badges and Competency-Based Education

In the aggregate and individually, colleges and universities are "internally pluralistic" fields in which multiple institutional logics contend (Kraatz and

Block 2008). Purely "academic" values are "precarious" (Kraatz, Ventresca, and Deng 2010) and—as evidenced from transformations in academic science (Berman 2012), enrollment management practices (Kraatz, Ventresca, and Deng 2010), and the incorporation of undergraduate business courses into liberal arts colleges (Kraatz and Zajac 1996)—they face challenges from market logics.

But while commercialization of academic science changed practices related to publication, access to data, the kinds of research undertaken, and the personnel involved, it did not change what science *means* or what "doing science" *is*. While management enrollment conflicted with the values previously guiding the awarding of financial aid, and thus affected the composition of entering classes of students, it did not change the fact that colleges served "students." And, while the establishment of business courses in liberal arts colleges may have introduced elements of professional or vocational education unwelcome to some, it did not recognizably change what "courses" and "classes" *are*.

What makes the challenges posed by badging and competency-based education perhaps unique is that these innovations could change the institutional categories that define and constitute structures, practices, identities, and social relations at the core of educational processes. These include the organization and forms of knowledge; what teaching, learning and knowing *mean*; to what ends they are directed; how they are accomplished; and how they are evidenced and represented.

In doing so, digital badging and competency-based education potentially challenge the already besieged autonomy and authority of higher education in the United States. By autonomy of higher education, I mean the capacity of higher education to order its practices and social relations according to values, principles, and categories originating from within the institution itself (Maton 2005). By authority, I mean the capacity of higher education to maintain the societal value of its organizational forms and practices, its forms of learning and knowledge, its institutionalized values, and its credentials.

Through application of Basil Bernstein's concept of "pedagogic code" and his other concepts that elaborate and build on this idea, we can better understand the nature and magnitude of the challenge that badging and competency-based education may pose to institutionalized "higher education."

Bernstein's (1977, 1990, 2000) model of "pedagogic codes" locates the play of power and control in the very core of educational processes, including knowledge (curriculum), pedagogy, and evaluation (assessment).

For Bernstein, power inheres in and is exercised by "classification." Classification pertains to the strength of the boundaries, or the degree of insulation, between categories of knowledge (e.g., among school subjects; between "esoteric" and "mundane" knowledge, or, put otherwise, between uncommonsensical and commonsensical, everyday knowledge), between agencies (e.g., between various levels of schooling; between education, state, and production), and between categories of agents (e.g., between students and instructors). The creation, reproduction, and legitimation of boundary strength, and thus of categories, presupposes relations of power (1990: 24). Strong classification is characterized by strict separations between subject matter, between categories of students, between kinds of institutions, and between those who are authorized to teach and those who are not, at each kind of institution. The crossing of boundaries is highly regulated and limited.

Control establishes the legitimate forms of communication between the transmitters of education knowledge and acquirers—those who, in badging parlance are "learners." "Control carries the boundary relations of power and socialises individuals into these relationships" (2000: 5). Power refers to *what* is to be reproduced, and control refers to *how* reproduction is accomplished.

While power is manifested in classification, control is indexed in "framing." Framing defines the "the form of the *context* in which knowledge is transmitted and received," and constructs "the specific pedagogic relationship of teacher and taught" (1977: 88; emphasis in original). Framing maintains "the strength of the boundary between what may be transmitted and what may not be transmitted, in the pedagogical relationship" (1977: 88). *"Thus frame refers to the degree of control teacher and pupil possess over the selection, organization, pacing and timing of the knowledge transmitted and received in the pedagogical relationship"* (1977: 89; emphasis in original).

To account for the character of, and changes in, pedagogic codes, Bernstein introduced the concept of "pedagogic device" (1990), meaning the fields in which education discourses and knowledge are originated ("primary field"), translated into pedagogical form (the field of "recontextualization"), and transmitted ("secondary field"). Within the primary field, "distributive rules" operate with respect to those to whom valued discourses and knowledge are made accessible. Within the secondary field, "evaluative" or "realisation" rules are applied to assess whether knowledge has been acquired in its valid form.

Bernstein (1977:188) defines the relative autonomy of education by the strength of classification between education and production. This does not mean that the fields of higher education and production are necessarily disconnected. Even under conditions of strong autonomy, extended "systemic relations" between education and production can exist (1977:185–186). The distribution of categorical outcomes of each field can correspond, specific categorical outcomes in one field can correspond to those in the other, and education can socialize individuals into the skill and dispositional requirements of the field of production. On the other hand, diminished autonomy of higher education, or weakening of classification between education and production, certainly creates the opportunities for "systemic relations" between education and production to be extended and intensified on terms favorable to the field of production.

Historically, the demarcation between the field of higher of education and the field of production in the United States has been strong—stronger, for example, than in Germany, with its close relationship between firms and post-secondary schooling under the apprentice system (Crouch, Finegold, and Sako 1999). This does not mean that higher education and production have been disconnected, as the use of academic degrees as labor market credentials attests (Collins 1979; Labaree 1997). But it does mean that the boundaries and distinctions between the fields of education and production have been recognizably strong. The terms on which higher education has engaged with political demands for relevance, as in the field of agricultural education,have been largely determined by dynamics internal to the field (Rawlings and Bourgeois 2004). And the terms on which higher education has dealt with expanding markets for its credentials have been largely determined by the interests and actions of actors within the field, as exemplified by the "institutional entrepreneurs" (Hardy and Maguire 2008) responsible for the development of community colleges (Brint and Karabel 1989).

The autonomy of higher education relies not only on the strong classification between education and other social spheres, but also on strong classificatory systems *within* higher education whose meanings are given by internal categories and practices. These include, for example, classifications of fields of study (subjects), credit-bearing and non–credit bearing courses and activities, "academic" *versus* "vocational" curricula, and "students" as distinct from "professors."

In Bernstein's terms, the badge and competency-based education movements diminish the autonomy of higher education. They do this by challenging the boundary between the fields of education and production *and* by challenging the classifications internal to higher education. They do it also by altering the frame values of education transmissions in ways that diminish the authority of faculty and strengthen the systemic relations between education and production. Finally, they change the configuration of, and composition of agents active in, what Bernstein (1990: 59–61) calls the "primary" field, the field of "recontextualization," and the "secondary" field. The "primary" field is the field of production of education discourses. The field of recontextualization is the field in which discourses originating in primary fields of symbolic production are refashioned for incorporation and use in the secondary fields in which students—or, more expansively, "learners"—engage "education," classrooms being the most prominent example.

The autonomy and authority of higher education rest on the assumption that the learning in colleges and universities and the knowledge acquired by formal study there are distinct from learning undertaken and knowledge acquired elsewhere. This is an example of how the legitimacy of highly institutionalized sectors entails assumptions about distinctive expertise being created that is unavailable elsewhere (DiMaggio 1988). DiMaggio (1988) offers the example of knowledge available through university attendance that is unavailable through apprenticeships. Badge advocates reject this assumption, and dispense with the strong classification between the knowledge worthy of being taught and learned in "academic" institutions, and everyday knowledge not worthy of inclusion in the curriculum. Instead, they advance the claim that learning happens "anywhere," "everywhere," and "any time." Moreover, they insist that learning acquired outside of schooling is equally worthy of being recognized *and* credentialed as is academically defined and transmitted knowledge. Erin Knight (2012), formerly of Mozilla, maintains that learning is "so much more than [formal education]—it's any experience where people learn something and that can happen inside a classroom but can also happen in a seemingly limitless amount of ways outside of classroom, and across lifetimes. It's all that other learning that isn't currently consistently recognized or valued." Badge advocates want, Knight explains, "to open up and legitimize learning that's happening everywhere" (Ash 2012).

Badge advocates object not merely that much important learning is generally unrecognized in formal higher education, but that any informal, peer-based, and self-directed learning which is recognized "is only acknowledged to the degree that it supports the formal curriculum" (Mozilla Foundation and Peer 2 Peer University 2012: 2). The prescriptive character of academic knowledge and learning—in Bernstein's terms, the strong classifications and frames which organize and regulate practices within higher education—is viewed as a flaw. Erin Knight explained, "One of the problems we're trying to solve is that a lot of the way learning is defined right now is incredibly prescribed, and the learning that counts is top-down decided" (Ash 2012). Carla Casilli and Erin Knight argue, "Badges could represent an opportunity for higher education to rethink what is of value and recognize achievements that could be codified but currently are not" (Casilli and Knight 2012).

In valuing learning equally wherever it is acquired, badge advocates are concomitantly advocating that similarly capable individuals be equally valued irrespective of where they have acquired their skills, knowledge, and abilities. They are thus rejecting the meaningfulness of the most basic category that the higher-education system produces for society, the one that separates "graduates" from nongraduates. John Meyer (1977) long ago argued that the effect of education as an institution is to construct and legitimate categories of knowledge *and* personnel. Schooling, Meyer (1970) argued, enjoyed a socially recognized "charter" to identify those who were to be entitled to preferred positions in society.[8] Pierre Bourdieu (1986) characterized academic qualification as an institutionalized form of cultural capital which protects its holders from the devaluation to which the autodidact is subject. Badging presumes that the competent autodidact should stand on an even par with the college graduate. As Cathy Davidson of HASTAC observed, "If I am engaged in a project with someone who does an exemplary job, I can award credit whether that person happens to have a Ph.D. from MIT or be a brilliant sixteen-year-old programmer in Gary, Indiana or Nairobi." (Cummings 2012).

Badge advocates do not only want learning and knowledge, whatever its source, to enjoy value equal to that associated with formal education. They also want to weaken classification to the point that all learning and knowledge are "connected." In their vision, badges help to construct an "ecosystem" of learning, in which learning acquired from multiple contexts and activities is integrated and rendered "interoperable" (Boston University 2014), rather than, in Connie Yowell's words, "incredibly fragmented" (Ash 2012). Learning, whatever its sources, should, according to Erin Knight, "work together" (Boston University, 2014). As we will see below, "interoperability" is to be facilitated by badging "competencies," and by "connecting credentials."[9]

In insisting that credentials convey competencies or "learning outcomes," proponents of badges and competency education are rejecting not only the necessity of a "degree," but the academic language in which degrees and transcripts are formulated as well. Rather than expressing deference toward academic degrees, badge advocates critique the informational value that degrees carry. They often dismissively claim that academic credentials fail to communicate what individuals actually know and can do, and assert that employers are now much more interested in the "skill sets" prospective employees possess than in what courses they have taken, or from where they have graduated. "Employers and other badge consumers are recognizing the value of the detailed information and evidence of skills that badges provide. This is in stark contrast to the opaque, rudimentary information provided in resumes and transcripts" (Everhart 2014b). Thus, badge advocates are rejecting the "logic of confidence" (Meyer and Rowan 1978) which has heretofore permitted colleges and universities to use their own categories—courses completed, grades, and credits—to attest that a "graduate" deserves a "degree" and access to ensuing advantages. Instead, they are insisting that *all* credentials specify the knowledge and skills exhibited in order for the credential to be earned (see, e.g., Lumina Foundation 2015a, 2016). The dismissal of diplomas on the instrumental grounds that they fail to convey sufficient information about what degree-holders "know and can do" speaks to an erosion of the legitimacy of academic credentials and the dilution of their symbolic authority.

It speaks as well to the erosion of rationales for learning other than profitable exchange. The priority that badge advocates assign to the exchange value of knowledge is evident in their insistence that learning that is not assessed, documented, and made systematically visible to others is of little value. In the absence of recognition of learning acquired outside the confines of formal education institutions, there is "less chance for young people to turn their achievements into new opportunities—whether in employment, as an alternative to formal accreditation, or as a standout accomplishment for university applicants" (Molineaux, 2012). Badge advocates envision badging as something that enables individuals to purposefully put their ubiquitous and now credentialed learning *to use* in attaining personal goals. By helping to solve the problem of unrecognized learning, and "making it easy to issue, earn and display badges across the web," Mozilla claims that its Open Badge Project will "unlock . . . career and educational opportunities, and help . . . learners everywhere level up in their life and work" (Mozilla Wiki 2014).

The specification of what individuals learn as discrete "competencies" aligns with the increasing general marketization and commodification of education, to which Mehta and Davies alluded in chapter 1 of this book. Commodification, in the words of the critical discourse analyst Norman Fairclough, refers to "the process whereby social domains and institutions, whose concern is not producing commodities in the narrower economic sense of goods for sale, come nevertheless to be organized and conceptualized in terms of commodity production, distribution and consumption"

(Fairclough 1992: 207). Education increasingly takes the form of "goods for sale." It is now common to describe education as an "industry," and to refer to education "providers" or "vendors" who "market" and "deliver" educational "products" to their "customers" (see, e.g., Gumport 2000). As early as the mid-1970s, Bernstein detected the weakening of the legitimating myths of education's autonomy in terms of education for the "mind," for "life," or for the development of the "self" (1977: 188)—or, in Michael F. D. Young's (1998) terms, knowledge for "its own sake." Knowledge, Bernstein lamented, "is [now] not just like money; it *is* money" (Bernstein 1990: 155; emphasis in original).

Fairclough recognizes the relationship between commodification of education and the construction of learning around "skills" and competencies": "Commodified educational discourse is dominated by a vocabulary of skills, including not only the word 'skill,' and related words like 'competence,' but a whole wording of the processes of learning and teaching based upon concepts of skill, skill training, use of skills, transfer of skills, and so forth . . ." (Fairclough 1992: 209).

The social philosopher Ronald Barnett (1994: 13) concurs, writing that the university has become less a place of broad educational and personal development accomplished through interaction, valuable in itself, but "more a place in which knowledge is viewed as a commodity, picked up by those who pass through in acquiring the latest technical competences and analytical capacities." As the state and the public have sought to bring education closer to other societal spheres, and to incorporate it as among the forces and relations of production, the ideology of "academic competence," Barnett (1994) argues, is under threat from the ideology of "operational competence." The ideal of contemplation yielding understanding is challenged by the ideal of operational knowledge. An older vocabulary of intellect, knowledge, truth, and objectivity is challenged by a new vocabulary of competence, outcomes, skills, and transferability. Older purposes of "understanding," "critical thought," "interdisciplinarity," and "wisdom," Barnett (1994) claims, are fading from public discourse around higher education.

The identification of competencies as an outcome of formal education undermine the knowledge bases of academic and professional identities (Jones and Moore 1993; Beck and Young 2005) and thus further dilutes the autonomy of higher education. The autonomy of higher-education institutions requires that their self-proclaimed purposes be credible to others on whom they depend for legitimacy and resources. Legitimacy cannot be self-conferred (Suchman 1995). Bernstein (1977) observed that under deteriorating economic circumstances, internal classifications sustaining maximum numbers of subjects would be weakened, offerings curtailed, and that "applied" categories of subject matter would ascend the hierarchy at the expense of "pure" categories. Observing education in Thatcherite Britain, Bernstein foresaw that "Education is to be vocationalized and to become more dependent upon the needs of the economic field and more ruled by principles derived from that field" (1990: 153). Moreover, the authority of professionals in the field of symbolic control, where he located education, was to be curtailed, and a thoroughly "secular" conception of knowledge in which knowledge served the market was to prevail.

Commodification in education changes not only the nature of valued knowledge, but also the *ideal* pedagogic relationship. Commodified education is understood as primarily a commercial transaction in which all parties invest less of themselves, and in which mutual commitments are diminished. While conventional education certainly entails elements of commodification, what neoliberalism does is elevate this to a valued norm.

Elevating the value of competencies diminishes the value of academic subject matter *as such*, and assumes a solely utilitarian view of learning. While some competencies may be specific to academically defined subject matter, many may be acquired through any number of courses, and, as we have seen, beyond the confines of academic institutions. In that case, diverse subjects may be unable to identify distinctive *use* values, and may be regarded as subject to substitution, or as dispensable. As Zygmunt Bauman (2005: 316) observes, under contemporary circumstances, "centres of teaching and learning are subjected to 'de-institutionalizing' pressure and prompted to surrender their loyalty to 'canons of knowledge' (whose very existence, not to mention utility, is increasingly cast in doubt), thus putting the value of flexibility above the surmised logic of scholarly disciplines" (Bauman 2005: 316). In some cases, advocates of competency-based learning and of badges recognize that their projects would constrain the autonomy of higher education faculty to determine what is taught. Michelle Weise (2014) objects to the "turf warfare" in which faculty engage, and to the "extreme territoriality over student learning" they exhibit. "Despite philosophical concerns regarding the purpose of a college education," Weise insists, "faculty members must acknowledge that students are and will be looking for the direct economic relevance of their studies" (ibid.: 34). Pearson Education (2013), in arguing for the benefits of digital badges to "unlock" job opportunities, notes that "educators and training providers must become more comfortable with unbundling diplomas and embracing outcomes-driven learning design" (Pearson Education 2013: 6). "College faculty will resist badges initially," Pearson concedes. "For some, the adaptation may be difficult because it requires—

perhaps for the first time—examining and defining the marketable job skills that students will develop in their courses" (ibid.). While Pearson and other companies cannot directly impose these demands on faculty, outside pressures for colleges and universities to demonstrate their "value" and return on investment may create a welcome for them among administrators.

Redefinition of academic subject matter into "learning outcomes" that are specified as "competencies" can carry implications for the organization of academic work and identities. Rather than "professors," one can in principle, have "subject matter specialists," "instructional design" specialists, and assessment specialists. Western Governor's University, for example, which offers an online, competency-based program, does not have "traditional professors," and relies instead on PhD. "course mentors" and on "person mentors" to assist students (Kamenetz, 2015). Lipscomb's CORE program relies on "faculty competency coaches" to serve as "a thinking partner who helps students work through the self-paced only course" (Lipscomb University, n.d.) and on "assessors" (Council for Adult & Experiential Learning 2014).

The idea that learning and knowledge may be equally valued and connected, irrespective of their source, is predicated on the belief that those things may be rendered qualitatively commensurate across institutional sites, as well as across category boundaries within institutional sites. Through the formulation of "competencies," strong classifications between education and other spheres and within education would be weakened, as would the classifications between various subjects and between areas of expertise. Diverse kinds of credentials, including traditional academic degrees, professional and industry-recognized certificates, and nontraditional and experimental credentials, are to be "connected" through the "common language" of "competencies," and "translated" or converted into a common "currency" (Everhart, Bushway, and Schejbal 2016; Everhart et al. 2016).[10] The Connecting Credentials project, for example, aims to develop a "clear language . . . for explaining what credentials mean in terms of knowledge and skills" that is mutually intelligible to educators, learners, and employers (Lumina Foundation 2015b 2). The project intends to provide a "universal translator" (Lumina Foundation 2016), and to provide common units and metrics of learning, irrespective of the source of learning (Lumina Foundation 2015b: 5).

"Competencies," it should be noted, are like "academic achievement" in that they are not naturally occurring phenomena but, rather, are discursive expressions of organized social practices that are given meaning by the practical contexts which they produce and in which they reside. "Competencies" are a category of practice. As Bowker and Star (1999) observe, "categories are tied to the things people do; to the worlds to which they belong." Within that category, particular behaviors or performances are recognized as specific competencies. They provide classifications or categories to "sort out" (Bowker and Star 1999) social practices *and* persons. As such, they are power-laden and interest-laden. Bowker and Star (1999: 5) observe, "Each standard and each category valorizes some point of view and silences another."

"Competencies" are, above all, assumed to be *useful* and *applicable*. In 2002, the National Postsecondary Education Cooperative Working Group on Competency-Based Initiatives defined a "competency" as "the combination of skills, abilities, and knowledge *needed to perform a specific task*" (US Department of Education 2002: vii; my emphasis). Competencies refer to "what a person knows and is able to do" (Lumina n.d.: 2), with the emphasis on "able to do." Competencies comprise knowledge and skills that "can be identified, measured and applied within educational and business and industry settings" (ibid.: 2). Paul LeBlanc, president of Southern New Hampshire University, which offers a competency-based degree program, defines competency as a "'Can do' statement representing observable and measurable behavior" or a "claim we would like to make about what a student knows and can do . . ." (LeBlanc 2013: slide 12). The American Council of Education, in cooperation with Blackboard, recently defined a "competency" as "a specific skill, knowledge, or ability that is both observable and measurable" (Everhart et al. 2014: 5). Competencies, thus, entail *application*, and are evidenced by *behavioral* performances, not merely by evidence of understanding.

According to badge and competency-based education advocates, "competencies" are the *same* across and within institutional sites, and the language of "competencies" can be used as a lingua franca across institutional boundaries. Most importantly, the very definition of the competencies higher education is asked to teach could well originate in the world of work, *not* within academic institutions. Carla Casilla, then of the Badge Alliance, speaks of using patterns of categories within the world of work, "existing taxonomies and emerging folksonomies," in order to define badged competencies that would serve as "a strong social currency that is understandable" (Casilli 2014). Evelyn Ganzglass, a senior fellow at the Center for Law and Social Policy, argues for the importance of "cross walking" the different standards and metrics on which industry and education credentials are based: in the first case, competencies, in the second, time-related course credits. "Thus, aligning curricula with industry requirements and determining equivalencies between industry and educational credentials requires ongoing communication and reassessment. Creating crosswalks helps students, educators, job seekers, and government understand what these credentials actually represent and promotes portability of credentials across boundaries (Ganzglass 2014: 8).

For those who are eager that credentials "connect," the distinctions between what words and ideas might mean in academia and in the workplace are a nonproblem or a problem to be overcome, not a boundary to be respected. When asked whether he was concerned that badges tailored to the expressed needs of employers might work to displace academic values, Pearson's Peter Janzow, who is responsible for the company's badge platform, Acclaim, answered that employers are most concerned with the "Four C's," which are creativity, communication, collaboration, and critical thinking. "So," Janzow continued, "it's not as if those liberal arts competencies are being ignored or downplayed . . ." (Janzow 2014). Similarly, for Charla Long, the former dean of the College of Professional Studies at Lipscomb University, "problem solving" and "decision-making" in jobs *are* what academics call "critical thinking." "*We* [faculty and employers] *just use different words*" (Long 2014; my emphasis).

This claim is, as Ronald Barnett (1994) observes, problematic. Barnett (1994) questions whether nominally identical terms and ideas valued in academia and in the labor market—communication, problem-solving, creativity, flexibility—*mean* the same thing, and he voices doubt that at workplaces there will be the autonomy and capabilities for real reciprocity in communication of the kind valued in the university. Based on findings from its 21st Century Skills Badging Challenge, the Education Design Lab reports that "critical thinking" is "one example of where employers and universities really diverge in how they define this" (Education Design Lab 2015). For example, the Association of American Colleges and Universities' Liberal Education and America's Promise (LEAP) project defines "critical thinking" as "a habit of mind characterized by the comprehensive exploration of issues, ideas, artifacts, and events before accepting or formulating an opinion or conclusion" (Association of American Colleges and Universities, n.d.). In contrast, employers interviewed by the EDL project associated critical thinking with the ability to solve problems over the steps necessary to complete an assigned task (Fraser 2015).

What facilitates the alignment between competencies acquired through education and those required in the workforce is that competencies "have a unique architecture [that] break[s] learning into discrete modules that are not inextricably tied to courses or topics" (Weise 2014: 30). Modularization "privilege[s] movement across departments, disciplines and institutions" (Naidoo and Jamieson 2005: 275–276). This permits students to acquire flexible and diverse combinations of competencies suitable to the occupations or jobs to which they aspire. "When learning is broken down into competencies—rather than by courses or by subject matter—modules of learning can be easily arranged, combined, and scaled online into different programs for very different industries. . . . Because learning is not broken down by subject matter, an online competency-based education provider can easily combine and stack learning modules together in different ways for various students" (Weise 2014: 30).[11]

For Bernstein, the significance of modularization in higher education is the succession of "singulars" by "regions" it facilitates. "Singulars are knowledge structures whose creators have appropriated a space to give themselves a unique name, a specialised discrete discourse with its own intellectual field of texts, practices, rules of entry, examinations . . ." (Bernstein 2000: 52), and so on—in short, academic fields and subjects. "Regions are constructed by recontextualizing singulars into larger units, which operate both in the intellectual field of disciplines and in the field of external practice" (ibid.: 52).

Modularization, Bernstein recognized, furthers regionalization. Two consequences follow, both of which accord with my analysis of the weakening of academic autonomy and authority. First, "regionalization necessarily weakens both the autonomous discursive base and the political base of singulars" (Bernstein 2000: 52). Second, regionalization leads to greater centralization of control that insists on greater responsiveness to, and produces greater dependence on, external markets.

While badges and competencies may well be associated with what Bernstein (2000) refers to as regions, in, for example, applied fields like nursing and teaching, they may also be associated with less coherent arrays of knowledge and skills. Indeed, the flexibility that individuals will need to acquire competencies that are required for impermanent or "precarious" employment (Kalleberg 2011), for their need to maintain "employability" (Brown and Hesketh 2004) and for exhibiting "trainability" (Bernstein 2000: 53) suggests that modularization, rather than regionalization, will be most closely associated with the inculcation and acquisition of generic competencies.

The effort to "connect credentials" entails the effort to construct a systematic, unified market for credentials that are aligned with industry and occupational standards, have been endorsed by credible third parties, are "portable" and "transparent," and convey credential-holders' competencies as well as communicating the credential's market value (Corporation for a

Skilled Workforce n.d.). Those who attempt to construct this market amalgamate higher education into an "ecosystem" of diverse credentials "issuers," and seek to place colleges and universities in competition with other education "providers," posing them with the imperative to demonstrate the economic value of academic degrees—or, in the words of General Assembly's CEO, Jake Schwartz (2016), "put[ting] them all against each other." It is assumed that credential issuers, among them colleges and universities, seek "to maintain and improve their reputations, attract new credential earners, meet the requirements of authorizing bodies, and adapt to meet the changing needs of stakeholders. Connected credentials help them address these needs by more clearly defining and enabling comparisons of the value, quality, and effectiveness of their credentials" (Everhart et al. 2016: 17).

Unification of the credentials/competencies market is to proceed not merely by placing academic degrees in competition with other kinds of credentials, but by blurring the boundaries between different kinds of credentials issuers by embedding diverse credentials within one another. As Bob Sheets, codirector of the Credentials Transparency Initiative at George Washington University, put it, with the variety of kinds of credentials being embedded within one another, it is becoming less possible to claim that "we have higher education credentials, we have 'other' credentials" (Sheets 2016). Burk Smith, CEO of StraighterLine, was even more emphatic, saying, "We don't really know what college is anymore" (Smith 2012).[12] Even if an individual has not earned a cumulative credential like a degree or certification, once "unbundled" from courses, individual competencies, irrespective of where they have been acquired, can be awarded badges; and combinations of competencies, whether badged or not, can be aggregated and "stacked" into credentials that can be used to represent an individual's distinctive "package" of skills and abilities. Individuals could be encouraged to acquire only the parts they want or need from the previously integrated offerings which a residential college or university with a full panoply of courses, majors, requirements, recreational facilities, extracurricular activities, housing, board, and intercollegiate spectator sports provides (see Craig 2015). They could assemble their learning from diverse "providers," some recognizably traditional institutions of higher education—although perhaps from multiple such institutions, especially those offering online learning, as well as from such providers as online "learning companies," for-profit online "universities," and coding boot camps.

Modularized competencies and stacked credentials can construct individualized pathways, diversify branching points, and facilitate periods of exiting from and resuming pursuit of credentials. Modularized competencies also allow for "just-in-time learning" that can respond to an employer's needs and to an individual's limited time commitments (Derryberry 2014). Julia Freeland at the Clayton Christensen Institute for Disruptive Innovation foresees that the "unbundling" of higher education and workplace education will continue to further *remove students from traditional perceptions of what a university means*" (Plater 2014; my emphasis).

In an extreme vision of unbundling education products, education providers, colleges and universities included, would disaggregate their offerings to the level of competencies, and compete in a "competency market" (Craig and Williams 2015). Following the music industry, "education" could be purchased in single units, as on iTunes. Analogous to software-as-a-service (SaaS),[13] "colleges and universities may soon transition from the bloated degree model to an 'Education-as-a-Service' (EaaS) model. Successful providers will sell students what they need when they need it: a 'just-in-time' educational model that is much closer to today's coding schools than current degree programs" (Craig and Williams 2015: 22).

Championing the practical benefits of modularization and unbundling is aligned with badge advocates' commitment to the individually empowered "learner." "Learner," as I noted earlier, is the term often substituted for "student." Increased visibility and centrality of the "learner" is part of recent worldwide discourses which "disassemble . . . and reassemble . . . education processes and systems" (Singh 2015: 363–364). In the rhetoric and iconography of badging, individual learners are depicted as availing themselves of multiple sources—"providers"—of learning, and then are shown as displaying their various badges as they see fit to different audiences: prospective employers, admissions officers, LinkedIn participants, organizations whose interests dovetail with the badge earner's, and so on.

Learners are characterized as "empowered" because they can choose what and from whom they learn, can construct unique combinations of learning experiences, and can forge "their own pathways" and "self-direct their lifelong learning." They can "take charge of their online identities and reputations." Learners, as Mozilla's Sunny Lee points out, own and control their own badges, through which they can "curate and manage the image that they want to represent to the rest of the world" (Ash 2012). Tuschling and Engemann's (2006) analysis of lifelong learning discourse suggests, however, that this may be less authentically empowering, and more a matter of individuals being subjected to new forms of surveillance and governance.

The individualization of learning and credentialing structured into competency-learning and badging is part and parcel of what Ulrich Beck (1992) has characterized as the "individualized society," in which "*the indi-*

vidual himself or herself becomes the reproduction unit of the social in the lifeworld" (ibid., 90; emphasis in original). In the individualized society, personal identities are underdetermined, self-constructed, changeable (Bauman 2012), and even "disposable" (Bauman 2009). Identity is an ongoing, unfinished, and fluctuating accomplishment (Bauman 2007), a series of self-focused flexible responses to the individualized forms and conditions of life (Beck 1992).

Pursuit of badges and competency education is a highly personalized and individualized endeavor, with little or nothing in common with nineteenth- and twentieth-century purposes of cultivating common identities—for example, national identities—or setting out normative models of being an educated person, as in the German concept of *Bildung*.

To craft viable identities requires being a competent "consumer." Bauman (2012: 73–74) claims that "the code in which our 'life policy' is scripted is derived from the pragmatics of shopping." "There are so many areas in which we need to be more competent," Bauman (2012: 74) argues, "and each calls for 'shopping around.' We 'shop' [for example], for the skills needed to earn our living and for the means to convince would-be employers that we have them." New modernity is an epoch of universal competitive comparison (Bauman 2012). Through the ways in which we consume to craft our identities, we become *ourselves* sellable "commodities" (Bauman 2012).

Given the limitless and perpetual opportunities for adding credentialed competencies, individuals will be called upon to be discerning consumers. Facing the myriad of educational experiences that the "connected credentials 'ecosystem'" will offer, individuals will require substantial informational and cultural capital to discover, identify, and evaluate the opportunities they confront. And they will have to assess the preferences of those to whom they "display" their credentials, so as to "curate" or tailor their identities most effectively. In doing so, they are likely to acquire a view of themselves as a "bundle of skills" (Urciuoli 2008; see also Collin 2011).

A possible consequence of the increased diversification of education credentials, the proliferation of education "providers," the "unbundling" and "stackability," the multiple and open-ended "connections" that contemporary credentials may facilitate, and the lifelong pursuit of further credentials, is that education will no longer define well-demarcated positions in the social structure, and will contribute to fractured identities rather than provide recognizable classifications that can contribute to stable and secure identities. Rather than help define "who you are," credentials in the future may refer only to a catalogue of "what you can do." In the context of my argument, this radical individualization of learning and learners, the disassembling of learning, and the relegation of academic institutions to just one among many sites from which to acquire recognized learning, is significant for the dilution of academic experiences as a source of identity for individuals. In writing about "identity," Bernstein was concerned not with intrapsychological answers to the question of "who am I?" but with the question of how pedagogic codes organized experience in ways that led individuals to locate themselves vis-à-vis education categories and with respect to the relationship between education, self, and time. Strongly framed and strongly classified "collection codes," for example, produce specific identities acquired from the characteristically hierarchical nature of authority relationships, the systematic ordering of differentiated knowledge, and an explicit examining process (Bernstein 1977). Weakly classified and weakly framed "integrated codes" led to correspondingly weakened identities (ibid.).

Bernstein explained that "the identity arises out of a particular social order through relations which the identity enters with other identities of reciprocal recognition, support, mutual legitimisation and finally through a negotiated collective purpose" (2000: 59). In the period that his later work treated—a period anticipating our own, in which "trainability"[14] is the object and mode of education—the identity produced is, according to Bernstein, socially "empty," characterized by eroded commitment, dedications, and coherent time (Bernstein 2001a: 366). Actors recognize one another not through shared identities grounded in shared experience of education institutions, but "by the materialities of consumption, by its distributions, by its absences" (Bernstein 2000: 59).

What makes digital badges particularly interesting in light of Bernstein's analysis of contemporary identity is that they are *among* the "materialities of consumption" made available through "the supplier-client, or shopping-mall-shopper pattern," which is replacing the "orthodox teacher-student relationship" (Bauman 2005: 317). Identity is augmented by further "consumption," and is available for display, but is not constructed from the introjection of the categories provided by institutionalized education.

The instability of identity in the "individualized society" is in part a consequence of that society tending toward being organized on the basis of network structure (Castells 1996). The network and networking logic not only characterize social structure and patterns of collective action but extend to the cultural logic upon which actors in society draw, modifying "the operation and outcomes in processes of production, experience, power, and culture" (Castells 1996: 469), "reaching objects and habits in everyday life" (ibid.: 21). Because network structures are not fixed or completed, and because connecting and disconnecting are characteristic processes, they facilitate temporary attachments and commitments (Bauman 2009). Networks facilitate multiplicity and fluidity of contacts and connections (ibid.). While in earlier times inclusion in stable networks contributed to firm and unambiguous identities, the unstable networks of new modernity fail to provide subjects or actors with the firm boundaries that enable stable identities (Beck, Bonss, and Lau 2003).

Unsurprisingly, "flexibility" is highly valued in the network society. "Flexibility has replaced solidity as the ideal condition to be pursued of things and affairs" (Bauman 2012: ix). Flexibility, as a feature of networks, facilities the ability to reconfigure selves, organizations, projects, activities. ". . . In a society characterized by constant change and organizational fluidity," the ability to reconfigure is "a decisive feature" (Castells 1996: 62).

Flexibility is among the chief virtues attributed to "connected credentials." Credentials from diverse providers may be combined and recombined, depending upon the needs of the ultimate "consumer"—for example, employers seeking variable combinations of skills, knowledge, and know-how. Nano-credentials associated with delimited skill and knowledge sets may be pursued and added on schedules suitable to learners' needs. The modular structure of competency education permits novel, open-ended combinations in learning.

Flexibility is characteristic of the organization of work and labor markets in the network society. ". . . *The business project, enacted by a network,* rather than individual companies or formal groupings of companies [become] the *actual operating unit of enterprises* (Castells 1996: 165; emphasis in original). This "looser form . . . of organization [can] be put together, dismantled and reassembled at short notice or without notice" (Bauman 2012: 154). Insofar as badges and credentialed competencies index relatively narrow and specific competencies, they will facilitate flexible, "just in time" assembling—and disassembling—of temporary teams of workers.

Work processes themselves are "increasingly individualized[;] labor [is] disaggregated in its performance, reintegrated in its outcome through a multiplicity of interconnected tasks in different sites, ushering in a new division of labor based on the attributes/capacities of each worker rather than on the organization of the task" (Castells 1996: 471). Wage earners are "treated as so many separate individuals, capable of different, unequal performances" (Boltanski and Chiapello 2007: 217), and are held responsible for their own employment futures. "When a project is over (perfected) they must be willing to move on to develop their own 'portfolio' of skills and achievements" (Gee, Hull, and Lankshear 1996: 30). Under this regime, there is less job security, a greater rate of job changing, and more time out of employment. In such uncertain circumstances, work does not provide a firm grounding for identity or commitment (Bauman 2012), which in turn makes more problematic the owners' and managers' ability to secure the willing collaboration of workers (Boltanski and Chiapello 2007). The solution is to promote "a project of self-realization, linking the cult of individual performance and extolment of mobility to reticular conceptions of the social bond" (ibid. 217).

These characteristics of the labor market and the workplace are recognized by education and credential providers, and are identified as reasons for learners and employers to avail themselves of the wares on offer. As one Pearson report observed, "The economic disruptions of the last two decades have made workers responsible for managing their own career development through learning that starts in secondary school and college but continues throughout their careers" (Pearson Education, Inc. 2013: 5). The publication in which this sentence appears is optimistically entitled *Open Badges Are Unlocking the Emerging Jobs Economy*.

An important consequence of the new workplace and employment regime, coupled with the requirement of self-responsibility, is that education is increasingly important to workers who are navigating turbulent and unchartered waters. In its increasingly variegated forms, it provides the credentials that workers need to compete in a labor market which requires that they distinguish themselves as much as possible from others (Beck 1992). "The employee of the future," as Munch (2012: 63) depicts, "is his/her own entrepreneur, is permanently under way, is at home nowhere and always eager to undergo further education." Further education, or "lifelong learning," contributes as well to the ongoing construction of always unfinished and impermanent identity, discussed earlier (Bauman 2009).

Conclusion

In sum, guided by Basil Bernstein's analyses of pedagogic codes, pedagogic discourses, and the pedagogic device, I have argued that digital badges, accompanied by competency-based education, have the potential in a number of ways to challenge both the autonomy and authority of traditional, academic higher education. These include, most significantly, weakening the classification between the economic field and the field of higher education, and extending the systemic relationships between education and production. Badging and competency-based education erode nonutilitarian rationales for learning, and attempt to redefine and reorganize content and forms of learning and knowledge as generic competencies that are identical across institutional boundaries. They reject claims for the superiority and uniqueness of academically acquired knowledge, diminish the claims of academically credentialed individuals, and reconstitute the contexts or fields within which educational discourses and practices are produced, recontextualized, and enacted and evaluated. Finally, badges and competency-based education further an identity that is oriented toward consumption, and diminish the contribution of education institutions to identity.

It remains an open question whether the subordination of education to the labor market and productive sphere which I have argued that badging and competency education advance will be as complete as my analysis might suggest. Higher education is, as noted above, *internally* a "pluralistic field" having "the potential for fragmentation, incoherence, conflict, goal-ambiguity, and organizational instability" (Kraatz and Block 2008: 243–244). The outcome of contemporary struggles over which institutional logics and which vocabularies of organization will shape universities and colleges remains at least somewhat uncertain. Historically, when colleges and universities have incorporated vocational, professional, and applied content, at least higher status institutions have given it an academic hue (Labaree 2006). In contexts where academic credential inflation spurred more vocationally oriented competitors, those competitors over time came to emulate more "academic" forms (Collins 2002). Because, as Michael Eraut (2004: 201) observes, "performance in the workplace typically involves the integration of several different forms of knowledge and skill, under conditions that allow little time for the analytic/deliberative approach favoured in higher education," the transfer of learning from education sites to the workplace is difficult and problematic. That may cause efforts like Connecting Credentials to founder in practice.[15] Nonetheless, in Basil Bernstein's (1977) terms, digital badging and competency education clearly diminish the strength of "classification" between education and the field of production. They construct "symbolic homologies" between the worlds of education and work (Maroy and Doray, 2000). Badges and measured competencies provide "instruments and approaches used by actors (educational and productive) to shape practical links between the educational and productive spheres" (ibid., 179), and are indicative of "power shifts, the changes in regulation methods and control of the spaces concerned, the professional identities advanced, and the nature of the knowledge mobilised and transmitted by the new practices" (ibid. 180).

The translation of "workplace requirements" and "employers' needs" into "competencies" that can be assessed and badged entails complex processes which warrant close study in the future. The translation will not be exact, and the ways in which the translations will be recognizably "academic" remain to be seen. What can be said is that the boundaries and composition of the fields which Bernstein (1990; 2001a,b) identified as sites for the production and recontextualization of educational discourses, and the sites for the evaluation of performances subject to evaluation, are shifting. We can anticipate that the field of symbolic control, comprising agents and agencies distinct from the economic field or field of production, will contract, and that agents and agencies within the economic field engaged in symbolic work—what Bernstein refers to as the "cultural field"—will expand in authority and effect. These will include "education firms," "learning companies," and others within the massive and complex field of education technology (Eduventures 2014). These firms do not merely provide academic institutions with technological devices and infrastructure to more effectively engage in traditional academic instruction, but offer the means to re-form the substance of "education."

Because the discourses of badging and competency-based education, as well as the broader discourse of lifelong learning in which those discourses participate, proclaim progressive themes like relevance, individualization, democratization, inclusion, personal fulfillment, and self-direction (Gewirtz 2008; Wheelahan 2010), it is tempting to hear echoes in these movements of earlier, even radical, critiques of education institutions and academic knowledge such as those offered in Ivan Illich's (1970) *DeSchooling Society* or even A. S. Neil's (1960) *Summerhill*. Illich's "learning webs," for example, might be likened to online "learning communities" (Davidson and Goldberg 2010). While Davidson and Goldberg's (2010) vision, and that of other early proponents of badging, may resurrect themes associated with Illich, the context of neoliberal society is one of disciplining and investing in the self, not one of communal values other than, perhaps, those underlying instrumental "teamwork" (Gee, Hull, and Lankshear 1996). Contemporary neoliberal individualization is associated less with older conceptions of "competence"-based pedagogic models,[16] stressing self-development, and more with "generic" pedagogic models, associated with "trainability" (Bernstein 2000).

Given that the history of American education expansion is also a history of differentiated practices and institutions (Scott 2015a,b), I think it is likely that both badging and competency-based education will become more characteristic of some kinds of institutions than of others. On the basis of Craig Rawlings' (2012) account of how status differences among education organizations shape their strategies, I would expect that lower-tier institutions that emphasize "what we do," and which try to establish niches by differentiating themselves from other lower-tier institutions, will be more likely than upper-tier institutions, which emphasize "who we are," to incorporate digital badging and competency-based education into the core of their processes. This conclusion accords with Bernstein's own conclusion that the new forms of knowledge and pedagogy associated with promoting "trainability" were more likely to be adopted by less privileged institutions, whereas elite institutions would remain "more selective of their preferred knowledge, manner of transmission, and evaluation of staff and students," and the diversification of education forms would "be filtered through the existing reproductive structures, and so the present hierarchy of privileging institutions will be maintained. Plus ca change . . ." (Bernstein 2001a: 368).

While North American sociologists of education of the 1970s and 1980s concerned themselves with relationships between education and economic structures, and some examined how tracking and ability grouping assigned higher-placed students more sophisticated academic fare (see, e.g., Oakes 1985) none posed the question of how knowledge forms per se might be important to the interpenetration of the education and economic fields, or for the autonomy and authority of higher education. Preliminary application of Basil Bernstein's theory of pedagogic codes and pedagogic devices to an analysis of digital badging and competency-based education has enabled me to explore those questions. More formal explication in terms of Bernstein's classification and framing values awaits, as does application of institutional logics and post-neoinstitutional field theories to an analysis of the contours and dynamics of the fields that Bernstein identifies as primary, recontextualization, and secondary. Such work will, I hope, suggest further paths of inquiry into education in a new society.

Notes

1. http://www.tiki-toki.com/time line/entry/216462/Open-Badges-in-2013/#vars!panel =2137335!; http://www.tiki-toki.com/time line/entry/388116/Open-Badges-in-2014/.
2. Despite the rhetoric of education democratization and personal empowerment used by badge proponents, digital badges might offer further advantages to those already advantaged. If, for example, badge earners are drawn from the same populations as those who pursue occupational certificates, or those whose further training employers have traditionally supported, they will be individuals who are already relatively well trained, older, more likely to be male, and more likely to be employed in positions with higher skill demands (Bills and Wacker 2003; Bills 2004; Fourage et al. 2010; Desjardins and Rubenson 2011).
3. If not accompanied by diplomas or degrees, digital badges may deepen employer control over employees. While badges *can* be used in dismantling visible workplace hierarchies with which conventional education credentials are associated (Bowles

and Gintis 1976), they can also undermine notions of career stages upon which employees have heretofore relied (Hefler and Markowitsch 2012), and contribute to employee insecurity under regimes of flexible, precarious employment (Crouch, Feingold, and Sako 1999; Kalleberg 2011).

4. Institutional logics are "the socially constructed, historical patterns of cultural symbols and material practices, including assumptions, values, and beliefs, by which individuals and organizations provide meaning to their daily activity, organize time and space, and reproduce their lives and experiences" (Thornton, Ocasio, and Loundsbury 2012: 2; citing Thornton and Ocasio 2008).
5. Vocabularies of organizing are "structured systems of words developed within social systems to articulate a specialized domain of practice or activity" (Lowenstein and Ocasio 2002: 4). They "provide organizational members with specific categories with which to think and act. . . ." (Lowenstein and Ocasio 2002: 9), and provide the semantic material through which institutional logics are articulated.
6. "Realisation rules" govern and enable speaking [enacting] the expected legitimate text. "The recognition rule, essentially, enables appropriate realisations to be put together. The realisation rule determines how we put meanings together and how we make them public. The realisation rule is necessary to produce the legitimate text," where "text" refers to anything which attracts evaluation" (Bernstein 2000: 17–18).
7. Alan Sadovnik's work stands as an exception to the neglect of Bernstein's corpus. Sadovnik's (1991) article in *Sociology of Education*, "Basil Bernstein's Theory of Pedagogic Practice: A Structuralist Approach," was awarded the American Sociological Association Sociology of Education Section's 1993 Willard Waller Award for the best published article in the field in the previous three years.
8. Meyer did concede that if "actual role training" were to gain in stature, we might expect "the university [to] indeed weaken and fragment, and more efficient competitors [to] win out" (Meyer et al. 2007: 25). That "actual role training" may well be growing in stature is evident in public officials disparaging nonapplied fields of study, and colleges and universities experiencing pressure to assess and report their "value added" and "return on investment."
9. As a common noun, "connecting credentials" describes long-standing aspirations of those advancing digital badging and competency education. As a proper noun, "Connecting Credentials" refers to a project undertaken by the American Council on Education, funded by the Lumina Foundation. By "connected credentials," project participants "refer . . . broadly to multiple aspects of connectedness, including connections and relationships among credentials, connections to purpose and value in multiple contexts, and connections to opportunities for credential earners" (Everhart, Ganzglass, Casilli, Hickey, and Muramatsu, 2016: 7).
10. When used to recognize learning outcomes *and* as credentials in hiring, badges and credentialed competencies are serving as "boundary objects" (Star and Griesemer 1989). Boundary objects are "classifications" which are "objects for cooperation across social worlds. . . . We define boundary objects as those objects that both inhabit several communities of practice and satisfy the informational requirements of each of them. In working practice, they are objects that are able both to travel across borders and maintain some sort of constant identity. . . . They can be tailored to meet the needs of any one community (they are plastic in this sense, or customizable). At the same time, they have common identities across settings. This is achieved by allowing the objects to be weakly structured in common use, imposing stronger structures

in the individual-site tailored use. They are thus both ambiguous and constant; they may be abstract or concrete" (Bowker and Star 1999: 15–16).

11. While not referring explicitly to competencies and modularization, Bauman, in describing "contemporary knowledge handling-and deploying practices," offers this apt characterization: "Instead of an image of an edifice erected floor by floor, from the foundations up to the roof, signalling the completion of building, it is better to think of knowledge as offered and consumed in small bites, each one separately cooked and quickly chewed and digested, and then as quickly vacated from the digestive tract, clearing the space for further portions. It is better as well not to think of the whole intake as ordered in any specific menu-like sequence" (Bauman 2005: 315–316).
12. StraighterLine is a private education "provider" which offers college level courses in several fields. Smith expressed the fuzziness of the higher education field when he wrote that "college is not well-defined now. It is not a residential environment where people go to one place and stay there for four years. At least, not for the majority of students.... It is not time-delimited in many cases. Students are transferring credits from place to place to place. There are very different modalities, with different cost structures associated with them, and we don't really even know what it should be. There are certificates that are being offered by colleges. There are adult-ed programs. There are online programs. *We don't really know what college is any more.* Or to put it another way, there are lots of different options for it" (Smith 2012; my emphasis).
13. "Software as a service (SaaS; pronounced /sæs/ ...) is a software licensing and delivery model in which software is licensed on a subscription basis and is centrally hosted.... It is sometimes referred to as 'on-demand software.' ..." Accessed March 30, 2016, at https://en.wikipedia.org/wiki/Software_as_a_service.
14. "Trainability" is "the ability to be taught, the ability to respond effectively to concurrent, subsequent, or intermittent pedagogies" (Bernstein, 2001a: 365–366).
15. While not an exact comparison to competency education and badges, the case of "University Business School" in the United Kingdom may nevertheless be apt. The school's curriculum was recast as "a 'business project' in which programmes were constructed as 'products' for the higher education market. The associated pedagogy was largely confined to behaviourist problem—solution routines based on narrow projections of the 'real world' of business. [The] UBS undergraduate programmes were designed in a generic mode in response to the material and discursive influences of marketisation. As a consequence, 'epistemic chaos' had arisen in which knowledge and pedagogy had become fragmented and amorphous" (Brady 2015: 1236).
16. Bernstein is using the term "competence model" in a developmentally oriented sense, associated with primary school and preschool pedagogy in which students are active creators of meanings and practice (Bernstein 2000: 42–43). "Competencies," as I have used the term throughout this chapter, are more associated with what Bernstein calls a "performance model." "... A performance model of pedagogic practice and context places the emphasis upon a specific output of the acquirer, upon a particular text the acquirer is expected to construct and upon the specialised skills necessary to the production of this specific output, text or product" (Bernstein 2000: 44).

References

Apple, Michael W. 1979. *Ideology and Curriculum*. London: Routledge and Kegan Paul.

———. 1982. *Education and Power*. Boston: Routledge and Kegan Paul.

———. 1993. *Official Knowledge: Democratic Education in a Conservative Age*. New York: Routledge.

———. 1999. *Power, Meaning, and Identity: Essays in Critical Educational Studies*. New York: Peter Lang.

———. 2013. *Can Education Change Society*? New York: Routledge.

Ash, Katie. "'Digital Badges' Would Represent Students' Skill Acquisition." *Education Week*, June 13, 2012. Accessed August 8, 2012, at http://www.edweek.org/dd/articles/2012/06/13/03badges.h05.html?tkn=VVTFxfZmUnTrwnZw9greLk0bnLLzPz5qEvsj&cmp=ENL-EU-EWS1& amp;intc=es&print=1.

Ashby, Iryna, Marisa Extr, Sorin Adam Matei, and Jeffrey Evans. 2016. "Lifelong Learning Starts at School." In *Digital Badges in Education: Trends, Issues, and Cases*, edited by Lin Y. Muilenburg and Zane L. Berge, 166–175. New York: Routledge.

Association of American Colleges and Universities. N.d. "Critical Thinking VALUE Rubric." Accessed June 26, 2015, at https://www.aacu.org/sites/default/files/files/VALUE/CriticalThinking.pdf.

Baker, David P. 2018. "Social Theory and the Coming Schooled Society." Chapter 2 in this volume.

Barnett, Ronald. 1994. *The Limits of Competence: Knowledge, Higher Education and Society*. Buckingham, UK: Open University Press.

Bauman, Zygmunt. 2005. "Education in Liquid Modernity." *Review of Education, Pedagogy, and Cultural Studies* 27: 303–317.

———. 2007. *Consuming Life*. Cambridge, UK: Polity.

———. 2009. "Education in the Liquid-Modern Setting." *Power and Education* 1 (2): 157–166.

———. 2012. *Liquid Modernity*. Cambridge, UK: Polity Press.

Beck, John, and Michael F. D. Young. 2005. "The Assault on the Professions and the Restructuring of Professional Identities: A Bernsteinian Analysis." *British Journal of Sociology of Education* 26:183–197.

Beck, Ulrich. 1992. *Risk Society: Towards a New Modernity*. Los Angeles: SAGE Publications.

Beck, Ulrich, Wolfgang Bonss, and Christoph Lau. 2003. "The Theory of Reflexive Modernization: Problematic, Hypotheses and Research Programme." *Theory, Culture & Society* 20:1–33.

Berman, Elizabeth Popp. 2012. *Creating the Market University: How Academic Science Became an Economic Engine*. Princeton, NJ: Princeton University Press.

Bernstein, Basil. 1977. *Class Codes and Control: Volume 3 Towards a Theory of Educational Transmissions*. London: Routledge and Kegan Paul.

———. 1990. *The Structuring of Pedagogic Discourse: Volume 4 Class, Codes and Control*. London: Routledge.

———. 2000. *Pedagogy, Symbolic Control and Identity: Theory, Research, Critique*. Lanham, MD: Rowman & Littlefield.

———. 2001a. "From Pedagogies to Knowledges." In *Towards a Sociology of Pedagogy: The Contribution of Basil Bernstein to Research*, edited by Ana Morais, Isabel Neves, Brian Davies, and Harry Daniels, 363–368. New York: Peter Lang.

———. 2001b. "Symbolic Control: Issues of Empirical Description of Agencies and Agents." *International Journal of Social Research Methodology* 4:21–33.

Bills, David B. 2004. *The Sociology of Education and Work*. Malden, MA: Blackwell.

Bills, David B., and Mary Ellen Wacker. 2003. "Acquiring Credentials When Signals Don't Matter: Employers' Support of Employees Who Pursue Postsecondary Vocational Degrees." *Sociology of Education* 76:170–187.

Boltanski, Luc, and Eve Chiapello. 2007. *The New Spirit of Capitalism*. London, UK: Verso.

Boston University. 2014. Alternate Credentialing Forum, College of Advancing and Professional Studies, June 18. Accessed June 18, 2015, at https://www.youtube.com/watch?v=ioZBsAbukp4.

Bourdieu, Pierre. 1984. *Distinction: A Social Critique of the Judgement of Taste*. Cambridge, MA Harvard University Press.

———. 1986. "The Forms of Capital." In *Handbook of Theory and Research for the Sociology of Education*, edited by John G. Richardson, 241–258. New York: Greenwood Press.

———. 1991. *Language and Symbolic Power*. Cambridge, MA: Harvard University Press.

———. 1996. *The State Nobility: Elite Schools in the Field of Power*. Stanford, CA: Stanford University Press.

Bowker, Geoffrey C., and Susan Leigh Star. 1999. *Sorting Things Out: Classification and Its Consequences*. Cambridge, MA: MIT Press.

Bowles, Samuel, and Herbert Gintis. 1976. *Schooling in Capitalist America: Educational Reform and the Contradictions of Economic Life*. New York: Basic Books.

Brady, Norman. 2015. "'Epistemic Chaos': The Recontextualization of Undergraduate Curriculum Design and Pedagogic Practice in a New University Business School." *British Journal of Sociology of Education*. 36:1236–1257.

Brint, Steven. 2013a. "A Priori and Empirical Approaches to the Classification of Higher Education Institutions: The United States Case." *Pensamiento Educativo: Revista de Investigación Educacional Latinoamericana* 50: 96–114.

———. 2013b. "The 'Collective Mind' at Work: A Decade in the Life of U.S. Sociology of Education." *Sociology of Education* 86:273–279.

Brint, Steven, and Jerome Karabel. 1989. *The Diverted Dream: Community Colleges and the Promise of Educational Opportunity in America, 1900–1985*. New York: Oxford University Press.

Brint, Steven, Mark Riddle, and Robert A. Hanneman. 2006. "Reference Sets, Identities, and Aspirations in a Complex Organizational Field: The Case of American Four-Year Colleges and Universities." *Sociology of Education* 79:229–252.

Brown, David K. 1995. *Degrees of Control: A Sociology of Educational Expansion and Occupational Credentialism*. New York: Teachers College Press.

Brown, Phillip, and Anthony Hesketh. 2004. *The Mismanagement of Talent: Employability and Jobs in the Knowledge Economy*. Oxford, UK: Oxford University Press, 2004.

Casilli, Carla. 2014. Presentation to "Year in Review." Session 13, #openbadgesMOOC "New Currency for Professional Credentials," December 12. Accessed June 26, 2015, at https://www. youtube.com/watch?v=vzhs9p81wGA.

Casilli, Carla, and Erin Knight. 2012. "Seven Things You Should Know About Badges." Educause, June 11. Accessed June 27, 2013, at http://net.educause.edu/ir/library/pdf/ELI7085.pdf.

Castells, Manuel. 1996. *The Rise of the Network Society. The Information Age: Economy, Society and Culture, Volume I*. Malden, MA: Blackwell Publishers.

Collin, Ross. 2011. "Selling the Self: Career Portfolios and the New Common-Sense of Immaterial Capitalism." *Social Semiotics* 21:615–632.

Collins, Randall. 1979. *The Credential Society: A Historical Sociology of Education and Stratification*. New York: Academic Press.

———. 1981. "Crises and Declines in Credential Systems." In *Sociology since Midcentury: Essays in Theory Cumulation*, 191–215. New York: Academic Press.

———. 2002. "Credential Inflation and the Future of the Universities." In *The Future of the City of Intellect*, edited by Steven Brint, 23–46. Stanford, CA: Stanford University Press.

Corporation for a Skilled Workforce. n.d. *Making a Market for Competency-Based Credentials*. Ann Arbor, MI: Corporation for a Skilled Workforce.

Council for Adult & Experiential Learning. 2014. "Customized, Outcome-based, Relevant Evaluation (CORE) at Lipscomb University." Accessed June 26, 2015, at http://www.cael.org/cael_lipscomb_case_study.

Craig, Ryan. 2015. *College Disrupted: The Great Unbundling of Higher Education*. New York: St. Martin's Press.

Craig, Ryan, and Allison Williams. 2015. "Data, Technology, and the Great Unbundling of Higher Education." *EDUCAUSE Review*, September/October 2015. Accessed March 16, 2016, at http://er.educause.edu/articles/2015/8/data-technology-and-the-great-unbundling-of-higher-education.

Credly. 2015. "Brandman University Teams Up with Credly to Issue Digital Badges as Part of Competency-Based Education Degrees." Blog.Credly.Com, January 7. Accessed June 26, 2015, at http://blog.credly.com/brandman-cbe-badges/.

Crouch, Colin, David Finegold, and Mari Sako. 1999. *Are Skills the Answer? The Political Economy of Skill Creation in Advanced Countries*. Oxford, UK: Oxford University Press.

Cummings, Jean. 2012. "How a 'Badge' System Could Revolutionize Your Brand and Job Search." Career Hub, March 28. Accessed June 18, 2015, at http://www.careerhubblog.com/main/2012/03/how-a-badge-system-could-revolutionize-your-brand-job-search.html.

Davidson, Cathy N., and David Theo Goldberg. 2010. *The Future of Thinking: Learning Institutions in a Digital Age*. Cambridge, MA: MIT Press.

Davies, Scott, and Jal Mehta. 2018. "The Deepening Interpenetration of Education in Modern Life." Chapter 3 in this volume.

Derryberry, Anne. 2014. "Assessment Strategies for Effective Badge Systems." Session 8, #openbadgesMOOC, "New Currency for Professional Credentials," February 24. Accessed June 18, 2015, at https://sas.elluminate.com/site/external/playback/artifact?psid=2014-02-24.1102.M.63161603E242CD007FD9802B7B3F01.vcr&aid=91192.

Desjardins, Richard, and Kjell Rubenson. "An Analysis of Skill Mismatch Using Direct Measures of Skills." *OECD Education Working Papers*, no. 63 (2011). OECD Publishing. Accessed September 6, 2015, at http://www.oecd-ilibrary.org/education/an-analysis-of-skill-mismatch-using-direct-measures-of-skills_5kg3nh9h52g5-en.

DiMaggio, Paul. 1988. "Interest and Agency in Institutional Theory." In *Institutional Patterns and Organizations: Culture and Environment*, edited by Lynne G. Zucker, 3–21. Cambridge, MA: Ballinger Publishing.

DiMaggio, Paul J., and Walter W. Powell. 1983. "The Iron Cage Revisited: Institutional Isomorhpism and Collective Rationality in Organizational Fields." *American Sociology Review* 48:147–160.

———. 1991. Introduction to *The New Institutionalism in Organizational Analysis*, edited by Walter W. Powell and Paul J. DiMaggio, 1–38. Chicago: University of Chicago Press.

Education Design Lab. 2015. "Are Badges College Ready?" June 24. Accessed June 25, 2015 at http://eddesignlab.org/2015/06/are-badges-college-ready/.

Eduventures. 2014. *The Next-Generation Higher Education Technology Landscape*. Boston: Eduventures.

Eraut, Michael. 2004. "Transfer of Knowledge between Education and Workplace Setting." In *Workplace Learning in Context*, edited by H. Rainbird, A. Fuller and A. Munroe, 201–221. London, Routledge.

Everhart, Deborah. 2014a. "Badges and Competency-Based Learning." Session 7, #openbadgesMOOC "New Currency for Professional Credentials," January 27. Accessed June 22, 2015, at https://sas.elluminate.com/site/external/playback/artifact?psid=2014-01-27.1050.M.63161603E242CD007FD9802B7B3F01.vcr&aid=77816.

———. 2014b. "Badges: Bridging the Gap between Higher Ed and the Workforce," March 19. Accessed June 18, 2015, at http://blog.blackboard.com/badges-bridging-gap-higher-ed-workforce/.

Everhart, Deborah, Deb Bushway, and David Schejbal. 2016. *Communicating the Value of Competencies*. Washington: American Council on Education.

Everhart, Deborah, Evelyn Ganzglass, Carla Casilli, Daniel Hickey, and Barandon Muramatsu. 2016. *Quality Dimensions for Connected Credentials*. Washington: American Council on Education.

Everhart, Deborah, Cathy Sandeen, Deborah Seymour, and Karen Yoshino. 2014. *Clarifying Competency Based Education Terms*. American Council on Education, and Blackboard, Washington. Accessed June 26, 2015, at http://blog.blackboard.com/clarifying-competency-based-education-terms/.

Fairclough, Norman. 1992. *Discourse and Social Change*. Cambridge, UK: Polity Press.

Fligstein, Neil, and Doug McAdam. 2011. "Toward a General Theory of Strategic Action Fields." *Sociological Theory* 29:1–26.

———. 2012. *A Theory of Fields*. Oxford, UK: Oxford University Press.

Fouarge, Didier, Trudie Schils, and Andries de Grip. "Why Do Low-Educated Workers Invest Less in Further Training?" Forschungsinstitut zur Zukunft der Arbeit, no. 5180, 2010. Bonn: Institute for the Study of Labor. Accessed September 6, 2015, at http://www.econstor.eu/handle/10419/46030.

Frank, David John, and Jay Gabler. 2006. *Reconstructing the University: Worldwide Shifts in Academia in the 20th Century*. Stanford, CA: Stanford University Press.

Frank, David John, Suk-Ying Wong, John W. Meyer, and Francisco O. Ramirez. 2000. "What Counts as History: A Cross-National and Longitudinal Study of University Curricula." *Comparative Education Review* 44:29–53.

Fraser, Don, Jr. 2015. Personal conversation, June 26.

Ganzglass, Evelyn. 2014. "Scaling 'Stackable Credentials' Implications for Implementation and Policy." Washington: Center for Law and Social Policy. Accessed June 26, 2015, at http://www.clasp.org/resources-and-publications/files/2014-03-21-Stackable-Credentials-Paper-FINAL.pdf.

Gee, James Paul, Glynda Hull, and Colin Lankshear. 1996. *The New Work Order: Behind the Language of New Capitalism*. Boulder, CO: Westview Press.

Gewirtz, Sharon. 2008. "Give Us a Break! A Sceptical Review of Contemporary Discourses of Lifelong Learning." *European Educational Research Journal* 7:414–424.

Grant, Sheryl. 2014. "What Counts as Learning: Open Digital Badges for New Opportunities." Digital Media and Learning Research Hub, Kindle edition.

Greenwood, Royston, Roy Suddaby, and C. R. Hinings. 2002. "Theorizing Change: The Role of Professional Associations in the Transformation of Institutionalized Fields." *Academy of Management Journal* 45: 58–80.

Gumport, Patricia. 2000. "Academic Restructuring: Organizational Change and Institutional Imperatives." *Higher Education* 39:67–91.

Hardy, Cynthia, and Steve Maguire. 2008. "Institutional Entrepreneurship." In *SAGE Handbook of Organizational Institutionalism*, edited by Royston Greenwood, Christine Oliver, Roy Suddaby, and Kerstin Sahlin-Andersson, 198–217. London: SAGE Publications.

Hefler, Gunter, and Jorg Markowitsch. 2012. "Bridging Institutional Divides: Linking Education, Careers, and Work in 'Organizational Space' and 'Skills Space' Dominated Employment Systems." In *Changing Spaces of Education: New Perspectives on the Nature of Learning*, edited by Rachel Brooks, Alison Fuller, and Johanna Waters, 160–181. New York: Routledge.

Hickey, Daniel T., James E. Willis III, and Joshua D. Quick 2015. "Where Open Badges Appear to Have Worked Better: Findings from the Design Principles Documentation Project." Accessed June 27, 2017 at https://library.educause.edu/~/media/files/library/2015/6/elib1503-pdf.pdf.

Hinings, C. R., Royston Greenwood, Trish Reay, and Roy Suddaby. 2004. "Dynamics of Change in Organizational Fields." In *Handbook of Organizational Change and Innovation*, edited by Marshall Scott Poole and Andrew H. Van de Ven, 304–323. New York: Oxford University Press.

Ifenthaler, Dirk, Nicole Bellin-Mularski, and Dana-Kristin Mah, eds. 2016. *Foundations of Digital Badges and Micro-Credentials*. Switzerland: Springer.

Illich, Ivan. 1970. *Deschooling Society*. New York: Harrow Books.

Inside Higher Education. 2016. "The Rise of Competency-Based Education." Accessed November 14, 2016, at https://www.insidehighered.com/quicktakes/2016/01/26/rise-competency-based-education.

Janzow, Peter. 2014. "From Colleges to Careers: Sharing Competencies through Open Badges." Pearson webinar, November 12. Accessed June 18, 2015, at http://www. brainshark.com/pearsonschool/vu?pi=zGazWoHOJzE 38yz0.

Jencks, Christopher, Susan Bartlett, Mary Corcoran, James Crouse, David Eaglesfield, Gregory Jackson, Kent McClelland, Peter Mueser, Michael Olneck, Joseph Schwartz, Sherry Ward, and Jill Williams. 1979. *Who Gets Ahead? The Determinants of Economic Success in America*. New York: Basic Books.

Jencks, Christopher, Marshall Smith, Henry Acland, Mary Jo Bane, David Cohen, Herbert Gintis, Barbara Heyns, and Stephan Michelson. 1972. *Inequality: A Reassessment of the Effect of Family and Schooling in America*. New York: Basic Books.

Jones, Lynn, and Rob Moore. 1993. "Education, Competence and the Control of Expertise." *British Journal of Sociology of Education* 14:385–397.

Kalleberg, Arne L. 2011. *Good Jobs, Bad Jobs: The Rise of Polarized and Precarious Employment Systems in the United States, 1970s–2000s*. New York: Russell Sage Foundation.

Kamenetz, Anya. 2015. "DIY U: Higher Education Goes Hybrid." In *Remaking College: The Changing Ecology of Higher Education*, edited by Michael W. Kirst and Mitchel L. Stevens, 39–60. Stanford, CA: Stanford University Press.

Kamens, David H., John W. Meyer, and Aaron Benavot. 1996. "Worldwide Patterns in Academic Secondary Education Curricula." *Comparative Education Review* 40:116–138.

Karabel, Jerome, and A. H. Halsey, eds. 1977. *Power and Ideology in Education*. New York: Oxford University Press.

Kelchen, Robert. 2015. *The Landscape of Competency-Based Education: Enrollment, Demographics, and Affordability*. Center on Higher Education Reform, American Enterprise Institute, Washington.

Knight, Erin. 2012. "Reflections on Reflections on Badges." Accessed June 17, 2015, at http://erinknight.com/post/20348999445/reflections-on-reflections-on-badges.

Kraatz, Matthew S., and Emily S. Block. 2008. "Organizational Implications of Institutional Pluralism." In *The SAGE Handbook of Organizational Institutionalism*, edited by Royston Greenwood, Christine Oliver, Roy Suddaby, and Kerstin Sahlin-Andersson, 243–275. London: SAGE Publications.

Kraatz, Matthew S., Marc J. Ventresca, and Lina Deng. 2010. "Precarious Values and Mundane Innovations: Enrollment Management in American Liberal Arts Colleges." *Academy of Management Journal* 53:1521–1545.

Kraatz, Matthew S., and Edward J. Zajac. 1996. "Exploring the Limits of the New Institutionalism: The Causes and Consequences of Illegitimate Organizational Change." *American Sociological Review* 6:812–836.

Labaree, David F. 1997. *How to Succeed in School without Really Learning: The Credentials Race in American Education*. New Haven: Yale University Press.

———. 2006. "Mutual Subversion: A Short History of the Liberal and the Professional in American Higher Education." *History of Education Quarterly* 46:1–15.

LeBlanc, Paul. 2013. "College for America." Slide presentation accessed June 22, 2015, at http://www.slideshare.net/DemandEngine/le-blanc-college-for-america-full-presentationfinalshorter?qid=57a32a2f-768b-4dbe-bd7d-cd680437b0be&v=default&b=&from_search=2.

Libscomb University. n.d. "Competency Coaches, Adjunct Positions." Formerly available at http://www.lipscomb.edu/hr/filter/item/0/28569. Date accessed unknown.

Long, Charla. 2014. Telephone interview, July 7.

Long, Charla, and Teresa Bagamery Clark. 2013. "Badges, Competencies, and Credit: Moving Toward a Competency-Based Bachelor's Degree." Accessed November 21, 2016, at https://unbound.upcea.edu/innovation/alternative-credentialing/badges-competencies-and-credit-moving-toward-a-competency-based-bachelors-degree/.

Loewenstein, Jeffery, and William Ocasio. 2002. "Vocabularies of Organizing: How Language Links Culture, Cognition, and Action in Organizations." Revision of paper presented at the 2002 meeting of the Academy of Management.

Lumina Foundation. N.d. *The Beta Credentials Framework Guidebook: A Universal Credentials Translator*. Accessed March 29, 2016, at http://connectingcredentials.org/aacc-rfp/.

———. 2015a. *Connecting Credentials: A Beta Credentials Framework*. Indianapolis: Lumina Foundation.

———. 2015b. *Connecting Credentials: Making the Case for Reforming the U.S. Credentialing System*. Indianapolis: Lumina Foundation.

———. 2016. *Connecting Credentials: Lessons from the National Summit and Next Steps in the National Dialogue*. Indianapolis: Lumina Foundation.

Maroy, Christian, and Pierre Doray. 2000. "Education-Work Relations: Theoretical Reference Points for a Research Domain." *Work, Employment & Society* 14:173–189.

Martin, John Levi. 2003. "What Is Field Theory?" *American Journal of Sociology* 109:1–49.

Maton, Karl. 2005. "A Question of Autonomy: Bourdieu's Field Approach and Higher Education Policy." *Journal of Education Policy* 20:687–704.

McEneaney, Elizabeth H., and John W. Meyer. 2000. "The Content of the Curriculum." In *Handbook of the Sociology of Education*, edited by Maureen T. Hallinan, 189–211. New York: Kluwer Academic / Plenum Publishers.

Mehta, Jal, and Scott Davies. 2018. "Introduction: Education in a New Society." Chapter 1 in this volume.

Meyer, Heinz-Dieter, and Brian Rowan. 2006. *The New Institutionalism in Education*. Albany: State University of New York Press.

Meyer, John W. 1970. "The Charter: Conditions of Diffuse Socialization in Schools." In *Social Processes and Social Structures: An Introduction to Sociology*, edited by W. R. Scott, 564–578. New York: Holt, Rinehart and Winston.

———. 1977. "The Effects of Education as an Institution." *American Journal of Sociology* 83: 55–77.

Meyer, John W., Francisco O. Ramirez, David John Frank, and Evan Schofer. 2007. "Higher Education as an Institution." In *Sociology of Higher Education*, edited by Patricia Gumport, 187–221. Baltimore: Johns Hopkins Press.

Meyer, John W., and Brian Rowan. 1978. "The Structure of Educational Organizations." In *Environments and Organizations*, edited by Marshall W. Meyer, 78–109. San Francisco: Jossey-Bass.

Molineaux, Sally. 2012. "Open Badges: The Future of Accreditation." November 22. Accessed June 24, 2015, at http://hastac.org/node/105584.

Mozilla Foundation and Peer 2 Peer University. 2012. "Open Badges for Lifelong Learning." Working Paper. Accessed June 17, 2015, at https://wiki.mozilla.org/images/5/59/OpenBadges-Working-Paper_012312.pdf.

Mozilla Wiki. 2014. "Badges." December 18. Accessed June 24, 2015, at https://wiki.mozilla.org/Badges.

Muilenburg, Lin Y., and Zane L. Berge, eds. *Digital Badges in Education: Trends, Issues, and Cases*. 2016. New York: Routledge.

Munch, Richard. 2012. *Inclusion and Exclusion in the Liberal Competition State: The Cult of the Individual*. London and New York: Routledge.

Naidoo, Rajani, and Ian Jamieson. 2005." Empowering Participants or Corroding Learning? Towards a Research Agenda on the Impact of Student Consumerism in Higher Education." *Journal of Education Policy* 20:267–281.

Neil, A.S. 1960. *Summerhill: A Radical Approach to Childrearing*. New York: Hart Publishing.

Oakes, Jeannie. 1985. *Keeping Track: How Schools Structure Inequality*. New Haven: Yale University Press.

Oliver, Christine. 1992. "The Antecedents of Deinstitutionalization." *Organization Studies* 13:563–588.

Olneck, Michael. 2013. "Why Are MOOCs Controversial, But Badges Are Not?" Accessed November 14, 2016, at https://www.hastac.org/blogs/molneck/2013/09/12/why-are-moocs-controversial-badges-are-not.

Pearson Education, Inc. 2013. *Open Badges Are Unlocking the Emerging Jobs Economy*. Accessed February 18, 2014, at http://www.pearsonvue.com/sponsors/acclaim/open_badges_unlock_jobs.pdf.

Plater, Michael. 2014. "Three Trends Shaping Learning." Accessed June 26, 2015, at http://www.clomedia.com/articles/5644-three-trends-shaping-learning.

Rawlings, Craig. 2012. "Status Reproduction in Uncertain Environments: Undergraduate Program Differentiation by U.S. Colleges and Universities, 1970–1990." Unpublished paper. Department of Sociology, University of California-Santa Barbara.

Rawlings, Craig M., and Michael D. Bourgeois. 2004. "The Complexity of Institutional Niches: Credentials and Organizational Differentiation in a Field of U.S. Education." *Poetics* 32:411–446.

Roome, Benjamin, and James Willis. 2015. "Competency-Based Education, Badges, and Professional Development." Re-Mediating Assessment, May 19. Accessed June 11, 2015, at http://remediatingassessment.blogspot.com/2015/05/competency-based-education-badges-and.html.

Ruef, Martin, and Manish Nag. 2015. "The Classification of Organizational Forms: Theory and Application to the Field of Higher Education." In *Remaking College: The Changing Ecology of Higher Education*, edited by Michael W. Kirst and Mitchel L. Stevens, 84–109. Stanford, CA: Stanford University Press.

Sadovnik, Alan R. 1991. "Basil Bernstein's Theory of Pedagogic Practice: A Structuralist Approach." *Sociology of Education* 64:48–63.

Schwartz, Jake. 2016. Comments made at panel on "The New Language of Credentials: Unbundling and Stacking," at the Parchment Summit on Innovating Academic Credentials, February 17. Author's notes.

Scott, W. Richard. 2008. *Institutions and Organizations: Ideas and Interests*. Third edition. Los Angeles: SAGE Publications.

Scott, W. Richard. 2015a. "Higher Education: A Field in Ferment." In *Emerging Trends in the Social and Behavioral Sciences*, edited by Robert Scott and Stephen Michael Kosslyn, 1–14. Wiley Online Library.

Scott, W. Richard. 2015b. "Higher Education in America: Multiple Field Perspectives." In *Remaking College: The Changing Ecology of Higher Education*, edited by Michael W. Kirst and Mitchell L. Stevens, 19–38. Stanford, CA: Stanford University Press.

Scott, W. Richard, and Manuelito Biag. 2016. "The Changing Ecology of U.S. Higher Education: An Organization Field Perspective." *Research in the Sociology of Organizations* 46:25–51.

Seymour, Deborah, Deborah Everhart, and Karen Yoshino. 2015. *The Currency of Higher Education: Credits and Competencies*. American Council of Education, and Blackboard, Washington. Accessed June 11, 2015, at http://www.luminafoundation.org/files/resources/currency-of-he.pdf.

Sheets, Robert. 2016. Developing a Common Language for Connecting Credentials. February 19. Webinar accessed March 29, 2016, at http://connectingcredentials.org/media/developing-a-common-language-for-connecting-credentials/.

Singh, Parlo. 2015. "Performativity and Pedagogising Knowledge: Globalising Educational Policy Formation, Dissemination and Enactment." *Journal of Education Policy* 30:363–384.

Smith, Burk. 2012. "Burk Smith on the Changing Model of Education." November 10. Accessed March 16, 2016, at http://www.straighterline.com/blog/burck-smith-on-the-changing-model-of-education/.

Star, Susan Leigh, and James R. Griesemer. 1989. "Institutional Ecology, 'Translations' and Boundary Objects: Amateurs and Professionals in Berkeley's Museum of Vertebrate Zoology, 1907–39." *Social Studies of Science* 19:387–420.

Suchman, Mark C. 1995. "Managing Legitimacy: Strategic and Institutional Approaches." *Academy of Management Review* 20:571–610.

Thornton, Patricia H., and William Ocasio. 2008. "Institutional Logics." In *The SAGE Handbook of Organizational Institutionalism*, edited by Royston Greenwood, Christine Oliver, Roy Suddaby, and Kerstin Sahlin-Andersson, 99–129. London: SAGE Publications.

Thornton, Patricia H., William Ocasio, and Michael Loundsbury. 2012. *The Institutional Logics Perspective: A New Approach to Culture, Structure and Process*. Oxford, UK: Oxford University Press.

Tuschling, Anna, and Christoph Engemann. 2006. "From Education to Lifelong Learning: The Emerging Regime of Learning in the European Union." *Educational Philosophy and Theory* 38:451–469.

Urciuoli, Bonnie. 2008. "Skills and Selves in the New Workplace." *American Ethnologist* 35: 211–228.

US Department of Education, National Center for Education Statistics. 2002. *Defining and*

Assessing Learning: Exploring Competency-Based Initiatives, NCES 2002–159, prepared by Elizabeth A. Jones and Richard A. Voorhees with Karen Paulson, for the Council of the National Postsecondary Education Cooperative Working Group on Competency-Based Initiatives, Washington.

Weise, Michelle. 2014. "Got Skills? Why Online Competency-Based Education Is the Disruptive Innovation for Higher Education." *Educause Review*, November/December. Accessed June 26, 2015, at http://www. educause.edu/ero/article/got-skills-why-online-competency-based-education-disruptive-innovation-higher-education.

Wheelahan, Leesa. 2010. "The Structure of Pedagogic Discourse as a Relay for Power: The Case of Competency-Based Training." In *Toolkits, Translation Devices and Conceptual Accounts: Essays on Basil Bernstein's Sociology of Knowledge*, edited by Parlo Singh, Alan R. Sadovnik, and Susan F. Semel, 47–63. New York: Peter Lang.

Whitty, Geoff. 1985. *Sociology and School Knowledge: Curriculum, Theory, and School Knowledge*. London: Methuen.

———. 2010. "Revisiting School Knowledge: Some Sociological Perspectives on New School Curricula." *European Journal of Education* 45:28–45.

Wooten, Melissa, and Andrew J. Hoffman. 2008. "Organizational Fields: Past, Present, and Future." In *The SAGE Handbook of Organizational Institutionalism*, edited by R. Greenwood, C. Oliver, K. Sahlin, and E. Suddaby, 130–147. London: SAGE Publications.

Young, Michael F. D. 1971a. "An Approach to the Study of Curricula as Socially Organized Knowledge." In *Knowledge and Control: New Directions for the Sociology of Education*, edited by M. F. D. Young, 19–46. London: Collier-Macmillan.

———. 1998. *The Curriculum of the Future: From the "New Sociology of Education" to a Critical Theory of Learning*. London: Falmer Press.

Young, Michael F. D., ed. 1971b. *Knowledge and Control: New Directions for the Sociology of Education*. London: Collier-Macmillan.

TEN

Research Universities and the Global Battle for the Brains

JOHN D. SKRENTNY AND NATALIE M. NOVICK

Across the globe, national governments and research universities are trying to attract foreign students to their universities. A special though not exclusive focus of this "battle for the brains" is on science and engineering talent, including graduate students and postdoctoral researchers. As David Baker highlights in chapter 2 of this volume, the increasing role of science, technology, engineering, and math (STEM) in academia has coincided with increasing demands for international students. This demand for international students in STEM has especially transformed graduate education, with some fields in the US averaging enrollments of more than 70 percent foreign-born.

In other contexts, large numbers of incoming migrants lead to concern, and even alarm or panic, as native populations fear they will lose their community or job opportunities. Governments respond by seeking to restrict immigration. Yet in many countries, foreign *students* are welcomed, and governments as well as universities seek to increase their numbers.

These policy elites must see international students as the solution to one or more problems—they see it as rational to attract and enroll them in universities. Our question is simple: Why? Why not focus on serving local populations, including those whose tax money (in the case of public institutions) helps to support the universities?

Part of the reason is simply that there are more foreign students, in STEM and other fields, than ever before. There are students in developed countries willing to move for their education, but there are even greater numbers of talented people in poorer countries who perceive limited opportunities or low wages at home. As migration theory would predict, the growing number of college-educated persons, especially in populous countries such as China and India, have been a boon for graduate programs across the world.[1] At the same time, some college age cohorts, such as in the United States, have actually shrunk.[2] In short, there are more qualified students in the world, and fewer at home.

But we focus here on the demand side. Education scholars have identified a long list of potential sources of the demand for international students.[3] One of the problems that international students help to solve is age-old: how to attract the most talented students available and to improve the educational experience on campus. This problem, though real, has always existed. Universities, especially those focused on research, want the best. What are more interesting from the perspective of the sociology of education are the problems that have developed in more recent decades, and which are particular to the current age—an age with a distinctive institutional environment, and thus distinctive goals and aspirations for those who make educational policy.

With this in mind, we identify three separate problems for which international students have come to be understood as the solution, fueling the battle for the brains in the world's research universities. Our approach is guided by neoinstitutional theory in organizations,[4] historical institutional theory in politics,[5] and especially the understanding that there are historical contingencies and strategic choices, shaped by taken-for-granted scripts, rules, and institutional arrangements. Our focus is on the United States, but we discuss other states to show that this is a global phenomenon. Our goal is to show why policymakers came to see enrollment of international students, especially STEM students, as rational, why they did not make other choices, and why international student enrollment came to be taken for granted as the rational course of action.

One problem to be solved was: How to create a "world-class university"? This term, used often by scholars and policymakers, has no set meaning, but typically refers to a bundle of qualities relating to an institution's resources, recruitment, and overall quality.[6] It is part of a series of changes, highlighted by Davies and Mehta in chapter 1 of this volume, that has raised the stakes for success and made recruiting the best students even more competitive. Having a world-class university has become especially important to newly industrialized nations that are concerned about their status and want to raise their reputation on a global scale. These countries evince eagerness to show their excellence in education and highlight the modernity of their intellectual development. A reasonable way to show off a university to the world is to have the world come visit it. The basic ideas here have been developed in a series of studies on world culture and the expansion and standardization of higher education, especially curricula.[7] In a process that had different start dates in different countries but is now widely established, universities and states perceived international students as a signal of their legitimacy and status in the global community. Global ranking services (see chapter 3 in this volume) then helped spread this "internationalization" of student bodies when they explicitly made it a part of their calculations—a high ranking was another signal of world-class status.

The second problem to be solved focused on domestic audiences: How to justify a university in neoliberal times? By "neoliberal," we mean the recent emergence of market rationalities in disparate and diverse social relations. Whatever the original justification for universities, and there have been many,[8] there can be little doubt that policymakers and education leaders have increasingly justified universities and education funding by reference to their contributions to economic growth, and thus to revenue generation.[9] Since many policymakers have come to see highly-educated STEM workers as the source of innovation, and innovation as the key to economic growth, attracting international STEM students has become part of this general economic orientation. The competition for STEM students has emerged as a response to the postindustrial economy long ago identified by Daniel Bell.[10]

The third problem that international students solve is related to these same changes in advanced industrial economies: How to pay the bills? Universities in many countries face decreasing proportions of government support for their expanding budgets. One obvious way that international students contribute to the solution is by paying tuition. The attraction to these students is especially pronounced in STEM, for complex reasons. Running a major research university is expensive, and maintaining labs and hiring the world-class faculty to staff them has become even more challenging than in the past. At the same time, funding for specific scientific projects with defined endpoints and deliverables is still plentiful. Rather than fight for more government core support, universities have adapted to the new fiscal environment, seeking to cut costs and generate revenue while still accepting project-based research funds. This has led universities to use international students (and here we include postdoctoral researchers, who are still being trained) for tuition funding and as inexpensive scientific labor. Another attractive feature of foreigners, at least doctoral students and PhDs in some STEM fields, is that they are willing to supply research labor power at low rates of pay as postdoctoral researchers in American university science laboratories. Universities pursue the international STEM students and postdocs, and governments create visa policy to enable this pursuit.

These choices that education policymakers are making are of great significance, and relate to larger themes in this volume. One of these themes is inequality. When the willingness of international students to "pay to play" becomes a major pillar of university financing, local students may be squeezed out of opportunities simply because there are fewer spaces available to them. In other words, the local democratizing mission of some public institutions becomes compromised, and higher education is cast as an ostensibly public good that is most readily available to those who can pay.

We also wish to underscore the political "taken-for-granteds" that make these policy choices rational, and to establish limits and boundaries to the notion of international students as solutions, especially in STEM. One of these taken-for-granteds is the globalization of science, and an acceptance of advancing science and engineering in international teams financed in single countries, like the United States. This is rational only if policymakers perceive no national security threats, but those perceptions are subject to change. Consider, for example, the reevaluation of international student policies in the aftermath of the terrorist attacks of September 11, 2001.[11] The Department of State has maintained a "technology alert list" that limits the exposure of international students from countries determined to be sponsors of terrorism, including a major STEM-student sender, Iran.[12] If China were to be determined to be a similar threat, it could have major implications for American higher education, for reasons that will become clear below.

In this chapter, we first show that this battle for the brains is in fact occurring in universities in different countries in the world. We then explore the different ways that international students, especially though not exclusively in STEM, have become solutions to problems and are sought after in different countries. Our overall conclusion suggests that the contemporary pursuit of these students was not inevitable, and that it is shaped by strategic decisions in specific historical and institutional contexts.

Is There a Competition for Foreign Students?

Universities have commonly been international meeting places for both scholars and students.[13] The institutional environment spurring the contemporary and growing pursuit of international students began after World War II. As the historian Margaret O'Mara has shown, American efforts to attract international students were based on the notion that their presence in the United States would encourage cross-cultural understanding and contribute to peaceful relations. This was a major rationale of the Fulbright Act of 1946. But it was not all about sharing; foreigners studying in the United

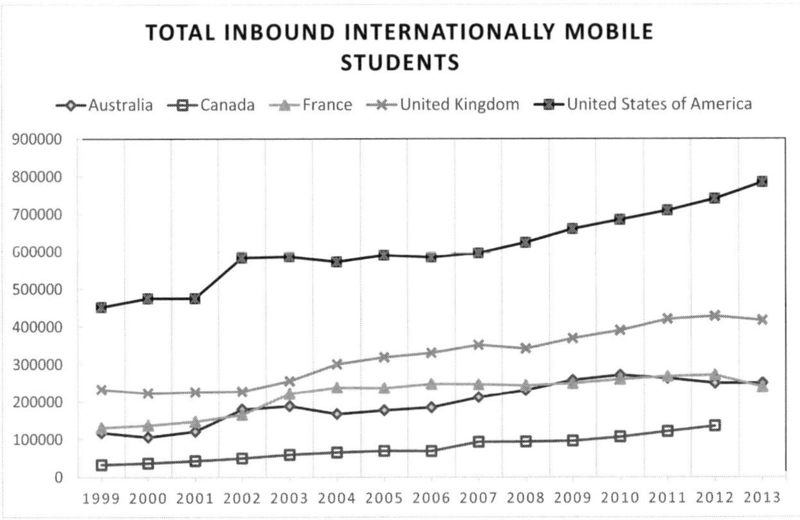

Figure 10.1. Source: UNESCO Global Flow of Tertiary-Level Students. Indicator: inbound internationally mobile students by continent of origin. Data accessed at http://data.uis.unesco.org/.

States, policymakers hoped, would see firsthand the superiority of American ways.[14] During the Cold War, the Soviet Union also sought to demonstrate openness to and build ties with other countries, especially in the developing world. To achieve this end, the government created the University of the Friendship of the Peoples, enrolling students primarily from Africa, Asia, and Latin America.[15]

Since the 1950s, the interest in recruiting international students has grown and spread. Their number is increasing worldwide, with some destinations seeing great increases in enrollments. As figure 10.1 shows, the United States remains the world leader in attracting international students, and despite a dip following the terrorist attacks of September 11, 2001, when visa policy tightened, the numbers have continued an upward trajectory, increasing from about half a million to nearly three-quarters of a million by 2008. Meanwhile, other key Anglophone destinations, the United Kingdom and Canada, have seen their numbers double over the decade.

Other data show the rise of multiple destinations for international students. Even while increasing in total numbers, the US share of the world total of international students declined by more than 5 percent in the first decade of the 2000s (see figure 10.2 and table 10.1). Other states increased their share, as the United Kingdom, the Russian Federation, and New Zealand made significant moves into this space.

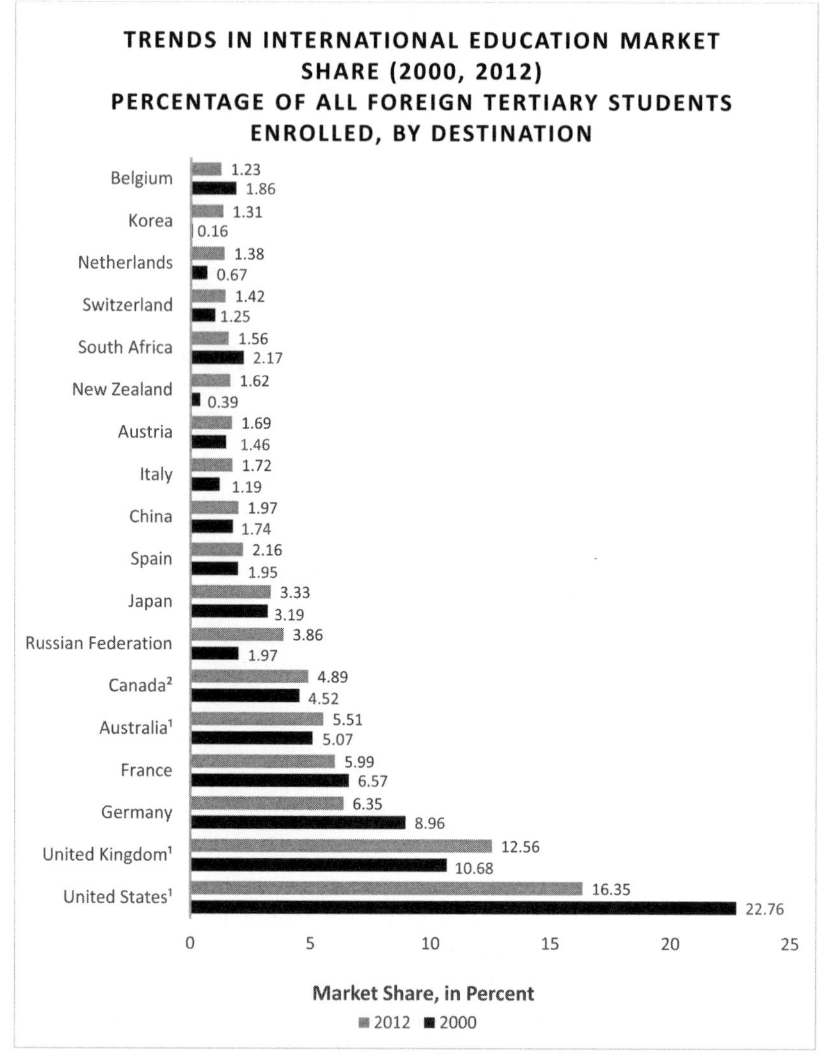

Figure 10.2. (1.) Data relate to international students defined on the basis of their country of residence. For the UK, data for 2012 is based on citizenship. (2.) Year of reference 2011 instead of 2012. Countries are ranked in descending order of 2012 market shares. Generated from "Education at a Glance, 2014." Organization of Economic Co-Operation and Development, OECD Publishing. Accessed at http://dx.doi.org/10.1787/eag-2014-en.

Table 10.1 Trends in International Education Market Share (2000–2012); percentage of all foreign tertiary students enrolled, by destination

	2000	2012		2000	2012
United States[1]	22.76	16.35	China	1.74	1.97
United Kingdom[1]	10.68	12.56	Italy	1.19	1.72
Germany	8.96	6.35	Austria	1.46	1.69
France	6.57	5.99	New Zealand	0.39	1.62
Australia[1]	5.07	5.51	South Africa	2.17	1.56
Canada[2]	4.52	4.89	Switzerland	1.25	1.42
Russia	1.97	3.86	Netherlands	0.67	1.38
Japan	3.19	3.33	South Korea	0.16	1.31
Spain	1.95	2.16	Belgium	1.86	1.23

Notes: (1.) Data relate to international students defined on the basis of their country of residence. For the UK, data for 2012 is based on citizenship. (2.) Year of reference 2011 instead of 2012.
Countries are ranked in descending order of 2012 market shares. Source: OECD, "Education at a Glance, 2014," Organization of Economic Co-operation and Development, OECD Publishing, accessed at http://dx.doi.org/10.1787/eag-2014-en.

Figures 10.3 and 10.4, focusing on the United States, provide understanding regarding the origins of these students. China, India, South Korea and Saudi Arabia are the major sending states of international students overall, while China towers above the rest if we focus only on doctoral students.

What do these students study? That depends on what level of student we are examining. Figures 10.5 and 10.6 show that undergraduate and master's international students focus mostly on business, with engineering in a distant second place. Figure 10.7 illustrates the focus of international doctoral students on—not surprisingly—engineering, with physics leading a crowded field of lesser choices.

Efforts to attract international students can be found across the globe, though we focus here on the major players by virtue of their success at attracting students from abroad. Other nations, though sometimes less successful, are nonetheless also notable for their major efforts to attract more students. In all cases, international students come not just because doors are opened, but because the students are actively courted.

For example, in 2011, the Canadian government announced funding to develop an international education strategy that sought to "reinforce Canada as a country of choice to study and conduct world-class research."[16] The subsequent report, "International Education: A Key Driver of Canada's Future Prosperity," culminated in a broad education strategy launched in 2014, a key priority of which aims to increase international student numbers.[17] Britain has been engaged with international student attraction for

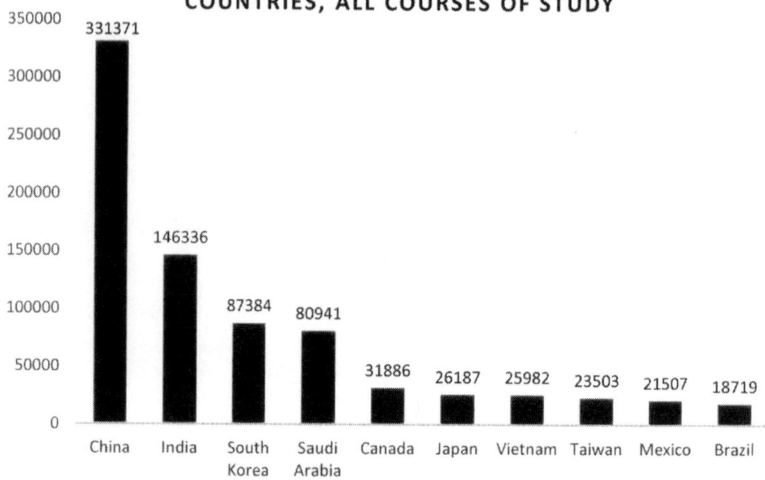

Figure 10.3. Generated from "SEVIS by the Numbers, February 2015: Real-Time SEVIS Data from February 6, 2015," US Department of Homeland Security. Accessed at http://studyinthestates.dhs.gov/sevis-by-the-numbers/february-2015.

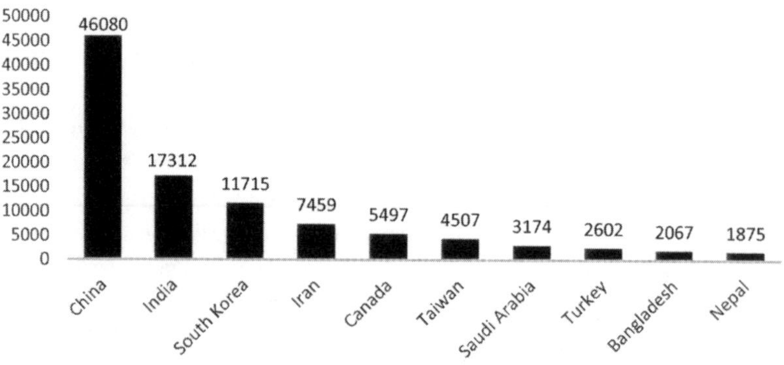

Figure 10.4. Generated from "SEVIS by the Numbers February 2015: Real-Time SEVIS Data from February 6, 2015." Accessed at http://studyinthestates.dhs.gov/sevis-by-the-numbers/february-2015.

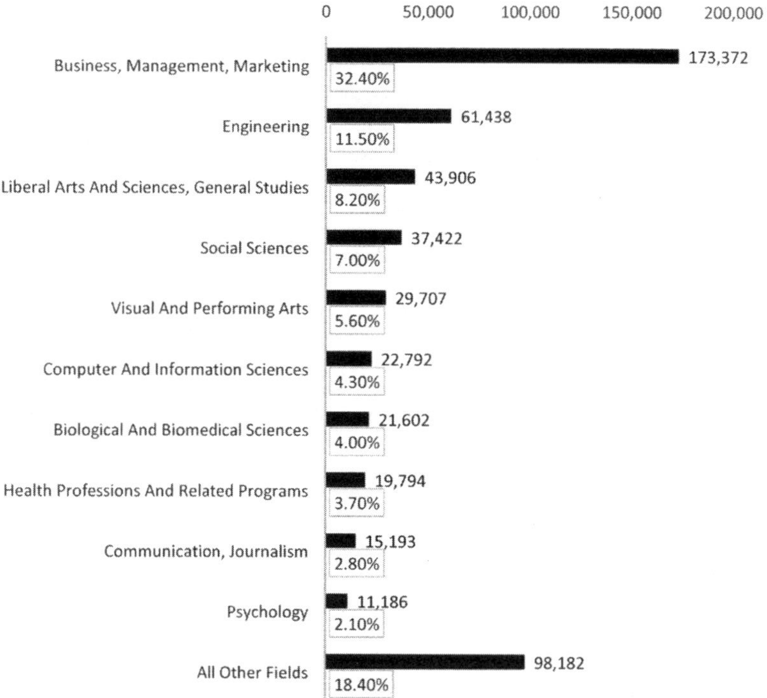

Figure 10.5. Generated from Neil G. Ruiz, "The Geography of Foreign Students in U.S. Higher Education: Origins and Destinations," Brookings Institution, August 29, 2014. Accessed at http://www.brookings.edu/research/interactives/2014/geography-of-foreign-students#/M10420.

years: in 2006, British Prime Minister Tony Blair launched a £7,000,000 drive to attract a hundred thousand more international students to the United Kingdom by 2011. It followed a successful 1999 initiative that aimed to increase the number of international students in the UK's universities and colleges to seventy-five thousand by 2005.[18] France has also sought to increase the presence of foreign students and researchers in the country's higher education institutions. It has implemented a multipronged "strategy for attractiveness" by developing a national research agency to coordinate a nationwide international research program, significantly increasing the amount of funding for higher education and research.[19] The strategy aims to give French institutions of higher education greater autonomy to recruit

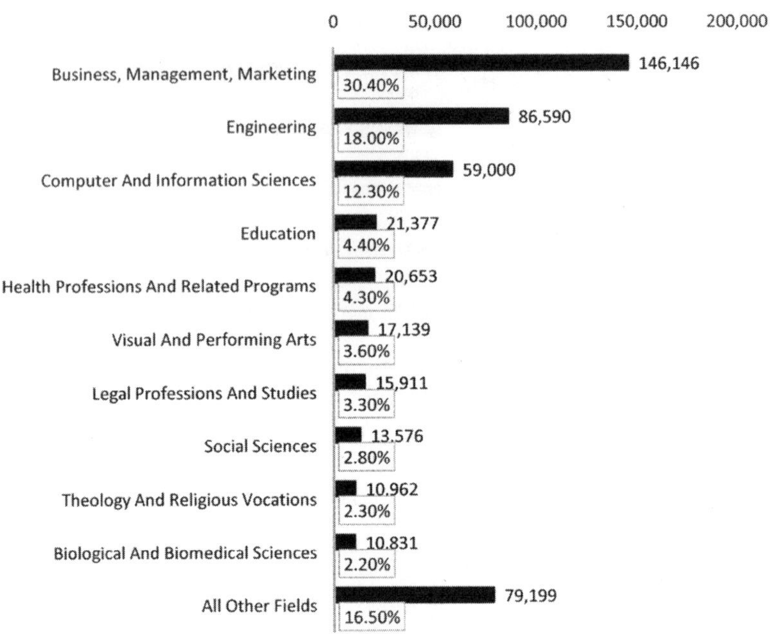

Figure 10.6. Generated from Neil G. Ruiz, "The Geography of Foreign Students in U.S. Higher Education: Origins and Destinations," Brookings Institution, August 29, 2014. Accessed at http://www.brookings.edu/research/interactives/2014/geography-of-foreign-students#/M10420.

the best talent, both domestically and from abroad, and to support foreign researchers at the country's national institutes.[20]

Similarly, in the early 2000s, an increasingly international turn in Australia aimed to make Australian institutions of higher education more competitive worldwide. More than three million international students have studied in Australia since the 1950s, and as of April 2015, 433,936 full-fee-paying international students were enrolled in Australia.[21] While successful marketing procedures have long lured international students to study in Australia, a new emphasis on bringing in higher-postgraduate students, paired with new visa opportunities extending additional points (Australia allocates visas on a point system to select the most desired visa applicants) to advanced-degree graduates from Australian institutions, has helped make Australia a destination for further study.[22]

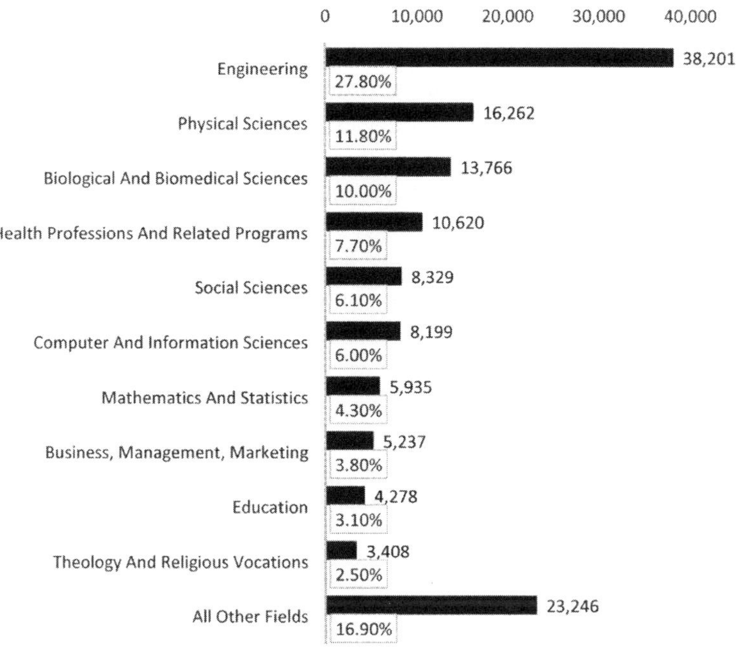

Figure 10.7. Generated from Neil G. Ruiz, "The Geography of Foreign Students in U.S. Higher Education: Origins and Destinations," Brookings Institution, August 29, 2014. Accessed at http://www.brookings.edu/research/interactives/2014/geography-of-foreign-students#/M10420.

Though Asian states are especially prominent as senders of students, a growing number also seek to attract international students. For example, since the 1990s, the Singapore government has sought to make Singapore an education hub in Asia, or the "Boston of the East."[23] The "Global Schoolhouse" strategy, implemented in 2002, aimed to attract 150,000 international students by 2015, and to increase education's share of the GDP from 1.9 percent to 5 percent.[24] Singapore now requires institutions of higher education to maintain a foreign enrollment rate of over 20 percent to promote international education and exchange.[25] As one observer has commented, "No institution is more effectively focused on global competition than the National University of Singapore."[26]

Malaysia has also sought to become a major player in international higher education over the last two decades. It has gone from being the world's third greatest exporter of international students in 1985 to being one of today's most promising destinations for international students.[27] In 2004, Malaysia hosted 32,000 international students, and by 2014, that number had jumped to 108,000.[28] Of these, 74 percent are undergraduates and 28 percent are postgraduate students. According to the government's official strategy, the "Malaysia Education Blueprint 2015–2025 (Higher Education)", the country aims to become a world leader in higher education by hosting 200,000 international students by 2020, and 250,000 by 2025.[29] In contrast to other countries that have looked to China and India for their traditionally high numbers of international students, Malaysian has specifically targeted countries of the Middle East and the Gulf states, with which it shares a Muslim heritage and which have newly mobile student populations.[30]

International Student Enrollment as a Signal of World-Class Status

To account for the rise of international students in the United States and in the world, we must first understand that some universities perceive international students as valuable because their presence signals legitimacy and membership in a global community. Work by John Meyer, Francisco Ramirez, and David John Frank, among others, has shown that universities have tended to follow cultural scripts that guide development in similar ways over time.[31] In the 2000s, having a robust international student body is part of the script to be followed if one wants to have a world-class university—and there is now a global rush to be a world-class university.[32] For many policymakers, having a world-class university benefits not only the university, but the entire country.

While this factor can be found worldwide, it may be especially prominent in countries that aspire to First World status and hope to rebrand themselves. For example, the Malaysia Education Blueprint suggests that increasing the number of international students contributes to developing Malaysia's "global prominence." As more students worldwide recognize Malaysia's high quality of institutions and value for money, the thinking goes, the country's higher-education institutions gain international respect. To achieve this, the country aims to further improve its course offerings for international students, and to develop a "green lane" immigration track for successful students, to give them an option to remain in the country after their graduation. As international students choose Malaysia for their studies, they further validate these institutional investments and burnish Malaysia's academic brand overseas.

Who is the audience for this signaling? Potential students, obviously, but others as well. One key audience is made up of the various organizations that rank the world's universities. In a commensuration process common in modern societies,[33] global university ranking systems have encouraged and focused desires of some states to have a world-class university.[34] They provide incentives to create research universities, since those are prioritized in global rankings, and the top ones tend to have large percentages of foreign graduate students, as well as foreign staff.[35] The ability to attract foreign students can also be a signal or indicator of the quality of research occurring at a university.[36]

Some prominent ranking systems therefore include the percentage of foreign students in their calculations.[37] For example, the QS World University Rankings bases five percent of its scoring on the international student ratio.[38] Similarly, the Times Higher Education World University Ranking bases 7.5 percent of its score on "international outlook: staff, students and research." Its methodology explains, "The ability of a university to attract undergraduates and postgraduates from all over the planet is key to its success on the world stage: this factor is measured by the ratio of international to domestic students and is worth 2.5 percent of the overall score."[39] When a razor-thin margin can determine top-ten or -twenty or -fifty status, even 2.5 percent is huge.

In a feedback loop, international students tend to rely on these rankings when they choose a university: "Rankings are a particularly critical factor when international students choose to study abroad because they may find it difficult to visit an institution in another country prior to making a college decision. Students, especially from Asian countries, are sensitive to rankings when they choose an international institution."[40] The more international students an institution has, the higher its ranking, and then the more international students it can attract.

The case of Taiwan illustrates how these institutional rules or scripts can affect an ambitious state or university's effort to become world-class. Aware of the importance of internationalization in global rankings of universities, the Taiwanese government sought to raise its visibility and global reputation by enhancing its position in the rankings. It therefore included the recruitment of international students in its 2003 National Development Plan. In 2004 the Taiwanese Ministry of Education created a "programme for expanding overseas student population" that subsidized university efforts to recruit international students—and then used international student recruitment as a measure of its own ranking of Taiwanese universities.[41]

International Students as a University Contribution to Economic Growth

International students, especially in STEM, also provide an answer to the problem of how universities can justify themselves in an era dominated by neoliberal (that is, market-based) rationalities and assumptions. Emphases on providing well-rounded, critically thinking citizens, or on enabling national defense, are not adequate. Universities must contribute something substantial to the economy, and policymakers in government and universities themselves have converged on the belief that students can contribute to future economic growth.[42] This perception may be more common in wealthier countries with postindustrial/knowledge economies, where innovation, and *technological* innovation in particular, is understood as the key to economic vitality.

In the context of knowledge-intensive, high-tech economies, universities or governments recruiting international students tend to focus on those majoring in STEM subjects.[43] As we have shown elsewhere,[44] this may appear uncontroversial and perfectly sensible, but on closer look, it appears to be guided more on faith or on a cultural script rather than on any empirical analysis or scientific basis.

First, even in the United States, a pioneer in the modern era in attracting international students, there is no research by the government or by social scientists that illuminates precisely how, which, or how many foreign students lead to economic growth. The causal linkage is certainly plausible, and these linkages are clear in basic science research, as all six US-based academic winners of Nobel Prizes in 2016 were foreign-born (two of these were former international students to the United States),[45] but the evidence to support this claim about economic growth and job creation remains unclear.

The basic theory that drives this economic growth argument for international students is "The more, the better."[46] This is a continuation of an old argument related to national security; during the 1950s and later, US government officials would count the number of scientists and engineers in the United States and compare that number, often unfavorably, with the number in the Soviet Union. There was never any proof that the number correlated with national security. Quality, rather than quantity, is the likely key variable.

Over the course of the 1980s, the threat changed from Soviet military power to Japanese economic power, and the goal of STEM policy became economic growth.[47] The notion of international STEM students being keys for growth has been promoted by the high-profile 2005 report of the National Academies of Sciences, Engineering, and Medicine, which focused on American competitiveness and was ominously titled *Rising above the Gathering Storm*. The report stated, "Another challenge for US research institutions is to attract the overseas students on whose talents the nation depends."[48] It warned of other nations attracting STEM students, and argued for more efforts to bring them to the United States. The committee authoring the report included leaders of industry, STEM faculty from several other universities, and the presidents of Texas A&M University, Renssalaer Polytechnic Institute, Yale University, University of Maryland at College Park, and the past president of MIT.

Other states are indeed seeking international students, especially in STEM, for the same reasons. The United Kingdom, which is the United States' closest competitor in attracting international students, works to attract them for similar reasons. British Council chair Lord Kinnock, a former president of Cardiff University, emphasized the importance that the push for international students at the undergraduate and graduate levels had toward providing a "direct contribution to . . . economic and technological development."[49] At the time, Kinnock reported 39 percent of all postgraduate research in the United Kingdom was done by non-UK postgrads, and that their research and teaching contributed significantly to that nation's "knowledge economy."[50]

In early 2014, Canadian Prime Minster Stephen Harper launched Canada's International Education Strategy," which was subtitled "Harnessing our Knowledge Advantage to Drive Innovation and Prosperity." The fact that this initiative was launched by the Canadian minister for international trade, and not the country's minister of education, suggests that universities may be assigned their economic role in admitting international students as much as choosing it themselves. International Trade Minister Ed Fast described the international education strategy as the "blueprint to attract talent and prepare our country for the 21st century."[51]

The strategy of recruiting international students to augment economic growth is also prominent in countries trying to move into the ranks of the most developed. For example, it figures prominently in up-and-coming Malaysia's rationale for increasing international student enrollments. According to the Malaysia Education Blueprint, international students, especially PhDs, will help develop a greater in-country supply of talent that can contribute toward Malaysia's innovation ecosystem. Maintaining that country's growing innovation sector requires the acquisition and development of human capital talent, including international students.[52]

A final way in which international students help justify universities is through simple consumption power: they spend a lot in host economies. A report by the National Association of International Educators on the 2013–2014 academic year found that the 886,000 international students and their families supported 340,000 jobs and contributed $26.8 billion to the US economy.[53] International education is a significant driver for the Australian economy, and is the country's largest services export. Education exports are the country's fourth largest export, following iron ore, coal, and gold.[54] Education for international students contributed A$16.3 billion to the Australian economy in 2013–2014, and supported 130,000 jobs nationally.[55] In 2012, the Canadian government estimated the country's 265,400 international students spent a total of C$8.4 billion in local communities, and generated $455 million in federal and provincial tax revenues. Furthermore, these students helped to sustain nearly 87,000 Canadian jobs.[56]

International Students as Tuition Payers and Inexpensive Scientific Labor

The third major problem for which international students are the solution is how to pay the campus bills. It is beyond the scope of this chapter to explore why higher education now costs so much, and why state government expenditures have not grown with the costs. The key point is that both public and private research universities have responded to the tight fiscal environment and limitations created by existing political institutions by seeking other sources of revenue and ways to cut costs—all while continuing and increasing their research missions.

In recent years, the pursuit of undergraduate students from China has become a growth industry in the United States, as these students pay high fees and may help support campuses.[57] Graduate students are also major sources of revenue.[58] Australia provides a dramatic example: over the past five years, international students have contributed A$18.5 billion towards Australian universities, which helps to support staff, teaching, and research outputs. These fees further help to provide university access to domestic Australian students by lowering education costs, contributing 16 percent of all university revenues in 2012.[59]

The other way in which international students (and, increasingly, postdocs) help pay bills is more complex, and reflects changes developing over several decades in the cost structures of universities, the willingness of different populations to seek education and training in STEM, and the availability of funding for research. Put simply, the problem is that universities are engaging in more research than ever before (though federal funds have declined, industry funds have increased),[60] but the chances of achieving a full-time faculty post in science and engineering are increasingly small. Given the funding-rich research environment, this means that students and postdocs must do more work, mostly for existing faculty, even while they face uncertain futures in academia.

If that is the simple explanation, understanding why the academic job market is so weak is complex. Economist Paula Stephan notes four main reasons.[61] First, the pool of PhDs in science and engineering has grown, both in the United States and abroad. While the number of male American citizens earning STEM PhDs has been stable or declining, that number has been going up among women citizens and temporary and permanent residents. If both US and other universities are producing PhDs at greater numbers, then there will simply be more candidates chasing a very few full-time tenure-track employment opportunities.

Second, universities have chosen to rely on non–tenure-track faculty, who receive low pay and benefits, over expensive tenure-track faculty.[62] This trend has occurred over several decades, but by 2001, 35 percent of faculty at public universities and 40 percent of faculty at private universities were non–tenure-track.

Third, hiring dried up because state governments fund public institutions less generously than they used to. Part of the problem was the 2008 financial crisis, which choked off tax revenues as incomes declined and people lost their jobs. But some of these wounds are self-inflicted, and reflect political choices: states have responded to political incentives to put more money in popular investments such as prisons and health care. Stephan reports that state funds for universities, adjusted for inflation and enrollments, fell by 11 percent between 1970 and 2005. This trend has continued in the wake of 2008's Great Recession. In 2016, state appropriations for higher education average 18 percent less per student than they did before the recession hit, and only four states—Montana, North Dakota, Wisconsin, and Wyoming—were spending more.[63] In what some observers have called a privatization of public higher education,[64] state funds have declined so that they only support 4 percent of the budget at the University of Washington, 6.3 percent at the University of Michigan, and 9.4 percent at Pennsylvania State University.

Finally, start-up packages for new STEM hires can be very high, and so each new scientist is a major investment. The University of California, San Francisco, for example, informs its new hires what to expect and what to request: start-up funds for new assistant professors of biology average between $308,000 (at public universities) and $403,000 (at private universities).[65] If every new professor is a major investment, and if universities do not have resources to make many such investments, then they will hire fewer of them.

While this is primarily a story for the United States, Stephan notes that universities abroad have not increased their hiring to pick up the slack. For example, the average age of assistant-professor equivalents in Italy is forty-five. In 2010, comprehensive reforms to the Italian university system largely removed opportunities for tenure for new academic staff, resulting in a 12-percent decline in tenured faculty from 2008 to 2012.[66] Further educational reforms elsewhere in Europe have contributed to an increasing share of temporary contracts and part-time positions for new academic staff. In South Korea, part-time faculty outnumber full-time faculty.[67]

The great number of openings for graduate students and postdocs, coupled with the scarcity of faculty positions, has created a bottleneck at the postdoc stage as STEM workers increasingly have long postdoc positions, or multiple postdocs, before they can get a full-time job.[68] According to one recent National Academies report, the situation is gloomy, has been for a long time, and is getting worse. The problems are many: a lack of visibility on campus, a lack of prestige, a lack of research independence, a lack of adequate pay, and a lack of adequate mentoring. In 2010, median pay for postdocs in science, engineering, and health up to five years after earning a degree was $43,000; for comparable workers *not* in postdoc positions, it was $76,000.[69]

A major problem with the increase in postdoctoral fellowships is that it is increasingly common for PhDs to do not just one but multiple postdocs in the hope of attaining a full-time job in science. This means that the low wages associated with academic postdocs may continue for several years after the PhD, leading to lost wages and delayed lives; the average age of someone hired for their first tenure-track job has been in the range of thirty-five to forty for several years.[70] The issue was a focus of another dreary and pessimistic National Academies report on "the arc of the academic research career"—dreary because, though most PhDs surveyed knew that only about 15 percent of PhDs in science and engineering had tenure-track jobs five years after receiving their degrees, about half or more (depending on the field) of those who preferred academic careers thought they would be one of the lucky ones.[71]

In this context, migration theory predicts that foreigners who face blocked opportunities and poor wage prospects will move to open and better opportunities. That appears to be what has happened. In the United States, foreign students and postdoctoral researchers comprise a sizable per-

Table 10.2 Top ten most popular graduate courses of study, by citizenship 2013

US citizens and permanent residents		Temporary residents	
Political science	42,018	Computer science	32,148
Psychology, other	26,441	Electrical engineering	30,670
Computer science	24,191	Mechanical engineering	11,296
Preventive medicine and community health	21,414	Chemistry	8,683
Psychology, general	15,041	Civil engineering	8,662
Electrical engineering	14,892	Economics (except agricultural)	8,172
Chemistry	14,266	Mathematics and applied mathematics	6,792
Social sciences, other	14,097	Physics	6,407
Speech pathology and audiology	13,717	Political science	6,393
Mechanical engineering	12,791	Industrial engineering	6,357
Agricultural sciences	12,773	Chemical engineering	5,068

Data source: NSF-NIH survey of graduate students and postdoctorates in science and engineering, info via WebCaspar. Analysis variable: number of graduate students, academic discipline (detailed).

centage of all STEM enrollments and research positions, showing higher numbers in STEM than in non-STEM fields, and outnumbering native students considerably in certain fields (see table 10.2). Between 1970 and 2005, the number of US citizens earning PhDs in engineering declined 23 percent, in the physical sciences 44 percent, and in math 50 percent. The overall numbers of Americans earning STEM PhDs in this period fell from 3,547 in 1970 to 1,986. The best students appeared to leave STEM for fields where wages were 5 to 15 percent higher, such as finance and accounting.[72] Meanwhile, temporary US visa holders came to comprise a majority of graduate students in a number of fields. For example, in 2013, foreign graduate students made up 51 percent of all graduate engineering students, and within some fields the numbers are even higher. Foreign graduate students comprise 73 percent of all enrolled petroleum engineers, and 67 percent of all electrical engineers. Temporary visa holders are 57 percent of all computer science graduate students.[73]

The federal government has also created numerous visa categories that can be used to fill postdoc positions, thus making it difficult to assess the dependence on immigrants.[74] With this caveat in mind, some data indicate that the United States has seen a steady increase in its postdoctorate population, from 19,000 in 1982 to more than 40,000 in 2001 (see figure 10.8).[75] By 2013, the National Science Foundation's comprehensive Survey of Graduate Students counted 61,942 postdoctoral appointees in science, engineering and health fields.[76] Of that total, less than half, 29,546, were US citizens or permanent residents. The remainder were temporary visa holders.

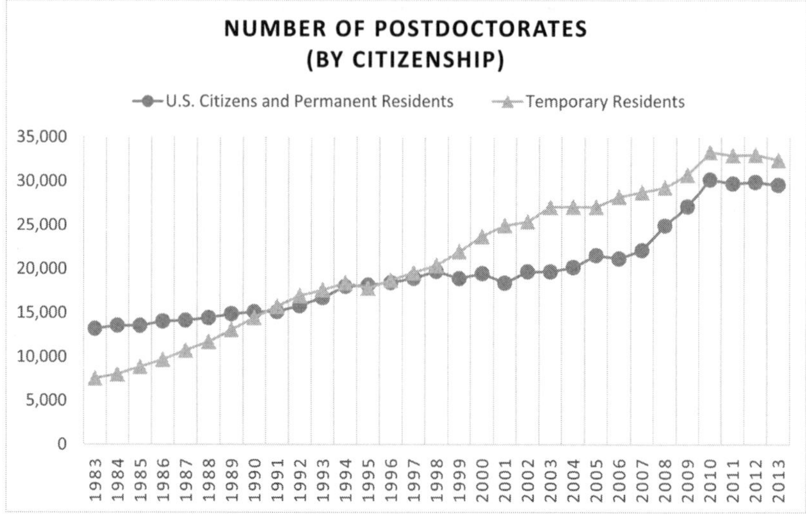

Figure 10.8. Data Source: NSF-NIH Survey of Graduate Students & Postdoctorates in Science and Engineering Info, via WebCaspar. Analysis variable: number of postdoctorates (type of doctorate degree, by citizenship) [sum].

Conclusion

We have argued that increasing international student enrollments serves several goals in the contemporary era. It is an indicator of "world-class" status, and an entrée into the global community of advanced nations. It is a way to show that universities are contributing to the local and state economies and are propelling future growth, especially if the students study STEM subjects. Finally, international students and postdoctoral researchers are simply a way to pay the bills and maintain the research enterprise, given the funding environment and the costs of doing science.

Given these institutional forces shaping the drive for international students, it is likely that this pursuit will continue for the foreseeable future. We have shown how universities around the world have adopted common scripts for international success, and how foreign students can contribute toward addressing specific challenges. In a globalized world, universities that teach and train only local students will look parochial and backward. And, given perceptions of the importance of economic growth and how to achieve it, as well as cost pressures, international students will likely serve domestic goals as well.

We also emphasize that the rationality of these policy choices is contingent upon historical context and therefore could change. In the 2010s, public institutions in the United States find it acceptable to leverage the willingness of international students to pay their way, thus limiting the opportunities of local students to enroll—but a political movement could close off this acceptability. Similarly, research universities' reliance on international students to conduct cutting-edge research in STEM fields could end if policymakers render this globalized science approach to be a threat to national security.

For sociologists studying higher-education policy, the lesson of neo-institutional theory in organizations and of historical institutional theory in the study of politics is that policymakers operate in historically bounded cultural and relational contexts. The job of the sociologist is to reveal why choices appear rational to those making the choices, and why patterns repeat across seemingly diverse contexts.

Notes

1. Richard B. Freeman and Daniel L. Goroff, Introduction to Freeman and Goroff, eds., *Science and Engineering Careers in the United States: An Analysis of Markets and Employment* (Chicago: University of Chicago Press, 2009), 1–16.
2. John Bound, Sarah Turner, and Patrick Walsh, "Internationalization of U.S. Doctorate Education," in Richard B. Freeman and Daniel L. Goroff, eds., *Science and Engineering Careers in the United States: An Analysis of Markets and Employment* (Chicago: University of Chicago Press, 2009), 59–97.
3. For a review, see Hans de Wit, *Internationalization of Higher Education in the United States and Europe: A Historical, Comparative, and Conceptual Analysis* (Westport, CT: Greenwood Press, 2002), chapter 5.
4. John W. Meyer and Brian Rowan, "Institutionalized Organizations: Formal Structure as Myth and Ceremony," *American Journal of Sociology* 83, no. 2 (September 1977), 340–363; Frank Dobbin, *Forging Industrial Policy: The United States, Britain and France in the Railway Age* (New York: Cambridge University Press, 1994).
5. See, for example, Theda Skocpol and Paul Pierson, "Historical Institutionalism in Contemporary Political Science," in Ira Katznelson and Helen V. Milner, eds., *Political Science: State of the Discipline* (New York: W. W. Norton; 2002), 693–721.
6. Rui Yang and Anthony Welch, "A World Class University in China? The Case of Tsinghua," *Higher Education* 63 (2012): 645–666.
7. David John Frank and Jay Gabler, *Reconstructing the University: Worldwide Shifts in Academia in the 20th Century* (Stanford, CA: Stanford University Press, 2006).
8. Clark Kerr, *The Uses of the University*, Fifth Edition (Cambridge, MA: Harvard University Press 2001 [1963]).
9. Derek Bok, *Higher Education in America* (Princeton, NJ: Princeton University Press, 2013); Sheila Slaughter and Gary Rhoades, *Academic Capitalism and the New Economy: Markets, State, and Higher Education* (Baltimore: Johns Hopkins University Press, 2004); Steven Brint, "Creating the Future: 'New Directions' in American Research Universities." *Minerva* 43 (2005): 23–50.
10. Daniel Bell, *The Coming of Post-Industrial Society* (New York: Basic Books, 1973).

11. James H. Johnson Jr., "U.S. Immigration Reform, Homeland Security, and Global Economic Competitiveness in the Aftermath of the September 11, 2001 Terrorist Attacks," *North Carolina Journal of International Law and Commercial Regulation* 419 (2002): 419–464.
12. Janice Jacobs, "Foreign Students and Scholars in the Age of Terrorism," testimony before the Committee on Science US House of Representatives, March 26, 2003, accessed at https://2001-2009.state.gov/r/pa/ei/othertstmy/33002.htm.
13. Edward Charnwood Cieslak, *The Foreign Student in American Colleges: A Survey and Evaluation of Administrative Problems and Practices* (Detroit: Wayne State University Press, 1955).
14. Margaret O'Mara, "The Uses of the Foreign Student," *Social Science History* 36 (2012): 583–615.
15. Martin Ebon, *The Soviet Propaganda Machine* (New York: McGraw-Hill, 1987), 275–276.
16. Advisory Panel on Canada's International Education, "International Education: A Key Driver of Canada's Future Prosperity" (Foreign Affairs, Trade, and Development Canada), accessed at http://www.international.gc.ca/education/advisory-consultation.aspx?lang=eng.
17. "Canada's International Education Strategy: Harnessing Our Knowledge Advantage to Drive Innovation and Prosperity" (proposal by Foreign Affairs, Trade, and Development Canada, 2014), 4. Accessed at http://international.gc.ca/global-markets-marches-mondiaux/assets/pdfs/overview-apercu-eng.pdf.
18. Elaina Loveland, "Opening Doors to the United Kingdom: An Interview with British Council Chair Lord Kinnock," *International Educator* (November-December 2006): 20–24. Accessed at https://nafsa.org/_/File/_/lordkinnockvoices111206.pdf.
19. "A Strategy for Attractiveness: Incentive Pprograms Implemented" (proposal by France Diplomatie 2010). Accessed at http://www.diplomatie.gouv.fr/en/coming-to-france/studying-in-france/receiving-foreign-students-in/a-strategy-for-attractiveness/.
20. http://www.agence-nationale-recherche.fr/en/project-based-funding-to-advance-french-research/.
21. Australian Government Department of Education and Training, "Monthly Summary of International Student Enrolment Data1—Australia—YTD April 2015." Accessed at https://internationaleducation.gov.au/research/International-Student-Data/Documents/Monthly%20summaries%20of%20international%20student%20enrolment%20data%202015/04_April_2015_MonthlySummary.pdf.
22. Christopher Ziguras and Siew Fang Law, "Recruiting International Students as Skilled Migrants: The Global 'Skills Race' as Viewed from Australia and Malaysia," *Globalisation, Societies and Education* 4 (2006): 59–76.
23. Hena Mukherjee and Poh Kam Wong, "The National University of Singapore and the University of Malaya: Common Roots and Different Paths," in Philip G. Altbach and Jamil Salmi, eds., *The Road to Academic Excellence: The Making of World-Class Research Universities* (Washington: World Bank, 2011), 129–166, 148.
24. Drewe, Vicki. "Singapore's Global Schoolhouse Strategy: The first Ten Years." Presentation at the Australian International Education Conference 2012. Accessed at http://aiec.idp.com/uploads/pdf/2012_drewe_thu_1140_219.pdf.
25. *The International Mobility of Students in Asia and the Pacific* (Paris: United Nations Educational, Scientific and Cultural Organization, Bangkok Office, 2013). Accessed at

http://www.uis.unesco.org/Library/Documents/international-student-mobility-asia-pacific-education-2013-en.pdf.

26. Simon Marginson, "Dynamics of National and Global Competition in Higher Education," *Higher Education* 52 (2006): 20.
27. *"The International Mobility of Students in Asia and the Pacific* (Paris: United Nations Educational, Scientific and Cultural Organization, Bangkok Office, 2013), 49. Accessed at http://www.uis.unesco.org/Library/Documents/international-student-mobility-asia-pacific-education-2013-en.pdf.
28. "The Malaysia Education Blueprint 2015–2025 (Higher Education)," Kementerian Pendidikan Malaysia, April 2015. Accessed at http://hes.moe.gov.my/event/docs/3.%20Malaysia%20Education%20Blueprint%202015–2025%20%28Higher%20Education%29.pdf.
29. "The Malaysia Education Blueprint 2015–2025 (Higher Education)."
30. *The International Mobility of Students in Asia and the Pacific*, 57. Accessed at http://www.uis.unesco.org/Library/Documents/international-student-mobility-asia-pacific-education-2013-en.pdf.
31. See, for example, John W. Meyer, Francisco Ramirez, David John Frank and Evan Schofer, "Higher Education as an Institution," in Patricia J. Gumport, ed., *Sociology of Higher Education: Contributions and the Contexts* (Baltimore: Johns Hopkins University Press, 2007), 187–221.
32. David P. Baker, *The Schooled Society: The Educational Transformation of Global Culture* (Stanford, CA: Stanford University Press, 2014), 87.
33. Wendy Nelson Espeland and Mitchell L. Stevens, "Commensuration as a Social Process," *Annual Review of Sociology* 24 (1998), 313–343.
34. Ka Ho Mok and Kar Ming Yu, "Introduction: The Quest for Regional Hub Status and Transnationalization of Higher Education: Challenges for Managing Human Capital in East Asia," in Ka Ho Mok and Kar Ming Yu, eds., *Internationalization of Higher Education in East Asia: Trends of Student Mobility and Impact on Education Governance* (New York: Routledge, 2014), 1–26, 22.
35. Hugo Horta, "Global and National Prominent Universities: Internationalization, Competitiveness, and the Role of the State," *Higher Education* 58, no. 3 (2009): 387–405.
36. Simon Marginson, "Dynamics of National and Global Competition in Higher Education," *Higher Education* 52, no. 1 (2006): 1–39.
37. For a discussion, see Jamil Salmi, *The Challenge of Establishing World-Class Universities* (Washington: World Bank Publications, 2009), 5–6.
38. Quacquarelli Symonds, "QS World University Rankings: Methodology," last modified September 12, 2014. Accessed at http://www.topuniversities.com/university-rankings-articles/world-university-rankings/qs-world-university-rankings-methodology.
39. Times Higher Education, "World University Rankings 2014–15." Accessed at https://www.timeshighereducation.co.uk/world-university-rankings/2015/world-ranking#tab-ranking-methodology.
40. Jung Cheol Shin and Robert K. Toutkoushian, "The Past, Present, and Future of University Rankings," in Jung Cheol Shin, Robert K. Toutkoushian and Ulrich Teichler, eds., *University Rankings: Theoretical Basis, Methodology and Impacts on Global Higher Education*. Volume 3 (New York: Springer Science & Business Media, 2011), 1–16.
41. William Yat Wai Lo, *University Rankings: Implications for Higher Education in Taiwan* (New York: Springer, 2014).

42. Roger L. Geiger, *Knowledge and Money: Research Universities and the Paradox of the Marketplace*. Stanford, CA: Stanford University Press, 2004).
43. Jane Knight, "Education Hubs: Focus on Student Mobility, Human Resource Development and Knowledge Production," in Ka Ho Mok and Kar Ming Yu, eds., *Internationalization of Higher Education in East Asia: Trends of Student Mobility and Impact on Education Governance* (New York: Routledge, 2014), 27–41.
44. John D. Skrentny and Natalie Novick, "From Science to Alchemy? The Progressives' Deployment of Expertise and the Contemporary Faith in Science to Grow the Economy and Create Jobs," in Stephen Skowronek, Bruce Ackerman and Stephen Engel, eds., *The Progressives' Century: Democratic Reform and Constitutional Government in the United States* (New Haven: Yale University Press, forthcoming).
45. Elizabeth Redden, "America's Immigrant Laureates," *Inside Higher Education*, October 11, 2016. Accessed at https://www.insidehighered.com/news/2016/10/11/foreign-born-professors-account-us-nobel-haul.
46. On the "myth of infinite benefit" of science, see Daniel R. Sarewitz, *Frontiers of Illusion: Science, Technology, and the Politics of Progress* (Philadelphia: Temple University Press, 1996), chapter 2.
47. Skrentny and Novick, "From Science to Alchemy?"
48. Committee on Prospering in the Global Economy of the 21st Century and Committee on Science, Engineering, and Public Policy, *Rising Above the Gathering Storm: Energizing and Employing America for a Brighter Economic Future* (Washington: National Academies Press, 2007), 78–79.
49. Loveland, Elaina, "Opening Doors to the United Kingdom." *International Educator* (2006): 20–24.
50. Loveland, "Opening Doors to the United Kingdom," 20–24.
51. "Canada's International Education Strategy: Harnessing Our Knowledge Advantage to Drive Innovation and Prosperity" (proposal by Foreign Affairs, Trade, and Development Canada, 2014). Accesssed at http://international.gc.ca/global-markets-marches-mondiaux/assets/pdfs/overview-apercu-eng.pdf.
52. "The Malaysia Education Blueprint 2015–2025 (Higher Education)."
53. NAFSA (National Association of Foreign Student Advisers) International Student Economic Value Tool, accessed at http://www.nafsa.org/Explore_International_Education/Impact/Data_And_Statistics/NAFSA_International_Student_Economic_Value_Tool/. On student spending in the UK, see "The Economic Costs and Benefits of International Students" (2013), a report by Oxford Economics for the University of Sheffield. Accessed at https://www.shef.ac.uk/polopoly_fs/1.259052!/file/sheffield-international-students-report.pdf.
54. Group of Eight Australia, "International Students in Higher Education and Their Role in the Australian Economy,", March 2014. Accessed at https://go8.edu.au/sites/default/files/docs/publications/international_students_in_higher_education_and_their_role_in_the_australian_economy.pdf.
55. "Draft National Strategy for International Education (for Consultation)," report by the Australian Ministry for Education and Training (April 2015), 5. Accessed at https://internationaleducation.gov.au/International-network/Australia/InternationalStrategy/Documents/Draft%20National%20Strategy%20for%20International%20Education.pdf.
56. "Canada's International Education Strategy: Harnessing our knowledge advantage to drive innovation and prosperity," 7. Accessed at http://international.gc.ca/global-markets-marches-mondiaux/assets/pdfs/overview-apercu-eng.pdf.

57. Matt Schiavenza, "The Tenuous Relationship between American Universities and Chinese Students," *Atlantic*, May 30, 2015. Accessed at http://www.theatlantic.com/education/archive/2015/05/american-universities-are-addicted-to-chinese-students/394517/#chinese%20students. However, international students can raise costs as well, as they have special needs and not all universities and colleges make money from them. See also Brendan Cantwell, "Are International Students Cash Cows? Examining the Relationship between New International Undergraduate Enrollments and Institutional Revenue at Public Colleges and Universities in the US," *Journal of International Students* 5, no. 4 (September-October 2015): 512–525.
58. "The Economic Costs and Benefits of International Students," report by Oxford Economics for the University of Sheffield (2013). Accessed at https://www.shef.ac.uk/polopoly_fs/1.259052!/file/sheffield-international-students-report.pdf.
59. Group of Eight Australia, "International Students in Higher Education and Their Role in the Australian Economy," March 2014. https://go8.edu.au/sites/default/files/docs/publications/international_students_in_higher_education_and_their_role_in_the_australian_economy.pdf.
60. Roger L. Geiger, *Knowledge & Money: Research Universities and the Paradox of the Marketplace* (Stanford, CA: Stanford University Press, 2004), chapter 4; see also David P. Baker, *The Schooled Society: The Educational Transformation of Global Culture* (Stanford, CA: Stanford University Press, 2014).
61. Paula Stephan, *How Economics Shapes Science* (Cambridge, MA: Harvard University Press, 2012), 170–171.
62. On this point, see also James D. Adams, "Is the United States Losing Its Preeminence in Higher Education?" in Charles T. Clotfelter, ed., *American Universities in a Global Market* (Chicago: University of Chicago Press and National Bureau of Economic Research, 2010), 33–68.
63. Michael Mitchell, Michael Leachman, and Kathleen Masterson, "Funding Down, Tuition Up," Center on Budget and Policy Priorities, August 15, 2016. Accessed at http://www.cbpp.org/sites/default/files/atoms/files/5-19-16sfp.pdf.
64. Thomas G. Mortenson, "State Funding: A Race to the Bottom," American Council on Education, Winter 2012. Accessed at http://www.acenet.edu/the-presidency/columns-and-features/Pages/state-funding-a-race-to-the-bottom.aspx.
65. "Negotiating your Start Up Package," Office of Career & Professional Development, University of California, San Francisco. Accessed at https://career.ucsf.edu/sites/career.ucsf.edu/files/PDF/ResearcherNegotiatingStartupPackage.pdf.
66. Davide Donina, Michele Meoli, and Stefano Paleari. 2015. *Higher Education Policy*. Springer. 28:215–234.
67. Stephan, *How Economics Shapes Science*, 171–172.
68. Michael S. Teitelbaum, *Falling Behind? Boom, Bust & the Global Race for Scientific Talent* (Princeton, NJ: Princeton University Press, 2014), 164.
69. Committee to Review the State of Postdoctoral Experience in Scientists and Engineers and Committee on Science, Engineering and Public Policy, *The Postdoctoral Experience Revisited* (Washington: National Academies Press, 2014), 27.
70. Beryl Lieff Benderly, rapporteur, and Committee on Science, Engineering and Public Policy, *The Arc of the Academic Research Career: Issues and Implications for U.S. Science and Engineering Leadership: Summary of a Workshop* (Washington: National Academies Press, 2014), 19. See also P. E. Stephan and J. Ma, "The Increased Frequency and Duration of the Postdoctorate Career Stage," *American Economic Review* 95, no. 71 (2005).
71. Benderly and Committee on Science, Engineering and Public Policy, *Arc of the Aca-*

demic Research Career, 21–22. Here the report discussed the important work of Henry Sauermann and Michael Roach, "PhD Students' Plans to Pursue Postdoctoral Training and Subsequent Transitions Into Postdoc Positions," unpublished manuscript.

72. Eric Bettinger, "To Be or Not to Be: Major Choices in Budding Scientists," in Charles T. Clotfelter, ed., *American Universities in a Global Market* (Chicago: University of Chicago Press and National Bureau of Economic Research, 2010), 69–98.
73. "Graduate Students in Science, Engineering, and Health in All Institutions, by Detailed Field, Citizenship, Ethnicity, and Race: 2013," Fall 2013 Survey of Graduate Students and Postdoctorates in Science and Engineering, National Science Foundation. Accessed at http://ncsesdata.nsf.gov/datatables/gradpostdoc/2013/html/GSS2013_DST_21.html.
74. For examples of how universities navigate hiring postdoctorate researchers, see University of Wisconsin https://www.ohr.wisc.edu/polproced/UPPP/0102_D.pdf or Stanford http://icenter.stanford.edu/docs/scholars/H1-J1-Visa-Comparison.pdf and http://postdocs.stanford.edu/admin/how-to/visas.html#h1b.
75. Philippe Moguérou, "Doctoral and Postdoctoral Education in Science and Engineering: Europe in the International Competition," *European Journal of Education* 40 (2005): 367–392.
76. National Science Foundation, "Postdoctoral Appointees in Science, Engineering, and Health in All Institutions, by Field, Citizenship, Ethnicity, and Race: 2007–13," Fall 2013 Survey of Graduate Students and Postdoctorates in Science and Engineering. Accessed at http://ncsesdata.nsf.gov/gradpostdoc/2013/html/GSS2013_DST_34.html.

PART THREE

Old Themes, New Perspectives

ELEVEN

The Expansion of the "School Form" and Deepening Inequality

DAVID KAREN

This volume raises the question of how, in the forty years since sociology of education received new theoretical lenses from the likes of Bell, Bowles and Gintis, Bourdieu, and Collins, education and its relationship to other social institutions has changed. The "new" theoretical insights were often framed in terms of whether and how education provided opportunities for mobility (on a level playing field, everyone was competing equally in a meritocratic contest) or was reproductive of the status quo ante (the poor were highly disadvantaged in a rigged game). As Davies and Mehta suggest in chapter 3, one of the major changes since the 1970s is the spread of the "school form"—organizational arrangements that mimic teacher-student relationships, including curricula and certifications—to many new domains. In this chapter I will address the expansion of the school form to new fields. Specifically, I will begin with a comment about the meaning and implications of meritocracy before addressing the degree to which inequality has worsened and risk has increased since the 1970s (see Hacker 2008). I discuss this in the context of changing community relationships and high levels of insecurity and status anxiety. I conclude with a brief comment about Bell's postindustrial society.

A Comment on Meritocratic Practice and Ideology

A key element in assessing the fairness and openness of a given society is the degree to which all members of the society have access to the resources and rewards available. In capitalist democracies, the educational system has been the locus of opportunity for mobility: education was deemed the escalator to which all had access and within which all had equal opportunity to demonstrate and prove their meritorious accomplishments. Success on the level playing field of education would lead to success in the occupational sector, providing just rewards for the highly talented.

This issue connects to arguments that my colleague, Bob Washington, and I have been developing on the *sports contest* as a model of meritocracy (see Karen and Washington 2015). In brief, we argue that the sports contest is a unique space where *transparency and publicity* frame a competition on a level playing field. In US professional sports, the audience members, *who can closely observe the entire competition*, generally accept the outcome of a given contest because we trust that it was fairly officiated—the officials are committed to fairness and are not being bribed or paid off by gamblers—and that everyone has played by the rules. There is an expectation that the coaches are employing their most effective strategies, that the players are there because they are the most meritorious, and that the teams are competing in order *to win*. With gambling out of the picture, we assume that the competitors are vying for victory for their own team, and that the officials are guaranteeing a level playing field.

We frame meritocracy both as a practice and as an ideology. As practice, meritocratic orientations in sport produce strategies, selection processes, and types and levels of effort that are necessary for success—the clearly defined goal of winning. This practice is analogous to—though less transparent and public than—the way we talk about meritocracy in education: we assume that the standardized test is a level playing field, and that everyone is doing their best to score the highest. Meritocracy, however, is also an ideological notion that privileges a very specific notion of fairness. We like to think that the educational system runs at least quasi-meritocratically, insofar as it focuses on achievement rather than ascription, transcending nepotistic, corrupt, family-, race/ethnic-, and class-based biases of unstandardized and informal systems of assessment. But it's also important to see how this narrow version of meritocratic assessment—even as it mistakenly presents standardized testing as a level playing field—systematically limits the realization of greater inclusiveness and greater participation because there are vast resource differences among schools and among various social groups (race/ethnic and class groups) that help reproduce unequal opportunities for different kinds of talent development. So even if everyone is equally equipped with a number two pencil when they confront the bubbles on the standardized test, and it appears that everyone is being treated equally (here's the level playing field!), there are vast differences in the nature and amount of talent development that occurred prior to the test administration.

To concretize how unlevel the playing field really is, it may help to clarify our conception of fairness in the sports field. We focus on four dimensions of fairness: (1) contest fairness (elimination of players' and officials' corruption), (2) access fairness (inclusion of all with adequate talent), (3) resource fairness (equal financial capacity for all teams within leagues to compete), and (4) pipeline fairness (opportunity for all to develop their talents). Much sociology of education assumes that we have contest fairness on the day of the test; given differences in nutrition, medical care, and basic school comforts during test administration, even this is highly problematic. Scholars subsequently have examined "access fairness" in terms of whether given test scores mean the same thing for different peoples (race/ethnic, region, class, etc.). Sociologists of education have explored "resource fairness" in terms of school spending, neighborhood resources, and so on. And finally, we have examined the fourth dimension in terms of whether students have the cultural capital necessary to acquire what is taught in school; in other words, do students have the "tools of appropriation," as Bourdieu has termed them. Pipeline fairness also involves the question of how narrowly or broadly defined are the talents that are rewarded. If we wished to maximize pipeline fairness in sports, we would advocate an "all sports for all" model, which would be a broad funnel for developing talent in many sports. In education, we would expect a broad appreciation for cultivating and rewarding many forms of cultural and linguistic expression. The analogy to sports is useful because the popularity of sports means that "the world" is interested in these violations of fairness and can actually witness immediately—often instantly, via available video—the violations on the very fields that gave the "level playing field" its name. In education, those violations are only discovered and understood through painstaking research by sociologists of education.

One implication of some of the chapters in this volume (especially chapters 3 and 9) is that, even if one acknowledges various non- or antimeritocratic processes, it may be especially difficult to untether—ideologically if not practically—success in school from success in life, given how ubiquitous school forms, badging, and credentials have become. As school forms proliferate and connect to subsequent career outcomes, schooling becomes even more highly legitimated as an engine of mobility, opportunity, and fairness. Indeed, it becomes impossible to find successful outcomes in given fields without educational certification. So a key aspect of the deeper interpenetration of education in modern life (Davies and Mehta, chapter 3) has to do with reinforcing the tight bond between education and conceptions of fairness. If meritocratic practice for a given organizational form can be claimed (as it has for the "school form"), it gains immediate legitimacy as reflecting equal opportunity and confers a baseline "default legitimacy" for any resulting credential, and for subsequent conversion processes in the labor market. Given these tight potential bonds, it is important to examine resistance to what are seen as meritocratic practices, as such critical examinations may lead to broadening conceptions of talent (what kinds of knowledge are rewarded) and broadening patterns of participation (who can demonstrate the knowledge). Ultimately, this kind of resistance—new and different forms of talent from marginalized sectors of the population—can be seen as leading potentially to more social-democratic forms of conceptions of fairness. Even if this development doesn't delegitimize old forms of knowledge and their acquisition, it opens up the possibility that new forms in different fields can be legitimated and rewarded. These third and fourth dimensions of fairness are especially ripe for exploration.

The Post-1970s Context

Interestingly, it was in the same decade—the 1970s—that sociologists of education such as Bowles and Gintis, Collins, and others published their overviews of education-society relations that the pattern of wage growth fundamentally changed. Of course, other key trends were also in play in the post–WWII period, such as women's increased entry into the labor force, rising divorce rates, and increased age at first marriage. But it was in 1973 that wage growth simply stopped. In fact, it appears that 1973 represents the low point of our poverty rate for adults between the ages of eighteen and sixty-four; it's never been as low since. (To offer another data point, 1968 represented the high point for the inflation-adjusted value of the minimum wage, when it was $8.54 in 2014 dollars. In 2014 the minimum wage was $7.25, also in 2014 dollars.)

Based on data from the Economic Policy Institute (EPI), between 1948 and 1973, average incomes grew about $22,000, and each income quintile shared roughly equally in that growth (though the richest 10 percent got about one-third of the growth). Between 1973 and 2008, average incomes grew by about $9300. *All* of the growth went to the richest 10 percent, while income for the bottom 90 percent declined. Taking a slightly different angle on the more recent period, between 1979 and 2005, those in the bottom fifth of the income scale received an average of a $200 increase over the course of those twenty-six years (a $7.69 increase per year!) while those in the top 0.1 percent received almost a $6 million increase over that same period (or about a $230,000 increase per year). Concentration of wealth dramatically increased: in 1962, the top 1 percent had approximately 125 times the net worth of the median household, while by 2009 that ratio had risen to 225. And at the same time, marginal tax rates on the wealthy declined precipitously.

The EPI's *State of Working America* reviews some of the major structural changes in the economy during the same period: decline of manufacturing and rise of finance, growing integration into the world economy, increased growth of the labor force (especially women) and higher education, massive decline in unionization and massive decline in real value of minimum wage, and decline since the Reagan era in public investment which keeps unemployment high (remember that, upon entering office, Reagan quite self-consciously traded double-digit interest rates for double-digit unemployment). As EPI summarizes:

> The focus instead has been on policies that claimed to make consumers better off through lower prices: deregulation of industries, privatization of public services, the weakening of labor standards such as the minimum wage, erosion of the social safety net, expanding globalization, and the move toward fewer and weaker unions. These policies have served to undercut the bargaining power of most workers, widen wage inequality, and deplete access to good jobs. In the last 10 years, even workers with a college degree have failed to see any real wage growth. (http://www.epi.org/economic_snapshots/entry/what_workers_gave_and_what_they_got/).

So many of the changes in education that we've witnessed—in particular, much of the horizontal, vertical, and metaphorical expansion of education that Davies and Mehta discuss—is tied to massive changes in inequality: in wealth, income, and time and massive changes in overall levels of *anxiety about status and basic security*.[1]

Education has been *the* answer for questions about status and security for a long time. From the 1960s television ads in which a young Abraham Lincoln tells the job counselor that he's qualified because he's "read a lot," and is told, "You ain't going nowhere without that sheepskin," to the continual bombardment from within school and without that more education means more opportunity and more income, the notion that education is a universal good has become ubiquitous. Yes, the recent flattening of the returns for a college degree is of concern,[2] but this has done little to dampen the demand for formal education and formal credentials (the Obama administration disagrees with James Rosenbaum's claims that "college for all" is a bad policy choice). And while the payoff of education for individuals has declined, the added benefits to private companies of this "socialization of training costs" continue to be enhanced. Ultimately, through private appropriation of profits, such arrangements contribute to the further generation of inequality and associated anxieties.

From many different studies, with Robert Putnam's (2000) work and the Saguaro Seminar leading the way, we see the decline of community, of real neighborhoods, of civic engagement, and of rich public spaces. Perhaps the spread of these school forms is a somewhat feeble attempt to compensate for these declines. Let me point to one example of the changing nature of community. Sherri Grasmuck's (2005) book on Little League baseball, *Protecting Home: Class, Race, and Masculinity in Boys' Baseball*, documents the different ways in which the old, longtime neighborhood residents from the working class and the newly arrived upper-middle-class residents orient to a community Little League. The working-class men who coach Little League teams coach the eight-year-olds year in and year out, independent of whether or where in the league their own kids play. The upper-middle-class father-coaches follow their kids through the league, coaching their own kids' teams, moving up an age/grade-level year after year. Needless to say, these different coaching "careers" are associated with developing very different relationships in the community in terms of breadth and meaning. Following Davies and Mehta's "metaphorical expansion" of school forms, the later father-coaches are "promoted" with their sons from age grade to age grade. So, on many different levels and in many different ways, "school forms" are stepping into a void created by the changing nature of community, neighborhoods, and networks. Specifically, the "old heads" increasingly are no longer available, and the stay-at-home moms who organized all sorts of local activities are not around; people are cobbling together two and three full or part-time jobs to make a living; and there is increased geographical mobility and an attendant decline of intergenerational sharing (except, perhaps, among the poor, who lack other kinds of resources to enrich the lives of kids). Due to these changes, families and communities have less time and capacity to provide training in literacy, social capital accumulation and activation, leisure, and communication (especially the ability to code switch between, say, neighborhood talk and talking to professionals, as Lareau [2011] demonstrates) . . . *except in school forms*.[3]

On the supply side, of course, we have massive numbers of credentialed people who are either forced or happy to hang out a shingle to engage clients and customers in a school form to provide many of the services that the government neglects, or which the community can no longer provide. These services are often basic necessities, such as child care, as well as new needs (youth centers, new forms of job training, etc.), but they are tied to addressing the anxieties of living in an economy in which jobs and wages are increasingly uncertain. In such a situation, and in a context in which school forms have legitimacy, almost any "course offering" can be packaged in ways that make it seem like a good leg up in a competitive world. From sports lessons oriented toward helping enrollees get D-I scholarships (some kids change sports in relation to perceived changes in opportunities for scholarships) to SAT prep courses, or to the many language, computing, leadership, or "image" classes that promise to help adults feel indispensable on the job and ripe for promotion, school forms are indeed ubiquitous. In the context of massive food and positional insecurity and high levels of status anxiety, the offering of resources in forms that resemble schools—those providers of equal opportunity and convertible credentials—can attract great interest. As Cooper (2014: 45) put it, "Americans are struggling to forge security in an insecure age."

Bourdieu's concepts of habitus, capital, and fields can help us get a handle on these various dynamics. Some of them can also be explained by a DiMaggio-Powell (1983) organizational field perspective. Both perspectives direct us to understanding the dynamics of competition, regulation, and resources, so as to better understand pressures toward particular outcomes. Both perspectives direct us to understanding better how actors develop particular taken-for-granted orientations toward the world that then motivate action in particular resource-dependent contexts. As we attempt to understand the spread of school forms to new arenas, and the desire of the populace to sign on, we need to understand better the *field* within which these struggles/contests are occurring. Such an analysis would focus on both supply and demand for these products: one would have to account for the social locations in the relevant fields of the contenders, the nature of the competition, the capital and resources available, and the perceptions of the opportunity structure (habitus).

It would be worthwhile to think about how organizations and industries that are beginning "to badge" position themselves in relation to one another, and in relation to other types of credentials. Olneck (chapter 9 in this volume) discusses these contestations and reminds us that the expansion of badges should signal to us how struggles for these emergent credentials may take many forms at different levels of analysis. Even as individuals attempt to obtain "better" badges, employers are deciding what they mean. Do they reflect particular competencies, or are they convertible primarily for their symbolic value? In other words, what kind of capital is being accumulated and how is it being converted? As the badges become more common, how does inflation affect their value within and across fields?

Finally, in the context of this expansion of school forms, it would be useful to think about what particular combinations of interests, practices, and ideologies might lead to *greater* inclusiveness and a more robust public space. What if this expansion took the form of claims for greater equality of access to a wider variety of talents and skills, so as to support fairer competition (say, equal funding of schools) and development of a wider range of capacities? Movements that seek to expand the conflict in this way broaden our conception of fairness well beyond meritocratic practice and ideology. The question is whether such arguments can be successful when inequality, insecurity, and anxiety are so high.

Additional Comment on Daniel Bell and the Technocracy

This leads me, finally, to comment on a point that Davies and Mehta raise about Bell's postindustrial society. In their discussion of the 1970s sociology of education theorizing, they discuss Bell's claim that the United States was becoming a "knowledge society." They claim correctly, in my opinion, that the United States is becoming a "schooled" society to a much greater extent than it is becoming a "knowledge" society. But there is one place where Bell got it both very right and very wrong. Bell expected greater development in science and technology, greater legitimacy *for* science and technology, and greater power for the scientific and technological elite. However, the one place where he probably didn't expect science and technology to win out—business—is the institutional locus where it has attained its most unquestioned superiority. The folks with the best equations rose quickly within financial firms, and were able to make millions and billions along the way. Certainly, within that sector, technical expertise continues to have enormous legitimacy. Yet the index of *The Coming of Post-Industrial Society* has no entries for banking, Wall Street, stocks, or finance, and only one for economic forecasting. So Bell was right about the power of science, but he didn't know where it would emerge. And then, because he couldn't believe that any sector could overtake the political sphere's authority—lest there be a Mills-type power elite—he insisted that in the end, the politicians would control the technocrats. Here, I wish he were more correct. Through harnessing the power of the technocrats, capital and business were able not only to maintain but to expand their power and, contrary to Bell's prediction, to circumvent political controls to an alarming extent. So capitalist class alignments with the technocracy and political elites lead us to our current state of massive inequality.

Final Query

Is the spread of all these school forms simply a continuation of the use of "schooling," broadly conceived, to solve all the problems of US society? Schools have been asked to "Americanize" any and every group thought not to be sufficiently so, to integrate "commercial" subjects into the high school, to develop the talent necessary to beat the Soviets to the moon, to ensure that our children are physically fit and avoid drugs and alcohol (and, often, sex), to drive well (!), and so on. In many ways, this book challenges us to think through the institutional pressures that conduce to these "solutions" under different historical conditions and even greater expansion of school forms. One is pushed to think about whether and how the United States is continuing, as has been its practice, to *substitute* equality of opportunity for social welfare (see Wilensky 1975; Heidenheimer, Heclo, and Adams 1975). Such a substitution narrows our conception of fairness and keeps us focused on meritocratic practice and ideology when broader conceptions of social justice are available.

Notes

1. In *Cut Adrift,* Marianne Cooper (2014) details the changes that have moved us to a society in which risk is felt throughout the class structure. Her book reports on the *emotional underpinnings* of the experience of this risk.
2. At the same time, part of the continued demand has to do with college still being the "best game in town." Even as the pattern of returns has flattened, those with less than a college education have seen *declines* in returns.
3. Or, within families. Lareau (2011) and Grasmuck (2005) both show the ways in which these behaviors and ways of being are class-based and rooted in different family practices in different classes.

References

Cooper, Marianne. 2014. *Cut Adrift: Families in Insecure Times.* University of California Press.

DiMaggio, Paul J., and Walter W. Powell. 1983. The Iron Cage Revisited: Institutional Isomorphism and Collective Rationality in Organizational Fields. *American Sociological Review* 48, no. 2 (April); 147–160.

Economic Policy Institute. "State of Working America." Accessed June 3, 2017, at http://www.stateofworkingamerica.org/.

Grasmuck, Sherri. 2005. *Protecting Home: Class, Race, and Masculinity in Boys' Baseball.* New Brunswick, NJ; Rutgers University Press.

Hacker, Jacob S. 2008. *The Great Risk Shift: The New Economic Insecurity and the Decline of the American Dream.* Revised updated edition. Oxford, UK: Oxford University Press.

Heidenheimer, Arnold, Hugh Heclo, and Carolyn Teich Adams. 1975. *Comparative Public Policy: The Politics of Social Choice in Europe and America*. New York: St. Martin's Press.

Karen, David, and Robert E. Washington. 2015. *Sociological Perspectives on Sport: The Games Outside the Games*. London and New York: Routledge.

Lareau, Annette. 2011. *Unequal Childhoods: Class, Race, and Family Life, 2nd Edition with an Update a Decade Later*. Berkeley: University of California Press.

Putnam, Robert D. 2000. *Bowling Alone: The Collapse and Revival of American Community*. New York: Simon and Schuster.

Saguaro Seminar: Civic Engagement in America. 2017. Kennedy School of Government, Harvard University. Accessed June 3, 2017, at http://www.hks.harvard.edu/programs/saguaro/.

Wilensky, Harold. 1975. *The Welfare State and Equality*. Berkeley: University of California Press.

TWELVE

Reopening the Black Box of Educational Disadvantage: Why We Need New Answers to Old Questions

JANICE AURINI AND CATHLENE HILLIER

Sociologists have long documented educational disparities. The emergence of large-scale data sets and new quantitative techniques in the 1960s and 1970s allowed researchers to trace the multiple ways in which the offspring from higher-class backgrounds outpaced their lower-class counterparts at every level and every facet of formal schooling. Their analyses showed that variables such as parental education and income predicted outcomes including receiving good grades, graduating high school, and entering postsecondary (for a classic discussion, see Karabel and Halsey 1977).

The inability of such data to fully answer *how* and *why* questions related to educational inequality did not discourage academics from speculating about structural and cultural origins (for discussions see Gamoran, Secada, and Marrett 2000; Hallinan 2006). At that time, competing explanations tended to polarize between those that traced inequality directly to teacher discrimination and curricular bias, and those that focused on the cultures of the poor and working classes. In the case of the former, prevailing structural explanations portrayed lower-class families as victims of a school system (Bowles and Gintis 1976). Teachers were accused of "misrecognizing" class cultures as intelligence (Bourdieu and Passeron 1977); lower-class and minority parents were "frozen out" of educational decision making (Connell et al. 1982); and working-class children were "cooled out" and channeled into less advantageous educational tracks (Clark 1960). In the case of the latter, cultural deprivation explanations directed our attention to the contexts of families and neighborhoods. According to this literature, lower-class families did not place the same value on education; they provided inferior learning environments for their children, and in some cases their children actively "resisted" schooling (Ryan 1976; Willis 1977). Subsequent research in the sociology of education extended these explanations to examinations of race and gender (e.g., American Association of University Women 1992; for a discussion see Hallinan 2006). Both literatures claimed to "open the black box" by exposing deep structural (e.g., Rist 1977) and cultural biases (e.g., Bourdieu 1977).

Since the 1970s, educational institutions have changed in many ways, offering more accommodations and choices. Parents also have more opportunities to participate in their children's schooling (for examples, see Lubienski and Lubienski 2013; Ong-Dean 2009; Powell, Cohen, and Farrar 1985). Aggregate attainment levels have also risen markedly at all levels of schooling (US Department of Education, National Center for Education Statistics 2014c). Despite these developments, new research also shows us that social class gaps in educational achievement are growing. This paradox—education expansion and accommodation on one hand, and widening achievement and attainment gaps on the other—represents a new "black box."

This chapter draws on three promising avenues of research that have started to provide answers to what are now fairly old questions about the antecedents, processes, and mechanisms of educational inequality. We do not claim to provide a comprehensive survey of the field. Rather, our intention is to highlight viable directions from which new insights into emerging educational inequality can be developed. Drawing on a diverse range of topics and methodologies, what this research shows is that while institutional and cultural changes have helped lower-class students finish high school and enter postsecondary, they rarely lead to the upper tiers of credential competition (e.g., Armstrong and Hamilton 2013; Mullen 2010; Radford 2013). Lower-class students are gaining traction, but arguably at less challenging and therefore less advantageous lower-end and middle-range educational contests. By way of contrast, higher-class parents have greatly intensified their parenting strategies, including navigating their children through increasingly complex educational pathways.

This research also shows that, in some cases, new forms of social inequality are reproduced by the very organizational and cultural contexts that encouraged widening access, accommodation, and parental and student involvement in the first place (e.g., Demerath 2009; Ong-Dean 2009). These contexts afford opportunities for some parents and students to adapt to changing educational contests, compensate for academic or intellectual shortcomings, and exert authority at key organizational decision-making points in ways that sometimes undermine well-intentioned efforts to mitigate social class disparities (see also Cherlin, Talbert, and Yasutake 2014; Reardon and Bischoff 2011; Thompson and Smeeding 2014).

Newer Answers to Classic Questions in the Sociology of Education

Such foundational questions about schooling outcomes have endured in our field, but the nature of educational inequality has evolved considerably. A growing body of literature in the sociology of education has altered our understanding of reproduction by highlighting environmental and organizational processes that have transformed the contours of educational inequality. Importantly, this research provides us with new answers to why efforts to widen opportunity and alter parenting practices have failed to close social class gaps in educational achievement (Conley and Albright 2004; Furstenberg 2011). In such explanations, schools and families are still at least partially responsible; however, this research shows that they sometimes contribute to the reproduction of privilege in unintended and surprising ways. We first highlight the research that foreshadows more recent advancements in the literature. Next, we turn to promising directions in the sociology of education. We conclude by discussing the generic methodological and theoretical principles that inform these developments.

Beyond the School Gate

One of the most consistent finding in the sociology of education literature is the strong association between family social class and educational achievement (e.g., Conley and Albright 2004; Roscigno, Tomaskovic-Devey, and Crowley 2006). Since the Coleman report (1966), researchers have found that a variety of nonschool factors influence academic outcomes more than do school resources. In fact, a substantial body of research shows that variations in student achievement are far better predicted by family resources such as income, wealth, and parental education than by school resources like spending per student, student-teacher ratios, physical equipment, and teacher experience (Coleman et al. 1966; Conley and Albright 2004; Heyneman and Loxley 1982, 1983).

The focus on non-school factors is not new. Yet there has been a general tendency among academics to avoid explanations that may cast them as "blaming the victim" (Ryan 1976; for a discussion see Brint [chapter 4 in this volume]; and Small, Harding, and Lamont 2010) or, perhaps even worse, as structural functionalists (e.g., Davis and Moore 1945)! These fears have likely contributed to the underdevelopment of examination of nonschool factors related to educational achievement.

Fortunately, as research about the shifting nature of inequality evolves, examinations of factors beyond the school gate have bridged classic and contemporary research in the sociology of education. Importantly, this research finds that many differences between higher-class and lower-class students emerge before children even start school and continue to grow over time. At the most basic level, there is evidence that poverty and related environmental stress have a more significant impact on children's brain development than does genetics. According to one study, while only 3 or 4 percent of children are born with observable cognitive differences, by kindergarten more than 25 percent are "developmentally vulnerable at school entry" (Hertzman 2004: 4). Examinations of children's brain development using magnetic resonance imaging (MRI) have also found socioeconomic (SES) differences related to the parts of the brain that are conducive to educational achievement, including memory, attention span, inhibition, complex learning, and emotional regulation (Hanson et al. 2012). In this sense, genes "listen to the environment" and change in ways that have a profound effect on children's ability to learn and function in school settings (Sokolowski 2013; see also Hertzman 2004 and Nelson III and Sheridan 2011).[1]

A second source of inequality emerges once children are of school age. A variety of research traditions, such as studies of cultural capital in sociology, find that middle- and higher-class children are more likely to be continually exposed to literacy and numeracy-enhancing activities outside school hours; they hear more enriched conversation at home, are read to more often; engage in more informal activities that promote language, reading, and counting; and receive more parental help with homework (Guryan, Hurst, and Kearney 2008; Hart and Risley 1995; Lareau 2011; Phillips and Lowenstein 2011).[2]

This research also identifies summertime as a key source of education achievement gaps between higher- and lower-class youth, particularly if those patterns compound over several summers. "Seasonal learning" studies find that learning rates by social class are roughly equal during the school year, but then diverge in the summer. Disadvantaged children tend to lose numeracy and literacy skills in July and August, while middle- and higher-class children tend to gain skills. In Baltimore, longitudinal research attributes disparities in summer learning to *most* of the SES gap in high school achievement, high school completion, and university attendance (Alexander, Entwisle, and Olson 2007; Alexander, Pitcok, and Bouley 2016; Davies and Aurini 2013; Downey, von Hippel, and Broh 2004; see also Heyns's [1978] groundbreaking research).

Are All Boats Rising? Greater Accommodations, Rising Levels, and Widening Social Class Gaps

> ". . . . The fact that working class youth may be holding steady or making modest progress is inconsequential if upper/middle class youth are pulling even further ahead."
>
> (Putnam, Frederick, and Snellman 2012: 4)

The research described above has altered the landscape of public policy and practice. A wide variety of initiatives attempt to overturn institutional processes that are seen to limit learning opportunities for lower-class and minority students. Far-reaching reforms in the United States seek to retain students, detrack schools, expose all students to an academically rigorous curriculum, extend postsecondary opportunities, and ensure that "no child is left behind" (for a historical overview see Labaree 2010). Parental involvement has also been formalized in educational policy, most notably in the areas of special education, school choice, and parent-school partnerships (see Lubienski and Lubienski 2013; Ong-Dean 2009; Robinson and Harris 2014). Since the 1960s, several programs such as Head Start and No Child Left Behind attempt to teach parents how to stimulate their children's development, connect to schools, and advocate for resources.[3] In K–12 education, advanced placement (AP), international baccalaureate (IB), and supplementary education services are just a few other examples of education options that cater to students' and parents' pedagogical preferences and learning needs (for an earlier discussion see Powell, Cohen, and Farrar 1985).[4] All of these program and policy changes—more accommodation, inclusivity, choice, and parent involvement—are realized in a rise in two key areas: educational attainment and parent involvement.

First, rising levels of educational attainment suggest that these reforms are having a positive impact. In the early part of the twentieth century, only 6 percent of students graduated high school, and only 3 percent entered postsecondary (Duncan and Murnane 2011: 3). Today, 90 percent of Americans over the age of twenty-five have received a high school diploma or its equivalent. Undergraduate enrollment grew by 31 percent over the past decade, 34 percent have completed a bachelor degree, and 7 percent have completed a master's degree or higher (US Department of Education, National Center for Education Statistics 2013b; see also the Association of Universities and Colleges Canada 2011). The United States now boasts 4,300 postsecondary institutions and colleges. These institutions continue to expand their enrollment targets, programs, and accommodations for nontraditional students (e.g., online and part-time options; Alon 2009). These developments have encouraged some to use terms such as "demographic uplift" to describe the character of schooling in the United States (Brint 2006; see also Arum and Roksa 2010; Rosenbaum 2004; Zarifa 2012).

Second, efforts to recalibrate parenting practices also appear to have "trickled down" to the mainstream (Aurini 2015). Today, parents from all social classes invest more money and time on their children's cognitive, social, and emotional development (Gauthier, Smeeding, and Furstenberg 2011; Kornrich and Furstenberg 2013; Ramey and Ramey 2010). Not only has parents' time with children increased, but so has the quality of parent-child interactions. All parents now spend more time and money on activities that are believed to improve children's school readiness, including reading and teaching letters, words, and numbers (Schaub 2015). When lower-class parents receive additional money, they increase their spending on items such as after-school and educational activities (Duncan, Huston, and Weisner 2007). These investments are part of a more general "revolution of expectations" in which most parents no longer hope but *expect* their children to do well in school, graduate high school, and attend postsecondary education (Davies 2004; see also Domina, Conley, and Farkas 2011; Jacob and Wilder Linkow 2011).[5]

Despite these significant developments, a variety of indicators suggest that academic disparities by social class are getting worse. Researchers are tracing widening social class gaps on measures such as reading and math scores (Reardon 2011). While almost 60 percent of lower-class students enter postsecondary schooling, they are more likely to attend two-year college institutions (Pell Institute 2015; Wyatt and Mattern 2011). In fact, the expansion of two-year colleges and programs accounts for most of the expansion at the postsecondary level (Alon 2009), and only a few students transition to four-year colleges (see Brint 2003). As Reardon, Baker, and Klasik (2012: 1) show, students "from top income quintile families are seven to eight times more likely to enroll in a highly selective college than students from bottom quintile families"—a difference that has grown in recent decades.

The college graduation gap between lower-class and higher-class students has also widened over time. In the past two decades, college graduation rates have climbed 18 percent for higher-class students, but only 4 percent for lower-class students (Bailey and Dynarski 2011; see also Dickert-Conlin and Rubenstein 2007).[6] Qualitative researchers have also documented how social origins continue to shape several aspects of the college experience, including the application process, student life, and the meaning and consequences of academic and extracurricular choices (Armstrong and Hamilton 2013; Espenshade and Radford 2009; Lehmann 2014; Mullen 2010).

In short, while all boats are rising, the educational fortunes of higher-class students are rising more.[7] Why? Widening accommodation, expansion, and rising levels of education attainment cast doubt on explanations that focus on the biases of schools and the "pathologies" of the lower classes. Such theories are no longer adequate, given the structural changes to the organization of schooling, the rising levels of attainment, and the evidence that lower-class parents now devote significantly more time and money on their children's development, and expect their children to go on to postsecondary. Instead, emerging research in the sociology of education identifies three ways by which new forms of reproduction are occurring that parallel widening income, marriage, and other social class gaps (e.g., Cherlin, Talbert, and Yasutake 2014; Kornrich and Furstenberg 2013; Putnam 2015; Reardon 2011; Reardon and Bischoff 2011; Snellman et al. 2015).

Buffering Environmental Uncertainty: Investment and Compensatory Strategies among Middle- and Higher-Class Families

The first new set of answers to emerging forms of educational inequality suggests the following hypothesis: *Any additional investments made by lower-class parents are surpassed by the considerable increase in time, money, and compensatory investments now made by middle- and higher-class parents.* As a consequence, the equalization benefits of attending parent-teacher meetings, volunteering, and helping with homework—practices that are promoted as a way to improve lower-class children's academic outcomes—are compromised in the wake of ever more elaborate and intensive practices engaged by higher-class parents (e.g., for discussions of parent involvement see Epstein 2005; but also McNeal 2012).

How are these responses different from previously reported trends in parenting? For several decades, researchers have documented the intensification of parenting practices (e.g., Hays 1996; Zelizer 1985). Such intensive parenting practices are no longer "new" or practiced exclusively by higher-class parents (Dermott and Pomati 2015; Schiffrin et al. 2013). What *is* new is the sheer escalation of investments and compensatory strategies adopted by middle- and higher-class parents, often in the name of a preparing children for an academic and job market that is perceived to be more competitive and unstable (Urist 2014; see also Ehrenreich, 1990).

Some of these strategies are quite observable to the naked eye. The most obvious measures of widening social class gaps are time and financial investments. According to one study, since the early 1970s the spending gap between children from lower-income and higher-income tripled (Duncan and Murnane 2011: 11). Kornrich and Furstenberg (2013) found an even larger growth in the spending gap. According to their study, high-income families spend nearly seven times as much on their children's development as low-income families, up from a ratio of four times in 1972. Similarly, while all parents now spend more time with children, the increase in child-related time use since the mid-1990s has been twice as great for college-educated parents (Ramey and Ramey 2010).

It is not just the amount of money and time, but the quality and variety of investments that vary. According to Kornich and Furstenberg (2013: 11), additional financial investments made by higher-class families between 1970 and 2000 were largely directed at human-capital-building activities such as child care and education. Similarly, others have found that the largest spending differences between lower-income and higher-income families include music lessons, travel, and summer camps (see Kaushal, Magnuson, and Waldfogel 2011). Higher-class parents spend approximately one more hour per day directly involved with their children (Putnam, Frederick, and Snellman 2012: 13), and by six years of age children from higher-income homes spend 400 more hours in literacy-related activities and 1,300 more hours with their parents in "nonroutine" contexts outside of a home or school environment (e.g., parks, libraries; see Phillips and Lowenstein 2011). Higher-class children also spend more time engaged in sports, clubs, and volunteering, while lower-class children's participation in such activities has either remained stable or declined over time (Putnam, Frederick, and Snellman 2012).

Longitudinal data on other indicators are in shorter supply, but we do have very good data that suggest that middle- and higher-class children participate in a number of other activities that may boost their overall grades and test scores. Tutoring is one example of a way in which these parents are better equipped, financially or otherwise, to improve their children's academic profiles or compensate for their children's learning difficulties. Buchmann, Condron, and Roscigno (2010) find that children from families with higher incomes are more likely to use test preparation, and are significantly more likely to use the most expensive forms of test preparation (private courses and private tutors). They also find that students from higher-class backgrounds are more likely to use test preparation for enrichment, rather than for remedial purposes. These results suggest that already financially and educationally advantaged students use test preparation to enhance their academic profiles even more, which in turn may increase their chances of attending the most selective colleges (Buchmann, Condron, and Roscigno 2010; see also Aurini, Davies and Dierkes, 2013; Baker and LeTendre 2005).

Any single particular additional investment is small and inconsequential. A few extra minutes of reading every night do not guarantee academic success, just as the absence of any one activity rarely predicts academic failure. However, small differences accrue over time, and lead to cumulative advantages and disadvantages by contributing to a student's stock of knowledge, self-concept, and noncognitive behaviors (e.g., good work habits) over the school year (Potter and Roksa 2013; see also Furstenberg 2006: 7; Lleras 2008) and summer months (e.g., Alexander, Entwisle, and Olson 2007).[8] The extra participation in sports, music, and clubs also favors higher-class children in academic contests and labor markets because they are used by college admission boards and employers as a "proxy" for less tangible qualities such as leadership (e.g., Snellman et al. 2015: 196). Perhaps not surprisingly, some research has also found that participation in such activities predicts educational attainment and future earnings (Kosteas 2010; see also Buchmann, Condron, and Roscigno 2010; Snellman et al. 2015).

Time, spending, and participation patterns are broadly consistent overall with a growing intensive parenting gap: lower-class parents have increased their amount of time, money, and participation in various enrichment activities, but such additional investments have not kept pace with the significant increase in investments made by middle- and higher-class parents. Consequently, the potential benefits of structural (e.g., detracking) and cultural changes (e.g., adoption of practices associated with concerted cultivation) are likely compromised by the sheer escalation of time and money spent by higher-class families. Not only are higher-class parents continually intensifying the lengths by which they help their children succeed at any given level of schooling, but they are particularly adept at mitigating potential problems.

Adaptation: Responses to the Changing Academic and Labor Market

> Adaptation is the "process of change by which an organism or species becomes better suited to its environment."
>
> —Oxford Dictionaries 2015

The second set of answers to emerging forms of educational inequality points to ways in which higher-class families strategically adapt to changing educational contests. This research supports the following generalization: *While lower-class parents are significantly more aligned with the standards of educational institutions than in the past, middle- and higher-class parents more effectively adapt to new environmental conditions.* What this research shows is that middle- and higher-class families have transformed their practices to match current educational circumstances. Parental resources—economic, academic, cultural or otherwise—provide middle- and higher-class families with the flexibility to recalibrate their practices and optimize opportunities for their children.

First, as lower-class families "learn the ropes" of educational processes, middle- and higher-class families strategically change their tactics to secure limited space in various educational arenas (e.g., selective postsecondary institutions and special education resources; also see MMI and EMI research below). A key principle of cultural capital is that the manners, predispositions, cultural tastes, and habits of the dominant culture (middle- and upper-class)—forming habitus or a "way of being"—are passed on and developed in the home environment (Bourdieu 1998; Bourdieu and Passeron 1977). For Bourdieu, capital is what the individual brings to the situation, and this is influenced by cultural, socioeconomic, and intellectual attributes. In relation to schooling, cultural capital theory asserts that middle- and upper-class families have the knowledge and resources to not only do relatively well, but also to help shape the system in a way that reflects their strengths and qualities. Building on Bourdieu's (1998) theory, Annette Lareau's (2011) work demonstrates the manner in which middle-class parents effectively navigate institutional processes and align their practices with the evolving standards of schooling. Similarly, Chin's (2000) analysis of the competitive private high school application process shows how higher-class parents use their "class capital" (a combination of financial, human, social, and cultural capital) to create the "perfect applicant." This process is not only about preparing children academically (e.g., tutoring), but is also about preparing children emotionally to handle the pressure of high-stakes tests and admission interviews.

The terms "pushy parents," "helicopter parents," and "snowplow parents" have been used in popular vernacular to describe overly involved parents (see Hunsaker 2013). These terms are not only applied to the parents of very young children; rather, researchers show how "intensive parenting" has made its way into university and colleges (e.g., Coburn 2006; Fingerman et al. 2012; Schiffrin et al. 2014). College and university professors receive phone calls and e-mails from parents concerned about their child's progress in class, and residence administrators handle complaints from parents about dorm accommodations (Coburn 2006). Even in the college application process, advantaged parents can help pave the way for their children not only to receive admittance to their school of choice, but to obtain the highest return on academic funding. Stuber (2011) describes a student who, at the recommendation of his father, applied to several schools and used the offers from other schools to negotiate with his school of choice.

Similarly, Demerath's (2009) four-year ethnography of Wilton, a public high school in an affluent neighborhood in the US Midwest, details how higher-class parents adapt to the changing competitive landscape of higher education. In his study, higher-class parents frequently asked teachers to justify grades, and routinely excused their children from school on test days or when an assignment was due. To secure additional accommodations for their children (e.g., extra time on tests), higher-class parents also successfully sought out individual education plans (IEP). As one teacher explained, ". . . There are no average kids in Wilton. You are either gifted or special ed. And special ed is a good thing here" (56). Demerath also documents how schools like Wilton actively construct the very symbolic capital that is rewarded by postsecondary institutions and labor markets. Near the end of his data collection, there were no less than forty-seven valedictorians, and almost half of the graduating students that year received an award at one of three recognition ceremonies.

Even within institutional processes (e.g., establishing an IEP) higher-class parents go beyond simply advocating for their children to obtain special-education status. Trainor (2010) observes that lower-SES parents adopt a more "intuitive" approach to special-education processes, since they "know their child" (Trainor 2010: 40). Conversely, higher-SES parents are more likely to research educational policies, document their children's academic and emotional growth in the classroom, and become everyday presences at school (see also Demerath 2009; Duquette et al. 2011; Ong-Dean 2009). In initial placement meetings, higher-class parents are more likely to come armed with the latest research and a solid understanding of educational policies about their children's rights. Some of these parents bring lawyers or representatives from the local association for gifted children (Bacon and Causton-Theoharis 2013; Duquette at al. 2011; Ong-Dean 2009). Certainly, cultural capital can be applied here to explain why middle- and higher-class parents feel entitled to make themselves such a visible and vocal presence in schools. However, as demonstrated above, parents also use their social capital (see Bourdieu 1998; Coleman 1988)—their networks with other parents and professionals—to leverage beneficial positions for their children.

Second, in line with Bourdieu's (1977) notion of habitus, higher-class parents and students tend to have a very different orientation toward schooling. Higher-class parents instill in children a sense of "belonging" and entitlement in educational settings. For example, Calarco's (2011, 2014) research demonstrates how children's social class largely determines the strategies they use to obtain help in the classroom. She illustrates how middle-class children—often coached by their parents—are more persistent and vocal in asking for help from their teachers, and how, as a result, they create advantages for themselves that further generate classroom inequalities.

In postsecondary, research suggests that higher-class students are simply better at adapting to competitive processes in schooling organizations and the labor market. Higher-class students are in a position to secure internships and high-quality volunteer opportunities. They also have more extracurricular experiences than their lower-class peers. These "résumé builders" advantage students in the labor market (Stuber 2011). As one elite student states: "My parents always said, you know, 'You don't go to undergraduate to get a job. You go to undergraduate to kind of make yourself a more educated person in a sense, a richer person'" (Mullen 2010: 133). These studies also illustrate that elites have adopted new ways to reproduce their privilege, learning the language and practices of meritocracy and diversity. Such skills endow students with the cultural and mental dexterity to straddle multiple social settings (Khan 2011).

Strategic Management of Choice

> ". . . the reliance on consensual language such as 'partnership,' 'involvement' and 'dialogue,' which features strongly in the home-school literature, edits out tension and conflict, as well as the inequalities underlying them."
>
> (Reay 1999; 160; paraphrasing Vincent 1996; 73)

The third set of answers to emerging forms of educational inequality points to the following: *Expanded structural differentiation and choice are more likely to be used and effectively managed by middle- and higher-class families.* Since the 1970s, reform efforts from across the political spectrum have called for enhanced grass-roots decision-making power and choice in public schooling.[9] Indeed, the language of parent-school "partnerships" now dominates the landscape of education (for examples see Epstein 2005; McNeal 2012; Ong-Dean 2009). The intention of these efforts varies widely—from encouraging market competition to expanding parent involvement—but it asserts the principles of individual rather than collective rights and responsibilities.[10]

Before children enter postsecondary education, middle- or higher-class parents strategically opt or petition for the most advantageous educational positions for their children; these may take the form of particular schools (e.g., prestigious private schools) or programs (e.g., IB courses; for an early discussion, see Collins 1979). In the spirit of individualization and choice, schools have continued to expand and diversify their curricular, program, and institutional offerings. Within the public education sector, parents can now find schools that cater to children's scholastic, artistic, or special education preferences (e.g., Ong-Dean 2009);[11] and optional programs such as AP, IB, and "immersion" language programs have become standard offerings.[12] Across schools, researchers document the steady increase in alternatives to traditional public schooling including magnet, charter schools, and homeschooling.[13] Parents can also choose from a growing number of private schools, tutoring options, summer programs, and academic coaching services (for discussions, see Aurini, Davies, and Dierkes 2013; Lubienski and Lubienski 2013); and postsecondary institutions now cater to a wide range of academic and extracurricular interests (e.g., Armstrong and Hamilton 2013).

The expansion of "voice" and "choice" is often discussed in the context of market forces, parent engagement, or intensive childrearing (e.g., Friedman Foundation 2014; Lubienski and Lubienski 2013); it is also frequently invoked in discussions about financial barriers to participation (e.g., the cost of private schooling). Yet, these changes are also altering the organizational context of educational inequality in ways that have more to do with the strategic management of choices than with the question of whether parents have the "right" or the economic power to access them.

There are two notable streams within this literature. The first body of work examines how parents vary in their ability to navigate the labyrinth of choices and exploit situational discretion in education institutions. Drawing on ethnography and mixed methods, this branch of research documents a variety of hidden processes, including the "systematic preferencing" of guidance counselors (Stevens 2009), the ways in which schools manage choice (Jennings 2010), and the ways in which social class informs the consequences of various academic, social, or cultural pursuits (Armstrong and Hamilton 2013; Khan 2010).

Special education is a particularly good example of this emerging body of research. Ong-Dean's (2009) work details how expanded decision-making power benefits parents with higher levels of education and better advocacy skills by providing them with an opportunity to negotiate higher-quality services, programs, and placements for their children. Research on school discipline policy yields similar findings. In their analysis of progressive discipline policies, Milne and Aurini (2015) find that middle- and higher-class parents are particularly adept at negotiating more favorable disciplinary outcomes for their children. These parents are more likely to participate in disciplinary proceedings, and to challenge principals and teachers. They also tend to have more experience in negotiating institutional rules. As a consequence, lower-class students tend to have less positive outcomes (e.g., suspensions)—not because teachers or principals favor middle- and higher-class students, but rather because opportunities to participate in program and placement decisions tend to advantage parents who are better equipped to make demands of schooling institutions.

The second body of research expands on Raymond Boudon's (1974) early insights about the relationship between structural differentiation and unequal education outcomes. Like Boudon, this research illustrates how social class continues to shape the "pathways" students take in highly differentiated systems, and the meaning and consequences of these choices. The research on "maximally maintained inequality" (MMI) and "effectively maintained inequality" (EMI) shows how middle- and higher-class families use their superior education and capital to channel their children into the most strategic "branches" in the system. Research on MMI empirically maps how privileged groups pursue the next tier of education as access to higher education expands and enrollment in the lower tiers grows (Raftery and Hout 1993). EMI describes a similar process, but documents the ways in which higher-class children enter into more selective fields or institutions *within* any one particular tier (Lucas 2001). As a consequence, while lower-class students are increasingly finishing high school and entering postsecondary, they tend to be situated within less competitive levels of schooling, institutions, and fields of study than their more advantaged counterparts (see also Davies and Guppy 1997; Mullen 2010; Radford 2013).

While this largely quantitative research shows us which students end up where, qualitative research perhaps best illustrates how expanded choice and voice reproduces inequality in new and surprising ways. This body of research documents how lower-class students, even those who technically "make it," still fail to realize the same benefits as higher-class students. Armstrong and Hamilton (2013) show how social class alters not only how students experience college, but the relative meaning and consequences of the choices they make (see also Mullen 2010). They identify three different pathways: those based on "partying," "mobility," and "professional attainment." In their effort to attract affluent students, colleges tend to cater to the "party pathway," offering less rigorous majors that provide students with more time to have fun and participate in sorority life (see also Arum and Roksa 2011). Armstrong and Hamilton find that this pathway disadvantages lower-class students. These students simply cannot afford to leave college with little more than crushing debt, low GPAs, and hollow degrees. Indeed, the consequences of partying and studying majors such as "event planning" are profoundly different for more affluent students who leave college with no debt while also having family and friends who can bear the costs associated with hiring someone to plan a wedding. Even among the more ambitious lower-class women in their study, only one managed to achieve upward mobility. As they observe, "The three pathways required varying levels of class resources to translate a college experience into socioeconomic success" (Armstrong and Hamilton 2013: 209).[14]

Broadly, this body of research traces how the expanded structure of decision making provides some families with a significant advantage: middle- and higher-class parents are better equipped to exploit opportunities, promote their children's interests, and manage their children's movement through the school system. This research also shows us that some of our measures can mask emerging forms of inequality. By all accounts, the lower-class students in Armstrong and Hamilton's (2013) study exemplify the triumph of egalitarianism and meritocracy. These students graduated high school and entered the same school, programs, and in some cases social circles as their more advantaged counterparts. Many, however, struggled in various ways during their time at university, and some were forced to drop out.

We do not interpret this body of research as suggesting a return to older "cultural deficit" theories of inequality. That is, we do not assume that lower-class students' comparably worse outcomes are somehow a by-product of insufficient preparation or ability. Instead, newer sources of schooling inequalities are rooted in parents' and students' different abilities to navigate institutional processes. Parents help their children enter the most advantageous pathways (e.g., guidance on which institution to attend, which subjects to take), "work" educational policies to their benefit (e.g., students learn how to negotiate extended deadlines for assignments), and the type of support families can offer during and after schooling (e.g., job opportunities, social connections; see also Demerath 2009; Lareau 2011; Khan 2010).

Conclusion

Rising aggregate levels of attainment suggest that meaningful gains have been realized, particularly for women, minorities, and lower-class students. Any lower levels of education could be interpreted as a "phase" *if* these groups were merely playing "catch-up" with those who historically have been educationally advantaged. But a growing body of research shows that attainment and achievement gaps are widening even as all boats are rising. Research on educational inequality has produced a wealth of knowledge about the kinds of people who generally do better in various educational contests. Until more recently, however, there was a dearth of research that captured the mechanisms of newer and perhaps more empirically accurate forms of educational inequality.

In this chapter, we present three promising directions in the sociology of education that offer new answers to the antecedents, processes, and mechanisms of emerging forms of educational inequality. While much of this emerging research has started to articulate how characteristics such as gender, race, and social class affect these processes and why, we focus on the intricacies of social class as the main driver of newer forms of inequality in education. All things being equal, even with increased participation from parents and students, individual outcomes can still vary widely (e.g., Espenshade and Radford 2009). The compensation and adaptation strategies of higher-class parents, described above, are concrete examples of how such parents actively construct meanings within the current context of academic and labor-market uncertainty. Similarly, the work of Armstrong and Hamilton (2013) tells us why lower-class students have worse outcomes, even though they are increasingly situated in the same institutional "pathways" as their more affluent counterparts. The ever-changing contexts of schooling mean that more and more lower-class students are attending postsecondary education. However, as the cited research demonstrates, those environments and institutional processes are increasingly intricate, and require considerable skill to navigate.

As we have argued in this chapter, understanding the contours of this new educational inequality involves looking into the black box, but also thinking outside of it. Research like that presented in this chapter has started to provide new answers to the evolving and often surprising context of emerging forms of education inequality.

Notes

1. Research has also found that early socialization experiences affect children's transition into school. By kindergarten, children from middle- and higher-class families tend to be more "school ready" than are lower-class children, as indicated on a range of early cognitive and language tests (Condron 2009; Davies and Janus 2009; Downey, von Hippel, and Broh 2004; Farkas and Hibel 2008; Fryer and Levitt 2006; Heckman 2008; Hertzman 2004; Hertzman and Williams 2009; Janus and Duku 2007).
2. In their now famous study on daily exchanges between children and parents, Hart and Risley (1995) found that children whose parents were professionals were exposed to a far greater number of words than children whose parents were on welfare—a difference of more than 1,500 words per hour. By age three, children from professional homes heard a whopping thirty million more words than children from poor or welfare homes.
3. The No Child Left Behind Act of 2001, for example, specifies shared accountability between parents and schools and expanded parental involvement (US Department of Education 2004: 1).
4. Just under 6 percent of publically funded schools are charter schools, 13 percent of children received special education services in the 2011–2012 school year, and 69 percent of high schools have students enrolled in advanced placement or international baccalaureate programs (US Department of Education, National Center for Education Statistics 2013a, 2013c, 2014a).
5. The "expectation gap" has narrowed considerably. According to the Monitoring the Future (MTF) survey, in the 1970s fewer than half of girls and boys with parents with less than a BA degree expected to obtain a BA. By the mid-2000s, 82 percent of grade-twelve girls and 70 percent of grade-twelve boys whose parents had not completed college expected to do so (Jacob and Wilder Linkow 2011).
6. Students who received Pell Grants are less likely to attend four-year degree granting or doctoral granting institutions. While bachelor degree attainment among students from the highest income quartile has almost doubled since the 1970s, from 40 to 77 percent, attainment among students from the bottom income quartile has remained fairly stagnant during that same time period, moving from 6 to 9 percent (Pell Institute 2015).
7. Equally disturbing is that many of these education trends parallel rising levels and widening social class gaps on a range of indicators including income (Reardon 2011), housing segregation (Reardon and Bischoff 2011), volunteerism (Putnam, Frederick, and Snellman 2012), and marriage "homophily" and fertility patterns (Cherlin, Talbert, and Yasutake 2014).As Andrew Cherlin and his colleagues (2014: 3) point out, these "recent demographic trends have produced a distinctive fertility regime in early adulthood that reinforces the growing social class differences."
8. Potter and Roska's (2013: 1016) research found that the differences in children's

family life accrue over time and "account for a substantial proportion of the growing inequality in academic achievement" between more and less advantaged children (see also Lareau 2011).

9. Enhanced "voice" and "choice" in educational institutions are relatively new. As Lareau observed in the late 1980s, "Until two decades ago, there were few indications that teachers expected or asked parents to take on an aggressive educational role at home or that parents acted in this fashion" (1989: 175).
10. Title 1 funding is contingent on parents' involvement in decision-making and on the development of "family compacts in which families and schools declare their mutual responsibility for children's learning" (Kessler-Sklar and Baker 2000: 102).
11. In the 2010–2011 school year, 13 percent of students received federally supported special education services (US Department of Education, National Center for Education Statistics 2014b).
12. In 2010 and 2011, 82 percent of high schools reported students who were in dual credit courses, and close to 70 percent of high schools reported students who were enrolled in AP or IB courses (US Department of Education, National Center for Education Statistics 2013a).
13. Of the close to 99,000 public elementary and secondary schools, 2,206 were special education, 1,485 were vocationally focused, 6,197 offered alternative education, and 5,274 and 2,722 were charter or magnet schools respectively (US Department of Education, National Center for Education Statistics 2012). The percentage of parents selecting alternatives to their assigned public school has grown slightly. In 1999, 74 percent of children aged five to seventeen were enrolled in their assigned public schools, 14 percent were in public schools of choice, 4 percent were in private schools, and 1.7 percent were homeschooled. In 2007, the proportion of children enrolled in their assigned public schools dropped to a little over 70 percent, and 15 percent were in public schools of choice, while more than 11 percent were in private schools, and almost 3 percent were homeschooled (US Department of Education, National Center for Education Statistics 2013d).
14. What is also clear in their analysis is the substantial role parents play in shaping their children's movement through postsecondary. Lower-class students who were more successful tended to have parents who intervened or provided support at critical junctures.

References

Alexander, Karl L., Doris R. Entwisle, and Linda S. Olson. 2007. "Lasting Consequences of the Summer Learning Gap." *American Sociological Review* 72 (2): 167–180.

Alexander, Karl L., Sarah Pitcok, and Matthew Bouley. 2016. *The Summer Slide: What We Know and Can Do about Summer Learning Loss*. Baltimore: Teachers College Press.

Alon, Sigal. 2009. "The Evolution of Class Inequality in Higher Education Competition, Exclusion, and Adaptation." *American Sociological Review* 74 (5): 731–755.

American Association of University Women, The. 1992. "How Schools Shortchange Girls: Executive Summary." http://www.aauw.org/files/2013/02/how-schools-shortchange-girls-executive-summary.pdf.

Armstrong, Elizabeth, and Laura Hamilton. 2013. *Paying for the Party*. Cambridge, MA: Harvard University Press.

Arum, R., and J. Roksa. 2010. *Academically Adrift: Limited Learning on College Campuses*. Chicago: University of Chicago Press.

Association of Universities and Colleges Canada. 2011. "Volume 1—Enrolment: Trends in Higher Education." http://www.aucc.ca/wp-content/uploads/2011/05/trends-2011-vol1-enrolment-e.pdf.

Aurini, J. 2015. *Why the Adoption of Middle-Class Practices Fails to Help Lower-Class Children Catch Up: The Limits of 'Trickle-Down' Parenting Culture* (book proposal).

Aurini, Janice, Scott Davies, and Julian Dierkes, eds. 2013. *Out of the Shadows: The Global Intensification of Supplementary Education*. Bingley, UK: Emerald Group Publishing.

Bacon, Jessica K., and Julie Causton-Theoharis. 2013. "'It Should be Teamwork': A Critical Investigation of School Practices and Parent Advocacy in Special Education." *International Journal of Inclusive Education* 17 (7): 682–699.

Bailey, Martha J., and Susan M. Dynarski. 2011. "Gains and Gaps: Changing Inequality in US College Entry and Completion." No. w17633. National Bureau of Economic Research. http://www.nber.org/papers/w17633.

Baker, David P., and Gerald T. LeTendre. 2005. *National Differences, Global Similarities: World Culture and the Future of Schooling*. Stanford, CA: Stanford University Press.

Boudon, Raymond. 1974. *Education, Opportunity, and Social Inequality*. New York: Wiley-Interscience Publication.

Bourdieu, Pierre. 1977. "Cultural Reproduction and Social Reproduction." In *Power and Ideology in Education*, edited by J. Karabel and A. H. Halsey, 487–510. New York: Oxford University Press.

Bourdieu. P. 1998. "The Forms of Capital." In *Education: Culture, Economy and Society*, edited by A. H. Halsey, Hugh Lauder, Philip Brown, and Amy Stuart Wells, 46–58. Oxford, UK: Oxford University Press.

Bourdieu, Pierre, and Claude Passeron. 1977. *Reproduction in Education, Society, Culture*. Beverly Hills, CA: Sage.

Bowles, Samuel, and Herbert Gintis. 1976. *Schooling in Capitalist America*. London: Routledge.

Bowman, B. T. 2015. Quoted in "Key to Vocabulary Gap is Quality of Conversation, Not Dearth of Words," by Sarah D. Sparks. *Education Week*, April 21, 2015. http://www.edweek.org/ew/articles/2015/04/22/key-to-vocabulary-gap-is-quality-of.html.

Brint, Steven G. 2003. "Few Remaining Dreams: Community Colleges since 1985." *Annals of the American Academy of Political and Social Science* 586 (March): 16–37.

———. 2006. *Schools and Societies*. Redwood City, CA: Stanford University Press.

Buchmann, Claudia, Dennis J. Condron, and Vincent J. Roscigno. 2010. "Shadow Education, American Style: Test Preparation, the SAT and College Enrollment." *Social Forces* 89 (2): 435–461.

Calarco, Jessica McCrory. 2011. "'I Need Help!' Social Class and Children's Help-Seeking in Elementary School." *American Sociological Review* 76 (6): 862–882.

———. 2014. "Coached for the Classroom: Parents' Cultural Transmission and Children's Reproduction of Educational Inequalities." *American Sociological Review* 79 (5): 1015–1037.

Cherlin, Andrew J., Elizabeth Talbert, and Suzumi Yasutake. 2014. "Changing Fertility Regimes and the Transition to Adulthood: Evidence from a Recent Cohort." In *Annual Meeting of the Population Association of America*, Boston, May 2014. http://krieger.jhu.edu/sociology/wp-content/uploads/sites/28/2012/02/Read-Online.pdf.

Chin, Tiffani. 2000. "'Sixth Grade Madness': Parental Emotion Work in the Private High School Application Process." *Journal of Contemporary Ethnography* 29 (2): 124–163.

Clark, Burton R. 1960. "The 'Cooling-Out' Function in Higher Education." *American Journal of Sociology* 65 (6): 569–76.

Coburn, K. L. 2006. "Organizing a Ground Crew for Today's Helicopter Parents." *About Campus* 11 (3): 9–16.

Coleman, J. S., E. Q. Campbell, C. J. Hobson, J. McPartland, A. M. Mood, F. D. Weinfeld, and R. L. York. 1966. *Equality of Educational Opportunity*. Washington: US Department of Health, Education, and Welfare. Office of Education (OE-38001 and supp.).

Coleman, James S. 1988. "Social Capital in the Creation of Human Capital." *American Journal of Sociology* 94:s95–s120.

Collins, Randall. 1979. *The Credential Society*. New York: Academic Press.

Condron, Dennis J. 2009. "Social Class, School and Non-school Environments, and Black/White Inequalities in Children's Learning." *American Sociological Review* 74 (5): 685–708.

Conley, Dalton, and Karen Albright, eds. 2004. *After the Bell: Family Background, Public Policy and Educational Success*. New York: Routledge Press.

Connell, R. W., Dean Ashenden, Sandra Kessler, and Gary Dowsett. 1982. *Making the Difference: Schools, Families and Social Division*. Sydney: George Allen & Unwin.

Davies, S., and J. Aurini. 2013. "Summer Learning Inequality in Ontario." *Canadian Public Policy* 39 (2): 287–307.

Davies, S., and M. Janus. 2009. "A Systematic Review of Longitudinal Effects of Family SES on Child Cognition and Social-Emotional Well-Being." Ottawa: HRSDC.

Davies, Scott. 2004. "School Choice by Default? Understanding the Demand for Private Tutoring in Canada." *American Journal of Education* 110 (3): 233–255.

Davies, Scott, and Neil Guppy. 1997. "Fields of Study, College Selectivity, and Student Inequalities in Higher Education." *Social Forces* 75 (4): 1417–1438.

Davis, Kingsley, and Wilbert E. Moore. 1970 [1945]. "Some Principles of Stratification." *American Sociological Review* 10 (2): 242–249.

Demerath, Peter. 2009. *Producing Success: The Culture of Personal Advancement in an American High School*. Chicago: University of Chicago Press.

Dermott, Esther, and Marco Pomati. 2015. "'Good' Parenting Practices: How Important are Poverty, Education and Time Pressure?" *Sociology* doi: 10.1177/0038038514560260.

Dickert-Conlin, S., and R. Rubenstein, eds. 2007. *Economic Inequality and Higher Education: Access, Persistence, and Education*. New York, NY: Russell Sage.

Domina. T., A.M. Conley, and G. Farkas. 2011. "The Link between Educational Expectations and Effort in the College-for-all Era." *Sociology of Education* 84 (2): 93–112.

Downey, Douglas B., Paul T. von Hippel, and Beckett A. Broh. 2004. "Are Schools the Great Equalizer? Cognitive Inequality during the Summer Months and the School Year." *American Sociological Review* 69 (5): 613–635.

Duncan, G. J., Aletha C. Huston, and Thomas S. Weisner. 2007. *Higher Ground: New Hope for the Working Poor and their Children*. New York: Russell Sage Foundation.

Duncan, G. J., and R. J. Murnane, eds. 2011. *Whither Opportunity? Rising Inequality, Schools and Children's Life Chances*. New York: Russell Sage Foundation.

Duquette, Cheryll, Shari Orders, Stephanie Fullarton, and Kristen Robertson-Grewal. 2011. "Fighting for their Rights: Advocacy Experiences of Parents of Children Identified with Intellectual Giftedness." *Journal for the Education of the Gifted* 34 (3): 488–512.

Ehrenreich, Barbara. 1990. *Fear of Falling: The Inner Life of the Middle Class*. New York: Harper Perennial.

Epstein, J. 2005. "A Case Study of the Partnership Schools Comprehensive School Reform (CSR) Model." *Elementary School Journal* 106 (2): 151–170.

Espenshade, Thomas J., and Alexandria Walton Radford. 2009. *No Longer Separate, Not Yet Equal: Race and Class in Elite College Admission and Campus Life*. Princeton, NJ: Princeton University Press.

Farkas, George, and Jacob Hibel. 2008. "Being Unready for School: Factors Affecting Risk and Resilience." *Disparities in School Readiness: How Families Contribute to Transitions into School*, edited by Alan Booth and Ann C. Crouter, 3–30. New York: Psychology Press.

Fingerman, Karen L., Yen-Pi Cheng, Eric D. Wesselmann, Steven Zarit, Frank Furstenberg, and Kira S. Birditt. 2012. "Helicopter Parents and Landing Pad Kids: Intense Parental Support of Grown Children." *Journal of Marriage and Family* 74 (4): 880–896.

Friedman Foundation. "What is School Choice?" Accessed December 18, 2014 at http://www.edchoice.org/School-Choice/What-is-School-Choice.aspx.

Fryer, Roland G., and Steven D. Levitt. 2006. "The Black-White Test Score Gap through Third Grade." *American Law and Economics Review* 8 (2): 249–281.

Furstenberg, Frank F. 2006. "Diverging Development: The Not-So-Invisible Hand of Social Class in the United States." *Network on Transitions to Adulthood Research Network*. http://transitions.s410.sureserver.com/wp-content/uploads/2011/08/invisiblehand_final.rev_.pdf.

———. 2011. "The Challenges of Finding Causal Links between Family Educational Practices and Schooling Outcomes." In *Whither Opportunity? Rising Inequality, Schools and Children's Life Chances*, edited by G. J. Duncan and R. J. Murnane, 465–482. New York: Russell Sage Foundation.

Gamoran, A., W. G. Secada, and C. B. Marrett. 2000. "The Organizational Context of Teaching and Learning: Changing Theoretical Perspectives." In *Handbook of Sociology of Education*, edited by M. T. Hallinan, 37–63. New York: Springer.

Gauthier, Anne H., Timothy M. Smeeding, and Frank F. Furstenberg. 2004. "Are Parents Investing More or Less Time in Children? Trends in Selected Industrialized Countries." *Population and Development Review* 30 (4): 647–672.

Guryan, Jonathan, Erik Hurst, and Melissa Schettini Kearney. 2008. "Parental Education and Parental Time with Children." No. w13993. National Bureau of Economic Research. http://www.researchgate.net/publication/4981817_Parental_Education_and_Parental_Time_with_Children.

Hallinan, Maureen. 2006. "On Linkages between Sociology of Race and Ethnicity and Sociology of Education." In *Handbook of Sociology of Education*, edited by M. T. Hallinan, 65–84. New York: Springer.

Hanson, J., N. Hair, A. Chandra, E. Moss, J. Bhattacharya, S. D. Pollack, and B. Wolfe. 2012. "Brain Development and Poverty: A First Look." In *The Biological Consequences of Socioeconomic Inequalities*, edited by B. Wolfe, W. Evans, and T.E. Seeman, 187–214. New York: Russell Sage Foundation.

Hart, Betty, and Todd R. Risley. 1995. *Meaningful Differences in the Everyday Experience of Young American Children*. Baltimore: Paul H. Brookes Publishing.

Hays, Sharon. 1996. *The Cultural Contradictions of Motherhood*. New Haven: Yale University Press.

Heckman, James J. 2008. "Schools, Skills, and Synapses." *Economic Inquiry* 46 (3): 289–324.

Hertzman, Clyde. 2004. "Making Early Childhood Development a Priority: Lessons from Vancouver. Canadian Centre for Policy Alternatives." Canadian Centre for Policy Alternatives, BC Office. http://www.policyalternatives.ca/sites/default/files/uploads/publications/BC_Office_Pubs/early_childhood.pdf.

Hertzman, Clyde, and Robin Williams. 2009. "Making Early Childhood Count." *Canadian Medical Association Journal* 180 (1): 68–71.

Heyneman, S. P., and W. A. Loxley. 1982. "Influences on Academic Performance across High and Low-income Countries: A Re-Analysis of IEA Data." *Sociology of Education* 55:13–21.

———. 1983. "The Effect of Primary School Quality on Academic Achievement across Twenty-nine High- and Low-income Countries." *American Journal of Sociology* 88: 1162–1194.

Heyns, Barbara. 1978. *Summer Learning and the Effects of Schooling.* Waltham, MA: Academic Press.

Hunsaker, Scott L. 2013. "High Involvement Mothers of High Achieving Children: Potential Theoretical Explanations." *Forum on Public Policy*. http://www.forumonpublicpolicy.com/vol2013.no1/vol2013archive/hunsaker.pdf.

Jacob, Brian A., and Tamara Wilder Linkow. 2011. "Educational Expectations and Attainment." In *Whither Opportunity? Rising Inequality, Schools and Children's Life Chances*, edited by G. J. Duncan and R. J. Murnane, 133–163. New York: Russell Sage Foundation.

Janus, Magdalena, and Eric Duku. 2007. "The School Entry Gap: Socioeconomic, Family, and Health Factors Associated with Children's School Readiness to Learn." *Early Education and Development* 18 (3): 375–403.

Jennings, Jennifer L. 2010. "School Choice or Schools' Choice? Managing in an Era of Accountability." *Sociology of Education* 83 (3): 227–247.

Karabel, J., and A. H. Halsey, eds. 1977. *Power and Ideology in Education*. New York: Oxford University Press.

Kaushal, Neeraj, Katherine Magnuson, and Jane Waldfogel. 2011. *How Is Family Income Related to Investments in Children's Learning?* New York: Russell Sage Foundation.

Keller, S., and M. Zavalloni. 1964. "Ambition and Social Class: A Respecification." *Social Forces* 43 (1): 58–70.

Kessler-Sklar, Susan L., and Amy J. L. Baker. 2000. "School-District Parent Involvement Policies and Programs." *Elementary School Journal* 101 (1): 101–118.

Khan, Shamus Rahman. 2011. *Privilege: The Making of an Adolescent Elite at St. Paul's School.* Princeton, NJ: Princeton University Press.

Kornrich, S., and F. Furstenberg. 2013. "Investing in Children: Changes in Parental Spending on Children, 1972 to 2007." *Demography* 50 (1): 1–23.

Kosteas, Vasilios D. 2010. "High School Clubs Participation and Earnings." Working Paper Series. *Social Science Research Network*. http://ssrn.com/abstract=1542360.

Labaree, David F. 2010. *Someone Has to Fail: The Zero-Sum Game of Public Schooling*. Cambridge, MA: Harvard University Press.

Lareau, Annette. 1989. *Home Advantage: Social Class and Parental Involvement in Elementary Education*. London: Falmer.

———. 2011. *Unequal Childhoods: Class, Race, and Family Life, Second Edition with an Update a Decade Later*. Berkeley: University of California Press.

Lehmann, W. 2014. "Habitus Transformation and Hidden Injuries: Successful Working-Cclass University Students." *Sociology of Education* 87 (1): 1–15.

Lleras, Christy. 2008. "Do Skills and Behaviors in High School Matter? The Contribution of Noncognitive Factors in Explaining Differences in Educational Attainment and Earnings." *Social Science Research* 37 (3): 888–902.

Loveless, T. 2009. "Tracking and Detracking: High Achievers in Massachusetts Middle Schools." Thomas Fordham Institute. Accessed at http://edex.s3-us-west-2.amazonaws.com/publication/pdfs/200912_Detracking_7.pdf.

Lubienski, C., and S. Lubienski. 2013. *The Public School Advantage: Why Public Schools Outperform Private Schools*. Chicago: University of Chicago Press.

Lucas, Samuel R. 2001. "Effectively Maintained Inequality: Education Transitions, Track Mobility, and Social Background Effects." *American Journal of Sociology* 106 (6): 1642–1690.

Maggi, Stefania, Lori J. Irwin, Arjumand Siddiqi, and Clyde Hertzman. 2010. "The Social Determinants of Early Child Development: An Overview." *Journal of Paediatrics and Child Health* 46 (11): 627–635.

McNeal, Ralph B., Jr. 2012. "Checking In or Checking Out? Investigating the Parent Involvement Reactive Hypothesis." *Journal of Educational Research* 105 (2): 79–89.

Milne, Emily, and Janice Aurini. 2015. "Schools, Cultural Mobility, and Social Reproduction: The Case of Progressive Discipline." *Canadian Journal of Sociology* 40 (1): 51–74.

Mullen, Ann L. 2010. *Degrees of Inequality: Culture, Class and Gender in American Higher Education*. Baltimore: John Hopkins University Press.

Nelson III, Charles A., and Margaret A. Sheridan. 2011. "Lessons from Neuroscience Research for Understanding Causal Links between Family and Neighborhood Characteristics and Educational Outcomes." In *Whither Opportunity? Rising Inequality, Schools and Children's Life Chances*, edited by G. J. Duncan and R. J. Murnane, 27–46. New York: Russell Sage Foundation.

Ong-Dean, Colin. 2009. *Distinguishing Disability: Parents, Privilege, and Special Education*. Chicago: University of Chicago Press.

Oxford Dictionaries. 2015. "Adaptation." http://www.oxforddictionaries.com/definition/english/adaptation.

Pell Institute. 2015. "Indicators of Higher Education Equity in the United States." http://www.pellinstitute.org/downloads/publications-Indicators_of_Higher_Education_Equity_in_the_US_45_Year_Trend_Report.pdf.

Phillips, Deborah A., and Amy E. Lowenstein. 2011. "Early Care, Education, and Child Development." *Annual Review of Psychology* 62:483–500.

Potter, D., and J. Roksa. 2013. "Accumlating Advantages Over Time: Family Experiences and Social Class Inequality in Academic Achievement." *Social Science Research* 42 (4): 1018–1032.

Powell, A. G., D. K. Cohen, and E. Farrar. 1985. *The Shopping Mall High School: Winners and Losers in the Educational Marketplace*. Boston: Houghton Mifflin.

Putnam, R. D. 2015. *Our Kids: The American Dream in Crisis*. New York: Simon & Schuster.

Putnam, R. D., C. B. Frederick, and K. Snellman. 2012. "Growing Class Gaps in Social Connectedness among American Youth." Cambridge, MA: Harvard Kennedy School of Government. http://www.hks.harvard.edu/saguaro/pdfs/SaguaroReport_DivergingSocialConnectedness.pdf.

Radford, Alexandria Walton. 2013. *Top Student, Top School?: How Social Class Shapes Where Valedictorians Go to College*. Chicago: University of Chicago Press.

Raftery, Adrian E., and Michael Hout. 1993. "Maximally Maintained Inequality: Expansion, Reform, and Opportunity in Irish Education, 1921–75." *Sociology of Education* 66 (1): 41–62.

Ramey, G., and V. A. Ramey. 2010. "The Rug Rat Race." *Brookings Papers on Economic Activity* (Spring): 129–176.

Reardon, S. F. 2011. "The Widening Academic Achievement Gap between the Rich and the Poor: New Evidence and Possible Explanations." In *Whither Opportunity? Rising Inequality, Schools and Children's Life Chances*, edited by Greg J. Duncan and Richard J. Murnane, 91–116. New York: Russell Sage Foundation.

Reardon, S. F., R. Baker, and D. Klasik. 2012. "Race, Income, and Enrolment Patterns in Higher Selective Colleges, 1982–2004." https://cepa.stanford.edu/sites/default/files

/race%20income%20%26%20selective%20college%20enrollment%20august%20 3%202012.pdf.

Reardon, S. F., and K. Bischoff. 2011. "Growth in Residential Segregation of Families by Income, 1970–2000." http://www.s4.brown.edu/us2010/Data/Report/report111111.pdf.

Reay, Diane. 1999. "Linguistic Capital and Home: School Relationships: Mothers' Interactions with Their Children's Primary School Teachers." *Acta Sociologica* 42 (2): 19–168.

Rist, R. C. 1977. "On Understanding the Processes of Schooling: The Contributions of Labeling Theory." In *Power and Ideology in Education*, edited by J. Karabel and A. H. Halsey, 292–305. New York: Oxford University Press.

Robinson, K., and A. L. Harris. 2014. *The Broken Compass: Parental Involvement with Children's Education*. Cambridge, MA. Harvard University Press.

Roscigno, Vincent J., Donald Tomaskovic-Devey, and Martha Crowley. 2006. "Education and the Inequalities of Place." *Social Forces* 84 (4): 2121–2145.

Rosenbaum, James E. 2004. *Beyond College for All: Career Paths for the Forgotten Path*. New York: Russell Sage Foundation.

Ryan, William. 1976. *Blaming the Victim* (revised edition). New York: Vintage Books.

Schaub, M. 2015. "Is There a Home Advantage in School Readiness for Young Children? Trends in Parent Engagement in Cognitive Activities with Young Children, 1991–2001." *Journal of Early Childhood Research* 13 (1): 47–63.

Schiffrin, H. H, M. Liss, K. Geary, H. Miles-McLean, T. Tashner, C. Hagerman, and K. Rizzo. 2013. "Mother, Father, or Parent? College Students' Intensive Parenting Attitudes Differ by Referent." *Journal of Child and Family Studies* 23 (6): 1073–1080.

Schiffrin, Holly H., Miriam Liss, Haley Miles-McLean, Katherine A. Geary, Mindy J. Erchull, and Taryn Tashner. 2014. "Helping or Hovering? The Effects of Helicopter Parenting on College Students' Well-Being." *Journal of Child and Family Studies* 23 (3): 548–557.

Schneider, B. L., and V. A. Keesler. 2007. "School Reform 2007: Transforming Education into a Scientific Enterprise." *Annual Review of Sociology* 33:187–217.

Simon, Marc H., and Matthew Makar (directors). 2008. *Nursery University* (documentary film). http://www.imdb.com/title/tt1213832/.

Sirin, Selcuk R. 2005. "Socioeconomic Status and Academic Achievement: A Meta-analytic Review of Research." *Review of Educational Research* 75 (3): 417–453.

Small, Mario Luis, David Harding, and Michèle Lamont. 2010. "Introduction: Reconsidering Culture and Poverty." In *The Annals of the American Academy of Political and Social Science: Reconsidering Culture and Poverty*, edited by David Harding, Michèle Lamont, and Mario Luis Small, 6–27. Thousand Oaks, CA: Sage. http://scholar.harvard.edu /files/lamont/files/reconsidering_culture_and_poverty_2.pdf.

Snellman, K., J. M. Silva, C. B. Frederick, and R. Putnam. 2015. "The Engagement Gap: Social Mobility and Extracurricular Participation among American Youth." *Annals of the American Academy* 657 (1): 194–207.

Sokolowski, M. 2013. Quoted by Ivan Semeniuk in "How Poverty Influences a Child's Brain Development." *Globe and Mail*, Friday, January 25, 2013. http://www.theglobeandmail .com/technology/science/brain/how-poverty-influences-a-childs-brain-development /article7882957/?page=all.

Sperber, M. A. 2000. *Beer and Circus: How Big-Time College Sports is Crippling Undergraduate Education*. New York: Henry Holt.

Stevens, Mitchell L. 2009. *Creating a Class: College Admissions and the Education of Elites*. Cambridge, MA: Harvard University Press.

Stuber, Jenny M. 2011. *Inside the College Gates: How Class and Culture Matter in Higher Education*. Lanham, MD: Lexington Books.

Thompson, J., and T. Smeeding. 2014. "Income Inequality." *National Report Card: The Stanford Center on Poverty & Inequality*. http://web.stanford.edu/group/scspi/sotu/SOTU_2014_CPI.pdf.

Trainor, Audrey A. 2010. "Diverse Approaches to Parent Advocacy during Special Education Home-School Interactions: Identification and Use of Cultural and Social Capital." *Remedial and Special Education* 31 (1): 34–47.

US Department of Education. 2004. "Parental Involvement: Title I, Part A: Non-Regulatory Guidelines." www2.ed.gov/programs/titleiparta/parentinvguid.doc.

US Department of Education, National Center for Education Statistics. 2013a. "Dual Credit and Exam Based Courses in U.S. Public High Schools: 2010–11." http://nces.ed.gov/pubs2013/2013001.pdf.

———. 2013b. "Fast Facts: Postsecondary Enrollment Rates." *Digest of Education Statistics, 2012* (NCES 2014–015), chapter 3. http://nces.ed.gov/fastfacts/display.asp?id=98.

———. 2013c. "Fast Facts: Students with Disabilities." *Digest of Education Statistics, 2012* (NCES 2014–015), table 48. https://nces.ed.gov/fastfacts/display.asp?id=64.

———. 2013d. "Percentage Distribution of Students Ages 5 through 17 Attending Kindergarten through 12th Grade, by School Type or Participation in Homeschooling and Selected Child, Parent, and Household Characteristics: 1999, 2003, and 2007." http://nces.ed.gov/programs/digest/d13/tables/dt13_206.20.asp.

———. 2014a. "The Condition of Education 2014 (NCES 2014–083), Charter School Enrollment." http://nces.ed.gov/programs/coe/indicator_cgb.asp.

———. 2014b. "The Condition of Education: Children and Youth with Disabilities." https://nces.ed.gov/programs/coe/indicator_cgg.asp.

———. 2014c. "The Condition of Education 2014 (NCES 2014–083), Educational Attainment." http://nces.ed.gov/fastfacts/display.asp?id=27.

———. 2014d. "The Condition of Education 2014 (NCES 2014–083), Public School Expenditures." https://nces.ed.gov/fastfacts/display.asp?id=66.

Urist, J. 2014. "Is College Really Harder to Get Into Than It Used to Be?" *Atlantic*, April 4, 2014.

Willis, Paul. 1977. *Learning to Labor: How Working Class Kids Get Working Class Jobs*. Farnborough, UK: Saxon House.

Wyatt, J. N., and K. D. Mattern. 2011. "Low-SES Students and College Outcomes: The Role of AP Fee Reductions." *Research Report Prepared for The College Board*. https://research.collegeboard.org/sites/default/files/publications/2012/7/researchreport-2011-9-low-ses-college-outcomes-ap-fee-reductions.pdf.

Zarifa, D. 2012. "Higher Education Expansion, Social Background and College Selectivity in the United States." *International Journal of the Sociology of Education* 1 (3): 263–291.

Zelizer, V. 1985. *Pricing the Priceless Child: The Changing Social Value of Children*. Princeton, NJ: Princeton University Press.

THIRTEEN

Schools as Great Distractors: Why Socioeconomic-Based Achievement Gaps Persist

DOUGLAS B. DOWNEY

Over the last several decades, income and wealth inequality have grown in the United States to the point where the general public has taken notice. The Occupy Wall Street movement of 2011 and subsequent discussions of both inequality and insufficient social mobility raise serious questions about the American opportunity structure (Beller and Hout 2006). Central to that discussion is the role of schools.

The pervasive view is that schools are a key engine of inequality. Rather than serving as a vehicle for social mobility, schools end up reproducing or even exacerbating existing social status differences because they are so uneven in quality. High-income Americans know this; it is part of why they seek housing in good school districts, or send their children to private schools. Low-income Americans know this too. It is why they seek more equal funding formulas and enter their children in lotteries for a chance in an esteemed charter school. To fix inequality, the thinking goes, America needs to fix the schools that serve disadvantaged children. Of course, not everyone agrees on the best strategy for improving those schools. Liberals tend to argue that the problem is one of resources; more equal funding is key. In contrast, conservatives tout the promise of market-based reform, believing that inefficiency is the real culprit. But while they may disagree on method, both groups agree that schools are key to the problem. Improving the schools that serve disadvantaged children is thought to be the best way to advance the lot of those on the bottom of the socioeconomic ladder.

But in this essay, I challenge this understanding of schools. I point out weaknesses in the evidence that allegedly supports this position, and I describe a line of research that more accurately identifies how schools matter. The research I rely on employs stronger methods—comparing children's learning rates when they are out of school (summer) to those in the period when they are in school. This seasonally collected evidence upends the belief that differences in school quality drive achievement gaps. Indeed, American schools are probably an equalizing force, reducing the level of inequality we would observe in their absence. And when school effectiveness is measured fairly, there are only modest differences, or even no differences at all, in the degree to which schools serving high- versus low-income children promote learning. Schools are also targeted as the culprit for other problems, like childhood obesity, but seasonal methods demonstrate that this too is unfair. My thesis is that schools have become a distraction from the more central sources of income-based achievement gaps.

Schools and Inequality: The Evidence

On its surface it appears that schools are an engine of inequality. Disadvantaged children perform substantially less well on math and reading tests than do advantaged children at all stages of schooling. In addition, the schools that disadvantaged children attend spend less money, have poorer facilities, and endure more discipline problems than the schools serving advantaged children. And schools that serve advantaged children likely attract and retain better teachers. Finally, international comparisons confirm that American schools, while outspending our foreign counterparts, produce only mediocre math, reading, and science scores (Merry 2013). Taken together, the evidence appears so overwhelming and consistent that there is little debate about the assumption that school inequality contributes to societal inequality.

But there should be debate. The problem with this evidence is a classic one in social science: Correlation does not equal causation. Because children are not randomly assigned to schools, the kinds of children whom schools happen to serve vary in important ways. Some schools serve children who mostly enjoy stable families with educated parents, plentiful learning opportunities, and consistent access to health care. Other schools serve children who endure unstable families, poor nutrition, and parents who abuse drugs or alcohol. Disadvantaged children's learning may be held back in important ways by something as simple as lack of eyeglasses (Rothstein 2004). Differences in reading or math skills may represent differences in school quality, or they may represent the powerful effects of children's families. Most research does not adequately separate the effects of these competing sources.

A key empirical pattern makes the school-based explanation for socioeconomic achievement gaps especially awkward: gaps in math and reading skills are large at kindergarten entry, and do not grow appreciably during the school years (Reardon 2011). This sobering pattern should immediately direct most of our attention to the early childhood years, the period when achievement gaps emerge.

Of course, it still leaves us wondering what role schools play. Some achievement gaps increase a little during the school years, consistent with the possibility that schools are a culprit. For example the ninetieth versus the tenth income-based achievement gap in reading may increase by about 10 percent between kindergarten and eighth grade, but it is hard to know whether even this modest growth is due to schools. The same nonschool forces that created the large gap at kindergarten entry surely persist during the school years too. How can we tell how schools matter when children's development is influenced by both school and nonschool environments?

The traditional approach to this problem is to isolate school effects by statistically controlling for indicators of children's nonschool environments. For example, scholars who compare the reading skills of children in school A versus B might statistically control for children's socioeconomic status, family structure, race, and gender. They might also predict children's *learning* rather than their skills at one point in time, because the children may have arrived at the schools with different levels of skill. The scholars then attribute differences in cognitive learning between the two schools to school processes.

But this approach assumes that we have successfully created an "apples to apples" comparison, in which the children in the two schools are similar in all ways, and any differences in learning can be attributed to the schools. This assumption is likely wrong in a number of ways. First, these models typically predict students' learning during a calendar year, like between the end of third grade and the end of fourth grade. If schools were the only thing that influenced children's learning during that period, these models would provide a reasonable gauge of school's effectiveness. But children's growth, even when isolated to a single year, is still influenced heavily by nonschool factors. So between the end of third and fourth grades, children will spend the vast majority of their waking hours in nonschool environments, which vary dramatically. Of course, traditional models attempt to address this problem by statistically controlling for some indicators of the non-school environment, an approach that might work if these observable differences among children were largely responsible for explaining variation in learning. But the typical statistical controls (e.g., socioeconomic status, family structure, race, and gender) account for less than 10 percent of the variation in children's learning. The big problem with the traditional approach to understanding schools is straightforward: most of the reasons why some children learn math and reading faster than others are unknown (Downey et al. 2004). The reason why this is so important is that the unmeasured factors that influence learning are distributed in a predictable way; they favor the advantaged. As a result, typical models attempting to estimate school effects this way are biased toward making schools appear to favor the advantaged more than they really do.

For our purposes, a general observation of value-added models is relevant; as the model more persuasively isolates school from nonschool factors, the evidence that disadvantaged children endure poorer schools weakens. Seasonal comparison research, a particular type of value-added model, reveals this pattern clearly.

Seasonal Comparison Research

The seasonal nature of the American school calendar—nine months of school, followed by a three-month summer break—provides leverage for understanding how schools matter independently of nonschool factors (Heyns 1978). Comparing what happens when school is in to what happens when it is out, with each student serving as their own control, is comparable to the crossover designs performed in medical research. The primary advantage of this method is that it circumvents the main weakness of the traditional studies: trying to identify and measure all of the school and nonschool characteristics that matter (Downey et al. 2004; Entwisle and Alexander 1992).

What do we learn when we look at inequality across seasons? The big news is that gaps in skills across socioeconomic groups grow faster when school is out than when it is in—not the pattern we should observe if schools serving the advantaged are dramatically better (Heyns 1978; Entwisle and Alexander 1992; Downey et. al. 2004). This pattern is not what most of us would have predicted, and it is only revealed through seasonally collected data that allows us to compare summer and school-year learning. In addition, when this seasonal approach is extended to other dependent variables, like children's body mass index (von Hippel, Powell, Downey, and Rowland, 2007; von Hippel and Workman 2016), we find similar patterns: schools equalize outcomes by benefitting the disadvantaged the most.

Of course, children's development and success in life depend on more than math and reading skills or their BMI, and so it is difficult to know *how* compensatory schools are until seasonal comparison work is expanded to a much broader range of dependent variables. It may be that schools are compensators with respect to children's cognitive skills and their BMI, but act as culprits in other ways. For example, it is possible that when it comes to promoting children's social and behavioral skills (e.g., their ability to pay attention, persevere, and get along with others), teachers favor children from advantaged backgrounds, and therefore facilitate their growth more than that of children from disadvantaged backgrounds. These skills are subjectively determined and thus may be more vulnerable to cultural mismatches between teachers and students. Black, poor, and male children have been especially vulnerable to disciplinary measures in schools, so these groups may also struggle to mature across the social and behavioral dimensions because of strained relationships with teachers (Farkas, Grobe, Sheehan, and Shuan 1990; Jennings and DiPrete 2010).

But it is also possible that schools play a compensatory role with respect to social and behavioral skills much as how they operate with respect to reading and math skills. One can imagine that social and behavioral skill gaps across social groups may be large at kindergarten entry, and on a strong trajectory shaped by the home and neighborhood environment. And teachers, rather than making these gaps worse, may provide greater attention to children who struggle to fit the "student role." There is some evidence consistent with this position. For example, a national survey of teachers found that, when asked who was most likely to receive one-on-one attention, 80 percent of teachers said "academically struggling students," while just 5 percent said "academically advanced" students (Duffett, Farkas, and Loveless 2008). And even if schools do not provide disadvantaged children with greater opportunities for social and behavioral growth, they may provide a more "common" environment than the family and neighborhood.

Scholars are just beginning to assess how gaps in social and behavioral skills change when school is in versus when it is out. Preliminary work with the ECLS-K:2011 suggests that there are large socioeconomic, racial, and gender-based gaps at kindergarten entry, but that these gaps do not clearly increase more quickly or slowly when school is out than when it is in, up until the end of second grade (Downey, von Hippel, and Workman 2016). If these patterns turn out to be robust, then schools play a mostly neutral role with respect to gaps in students' social and behavioral skills.

International Test Scores

While these domestic analyses produce a more favorable picture of schools than the one we traditionally know, surely the fact that American test scores are consistently mediocre highlights the inefficiency of our education system. But international test scores are also a product of both school and nonschool factors. Joe Merry documents how Canadians are ahead of Americans by the sizeable margin of .31 standard deviation units on the PISA reading test given to fifteen- and sixteen-year olds. But he also compared four- and five-year-old Canadian and American children from the same cohort on the PPVT reading test before their formal schooling had started, and found that the gap at that age was nearly the same: .30 standard deviation units (Merry 2013). One has to wonder how much of the American childrens'mediocre performance had to do with forces outside the control of the education system (e.g., low birth weight, lack of access to health care, income inequality, family structure, immigrant status, racial and ethnic inequality). Perhaps all of it?

Schools as Great Distractors

To be fair, it may be premature to accept the patterns from seasonal data and these international studies unequivocally. The empirical basis for this work remains modest. But seasonal comparison research has been widely praised for its methodological advantages over traditional studies (Farkas 2003; Firebaugh 2008; Gangl 2010), and to date there has been virtually no serious criticism of the work. So why have the patterns failed to redirect attention away from schools as the source of social problems?

One reason may be that the dominant narrative about schools—that they are a driving engine of inequality—is simply too powerful to overcome with something like evidence. Scholars and the general public may also require an appealing alternative cognitive framework that provides a different understanding of how schools matter. Given what we see with our own eyes when we look at schools—different quality resources, curriculums, and learning environments—the notion that schools are compensatory faces a tough marketing challenge, regardless of its validity. We can dismiss the correlation between storks and birth rates as spurious because the causal relationship is implausible, but the correlation between schools and inequality is not only plausible, but something that seems likely. And we have spent decades describing the school mechanisms that exacerbate inequality (e.g., ability grouping, unequal funding, teacher expectations, curriculum differentiation, cultural capital).

These distractions have led us down the wrong path in terms of policy. Perhaps one of the best investments we could make would be to move away from the agriculturally based school calendar and extend the school year. Policymakers distracted by the popular school-based rhetoric reasonably ask, "Why spend money increasing the quantity of school when the quality is so poor?" But a longer school year would improve the skills of American children in general, and would benefit disadvantaged children the most. In addition, the evidence that early childhood is very important grows. While it may be possible to overcome a poor childhood with extraordinary school efforts later in life, surely it is more cost-effective to start earlier, before problems emerge.

During the growth of schooling in American society over the last century, we have come to expect more and more from schools and see them as a key lever of social policy. It turns out that when it comes to inequality, this lever is working the way we want: schools are more part of the solution than part of the problem. Without them, inequality would be much worse. Perhaps schools could do more—that is a discussion worth having—but any conversation about schools and inequality should start by noting that schools' overall effect on socioeconomic achievement gaps is an equalizing one.

But continuing to focus the majority of our attention toward school-based solutions is a distraction from the more central sources of inequality. It might feel more comfortable to fiddle with school levers, but that does not make them the right policy levers. We need to understand why young American children are so far behind their Canadian counterparts in reading skills before they even begin formal schooling. And we need to know how our growing economic inequality is shaping children's ability to learn. Rather than providing the answer to those questions, schools distract us from their source.

How Should Sociologists of Education Study Inequality?

The best evidence currently suggests that schools do not operate as many social scientists assume with respect to socioeconomic achievement gaps. And it is possible that, as the seasonal comparison method is expanded to a broader range of dependent variables, we will learn that schools are even more compensatory than previously thought. After all, we never suspected that schools were compensatory with respect to cognitive skills until we analyzed the patterns across seasons. If schools really are compensatory in a much broader sense than was previously appreciated, then we should think about what that means for the field, and how sociologists of education should approach inequality. With this possibility in mind, I have several suggestions for the kinds of questions scholars should explore with greater urgency.

(1) What are the social conditions that produce large socioeconomic-based achievement gaps before the onset of formal schooling? It appears that most of the "action"—maybe all of it—is concentrated in early childhood. There is great value, therefore, in understanding the social conditions that produce these gaps in the first place, and sociologists of education are well placed to do this kind of contextual research. Historical and cross-cultural studies may provide the leverage for understanding which social conditions matter most. For example, Reardon (2011) finds that the ninetieth/tenth income-based gap in reading has increased by 40 percent since the 1970s. One has to wonder what were the social conditions outside school that produced this large change. And why are Canada's four- and five-year olds significantly ahead of US children in reading skills? Canada's advantage is most notable at the bottom end of the distribution, among the lowest socioeconomic group. Why are Canada's low performers so much better than those of the United States? Many possibilities come to mind, such as how Canadian families enjoy universal health care, more generous unemployment benefits, and more generous public housing and transportation systems than their American counterparts—but which of these social conditions are most responsible for the reading gaps between the two countries? If Americans chose to combat achievement gaps via broader social reform, what kinds of reforms would be most effective?

(2) How are schools compensatory? Schools are probably compensatory with respect to socioeconomic gaps in cognitive skills, operating in the opposite way from what most scholars have assumed, but how are they compensatory? We need to spend more time considering which school mechanisms are responsible for the compensatory patterns. These processes have been undertheorized, leaving us with little understanding of the way in which dominant school mechanisms influence children's life chances. This is not to say that the exacerbatory processes (those favoring high-SES children) do not exist, but rather that they are likely countered by compensatory processes of equal or greater magnitude. Scholars focusing only on exacerbatory (or only on compensatory) processes provide a less useful picture than those who study both.

Most seasonal comparison research has observed achievement gaps from a thirty-thousand-foot perspective, simply describing their overall patterns. This has been an effective way of understanding how schools matter, but it has told us little about the school mechanisms that influence inequality. We could take seasonal comparison methods, however, and use them to identify the school characteristics associated with reducing or increasing achievement gaps.

In addition, how has schools' compensatory power changed as conditions outside schools have become more unequal over the last few decades? And most important, if we generalize the seasonal comparison method to a broader range of dependent variables, do we still find evidence that schools are compensatory—or at least neutral?

(3) How do schools matter for racial and ethnic gaps? This chapter has focused on socioeconomic gaps, but the seasonal evidence for racial gaps in cognitive skills merits further study. Whereas schools appear to be reducing achievement gaps across socioeconomic status, the bulk of evidence is less encouraging for race. Black/white gaps, originally thought to grow faster during the summer than during the school year (Heyns 1978), show the opposite pattern in the nationally representative ECLS:K (Downey et. al. 2004), thus suggesting that schools may play a role in exacerbating the black/white gap. And there is provocative evidence from the ECLS-K and NWEA surveys that schools may undermine the performance of Asian-American students too (Downey et al. 2004; Yoon and Merry 2016). Sociologists of education could explore why schools seem to hold back the learning of black and Asian students, but I encourage them to do so using methods that rigorously separate school and nonschool factors.

(4) How do schools influence overall variation in skills? So far, seasonal comparison scholars have looked at how SES- or race-based gaps have changed across season, but they have said little about how variation in children's skills changes in general (Meyer 2016). This is unfortunate, because it turns out that most inequality in learning is unrelated to socioeconomic status, race, gender, family structure, or the other measurable characteristics typically available to scholars in large data sets. Indeed, in models predicting summer learning, all of these observable characteristics typically explain less than 10 percent of the variation (Downey et. al 2004; Burkam et. al 2004). Downey et. al. (2004) briefly mention that overall variation in skills grows faster during the summer than during the school year, but this pattern merits more attention if we want to know how schools really influence the inequality of skills.

(5) Why do Americans view schools as the legitimate policy lever while eschewing policy aimed at broader social reform? The inconvenient truth is that schools do not generate socioeconomic achievement gaps. If the prob-

lem was mostly the kinds of schools that the poor attend, then we could target school reform as the answer. Sure, there would still be challenges in identifying the best school practices and scaling them up to the societal level, but the problem would be identified. Unfortunately, the problem is bigger than school reform; it resides in the dramatically unequal social conditions that children experience outside of school. This means that the solution requires reducing inequality outside schools, in an arena where there is considerably less political support for action.

In American society, schools have become the legitimate means by which the state is allowed to shape the opportunity structure while other redistributive acts are viewed with greater suspicion. This puts us in a peculiar position: the real source of the problem (broad inequality outside of schools) is precisely the area that Americans are reluctant to address via policy change. Scholars need to understand more about why Americans favor school policy over broader social policy.

Finally, scholars can provide the public with a better understanding of how children's lives outside school shape the achievement gaps observed in schools. If scholars more accurately portrayed achievement gaps and the role of schools in generating them, there might exist greater public support for broader social reform. Growing income inequality presents a major obstacle to reducing achievement gaps, but education scholars have hardly noticed. They've been distracted by schools.

References

Beller, Emily, and Michael Hout. 2006. "Intergenerational Social Mobility: The United States in Comparative Perspective." *The Future of Children* 16 (2):19–36.

Brooks, Ryan C. 2011. "Are Schools the Great (Noncognitive Skills) Equalizer?" Master's thesis, Ohio State University.

Downey, Douglas B., Paul T. von Hippel, Beckett A. Broh, and Paul T. Von Hippel. 2004. "Are Schools the Great Equalizer? Cognitive Inequality during the Summer Months and the School Year." *American Sociological Review* 69 (5):613–635.

Duncan, Greg J., and Katherine Magnuson. 2011. "The Nature and Impact of Early Achievement Skills, Attention Skills, and Behavior Problems." In *Whither Opportunity: Rising Inequality, Schools, and Children's Life Chances*, edited by Greg J. Duncan and Richard J. Murnane, 47–69. New York: Russell Sage Foundation.

Entwisle, Doris R., and Karl L. Alexander. 1992. "Summer Setback: Race, Poverty, School Composition, and Mathematics Achievement in the First Two Years of School." *American Sociological Review* 57 (1):72–84.

Farkas, George. 2003. "Racial Disparities and Discrimination in Education: What Do We Know, How Do We Know It, and What Do We Need to Know?" *Teachers College Record* 105 (6):1119–1146.

Farkas, G., R. P. Grobe, D. Sheehan, and Y. Shuan. 1990. "Cultural Resources and School

Success: Gender, Ethnicity, and Poverty Groups within an Urban School District." *American Sociological Review* 55 (1): 127–142.

Firebaugh, Glenn. 2008. *Seven Rules for Social Research*. Princeton, NJ: Princeton University Press.

Gangl, Markus. 2010. "Causal Inference in Sociological Research." *Annual Review of Sociology* 36:21–47.

Heyns, Barbara. 1978. *Summer Learning and the Effects of Schooling*. New York: Academic Press.

Jennings, J. L., and T. A. DiPrete. 2010. "Teacher Effects on Social and Behavioral Skills in Early Elementary School." *Sociology of Education* 83 (2): 135–159.

Lee, Valerie E., and David T. Burkam. 2002. *Inequality at the Starting Gate: Social Background Differences in Achievement as Children Begin School*. Washington: Economic Policy Institute.

Merry, Joseph J. 2013. "Tracing the U.S. Deficit in PISA Reading Skills to Early Childhood: Evidence from the United States and Canada." *Sociology of Education* 86 (3):234–252.

Meyer, J. W. 2016. "Meyer Comment on Downey and Condron." *Sociology of Education* 89 (3): 227–228.

Reardon, Sean F. 2011. "The Widening Socioeconomic Status Achievement Gap: New Evidence and Possible Explanations." In *Whither Opportunity: Rising Inequality, Schools, and Children's Life Chances*, 91–115. Washington: Brookings Institution.

Rothstein, Richard. 2004. *Class And Schools: Using Social, Economic, And Educational Reform To Close The Black-White Achievement Gap*. Washington: Economic Policy Institute and Teachers College.

Von Hippel, P. T., B. Powell, D. B. Downey, abd N. J. Rowland. 2007. "The Effect of School on Overweight in Childhood: Gain in Body Mass Index during the School Year and during Summer Vacation. *American Journal of Public Health* 97 (4): 696–702.

Von Hippel, P. T., and J. Workman. 2016. From Kindergarten through Second Grade, US Children's Obesity Prevelance Grows Only during Summer Months. *Obesity* 24 (11): 2296–2300.

Walberg, Herbert J. 1984. "Families As Partners in Educational Productivity." *Phi Delta Kappan* 65 (6): 397–400.

Yoon, Aimee, and Joseph Merry. 2015. "Understanding the Role of Schools in the Asian-White Gap: A Seasonal Comparison Approach." Paper presented at the American Sociological Association Meetings, Chicago.

FOURTEEN

Race and White Supremacy in the Sociology of Education: Shifting the Intellectual Gaze

JOHN B. DIAMOND

Race and racial inequality are central issues in the sociology of education. The addition of the *Sociology of Race and Ethnicity* as one of the fourteen American Sociological Association journals, the resurgence of theoretical and empirical work on evolving patterns of racism in the post-civil rights era (Bonilla-Silva 2010), and the increasing multidisciplinary appreciation for the ongoing importance of race across various institutions (Pager and Shepherd 2008) all highlight the importance of this area of scholarship. The emergence of the Black Lives Matter movement, the continued struggles between US government officials and indigenous nations over land and water rights (e.g., the Dakota Access Pipeline conflict), contentious discourses about Latinx immigration, and the election of Donald Trump, a white supremacist sympathizer, as president further highlight the continuing centrality of the color line in the United States (Du Bois 1903).

While the study of race and education has produced important insights, broader research on race has not been fully incorporated into the mainstream sociology of education. This oversight has limited our ability to develop a complete understanding of how race matters in education. In this chapter, I identify three limitations of research on race in the mainstream sociology of education, and make suggestions for how the field can move forward most productively. First, as sociologists of education, we tend to treat race as a statistical variable or set cultural characteristics (O'Connor, Lewis, and Horvat 2007; Zuberi, Patterson, and Stewart 2015; Zuberi 2001) rather than a socially constructed, interactive process of categorization, resource allocation, and opportunity hoarding (Lewis-McCoy 2014; Lewis and Diamond 2015; Massey 2007).

Second, while we have documented race-based structural and organizational patterns of inequality, we have been less effective in understanding the importance of symbolic inequalities (rooted in social status) that are key mechanisms in the reproduction of racial inequality in education and society. As Ridgeway (2014) stated in her 2013 American Sociological Association presidential address:

> In contrast to resources and power, status is not seen as an *independent* mechanism by which inequality between individuals and groups is *made* . . . This, I argue, is a major misjudgment that greatly limits our ability to understand how stratification actually works in an advanced industrial society like our own (p. 2, emphasis in original).

Finally, while we have captured organizational patterns that are tied to racial disparities in outcomes (e.g., tracking and school segregation), we've been less effective at understanding how and why structural and symbolic inequalities become embedded in organizations. Analyzing these processes will help us better understand the multilevel process that undergirds the reproduction of racial inequality.

This chapter proceeds as follows. I begin by defining race as it emerged in the United States as a social construction designed to establish, justify, and sustain white supremacy. I then draw on scholarship in social psychology to highlight how race shapes social interactions in ways that advantage whites and disadvantage people of color. Following this, I discuss the consequences of racially biased beliefs and treatment, drawing on work using critical race theory, black feminist theory, psychology, social psychology, public health, and biosociology. I then discuss how structural and symbolic racial inequalities become embedded in organizational routines. Finally, I conclude with a discussion of the implications of these arguments for scholarship in the sociology of education.

What is Race?

The popular conception of race emphasizes biological or essentialist understandings of racial categories (Morning 2011).[1] However, as social scientists, most of us know that race is a socially constructed system developed by Europeans to support white supremacy and to justify the economic, social, political, and physical exploitation of people defined as nonwhite (Smedley and Smedley 2005). While social scientists at various periods have tried to identify a biological or genetic categorization of racial groups through pseudoscientific studies (Golash-Boza 2016), no meaningful categorization exists. Race is a biological fiction but a social reality, in large part because people attach meaning to those who have been positioned in racialized categories (Smedley and Smedley 2005).

As Golash-Boza (2016) writes: "The idea of "race" . . . is inextricably linked to notions of white or European superiority that became concretized during the colonization of the Americas and the concomitant enslavement of Africans. Race is a modern concept and a product of colonial encounters" (p. 130). To justify the brutal treatment and murder of those defined as nonwhite, Europeans developed racial ideologies that espoused their intellectually and morally superiority over other groups (Bonilla-Silva 2010; Collins 1990). While race is based on arbitrary physical characteristics, it shapes social structures, institutions, laws, and interpersonal interactions in ways that perpetuate white supremacy (Bonilla-Silva 2010; Diamond 2006). As Bonilla-Silva (2010) argues, societies like the United States form "racialized social systems" across all dimensions of social life, which contribute to the reproduction of white supremacy. Other scholars have spoken to what Mills refers to as "global white supremacy" as both an ideology and a social system (Du Bois 1915; Mills 1997). This is not to suggest that race is the only form of stratification. Class and gender exist simultaneously, and interlock with race in an intersectional matrix of domination (Crenshaw 1989; Collins 2004).

While race is about how people attach meaning to human bodies, racial thinking helps to create, justify, and sustain a racialized social structure by determining which people have access to social rewards like jobs, housing, medical care, bank loans, civil liberties, voting rights, and freedom of movement. Race is a *relational* phenomenon that advantages whites and disadvantages everyone else. Whites, for example, receive structural advantages by gaining easier access to income and wealth-generating resources like jobs and homes (Oliver and Shapiro 1995; Shapiro 2004; Du Bois 1915, 1935). During the early to mid-twentieth century, the federal government subsidized the creation and growth of suburban communities through providing low-interest-rate Federal Housing Administration (FHA) loans almost exclusively to whites and simultaneously undermining black communities in central cities through redlining (Shapiro 2004; Katznelson 2005). This led to housing values appreciating more rapidly in the suburbs than in cities (and more rapidly in white communities than in black ones), which in turn has contributed to stark wealth disparities between black and white communities in the United States,which have continued to grow even when income is held constant (Shapiro et al. 2013; Shapiro 2004; Oliver and Shapiro

1995). Shapiro et al. (2013) demonstrates that the gap in median wealth between African American and white families was $236,500 in 2009 (triple what it was in 2009). Likewise, the United States has functioned as a white supremacist settler colonial power in relation to the pre-existing indigenous nations that existed prior to the arrival of Europeans. White supremacy was a foundational racial ideology supporting the genocide of indigenous people, violation of hundreds of treaties with indigenous nations, and land theft during the westward expansion of the United States.

Whites also receive the psychic advantages of white privilege (Du Bois 1935; Roediger 2007). As Du Bois wrote in 1935, "It must be remembered that the white group of laborers, while they received a low wage, were compensated in part by a sort of public and psychological wage. They were given public deference and titles of courtesy because they were white." This helps explain why various European groups in the United States, including Irish, Italians, and Jews, worked hard to attain white status.

Because of its structural and symbolic value, whites have actively worked to maintain the social advantages of whiteness through opportunity hoarding (Massey 2007; Lewis and Diamond 2015; Lewis-McCoy 2014; Tilly 1998). Du Bois demonstrates the role of the whites in opportunity hoarding in his analysis of race and class in the United States.

> The black proletariat is not part of the white proletariat. . . . while Negro labor in America suffers because of the fundamental inequities of the whole capitalist system, the lowest and most fatal degree of its suffering comes not from the capitalists but from fellow white laborers. It is white labor that deprives the Negro of his right to vote, denies him education, denies him affiliation with trade unions, expels him from decent houses and neighborhoods, and heaps upon him the public insults of open color discrimination (Du Bois, 1933; cited in Thompson 2016).

Here we see that race is reproduced in part through the active participation of whites who gain material and symbolic advantages from the perpetuation of white supremacy (also see Du Bois 1915; 1935; Bonilla-Silva 2003). In education this has been done through the creation of laws that regulate the distribution of education, differential allocation of resources through segregation (*Brown v. Board of Education*, 1954), institutionalized processes of residential segregation, and monopolization of privileged positions in integrated schools through tracking (Oakes 2005; Mickelson 2001; Lewis and Diamond 2015). The active work of creating group advantage through individual, institutional, and governmental action is a core feature of the interactive process through which whites have worked to establish and maintain white supremacy. Therefore, race is not an individual characteristic in a sociological sense, but instead a social position that determines how one is treated and rewarded in a racial hierarchy that privileges whiteness.

Treating Race as a Socially Constructed, Interactive Phenomenon

Most work in the sociology of education has treated race as a characteristic of individuals. It is operationalized as a variable in statistical analyses or as a set of cultural characteristics that resides within a person (Zuberi 2001; O'Connor, Lewis, and Horvat 2007). This is a particular problem in quantitative analyses of race (the dominant methodology in the sociology of education; see chapter 1) that draw on the limited number of available data sets. Race, however, is a socially constructed category along which resources are allocated and interactions are shaped. Saying that outcomes are caused by race, when race is measured as an individual characteristic, does little to capture the significance of race or how and why it matters. Because race is often undertheorized, the sociology of education has often missed the opportunity to develop more sophisticated racial analyses. We need work that takes race as a socially created, actively constructed process and operationalizes it as such.

Some work points to useful strategies for moving in this direction. One challenge of sociological research on race is the use of single quantitative methods. As Stewart and Sewell (2011) write, "The dilemma is that our methods, when used singularly, undermine our ability to clearly identify the range of mechanisms behind race and racial inequality. We can overcome the limitations in one method by supplementing our analyses with complimentary methods" (pp. 227–228). For instance, they argue that the triangulation of multiple quantitative methods has the potential to help us shed new light on the mechanisms that contribute to the reproduction of racial inequality.

In contrast to the static and individual conception that shapes much of our research, race is a dynamic and relational social process that can be understood using Weberian notions of social status (Ridgeway 2014, 2000; Weber 1978). Social status is an important mechanism of social stratification, but is often treated as less powerful than structural mechanisms (Ridgeway 2014). Ridgeway and her colleagues have demonstrated that status distinction can lead to status beliefs or "widely shared cultural beliefs that people who belong to one social group are more esteemed and competent than those who belong to another social group" (Ridgeway and Erickson 2000: 580). These status beliefs "construct and justify social inequality between categories of people" (Ibid.: 580). She further elaborates thus:

> Contemporary U.S. status beliefs assert that people in a particular category, say whites, men, or the middle or upper class, are not only more respected but also presumed to be more *competent*, especially at what "counts most" in society, than are people in contrasting categories, such as people of color, women, or the working class" (Ridgeway 2014: 3).

A large and growing body of work in sociology, social psychology, psychology, and education provides important insights into how these status beliefs influence social interactions. Because of the dominant white supremacist and anti-black ideology in the United States, when someone is identified as "black," there is a semi-automatic set of negative beliefs that are triggered in most whites (Banaji et al. 2015; McAfee, 2014; Ridgeway 2014; Banaji and Greenwald 2013). Ridgeway's work on performance expectations demonstrates how stereotypes about gender, race, and intelligence are productive of structural inequality.

Such race-based status beliefs, and subsequent behaviors, lead to multiple results. For instance, we know that a large majority of whites hold negative associations toward African Americans on the Implicit Association Test. These unconscious biases are therefore associated with conscious beliefs and behaviors. As Banaji et al. (2015) write, "A signature result from research using the IAT is that people who have no intention to discriminate may still do so in their behavior toward others" (2015: 183). This work has shown that those with more anti-black biases behave in ways that detrimentally affect African Americans in medical care, criminal justice, and attitudes toward race-based public policies (Banaji, Bhaskar, and Brownstein 2015). Likewise, negative associations with Latinx are associated with attitudes toward legal and illegal immigration (Ibid.).

While sociologists who study racial attitudes have documented declines in overt racial antipathy among whites (as expressed on traditional surveys), they continued to document anti-black racism. For instance, a large percentage of whites prefer mostly white schools, hold negative racial stereotypes about African Americans, and believe that blacks are less hardworking and intelligent than whites (Bobo, Charles, Krysan, et al. 2009). However, in contrast to the Jim Crow–era expression of racism, current racial beliefs have shifted from biological innate characterizations to being seen as a manifestation of group culture (Ibid.) or what Bonilla-Silva refers to as the biologization of culture (Bonilla-Silva 2010). Other work on racial attitudes also highlights how new and more elusive forms of racism, including color-blind racism (Bonilla-Silva 2010) and racial apathy (Forman 2004) have emerged and serve as mechanisms for the reproduction of racial inequality in the contemporary racial environment. Unfortunately, these insights about the evolving nature of racism, even as they emerge in the contemporary sociology of race, have failed to penetrate deeply into the mainstream sociology of education.

The fact that negative stereotypes about people of color persist among whites is clearly an important issue given that the current US teaching force is overwhelmingly white and the student population is increasingly African American, Latinx, Asian, Native American, or biracial (Warikoo, chapter 15 in this volume). We have several studies that demonstrate the significance of this racial mismatch between teachers and students. White teachers, for instance, judge black students more harshly in terms of behavior and academic potential than they do white students (Fox 2016; Downey and Pribesh 2004) and these expectations can have negative implications on students' outcomes. There is also a more general body of work on race and ethnicity-based expectations that demonstrates teachers' lower expectations for black and Latinx students.

We also have good evidence that race shapes how students' behavior is interpreted (Ferguson 2000). The disproportionate suspension and expulsion rates of black and Latinx students emerges from teacher referrals for behaviors that are often subjective (e.g., defiance) rather than objective (e.g., drug possession), thus making these students highly susceptible to (mostly) white teachers' implicit or explicit racial biases. One indication of the power of these school discipline experiences to shape students' academic perceptions is the finding that on national surveys, black students are more proschool than are white students on all indicators except the perception that discipline is fair (Downey, Ainsworth, and Qian 2009). There is a clear link between exclusionary discipline and racial disparities in educational outcomes (Morris and Perry 2016; Gregory, Skiba, and Noguera 2010).

What Are the Implications of Racially Biased Beliefs and Treatment?

The perpetuation of the myth of white supremacy has negative implications for the academic performance of black and Latinx students. A substantial body of this research has focused on the implications of experiencing discrimination. The work on stereotype threat, for example, emphasizes how stigmatized group members perform less well on academic tasks because of the desire to disprove negative stereotypes about their group (Steele 2011). Research in this area demonstrates that the stereotype threat condition leads to a measurable stress reaction on the part of target group members. Black college students placed in a stereotype threat condition experienced physical and cognitive reactions including increased blood pressure, reduced memory capacity, increased heart rate variability, and taxed self-regulation ability. Thus, trying to disprove a stereotype takes away from one's cognitive capacity to do so. There is also evidence of the opposite effect known as *stereotype lift*, in which beliefs about white intellectual superiority can enhance white students' academic performance. Again, race is a relational phenomenon, not simply an individual characteristic. The psychological impact of status beliefs can have direct and indirect impacts of educational performance.

Critical race theory (CRT) scholarship, which emerged in law schools in the 1980s (Bell 1987) and later in education scholarship in the 1990s has contributed a key theoretical framework to understanding how racism in experienced. It has done so by adding empirical evidence for the idea of racial microaggression (Pierce 1970; Huber and Solorzano 2015). Chester Pierce (1970) defined microaggressions as "subtle and stunning" offensive actions that have implications because of their cumulative nature. The work in this area has been taken up by critical race scholars who have demonstrated how ideas about the intellectual inferiority and inherent criminality of people of color in educational contexts lead them to experience microaggressions that impact students' sense of safety and connection to educational institutions, and demonstrate the psychosocial implications of discrimination, including what Smith has called "racial battle fatigue," in higher education contexts (Smith et al. 2007). Much of this work has been conducted by psychologists and sociologists in higher education settings which suggests the need for more work in K–12 settings.

The literature on microaggression also points to the patterns of biased treatment that exit at the institutional and societal levels—what Sue et al. (2007) call environmental microaggressions—"racial assaults, insults and invalidations which are manifested on systemic and environmental levels" (Sue et al. 2007). These are features of social context beyond the interpersonal level. In education, many colleges and universities have buildings named almost exclusively after white heterosexual men. Such practices can send the message that students who do not fit those categories do not belong in the institution (Sue et al. 2007; Solorzano, Ceja, and Yosso 2000). Likewise, integrated schools, racial disproportionality in honors, Advanced

Placement, and regular level classes in which whites are positioned in upper-level classes and Blacks and Latinx students are in lower-level classes is another form of environmental microaggressions (Lewis and Diamond 2015; Tyson 2011).

The originators of work on microaggressions argue that it is their cumulative impact that makes them powerful factors that influence people's experiences and outcomes. Important work has emerged on race and health that relates to the implications of experiencing discrimination such as racial microaggressions. A growing body of work drawing on the biopsychosocial model of racism as a stressor demonstrates that experiencing discrimination leads to negative health outcomes (Clark et al. 1999; Goosby and Heidbrink 2013; Williams 2012). For example, African Americans who experience more discrimination develop bodily inflammation (in the form of increased C-reactive protein) and have higher blood pressure (Goosby et al. 2015) than African American students who attend predominantly white schools. They also report more early adult depression, stomach aches, headaches, and nausea than those who do not attend such schools. Other work shows that writing about personal experiences of discrimination inhibits the body's ability to response to flu vaccinations. Scholars like David Williams at Harvard and Bridget Goosby at Nebraska are continuing important work in this area which captures the cumulative impact of racial oppression as a set of experiences.

Another important contribution of CRT, drawing on black feminist scholarship, is the idea of intersectionality. As Crenshaw (1989) writes, "The intersectional experience is greater than the sum of racism and sexism; any analysis that does not take intersectionality into account cannot sufficiently address the particular manner in which Black women are subordinated." While intersectionality has emerged as an important theoretical advancement in understanding stratification, and a section on race, class, and gender intersections exists in the American Sociological Association, work in the sociology of education has not fully incorporated these insights. In fact, given its heavy reliance on regression analysis in status attainment studies (Mehta and Davies, chapter 1) most mainstream quantitative work still treats the contributions of race and gender as distinct variables (race or gender) or in an additive fashion (race + gender). However, recent work suggests using alternative methods that are more consistent with an intersectional approach such as fuzzy-set qualitative comparative case studies.

An interesting insight from the work on microaggressions and intersectionality is that bringing cross-disciplinary insights and methodological approaches together can yield more sophisticated ways of understanding the implications of race. Work on racial microaggressions, when linked with work in psychology, social psychology, education, and health, can lead to more robust theoretical, methodological, and practical advancements in the examination of race.

Unfortunately, much of this work has failed to penetrate the mainstream sociology of education. This could result in part from patterns of subdisciplinary specialization within sociology, the preponderance of quantitative articles published in mainstream journals, and the lingering issue of the marginalization of both critical scholarship and what Mehta and Davies call "studies" units (e.g., African American Studies, Latino/a Studies, Women's Studies; Mehta and Davies, chapter 1 in this volume).

To this I would add the marginalization of scholars of color from inclusion in our most prominent venues. This exclusion dates back to the founding of US sociology. W. E. B. Du Bois, the scholar who founded the first school of sociology in the United States at Atlanta University (Morris 2015), was largely written out of the history of the field because of white supremacist beliefs and structures. Du Bois laid the foundation for several sociological subdisciplines, including urban sociology (Du Bois 1899), the sociology of race (Du Bois 1903), and whiteness studies (Du Bois 1920). He conceptualized race as a social construct (challenging the scientific racism of the early twentieth century), analyzed race and class as interactive processes, engaged in intersectional analysis (Morris 2015) and introduced various methodological innovations including data triangulation, qualitative/quantitative mixed-method approaches, and participant observation. His exclusion from the mainstream of sociology is perhaps the quintessential example of the perils of white supremacy for the discipline's development.

But How Do These Status Beliefs Matter in Education?

The sociology of education has documented structural and organizational processes related to the reproduction of racial inequality. This work has provided important insights into how race-based structural inequality related to social class and wealth (Johnson 2014; Shapiro 2004), residential and school segregation (Shapiro 2004) *and* organizational processes and characteristics like tracking (Oakes 1985; Tyson 2011), teacher quality (Darling-Hammond 2010), and disproportionate suspension and expulsion (Skiba, Gregory, and Noguera 2005) contribute to the reproduction of inequality.

However, we need to better understand how racial inequality becomes embedded in organizational routines that are ostensibly designed to produce more equitable outcomes. I argue that borrowing from work on organizational routines can help illustrate how structural and symbolic racial inequality is perpetuated through organizational processes.

Schools (and all organizations) partly function through the operation of organizational routines (Feldman and Pentland 2003). These routines include the collective daily practices that people engage in to get things done. We can think about the typical morning ritual at a school, the changes of class on the hour, or teacher-faculty meetings as examples of organizational routines. Discipline practices like teacher referrals are also organizational routines. Recent work has identified two key "aspects" of these routines—the *ostensive aspect* or the ideal of the routine, and the *performative aspect* or the routine as practiced (Feldman and Pentland 2003; Sherer 2007). As Feldman and Pentland (2003: 101) put it, "The ostensive aspect is the . . . abstract, generalized idea of a routine or the narrative in the organization about how things *should* be done." They continue, "The performative aspect of the routine consists of specific actions, by specific people, in specific places and times." It consists of how the routine is *actually* performed in everyday practice. The performative aspect of a routine may be highly aligned with the implicit intentions of the ostensive aspect, or it may diverge dramatically.

For instance, Feldman and Pentland (2003) use the example of the hiring routine to illustrate this distinction. Hiring is usually broken down into three related activities: attracting candidates, screening applicants, and hiring the most qualified candidate. However, the performance of the hiring routine is much more complicated. An informative study by Pager, Western, and Bonikowski (2009) sent black, Latinx, and white field testers to interview for jobs with the same credentials. Whites were more likely to be called back for a second interview than were black and Latinx people, even when whites reported felony records and blacks reported clean records. In this case, it is critical to distinguish between the ideal of the routine and how it is actually practiced.

Other studies have shown a disjuncture between the ostensive and performative aspects of the hiring routines. Employers with more inclusive diversity statements are no more likely to hire applicants of color than those with less inclusive statements (Kang et al. 2016) and employers who expressed an equal likelihood of hiring black and white ex-offenders are still more likely to hire whites over blacks (Quillian and Pager 2005).

In my recent book with Amanda Lewis about race and education in an integrated high school (Lewis and Diamond 2015), we argue that it is important to understand how everyday interpersonal interactions are shaped by the structural and symbolic racial inequalities (Lewis and Diamond 2015). For example, school discipline practices can be thought of as an organizational routine with ostensive and performative aspects. All schools have rules of conduct that dictate how students interact with each other and with teachers and administrators. These rules and regulations form the ostensive aspect of disciplinary routines and are written as if they apply equally to all students, regardless of background.

While discipline routines are stated in race-neutral terms, their practice can deviate from the ideal. This is because of the way race works symbolically (the meaning and values people attach to members of different racial groups) and structurally (affecting who has access to certain kinds of resources) when real people interact in specific contexts. Rather than a discrete moment, discipline is a process (Gregory, Skiba, and Noguera 2010). This process includes at least three components: selection for discipline, movement through the discipline process, and enforcement of consequences (Piquero 2008; Gregory, Skiba, and Noguera 2010). Racial differences in disciplinary experiences can emerge at any moment during the process, from *differential selection* (institutional practices that might lead minorities to get picked out for wrongdoing more often despite episodes of misbehavior similar to those of white students) to *differential processing* (institutional practices that might lead minorities, once picked out for wrongdoing, to get different sanctions despite transgressions similar to those committed by white students; Gregory, Skiba, and Noguera 2010; Piquero 2008; Skiba et al. 2011).[2]

In our study, we found that black and Latinx students were more likely to be singled out for intervention even when white students engaged in similar behavior. This was because of the performance expectations of black and Latinx students tied to racial status beliefs. For example, students were expected to have hall passes when they were not in class during class periods. However, race determined the extent to which students were scrutinized during these periods. This pattern repeated itself and was identified by students, teachers, and administrators of all races.

Black and Latinx students were also treated differently from white students once they were cited for disciplinary infractions. Because of their structural and symbolic advantages, white parents had access to valued resources (economic, social, cultural, and symbolic) that led white students to receive less punitive treatment. White parents were able to use their social position to negotiate favorable outcomes for their children. Here, whiteness served as a form of symbolic capital that shaped students' experiences with the discipline process. As a result, black and Latinx students were more likely to be sanctioned for their behavior *and* to receive more punitive sanctions when they did receive them. Our work points to the simultaneous functioning of structural and symbolic inequality in the reproduction of racial stratification.

Conclusion

I have argued that mainstream sociology of education has been limited by its failure to fully engage with the broader work on race in sociology and across the social sciences. This has limited the theoretical and empirical sophistication of work on race in the sociology of education. To address these limitations, I argue that educational sociologists need to conduct research that treats race as a socially constructed category designed to promote white supremacy through the unequal distribution of structural and symbolic resources. This system is maintained through conscious and unconscious practices of opportunity hoarding in which whites seek to maintain interpersonal, institutional, and structural advantages and to exclude people of color from those advantages.

While we have a large body of work that documents structural and institutional patterns of racial inequality (e.g., income and wealth disparities, residential and schools segregation, ability grouping/tracking), we have been less successful in documenting how race functions symbolically to reproduce educational inequality, and how structural and symbolic inequality become embedded in routine organizational practices.

In order to move the sociology of education forward, I argue that we need to reinvigorate work on social status—drawing on the work of social psychologists who have provided powerful insights into how status beliefs influence performance expectations and intergroup dynamics (Ridgeway 2011). In particular, we need to understand how daily social interactions are shaped by race-based performance expectations that are dynamic and cumulative. We also need work that critically analyzes the implications of navigating racially hostile schools where broader racial ideologies question the intellectual and behavioral competence of students of color. I have discussed the biological and psychological implications of white supremacist ideologies on the health of people of color; we need more work that attends to these dynamics and tracks them over time with a focus on education and the interactions between physical and psychological well-being and educational experiences and outcomes.

In light of the interactive nature of racial ideologies, more attention needs to be paid to the implications of status beliefs for white students' achievement. Work on stereotype lift has demonstrated that white students' performance is boosted by positive beliefs about their capacity. The kind of work I believe is needed would include the analysis of national and international data sets, but would not be as limited to them as it has been. Such data sets provide key information, but they are limited in their ability to capture how race operates in schools. Future work will benefit from multimethod studies that combine qualitative and quantitative work, as well as work that brings multiple quantitative approaches to bear on specific race-based educational issues. Many of the most powerful insights on contemporary racial inequality require studies that document actual practices rather than just statements about race (e.g., audit studies), that draw on social psychological experiments (Ridgeway 2011; Steele 2011), and which build upon biopsychosocial models of racism (Goosby and Heidebrink 2013). Our work in the sociology of education needs to treat race as a category that is meaningful because it shapes how people are treated and the opportunities to which they have access, rather than as a characteristic that individuals carry with them into educational contexts.

Likewise, most work in the sociology of education fails to interrogate how whites actively maintain their educational advantages though opportunity hoarding. The intellectual gaze of sociologists is too often focused on black and Latinx students and families who are perceived to lack some form of cultural and intellectual know-how or investment in education, rather than on whites who have worked tirelessly to monopolize educational advantages. Promising work has begun to shed light on the reproduction of elite status, but more studies of the interactive, relational nature of racial privileges and penalties is needed.

Finally, with regard to methodology, we need to expand how we study race. Mainstream sociology of education has been dominated by quantitative studies relying on surveys that treat race as a variable. The most innovative work discussed here expands beyond single methods to utilize qualitative/quantitative mixed-method approaches, multiple quantitative methods, experiments, and other forms of analysis. It also takes seriously the theoretical insights from work in psychology, social psychology, public health, critical race theory, and black feminist epistemology. Taking race seriously in the sociology of education means seriously revising how we conceptualize and study it.

Notes

1. In this chapter, race is discussed in the context of the United States because of this volume's emphasis on the sociology of education in the United States.
2. Of course, while race mattered, it did not function in isolation. Instead, as we will

discuss further, there was an intermingling of race, class, gender, and cultural style that "colored" students' interactions with school officials.

References

Anderson, K. F. 2013. Diagnosing Discrimination: Stress from Perceived Racism and the Mental and Physical Health Effects. *Sociological Inquiry* 83 (1): 55–81.

Banaji, M. R., R. Bhaskar, and M. Brownstein. 2015. When Bias Is Implicit, How Might We Think about Repairing Harm? *Current Opinion in Psychology* 2015 (6): 183–188.

Banaji, M. R., and A. G. Greenwald. 2013. *Blindspot: Hidden Biases of Good People*. New York: Delacorte Press.

Bell, D. 1987. *And We Are Not Saved: The Elusive Quest for Racial Justice*. New York: Basic Books.

Bobo, Lawrence D., Camille Z. Charles, Maria Krysan, and Alicia D. Simmons. 2012. The Real Record on Racial Attitudes. In *Social Trends in the United States: Evidence from the General Social Survey since 1972*, edited by P. V. Marsden, pp. 38–83. Princeton, NJ: Princeton University Press.

Bonilla-Silva, E. 2003. *Racism without Racists*. Third edition. Lanham, MD: Rowman & Littlefield.

Clark, R., N. B. Anderson, R. Clark, and D. R. Williams. 1999. Racism as a Stressor for African Americans: A Biopsychosocial Model. *American Psychologist* 54 (10): 805–816.

Collins, P. H. 1990. *Black Feminist Thought: Knowledge, Consciousness, and the Politics of Empowerment*. New York: Routledge.

———. 2004. *Black Sexual Politics: African Americans, Gender, and the New Racism*. New York: Routledge.

Crenshaw, K. W. 1989. Demarginalizing the Intersection of Race and Sex: A Black Feminist Critique of Anti-Discrimination Doctrine, Feminist Theory and Antiracist Practices. *University of Chicago Legal Forum* (1).

Darling-Hammond, L. 2010. *The Flat World and Education: How America's Commitment to Equity Will Determine Our Future*. New York: Teachers College Press.

Diamond, J. B. 2006. Still Separate and Unequal: Examining Race, Opportunity, and School Achievement in "Integrated" Suburbs. *Journal of Negro Education* 75 (3): 495–505.

Downey, D., J. W. Ainsworth, and Z. Qian. 2009. Rethinking the Attitude Achievement Paradox among Blacks. *Sociology of Education*, 82:1–19.

Downey, D. B., and S. Pribesh. 2004. Missing When Race Matters: Teachers' Evaluations of Students' Classroom Behavior. *Sociology of Education* 77 (4): 267–282.

Du Bois, W. E. B. 1903. *The Souls of Black Folk*. Chicago: A. C. McClurg.

———. 1915. The African Roots War. *Atlantic Monthly*, 707–714.

———. 1935. *Black Reconstruction in America: An Essay toward a History of the Part Which Black Folk Played in the Attempt to Reconstruct Democracy in America, 1860–1880*. New York: Harcourt Brace.

———. 1999. *Darkwater: Voices from within the Veil*. New York: Dover Publications.

Eze, Emannuel C. 1997. *Race and the Enlightenment: A Reader*. New York: Wiley-Blackwell.

Feldman, M. S., and B. T. Pentland. 2003. Reconceptualizing Organizational Routines as a Source of Flexibility and Change. *Administrative Science Quarterly* 48 (1): 94–118.

Ferguson, A. 2000. *Bad Boys: Public Schools in the Making of Black Masculinity*. Ann Arbor: University of Michigan Press.

Forman, T. 2004. Color-Blind Racism and Racial Indifference: The Role of Racial Apathy in Facilitating Enduring Inequalities. In *The Changing Terrain of Race and Ethnicity*, edited by M. Krysan and A. Lewis, pp. 43–66. New York: Russell Sage.

Fox, L. 2016. Seeing Potential: The Effects of Student–Teacher Demographic Congruence on Teacher Expectations and Recommendations. *AERA Open* 2 (1): 1–17.

Golash-Boza, T. 2016. A Critical and Comprehensive Sociological Theory of Race and Racism. *Sociology of Race and Ethnicity*. 2 (2): 129–141.

Goosby, B. J., and Chelsea Heidebrink. 2013. African American Health over the Life Course: The Transgenerational Consequences of Racial Discrimination. *Sociology Compass* 7:630–643.

Goosby, Bridget J., Sarah Malone, Elizabeth Richardson, Jacob E. Cheadle, and Deadric Williams. 2015. Perceived Discrimination and Markers of Cardiovascular Risk among Low-Income African American Youth. *American Journal of Human Biology* 27 (4): 546–552.

Gregory, A., S. J. Skiba, and P. A. Noguera. 2010. The Achievement Gap and the Discipline Gap: Two Sides of the Same Coin? *Educational Researcher* 39 (1): 59–68.

Huber, L. P., and D. Solorzano. 2015. Racial Microaggressions as a Tool for Critical Race Research. *Race, Ethnicity, and Education* 18:297–320.

Johnson, H. B. 2006. *The American Dream and the Power of Wealth: Choosing Schools and Inheriting Inequality in the Land of Opportunity*. New York: Routledge.

Kang, S. K., K. A. DeCelles, A. Tilcsik, and S. Jun. 2016. Whitened Resumes: Race and Self-Presentation in the Labor Market. *Administrative Science Quarterly* 61: 469–502.

Katznelson, I. 2005. *When Affirmative Action Was White: An Untold History of Racial Inequality in Twentieth Century America*. New York: W. W. Norton.

Lewis, A. E., and J. B. Diamond. 2015. *Despite the Best Intentions: How Inequality Thrives in Good Schools*. New York: Oxford University Press.

Lewis-McCoy, R. 2014. *Inequality in the Promised Land: Race, Resources, and Suburban Schooling*. Stanford: University of California Press.

Massey, D. S. 2007. *Categorically Unequal: The American Stratification System*. New York: Russell Sage Foundation.

McAfee, Myosha. 2014. The Kinesiology of Race. *Harvard Educational Review* 84 (4).

Mickelson, Roslyn. 2001. Subverting Swann: First and Second-Generation Segregation in the Charlotte-Mecklenburg Schools. *American Educational Research Journal* 38 (2): 215–252.

Mills, C. W. 1997. *The Racial Contract*. Ithaca, NY: Cornell University Press.

Morning, A. 2011. *The Nature of Race: How Scientists Think and Teach about Human Difference*. Berkeley: University of California Press.

Morris, Aldon D. 2015. *The Scholar Denied: W. E. B. Du Bois and the Birth of American Sociology*, Oakland: University of California Press.

Morris, E W., and B. L. Perry. 2016. The Punishment Gap: School Suspension and Racial Disparities in Achievement. *Social Problems* 63:68–86.

Oakes, Jeannie. 2005. *Keeping Track: How Schools Structure Inequality*. 2nd ed. New Haven, CT: Yale University Press.

O'Connor, C., A. E. Lewis, and E. Horvat. 2007. Researching "Black" Educational Experiences and Outcomes: Theoretical and Methodological Considerations. *Educational Researcher* 36 (9): 541–552.

Oliver, M., and T. Shapiro. 1995. *Black Wealth/White Wealth: A New Perspective on Racial Inequality*. New York: Oxford University Press.

Pager, D., and H. Shepherd. 2008. The Sociology of Discrimination: Racial Discrimination in Employment, Housing, Credit, and Consumer Markets. *Annual Review of Sociology* 34: 181–209.

Pager, D., B. Western, and B. Bonikowski. 2009. Discrimination in a Low-Wage Market: A Field Experiment. *American Sociological Review* 74 (5): 777–799.

Pentland, B. T., and M. S. Feldman. 2005. Organizational Routines as a Unit of Analysis. *Industrial and Corporate Change* 14 (5): 793–815.

Pierce, C. 1970. Offensive Mechanisms. In *The Black Seventies*, edited by F. Barbour, pp. 265–282. Boston: Porter Sargent.

Piquero. A. R. 2008. Taking Stock of Developmental Trajectories of Criminal Activity over the Life Course. In *The Long View of Crime: A Synthesis of Longitudinal Research*, edited by A. M. Liberman, pp. 23–78. New York: Springer.

Quillian, L. 2008. Does Unconscious Racism Exist? *Social Psychology Quarterly* 71:6–11.

Ridgeway, C. L. 2011. *Framed by Gender*. New York: Oxford University Press.

———. 2014. Why Status Matters for Inequality. *American Sociological Review* 79 (1): 1–16.

Ridgeway, C. L., and K. G. Erickson. 2000. Creating and Spreading Status Beliefs. *American Journal of Sociology* 106:579–615.

Roediger, D. R. 2007. *The Wages of Whiteness: Race and the Making of the American Working Class*. Chicago: Charles H. Kerr.

Shapiro, T. 2004. *The Hidden Cost of Being African American*. New York: Oxford University Press.

Shapiro, T., T. Meschede, and S. Osoro. 2013. The Roots of the Widening Racial Wealth Gap: Explaining the Black-White Economic Divide. Institute for Assets and Social Policy Research and Policy Brief.

Sherer, J. Z. 2007. The Practice of Leadership in Mathematics and Language Arts: The Adams Case. In *Distributed Leadership in Practice*, edited by J. Spillane and J. B. Diamond, pp. 106–138. New York: Teachers College Press.

Smedley, A., and B. Smedley. 2005. Race as Biology Is Fiction: Racism as Social Problem Is Real: Anthropological and Historical Perspectives on the Social Construction of Race. *American Psychologist* 60 (1): 16–26.

Smith, W. A., W. R. Allen, and L. L. Danley. 2007. "Assume the Position . . . You Fit the Description": Campus Racial Climate and the Psychoeducational Experiences and Racial Battle Fatigue among African American Male College Students. *American Behavioral Scientist* 51 (4): 551–578.

Solorzano, D., M. Ceja, and T. J. Yosso. 2000. Critical Race Theory, Racial Microaggressions, and Campus Racial Climate: The Experiences of African American College. *Journal of Negro Education* 69 (1/2): 60–73.

Steele, C. 2011. *Whistling Vivaldi: How Stereotypes Affect Us and What We Can Do*. New York: W. W. Norton.

Stewart, Q. T., and A. A. Sewell. 2011. Quantitative Methods for Analyzing Categorical Inequality, in *Rethinking Race and Ethnicity in Research Methods*, edited by J. Stanfield. Walnut Creek, CA: Left Coast Press.

Sue, D. W., C. M. Capodilupo, G. C. Torino, J. M. Bucceri, A. M. B. Holder, K. L. Nadal, and M. Esquilin. 2007. Racial Microaggressions in Everyday Life: Implications for Clinical Practice. *American Psychologist* 62 (4): 271–286.

Thompson, J. P. 2016. Capitalism, Democracy, and Du Bois's "*Two* Proletariats." Items: Insight from the Social Sciences. Accessed December 8, 2016, at http://items.ssrc.org/capitalism-democracy-and-du-boiss-two-proletariats/.

Tilly, C. 1998. *Durable Inequality*. Berkeley: University of California Press.

Tyson, K. 2011. *Integration Interrupted: Tracking, Black Students, and Acting White after Brown*. New York: Oxford University Press.

Weber, M. 1978. *Economy and Society: An Outline of an Interpretive Sociology*. Berkeley: University of California Press.

Williams, David R. 2012. Miles to Go before We Sleep: Racial Inequalities in Health. *Journal of Health and Social Behavior* 53:279–295.

Zuberi, T. 2001. *Thicker Than Blood: How Racial Statistics Lie*. Minneapolis: University of Minnesota Press.

Zuberi, T., E. J. Patterson, and Q. T. Stewart. 2015. Race, Methodology, and Social Construction in the Genomic Era. *Annals of the American Academy of Political and Social Science* 661 (1):109–127.

FIFTEEN

Race, Ethnicity, and Cultural Processes in Education: New Approaches for New Times

NATASHA KUMAR WARIKOO

The United States has undergone two dramatic changes with respect to race in education over the past fifty years. First, in the next five years a majority of all children in the United States will be black, Latino, Asian, Native American, or a combination of races (Federal Interagency Forum on Child and Family Statistics, 2015). Second, since the civil rights movement there has been increasing acceptance of diversity and multiculturalism in the United States, and a decline of overtly racist racial attitudes (Alba and Nee 2003; Schuman, Steeh, and Bobo 1997). At the same time, we have seen renewed attention in the recent past to antiblack violence, especially in the hands of the state, as well as mass incarceration and what some call a "school to prison pipeline" (Kim, Losen, and Hewitt 2010).

These shifts and their sometimes unexpected consequences raise important questions that sociologists of education have yet to answer. The existing scholarship in stratification documents important ongoing racial and ethnic disparities in education—important for public awareness that there *is*, in fact, a dramatic race problem in the United States. Still, it does not provide a path forward. In order to determine how to attack these carefully documented disparities, and to learn from the documented successes in reducing racial inequality, we need to understand the mechanisms by which they happen. Further, a deeper understanding of race, education, and the lives of young people should look beyond academic outcomes to broader social processes, which can contribute to our understanding of society overall. As labs for observing social dynamics, race relations, and status hierarchies, educational institutions showcase important social and cultural processes that sociologists of education can mine for a deeper understanding of social life.

I argue that methods that focus on underlying social and cultural processes in education will provide important insights related to these topics. This investigation requires methods that historically have not been at the core of the field of sociology of education, as defined by what is printed in the flagship journal *Sociology of Education*, such as investigating differences *within* racial and ethnic groups to illuminate how racial and ethnic forces influence education. Scholarship that employs these methods to reveal social and cultural processes related to youth and education should be taken more seriously by the core of the field. Further, I identify five rich areas for investigation in the sociology of race, ethnicity, and education related to our changed racial landscape:

1. How do individuals make meaning of race, and how do educational institutions influence that meaning-making?
2. How does race play into the often perceived tension between, on the one hand, access, inclusion, and democracy, and on the other, meritocracy? In other words, how does our racial history and changing demographics and culture shape and get shaped by struggles over meritocracy, inclusion, and opportunity? Relatedly, how does "diversity" shape school and university cultures and the consequent experiences of students, teachers, and staff?
3. How, if at all, is Asian American educational success changing dominant culture(s)?
4. How do elites from nondominant groups such as minorities and those from modest-income families navigate systems of privilege and racialized domination?
5. From an institutional standpoint the sociology of education needs to engage more deeply with the fields of critical race theory and critical pedagogy.

I conclude by suggesting that a greater emphasis on studies that employ the tools of the sociology of culture—developing theoretical arguments through in-depth, qualitative empirical research—will provide important insights into the sociology of education and race.[1] This means employing complex conceptions of culture that go beyond values and essentialized understandings of racial and ethnic groups. Mario Small, David Harding, and Michele Lamont (2010) highlight scholarship in the study of culture and poverty that moves beyond simplistic, sometimes racist "culture of poverty" explanations. They identify frames, repertoires, narratives, symbolic boundaries, cultural capital, and institutions as specific concepts that have been employed in important ways to engage questions of culture and inequality. Sociologists of education and race, too, should use these tools to illuminate important cultural processes that will provide insights beyond documenting inequality by race. In addition, the sociology of organizations can help inform our understanding of how racial meanings are produced in schools and universities.

For reasons of brevity, and because American sociology of education remains focused on the United States, I limit most of this discussion to race in the United States, where racial inequality is rooted in Native American genocide and displacement, African American slavery, and large waves of immigration, both legal and undocumented. In the conclusion I address the need for greater attention to non-US contexts.

A Changing United States

A slight majority of young children in the United States today are racial or ethnic minorities, compared to 38 percent of the total US population (US Census Bureau 2015). One driver of this shift is the fact that the United States is home to the largest number of immigrants in its history, with more than forty-one million immigrants residing in the country today, 13 percent of the US population (Migration Policy Institute n.d.-b). Among children, one in four has an immigrant parent, and about half of those children are immigrants themselves (Migration Policy Institute n.d.-a). Relatedly, the 2000 Census was the first time that African Americans were not the biggest minority group in the United States; they are now outnumbered by Latinos, so the black-white dichotomous way of treating race relations in prior years has shifted. Latinos already outnumber non-Hispanic whites in California (US Census Bureau n.d.). As a consequence, in California today and in many other parts of the country, "third-plus" generation Americans—those who are US-born with US-born parents—must contend with growing diversity in their communities and the changes that come with it (Jimenez 2017). Finally, one child in twenty identifies with two or more races, and that number is growing (Federal Interagency Forum on Child and Family Statistics 2015).

While the ethnic and racial composition in the United States has changed, so too have racial attitudes among ordinary Americans. Overtly racist attitudes in the United States have declined precipitously in the past half century, and overall, Americans are more likely to accept racial and ethnic differences, at least at a superficial level. For example, in the early 1940s nearly one-third of white Americans believed black and white children should attend separate schools; by the mid-1990s that percentage was less than 5 percent (Bobo, 2001). Relatedly, a cultural shift in recent decades has led to an embracing of multiculturalism and diversity. For example, today many school children celebrate the life of Martin Luther King and his moderate ideas about racial equality (but not many other, more radical racial justice leaders, or King's views on economic justice), and many urban schools host international nights that celebrate the cuisines and holidays of their students' countries of origin.

Shifts in immigrant incorporation are related to African American history. Richard Alba and Victor Nee (2003) have argued that the United States is more inclusive of ethnic and racial identities today than it was in the past. Alba and Nee redefine assimilation as a declining social distance between social groups, rather than minorities becoming part of a dominant white group as previously conceptualized. Overall, these changes stem in part from the victories of the African American–led civil rights movement, which highlighted the moral injustices of racial segregation and won legal protections for racial minorities, such as court-ordered school desegregation, the Civil Rights Act of 1964, the Voting Rights Act, and the Fair Housing Act. In addition, institutionalized supports for minorities developed in organizations, because segregation's moral illegitimacy was made clearer to many who had previously been opposed to integration. In other instances, organizations developed such supports to avoid legal vulnerability or racial unrest (Dobbin 2009; Stulberg and Chen 2014). Universities instituted affirmative action, and on many campuses student activists helped create minority students' groups, departments of African American and ethnic studies, and minority student centers (Rojas 2007; Stulberg and Chen 2014). Today, immigrants and their children benefit from many of these rights and institutions (Kasinitz, Mollenkopf, Waters, and Holdaway, 2008). Overall, then, the civil rights movement altered the legal and cultural context of race in the United States, changing the setting in which immigrants and their children navigate American society. Further, national legislation and Supreme Court decisions provided some legal recourse to ongoing racial discrimination and inequality.

Still, overt racism, brutal at times, continues as events of the recent past make very clear. Some argue that the criminal justice system in particular is "the new Jim Crow," given American mass incarceration and the disproportionate imprisonment of African Americans (M. Alexander 2010). Waters and Kasinitz (2015) argue that legal exclusion, whether for African Americans or undocumented immigrants, has come to define an individual's social life even more than race, at times excluding individuals from rights, civic participation, and humanity, as racial exclusion did prior to the civil rights era. In addition, civil rights legislation has led some to argue that we live in a colorblind era, even while racial injustice continues; some scholars describe this discourse of colorblindness amid racial inequality as colorblind racism (for example, see Bonilla-Silva 2003). Discourses of colorblindness allow some to view, for example, the disproportionate referral of black youth for special needs classrooms (Blanchett 2006), school suspension, and expulsion (Skiba, Michael, Nardo, and Peterson 2002) as being unrelated to race. Claims about colorblindness and a postracial society also ignore the ongoing impact of residential segregation and inequality, shaped by social policies of the past like redlining (Massey and Denton 1993). These policies led to today's urban poverty and racially stratified school experiences, which endure over generations (Sharkey 2013).

What does this racial landscape mean for the study of race and education in social life? I turn next to methods and scholarship that will allow researchers to understand the mechanisms of change and persistence.

New (and Old) Methods for New Times

While a complex portrait of immigrant and African American pathways to and through education is emerging from the scholarship on stratification, research investigating the mechanisms of inequality can deepen our understanding of the complex social processes in and out of schools that affect the lives of children and adult learners. Below I highlight recent work in the area of race and education that employs methods suitable for investigating mechanisms of racial change, meaning-making, and cultural and status processes. I highlight recent scholarship that employs two important but underutilized methodological strategies: selecting on the dependent variable, and explaining within-group differences. Taking seriously this work and work like it will refresh the field and enable it to say more about the relationships between race, ethnicity, education, and society.

Selecting on the Dependent Variable

In Statistics 101 we teach students never to select on the dependent variable, because this introduces selection bias. However, many important qualitative studies have done just that, providing deep insights into how uncommon but much-preferred outcomes emerge. These studies reveal the conditions and mechanisms through which, for example, youth succeed in low-performing schools, and college students develop cross-racial friendships that confront racial inequality. Indeed, textbooks of qualitative research often tell students to select cases for their uniqueness, rather than for their representativeness. In his groundbreaking *Global Ethnography*, Michael Burawoy (2009) argues for the "extended case method," whereby cases are chosen explicitly for their uniqueness rather than their generalizability. Similarly, Mario Small (2009) suggests that researchers choose cases or even interview respondents precisely for a set of characteristics that they hold.

Many insightful studies in the field of racial inequality in education select on the dependent variable to illuminate pathways to success. For example, Carla O'Connor (1997) and Dorinda Carter Andrews (Andrews 2009; D. Carter 2008) have written highly cited articles about African American high achievers, based on in-depth studies of only high achievers. They reveal the importance of particular forms of racial identity as well as family narratives about collective struggle in supporting those students' success. Robert Smith (2008) has done the same through an in-depth analysis of a single case study of a Mexican American student. Gloria Ladson-Billings's classic study of teachers who are successful in promoting their African American students' success, *The Dreamkeepers* (1994), provides an in-depth look at what those teachers do to promote their students' success. She finds that this work inevitably includes strengthening cultural identities and drawing from students' individual strengths. In higher education, Shaun Harper (2008) studies the experiences of high-achieving African American men; he describes, among other things, the ways in which they leverage social capital to further personal goals successfully. Together these studies of nonmodal occurrences demonstrate pathways beyond the structural barriers that prevent many from achieving success. As a consequence, beyond their theoretical implications the studies provide important insights into how to increase educational opportunities.

Other studies select on negative outcomes. For example, in his book *Punished*, Victor Rios (2011) reveals the troubled relationship between delinquent black and Latino youth and the criminal justice system, in which their criminality is assumed. Rios reveals, too, the spaces for resistance for the young men in that system.

Overall, the in-depth case study approaches of these studies allow the scholars to go deep, revealing complexity in the pathways to either desired or undesired outcomes. They all help us understand mechanisms through which students, teachers, schools, and even campus organizations sometimes promote positive experiences for minority groups. Some may quibble that these studies suffer from a lack of counterfactual evidence. As a scholarly community, we should respond by conducting further studies to test the insights of earlier studies that selected on the dependent variable, perhaps through quantitative measures of larger populations, rather than by dismissing the potentially groundbreaking insights the qualitative studies provide.

Beyond selecting on the dependent variable, studies that employ qualitative methods to look across groups can identify when behaviors, outlooks, and narratives are related to a particular group, and when they are not. For example, Karolyn Tyson's (2011; Tyson, Darity, and Castellino 2005) comparisons of schools with different racial makeups demonstrate that while black youth in integrated schools sometimes accuse high-achieving peers of "acting white"—a set of behavioral characteristics that includes styles of dress and comportment, but not achievement—white students, too, sometimes tease high-achieving white peers for "acting high and mighty." In addition, Tyson demonstrates how racialized tracking systems implicitly tell students that achievement is "white," because higher tracks are associated with white students, and lower tracks with minority students. This work reveals the mechanisms by which achievement sometimes is racialized as "white" even while almost all students, across race and achievement lines, aspire to succeed in school. Tyson shows that black students define achievement in racial terms in certain school contexts where most students in high tracks are white, but not in predominantly black schools, where high achievers are also black. In my own study of second-generation youth, I found that most youth attempted to gain status among their peers, but the markers of peer status differed across ethnic groups (Warikoo 2011). For example, while a taste for hip-hop gained status across groups, nonblack youth who exhibited stylistic markers of hip-hop were sometimes accused of "acting black," and consequently had to attenuate those styles or blend them with ethnic markers, such as gold necklaces in hip-hop style but with Sikh or Muslim religious symbols as the pendants. Both of these studies benefit from looking qualitatively across ethnic and racial groups.

Examining Variation within Groups

Studies of "the black-white test-score gap" (Jencks and Phillips 1998) emphasize the continued statistical significance of race after controlling for a host of measures, including socioeconomic status, parental education, and much more. These studies have been very important in raising the issue of racial inequality in education—in fact, they led Republican President

George Bush to include requirements that school accountability data be disaggregated by race (and disability and English as a second language status), to highlight when school achievement gains are stratified by race (U.S. Department of Education, 2002). However, in order to change those gaps and identify promising pathways to success for historically marginalized groups, we need to examine differences *within* race groups, rather than solely identifying trends along race lines. As with selecting on the dependent variable, looking at differences within groups highlights the mechanisms by which individual kids experience academic success, social status, and more.

In one such study, Nilda Flores-Gonzales (2002) demonstrates how a Chicago high school produces "school" and "street" identities among Puerto Rican students, leading those with "street" identities to drop out. Within-group differences need not be related to school completion or achievement. Carla Shedd's (2015) study of four predominantly minority Chicago high schools reveals how location and the distance between a high schooler's home and school can shape students' understandings of the police, justice, and equity. In her book on black and Latino young people living in public housing in Yonkers, New York, Prudence Carter (2005) outlines three orientations toward school that explain differences between her respondents' behaviors in school and their ethnic and racial identities. "Cultural mainstreamers," as Carter calls them, adhere to the dominant, adult-sponsored culture at school. "Noncompliant believers," on the other hand, want to succeed in school but do not always comply with the dominant school culture, sometimes landing them in trouble despite their desire for school success. Finally, "cultural straddlers" manage to both engage in behaviors and dispositions necessary to achieve school success while also maintaining strong ethnic or racial identities. Cultural straddlers are skilled in code-switching between the two social worlds in which they move. Similarly, my book on children of immigrants in diverse high schools illuminates the different ways in which kids perform "Balancing Acts" between school expectations and their desire for peer status (Warikoo, 2011). Some youth focus on their desire for peer status to the detriment of school success, despite their best intentions. Others have a more singular focus on academic success, and end up exhibiting cultural markers that mark them as low status among their peers, such as large backpacks, little socializing, and quiet demeanor. Finally, those successful in the balancing act manage to maintain peer status as well as school success. I illuminate in the book school rules, organizational aspects of the school, racialized expectations, and constraints that prevent more children from success in the balancing act.

Some scholars have examined variation by gender. For example, Nancy Lopez's (2002) study of Dominican students at a New York high school shows the different treatment young Dominican women and men experience in school. Young women are provided more flexibility with respect to school rules; their stereotype as teenaged mothers does not adversely affect teacher interactions as much as the stereotype of Dominican young men as dangerous and aggressive affects those young men. Teachers are consequently more strict and authoritarian with young men, with conflicts escalating more frequently and more dramatically between young men and school authorities. Simone Ispa-Landa (2013) studied the gendered experiences of black students participating in a busing program to bring urban minority youth to predominantly white, suburban schools. She finds that gendered constructions of beauty, masculinity, and athletics together led black boys to have an easier time integrating socially than their female peers (see also Holland, 2012).

Outside of schools, Maria Rendon's (2014) study of Latino young men living two high-poverty Los Angeles neighborhoods describes how some end up getting "caught up" in urban violence and as a result, end up dropping out of school, while others manage to avoid getting entangled in urban violence (see also Harding, 2010). Rendon identifies engaged fathers and attending a school outside of the neighborhood as protective factors that sometimes shielded young men from getting entangled in neighborhood violence.

Promising new work in higher education has unpacked differences in the experiences of students from nondominant backgrounds. For example, Maya Beasley (2011) demonstrates the role of university structures, including supports for minority students and the racial makeup of the student body, in her comparison of the career choices of black graduates of Berkeley and Stanford. Through her comparison of graduates of the two universities she is able to illuminate the social networks, campus activities, and campus experiences that shape career choices for graduates. Tony Jack's (2014) study of black students from low-income families attending an elite university reveals two kinds of experiences, marked by students' prior schooling. The "privileged poor" enter college with experiences in privileged high schools through magnet schools or through programs such as A Better Chance and scholarships to private schools, bringing to college insights and skills for navigating predominantly white institutions and social worlds. In contrast, the "doubly disadvantaged" come from urban high schools serving disadvantaged families, and consequently college is their first experiences with the academic demands, cultural expectations, and social world of privilege and majority white spaces, putting them at a greater disadvantage than their "privileged poor" peers. Smith and Moore (2000) identify factors shaping black students' feelings of inclusion in the black community on their college campuses.

The studies above examine variation within racial and ethnic groups. Some show variation along explicit lines such as gender and school-level characteristics, while others show that identity development, influenced by a variety of social and psychological experiences, as well as neighborhood effects, social networks, organizational processes, and institutional practices lead to different orientations among same-race students, even within the same local community and gender. The studies illuminate the pathways in and through education for students, which can inform teacher practices, leadership, and policymaking to improve school experiences for all children. While academic achievement is one aspect of these school experiences, identity development, social integration, and psychological well-being are some of the myriad other important domains addressed in this work.

Overall, the scholarship I have highlighted above demonstrates the kinds of research that will provide deeper understandings of the inner-workings of schools and universities, and of the impact of the new American racial landscape on education writ large. Future studies might select on the dependent variable or examine variation by, for example, studying variability in conceptions of race, and how those conceptions develop; studying high achievers across racial lines; examining differences in Asian American experiences in schools; and identifying measures of successful critical pedagogy and studying how they came about, what supports them, and their impact. I turn next to these and other new areas for inquiry, for which the tools of sociological analysis can uncover important insights.

New Topics for New Times

Numerous areas for fruitful inquiry in the sociology of education and race are emerging. Below I identify five areas of scholarship related to race and ethnicity that demonstrate the kinds of questions that will make for a broader, deeper sociology of education. These examples illustrate the complexity and rich insights to be gained by using qualitative methods, looking beyond academic outcomes, and borrowing tools from other fields, especially the sociology of culture and the sociology of organizations.

Schools, Universities, and the Production of Race

Schools are frequently taken for granted as the places in which children develop their understandings of the social world, including race. However, we do not yet know just how that racial meaning develops. How and when, for example, do schools reinforce or mute racial stereotypes as children develop their understandings of race? Sociologists of race and ethnicity have highlighted processes of racial formation (Cornell & Hartmann, 1998) and racial domination (Desmond & Emirbayer, 2009), and the racial attitudes literature has debated the origins of new racism (psychological, versus feelings of group threat, versus political views [see Sears, Hetts, Sidanius, and Bobo, 2000]). However, we need in-depth studies of the *production* of racial attitudes, whether in families, schools, or other institutions. This will require more ethnographic portraits of language and interaction in schools and in families, beyond survey measures of feelings of group threat or prejudice (see Skrentny, 2008 for a similar argument). Understanding individual meaning-making around race and the complex organizational influences on that meaning making will reveal how conceptions of race are reproduced, and, sometimes, how they shift.

Some new scholarship has started to develop this field. For example, Ann Morning (2011) has investigated how professors and undergraduates make meaning of what race *is* and what it *does*. Warikoo and de Novais (2015) analyze undergraduate understandings of the role that race plays in society, highlighting the influence of university cultures related to diversity on those understandings. In K–12 education, Amanda Lewis's (2003) ethnography of a predominantly white, suburban school illuminates how schools teach children about race, even while espousing a 'colorblind' stance (see also Carter, 2012; Pollock, 2004). Overall, the sociology of education can contribute important analyses of how educational organizations influence racial meaning-making, drawing tools from the sociology of organizations. This research is crucial if we want to identify the production of racial meanings that influence so much of social life in the United States.

Democracy and Meritocracy

The dual shifts over the past half century toward meritocracy and civil rights warrant further investigation. That is, how do organizations and ordinary people make sense of the quest for equality of opportunities alongside desires for meritocracy? How do these considerations shape conceptions of fairness, especially in the face of racially and socioeconomically unequal outcomes? Classic theories in sociology address the question of meritocracy. During the mid-twentieth century, Seymour Lipset and Reinhard Bendix (1992) argued that equal opportunity and mobility in fact characterize industrial societies. This mobility rests on a meritocracy to mete out rewards. Later, Daniel Bell (1973) described a new "post-industrial society" in which a system of social rewards based on merit and achievement rather than inherited status would allow leaders to solve the most pressing social problems. Max Weber (1968) further envisioned meritocracy as a tool for promoting equity and justice in modern societies. At the same time, during the latter half of the twentieth century, more white Americans began to recognize ongoing injustices toward African Americans as illegitimate. Racial discrimination—both interpersonal and structural—called into question the proper functioning of American meritocracy. Of course, racial oppression has characterized black/white relations for centuries. However, it was not until the latter half of the twentieth century that a majority of whites began to question this systematic exclusion and oppression. How do the institutionalized systems of meritocracy and mobility, which undergird American ideology about equal opportunity and justice, respond to the now recognized exclusion of African Americans from the American dream? More recently, renewed attention to antiblack violence has led more whites to recognize ongoing racial biases, thus calling the rhetoric of colorblindness into question. What new forms of democracy will ensue, given this recognition?

The most radical critiques of racial inequality in education related to merit call for the dismantling of merit-based systems altogether, in the belief that they are inherently undemocratic. This position was victorious at the City University of New York (CUNY) amid battles over admissions policies, and it led in 1970 to open admissions (Reuben 2001). A different solution to African American exclusion was to create mechanisms for (limited) social mobility among African Americans. This is what most selective colleges did. Unlike CUNY, they simply shifted their definitions of merit to accommodate concerns over racial inequality most commonly through affirmative action, thus maintaining the elite systems and restoring their legitimacy (Grodsky 2007; Reuben 2001).

Relatedly, after the 1960s, rationales for affirmative action shifted. Ellen Berrey (2015) demonstrates how universities and other institutional contexts developed understandings of race that centered on "diversity," with implications for the cost of that framing to advancing racial justice. In other words, in order to make affirmative action palatable to the old elites, it was increasingly couched as something beneficial to whites due to the inclusion of diverse perspectives, rather than as a form of redress in the name of racial justice and maintainance of the legitimacy of meritocracy. Affirmative action was no longer needed to restore faith in the American ideology of equal opportunity, now that civil rights legislation mandated equal opportunities and whites could adopt a "colorblind" ideology (see also Gallagher 2008; Moore and Bell 2011). All of this has happened while admission rates to elite colleges have declined steadily; today, admissions rates to top colleges in the US are well under 10 percent of those who even dare to apply—a fact highlighted frequently by universities, which implicitly suggest that those low admissions rates are measures of status and a flourishing meritocracy.

New research should analyze the implications of this relationship between race and meritocracy today. The literature in higher education on campus racial climate has examined the impact of affirmative action on minority and white students alike, seeking to understand the benefits of diversity on everything from students' racial attitudes to academic performance (see Harper and Hurtado 2007 for a review). Still, scholars have neglected the ensuing cultural processes. How, for example, do student understandings of affirmative action shape racial dynamics on campus? How do they shape conceptions of justice and merit? (see Warikoo 2016). How do schools promote the notion of opportunity and mobility to children for whom school inequality and racial segregation are obvious? These are just some of the important unanswered questions related to meritocracy and democracy that new scholarship in the sociology of education should address.

Asian American Educational Success

What happens when a minority group is more successful than the dominant majority group? Sociologists have much to contribute to public discussions about Asian American educational success. Asian Americans are overrepresented at many elite public schools that admit students on the basis of a standardized test, such as New York City's Stuyvesant High School, which is 74 percent Asian. The same is true at selective colleges, where Asian Americans represent 14 percent of the student body[2] as compared to 5.6 percent of the US population (Espenshade, Radford, and Chung 2009; US Census Bureau n.d.). Despite their overrepresentation, Asian American students' SAT scores are higher on average than those of their white peers at the same universities (Espenshade et al. 2009). Asian American excellence appears in academic extracurricular activities as well. For example, Indian Americans have dominated the national spelling bee in recent years (Basu 2015). These gains lead to the important empirical question of what happens when a minority group outperforms the majority group. Does the stratification system change, or does the minority group redefine the dominant culture? Asian Americans in traditionally white, advantaged communities may sometimes be perceived as changing local cultures so that academic achievement is marked as "Asian" and whiteness is marked as "slacker" (Jimenez and Horowitz 2013). Relatedly, how does Asian American success shape whites' definitions of merit and success? Frank Samson (2013) has demonstrated that when whites are reminded of Asian Americans' high GPAs, they downplay the importance of GPA in selective college admissions; on the other hand, when they are reminded of black Americans' low GPAs, they express strong belief in the use of GPA to judge applicants. This suggests that as Asian American successes continue, whites may shift their definitions of merit and success to maintain white privilege. Some have critiqued elite college admissions for supposed Asian American quotas, akin to the Jewish quotas of the 1920s, which were achieved by shifting the criteria for "merit" in admissions (Karabel 2005). All of this suggests that Asian American successes are beginning to chip away at white privilege; and as they do so, whites may find other ways to maintain their privileges and "group position" (Blumer 1958).

In addition to white responses to Asian American success, we need more studies of Asian Americans. In a study that goes well beyond the "model minority" debate, Jennifer Lee and Min Zhou (2015) show how Asian Americans' unique "success frames" play a role in their high achievement. Lee and Zhou (2015) also discuss Asian Americans' linking of Asian identity with certain forms of school success, with negative repercussions for Asian youth who cannot meet the high standards of success expected of Asian youth. Relatedly, worrisome mental health issues have emerged among Asian Americans (Bachman, O'Malley, Freedman-Doan, Trzesniewski, and Donnellan 2011; US Department of Health and Human Services Office of Minority Health n.d.). Sociologists of education should investigate social processes in schools and families explaining this growth.

Elites, Race, and Education

Beyond Asian Americans, greater attention to social processes among the advantaged in education is needed (see also Khan 2012). Missing from the emerging literature on the sociology of elites are, as Khan (2012) highlights, studies of "new" elites—that is, elite racial minorities, elite women, and elites of other underrepresented groups. In addition, how does the changing face of elites change the status processes and cultural practices that go hand-in-hand with being elite? Does an expanded elite, for example, change the nature of elite organizations to make them more inclusive and effective? Studies of new elites will allow scholars to better understand whether and how processes of status legitimation and racial identity, among others, change when women, individuals from working-class families, and racial minorities join the ranks of elites. Writing about students of color attending an elite boarding school, Gaztambide-Fernandez and DiAquoi (2010) highlight their experiences of what DuBois long ago labeled "double-consciousness": the students are "in, but not of" their elite school. Other work mentioned above contributes to this question, including Ispa-Landa's (2013) work on minority youth bused to wealthy suburban districts, and Jack's work on black students attending elite universities (2014). Beyond formal education, Lauren Rivera's (2015) study of elite firms' hiring processes shows that black and Latino candidates are often judged for lacking "polish," and are otherwise frequently bypassed based on subjective dislike on the part of white interviewers.

Relatedly, "omnivorous" tastes, including those related to minority taste cultures, have increasingly become markers of high status (Peterson and Kern 1996). This intervention into Pierre Bourdieu's theory of culture and social reproduction requires more work on the resulting cultural processes. That is, while scholarship in the sociology of culture has documented the taste preferences of elites, we know less about the effects of those taste preferences, and what role racialized understandings—for example, rap and hip-hop's identities as black—play in those effects. In addition, we need more work to illuminate not only how this shift changes racialized conceptions of status, but also how those shifts change the social world. For example, how do youth taste preferences change over time and across class lines? Where do changes start—among elites, among non-elites, or among minority groups overall? In addition, when multiculturalism is accepted as a moral and cultural framework for status (Voyer 2011), schools serving both elite and non-elite children attempt to school children in diversity, often through superficial "international potlucks" and related events. Sociologists of race and education should investigate this shift, and the meaning that children make of this understanding of diversity. Overall, shifting perspectives on the importance of racial diversity and its benefits to whites and minorities alike (Berrey 2015), along with unique institutional supports for diversity on college campuses in particular (Warikoo 2016), influence students in schools and universities in new ways that a new sociology of education can mine for a deeper understanding of the changing racial landscape in the United States.

Critical Race Theory

Finally, sociologists of education need to contend more deeply with scholarship that engages critical race theory (CRT), which emphasizes how racism is embedded in institutions in ways that are often invisible at first. Based on scholarly engagement as measured by citations, CRT is central to the sociology of education in the domain of race. A Google Scholar search of "sociology of education and race" yields articles related to three main topics: (1) introductions or reviews of the field, (2) work on racial stratification that employs quantitative data, and (3) work explicitly grounded in CRT. However, searches in the journal *Sociology of Education* for "critical race theory" and "critical theory" yield no results.[3] This suggests that mainstream scholarly engagement with CRT is strong, even if the flagship journal, as a gatekeeper, has not embraced this area.[4]

In education CRT scholars illuminate the ways in which schools perpetuate ideologies of colorblindness despite institutionalized racism embedded in schools (for a review, see Dixson and Rousseau 2005; for early examples, see Parker, Deyhle, and Villenas 1999). For example, CRT scholars argue that overtly race-neutral school funding policies and tracking have harmed African American youth and led to racially unequal access to high-quality teaching (Ladson-Billings and Tate IV 1995; Solorzano and Ornelas 2004). CRT critiques liberal individualist perspectives that emphasize ostensible equality of opportunities while ignoring unequal outcomes. CRT scholars also point out that gestures toward "multicultural education" do not address the institutionalized racism embedded in US society (Jay 2003; Ladson-Billings and Tate IV 1995). In higher education, Rashawn Ray (2012) finds that the organizational structure and "normative institutional arrangements" of predominantly white universities leaves white fraternities more able to avoid accountability for transgressions than are black fraternities; they also shape members' engagement with women (Ray and Rosow 2010). Critical race scholars have also critiqued the discourse of "diversity" as the rationale for affirmative action, for ignoring ongoing racial disparities, and for ignoring the rationale of restorative justice (Moore and Bell 2011; Yosso, Parker, Solarzano, and Lynn 2004).

Shaun Harper and his colleagues (2009) similarly push the field of higher education and race to employ CRT in analyzing access and equity. Overall, scholarship that engages CRT has grown in prominence, especially among students eager to understand ongoing racial disparity in US education. Empirical work that operationalizes CRT and tests its explanations empirically is a promising area of scholarship; perhaps it is this empirical analysis that will allow CRT to become more central in the sociology of race and education as defined by the flagship journal.

A group of scholars who would align themselves with the perspectives of CRT, even if they are more focused on *action*, are those who write about "critical pedagogy." These scholars, inspired by Paulo Freire's *Pedagogy of the Oppressed*, envision education that teaches children to learn about and engage with the world not only as it is, but also as it might become (for example, see Duncan-Andrade and Morrell 2008; Giroux 1983; Sleeter and McLaren 1995). Henry Giroux (1983) was an early proponent of critical pedagogy, placing it between an understanding of social reproduction, which seemed to lack room for building capacity in children for social change, and pluralist visions for education, which deemphasized power relations. Perhaps just as the civil rights movement and its aftermath in the 1960s fueled scholarly interest in social change and the sociology of social movements, so too might the field of critical pedagogy grow to occupy a corner of the sociology of education that outlines when and how children learn to become agents of social change through education. This understanding will require creative empirical scholarship that investigates the forms that critical pedagogy takes, its differences from "traditional" teaching, how and when it emerges, and its effects on children. This is an important and promising area for new research.

Conclusion

Above I have highlighted innovative work in the sociology of education and race that addresses growing diversity and the changed racial landscape in the United States, and I have further identified areas for deeper investigation. Overall, the sociology of culture has much to offer to the field of sociology of education, just as it has done for the study of poverty (see also Skrentny 2008; Small et al. 2010). When Mario Small, Michele Lamont, and David Harding (2010) wrote their review of how the tools of cultural sociology have been and can further be leveraged in the study of poverty, they brought their insights to Capitol Hill in an effort to reach policymakers. A similar effort in the study of racial inequality in education, corralling the tools of cultural sociology, would be fruitful.

In order to do this, we need to define the parameters of rigorous scholarship. Most of the work I have highlighted is qualitative, but there is less agreement among scholars about how to evaluate qualitative research. Social psychologists tell us that when criteria of evaluation are unclear, implicit biases tend to have a greater impact on judgement (Olson and Fazio 2009).

Given the relatively low status of qualitative studies compared to those that employ econometric tools, this is cause for concern. In order to attenuate those biases, we need shared understandings of high quality qualitative scholarship. Ten years ago, Michele Lamont and colleagues discussed the construction of interdisciplinary standards for qualitative research (Lamont and White 2005). Perhaps it is time to revisit that discussion.

Overall, sociologists of education should pay closer heed to qualitative studies that reveal the richness and complexity of race in society, rather than sticking too close to the historic bread and butter of our field, the study of stratification. Further, there is much to be gained by turning outward, in terms of both disciplinary boundaries as well as national boundaries. This means learning from rich qualitative studies of schools and youth by scholars of education in the United States who do not identify as sociologists. For example, see work cited above by young scholars who are trained and are teaching in education, including D. Carter and Gaztambide-Fernandez, as well as by others who are more established, such as Sara Lawrence-Lightfoot (1983) and Lois Weis (2014).

Looking outside of the United States allows us to see the impact of our racial and immigration history, along with related legal issues, bringing into full relief the specific qualities of the United States that matter (for some examples, see C. Alexander 2000; Dehanas 2013; Fong 2011; Hall 2002; Teeger 2015). The British sociologist Paul Willis's Learning to Labour (1977), a qualitative study of working-class boys in England, appears on many, perhaps most syllabi in the sociology of education; and yet, more recent work located in places outside the United States is much less common on those same syllabi. Questions related to the new topics I highlighted earlier that will benefit from comparative studies include: How do histories of enslavement, colonialism, and migration, along with political economies and laws, shape racial meaning, especially as it is produced in schools and universities? When and for which kinds of groups does affirmative action in higher education arise, and how does it get institutionalized or contested? What kinds of extracurricular preparation exist in China and India to improve students' chances of passing university entrance exams or of gaining entrée into top Western universities, and what are the experiences and pathways of students through those mechanisms? Beyond single-case studies, qualitative cross-national comparative research is promising for its ability to both provide a reference group while also addressing the complexity of sociocultural processes (for example, see P. L. Carter 2012; Warikoo 2011; Warikoo 2016). While comparative qualitative research is expensive and time-consuming, it does have a long tradition in education (see, for example, Tobin, Wu, and Davidson 1989; Whiting, Whiting, and Longabaugh 1975).

Finally, while many of the scholars cited above are young scholars of color, the general lack of racial diversity in the field of sociology of education, especially when compared to the field of education, may be a symptom of the emphasis on documentation of disparity rather than on documentation of mechanisms that can help us see a path forward. The popular but unrecognized field of CRT highlights the importance of voicing the perspectives of marginalized groups, who historically have not been the writers of history or the documenters of our social world (Dixson and Rousseau 2005; Solórzano and Yosso 2002). It also suggests that activism should be a central part of the work of scholars. While a new sociology of education may not fully embrace this direction, it must contend with the calls for greater inclusion regarding who does research, what they research, what they do with that research, and what kinds of research get labeled as "rigorous."

Notes

1. Interestingly, the one theoretical debate that Steven Brint finds in his review of ten years of articles in the journal *Sociology of Education* is the debate about anthropologist John Ogbu's theory of oppositional culture, a cultural theory about race and school success. Each of the articles on oppositional culture critiques the theory in some way, as have scholars in other venues (e.g., P. Carter 2005; Harris 2011; Warikoo 2011). While the debate is indeed theoretical and adjudicated through empirical studies, many have suggested that Ogbu's theory of culture is relatively weak. As the field moves ahead, scholars should identify new questions related to race, ethnicity, culture, and education that go beyond the oppositional culture debate.
2. Class of 2001. At Ivy League universities, Asian American enrollment has remained somewhat consistent since then (Unz 2012).
3. This issue is not endemic to the sociology of education. While two recent presidents of the American Sociological Association (Patricia Hill Collins and Evelyn Nananko), voted by the organization's full membership, have been scholars affiliated with critical theory, just *one* article in its flagship journal has referenced critical theory (J. M. Bell and Hartmann 2007).
4. Mehta and Davies discuss the historical roots of this disconnect in chapter 1.

References

Alba, R. D., and V. Nee. 2003. *Remaking the American Mainstream: Assimilation and Contemporary Immigration*. Cambridge, MA: Harvard University Press.
Alexander, C. 2000. *The Asian Gang: Ethnicity, Identity, Masculinity*. Oxford, UK: Berg.
Alexander, M. 2010. *The New Jim Crow: Mass Incarceration in the Age of Colorblindness*. New York: The New Press.

Andrews, D. J. C. 2009. "The Construction of Black High-Achiever Identities in a Predominantly White High School." *Anthropology & Education Quarterly* 40 (3): 297–317.

Bachman, J. G., P. M. O'Malley, P. Freedman-Doan, K. H. Trzesniewski, and M. B. Donnellan 2011. "Adolescent Self-Esteem: Differences by Race/Ethnicity, Gender, and Age." *Self and Identity: The Journal of the International Society for Self and Identity* 10 (4): 445–473.

Basu, M. 2015. "Why Indian-Americans Win Spelling Bees: P-R-A-C-T-I-C-E." Accessed July 14, 2015, at http://www.cnn.com/2015/05/29/us/spelling-bee-south-asians/.

Beasley, M. A. 2011. *Opting Out: Losing the Potential of America's Young Black Elite*. Chicago: University of Chicago Press.

Bell, D. 1973. *The Coming of Post-Industrial Society: A Venture in Social Forecasting*. New York: Basic Books.

Bell, J. M., and Hartmann, D. 2007. "Diversity in Everyday Discourse: The Cultural Ambiguities and Consequences of 'Happy Talk.'" *American Sociological Review* 72 (6): 895–914.

Berrey, E. 2015. *The Enigma of Diversity: The Language of Race and the Limits of Racial Justice*. Chicago: University of Chicago Press.

Blanchett, W. J. 2006. "Disproportionate Representation of African American Students in Special Education: Acknowledging the Role of White Privilege and Racism." *Educational Researcher* 35 (6): 24–28.

Blumer, H. 1958. "Race Prejudice as a Sense of Group Position." *Pacific Sociological Review* 1 (1): 3–7.

Bobo, L. 2001. "Racial Attitudes and Relations at the Close of the Twentieth Century." In *America Becoming: Racial Trends and Their Consequences*, Vol. I, edited by N. Smelser, W. J. Wilson, and F. Mitchell, 264–301. Washington: National Academy Press.

Bonilla-Silva, E. 2003. *Racism without Racists: Color-Blind Racism and the Persistence of Racial Inequality in the United States*. Lanham, MD: Rowman & Littlefield.

Burawoy, M. 2009. *The Extended Case Method: Four Countries, Four Decades, Four Great Transformations, and One Theoretical Tradition*. Oakland: University of California Press.

Carter, D. 2008. "Achievement as Resistance: The Development of a Critical Race Achievement Ideology among Black Achievers." *Harvard Educational Review* 78 (3): 466–497.

Carter, P. 2005. *Keepin' It Real: School Success beyond Black and White*. New York: Oxford University Press.

Carter, P. L. 2012. *Stubborn Roots: Race, Culture, and Inequality in U.S. and South African Schools*. New York: Oxford University Press.

Cornell, S. E., and D. Hartmann. 1998. *Ethnicity and Race: Making Identities in a Changing World*. Thousand Oaks, CA: Pine Forge Press.

Dehanas, D. N. 2013. "Keepin' It Real: London Youth Hip Hop as an Authentic Performance of Belief." *Journal of Contemporary Religion* 28 (2): 295–308.

Desmond, M., and M. Emirbayer. 2009. "What Is Racial Domination?" *Du Bois Review: Social Science Research on Race* 6 (02): 335–355.

Dixson, A. D., and C. K. Rousseau. 2005. "And We Are Still Not Saved: Critical Race Theory in Education Ten Years Later." *Race Ethnicity and Education* 8 (1): 7–27.

Dobbin, F. 2009. *Inventing Equal Opportunity*. Princeton, NJ: Princeton University Press.

Duncan-Andrade, J. M. R., and E. Morrell. 2008. *The Art of Critical Pedagogy: Possibilities for Moving from Theory to Practice in Urban Schools*. New York: Peter Lang.

Espenshade, T. J., A. W. Radford, and C. Y. Chung. 2009. *No Longer Separate, Not Yet Equal: Race and Class in Elite College Admission and Campus Life*. Princeton, NJ: Princeton University Press.

Federal Interagency Forum on Child and Family Statistics. 2015. "America's Children: Key

National Indicators of Well-Being," table POP3. Accessed 14 July 2015 at http://www.childstats.gov/pdf/ac2015/ac_15.pdf.

Flores-González, N. 2002. *School Kids/Street Kids: Identity Development in Latino Students*. New York: Teachers College Press.

Fong, V. L. 2011. *Paradise Redefined: Transnational Chinese Students and the Quest for Flexible Citizenship in the Developed World*. Stanford, CA: Stanford University Press.

Gallagher, C. A. 2008. "'The End of Racism' as the New Doxa." In *White Logic, White Methods: Racism and Methodology*, edited by T. Zuberi and E. Bonilla-Silva, 163–178. New York: Rowman and Littlefield.

Gaztambide-Fernandez, R. A., and R. DiAquoi. 2010. "A Part and Apart: Students of Color Negotiating Boundaries at an Elite Boarding School." In *Educating Elites: Class Privilege and Educational Advantage*, edited by A. Howard and R. A. Gaztambide-Fernandez, 55–78. New York: Rowman & Littlefield Education.

Giroux, H. A. 1983. *Theory and Resistance in Education: A Pedagogy for the Opposition*. London: Heinemann Education Books.

Grodsky, E. 2007. "Compensatory Sponsorship in Higher Education." *American Journal of Sociology* 112 (6): 1662–1712.

Hall, K. 2002. *Lives in Translation: Sikh Youth as British Citizens*. Philadelphia: University of Pennsylvania Press.

Harding, D. J. 2010. *Living the Drama: Community, Conflict, and Culture among Inner-City Boys*. Chicago: University of Chicago Press.

Harper, S. R. 2008. "Realizing the Intended Outcomes of Brown: High-Achieving African American Male Undergraduates and Social Capital." *American Behavioral Scientist* 51 (7): 1030–1053.

Harper, S. R., and S. Hurtado. 2007. "Nine Themes in Campus Racial Climates and Implications for Institutional Transformation." *New Directions for Student Services* 120:7–24.

Harper, S. R., L. D. Patton, and O. S. Wooden. 2009. "Access and Equity for African American Students in Higher Education: A Critical Race Historical Analysis of Policy Efforts." *Journal of Higher Education* 80 (4): 389–414.

Harris, A. L. 2011. *Kids Don't Want to Fail: Oppositional Culture and Black Students' Academic Achievement*. Cambridge, MA: Harvard University Press.

Holland, M. M. 2012. "Only Here for the Day: The Social Integration of Minority Students at a Majority White High School." *Sociology of Education* 85 (2): 101–120.

Ispa-Landa, S. 2013. "Gender, Race, and Justifications for Group Exclusion: Urban Black Students Bussed to Affluent Suburban Schools." *Sociology of Education* 86 (3): 218–233.

Jack, A. A. 2014. "Culture Shock Revisited: The Social and Cultural Contingencies to Class Marginality." *Sociological Forum* 29 (2): 453–475.

Jay, M. 2003. "Critical Race Theory, Multicultural Education, and the Hidden Curriculum of Hegemony." *Multicultural Perspectives* 5 (4): 3–9.

Jencks, C. and M. Phillips. 1998. *The Black-White Test Score Gap*. Washington: Brookings Institution Press.

Jimenez, T. 2017. *The Other Side of Assimilation: How Immigrants Are Changing American Life*. Berkeley: University of California Press.

Jimenez, T., and A. L. Horowitz. 2013. "When White Is Just Alright: How Immigrants Redefine Achievement and Reconfigure the Ethnoracial Hierarchy." *American Sociological Review* 78 (5): 849–871.

Karabel, J. 2005. *The Chosen: The Hidden History of Admission and Exclusion at Harvard, Yale, and Princeton*. Boston: Houghton Mifflin.

Kasinitz, P., J. H. Mollenkopf, M. C. Waters, and J. Holdaway. 2008. *Inheriting the City: The Children of Immigrants Come of Age*. Cambridge, MA: Harvard University Press.

Khan, S. R. 2012. "The Sociology of Elites." *Annual Review of Sociology* 38 (1): 361–377.

Kim, C., D. J. Losen, and D. Hewitt. 2010. *The School to Prison Pipeline: Structuring Legal Reform*. New York: New York University.

Ladson-Billings, G. 1994. *The Dreamkeepers: Successful Teachers of African American Children*. First edition. San Francisco: Jossey-Bass Publishers.

Ladson-Billings, G., and W. F. Tate. 1995. "Toward a Critical Race Theory of Education." *Teachers College Record* 97 (1): 47–68.

Lamont, M., and P. White. 2005. "Workshop on Interdisciplinary Standards for Systematic Qualitative Research." National Science Foundation. Accessed 14 July 2015 at http://www.nsf.gov/sbe/ses/soc/ISSQR_workshop_rpt.pdf.

Lawrence-Lightfoot, S. 1983. *The Good High School: Portraits of Character and Culture*. New York: Basic Books.

Lee, J., and M. Zhou. 2015. *The Asian American Achievement Paradox*. New York: Russell Sage Foundation.

Lewis, A. E. 2003. *Race in the Schoolyard: Negotiating the Color Line in Classrooms and Communities*. New Brunswick, NJ: Rutgers University Press.

Lipset, S. M., and R. Bendix. 1992. *Social Mobility in Industrial Society*. New Brunswick, NJ: Transaction Publishers.

López, N. 2002. *Hopeful Girls, Troubled Boys: Race and Gender Disparity in Urban Education*. New York: Routledge.

Massey, D. S., and N. A. Denton. 1993. *American Apartheid: Segregation and the Making of the Underclass*. Cambridge, MA: Harvard University Press.

Migration Policy Institute. N.d.-a. "Children in U.S. Immigrant Families. U.S. Immigration Trends." Accessed 14 July 2015 at http://migrationpolicy.org/programs/data-hub/us-immigration-trends#history.

———. N.d.-b. "U.S. Immigrant Population and Share over Time, 1850–Present: U.S. Immigration Trends." Accessed 14 July 2015 at http://migrationpolicy.org/programs/data-hub/us-immigration-trends#history.

Moore, W. L., and J. M. Bell. 2011. "Maneuvers of Whiteness: 'Diversity' as a Mechanism of Retrenchment in the Affirmative Action Discourse." *Critical Sociology* 37 (5): 597–613.

Morning, A. J. 2011. *The Nature of Race: How Scientists Think and Teach about Human Difference*. Berkeley: University of California Press.

O'Connor, C. 1997. "Dispositions toward (Collective) Struggle and Educational Resilience in the Inner City: A Case Analysis of Six African-American High School Students." *American Educational Research Journal* 34 (4): 593–629.

Olson, M. A., and R. H. Fazio. 2009. "Implicit and Explicit Measures of Attitudes: The Perspective of the MODE Model." In *Attitudes: Insights from the New Implicit Measures*, edited by R. E. Petty, R. H. Fazio, and P. Briñol, 19–63. New York: Psychology.

Parker, L., D. Deyhle, and S. A. Villenas. 1999. *Race Is—Race Isn't: Critical Race Theory and Qualitative Studies in Education*. Boulder, CO: Westview Press.

Peterson, R., and R. Kern. 1996. "Changing Highbrow Taste: From Snob to Omnivore." *American Sociological Review* 61 (5): 900–917.

Pollock, M. 2004. *Colormute: Race Talk Dilemmas in an American School*. Princeton, NJ: Princeton University Press.

Ray, R. 2012. "Fraternity Life at Predominantly White Universities in the US: The Saliency of Race." *Ethnic and Racial Studies* 36 (2): 320–336.

Ray, R., and J. A. Rosow. 2010. "Getting Off and Getting Intimate: How Normative Institutional Arrangements Structure Black and White Fraternity Men's Approaches toward Women." *Men and Masculinities* 12 (5): 523–546.

Rendón, M. G. 2014. "'Caught Up': How Urban Violence and Peer Ties Contribute to High School Noncompletion." *Social Problems* 61 (1): 61–82.

Reuben, J. A. 2001. "Merit, Mission, and Minority Students: A History of Debates over Special Admissions Programs." In *A Faithful Mirror: Reflections on the College Board and Education in America*, edited by M. C. Johanek, 195–243. New York: The College Board.

Rios, V. M. 2011. *Punished: Policing the Lives of Black and Latino Boys*. New York: New York University Press.

Rivera, L. A. 2015. *Pedigree: How Elite Students Get Elite Jobs*. Princeton, NJ: Princeton University Press.

Rojas, F. 2007. *From Black Power to Black Studies: How a Radical Social Movement became an Academic Discipline*. Baltimore: Johns Hopkins University Press.

Samson, F. L. 2013. "Multiple Group Threat and Malleable White Attitudes towards Academic Merit." *Du Bois Review: Social Science Research on Race* 10 (1): 233–260.

Schuman, H., C. Steeh, and L. Bobo. 1997. *Racial Attitudes in America: Trends and Interpretations*, Revised edition. Cambridge, MA: Harvard University Press.

Sears, D. O., J. Hetts, J. Sidanius, and L. Bobo. 2000. "Race in American Politics: Framing the Debates." In *Racialized Politics: The Debate about Racism in America*, edited by D. O. Sears, J. Sidanius, and L. Bobo, 1–43. Chicago: University of Chicago Press.

Sharkey, P. 2013. *Stuck in Place: Urban Neighborhoods and the End of Progress toward Racial Equality*. Chicago: University of Chicago Press.

Shedd, C. 2015. *Unequal City: Race, Schools, and Perceptions of Injustice*. New York: Russell Sage Foundation.

Skiba, R., R. Michael, A. Nardo, and R. Peterson. 2002. "The Color of Discipline: Sources of Racial and Gender Disproportionality in School Punishment." *Urban Review* 34 (4): 317–342.

Skrentny, J. D. 2008. "Culture and Race/Ethnicity: Bolder, Deeper, and Broader." *Annals of the American Academy of Political and Social Science* 619:59–77.

Sleeter, C. E., and P. McLaren. 1995. *Multicultural Education, Critical Pedagogy, and the Politics of Difference*. Albany: State University of New York Press.

Small, M. L. 2009. "'How Many Cases Do I Need?': On Science and the Logic of Case Selection in Field-Based Research." *Ethnography* 10 (1): 5–38.

Small, M. L., D. J. Harding, and M. Lamont. 2010. "Reconsidering Culture and Poverty." *Annals of the American Academy of Political and Social Science* 629 (1): 6–27.

Smith, R. C. 2008. "Horatio Alger Lives in Brooklyn: Extrafamily Support, Intrafamily Dynamics, and Socially Neutral Operating Identities in Exceptional Mobility among Children of Mexican Immigrants." *Annals of the American Academy of Political and Social Science* 620 (1): 270–290.

Smith, S. S., and M. R. Moore. 2000. "Intraracial Diversity and Relations among African-Americans: Closeness among Black Students at a Predominantly White University." *American Journal of Sociology* 106 (1): 1–39.

Solorzano, D. G., and A. Ornelas. 2004. "A Critical Race Analysis of Latina/o and African American Advanced Placement Enrollment in Public High Schools." *High School Journal* 87 (3): 15–26.

Solórzano, D. G., and T. J. Yosso. 2002. "Critical Race Methodology: Counter-Storytelling as an Analytical Framework for Education Research." *Qualitative Inquiry* 8 (1): 23–44.

Stulberg, L. M., and A. S. Chen. 2014. "The Origins of Race-Conscious Affirmative Action in Undergraduate Admissions: A Comparative Analysis of Institutional Change in Higher Education." *Sociology of Education* 87 (1): 36–52.

Teeger, C. 2015. "Ruptures in the Rainbow Nation: How Desegregated South African Schools Deal with Interpersonal and Structural Racism." *Sociology of Education* 88 (3): 226–243.

Tobin, J. J., D. Y. H. Wu, and D. H. Davidson. 1989. *Preschool in Three Cultures: Japan, China, and the United States*. New Haven: Yale University Press.

Tyson, K. 2011. *Integration Interrupted: Tracking, Black Students, and Acting White after Brown*. New York: Oxford University Press.

Tyson, K., J. W Darity, and D. Castellino. 2005. "It's Not 'a Black Thing': Understanding the Burden of Acting White and Other Dilemmas of High Achievement." *American Sociological Review* 70 (4): 582–605.

Unz, R. 2012. "The Myth of American Meritocracy." *American Conservative* 11:14–45.

US Census Bureau. N.d. "QuickFacts." Accessed 17 November 2016 at https://www.census.gov/quickfacts/table/PST045215/06,00.

US Census Bureau. 2015. "A More Diverse Nation." Accessed 14 July 2015 at http://census.gov/content/dam/Census/newsroom/releases/2015/cb15-113_graphic.jpg.

US Department of Education. 2002. "No Child Left Behind Act of 2001." Accessed 14 July 2015 at http://www2.ed.gov/policy/elsec/leg/esea02/107-110.pdf.

US Department of Health and Human Services Office of Minority Health. N.d. "Mental Health and Asian Americans: Minority Population Profiles." Accessed 22 May 2015 at http://minorityhealth.hhs.gov/omh/browse.aspx?lvl=4&lvlID=54.

Voyer, A. 2011. *Disciplined to Diversity: Learning the Language of Multiculturalism. Ethnic & Racial Studies* 34 (11): 1874–1893.

Warikoo, N. 2011. *Balancing Acts: Youth Culture in the Global City*. Berkeley, CA: University of California Press.

———. 2016. *The Diversity Bargain: And Other Dilemmas of Race, Admissions, and Meritocracy at Elite Universities*. Chicago: University of Chicago Press.

Warikoo, N. K., and J. de Novais. 2015. "Color-Blindness and Diversity: Race Frames and Their Consequences for White Undergraduates at Elite US Universities." *Ethnic and Racial Studies* 38 (6): 860–876.

Waters, M. C, and P. Kasinitz. 2015. "The War on Crime and the War on Immigrants: Racial and Legal Exclusion in 21st Century United States." In *Fear, Anxiety and National Identity: Immigration and Belonging in North America and Europe*, edited by N. Foner and P. Simon. New York: Russell Sage.

Weber, M. 1968. *Economy and Society: An Outline of Interpretive Sociology*. New York: Bedminster Press.

Weis, L., Cipollone, K., & Jenkins, H. (2014). *Class Warfare: Class, Race, and College Admissions in Top-Tier Secondary Schools*.

Whiting, B. B., J. W. M. Whiting, and R. Longabaugh. 1975. *Children of Six Cultures: A Psycho-Cultural Analysis*. Cambridge, MA: Harvard University Press.

Willis, P. E. 1977. *Learning to Labour: How Working Class Kids Get Working Class Jobs*. Farnborough, UK: Saxon House.

Yosso, T. J., L. Parker, D. G. Solarzano, and M. Lynn. 2004. "From Jim Crow to Affirmative Action and Back Again: A Critical Race Discussion of Racialized Rationales and Access to Higher Education." *Review of Research in Education* 28:1–25.

SIXTEEN

Claim No Easy Victories: Some Notes toward a Fearless Sociology of Education

CHARLES M. PAYNE

> "Hide nothing from the masses of our people. Tell no lies. Expose lies whenever they are told. Mask no difficulties, mistakes, failures. Claim no easy victories. . . ."
>
> —Amilcar Cabral

If only "Tell no lies. . . . Claim no easy victories" could be the watchword of scholars as well as revolutionaries.[1] Amilcar Cabral, though, only had Portuguese colonialists to worry about. Sociologists of education who want their work to contribute to improving the lives of marginalized children and families have to contend with Rush Limbaugh and Fox News. I suspect there are few of us who don't have the occasional anxiety attack over the thought that our work will be somehow taken up and used by the servants of Loot and Clout to the detriment of people we care about; this anxiety may well have been intensified by the election of Donald Trump. There may be a temptation to spin sensitive topics in ways that make them less palatable to conservative audiences, or to just stick to questions that feel safe, a point noted by Wilson (1996) and Alexander (2010), among others.

Similar pressures may come from sources which are less clearly ideological, and perhaps therefore more dangerous. The increasing rigor of educational research is an obviously welcome development, allowing unprecedented certitude on some points. Nevertheless, it may come at a cost. The preferred ways of constructing truth in the social sciences may actually narrow the questions themselves in ways that make it harder to get traction on the problems we study. More certain knowledge is not necessarily more useful knowledge. It may not be too much to say that much of the academic discourse on inequality, educational and otherwise, has been hijacked by two self-congratulatory elite discourses, both of which frame inequality in ways that don't give us as much real-world leverage as we might have.

Sociologists of education might matter more in these discussions if we were less timid about challenging the terms of the discourse itself. That may mean insisting on the right of poor people to mess up, without letting them be reduced to *the* problem. That may mean insisting that even when they are messing up, the marginalized have more potential than others see in them, often more than they see in themselves. Poor families can do better by their children, inner city fathers can do better, and schools and other social institutions can certainly do better. Sociologists can be a part of the process of figuring out the supports and policies needed to make those things happen, and we can do this while continuing to analyze the racism, sexism, class exploitation, and sheer disregard for the humanity of others that define our educational and family support systems. Doing that more effectively, though, almost certainly requires that we judge our work by tougher standards than we sometimes use.

Running from Rush

There is good reason to fear producing work that can be used to blame the victim. The idea that inequality is fundamentally explained by the attributes of individuals is central to American social thinking (Payne 1984).[2] Among the broader public, from about 1969 to 1990, almost 90 percent endorsed the idea that individual characteristics are the primary cause of poverty (Wilson 1996: 160). That number has since been dropping, with one recent poll finding just 44 percent endorsing a similar question (Wessler 2014). Still, a sizeable portion of the population remains predisposed to explanations of poverty that emphasize issues of character rather than structures of opportunity and exploitation, with the implicit corollary that distribution of resources doesn't matter much, given the power of character. Of course this includes many policymakers, as witnessed by the recent popularity of legislation intended to humiliate the poor (Milbank 2015). Social programs to alleviate poverty continue to be as unpopular as they were twenty years ago (McCall 2013), in a way that is reminiscent of the pattern of people endorsing school integration but opposing the means to achieve it. In racial terms, Moffatt (1989) has called the mindset that sees neither history nor structure "ahistorical individualism." In the language of Karl Mannheim (1936), this is a total rather than a particular ideology, and thus it is not easily refutable on the basis of evidence or logic.

Simply saying "no" to the traditional narrative, however, may be less useful than we think. Just inverting the arguments favored by the audience of Loot and Clout may not do much more than legitimate their framework, their right to question the moral fiber of the poor. The best we can hope for is a better answer to a bad question. Focusing solely on that question—staying on the intellectual plantation, if you will—can blind us to the struggles of the most oppressed. It can obscure important questions and potential pathways to change. It can lock us into a questionable set of assumptions about how social change is made. At a moment of looming unprecedented mean-spiritedness toward the poor, there are certainly situations in which one must speak out against persistent, shallow caricatures; but if that is all we do, we may produce work that fails both as scholarship and as advocacy.

In *The New Jim Crow*, Michelle Alexander suggested (p. 223) that many civil rights leaders had maintained an "awkward silence" around crime and punishment. This is part of a larger list of questions that the left finds uncomfortable, including questions about poor families, especially black poor families, and about the social behaviors of black men. The enduring example is the Daniel Moynihan report on the Negro family, or the reaction to it. Sara McLanahan and Christopher Jencks (2015) recently noted:

> Moynihan's claim that growing up in a fatherless family reduced a child's chances of educational and economic success was furiously denounced when the report appeared in 1965, with many critics calling Moynihan a racist. For the next two decades few scholars chose to investigate the effects of father absence, lest they too be demonized if their findings supported Moynihan's argument.[3]

It is a kind of left-handed compliment to Moynihan's work that, fifty years after the report was published, it still stirs passions. For a special issue on Moynihan, the conservative journal *Education Next* choose for the cover an image of a black couple posed in the style of Grant Wood's painting *American Gothic*, with the image of the man fading away. It was immediately denounced as blatant racism, leading one editor to apologize for insensitivity (Walsh 2015a; Walsh 2015b).

Shying away from touchy questions, of course, lets the wrong side drive the agenda; but, to put it harshly, it may also amount to selling out the most vulnerable members of disadvantaged communities. Much of what passed for historical analysis in the report was cartoonish. The sociological analysis was partly overstatement and gratuitous interpretation—famously, "At the heart of the deterioration of the fabric of Negro society is the deterioration of the Negro family. It is the fundamental source of the weakness of the Negro community at the present time" (p.5). Moynihan had no data supporting the assertion that family problems were more important than labor market discrimination or the concentration of poverty or racial isolation. This is to say nothing of the fact that language like "fundamental source of weakness" is just hubris. Social science data are seldom definitive enough to justify claims of that strength. The evidence would have been better served had Moynihan framed family instability as a very significant and widening problem, not as *the* problem. The attacks on him were often pitched at the same un-nuanced level, so that the important ideas at the core of his work drowned in critique.

These attacks were intended to be advocacy, but it was advocacy with a cost. One could imagine a response to Moynihan that would have pointed out the many weaknesses in the report but then gone on to discuss better supports for low-income black women and their children. Lyndon Johnson clearly wanted that discussion (Rainwater and Yancey 1967). What is normally lost in discussions of Moynihan is that his main policy proposal was to return to the days of twice-a-day mail deliveries in urban areas, in order to create a job market for men of modest educational attainment. What would we give now to go back to a moment when that was even a discussable possibility?[4] Instead, an idea that might really have meant something to poor families got lost in another iteration of the great debate about the moral worthiness of black people. Militant advocacy gets equated with defense of the group's image, which typically does little for the group's lower-ranking members. It says something profound about the operation of white supremacy and patriarchy that, fifty years after Moynihan, it is still hard to have a conversation that focuses squarely on the needs of poor black women trying to raise children in hostile, resource-poor environments, without running afoul of the (understandable) fear of reinforcing stereotypes. The race gets defended, and male privilege in the inner city goes unexamined.

Jody Miller's *Getting Played: African American Girls, Urban Inequality and Gendered Violence* is cognizant of the politics of image, but also suggests a framework for speaking to it. The book is a study of the violence that African-American girls in inner-city Saint Louis suffer at the hands of the men in their lives. At many levels, it is a study in invisibility. It is not well known that young African-American women and Latinas endure more and more serious sexual harassment than their counterparts in other demographic groups. Part of the reason for this may be the broader invisibility of black women; any narrative about them is hidden behind a national narrative about the more dramatic problems of black men and boys, compared to whom black girls seem like a success story.[5] (Seldom asked is the question of the price they pay for such success as they have achieved.) Black women can also be rendered invisible by the politics of image—in this case, the fear of reinforcing stereotypes against black men—and perhaps no such stereotype has a more fraught historical resonance than that of the black rapist.

Almost painfully aware of this problem, Miller is very careful to contextualize, analyzing the social factors that facilitate rape culture across time and societies. She stresses that we find the same behaviors among the most privileged men, and that we find wide variation among disadvantaged males in how they construct masculinity. She emphasizes how much destructive individual behavior is linked to structures of opportunity. She frames urban gangbangers and fraternity boys in a way that sees them both reacting to the same cultural imperatives, thus making it harder to reduce destructive behavior to a problem of ghetto culture.

But the ghetto is one setting where a particularly nasty case of the larger problem plays out. Boys and girls describe the neighborhoods they live in as sources of vulnerability, which they attribute to both trifling people and institutional neglect. One respondent described her neighborhood thus:

> Terrible. Every man for theyself. Ghetto in the sense of raggedy, people uncool to people, just outside, street light never come on, police don't come in after 4 o'clock. . . . Heavy drug dealing. They loud, they don't care about, you know, the old people in the neighborhood or nuttin'. It's been like females, it was a ten-year-old girl who got raped recently and kilt and didn't nobody . . . but didn't nobody, you know, even try to help the girl or nuttin' like that (p. 19).

Girls are almost as likely to be victims of nonlethal violence as boys, despite their strategies for navigating neighborhood dangers. With an average age of sixteen, half the girls report some form of sexual victimization. They essentially have no confidence in the institutions that are supposed to support them, including schools and police; the police can't be relied on even to show up, and schools are likely to see harassment of girls as boys being boys, just playin'. The lack of institutional response and the existence of strong norms of noninterference in the community—the idea that everyone should mind their own business—means that girls learn that they have to rely on themselves and few others. Both boys and girls use dehumanizing language—crackheads, alkies—to describe some of the victims around them, language that might imply that the victims deserve what they get.

Some girls apply a similar logic to sexual harassment, agreeing with the boys that the root of the problem is that girls are too provocative. The boys can describe their planning and participation in gang rapes, their techniques for manipulating girls and taking advantage of their trust, in perfectly callous terms; but at least some of them can then turn around and be impressively reflective and self-critical. Miller's presentation doesn't hide their brutality, but it also doesn't let the boys' brutality obscure their potential to do and be something else. Her discussion of what would make a difference, drawn largely from the youth themselves, leans toward the institutional, not the individual. It includes basic neighborhood improvements such as providing more for youth to do, stabilizing community agencies in which they can develop relationships with caring adults, holding relevant institutions to account, providing jobs, and helping young women develop solidarity with one another.

Fearful of a national discourse ever ready to pounce on new evidence of black moral deficiency, scholars may be reluctant to discuss morally reprehensible behavior among disadvantaged populations. But failing to discuss it can be considered a kind of complicity in which the most disadvantaged among the disadvantaged are left to fend for themselves when we might at least be able to bring attention to their issues and questions. Facing these issues may have more value than defending the image of the poor. Miller raises questions about what seemingly uncaring neighborhoods do to the social understanding of young people; about the consequences of girls internalizing responsibility for their own degradation; about the ideologies boys use to excuse that degradation; and about practical reforms, including building on what is positive in the boys. These questions matter, but we cannot give them adequate attention if we fear that they may be turned into conservative fodder.

Given the paradigmatic position of Marx in the development of radical social science, it is well to remember that Marxism offers tools for thinking about the possibility that oppressed and marginalized communities will sometimes reinforce their own oppression. One such tool is the idea of the unity of opposites: social forces that are fundamentally antagonistic to one another can nonetheless be temporarily dependent on and supportive of one another. At any given moment, workers, even though they are being exploited by capitalists, may need those capitalists to survive, so they cooperate with a system that ultimately is not operating in their best interest. Similarly, they may help the education system reproduce class stratification. Samuel Bowles, among the most influential of Marxist students of education, quotes Melvin Kohn with approval:

> Whether consciously or not, parents tend to impart to their children lessons derived from the condition of life of their own class and thus help to prepare their children for a similar class position.... The conformist values and orientation of lower- and working-class parents are inappropriate for training children to deal with the problems of middle-class and professional life.... The family, then, functions as a mechanism for perpetuating inequality. (Bowles 1972: 308)

Making an early version of an argument which has been recently revived (Heckman et al. 2014), Bowles notes that certain highly rewarded personality characteristics are more important than cognitive skills in explaining economic success, and adds, "These personality characteristics, originating in the work experiences of one's parents, transmitted in turn to children through early socialization practices and reinforced in school and on the job are an important vehicle of the reproduction of the social division of labor." A classic example would be Sennett and Cobb's (1993) discussion of working-class white ethnic men who respond to the class indignities that shape their lives by embracing a masculinity that valorizes physical work and denigrates anything intellectual or academic, thus leading their sons to think of such work as sissified, and helping to keep them at the same level as their fathers. Certainly, in much popular and some academic discourse, the way people react to the limitations placed on them becomes the "cause" of poverty. "Cut off my legs and call me Shorty!" Louis Armstrong used to sing. Nevertheless, if we are willing to think about the ways in which poor parents can help transmit disadvantage to their children, we may find situations where they are strategically placed to disrupt the process.

While we should be open to the idea that poor families help reproduce their own status, we should still be cautious about how working-class culture gets framed in these discussions. These discussions tend to assume that cultural influences are all pushing in one direction. In fact, they can be contradictory (e.g., Wilson 1996). We can be sure that some of the men Sennett and Cobb described were working overtime to keep their children in Catholic schools, which may have given those children certain competitive advantages. What about the inner-city mother who says all the right things about education to her children, but then clearly signals something else by avoiding contact with the school?

Ideas like the unity of opposites are one way to avoid either/or formulations, but we have had a number of warnings against seeing some fixed and immutable boundary between "culture" and "structure" (Massey and Denton 1993; Small, Harding, and Lamont 2010; Wilson 1996). Much that looks like value-driven behavior may be response to structures of opportunity. A particularly useful example, because it involves a privileged population, is offered by Powell and Driscoll (1973). Due to a downturn in the aerospace industry, a group of scientists and engineers faced long-term unemployment. Their initial reaction was to treat finding a job as if it were their job, putting in full days grinding out resumes and working their contact networks. As their separation from the labor market stretched on, they changed. They became moody and angry, and put less time into the job search. Their relationships with their wives deteriorated. They restricted their socializing, especially with friends who had jobs. They showed signs of cynicism, pessimism, and a general sense of powerlessness. This change all took place in less than a year. The authors conclude, "Much behavior characteristic of unemployed scientists and professional groups in [the final stages of unemployment]—malaise, cynicism, a sense of powerlessness—has been described as typical of the poor and minority group workers as well as of workers in other countries" (p. 26).

The removal of ordinary supports can make middle-class people look ghetto, and the presence of such supports can make poor people look respectable. There is considerable evidence that when the poor get a little money, some of them do family and child rearing more as the privileged do. The Minnesota Family Investment Program (MFIP), piloted from 1994 through 1998, included more than fourteen thousand welfare recipients and applicants, most of them single parents (Knox et al. 2000). Recipients were randomly assigned to MFIP, which made them eligible to keep any additional income they earned without giving up welfare benefits, or to Aid to Families with Dependent Children, which took a dollar from benefits for every dollar earned. Improving their economic status had the most dramatic and wide-ranging effect on single parents who were long-term recipients; they experienced more marriages and less domestic abuse, and their children saw improved reading scores in third grade. Among the most disadvantaged families, the effects were particularly large on the small number of children aged two to five, nearly doubling the proportion of them performing at grade level when they got to fifth grade (see also Miller et al. 2000). So what is bad culture and what is reaction to lack of resources? Whatever deeply seated beliefs parents may hold, some problems of family life and child development that are easily attributed to culture can be ameliorated by providing families with more resources.

The point is not that culture doesn't matter—I'll take odds that one could find families in the Minnesota study who weren't helped by income transfer—but that the ways in which it matters are complex and easily exaggerated. Perhaps more important, it is not clear that focusing on the culture of the poor helps us understand those schools and school systems that are in fact improving. The most convincing and best documented cases we have of large-scale improvement in outcomes include New York's small schools of choice (Bloom and Unterman 2013; Duncan and Murnane 2014); the school systems of Montgomery County, Maryland (Childress, Doyle, and Thomas 2009), and Charlotte-Mecklenburg, North Carolina (Clark 2014; Snipes, Doolittle, and Herlihy 2002); and the use of early-warning systems to raise graduation rates (Allensworth and Easton 2007; Roderick et al. 2014). It does not seem as though one could make a plausible case that any of them are addressing ghetto culture, however that term is defined.[6] One could make a plausible case that the places making the most progress in improving high school graduation and college enrollment rates or meaningful test scores are doing so through concentration and realignment of resources, increased personalization and rigor of instruction, better use of data, improvment and redistribution of professional capital, and investment of more resources in the children with the greatest need.

This doesn't mean that culture cannot leverage change. It seems clear enough that engrained patterns of behavior among some poor parents have a high probability of negative implications for children: avoiding contact with teachers and schools, modeling poor nutritional habits, not getting younger children to school or preschool, encouraging or allowing excessive television viewing, discouraging students from attending selective colleges, accepting low standards for academic achievement, and so on. There may be completely understandable reasons for all these habits, but that doesn't change their implications for children. Again, to pretend we can't find bad parenting in the inner-city is to sell out the most vulnerable population: children.

There are promising interventions organized at least partly around culture. Given low-cost interventions to help them understand language development, low-income parents can change their linguistic patterns in ways that are likely to help their children's development (Suskind and Leffel 2015). Training low-income parents in positive behavior supports seems to increase their children's self-regulation and kindergarten academic performance (Brotman et al. 2013). We may not know how scalable and sustainable these interventions are, or whether the good effects persist, but these interventions give us something to build on.

Suppose, for a moment, that we somehow were able to get a great many more fathers to participate positively in their families. We know that father absence is associated with an increase in aggression, rule breaking, delinquency, and drug use, and these associations are consistently stronger for boys than girls (McLanahan and Jencks 2015). What would that mean in terms of social mobility? Given the other issues in the lives of children, it is not easy to say how much difference might be made by changing parental behavior. Certainly we should expect that some children would be helped, just because there are always children who have almost everything they need to get over some of life's hurdles, so that just a little more invested in them at home or in school, can have a large payoff. Having better-functioning fathers, though, won't fix poor schools, or stop jobs from migrating away for the cities, or reduce labor market discrimination. Whether the system is capable of absorbing large numbers of such children, especially if they come from stigmatized minorities, is an open question. We can probably have more confidence that positive participation from fathers would mean a change in the quality of life of single mothers and children. Perhaps some children would grow up with less anger; perhaps some could be better citizens of their communities. Maybe fewer moms would get overwhelmed by life's stresses. Mobility is only one way to think about what children get from high-functioning family environments.

Suppose, again, that we knew in advance that changes in fathering would not make dramatic inroads against poverty. The predictable response from the proponents of a hard structural view is that small-scale interventions are distractions. Structural problems demand structural solutions, not band-aids that reach only a few; we can't fix schools until we fix poverty. On moral grounds alone, that argument should be suspect. It treats poor children as if they only matter in the mass, not as individuals. They matter as weapons in ideological warfare. No one applies that kind of reasoning to their own children. In practice, the hard structural position too often justifies doing nothing until the revolution comes: the easiest radicalism. While we continue to advocate for structural responses to poverty, we can also work to help parents develop higher educational standards, to challenge young men who have absorbed the larger society's most negative messages about the value of women (Wilcox 2008). How much good we can do that way can't be known in advance, but it should be more than we can do if we restrict ourselves to hurling critique at structure. Cabral (1966) again: "We are not going to eliminate imperialism by shouting insults against it. . . ."

We can be certain that Cabral, like many civil rights organizers in this country (Payne 2007), wanted to develop his base because he saw them as the ultimate source of change. To the extent that one sees the disenfranchised as significant drivers of change, it is less important what the privileged think of them, and more important that their own capacities be developed. Academics may make a more powerful contribution to these conversations by supporting the development of the human potential in marginalized communities, while continuing to critique and challenge structural inequities and their supporting ideologies and looking for short-term practices and policies that will at least ameliorate conditions for some people.

The hard structural position is embedded in a set of assumptions, which normally go unexamined, about how change is made. It can reflect both a simplistic either/or conception of the causes of social problems and a naive conception of the importance of understanding causation, if our primary purpose is to support change. It can deflect attention from the specific issues of the most vulnerable populations. It may actually reinforce the legitimacy of a discourse rooted in the preoccupations of elites. Certainly, we should always be aware of the engrained tendency to exaggerate and decontextualize the cultural dimensions, but we can still be open to investigating any possible lever that might help vulnerable children and families. Of the things we know that can make a difference, which ones make the most profound difference? Of those, which are more likely to be implementable and sustainable in the real world? A conversation in which the needs of the most vulnerable actually took center stage would be a revolutionary change.

More Fearsome Than Fox News

Perhaps the most important reason why it isn't a good idea to invest too much energy in worrying over whether culture causes poverty is that the issue of causation is itself overrated. If our primary purpose is improving the life outcomes of marginalized children, centering inquiry around the identification of causality is the long way around. If Rush Limbaugh is one icon of fear, another is your department chairperson, or whatever symbol you choose for the idols of the profession. Nothing is more prized in social science research right now than research that establishes strong grounds for causal inference; yet it would not be easy, based on the record, to demonstrate that research in that tradition has done very much to help children.

Probably no one work has done as much to shape the sociology of education as the 1966 report by James Coleman and colleagues, centered on the causes of achievement differentials by race and class. Five decades later, it is still cited in some discussions as if it were unproblematic. Thus, David Berliner (2013), a central figure in contemporary discussions of educational inequality, has compiled much recent research consistent with Coleman's central point about the modest effects of schools in shaping differences between groups, pointing out that years of research since Coleman show that school effects are associated with about 20 percent of the variation in achievement test scores, while out of school factors are associated with about 60 percent, the latter including such factors as "family income; the neighborhood's sense of collective efficacy, violence rate, and average income; medical and dental care available and used; level of food insecurity; number of moves a family makes over the course of a child's school years; whether one parent or two parents are raising the child; provision of high-quality early education in the neighborhood; language spoken at home."

It is true, but misleading. We might call this the Coleman fallacy, conflating correlation with causation and causation with change. A pattern that has been caused by one thing may be changed by another. In the broadest sense, poor children don't develop as well as others because we invest less in their development. By changing the way we invest at some critical points, we may be able to compensate for lack of investment at other points. A growing body of experience suggests that the rates of kids dropping out of high school can be substantially reduced if we give youngsters more support at key transitional points like ninth grade (Roderick et al, 2014). That doesn't mean we have addressed the root causes of dropping out, which presumably are many, and which develop over time.[7]

The Charlotte-Mecklenburg school system regularly posts some of the country's best performance figures for poor and minority children (TUDA 2013). Many leaders of that system attribute this to their commitment to systematically providing better human capital, including better leadership, to the children who are usually last in line for it (Clark 2014). If that is true, then they are not addressing homes with little educational strength, to invoke Coleman's useful phrase; they are not fixing dangerous neighborhoods or negative peer cultures. Saying that out-of-school factors are ordinarily very powerful is true beyond argument, but that doesn't tell us what more intentionally organized schools might do to counter them. (And it is inevitable that the relative success of some schools and systems will be misused to argue that resources don't matter. If they can do it. . . .).

In the last ten years, what body of research has had the most positive impact on the lives of poor children? The question invites an argument, but I would nominate the work that has led to a prolonged rise in the national graduation rate, which passed 80 percent for the first time in 2012. Minority students have improved considerably faster than others (Balfanz et al. 2014). The research supporting this work is mostly predictive, not causal, asking what factors allow early identification of dropouts and what interventions prevent them. It is hard to think of a body of research based on random assignment which has been associated with so much meaningful change.[8]

Random assignment can give us crucial information about which interventions matter, but not necessarily about *how* to do them. Consider New York's small high schools of choice. Since 2002 the city has opened more than 120 academically nonselective small high schools, serving some of New York's most distressed neighborhoods. The large neighborhood schools they replaced typically had graduation rates below 45 percent. These schools now serve more than twenty thousand students. A fifth of the incoming students were over age for eighth grade; 70 percent were below grade level in reading, while 63 percent were below in math. The schools stress rigorous learning and have curricular themes. They were designed through a competitive process involving many stakeholder groups, including teachers and community members. Part of the rationale for keeping the schools small was to facilitate deeper relations between adults and youth. Most had community partners who offered the students additional learning opportunities inside and outside the classroom, or provided organizational support. Both the teachers' union and the administrators' union were involved in the implementation. An evaluation (Bloom and Unterman 2013) of the first three graduating cohorts shows an average impact of 9.5 percent on graduation rates, while also increasing by 7.6 percent the numbers of students who meet a measure of college readiness in English (but not in math). The positive effects hold for several subgroups, including previously low-achieving students, males and females, blacks and Hispanics, and lower-income students. Black and Hispanic males are among the largest gainers. The positive effects seem to persist into college or junior college. Initially, there were concerns that these schools were having success by concentrating their resources in ways that helped them, but hurt the system. However, recent work looking at four cohorts of graduates in various types of schools suggests just the opposite (Stiefel, Schwartz, and Wiswall 2015).

Since students are chosen for these schools by lottery, we have strong grounds for believing that the outcomes reflect the schools' influence. While these are almost certainly school effects, there remains room for argument about just *how* the schools are having an impact. In order to get a handle on that, MDRC asked principals and teachers at some of the most successful schools to explain their success. They pointed to academic rigor and the personal relationships that students and teachers develop, along with staffs committed to being in that kind of environment and working with that kind of student. The personalization and rigor themes are consistent with a good deal of research on successful inner-city schools, but knowing that they seem to matter doesn't help much when it comes to trying to replicate these schools. It might help if we know more about the history of their creation. We know, for example, that when there was a national movement around intentional small schools, New York was deeply involved in it, perhaps more than any other city. The leaders of that movement constituted a whole subculture of people who shared or developed ways of thinking about good teaching, child development, school creation, and so on. Over a period of two decades, they worked on projects as small as professional development, and as large as creating networks of schools. Obviously they developed working relationships with one another, including knowledge about who was good at what. When the system gave them the opportunity to develop more schools, they brought stores of capital with them they had developed over the years. Thus, it is may be that this model fit particularly well with earlier stages of reform in New York City and would be a tougher (but not impossible) project elsewhere. If so, that's a type of knowledge we won't get from experimental research alone.

More broadly, it seems safe to say the current state of urban schools is the product of many decades of social, political and economic disinvestments in poor children and their neighborhoods. The result is an ongoing, self-reinforcing pattern of mutual disinvestment in which the various actors behave in ways that encourage other actors to disengage. The variablized representations of reality underlying most random assignment research can strip the problem of historical and social context. While resources may be part of the long-term root of the problem, simply providing more resources now may not be as effective as one would hope, if one doesn't do something to reverse the social and professional deterioration of the worst schools.

Shortly after the Institute for Education Sciences initiated a push to dramatically increase random assignment research in education, Murnane and Nelson (2007) argued that the new emphasis could help improve performance in the educational sector, but that it was important to realize that experimental models were most likely to be of use under limited conditions: when the treatment was well defined and easy to implement, when results manifested themselves in a relatively brief period of time, and when the effects of the treatment did not vary much across various subpopulations. This means that large-scale, multidimensional initiatives—the kinds of things that are associated with some of the most impressive cases of change—may not be appropriate. More recently, Schorr and Bryk (2015) have elaborated on the most effective way to think about experimental research:

> We must learn not only whether an intervention can work (which is what randomized control trials tell us), but how, why, and for whom—and also how we can do better. We must draw on a half-century of work on quality improvement to complement what experimental evidence can tell us. And, importantly, the learning must be done not alone by dispassionate experts, but must involve the people actually doing the work, as well as those whose lives the interventions are trying to enrich.

Schorr and Bryk emphasize the need to study variations in context and outcome, getting beyond the fixation on central tendency, and the importance of embedding the work in networks of academic researchers, practitioners, students, and others who develop hypotheses, try interventions based on them, and make adjustments based on the results. The process involves looking at what to do and how to do it in real-world contexts. It also involves broadening the conception of expertise beyond academic expertise, and broadening the conception of relevant evidence beyond the causal. "Achieving quality outcomes reliably, at scale, requires that we supplement carefully controlled, after-the fact program evaluations with continuous real-time learning to improve the quality and effectiveness of both systems and programs."[9]

This kind of long-term, continuous improvement research is not well matched to academic reward structures that privilege research that gets done quickly, is highly quantitative and experimentally based, and employs scientific rhetorics. Nor does that reward structure valorize the usability and accessibility of research, or collaboration with practitioners. Thirty-five years ago, the scholar-activist Ron Edmonds (1979) argued that the research establishment, including the American Educational Research Association, was not equipped to serve the equity interests of the poor, given the nature of conventional social science wisdom and its tendency to serve the interests of elites. We still grapple with that challenge. We cannot take it for granted that either mainstream epistemologies or hard structural critiques are going to point us to questions that give us the best chance of addressing Edmonds's concerns about the equity interests of the poor.

Whose Questions?

> We note, however, that one form of struggle which we consider to be fundamental has not been explicitly mentioned in this programme. . . . We refer here to *the struggle against our own weaknesses*. . . . Our experience has shown us that in the general framework of daily struggle this battle against ourselves—no matter what dif-

> ficulties the enemy may create—is the most difficult of all, whether for the present or the future of our peoples.
>
> —Cabral, "The Theory of Weapon"[10]

What weaknesses might sociologists of education who want to support the "downpressed" bring to their work? Our good intentions, probably. To the extent that we see ourselves as advocates, we claim a moral status. Our activism is itself a commodity. We should be ever-skeptical of the idea that the work which gives us the best payoff in terms of confirming our preferred identities is also the kind of work that creates the best basis for change. Things are seldom so convenient.

Sociologists are probably no better than others at penetrating total ideologies, but developing a different relationship with the people we write about might help. Patterson (2014) makes the point that we should pay more attention to how those from the social margins explain inequality and mobility. It goes too far to suggest, as Patterson does, that their explanations—or anyone else's—should be taken at face value, but making their thinking a more central part of the conversation is important partly because the complexity of their thinking often flies in the face of stereotypes (e.g., Young 2004), and partly because their biases may be a useful counterbalance to the biases in elite discourses. Freed of the need, or the possibility, of establishing either their moral or their professional bona fides, members of marginalized communities may be able to help us think with more nuance about the questions that matter most. The networked improvement communities proposed by Bryk and colleagues (2015) offer one way to think about how such relationships might be structured.

Although it might be a naive suggestion, we could try to treat the problem of which questions we should be pursuing when as an empirical one. If we think that certain kinds of questions and certain kinds of academic work best support more just social outcomes, what evidence can we adduce for that? Maybe evidence will matter little in the face of deep personal investments, but maybe that kind of discussion could help us be a little more aware of the self-serving component of what we do in the name of helping, and a little more modest in what we claim for whatever approach we take.

How any of this will be affected by the election of Donald Trump is an open question, but many of us expect that his election heralds an era of unprecedented assaults on the well-being of children and families. If so, we will have to wait to see what form those assaults take before we can say much about how concerned sociologists can best respond. It may be, though, that whatever leverage resided in the politics of image in the past will be greatly reduced in an era when public policy is likely to be driven by fixed ideological priorities. On the other hand, to the degree that any part of the conservative movement can be moved by evidence, it may well be that Big Data is the form of evidence most likely to be attended to, witness the support of some businesspersons for early childhood education.

George Washington, founding member of the Loot and Clout club, held among his slaves a young woman named Oney Judge. Upon learning that she might become a wedding gift to one of Washington's granddaughters, she fled, ending up in New Hampshire, leaving her owner incensed. Washington wrote to someone who had been sent to recapture her: "I regret that the attempt you made to restore the Girl (Oney Judge as she called herself while with us, and who, without the least provocation absconded from her Mistress) should have been attended with so little Success." Oney Judge offered to come back if given a promise of manumission, but Washington considered that out of the question, given her "unfaithfulness" (Washington 1796). Washington was clear; the problem was not the structure of slavery, but the character of this slave. Nothing in the historical record suggests that Judge tried to refute him. She did not engage him in a debate over the morality of slavery, or about what she did or did not deserve, or about who had provoked whom. She just left. There are times when it makes sense to argue over the self-delusions of the powerful, but there are also times when the right thing to do is to find the shortest road to Canada and start answering your own questions.

Notes

1. The author would like to acknowledge very helpful comments from Jeffrey Henig and the members of the Egalitarianisms seminar at the Institute for Advanced Study.
2. In education we are seeing a different framing, at least for the time being, as conservatives organize around the idea that the real problem in schools is the educational profession, not poor families and children. For the moment, parent bashing has yielded to teacher bashing.
3. This substance of this quote is almost certainly right, but the wording is suspect. The main assertion in Moynihan was that family instability was the fundamental problem in black communities, not that fatherlessness had negative consequences. By framing it in this way, MacLanahan and Jencks make Moynihan seem more reasonable, and his critics less so.
4. Steinberg (2015), though, sees this as just substituting one occupational caste for another.
5. At the more privileged end of the social spectrum, I have twice known of cases in

which black women in college who said they had been assaulted by black men were encouraged not to press charges, given how hard it was for black men to get to that level—the black male narrative thus totally devaluing black women.

6. For a possible exception, see Schwartz 2010.
7. The children most likely to drop out can be identified as early as first grade (Sparks 2013).
8. Another contender for most impactful research would be the work that has helped build something approaching a national consensus on the desirability of preschool for poor children (e.g., Heckman 2006). There, too, the research has largely been predictive, but with some important experimental work early on.
9. There is also problem of the language used in talking about change. Researchers, including Coleman, consistently refer to data that are only correlational as "explaining" or "accounting for" something; "causal modeling" is equated with "causal analysis."
10. Compare Cabral to Charlie Cobb, a veteran of the civil rights struggle in Mississippi in the early 1960s: "Every step in the fight against racism and discrimination was preceded by a deeper and more profound struggle that involved confronting oneself" (Cobb 1999: 135).

References

Alexander, Michelle. 2010. *The New Jim Crow: Mass Incarceration in the Age of Colorblindness*. New York: New Press.

Allensworth, E., and J. Easton. 2007. *What Matters for Staying On-Track and Graduating in Chicago Public Schools*. Chicago: Consortium on Chicago School Research.

Balfanz, Robert, John M. Bridgeland, Joanna Hornig Fox, Jennifer L. DePaoli, Erin S. Ingram, and Mary Maushard. 2014. *Building a Grad Nation: Progress and Challenge in Ending the High School Dropout Epidemic*. Baltimore: Everyone Graduates Center.

Berliner, David. 2013. "Effects of Inequality and Poverty vs. Teachers and Schooling on America's Youth." *Teachers College Record* 115:1–26.

Bloom, H. S., and R. Unterman, R. 2013. *Sustained Progress: New Findings about the Effectiveness and Operation of Small Public High Schools of Choice in New York City*. New York: MDRC.

Bowles, Samuel. 1972. "Getting Nowhere: Programmed Class Stagnation." *Society* 9:42–49.

Brotman, L., Spring Dawson-McClure, Esther J. Calzada, Keng-Yen Huang, Dimitra Kamboukos, Joseph J. Palamar, and Eva Petkova. 2013. "Cluster (School) RCT of ParentCorps: Impact on Kindergarten Academic Achievement," *Pediatrics* 5:1521–1529.

Bryk, Anthony, Louis Gomez, Alicia Grunow, and Paul G. LeMahieu. 2015. *Learning to Improve: How America's Schools Can Get Better at Getting Better*. Cambridge, MA: Harvard Educational Press.

Cabral, Amilcar. 1966. "The Weapon of Theory." Address to the First Tricontinental Conference of the Peoples of Asia, Africa and Latin America, Havana, Cuba. https://www.marxists.org/subject/africa/cabral/1966/weapon-theory.htm.

Childress, Stacey, Denis Doyle, and David Thomas. 2009. *Leading for Equity: The Pursuit of Excellence in Montgomery County Public Schools*. Cambridge, MA: Harvard Education Press.

Clark, Ann. 2014. "Getting Strong Educators to the Students Who Most Need Them." Presentation at the 2014 Conference of the Education Trust, Baltimore, MD.

Cobb, Charles. 1999. "Organizing Freedom Schools." In *Freedom Is a Constant Struggle: An*

Anthology of the Mississippi Civil Rights Struggle, edited by Susie Erenrich. Montgomery, AL: Black Belt Press.

Coleman, J. S., E. Campbell, C. J. Hobson, J. McPartland, A. M. Mood,, F. D. Weinfeld, and R. York. 1966. *Equality of Educational Opportunity*. Washington: Government Printing Office.

Duncan, Greg, and Richard Murnane. 2014. *Restoring Opportunity: The Crisis of Inequality and the Challenge for American Education*. Cambridge, MA: Harvard Education Press.

Edmonds, R. 1979. Effective Schools for the Urban Poor. *Educational Leadership* 37:15–24.

Heckman, J. J. 2006. "Skill Formation and the Economics of Investing in Disadvantaged Children." *Science* 312:1900–1902.

Heckman, J. J., J. E. Humphries, and T. Kautz, eds. 2014. *The Myth of Achievement Tests: The GED and the Role of Character in American Life*. Chicago: University of Chicago Press.

Knox, Virginia, Cynthia Miller, and Lisa Gennetian. 2000. *Reforming Welfare and Rewarding Work: A Summary of the Final MFIP Report*. New York: MDRC.

McCall, Leslie. *The Undeserving Rich: American Beliefs about Inequality, Opportunity, and Redistribution*. New York: Cambridge University Press, 2013.

McLanahan, Sara, and Christopher Jencks. 2015. "Was Moynihan Right?" *Education Next* 15, no. 2: 14.

Mannheim, Karl. 1936. *Ideology and Utopia: An Introduction to the Sociology of Knowledge*. New York: Harcourt, Brace and Company.

Massey, Douglas S., and Nancy A. Denton. 1993. *American Apartheid: Segregation and the Making of the Underclass*. Cambridge, MA: Harvard University Press.

Milbank, Dana. 2015. "The Rush to Humiliate the Poor." *Washington Post*, April 7.

Miller, Cynthia, Aletha C. Huston, Greg J. Duncan, Vonnie C. McLoyd, and Thomas S. Weisner. 2008. *New Hope for the Working Poor: Effects after Eight Years for Families and Children*. New York: MDRC.

Miller, Jody. 2008. *Getting Played: African American Girls, Urban Inequality, and Gendered Violence*. New York: New York University Press.

Moffatt, Michael. 1989. *Coming of Age in New Jersey: College and American Culture*. New Brunswick, NJ: Rutgers University Press, 1989.

Murnane, R. J., and R. R. Nelson. 2007. "Improving the Performance of the Education Sector: The Valuable, Challenging, and Limited Role of Random Assignment Evaluations." *Economics of Innovation and New Technology* 16 (5): 307–322. DOI: 10.1080/10438590600982236.

Payne, Charles M. 1984. *Getting What We Ask For: The Ambiguity of Success and Failure in Urban Education*. Westport, CT: Greenwood Press.

———. 2007. *I've Got the Light of Freedom: The Organizing Tradition and the Mississippi Freedom Struggle*. Berkeley: University of California Press.

Patterson, Orlando. 2014. "How Sociologists Made Themselves Irrelevant." *Chronicle of Higher Education*, December 10.

Powell, Douglas, and Paul F. Driscoll. 1973. "Middle-Class Professionals Face Unemployment." *Society* 10 (2): 18–26.

Rainwater, Lee, and William L. Yancey. 1967. *The Moynihan Report and the Politics of Controversy*. Cambridge, MA: MIT Press.

Roderick, Melissa, T. Kelley-Kemple., D. Johnson, and N. Beechum. 2014. *Preventable Failure: Improvements in Long-Term Outcomes When High Schools Focused on the Ninth Grade Year: Research Summary*. Chicago: Consortium on Chicago School Research.

Schorr, L. and A. Bryk. 2015. "To Achieve Big Results From Social Policy, Add This." Huffington Post, January 21. http://www.huffingtonpost.com/lisbeth-lee-schorr/to-achieve-big-results-fr_b_6510262.html.

Sennett, Richard, and Jonathan Cobb. 1993. *The Hidden Injuries of Class*. New York: Norton.

Small, Mario, David J. Harding, and Michele Lamont. 2010. "Reconsidering Culture and Poverty. *Annals of the American Academy of Political and Social Science* 629 (1): 6–27.

Snipes, J., F. Doolittle, and C. Herlihy. 2002. *Foundations for Success: Case Studies of How Urban School Systems Improve Student Achievement*. New York: MDRC.

Sparks, Sarah. 2013. "Dropout Indicators Found for 1st Graders." *Education Week*, July 29. http://www.edweek.org/ew/articles/2013/07/29/37firstgrade.h32.html.

Steinberg, Stephen. 2015. "The Moynihan Report at 50." *Boston Review*, June 24. http://bostonreview.net/us/stephen-steinberg-moynihan-report-black-families-nathan-glazer.

Stiefel, L., Amy Ellen Schwartz, Matthew Wiswall. 2016. "Does Small High School Reform Lift Urban Districts? Evidence from New York City." *Educational Researcher* 44:161–172.

Suskind, Dana, and Kristen Leffel. 2013. "The Thirty Million Words Project: A Randomized Controlled Pilot." Presentation at the Lena Conference, Denver, CO. http://www.lenafoundation.org/wp-content/uploads/pdf/LENA-Conf-2013/Presentations/LENA-Conference-2013-Dana-Suskind.pdf.

TUDA (Trial Urban District Assessment). 2013. "District Results for the 2013 Mathematics and Reading Assessments." http://www.nationsreportcard.gov/reading_math_tuda_2013/#/executive-summary.

Walsh, Mark. 2015a. "'Education Next' Cover on Moynihan Report Anniversary Raises Hackles," *Education Week*, March 4. http://blogs.edweek.org/edweek/education_and_the_media/2015/03/education_next_cover_raises_hackles.html.

———. 2015b. "From 'Education Next' Editors, Cover Sparks an Apology and a Defense," March 5. http://blogs.edweek.org/edweek/education_and_the_media/2015/03/From_Education_Next_editors_cover_sparks_an_apology_and_a_defense.html.

Washington, George. 1796. Letter to Joseph Whipple, November 28. http://founders.archives.gov/documents/Washington/99-01-02-00037.

Wessler, Seth Freed. 2014. "Poll: Fewer Americans Blame Poverty on the Poor." NBC News, June 20. https://www.broadwayworld.com/bwwtv/article/NBC-News-Poll-Finds-that-Fewer-Americans-Blame-Poverty-on-the-Poor-20140620.

Wilcox, Susan. 2008. "My Sister, My Brother, Myself: Critical Exploration of Sexism and Misogyny at the Brotherhood/Sister Sol." In *Teach Freedom: Education for Liberation in the African-American Tradition*, edited by C. Payne and C. Strickland. New York: Teachers College Press.

Wilson, William J. 1996. *When Work Disappears: The World of the New Urban Poor*. New York: Knopf.

Young, Alford A. 2004. *The Minds of Marginalized Black Men: Making Sense of Mobility, Opportunity, and Future Life Chances*. Princeton, NJ: Princeton University Press.

EPILOGUE

What Next for the Sociology of Education?

MITCHELL L. STEVENS

In the middle of the twentieth century, dramatic advances in computational capacity and the availability of national survey data created conditions for sociologists to build a rigorous statistical sociology of education. As I have argued in more detail elsewhere (Stevens 2015, 2008), this sociology conceived of education as a process that worked on individuals, who accumulated greater or fewer measurable assets tradable on labor markets as they moved through their educational careers. This way of conceptualizing education and assessing its benefits was enormously generative of empirical social science, but as Davies and Mehta have so ably showed in chapter 1, it placed strong limits on how education could be sociologically appraised. It virtually required scholars seeking visibility at the center of the discipline to operationalize education as precursor and preparation for paid work.

How this form of educational sociology is implicated in its historical context has yet to be fully explained. But here are some data points:

- Upon receipt of a now famous federal government commission, the organizationally focused, small-*n*, network-sensitive author of *The Adolescent Society* (1961) morphed into the national–data set, aggregate-inequality author of what came to be called the "Coleman Report" (1966). *The Adolescent Society* became a cult classic while the "Coleman Report" became the cornerstone of a huge scholarly edifice which has continually expanded ever since.
- Describing inequality in educational access, assets, and returns has been the main business of educational sociology from the 1960s onward. This is coincident with a national focus on racial inequality and its remediation in the 1960s and '70s in the wake of the civil rights movement. Educational sociologists addressing racial inequality during these decades have

given most of their attention to black/white differences in access, assets, and returns to education.

- With rare exceptions (e.g., Arum 2003) the idea of schooling as a moral enterprise, a notion central to the educational sociology of Emile Durkheim (1961) and Talcott Parsons (1959), became peripheral to social-science discourse on education after the 1960s.
- A view of schooling as a productive enterprise that adds value to lives and societies, rather than one that perpetuates inequality, was left largely to economists, who came to dominate national policy discourse about schooling in the 1990s. This is coincident with a shift in national attention from educational inequality to educational productivity and efficiency.

As I read it, a great challenge of the work assembled in this volume is to take the intellectual limitations of the current sociology of education as a worthy intellectual puzzle in its own right. How did we get here, and why? These are historical questions, and while I know that some sociologists are taking them up, I recognize that many of the readers of these pages would be happy to leave such questions to others. So what might ambitious sociologists of other stripes with careers ahead of them do?

First, they could conceive of education as a productive process as much as an inequality-perpetuating one. Education is one of the very few legitimate forms of social provision remaining in American political culture. Much of the current US national conversation about education is about how to extract as much value per unit of investment in education as possible. This approach can be hitched to equity/equality projects, and often is. But sociologists' professional predilection for emphasizing inequality does not oblige them always to provide unhappy accounts of the relationship between education and social stratification.

Second, they could talk about returns to schooling in more plural ways. A focus on individual, usually economic returns to schooling back in the 1960s made it difficult to talk later about other productive aspects of education. This has changed in recent years. Economists, demographers, psychologists, and sociologists are increasingly considering returns to education in marriage markets, timing of childbirth, physical and mental health and well-being, regional economic development, and sheer human happiness. My guess is that most social scientists believe that education has many more positive returns than the ones most prominently modeled and measured in academic sociology. Those more pluralistic beliefs can be translated into tractable research programs.

Third, they can recognize a current watershed moment in computational capacity and data availability which is akin to the 1960s, when the touchstone classics of the education stratification tradition were first published. Peter Blau and Otis Dudley Duncan's *American Occupational Structure* (1967), for example, was a truly massive technical undertaking in its time, requiring state-of-the-art machinery and data access. Now our undergraduates do regression analyses on their laptops for homework, and the digital mediation of instructional provision means that education can be quantitatively described in multiple ways (US Department of Education 2013; Waldrop 2013). Social scientists of education no longer need presume that schooling is an individual-level process or possession. The data sets and the math can be different now. The theorizing can be different too.

Fourth, they could think about education as a generic process of self-fashioning—and of working on people (Leidner 1993)—that is highly legitimate and increasingly pervasive in modern societies. As the editors of this book so convincingly argue in their chapters, we should study education not just in schools, but everywhere.

I would add this: There may be no institution of modern life in which education does not have a positive valence. The valence of education can be made negative—for example, when it is called indoctrination or brainwashing—but making education negative requires active rhetorical work, and is invariably an uphill climb. The default valence is positive. Savvy students of education could view the persistence of this fact as an important sociological problem in its own right. John Meyer and his colleagues wisely sourced the origins of educational optimism to the Enlightenment dream of reason, but a lot of history has happened since then, right here in the United States. The ambitious state-building that supported the massification of higher education and underwrote mass-scale educational social science during the middle of the last century gave way to a presumption of scarcity in social provision and new imperatives to use markets and competition to optimize the provision of public goods. "Government," always of questionable moral value in American political discourse, was demoted to an almost unequivocally bad word. Digitally mediated systems for educating and producing information about citizens arose fully within the private sector. Vast fortunes controlled by people living west of the Rocky Mountains have been put in the service of fundamental change in the provision and measurement of educational services. All the while, education retains its positive valence, but who is presumed to be responsible for education's force of good has been extraordinarily dynamic. Social scientists have scarcely even recognized this dynamism. Explaining it is a tantalizing opportunity for historical, political, and cultural sociologists.

Finally, sociologists could remember, and say out loud with conviction, that education is a moral enterprise. How societies go about provisioning education, what content they give it, and how they distribute it says a great deal about what they value. In the same vein, how social scientists study education, what components of its complexity we attend to, and which of its many outcomes we measure say a great deal about what we ourselves value. That is why I am so grateful that this book has come to fruition. Its existence challenges all of us who study education to be more ambitious, catholic, and humane.

References

Arum, Richard. 2003. *Judging School Discipline: The Crisis of Moral Authority*. Cambridge, MA: Harvard University Press.

Blau, Peter Michael, and Otis Dudley Duncan. 1967. *The American Occupational Structure*. New York: Wiley.

Coleman, James S. 1961. *The Adolescent Society*. Oxford, UK: The Free Press of Glencoe.

Coleman, James S., et al. 1966. *Equality of Educational Opportunity*. Washington: US Department of Health, Education, and Welfare, Office of Education.

Durkheim, Émile. 1961. *Moral Education*. Translated by Everett K. Wilson and Herman Schnurer. New York: The Free Press.

Leidner, Robin. 1993. *Fast Food, Fast Talk: Service Work and the Routinization of Everyday Life*. Berkeley: University of California Press.

Parsons, Talcott. 1959. "The School Class as a Social System: Some of Its Functions in American Society." *Harvard Educational Review* 29:297–313.

Stevens, Mitchell L. 2015. "The Changing Ecology of US Higher Education." In *Remaking College: The Changing Ecology of Higher Education*, edited by Michael W. Kirst and Mitchell L. Stevens, 1–15. Stanford, CA: Stanford University Press.

———. 2008. "Culture and Education." *Annals of the American Academy of Political and Social Science* 619:97–113.

US Department of Education. 2013. *Expanding Evidence Approaches for Learning in a Digital World*. Washington: US Department of Education, Office of Educational Technology.

Waldrop, M. Mitchell. 2013. "Campus 2.0." *Nature* 495 (14 March): 160–163.

INDEX OF AUTHORS

INDEX OF SUBJECTS